The transcript of t... ....

of the united parishes of S. Mary Woolnoth and S. Mary Woolchurch Haw, in the city of London, from their commencement 1538 to 1760.

To which is prefixed a short account of both parishes, list of rectors and churchwardens, chantries, &c. together with some interesting extracts from the churchwardens' accounts

J. M. S. Brooke,

A. W. C. Hallen

Alpha Editions

This edition published in 2019

ISBN : 9789389465297

Design and Setting By
Alpha Editions
email - alphaedis@gmail.com

THE

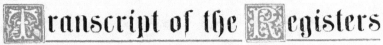 Transcript of the Registers

OF THE

United Parishes of

S. Mary Woolnoth

AND

S. Mary Woolchurch Haw,

IN THE CITY OF LONDON,

FROM THEIR COMMENCEMENT 1538 TO 1760.

TO WHICH IS PREFIXED

A SHORT ACCOUNT OF BOTH PARISHES,

LIST OF RECTORS AND CHURCHWARDENS,

CHANTRIES, &c.

TOGETHER WITH SOME INTERESTING

EXTRACTS FROM THE CHURCHWARDENS ACCOUNTS,

BY

J. M. S. BROOKE, M.A., F.R.G.S.

RECTOR OF UNITED PARISHES,

AND

A. W. C. HALLEN, M.A., F.S.A. SCOT., F. HUG. S., M. HARL. S.

" Quo baptizatus, nuptus sit, siue sepultus
tempore quis quæris? hæc liber iste docet.
Quo moriere die, caro mortua quoque resurget,
dicere quærenti pagina nulla potest.
Fixa tamen et certa manet mortalibus hora,
qua moriturus erit, quaque resurget homo.

ergo ~ ~ plus vigila semper.　　　　　Laus deo Amen."

LONDON :

PRINTED BY BOWLES & SONS, GEORGE STREET, E.C. (formerly Bearbinder Lane,)

IN THE PARISH OF S. MARY WOOLCHURCH HAW.

1886.

TO

THE RIGHT HONOURABLE

W. E. GLADSTONE, M.P., P.C.,

OF HAWARDEN CASTLE, FLINTSHIRE,

AND

ADMIRAL

SIR G. N. BROKE-MIDDLETON, BART., C.B.,

OF SHRUBLAND PARK, SUFFOLK,

THIS COMPILATION AND TRANSCRIPT

OF REGISTERS OF

S. MARY WOOLNOTH AND S. MARY WOOLCHURCH HAW,

ARE RESPECTFULLY DEDICATED,

IN GRATEFUL RECOGNITION OF A KINDLY INTEREST

BESTOWED BY THEM UPON THE WORK OF

THE EDITORS.

OFFICIALS

OF THE UNITED PARISHES IN 1886.

Rector :

JAMES MARK SAURIN BROOKE.

Curate :

CLEMENT RAYMOND PERRY.

Churchwardens :

THOMAS WEBBER, *Deputy.*

JOSEPH SAVORY, *Alderman.*

JOSEPH BOWLES.

JOSEPH BATTY.

Overseers :

FREDERIC HENDRIKS.

HENRY PUCKLE.

EDWARD FLETCHER.

WILLIAM NEELY.

Vestry Clerk :

HENRY DRUIT PHILLIPS.

Organist :

WILLIAM ESSEX.

Collector :

GEORGE LEEMING.

Beadle :

ROBERT MELVILLE.

NOTICE.

Only 300 Copies of this Work have been printed, none of which will be placed in the hands of the trade.

When Subscribers have been supplied the remaining Copies will be sold privately at an advanced price. Application to be made to

The Rev. J. M. S. BROOKE,

St. Mary Woolnoth Vestry,

Lombard Street,

London, E.C.

or to

The Rev. A. W. CORNELIUS HALLEN,

The Parsonage,

Alloa, N.B.

The importance of transcribing the valuable Church Registers of Parishes in London is now recognised, and the Rectors of several City Churches have already courteously permitted transcripts to be taken and printed by the Harleian Society or by individuals.

Mr. HALLEN (Mem. Har. Soc.) hopes to be able to issue yearly a Transcript of a London Parish Church Register, and will announce particulars as soon as he has made definite arrangements for the next volume, which will NOT be, as was formerly stated, St. Andrew Undershaft, that having now been undertaken, by mutual arrangement, by W. HARVEY, Esq.

Subscribers' names are still being received by him for the Transcript of the Muthill (Perthshire) Register of Baptisms (1697-1847).

Subscription 7s. 6d.

TABLE OF CONTENTS.

Preface.

IN a work like the present only a few words of explanation are necessary. After consulting some well-known authorities we decided to eliminate from the volume a large quantity of matter connected with the history and antiquities of the united parishes. We were borne out in this decision by the fact that a large percentage of those who manifested a practical interest in the work were more anxious to obtain copies of the Registers than the accompanying history.

We think it sufficient to print verbatim the Account of the two parishes given in "Newcourt's Repertorium,' to which we have added notes, some of which have been most kindly supplied by friends.

As the Church of St. Mary Woolnoth has been entirely rebuilt and St. Mary Woolchurch Haw has been destroyed, it does not seem advisable to enlarge on the style or appearance of the old Churches. Care has however been taken to give such entries from the Churchwardens' accounts, &c., as show that they were handsome and large edifices. These Accounts are so voluminous that great difficulty has been experienced in making a selection at once interesting and concise. Special attention has been paid to the earlier portions, as there the Archæologist will find most to interest him, while the student of history will note how the stirring events of the time affected the parochial life of the citizens.

The Inventory of Church Goods which strikes us as particularly full has been given in *extenso*.

It will be seen that the Registers of both parishes were transcribed in 1599—

"159⅞. Item paid for fair writing into the Parchment booke all the Christenings weddings and burials from anno 1538 until this year 1599 [Woolnoth Ch. Acc.] iij*li*."

The Title page of the Woolchurch Register (p. 297) shows that in the same year a transcript was made from an older volume which commenced in 1558. The Woolchurch volume was disused after the Great Fire except for a few occasional entries.

This wholesale transcribing of the earlier portions of both Registers led to clerical errors, the scribe apparently being puzzled as to some of the names. On careful consideration we have thought it best to give a simple transcript without venturing to suggest correct readings, except that in the index some of the more manifest errors have been noted—a very careful revisal convinces us that the printer has done his work with great exactness. At page 43 however the date 1639 should have been inserted between Feb. 24 and April 8.

The plan wisely adopted by our best transcribers has been followed, and though every entry and every name have been carefully copied, superfluous matter has been omitted; had this not been done the already bulky volume would have grown to an unwieldly size without any commensurate advantage. Many minute details are given in the original as to the exact position of graves which were doubtless intended to guide future sextons. Notices of Burials in the Chancel have been copied as they shew that the deceased held a superior social position. Also a few notices of burials in "the new Churchyard" or "Bethlehem" showing that the parishioners occasionally made use of the Cemetery which was provided by Lord Mayor Sir Thomas Rowe in 1568, by enclosing part of the site of the Priory of St. Mary of Bethlehem close to Bishopsgate Street. This burying place was called "The new Churchyard near Bethlehem."

Some events connected with the Royal Family will be found recorded.

It is singular that no notice of the great plague of 1665 appears in the Woolnoth books. In the Woolchurch volume "pl." has been written in blacker ink.

The Woolnoth Registers possess a feature which is almost entirely absent from those of Woolchurch, Trades and designations are very fully entered, and we may be allowed to say a few words on this subject. Very many "Strangers"* lived in the parish. The Genealogist will recognise many of the names given below and in the Index. There are some words which ask for an explanation such as "Weynerth Stranger" (p. 199), and "Zelzere Stranger" (p. 190). Some of the Trades mentioned in the Register and Church Accounts also require explanation such as "Pasteler," "Gongfarmer," "Poyntagger." A "Vergenal maker" named Cramor is found in the 16th century, and an early instance of a double Christian name (foreign however) at page 14. "The Writer of the Court letter" (p. 1 and elsewhere) was the designation of a Scrivener prior to the grant of the Royal Charter in 1616. John Fearne (Farnese ?) a "stranger," was a "Mylliner," while the son of an Italian Duke (p. 194) was laid to rest with this brief record of his rank. The term "Chrisom" is explained in a document (Sta. Pa. Dom. 1636), "It was an ancient custom at Basingstoke that women coming to be churched brought with them a piece of linen cloth which was called a Chrisom which was offered and given to the Vicar, but if any child died before the mother's churching it was buried in the same Chrisom." We give but a few instances of rare words and would refer the reader to the general index where we have endeavoured to collect all words of real interest.

Any value which this volume may be found to possess is largely due to the assistance which has been most kindly rendered by many

* The meaning of the term "stranger" is explained by the following extract—"I thought that a forrener and a straunger had been all one . . . Than remaine there none other forreners and straungers to be looked upon, but Dutchmen, Danes, Italians and frenchmenne." (Bales "Declaration," 1554, fo. 35). The following will be found in this volume designated as "strangers" or "foreigners ;" some of the names appear to have been Anglicised while some are evidently Scotch.—Ashby, Babham, Bagnall, Bare, Beesan, Beldon, Bissack, Bigwood, Blackford, Bodington, Bogenmaker, Bowdans, Brainger, Brian, Brunskill, Browne, Bugardte, Buggin, Bultell, Byoma, Caloone, Chaney, Clarke, Cokytt, Collard, Copanoll, Cornelius, Crawley, Dackellon, de Corano, de Dorper, Deggis, Delastat, Deloie, de Pive, Devielmo, Domicolo, du Mont, Durant, Eies, Ellyott (? Allett), Fearne, Finch, Frederigo, Fropp, Furrey, Gabriell, Gardner, Gildersleeve, Gills, Gossoin, Greene, Greye, Hall, Hill, Holland, Houbelon, Hovenor, Johnson, Jurion, King, Lant, Lanz, Locatteil, Lucas, Marishaw, Maurice, Meakins, Moicier, Moldeworth, Monge, Moone, Morgan, Morundo, Munns, Myskin, Oute, Patton, Paves, Pighte, Rote, Roukesby, Ryele, Sadler, Sandtman, Seggore, Selynge, Shalts, Shevaleare, Shipman, Sixty, Slany, Smith, Sparrow, Stenly, Sturtivant, Tailor, Torrentine, Tybault, Van Cowen Bargen, Van Cullen, Van Dunyseller, Van Hove, Van Seldt, Waker, Walton, Wayman, White, Woodcock. (For an important document concerning the Company of Merchant strangers see Sta. Pa. Dom. 163⅞, vol. cclxxij., § 12.)

friends, and our thanks are specially due first to the Worshipful Company of Goldsmiths who, owing to their long and close intimacy with the parish and with which they have been honourably connected for centuries, have handsomely and generously subscribed towards the cost of this work; also to the Rev. E. HOSKINS, Rector of St. Mary Magdelene and St. Gregory by St. Paul; J. JACKSON HOWARD, Esq., LL.D.; W. H. OVERALL, Esq.; WALFORD D. SELBY, Esq., Record Office; J. SHARPE, Esq., LL.D., Guildhall; J CHALONER SMITH, Esq., Somerset House; H. D. PHILLIPS, ESQ., and Messrs. NOBLE and ESSEX. We owe much to the taste and care shown by Messrs. BOWLES & SONS, our printers. We feel sure that Mr. J. BOWLES has taken special interest in these records as he is Churchwarden of St. Mary Woolchurch. The volume has been printed in the parish. Bearbinder Lane (now called George Street) was the direct communication between the two Churches and a relic of Old London is still to be met with in a cellar in this street.

As this volume has been the fruit of much labour we trust it may be appreciated by those who are desirous of preserving the annals of the past.

December, 1885.

J. M. S. B.
A. W. C. H.

Account

of the PARISH of ST. MARY WOOLNOTH,

Extracted from Newcourt's Repertorium Ecclesiasticum Parochiale
Londinense from the Conquest to A.D. 1700. London, 1708.

[The notes in small numerals have been supplied from various sources. Ed.]

St. Mary Woolnoth[1] Rectory *(page 461)*.

THIS Church, called *S. Mary Woolnoth of the Nativity*, Stow Surv. 223.
but the Reason thereof (*Stow* says) he hath not yet
learned, is situate on the South Side, and towards the West
end of *Lombard Street*, in *Langbourne* Ward. It is a
Rectory and subject to the Archdeacon.

This Church was new built about the year, 1438,
from the very foundation, as it seems; for I find a Com-
misson dated *March* 24 that year granted by *Robert* Gilbert 85.
Gilbert, then Bishop of *London* to the Bishop of *Enachdum*,
in *Ireland* (a Bishoprick now united to some other in that
Kingdom) for the Consecration thereof. By which Com-
mission he impowered the said Bishop to Consecrate, not
only the Church, but also two Altars in it; one to the
Honour of the Blessed Virgin *S. Mary* and *S. Anne*, and
the other to *S. John Baptist* and *S. John Evangelist*. And
further to assign the Feast of Dedication of this Church to
be on *Thursday* next after the Feast of *S. Anne* the Mother
of the immaculate Virgin which is *Thursday* next after
July 26.

Sir *Hugh Brice*, Goldsmith, Mayor in the First of Stow ut supra,
Hen. VII., Keeper of the King's Exchange at *London,* and
one of the Governors of the King's Mint in the *Tower of
London* under *William* Lord *Hastings* in the 5 *Edw.* IV.
deceased built in this Church a Chapel called the *Charnel*
as also part of the Body of the Church and of the Steeple,
and gave money towards the finishing thereof besides the
House that he had prepared. He died in 1496 and was
buried in the Body of this Church.

Sir *Simon Eyre* a famous Merchant sometime an Ibidem.
Upholster, then a Draper and Mayor of *London* in 1445,
the Founder of *Leaden* Hall and a Fair Chapel there, gave
the *Cardinal's Hatt* Tavern in *Lombard Street* with a Tenement annext on the East part of it, and a Mansion behind
the East Tenement together with an *Alley* from *Lombard
Street* to *Cornhill* with the appurtenances, all of which were

[1] Willmore alias Willnoth, in a Will 1443.

Ibid 163.

by him new built towards a Brotherhood of our *Lady* in this Church. He died *Sep.* 18, 1459, and was buried in the same.[2]

Ibid 223.

Geo. Lusken sometime Taylor to the Prince, built the Chapel of *S. George* in this Church.[3] Here was a per-

Baudake 85.

petual Chantry founded for the souls of *Gregory* de *Rakesley* and *Amicia* his Wife of which the Parishioners were Patron ; which Gregory was the same who was Mayor of *London* from the year 1275 to the year 1282 and dying not long after was buried in the *Grey Friars* Church in which Priory he built Dorters and Chambers and gave Bed to them.

Baybr, 188.

Another perpetual Chantry was founded here at the Altar of the *Blessed Virgin* and *S. Anne* about the year 1400 for the souls of *Tho. Noket, Gregory Norton* and their wives, and others their Relations of which the two Prioress and Convent of *S. Mary Clarkenwell* were Patrons. But these two Chantries it seems were afterwards united by reason whereof the Rector, Churchwardens and Chief of the Parishioners presented sometimes, and some-time the said Prioress and Convent of *S. Mary Clarkenwell* as appears by the *London Registry.*

The Advowson of this Church was all along in the gift of the Prioress and Convent of *St. Helen, London,* till their suppression in the reign of *Hen.* VIII. who soon after, *viz.,*

Stow Sur. 224.

in 31 of his Reign granted it to Sir *Martin Bowes* in whose family the Right of Patronage hath continued ever since. Which Sir *Martin Bowes*, Goldsmith and Mayor of *London* anno 1545, died *Aug.* 4, 1566, and with *Cecily,* Dame *Anne* and Dame *Elizabeth* his wives was buried under a goodly Marble close Tomb under the Communion Table here.

Ibidem.

There was a goodly Monument in the East end of the Chancel of this Church erected by the Executors of Sir *Thomas Ramsey,* Knight and Mayor of this City in 1577 in memory of the said Sir *Thomas* who died *May* 19, 1590, and of his two virtuous Ladies Dame *Alice* and Dame *Mary,* the latter of which was very remarkable for her Charity to several places, especially to *Christ's* Hospital.

Sion Col. MS.

In 1636 the yearly Profits of this Church were re-returned as followeth—

	£	s.	d.
Tythe	80	00	00
Casualties	02	18	00
A Parsonage House ...	00	00	00

This Church was not wholly consumed in the late dreadful Fire ; but the Steeple remained unburnt and part of the Walls of the Church which is now rebuilt chiefly on the old Walls except the North side which fronts *Lombard Street* and is wholly new, by the munificence (if I mistake not) of the late Worthy and Generous (but unfortunate) Sir *Robert Viner,* Knight and Baronet, deceased.[4] It is

---

[2] See burial of Joan Eyre. (Reg. p. 294.)

[3] See burial of George Lovekin. (Reg. p. 294.)

[4] This later Church falling greatly to decay, it was thought necessary to pull down the whole ; in consequence of which, it was rebuilt of stone, in the year 1719, in the manner in which it now appears. Lambert's His. Lon , vol. II, p. 454. Lambert is wrong here. The Church was finished in 1729. Ed.

made Parochial Church for this and the parish of *S. Mary Woolchurch* which is annext to it and both together are made of yearly value of £160 in lieu of Tythes to the Incumbent.

		£	s.	d.
In 1636, Tythes of *S. Mary Woolchurch* ...		50	16	06
Woolnoth ...		80	00	00
Total of both		130	16	6
Both now by Act of Parliament ...		160	00	00
Both now more than before... ...		29	03	06

In 1693 the Parsonage House was presented, burnt Reg. Lon. down in the late dreadful fire, but since rebuilt by Mr. *Crisp*, late Rector of this Church and leased out to him at £5 *per ann.* Ground rent for the term of 40 years.

Likewise Two Lectures, one to be preached about the 20th of November yearly, for which is paid *20s.* a sermon given by Sir *Martin Bowes* and constantly paid by the Goldsmiths' Company. The other on *S. Thomas* day yearly given by Mr. *Wites* for which is paid *20s.* a sermon by his Heirs Tenants.

		£	s.	d.
	Primitæ ...	25	00	00
Onera hujus Ecclesiæ	*Decimoe* ...	02	10	00
	Proc Epis ...	00	09	06
	Proc Archid	00	03	04

Rectores.

Sudbury.	58.	*a.*	John de Norton.	
			Joh. de Treenfield, pr. prid. Id. Nov. 1368.	
			Will Godeswayne.	
Grey.	25.		Jac. Forster, cl. 17 Jan. 1428, per mort Godeswayne.	
Kemp.	64.		Rog. Cheshire, pr. 14 Apr. 1459, per mort Forster.	Prioresssa et Conventus S. Helenæ, London.
	82.	*b.*	Nic. Goldwell, L.B., 21 Jul. 1462, per mort Cheshire.	
			Rog. Necton.	
Ibid.	199.	*c.*	Rob. Bradow, D.B., 17 Jul. 1484, per mort Necton.	
	12.	*d.*	Ric. Rawlins, S.T.P., 15 Mar. 1494 per mort Bradow.	
		e.	Joh. Watson.	
			Joh. Shedar.	
Bonner.	166.		Humfr. Edwards, A.M., 26 April 1549. per mort Shedar.	Martin Bowes Miles et Aldermanus London.
	471.		John Morris, cl. 21 Maii. 1557, per mort Edwards.	
	478.		Mil. Gerard, cl. 30 Nov. 1558, per mort Morris.	
Grindall.	163.	*f.*	Tho. Buckmaster, cl. 17 Oct. 1572.	Jasper Fisher arm pro hac vice Humf. Kail et alii pro hac vice.
	320.	*g.*	Joh. Childerley, S.T.B., 14 Maii 1599, per mort Buckmaster.	
Bancroft.	131.	*h.*	Tho. White, A.M., 14 Nov. 1609, per ref. Childerley.	Jac. 1. R. a ratione minor Tho. Bowes wardli sui.
	162.	*i.*	Josias Shute, A.M., 29 Nov. 1611, per mort White.	
Laud.	112.	*k.*	Tho. William, S.T.B., 19 Jul. 1643, per mort Shute.	Tho. Bowes, Miles.
		l.	Will Outram, S.T.P.	
Henchman.	120.		Andrew Crispe, A.M., 9 Jul. 1666, per ref. Outram.	Rob. Viner, pro hac vice.
Compton.	107.	*m.*	Sam Angier, A.B., 3 Maii 1689, per mort Crispe.	Sam Angier, gen. pro hac vice.

[For the later Rectors see below.]

a. *John de Norton* was parson of this Church 1355, for on *Octob.* 22 that year he had the King's License to exchange it for the Church of *St. Peter* in *Berkhamsted* with *Phill. de Legh* [Pat. 29, E. III., p. 3] but this exchange seems not to have taken effect because after, *viz., Nov.* 29 following the said *de Legh* gets the King's License to exchange his said Ch. of *Berkhamstead* for that of *St. Michael Queenhithe* [ib.] Neither is it likely that this took effect for on 22 of next *July* the said *de Legh* obtains another License to exchange the said Ch. of *Berkhamsted* for that of *St. Edmund Lombard* Street [Pat. 30, Ed. III., p. 2] and whether that was effectual I cannot find by the Registry.

b. *Nic. Goldwell* [vid *Roding Alta* (*Ess.*) inter *Rectores.*]
c. *Rob. Bradow* [vid *Markshall* (*Ess.*) inter *Rectores.*]
d. *Ric. Rawlins* [vid inter *Præb de Willsden.*]
e. *John Watson* [vid *Greensted juxta Colch Notley Alba* and *Waltham Magna* (*Ess.*) inter Incumb.]
f. *Tho. Buckmaster* [vid *Alhal the Wall* inter Rec.]
g. *Joh. Childerley* [vid *S. Dunstan East* inter Rec.]
h. *Tho. White* [vid *S. Dunstan West* inter Rec.]
i. *Josias Shute* [vid inter *Archid Colch.*]
k. *Tho. William* [vid *Mistley* (*Essex*) inter Rec.]
l. *Will Outram* was also Minister of *S. Margaret*, Westminster, which (if I mistake not) became void by his death.
m. *Sam Angier* The present Rector with that of *S. Mary Woolchurch* annexed 1700.

[End of Newcourt's Notes.]

The following have been Rectors since Mr. Angier :

1752.	Charles Plumtre.
1779.	John Newton.
1809.	Samuel Birch, D.D.
1848.	Robert Dear.
1872.	Josiah Irons, D.D.
1883.	James Mark Saurin Brooke, M.A.

THE following Notes are given to supplement Newcourt's List of Rectors and his notes thereon.

1314-15.	William le Mareschal, *Rector* (See Kent Fine, No. 384, Edw. ij).
1375.	William Dymmok, *Rector*, mentioned in the Will of Cecily Dod formerly Burstall.
1396.	William Cacchemayde, *Rector*, mentioned in the Will of Noket and again in 1399 (Close Rolls, No. 29, dorse Anno 23, Rich. ij).
1404.	Richard att the Hyde, *Rector* (Enrollment of Exchequer, pleas. Rec. Off., vide Vol. sub. Lon., page 153.)
1417.	John Clynton, *Capellanus*, made bequests to Drowda (Drogheda) and Dublin.
1419.	William Godeswayne, *Rector*, proved by the Will of John Megre.
1423.	Radulphus Dalby, *Capellanus*, "Cantariœ fundatœ" ordained in his Will to be buried in the Lady Chapel.
1433.	Sir John Hoo, *Chantry Priest*, administered to estate of Thos. Combe.
143⅚.	John Elm (?), *Chaplain of Chantry* (Vide Lay subs.: divers Counties, No. $\frac{240}{289}$, ao. 14, Hen. VI.)
1462.	Nicholas Goldwell, *Clerk*, *Parson of Blofield* (Norfolk), made his Will at Norwich, 1505.
1471.	Richard Bryde, *Capellanus*, ordained to be buried in the Chapel of St. Mary.
1509.	John Pynde, *Parish Priest*, mentioned in the Will of Van Uright.
1517.	Nicholas Rycardes, *Curate*, mentioned in the Will of John Tuk, and as *Parish Priest* in the Will of John Hilton, 1519.
1518.	Sir Laurence Waren, *Prest*, ordained to be buried near Sir John Percival, Knt., and in his Will mentioned.
1518.	Sir William Hilton, *Chantry Prest*.
1521.	Sir John Tempyll, *Divina celebrans*. Will in this year.
1522.	Peter Swake, or Swage, Batchelor of Law, *Parish Priest*. Will of A. Glaster.
1523.	The same, *Curate of the Parish*, Will of Richd. Peppis.
1524.	Christopher Stevynson, *Parish Priest*, Will of Sir. J. Skevington, Kt. 1525.
1531.	Dr. Watson was Rector in this year as proved by the Will of E. Warley.

1531. Sir Edmund Crispyn, *Priest*, "late Curate here," same Will.

1540. John "Shether," *Rector*, is mentioned in the Will of John Barnes, and in 1542 in the Will of John Mychell.

1543. Sir Robert Roys, *Curate*. Will of R. Vaughan.

1537. Sir John Morys, *Chantry Prest*. Will of W. Davy. (Vide also Extracts from Church Accounts and Woolnoth Burials, p. 185).

1537. Thomas Parcyvall, *Parish Priest*. Will of W. Davy.

1539. Sir Thobye, *Chantry Priest* (see Church Accounts and Woolnoth Burials, p. 178).

1539. Sir Atkynson, *Chantry Priest* (see Church Accounts).

1540. Sir Richard Dawson, *Chantry Priest* (Church Accounts).

1540. Sir Richard Stythefield, *Chantry Priest* (Church Accounts).

1540. Sir Stoke, *Chantry Priest*.

1566. Jan. 22, Thomas Buckmayster married Alice Reniger, *Widdow*, who had married Aug. 24, 1560, to Thomas Reniger, Rector of Allhallows in the Wall.

1643. June 12, "Mr. Josh. Shute, Preacher in Lombard Street, died" (Smyth's Obituary). 1670, June 11, "Old Mrs. Shute the *Widdow* of Mr. Jos. Shute, Preacher, died aged above 100 years" (Ibid).

Ezechiel Hopkins was *Rector* during the interregnum, (vide Reg. Mag. Col. Ox. Edited by Dr. Bloxam, vol. iii., p. 169).

1655. Ralph Robinson, *Preacher of the Gospel and Rector of St. Mary Woolnoth*. Will proved.

1655. Samuel Jacomb, admitted *Rector* 28 Nov. Patron, Sir Thomas Bowes (vide Lambeth MS., 996, p. 380). His Will is dated 1659.

1685. Francis Sclater, *Minister*, buried 12 May, 1685, at St. James, Clerkenwell, where his monument (Vide Hatton's His. London, Vol. I., p. 286). The M.I. states that he had been for two years before his death " Minister of S. Mary Woolnoth" (perhaps *Lecturer* is meant).

AUGMENTATION

Chantry Certificates

MIDDLESEX ROLL 34 No. 40.

ST. MARY WOOLNOTH.

Primo die Januarij anno Primo RR Edwardi vjti.

The paroche of St. Mary Wolnoth in Lombardstret.

To Wit.

Thomas Nocket gave unto the parsonne and churchwardens there to the mayntenance of two channtry prestes all those his tenement amountinge to the yerelie valew of xiij*li.* vj*s.* viij*d.* whereof

To Sir Willyam Wenters Channtry preste by yere	vj*li.* xiij*s.* iiij*d.*	
To Sir Richard Browne Channtry preste	vj*li.* xiij*s.* iiij*d.*	xiij*li.* vj*s.* viij*d.*
And then Remaynethe clere	*nil.*	

Hewe Brige Knight gave unto the parson and wardens to the maynetenance of one prest for ever w^t liij*s.* iiij*d.* as a rent charge going out of a Capitall Messuage in Lumberd stret wherin Sir Marten Bowes Knight inhabiteth lands by yere amounting to xiij*li.* xiij*s.* iiij*d.* whereof

To John Meres prest	vi*li.* xiij*s.* iiij*d.*	
To the Kinge for tenth	xiij*s.* iiij*d.*	vij*li.* viij*s.* viij*d.*
To the Kinge for quiterent	ij*s.*	
And then Remaynethe clere		vj*li.* iiij*s.* viij*d.*

Thomas Wymonnde gave unto the same parson and wardens after the death of Elizabeth his wife now deceased towards the finding of an obite and Clerk one Tenement in Shereborn lane by yere xl*s.* whereof

Spent upon Thobbite	v*s.*	
To the Clerke	xxxv*s.*	xl*s.*
And then Remayneth clere	*nil.*	

Dame Elizabeth Brice gave for the finding of an obite for ever one annuall rent by yere xx*s.*

Dame Emme Meger gave for the finding of v Taps for ever two Tenements by yere xxix*s.* iiij*d.*

Memor$^{D.}$

Ther is of howseling people within the same paroche the nombre of ccc.

Sir John Shether is parson of the same Churche and therly value of the same is xxvj*li.* and that no prests are founde ther by him but onely deputy and to the residue of tharticles ther is nothing to answer.

Extracts

From the *CHURCHWARDENS' BOOKS OF ST. MARY WOOLNOTH, LONDON.*

Memorandum that Sir Martyn Bowes Knight and Alderman of London parishioner of this Parish of his benevolence and goode will towards the said parish at his own proper costes and charges in the month of August in Anno domini 1556 in the iij*d* and iiij*th* yeres of oure sovraigne lord and lady kynge Philipp and queene Mary caused the roode and Mary and John and the cross to be gilden and paynted as by the same appereth.

Also the said Sir Martyn Bowes of his further benevolence at the Feast of Ester anno 1557 et seq. annis did gyve a faire cloth for the Sacremente to be used in this church which cloth is of cloth of gold and the Fower faire gilt buttons the same. [On fly leaf.]

1539

Item receyved of the Master and Wardens of the Merchint Tayllours for the beame light of this church according to the devyse of Dame Thomasyn Percyvall widow late wyf of Sir John Percyvall Knight deccased — xxvi*s*. viij*d*.

Item receyved more of the Master and Wardens of Merchint Tayllors for ij tapers thoon of vij*lb* and the other of v*lb* to brenne about the Sepulture in this Church at Ester ij*s* iiij*d* and for the churchwardens labor of this church to gyve attendance at the obit of Sir John Percyvall and otherwyse according to the devyse of Dame Thomasyn Percyvall his wyf iiij*s* — vi*s*. iiij*d*.

Item receyved of the said Master and Wardens of Merchint Tailors for the Repacions of the ornaments of this church according the will of the said Sir John Percyvall — vi*s*.

Item receyved of the Maister and Wardens of Merchint taillors for a hole yere for our Conduct for kepying the Antempur afore Saint John with his children according to the will of the said Dame Thomasyn Percyvall — xx*s*.

Item receyved of the Churchwardens of Saint Edmonde in Lombard Strete for the Pascall light at Ester according to the wille of Thomas Wette that is to say x*s* for the Pascall and iiij*d* for the parson or his deputie for xhorting the parysshens at Ester at their houses to say a pater noster and ave for the soule of the said Thomas Wette — x*s*. iiij*d*.

Item paid for Mr. Amada's obyt the vij day of Aprill that ys to say ij tapers from the Sepulture of my

Lady Parcyvall to the parson xij*d* to vi preists ij*s* to iij clarkes xij*d* for ryngyng viij*d* for drynkynge to preists and clarkes xviij*d* for our offering ij*d* given to pore folkes of the pisshe vi*s* viij*d* to us the churchwardens for our labour iiij*s* and to Robert Curry of almes iiij*d* summa — xvij*s*. iiij*d*.

Item for Holy and Ive against Chrystmas — iiij*d*.

Item paid to Emery the xxi day of Marche for the Empoures Dirige kept v day of June — iij*s*.

Item paid for this great boke of paper to write in the churche accomptes, and for a litill boke of paper — vij*s*.

Item paid on Ahalowen day for v herps for virgyns to play — ij*s*.

Item for garlandes for the same virgyns — ij*d*.

Item for lampes for the same virgyns — iiij*d*.

Item to the Waxchandler [a long account for tapers, &c.] — xlvij*s*. viij*d*.

Item paid on Palme Sunday for brede ale and wyne geven to the preists and clarkes at reding of the Passion — vij*d*.

Item paid for palme flowers and caks on Palme Sunday — vi*d*.

Item paid for a quarter of Coles against Ester — vi*d*.

Item paid for watching of the sepulture — viij*d*.

Item paid for the half of the Bybill in the Church which cost xiij*s* iiij*d* — vi*s*. viij*d*.

Item paid for Rose garlands on Corpus Xti day — ij*d*.

Item paid to Emery the xxi day of March for the Empours Dirige kept the v*th* day of June which James Stephyns should have paid to his accompt — iij*s*.

Item paid to Sir Thobye oon of the Chauntry preistes of this churche for Noketts foundacion to the augmentacion of his salary according to the wyll of the said Sir Hughe Bryce for a hole yere — vi*s*. viij*d*.

Item paid in lykewyse to Sir Atkynson his felowe for lyke intent for half a yere ending at Midsomer — iij*s*. iiij*d*.

Item paid to Sir John Moryce our Lady masse prest for his salary and wages for syngyng our Lady masse and helping nyghtly at the Salves that is to say for the fyrst foundacion vi*li* xiij*s* iiij*d* and to the augmentacion of his salary according to the will of the said Sir Hughe Brice vi*s* viij*d* for a hole yere — xij*li*.

Item paid to Thomas Eve our Conducte for lyke service doon by hym and his children for a whole yere ending at the said Later Mighelmas — xl*i*.

Item paid for thengrossing of this accompt (5 folios) — iij*s*. iiij*d*.

1540

Item paid for a basket for Holy bread — iij*d*.

Item paid for a Holy water sprynkill — iij*d*.

Item for chayne for the same sprynkill — i*d*.

Item for ix ells &c. of clothe for iiij surplices for children in the quire at vi*d* the ell — iiij*s*. vi*d*.

Item for making of the same iiij surplices — xvi*d*.

Item for setting up the railes upon the leds on Palme Sunday — iij*d*.

Item for makyng a deske to sett on the bibill — vi*d*.

Item for ij stapulls for the chayne of the said bibill — ij*d*.

Item for mendyng of the chest at St. Catheryns Altaur .... iiij*d*.

Item to Xrofer Fee for workmanship and stuff for the gilding paynting and trymmyng of the crucyfix with Mary and John in the Rode lofte .... xliij*s*. iiij*d*.

Item paid to Sir Stoke preist the xxi day of February for his quarters wages of Noketts fundacion as may appere by a bill of his hande .... xxxiij*s*. iiij*d*.

Item paid in lykewise to Sir Richard Dawson his felowe the iiij day of April as appereth by a bill .... x*lb*.

Item paid more to the same Sir Richard the xix day of August .... vi*s*. viij*d*.

Item paid more for there acquitances .... viij*d*.

Item paid for the paving of Sir Thoby grave .... vi*d*.

Item paid to William Franklyn glazier for mendyng and closying of the wyndowes in the churche and for mendyng the side wyndows in the quyer .... ix*s*. viij*d*.

Item paid to Sir Richard Stythefelde oon of the chantry preistes of Noketts foundacion to the augmentacion of his salary according to the will of Sir Hughe Brice for a hole yere ending at the said latter michelmas .... vi*s*. viij*d*.

1541

Item paid to Sir Richard Dawson oon of the Chantrie prestes of Noketts foundacion in this church to the augmentacion of his salary according to the wille of the said Sir Hugh Brice for a hole yere .... vi*s*. viij*d*.

Item paid to iiij Preists and ij clarks of this churche for kepyng of our Lady masse by note in the time of the vacation of a Conduct to evry one of them ij*s* summa .... xij*s*.

Item paid to our conduct for lyke since doon by him and his children for iij quarters of a yere ending at the said latter myghellmas .... vi*li*.

Robert Morecok our Conduct

1542

Item received for the crosse and candlestyks at the burying of Clement Webes wyf .... viij*d*.

Item paid for carying the Shryne to Westmyster and home again to Robard Emery .... viij*d*.

Item paid to Sir William Ventrys oon of the Chauntry preysts .... v*s*.

1543

Item paid for paynting of the lentyn clothes in Saint Georges Chapell .... ii*s*. viij*d*.

Item paid for a potation for preists and clarkes to help to rais upp rafters and bordes .... iiij*d*.

Item paid to Sir Richard Browne from the xth daye of August untill mighelmas after iiij*d* the daye .... xvi*s*. viij*d*.

Item paid for the pulpet .... iiij*s*. iiij*d*.

[N.B.—A memorandum at close of this year shows that the silver and gilt plate had been sold to raise money to make extensive repairs on the Church, which plate was to be replaced when possible.]

1544

Item paid for creacon [? recreation] at the Cardynalls Hatt for attonement between the p'son and the parisshoners bycause he wolde have had of the parishe to fynde hym a surples and it was agreed he should fynde yt hymself   iii*s.*

[Note in margin] Mr. p'son is to fynde hymself a surplus.

Item paid for iiij boks of Passion in English   viij*s.*

Item paid for pyns to make redy the prophecies   ij*d.*

Item paid in lykwise [for extraordinary and voluntary church work] to Sir Robert Rostell of benyvolence   iiij*s.*

Item paid more to Sir Ayryott [?] of benyvolence for lyke service   iiij*s*

William Squier Conduct.

1545

Item paid for setting up the railes for prophetes   ij*d.*

Item paid for pynns   i*d.*

1546

Paid for rynginge of the knyll and peales at the Dirige and Masse kept the vij day of February for our late sovrain Lord of famous memory King Henry viijth   xx*d.*

Paid for rynging at the frenche kings funrall   xx*d.*

Paid to a carpenter for taking down of the Image of Saint George   viij*d.*

Paid to a glazier for vi fote new glass at the ende of the church where Sant Mychell stode waying soules   ij*s.*

1547

Item received for the case of the tabernacle upon the high alter   vi.*s* viij*d.*

Item paid for taking downe the ij tabnacles the Body with Mary and John and other images in the church   viij*s.*

Item paid for the half of the paraphrase of Erasmus   v*s.*

Item paid for vi Salters in Englishe for the quyere   v*s.*

1549

For taking down of the highe Aulter

1552

Item payd to Gregorie the clerk for playing at the organes one hole yeare   xiij*s.* iiij*d.*

1553

Item paid to Robert Fryer for two antiphons ij grates ij masse boks one Legend one manuell one venite booke iii processyons, and one dirige booke   x*li.* xvi*s.* viij*d.*

Item paid for one manuell in print   iij*d.*

Item paid for a crosse of copper gilt   xv*d.*

Item paid for a pix and a crosse staffe a little crucifix
with a foote and a pax all being copper and gilt — xiiis. iiij*d.*

Item paid for a cristmetory and a little pax of tyn — viijs. iij*d.*

Item paid for a pair of candlesticks and a shyppe for
frankynsense of Latten — xiis. viij*d.*

Item paid for a paire of cruetts and a sarving bell — xvi*d.*

Item paied for a hole hyre and other charges at sundry
tymes to Westminster and againe for getynge of
certain ornaments of the churche — iis. i*d.*

Item paid in reward to Mr. Sturtons at the receyving of
ij Tabernnacles, and for expense goinge about to
seek for them in dyvers parishes — iis. v*d.*

Item paid for the building of the highe Altar [&c.]

1554

Item receyved more of Mr. George Eton by the Queenes
Majesties gyft remayning in his handes upon the sale
of churche goodes — xvi*li.* vs.

Item paid to Reynolds and Standish singinge men for
theyre paynes by the space of one moneth — vs. iiij*d.*

Item paid to Walton for a booke of masses and Antims
in Prick Songe — xs.

Item paid to John Morrys for a stole of grene clothe of
Bawdkyn — xii*d.*

Item paid for a thousand of brycke for the two syde alters — viijs.

Item paid iiij men for to helpe up with the alter stones — iiij*d.*

Item paid ix yeardes of heare for the thre alters at viij*d*
the yarde — vis. iiij*d.*

Item payed for a newe table fraymed upon the high alter — xxs.

Item paied to Uncle for workmanshipp of the clothe
over the high alter — xxvis.

Item paied for a crusifix — ixs.

Item paied for half passes one for the highe alter and
one for the syde alter — ijs.

Item paied for a drinkeing to them that dyd helpe the
quire on palme Sondaye — vi*d.*

Item paied for the making of the hole for the Judas crosse — viij*d.*

Item paied for a new quarter for the seputure and for
settinge up of the frame of it and takinge of it downe
to Standbacke — xij*d.*

Item paied to White for watching of yt — viij*d.*

Item paied for two knoppes for the banner of the crosse
[The word "staffe" delcted] — xii*d.*

Item paied for the office of the masse in nomine Jesu — viij*d.*

Item paied to Marchande-broderer for new mendinge of
of xvi copes, ii Surcingles and one chisible — v*li.* viijs.

Item paied for wax candles at ye consecration of ye alter — v*d.*

Item paied for the clothe for the Roode lofte — v*li.*

Item paied for tymbre and workmanshippe to pece one
of the arms of the crosse — xvi*d.*

1555

Item paied more to him [Anthony Pavyour] for ij*lb.* of
frankynsense — vi*d.*

Item paide for half an ell of bokram for to hange uppon
the steple on the generall churche hollydays — iiij*d*.
Item paid more to hym [Edward Sufford] for a booke
called the Omilyes — viij*d*.
Item paide to a carman for the caryinge of certain
powles and other necessaries for a scaffold for the
settying uppe of the crucifixe — iiij*d*.
For the fasteninge of the crosse for the roode
Item paide to Harman Cure and his brother for the
Roode the Mary John and for the fower evangelysts — vij*li*.
Item paide for a platter for the paschall — i*d*.
Item paide to the Somner for oyl and crysme for the
crysmatorie — iiij*d*.
Item paide to Uncle the paynter for payntyinge of the
said xxvi scutchons — xxxi*s*.
Item paide to Harman Cuer and hys brother for the
picture of oure lady the patroness of our churche — xlix*s*.

1556

Item paide for housinge breade at Easter — vi*d*.
Item paide for palme ewe and boxe an se cakes for
the churche — vi*d*.

1557

Item paide the viij daye of September, 1557, to Goodman
Stanbanke for seven clarkes hyghred at vi*d*. the pece — iij*s*. vi*d*.
Item paied the same daye to Tailour the clark master
of the syngynge chyldren of the hospitall for hym
and his children — xvi*d*.
Item paide to Maister parson for a boke called the
rosessaryes of the church — ij*s*. x*d*.
Item paide Edward Sutton, bok binder, for twoo bookes
called the twoo Antisymes — xl*s*.
Item paide more to him [Anthony Paviour] for a staf-
torche for christeninge — xij*d*.
Item paide more for synginge breade at Easter — iiij*d*.
Item receyved of Lanncellot Wytton for one hole yeares
rent of hys chamber over the Cloyster — xiij*s*. iiij*d*.
Item paide to Vaughan for repayring the copes and for
makinge a new kuchen — vij*s*. viij*d*.
Item paide the xiij day of Marche for the Latten candel-
styckes to stand before the Roode — vi*s*. viij*d*.
Item paid the xxix daye of Marche to Shute wyfe for
xiij yeardes of Sisters clothe to make surplesses, at
xiiij*d*. the yearde — xiij*s*.
Item paide to good wyfe Ventres for mendinge of foure
awbes two newe fanells, three surplesses for children
and two for men — ij*s*.

1558

Item paide the xvi*th* daye of Maye, 1558, to Mr. Clerke
and his sonnes to helpe to synge being Rogacion weke — xij*d*.
Item paide for caryage of the strand [?] iiij days — vi*d*.

Item paide for trashe and hookes to hange up the carpettes in the church — ij*d*.

Item paide father Groves and father Baker for keping the quier that daye, being churche holly daye — viij*d*.

Item paide to the same Anthonie [Pavior] for the trimdell agaynst cadlemas, 1558 — ii*s*. vi*d*.

Item paide to the same Antonie for ij*lb*. tennabell candells — ij*s*.

Item paied the vii daye of November to Walter Rake bell founder by the ordre of Mr. Alderman and others of the parishe at the Redinge of Mr. Atkinson's accompte for mendynge of the thyrde bell for a hope of Jron in the same and four dayes labour for hym and on other — vi*s*. viij*d*.

Item paied to Guillame Van de lip in full paymen for mendynge the chyme — xxx*s*.

Item paide to a stationer for wrytyinge xx leaves of parchement on bothe syds into ij antiphoners wherein is conteyned the service of St. Thomas of Canterburie, and the service of the iij days of Jesus in August and for the said parchment — x*s*. iiij*d*.

Item paide the viij daye of ffebruary for iiij bookes of the English service — viij*d*.

Item paide to Eton the carpenter and iiij men to help him to take downe the roode — vi*s*. viij*d*.

Item paide to iiij men for taking down the altares, and the alter stones — xvi*d*.

Item paide for ij labourers for ij dayes dyggynge downe the altares and conveying out the rubbishe — iiij*d*.

Item paide to a bricklayer for ij dayes work and his labourer for lettynge the alter stones into the ground and mendynge the hoale in the churche wall where the altare stoode — iij*s*. iiij*d*.

1559

Receyved more of Robert Fryer for copes vestments and ornaments as appear by a byll of sale solde to hym by the consent of the paryshoners for the repaarcyon of the churche the some of — c*li*.

Receyved of Robert Tayleboys for ij Chalcyses parcell gilt averyging xxv ounces at x*s*. the ounce, whererin was founde iij*lbs*. of Leade so was not of sylver xxiiij ounces — vi*li*. ij*s*.

Receyved more of hym for a gilt chalesse with a patent weying xxij ounces at v*s*. viij*d*. the ounce — vi*li*.

Payed to Robert Tayleboys for a comunion cuppe with a cover gilt weyinge xxxiij ouces at vi*s*. viij*d*. the ounce amounteth to — vi*li*. iij*s*. iiij*d*.

Item payed for ij psalme bookes in myter for the churche — xvi*d*.

Item payed to Robert Fryar the xth daye of Maye, 1560 for a cope of blewe velvet and gold and carpet for the comunion table of green velvet and gold — viij*li*.

Item payed for a booke of the prayers to Stanbacke — ij*d*.

Item for ij dayes and hys man for takinge downe the altar and the garnishinge in St. Georgey's Chappell — iiij*s*.

1560

Item receyved of Maister Atkinson for ij pieces of old
tymbre and v olde bordes that were of the Rood
lofte   v*s.*

Item touchinge the rest of the same Roodlofte part
was delyvred by the order of Syr Martyn Bowes
Knight to the Governours of Bethelem and the
pourcyous being xiij*li.* weare delyvered by lyke order
to the Governours of Bridewell and the rest ys to be
delyvered by this accomptant to the Churchwardens
now charged

Item receyved of a stacyioner for the lattyn service
bookes which weare sold by consent of the perishoners   xxvi*s* viij*d.*

Item receyved of a founder for xxxvij*lb.* and a halfe of
candlestycks metale and brasse at iij*d.* the pounde   x*s.* x*d.*

Item payed to the Bysshoppe of Londons Somoner for
a table of the comandements and a booke with
a calendr howe the chapters shall be redde in the
churche   xviij.

1561-2

Item paid to the children of Powles for helpeing the
quier at my lady Bowes daughters marriage   v*s.*

Item paid to the Cuerat for his wages for one whole
yere ending at the feaste of St. Michell tharchall,
1563   xiij*li.* vi*s.* viij*d.*

1562-3

Item paide to the Sumner for the copy of a prayer for
Frydays and wensdays in the church   ij*d.*

Item paide the xij of December 1562 for the Sumner
when he came to warne me and my fellowe to make
a booke of the names of the straungers dwelling in
this parish   iiij*d.*

The v day of April Anno 1563 for carryinge awaye
of a dead dogge laide at the church door   i*d.*

Item paide for ij lytell new bookes of Service for the
tyme of the plage the xxvij*th* of August 1563 for
the churche   vi*d.*

Item paide for francinsense to aire the church   i*d.*

1563-4

Item receyved more of Mr. Witton for lumber in the
scole house   xl*s.*

Item receyved of Roberte Taylboys for an olde chyme
in the vestery   iiij*s.* iiij*d.*

Item receyved of Edmund Sutton the same tyme for a
long stremer   vi*s.*

Item receyved more of hym for a canopy cloth and an
old cross case   vi*s.*

Item receyved of Thomas Watte the same time for a
vale cloth   vij*s.*

Item receyved more of Thomas Gyles for ij old vestments aubes and olde stoles — vij*s.*

Item receyved of Richard Bryseley for iij old aulter clothes of heare — ij*s.*

Item paide to Goodman Howe the organ maker the last day of Janeary 1563 for ij sprynges for the base pypes of the organ — vi*d.*

Item paide the same day [5 July, 1564] for a carr to bryng the harnesse from Sir Martyn Bowes house to the church dore for ij lode being the warde harnesse — vi*d.*

1564-5

Item paied for a whip to beate doggs owte of the churche — i*d.*

Item paied to John Holford gardener the xxiij of June 1565 for a daye and a halfe diggyng and leveling the church yarde — ij*d.*

1565-6

Item payd for the mendynge of the glasse wyndowes in the chamber where Goodman Grene dyd dwell — xij*d.*

Item payd the iiij of November 1565 for iiij lytle bookes of servyce of thankesgyvinge for the delyverance of Christendome from the Turke Som — vi*d.*

1566-7

Item paide the x*th* of December for a borde of tenne foote longe for the bench to kneel on before the Communyon table — ij*d.*

Item paid to Goodman Plommer the xxiiij*th* day of December for to buy holly for the churche and for packthryd to bynde up the same — ix*d.*

1568-9

Item paide to the Somner the iiij of January for the bill of reporte of Straungers — iiij*d.*

Item paide for a boke of Common Prayer for to be used in the church — iiij*d.*

1573-4

Item receyved the xxiiij day of December 1573 of Thomas Wate for a paynted clothe — ij*s.* vi*d.*

1576-7

Item receyved the same day of certain parishoners of this parish for olde surplices olde Lynnen a pawle clothe banners and bannerstaves [&c., &c.,] a small banner cloth — iij*li.* ij*s.* x*d.*

Item paid the xij of September to the joyner for mendyng the sworde case for the Lorde Maior to sett up in the church against the pewe and for removing Sir William Harpers sworde case — iiij*d.*

1577-8

Item paid to the Glasyers man for settinge up a clothe to keep awaye the sonne from the preacher [in the margin is written "objected"] — i*d.*

1578-9

Item paide for three balletts and books for the parson and clarke to sing on the daye of the Queens Maj. raigne — viij*d.*

1579-80

Item paide for three bookes of prayer for the Earthquake — xij*d.*
Item paide for twooe lynkes to lighte home the precher — viij*d.*

1589-90

Item paide for three prayer books for the good successe of the French Kinge — iij*d.*

1590-1

Item paide for xxiiij quarts and one pint of Muscadell for the comunion for one whole year endinge at the same time — xx*s.* v*d.*

1592-3

Item paide for carriage of three dead cats from the church wall — ij*d.*

1593-4

Item for setting a crosse upon one Allens dore in the sicknesse time — ij*d.*
Item paid for setting two red crosses upon Anthony Sound his dore — iiij*d.*

1594-5

Item for making cleane the plate belonging to the boundes of this parish — iiij*d.*

1595-6

Item paid the 7th of December 1595 unto John Knight and Robert Bridgewell paynter steyners for paynting the pullpets the three toumbes jaspering the pillers and paynting and amending the other writing and paynting work in the quier as by their bills appereth — v*li.* vi*s.*
Item paid for a book to write the particular receipts of the offerings at every communion — vi*d.*

1597-8

Item paid for the article for the suspected persons in our parish — viij*d.*

[List of old armour sold]—4 black billes ij*s*. 2 old cosselletes iiij*s*. 2 owld bowes xij*d*. 10 swordes xi*s*. viij*d*. 3 almain revetts xij*d*. 1 cossellet 2 bowes a brown bill iij*s*. vi*d*. 3 swordes and a gonne iiij*s*. vi*d*.

1599

Item paid for faire writing into the same parchment booke all the christenings, weddings and burialls from Anno 1538 untill this yeare 1599   iij*li*.

1600-1

Item paid for the whipping of two rogues   viij*d*.

1602-3

Paid for three dozen of points given to the children of this parishe on Ascension day   vi*d*.

Paide for two bookes of Thanksgiving for the Kinges delivry from his enemies in Scotland   xx*d*.

Paide for two bookes for fast and prayer on Wednesdaies   vi*d*.

Paid to the ringers on the day of the Kinges delivry from the Earle Gowrie   ii*s*.

1604-5

Item paid for a staffe for the warden for vagabonds and other pore   xviij*d*.

1605-6

Item paid to a paynter that wold have painted the Kinges armes in our church   xij*d*.

Item paid for another noate out of Mr. Holland's office*   xij*d*.

1607-8

Item paid more to Thomas Watton for payntinge the ten commandments the gallary the pulpetts, the two easte endes with the creede and the Lordes prayer the Three tombes and all the pillors of the church in oyl cullors as now they be and for tallowing the iron barrs in the church windows   xij*li*. x*s*.

1609-10

Item paid to Mr. Chesmore for mending the stocks   xiij*s*. iiij*d*.

Item paid to the pore of this parish which was received of John de Dorpes† by order of the Archbishopp of Canterbury for a licence to eat flesh   vi*s*. viij*d*.

1610-11

Item paid for setting upp of three scutchions in the church windows   iij*s*.

Item paid for a booke called Bishoppe Jewells workes by command from the Lord Bishopp of London   xxiij*s*.

* Mr. Holland's name appears elsewhere as a "stranger."
† John de Dorper's name appears elsewhere as a "stranger."

1611-12

Item paid for a booke directed unto us from the Lord Archbishopp to be read morning and evening every Sunday during the drought   iiij*d.*

Item paid for the new dressing of the carpett of the communion borde   xiiij*d.*

Item paid for a booke of common praier for the church   vij*s.* vi*d.*

1616-17

Item paid the ringers when the lady Elizabeth was delyvered of a sonne   ij*s.*

Item paid Mr. Munday for a booke of the survey of London   x*s.*

1622-23

Item paid the ringers the first of April, 1623 for ringing the bells for the prince his safe arrivall in Spayne   ij*s.*

1631-2

Paid for ringing at the birth of ye Princesse Maria   oo o2 o6

1633-4

Paid for ringing on the Prince's Birthday   oo o2 o6

Paid for half an ell of Sletia cloth for the communion plate   oo oo 10

Paid for ringing upon the Duke's Christening day   oo o1 o6

Paid for carving of some of the Angells and for some new made   o1 18 oo

Paid for the dove and monument over it   ooo 18 oo

1639-40

Paid ringers at the birth of the Young Prince   oo o2 o6

[Later items possess no particular interest.]

Exchequer Q.R. Church Goods

LONDON.

S. MARY, WOLNORTH $\frac{4}{96}$.

THE Certificate indented of John Reynolds, Goldsmith, and Jasper Fisher, Goldsmith, Churchwardens of the parish of St. Mary Wolnorth in Lombard Street, within the Ward of Langborne of London, made into the Lord Mayor and others our Sovereign Lord the Kings Commissioners within the City of London the 22 day of Sepr. in the sixth year of the reign of our Sovereign Lord King Edward the Sixth [1553] according to the commandment to them the said Churchwardens by the said Commissioners in articles given.

1. In primis as to the first article the said Churchwardens say that Hugh Ruck and Thomas Hancock were Churchwardens of the said Church in the first year of the reign of our said Sovereign Lord [1547.]

Item as to the second Article the same Churchwardens say that they have now in their custody and keeping belonging to the said Church All the goods plate and ornaments here under written and particularly mentioned that is to say

The Inventory of all the plate goods ornaments and bells belonging to the parish Church of St. Mary Wolnorth in Lombard Street of London.

IN THE VESTRY.

First a large chest with lock and key to the same with their parcels of plate and other things in the same as followeth.

Item a cross of silver with Mary and John all gilt and enameleyed weighing 43¾ oz.

Item a Monstrans of silver all gilt with a great birrall [beryl] in it weighing 32 oz.

Item a Pax of silver all gilt and enamiled, with a piece broken of it behind weighing 9½ oz. and ½ oz.

Item a round pix of silver with a cross broken of it all gilt weighing 4¼ oz.

Item four buttons or beades of silver parcel gilt, weighing one oz.

Item two cruetts of silver, parcel gilt weighing 7¾ oz. scant.

Item a Chalice with a patent of silver parcel gilt weighing 12¾ oz.

Item another Chalice of silver with patent parcel gilt weighing 12½ oz.

Item another Chalice of silver with a patent parcel gilt weighing 12 oz. scant.

Item the Bishops Miter garnished with silver perles and counterfet stones poized altogether 22¼ oz.

Item in broken silver 1¼ oz.

Item a Cristal garnished with gilt copper.

Item three pieces of Cristall.

Item a Crismatory of silver parcel gilt and certain oil in the same with
a string of silk to the same weighing altogether 6 oz.

Item four corpres cases of cloth of tissue and gold.

Item a sudray cloth of Turkey silk to bear the crismatory at Easter.

Item one Corporals cases of red tissue.

Item three Corporal clothes in the said cases.

Item three small pieces of cloth of gold which was parcel of St.
George's Cote.

Item a head stall of copper and gilt and enamayled for a horse.

Item three clothes which were for the Pix one of blue Sarcenet
embroided with vein of gold another of red Sarcenet with knops
of Venice gold of needlework and another of White Sarcenet.

Item a crown of copper and gilt with counterfet stones set in the same.

Item a helmet of Stele and two labels of black velvet with two buttons
of wood gilt with two tassels of silk.

Item a Cote Armor of Sarcenet paynted with Mr. Amadas arms.

Item 11 pieces of brodery work small and great which were riped off
the altar Clothes of Black Velvet.

IN A GREAT CHEST NEAR THE DESK IN THE VESTRY.

First fur [? four] vestments of red tissue complete saving a fannel of
needlework.

Item three other vestments of green cloth of Bandekin complete.

Item other vestments of white Damask complete.

Item the Scaring [? sacring] bell that was in the South Chapel.

Item two neither altar clothes of blue bokeram and three old
linen [?] clothes.

Item two hangings of black velvet for the high altar.

Item a pale cloth of black Damask with a cross of white Damask.

Item a front cloth for an altar of needlework and Bokeram.

Item 12 Corporal Cases of Cloth of gold and silk and three corporal
Clothes in the said cases.

IN THE PRESS IN THE VESTRY.

First three copies of white Damask Bokeram.

Item five copes of green Bokeram.

Item three copes of black worsted.

Item an old cope of bokeram with Tassels and byrdes.

Item an old cope of red satin with byrdes.

Item two old copes for children.

Item a sharyne [? shrine] for the Sepulture covered with cloth of
Tissue.

Item an old broken chyme which stood in St. George's Chapel.

Item a vestment of Green satin complete.

Item a vestment of red Baudekyn with a blue cross of Baudekyn.

Item a vestment and two tunycles of black worsted complete.

Item a Lenton vestment of white fustian complete.

Item another vestment of White fustian.

Item a vestment of purple sarcent with long strakes.

Item a vestment of red satin with a bordered cross of gold complete.

Item a vestment of green Bawdekyn with a cross of white Damask.

Item a vestment of red Bawdekyn with a cross of blue Bawdekyn.

Item two old vestments of green with white and red stripes.

Item a vestment of green Damask with a cross of green tissue complete.

Item a vestment of green Satin with a cross of red velvet complete.

Item a vestment of blue satin with a cross of red satin embroydered complete

Item a vestment of Red Dornick with a green cross embroydered complete

Item a vestment of blue Bawdekyn with a cross of red Bawdekyn complete.

Item a vestment of White fustian for Lent complete.

Item a vestment of red Doryck with a green cross.

Item two tunicles of old red Bawdekyn with blue crosses with fringes of silk.

Item four Albes and four Amyses of linen cloth for children.

Item seven old pillows.

Item six stayned clothes for Altars.

Item a herse cloth of red silk with a fringe of silk.

Item two stained clothes one of our Lady and the other of the Resurrection.

Item a great fire pan.

Item a double desk in the vestry with three Ambries in it.

Item six new Salter books printed in English.

Item two communion books in English.

Item a book of the Homilies.

Item a Bible and Paraphrase.

Item two old tubbes with broken glass.

Item four Cappie [? copper] stares paynted.

IN A CHEST NEXT THE VESTRY AND IN THE QUIRE.

First five towels of Diaper.

Item fifteen Altar clothes broken and hole.

Item four Altar clothes of dirap [? diaper] and two hand towels of the gift of Christopher Rainwick.

Item three empty chests.

Item a long empty chest without a key.

Item a great laten candlestick and two small and a little candlestick with two noses.

Item two Chests and a desk.

Item a pair of organs.

Item four desks upon the quire stalls with four foot spaces curtains and rods there.

Item sundry old chests about the quire and chapels.

IN THE RODE LOFT.

Item an old ship chest with pieces of old Bukeram and other trumpry in the same.

Item one other long chest with four painted banner clothes of cloth painted banner clothes of the passion of cloth eight streamers of silk stained five banners of silk stayned two cross banners of silk stained in the said chest.

Item four banner clothes and a streamer of silk stained and a white curtain of Sarcent fringed with silk and two cloths of silk with garters embroydered.

Item two painted Lenten Clothes for Altars one old great painted cloth and a painted cloth of St. George.

Item two borders of Bawdkyns fringed with silk.

Item eight painted clothes for Images and three rollars for banners.

Item a vaile for the Quire with curtain rings.

Item An old banner cloth of silk.

Item a canopy cloth and ten pendant sticks with seven pendants of silk.

Item an empty chest.

Item sixteen banner staves long and short.

Item an old pair of organs a table of wainscot and a desk of wood with a fawcoln.

Item an old settle two old books and a ladder with fourteen staves of boardes.

Item in the body of the Church two old chests with certain torches and ends of torches in the same.

Item a cuppord with a desk upon the same and two formes.

IN ST. GEORGE'S CHAPEL.

Item a Settill of Wainscott and form with a small banner staff.

Item a lantern of glass with a rack of Iron and a little seat or pew desk fashion and a piece of a tabernacle.

IN THE BELFRY.

Item a bench bord fixed and a table newly whited in a frame of wainscot.

Item in the steeple five great bells and a little bell with a clock and a chime and ropes to the same.

IN THE CLOISTERS AND CHURCHYARD.

Item a press of wainscot with 20 gilt hedds for torches and a little old chain.

Item a great coffin three coffins besides certain pieces of timber.

Item a long chest old in the schoolhouse.*

The rest of the document is too long for printing and is of no interest save that a list of vessels and vestments sold for £148 8s. 1d. is given; of the money received £60 was spent on repairs which included "pulling down of glass windows with Images," and the residue in "setting up new pews and a communion table."

---

* " 1616. To the Scole Mistress vs." Ch. Acc.

St. Mary Woolnoth.

THE Church of St. Mary Woolnoth forms a very conspicuous object in the City of London, and is situated at the apex of the angle formed by the junction of King William Street and Lombard Street. The late Bishop of London, in conversation with the present Rector, spoke of it as "the most prominent church in the City, and second in importance only to the Cathedral of St. Paul's." In this work, the history of the Church—for the very material reason given in the preface—must become a secondary matter; for the chief importance and interest of it lie in the transcription of its registers and those of the sister parish, which began more than 300 years ago, and must consequently transcend historical matter connected with the Church. NEWCOURT supplies sufficient information, an annotated copy of which will be found in the body of this work. It may here be remarked that the "Domesday Book" affords us no help, as London was exempted from the operation of its survey. In the preface in the edition by Vacher and Son there is the following extract, which seems to account for this omission : " The absence of any record of the many churches contained in it (Middlesex) may, however, be mentioned as one in which it stands nearly alone. It might be thought singular that the metropolis of the kingdom should be altogether unnoticed ; but it is understood that London and a few other chief cities were exempted from the survey by charters of immunity."

STOWE says he has " not yet learned" the reason why St. Mary's was called the Church of Our Lady of Woolnoth. Some say its name was derived from its closeness to the beam where wool was weighed in the Stocks Market, in the parish of Woolchurch Haw, and that it obtained its name from being *wool-neagh*, or *nigh ;* but Mr. Gwilt says that it may, with more probability, and with better approximation to the present orthography, be derived by the mere transposition of a single letter, from the words Wul-noht—a woolnought—as distinguishing it from the one in whose churchyard (Woolchurch) the wool-beam was actually placed. The site on which the Church is built has been for long ages dedicated to religious worship—longer, perhaps, than that of any other fabric in the kingdom. It is supposed—and with reason—that one of the earliest temples erected by the Romans in England, and dedicated to the Goddess Concordia, stood on this spot. In digging for the foundation of the present church, in 1715, some beautiful specimens of Roman pottery, bones and tusks of animals, tesselated pavement, Roman coins, and many other pieces of antiquity were discovered twenty feet below the surface , also a well, from which, when emptied, a pure and wholesome spring arose. The temple to which we have above alluded gave place in time to Christianity, and from its ruins a Christian church arose to the honour of the Blessed Virgin. In the year 1355 we have actual proof of the existence of a church on this spot, knowing, as we do, the name of its Rector at that date. This was the church which was rebuilt, of which, also, we have authentic information in 1438. Nearly 200 years later we find it was thoroughly restored and renovated, and in 1666 it was seriously damaged by the "great and dreadful fire," and was repaired again about ten years later; but this restoration does not appear to have been complete, for the old structure was entirely removed in 1715, and the present church rebuilt, finished, and opened on Easter Day, 1727, under the guidance and ingenuity of NICHOLAS HAWKES-MOOR, a pupil of Sir Christopher Wren. It is a very beautiful example of the Italian style, the interior of which is unrivalled by those of WREN himself, the instructor and master of the architect, and the defects are to be found only in detail, the chief of which, as Mr. GWILT remarks, and who is the principal authority on its architecture, is the "break in the entablature between the wider inter-columnations, yet the church has such exquisite beauties that it is irksome to dwell on its few and trifling faults." On the north side the elevation is composed of three large semi-circular rusticated niches, each standing on a lofty rusticated pedestal, relieved with blank recesses, which are repeated in the intervals below between the niches; and it may be mentioned that this side has been selected as a specimen of its order as a copy for the students at South Kensington. The three entrances at the west front are under lofty rusticated arches, through and at the sides of the tower. This is oblong and rusticated to the level of the cornice, above which is an unbroken pedestal for the support of six composite columns in the east and west elevations, and of two of the north and south sides. From this order rise two low towers, pierced and surmounted with balustrades. The South front is pierced with four semi-circular-headed windows, like the lantern in the upper storey. The whole walls are of stone, and the rustic grooves wide and deep.* The interior is very richly and beautifully decorated, and almost square, being built in the form of the Roman atrium. Twelve Corinthian columns, fluted and carrying an enriched entablature one-quarter of their height are placed three in each angle, at a distance from the walls about one-sixth of the width of the whole church; these support an entablature and clerestory above it, which latter takes the form of a large semi-circular window on each of the four sides. The ceiling is profusely ornamented with panels and carved mouldings, all in stone. The east end is recessed square for the altar-piece, under an oak baldachino, carried by two twisted columns, with Corinthian capitals.

MAITLAND says: "In Lombard Street was situate a magnificent Royal Palace, which I take to have stood in this parish, which EDWARD III., in the year 1348, conferred upon the Collegiate Church or Royal Chapel of St. Stephen, in his palace at Westminster; and on the west side of the church, and south side of Lombard Street, stood the City mansion of the Earl of Suffolk." From "Steven's History of Monasteries" (page 295), we find St. Helen's nunnery, which had the advowson of St. Mary Woolnoth, was founded 1216 (HENRY III.), dissolved Nov. 25th, 1539. The Abbey of Colchester had the advowson of St. Mary Woolchurch, dissolved in 1540. First abbot, 1104, and the last was hanged at Colchester in 1539, for refusing to acknowledge the King's supremacy. In 1638 the Rectory and glebe was worth £22 13s. 4d. Another source of revenue were two lectureships, one of which—founded by Sir MARTIN BOWES—still exists; the other—founded by Mr. WITES—is a thing of the past.

* Gwilt in loco.

In 1440 there was a crucifix in the church, with a gilded foot of hawthorn leaves, two amices of blue cloth of gold, with haws sitting on a perche.

We find mention by Stow in the old church of the following monuments, none of which are now remaining :—

Sir MARTIN BOWES, Lord Mayor, 1566.
Sir HUGH BRICE, Lord Mayor, 1485.
Sir SIMON EYRE, Lord Mayor, 1459.
Sir THOMAS RUMSEY, Lord Mayor, 1590.
Sir JOHN PERCIVAL, 1498.

Here are memorials of the family of VINER, and an inscription to the memory of Mr. JAMES HOUBLON, "who," as his descendant, Mr. PENNANT, expresses it, "was eminent for his plainness and piety," the following epitaph was composed for him by SAML. PEPYS, Esq., Secretary to the Admiralty in the reigns of CHARLES II. and JAMES II. :—

JACOBUS HOUBLON,
Londinas P.E.T.R.I. filius,
Ob fidem Flandria exulantis :
Ex. C. Nepotibus habuit LXX. superstites :
Filios V. videns mercatores florentissimos ;
Ipse Londinensis Bursæ Pater ;
Piissimè obiit Nonagenarius,
Ao. D. CLXXXII.

There are also thirteen mural tablets, only three of which are worthy of note—that of JOHN NEWTON, late Rector of the church ; that of HENRY FOURDRINIER; and that of GABRIEL SMYTH, grandson of the learned JOHN SMYTH, Esq., Nibley, Gloucestershire, the author of the lives of the Berkeleys, written in 1638.

The will of Sir JOHN PERCIVAL hangs in the church.

But we now pass on to give a short account of

THE ORGAN

THE earliest record we possess of such an instrument in the church of St. Mary Woolnoth appears from an extract from the Churchwardens' books, dated 1539, where we find the following items entered in their accounts for that and succeeding years :—

1539. Item paid to Howe the organ maker for his yearly fee ending at the said later Mychemas — iiijs.
1552. Item payd to Gregorie the Clerk for playing at the organ one whole yeare — xiijs. iiijd.
156½. Item received of Richard Tyrwhitt Vicar of Barking in Essex, the viij day of May 1562 for cijlb. of old organ pypes of lead which were viewed by John Wetherhill and Thomas Atkynson by the commandment of Sir Martyn Bowes and wayed by the prson and me, and sold for ijd. the pounde — xviijs.
156¾. Item payd to good-man Howe for ij sprynges for base pype of organ

The annual fee to JOHN HOWE from 1539 ceases in 1568. There is no mention of the organ afterwards.

1580. Oct 21. John Howe organ-maker (in 1570 "organ-player") receives a yearly fee. Sometimes he is called "Father Howe."

No mention of organ after 1570.

It would appear from these items that the then organ was a large and ancient instrument—worthy of a church which boasted of no less than three altars and a cloister, a large choir of singing clerks, chanting priests, the treble voices of many children, and a church which provided harps, garlands and lamps for seven virgins on each successive All-Hallow's Day. Probably, too, when part of it was sold, as we learn by one of the above-mentioned items, the rest of the pipes were stored away, and the case removed, though from what we can gather it is not at all improbable that some of these were utilised in the next organ by DALLAMS, and worked in again by Father SCHMIDT, and that these are now in the present one, having every appearance of rich decoration, careful diapering, and great age.

There is very little doubt but that, during the time of the Great Rebellion, almost everything, in the shape of ornamental church furniture, or what was interesting to the antiquarian and ecclesiologist, was ruthlessly mutilated or destroyed, and that this organ, to which we have alluded, shared the common fate of all things ecclesiastical. Soon after the restoration, when choral services were about to be revived, it was found that only four organ builders existed in this country, viz., DALLAMS, of London; LOOSEMORE, of Exeter; THAMAR, of Peterborough; and PRESTON, of York, the first-named of which, ROBERT DALLAMS, supplied the new organ for St. Mary's. It was this same DALLAMS—"Citizen and Blacksmith of London"—who built the large organ in York Minster, which was burnt in 1829.

But ROBERT DALLAMS' organ was not long destined to lead the praises of the worshipping congregation at St. Mary's, for it was almost irretrievably injured by the Great Fire of 1666. It then became palpably necessary to supply a new one. The four English builders were unable to meet all the demands of the country, and we find that premiums were offered to foreign builders to come and settle in London. Amongst the first and best of these were BERNARD SMITH (commonly called Father SCHMIDT), a German, who came to this country at the latter part of the 17th century; also RENATUS HARRIS, a Frenchman, tempted, no doubt, by the same ambitious spirit as his German rival. Their memorable contest respecting the Temple organ is well known; for a whole twelvemonth the battle continued, until the Lord Chief Justice JEFFRIES, who was appointed arbitrator, decided in favour of SCHMIDT. It may here be remarked that altogether SCHMIDT erected thirty-eight organs in England, amongst which were those of Durham and St. Paul's. In 1680 subscriptions were invited, from the parishioners and others, to procure a new organ, which SCHMIDT built during the year 1681; but it is probable that in building the new one, he made use of some, if not all, of the pipes contained in the old, as there are certain marks on some of them to prove it. There is another reason—SCHMIDT has always been credited with being most particular in making and finishing his pipes, especially those made of wood; and it so happens that the pipes of the stop diapason now in the organ (wood) are very roughly made; some also of the pipes of the principal (great organ) have traces of diaper work upon them, and the feet are of various lengths, showing that they were the front pipes of some previous organ. The pipes of these two stops below FF are of another make, so that was probably the lowest note of the one made by DALLAMS. SCHMIDT's organ had only one manual of what was termed short octaves, and the keys black-whites and white-blacks ; but it must have been a very good one of its kind, and with such a full complement of stops it must have produced a very fine chorus effect. It may here be remarked that this must have been the identical organ that JOHN READING (formerly organist of Winchester Cathedral, and composer of the celebrated old tune known as the Portuguese Hymn) played upon, as he was organist of St. Mary Woolnoth in the year 1682. The organ must have remained in its original state till about fifty years since, when it had a second manual added to it.

About the year 1850 the organ was greatly altered and modernised. New and complicated movements were added to SCHMIDT's action, which was old and worn, the result being that it was often out of order till the year 1868, when it was put into the hands of Messrs. GRAY and DAVISON to be reconstructed, at a cost of about £190. They, however, quite altered the rich old tone, by first taking certain stops out, and then putting on a heavier pressure of wind to make up. In 1875-6, when the church underwent a thorough re-arrangement, the organ was again altered, and its position changed.

The original organ stood in a small arch on the north side, over the tomb of Sir MARTIN BOWES, and underneath bore this inscription : "This organ was built by Father SCHMIDT in 1681."

Churchwardens

OF ST. MARY WOOLNOTH.

1539. John Gardyner, *Goldsm.*—John Robson, *Marchant Talyor.*
1540. John Robson, *Taillor*—George Webbe, *Goldsmith.*
1541. George Webbe—Stephen Hawkins, *Peuterer.*
1542. Stephen Hawkins—George Tadlove, *Habyrdassher.*
1543. George Tadlove—Christofer Salmon. *Barbourd Surgion.*
1544. Xrofer Salmon—William Humble, *Goldsmith.*
1545. William Humble—Hugh Ruck, *Scryvaner.*
1546. Hugh Ruck—Thomas Hancok, *Vynter.*
1547 Thomas Handcock—Thomas Wetherhill, *Goldsmyth.*
1548. Thomas Wetherhill—James Cross, *Goldsmythes.*
1549. James Crosse—James Stavely, *Vyntener.*
1550. James Staveley—John Reynolde.
1551. John Reynold—Jasper Fissher.
1552. Jasper Ffisher—Henry Boshall, *Goldsmythes.*
1553. Henry Bossall—John Keyll, *Goldsmythes.*
1554. John Keyle—Edward Sclater, *Haberdasher.*
1555. Edward Slater—Thomas Atkynson, *Scryvener.*
1556. Thomas Atkynson, *wryter of the news letter of London.*
1557. Thomas Atkynson and Thomas Wytton, *Wryters of the Courte letter of the citie of London.*
1558. Thomas Wytton—Robert Ffrier, *Goldsmyth.*
1559. Robert Ffryer —William Tracie, *Merchant Taylor.*
1560. Thomas Muschampe—Thomas Kelinge *Goldsmythes.*
1561. Thomas Kelinge—Robert Tailbushe, *Goldsmythes.*
1562. Robert Tayleboyes—William Abraham, *Vyntener.*
1563. William Abram—John Kettelwodd, *Goldsmyth.*
1564. John Kettylwoode—John Pekeryng, *Habberdasher.*
1565. John Pyckering—John Myiles.
1566. Robert Talboyes—Humfreye Stevens, *Goldsmythes.*
1567. Humfrey Stevyns—Edward Sutton, *Stacyoner.*
1568. Edwarde Sutton—Cuteberte Buckle, *Vyntener.*
1569. Cuthberte Buckell—Francis Barnarde, *Cooke.*
1570. Ffrancice Barnarde—Thomas Corbett, *Skynner.*
1571. Thomas Corbett—Thomas Watte, *Haberdasher.*
1572. Thomas Watte—Rowland Okeover, *Merchant Taylor.*
1573. Rowlande Okeover—William Charles, *Weaver.*
1574. William Charles—Hugh Keale, *Goldsmyth.*
1575. Hugh Keyle—Ffrancis Kydd, *Writer of the Courte letter of the citie of London.*
1576. Francis Kidd—George Kevall [or Revall] *Writer of the Courte letter of the citie of London.*
1577. George Kevall [or Revall]—William Cocknedge, *Goldsmyth.*
1578. William Cocknedge—Thomas Simpson, *Goldsmyths.*
1579. Thomas Simpson—Richard Offeley, *Merchant Tailors.*

1580. Richard Offley—Roger Tasker, *Goldsmith.*
1581. Roger Tasker—George Newbolde, *Goldsmythes.*
1582. George Newbold—Rowland Broughton, *Haberdasher.*
1583. Rowland Broughton—William Warde.
1584. William Warde—John Wilkyns.
1585. John Wilkyns—Clemente Webster.
1586. Clemente Webster—John Beaver.
1587. John Beaver—Nicholas Style.
1588. Nicholas Style—Patteryck Brewe.
1589. Pattrick Brewe—John Alderson.
1590. John Alderson—Henry Butler.
1591. Henry Butler—Willyam Franck.
1592. Willyam Franck—Edward Griffin.
1593. Edward Griffeth—Thomas Clarke.
1594. Thomas Clarke—Giles Simpson.
1595. Giles Simpson—John Leak.
1596. John Leake—George Samwell.
1597. George Samwell—Thomas Francknell—Richard Brooke.
1598. Richard Brooke—Richard Hadley—John Blakmore.
1599. John Blackmore—Ralphe Conyers.
1600. Ralphe Coniers—Franncis Shute.
1601. Franncis Shute—John Kerby.
1602. John Kirby—Simeon Sedgwick.
1603. Simeon Sedgwick—Thomas White.
1604. Thomas White—Richard Harrison.
1605. Richard Harrison—Simeon Sedgwick.
1606. Richard Harrison—William Dutton.
1607. William Dutton, *Haberdasher*—Richard Cheney, *Goldsmith.*
1608. Richard Cheney—Robert Mildmay, *Grocer.*
1609. Robert Mildmay—John Sudbury, *Leatherseller.*
1610. John Sudbury—Thomas Laurance, *Goldsmith.*
1611. Thomas Lawrence—Willyam Hamor, *Cloth Worker.*
1612. William Hamore—Charles Glascocke.
1613. Charles Glascocke—John Cote.
1614. John Cot—William Tirrey, *Goldsmith.*
1615. Willyam Tirrey, *Goldsmith*—Thomas Titeradge, *Grocer.*
1616. Thomas Tickeridge—William Sayle, *Marchant Taylor.*
1617. William Sayles—John Aston, *Goldsmith.*
1618. John Aston—George Humble, *Lether Seller.*
1619. George Humble—William Wood, *Goldsmith.*
1620 William Wood—Richard Ockould, *Stationer.*
1621. Paul Furrey—William Rolfe, *Goldsmith.*
1622. William Rolfe—Edward White, *Grocer.*
1623. Edward White—John Hill, *Goldsmith.*
1624. John Hill—George Bromley, *Grocer.*
1625. George Bromley—Walter Furser, *Goldsmith.*
1626. Walter Furser—Francis Chapman, *Goldsmith.*
1627. Francis Chapman—Raph King, *Vintner.*
1628. Raph King—Emanuel Castleman.
1629. Emanuel Castleman—Henry Blackmere.
1630. Henry Blackmere—Peter Sadler.
1631. Peter Sadler—Michaell Gardener.
1632. Michael Gardener—Thomas Vinor.
1633. Thomas Vinor—Adrian Evans.
1634. Adrian Evans—Samuel Dey.
1635. Samuel Dey—Henry Wollaston.

1636. Henry Wollaston—Thomas Willet.
1637. Thomas Willett—Bartholomew Gilman.
1638. Bartholomew Gilman—Roger Daniell.
1639. Roger Daniell—Thomas Nevett.
1640. Thomas Nevett—Richard Briggenshaw.
1641. Richard Briggenshaw—Anthony Pennystone.
1642. Henry Stutter—William White.
1643. William White—Charles Lathum.
1644. Charles Lathum—Thomas Watson.
1645. Thomas Watson—William Hubberd.
1646. William Hubberd—Alexander Holt.
1647. Alexander Holt—Francis Bishop.
1648. Francis Bishop—William Sanky.
1649. William Sankey.
1650. Alexander Pollington.
1651. Abraham Johnson, *Merchant*.
1652. John Steele, *Vintner*.
1653. Richard Butler.
1654. Samuell Moore.
1655. Hugh Gough.
1656. Nathanioll Cocke.
1657. Abraham Clarke.
1658. Clement Perry, *Goldsmith*.
1659. Samuell White.
1660. John Portman, *Upper Church Warden*.
1661. Thomas Canham.
1662. Robert Jones—Thomas Collet.
1663. John Shipman—Samuel Paine.
1664. John Sayer.
1665. Daniell Morris.
1666. Samuel Simonds.
1667. }
1668. } [*sic.*]
1669. John Colville—Samuell Simonds.
1670. Samuel Simonds—George Dixon.
1671. George Dixson—Michaell Weareing.
1672. Michael Weareing—Thomas Mottershed.
1673. Thomas Mottershed—William Gloster.
1674. William Gloster.
1675. Edmund Rolfe—Thomas Seymour.
1676. Thomas Seymour—Godfrey Beck.
1677. Godfrey Beck—Austin Ballow.
1678. Thomas Foley—Godfrey Bock.
1679. Godfrey Bock—Augustine Ballowe.
1680. Augusine Ballowe—Laurence Weld.
1681. Laurence Weld—Alexander Pollington.
1682. Alexander Pollington—Capt. John Hilman.
1683. Capt. John Hillman—John Hayward.
1684. Philip Scarth—Peter White.
1685. Peter White.
1686. Theophilus Dorrington.
1687. Theophilus Dorrington—John Jones.
1688. John Jones—Daunil Perkins.
1689. Daniel Perkins—John Coleman.
1690. John Coleman—Edward Gladwin.
1691. Bernard Eates—Johathan Miles.

1692. Jonathan Miles or Bernard Eates—Thomas Haywood.
1693. Jonathan Miles—Richard Guy.
1694. Richard Guy—John Sutton.
1695. Thomas Haywood—William Denny.
1696. John Sutton—Jeremy Stoakes.
1697. William Denny—Thomas Paine.
1698. Jeremiah Stoakes—Joseph Cozens.
1699. Joseph Cozens—James St. John.
1700. James St. John—Edward Drayner.
1701. Edward Drayner—Robert Batho.
1702. John Back—Edward Lloyd.
1703. Edward Lloyd—George Cooke.
1704. George Cook—Richard Mottershed.
1705. Peter Robinson—John Wellings.
1706. John Wellins—George Seigner.
1707. John Wellins—Ralph Gerrard.
1708. John Wellins—Robert Lowth.
1709. Robert Lowth—Richard Godman.
1710. Richard Godman—William Barwell.
1711. William Barwell—Stephen Ram.
1712. Stephen Ram—William Byrch.
1713. William Byrch—Thomas Tax.
1714. Thomas Tax—John Barker.
1715. Thomas Tax—Edward Meakins.
1716. Thomas Tax—Edward Meakins.
1717. Thomas Tax—Edward Meakins.
1718. Edward Parker—John Berney.
1719. John Berney—James Thomason.
1720. James Thomason—Thomas Falkingham.
1721. Thomas Falkingham—John Tipping.
1722. John Tipping—Thomas Tax.
1723. Thomas Tax.
1724. Thomas Tax—William Collins.
1725. William Collins—William Lowe.
1726. William Lowe—Joseph Lawe.
1727. William Lowe—Joseph Lawe.
1728. William Lawe—George Dawson.
1729. George Dawson—Samuel Cooke.
1730. William Stevens—Samuel Gibson.
1731. Samuel Gibson— Michael Cheltenham.
1732. Michael Cheltenham—Stephen Wiggin.
1733. Stephen Wiggin—Claude Edet.
1734. Claude Edet—John Martindale.
1735. John Martindale—John Best.
1736. John Best—Thomas Taft.
1737. Thomas Taft—John Edwards.
1738. John Edwards—Valentine Meaykin.
1739. Valentine Meaykin—Castle Thorpe.
1740. Castle Thorpe—Francis Collins.
1741. Francis Collins—Jacob Bell.
1742. John Best—Benjamin Wilding.
1743. Benjamin Wilding—Thomas Geary.
1744. Thomas Geary—William Barton.
1745. William Barton—John Smith.
1746. John Smith—William Cooke.
1747. William Cooke—William Webster.

1748. Joseph Wilson—John Langley.
1749. John Langley—William Collins.
1750. William Baker—John Beecroft.
1751. John Beecroft—Thomas Blamire.
1752. Thomas Blamire—William Mannings.
1753. William Mannings—John Waring.
1754. Jacob Marsh—John Boultby.
1755. John Griffith—Samuell Wood.
1756. Samuell Wood—Henry Quantilo.
1757. Henry Quantilo—John Attleborough.
1758. John Attleborough—James Waugh.
1759. James Waugh—Samuel Tucker.
1760. James Waugh—William Lawe.
1761. William Lawe—John Seymour.
1762. John Seymour—Robert Jones.
1763. Robert Jones—Walter Watkins.
1764. James Peto—Henry Fourdrinier.
1765. Henry Fourdrinier—Robert Todd.
1766. Robert Todd—John Gill
1767. John Gill—Benjamin Ray.
              (Imbezzled money and absconded.)
1768. Benjamin Ray.*
1769. Job Peachey—Rowland Stephenson.
1770. Rowland Stephenson—Christopher Corrall.
1771. Christopher Corrall—John Nightingale.
1772. John Nightingale—Peter Cargill.
1773. Peter Cargill—Richard Ayton Lee.
1774. Richard Ayton Lee—William Ayton.
1775. William Ayton—Thomas Dickens.
1776. Thomas Dickens—George Aubery.
1777. George Aubery—William Meadows.
1778. John Lewis—John Moffatt.
1779. John Moffatt—Richard Sillitoe.
1780. Richard Sillitoe—Joseph Monk.
1781. Joseph Monk—Thomas Blackford.
1782. Thomas Blackford—William Webster.
1783. John Fook—Richard Wynne.
1784. Richard Wynne—Robert Shuttleworth.
1785. Robert Shuttleworth—Henry Morrow.
1786. Henry Morrow—Nathaniel Phillips.
1787. Nathaniel Phillips—Miles Salterthwaite.
1788. Miles Salterthwaite—James Looker.
1789. James Looker—John Griffin.
1790. John Griffin—William Martin.
1791. William Martin—Owen Wynne.
1792. Owen Wynne—William Collins.
1793. William Collins—William Clarke.
1794. William Clarke—Richard Rankin.
1795. Richard Rankin—William Staddon Blake.
1796. William Staddon Blake—William Gibson.
1797. William Gibson—Richard Pugh.
1798. Richard Pugh—Richard Webster.
1799. Richard Webster—William Remington.
1800. William Remington—George Foote.

* It appears that Benjamin Ray was sole churchwarden in this year; this would partially account for the embezzlement of the church's funds

APPENDIX.

Since going to press we have fallen upon some additional information concerning St. Mary Woolnoth. As we are not able to embody it in our notes we subjoin references and abstract. Harl. MSS. 877. (Catalogue of Harl. MSS. vol. I, pp. 466, 467.)

i. Charter of foundacion of Nokets Chantry with two Chaplains William Caccheymayde Rector.—23. Ric. ij. (A.D. 1400.) (fo. 1.)

ij. Will of Emma Megre wife of late John Megre Citizen and Pewterer—legacy for maintaining "duos Torticios cere ponderis utriusq 13 Librorum ad standum in duobus Magnis Candelabris de Auricalco in summo choro . . . . coram summo Altare" also "tres cereos ardentes coram Imagine Sti Johannis Baptiste et alios tres cereos ardentes coram Imagine Sti Johannis Evangeliste."—A.D. 1435. (fo. 5b.)

iij. Will of John Megre Citizen and Pewterer. Legacy for the sustenance of two Chaplains to say masses for the soul of the said John Megre Emma his wife and their children. One priest at St. Mary Woolnoth the other at the Parish Church of St. Mary Trerewe Cornwall.—1419. (fo. 12.)

iv. Further Legacies of John Megre. (fo. 17.)

v. Indenture between Churchwardens and Sir Nicholas Savage Chantery Preste of the Chauntrye of Thomas Nokett witnessing delivery divers jewells &c. of the same Chauntrey.—A.D. 1440. (fo. 18b.)

vi. Will of Thomas Nokett "Civis et Pannarius."—A.D. 1396. (fo. 19.)

viii. Will of Sir Hugh Bryce Knight Alderman and Goldsmith mentions "the late Sir Symonde Eire and other well disposed persons being a guild or fraternity."—A.D. 1492. (fo. 21.)

viij. Will of Dame Elizabeth Bryce (widow of Sir Hugh Bryce) legacy for maintenance of two obits for ever, one in the Church of St. Mary Woolnoth; the other in the Parish Church of Ruston in Com : Ebor.—A.D. 1498. (fo. 30b.)

𝕬𝖈𝖈𝖔𝖚𝖓𝖙

OF THE

PARISH of ST. MARY WOOLCHURCH HAW,

Extracted from Newcourt's Repertorium Ecclesiasticum Parochiale
Londinense from the Conquest to A.D. 1700. London 1708.

St. Mary Woolchurch Rectory *(page 459)*.

THIS Church of *St. Mary* (which is a Rectory) stood near the *Stocks* in *Walbrook* Ward, and was called *St. Mary Woolchurch* of a beam placed in the Church yard which was thereof called *Woolchurch Haw* of the weighing of wool there used. And to the verifying of this, *Stow* tells us, that he found among the Customs of *London* written in French, in the reign of *Edward* ij a chapter entitled *Les Custoines de Woolchurch Haw*, wherein is set down what was there to be paid for every parcel of Wool weighed, which Custom there continued till the 6th of Ric. ij *John Churchmom* then building the Custom House upon the *Wool Key* to serve for that use. `Sto. Sur. 224.`

This Church (I guess) was built about the Conquerors time by one *Hubert de Ria*, Father of *Eudo*, Steward of the Household to King *William* the Conqueror, and Founder of the Abbey of St. *John*, in Colchester; for I find in the said *Eudo's* Charter of Foundation and Endowment of that Abbey, he gives to it *(inter Alia)* this Church by the name of *St. Mary de Westcheping, London quæ vocatur Niewecherche*, in these words viz., " Et Ecclesiam St. Mariæ de Westcheping, London quœ vocatur Niewecherche, concedente *Ailwardo Grosso* Presbytero, qui in eadem Ecclesia ct donatione Antecessoris mei *Huberti de Ria* Personatum consecutus fuerat." So that *Ailward* the Priest having this Church by the Gift of *Hubert de Ria*, it is plain, that the said *Hubert* was Patron thereof, and probably the Founder too, by its being then called *New Church*, as if then newly built. And hence, I think, that the *Street* which lies between *Cheapside* and *Cornhill*, and is now called the Poultry was in those days part of *Cheapside* or that which was then called *West Cheping*, on the South side of the upper end of which this Church stood. `Mon. Augl. 2 vol. 893.`

As this Church was given to the Abbot and Convent of *Colchester* by the said Founder of the said Abbey, so, for ought appears to the contrary, they continued Patrons thereof till their Suppression, upon which it came to the Crown and hath remained in it ever since. It is subject to the Archdeacon, saving only as to Wills and Administrations, which belong to the Commissary. `Archid. Com. Lon.`

ST. MARY WOOLCHURCH HAW.

Sto. Sur. 224. This was a reasonable fair and large Church and was new built by License granted in the 20th *Hen.* vi. with condition to be built 15 foot from the *Stocks Market* for sparing of Light to the said *Stocks.*

Ibedem. The Parson of this Church was to have four Marks the year for Tythes of the said *Stocks,* paid him by the Masters of the *Bridge House* by a Special Decree made 2 *Hen.* vii.

Ibidem. *John Wingar,* Grocer, Mayor of this City in 1504 was a great Helper to the building of this Church and was buried in 1505. He gave unto it by his Testament two large Basons in silver and £20 in Gold.

Ibidem. *Richard Shore,* Draper, one of the Sheriffs in 1505, was a great Benefactor to this Church in his Life time, and by his Testament gave £20 to make a porch at the westend thereof, and was there buried. The Church was richly repaired and beautified in 1629.

Tunstall 15. Here was a perpetual Chantry founded in the Chapel of *St. Nicholas* the Bishop and Confessor by *Ann Cawood* widow about the beginning of the Reign of King *Henry* viij of which the Parson and Parishioners were Patrons.

Sion. Coll. MS. In 1636 the yearly profits of this Church were returned as followeth—

	£	s.	d.
Tyths	50	16	06
Glebe	22	13	04
Casualties	13	06	08

This Church being burnt down in the late dreadful Fire, is since united to that of *St. Mary Woolnoth* which is made the Parochial Church for the Inhabitants of both the Parishes; but the site of this Church and also of the Churchyard are laid into the *Stocks Market* Place. And the profits of both these Churches in lieu of Tyths, are made of the yearly value of £160 to the Incumbent.

Reg. Lon. In 1693 the Churchwardens say in the Presentment, that they believe there was a Parsonage House belonging to the Rector before the same was burnt down in the late daeadful fire. And the present Rector says that he receives £16 12s. 4d. *per ann.* That the Glebe in 1636 was £22 13s. 4d. as above.

Onera hujus Ecclesiæ	£	s.	d.
Primitæ	18	13	04
Decimæ	01	17	04
Proc Episc	00	10	00
Proc Archid	00	4	00

xliv

Rectores.

Braybrooke.	8.	*a.*	John Dyne.	PATRONI.

Braybrooke. 8. *a.* John Dyne.   PATRONI.
8.   Will Tankervyle, pr 29 April 1382, per ref. Dync.
40.   Rob. Bolton, pr Nov. 1385, per mort Tankervyle.
44. *b.* Joh. Wyles, 23 Maii 1386.
84.   Will de Ragenhyll, 17 Feb. 1390, per ref. Wyles.
c. Ric. Chaundler.
Wal. P Fit. 12.   John Skypton, pr 9 Oct. 1432, per mort Chandler.
d. Ric. Chester.
Gilbert. 77. *e.* Rob. Kyrkham, 25 Maii 1447, per ref. Chester.   Abb. et Conv. St. Joh. Baptista Colchester.
7.   Tho. Knyght, D.B., 26 Jan. 1450, per ref. Kyrkham.
Kemp. 32. *f.* Joh. Bewet, 9 Jul. 1454, per ref. Knyght.
g. John Archer.
Hill. 50.   John Cowcd, D.B., 25 Dec. 1504, per mort Archer.
Fitzjames. 72. *h.* Will Capon, 9 Maii 1517, per mort Cowerd.
Stokesley. 16. *i.* Sim. Mathew, al. Cower, S.T.B., 1 Feb. 1532, per ref. Cap.
k. Galfr. Jones.
Bonner. 449.   Tho. Goldsborough, pr. 22 March, March 1554 per dep. Jones.   Mar. Reg. A.
113.   Tho. Jenkynson, cl. 22 Feb. 1559, per mort. ult. Rec.
280. *l.* John Hayward, A.M., 10 Jan. 1593, per mort Jenkynson.   Eliz. Reg. A.
*   Ric. Crooke.
106. *m.* Will Fuller, cl. 30 July 1641, per mort ult. Rec.
Laud. 107. *n.* Joh. Tireman, S.T.B., 16 Dec. 1641, per ref. Fuller.   Car. i. R.A.
116.   Joh. Whateley, cl. 9 Feb. 1645, per ref. ult. Rectoris.
o. ——— Ball, S.T.P.
Henchman. 17. *p.* Car. Mason, S.T.P., 15 Junii 1661, per ref. Ball.   Car. ii. R.A.

Pro cœteris vid St. Mary Woolnoth cum hœc Ecclesia est Annexa.

a. John Dyne [vid S. Alphege inter Rec.]
b. John Wyles [vid Purley Essex inter Rec.]
c. Ric. Chaundler [vid St. Nic. Acon. (Lond.) Laverpawe (Essex) inter Rec.]
d. Ric. Chester [vid inter Præb de Twyford.]
e. Rob. Kyrkham [vid inter Præb de Browneswood.)
f. Joh. Bewet [vid St. Margaret Lothbury, inter Rec.]
g. Joh. Archet [vid. S. Mary Abchurch, inter Rec.]
h. Will Capon [vid Barkway (Herts) inter Rec.]
i. Sim Mathew al. Cower [vid Præb de Sneating.]
k. Galf. Jones [vid St. Swithin London Stone, Notly Alba (Essex) inter Incumb.]
l. Joh. Hayward [vid Stepney (Mid.) inter Rec.]
* Ric. Crooke was Rector here in 1636 when the yearly profits were returned.
m. Will Fuller—whether he was the same as *Dr. Will Fuller* who was Vicar at *St. Giles Without Cripplegate*, I am not certain. If he was you may see more of him there.
n. John Tireman was for his Loyalty forced to forsake this Church in the late Rebellion [Mere Ruft. 225] vid Grandborough in Decand St. Albani inter vic.
o. ———Ball was (if I mistake not) of the University of Cambidge. He was Preacher in this Church towards the latter end of *Oliver Cromwell's* usurpation, and was much followed by the Loyal Party. After the Death of *Dr. Mathew Griffith* he was made Master of the *Temple*.
o. Car. Mason [vid inter Præb de Portpool,]

[End of Newcourt's Notes.]

THE following Notes are given to supplement Newcourt's List of Rectors and his notes thereon.

1395. John Dyne, Rector of "Sci Nichi ad Maceti" (St. Nicholas Shambles) in 1395. Rector of St. Alphege, 1396. Rector of St. Leonard, Eastcheape, 1413.

1385. William Tankervyle. His Will was proved in 1385. Archd. Crt of London.

1393. William de Ragenhyll is mentioned in 1393 in the Will of Petronilla de Middelburgh, and again in 1403 in the Will of Bechefonte, Rector of St. Stephen, Walbrooke.

1425. Richard Chandler is mentioned in the Will of ——Coldred, 1425.

1436. John Brooke, Brewer, Henry Skete and others, Grocers, Parishioners, devise land situated in Walbrook to John White, Chaplain.

1442. An old engraving exists of a broken slab on which is a floriated cross with arms of equal length and an inscription partly destroyed

Johes   Sturg *
Emanuel
iiij^o May a^o m^o cccc^o xlij
Fundata

the stone measured about 12 inches in height and 8 inches in width, at the foot of the engraving is the following :

"In digging the foundation of the Mansion House for the Lord Mayor of London in April 1739, a stone with this Devise and Inscription was taken out of the Remains of St. Mary Woolchurch which was destroyed by the general conflagration in 1666."

The engraving is, I am informed, to be met with in some of the Histories of London, but all trace of the stone has disappeared.

1442. John Skypton—his Will is dated 1442—directs to be buried in the Chapel of St. Nicholas.

1479. 1459, Mr. Robert Silvester "Parish Priest," is mentioned in the Will of J. Bonde.

1477. John Benet is mentioned in the Wills of Elizabeth Percyvale, 1477, and J. Clerk, 1479.

1516-7 John Cornard—his Will is dated 151⁶⁄₇—directs to be buried in the Quyre. Makes a bequest to the Abbot of Colchester who had presented him to the Rectory of St. Nicholas, Colchester.

1550. William Capon, S.T.P., Rector of North Stoneham, Hants, appears to have founded a School at Southampton. John, Bishop of Salisbury, was his Brother. He held the livings of Symsborough, Berkeley Harness, St. Mary Southampton, and Duxford, Co. Cambridge, and was Master of Jesus College, Cambridge, from 1516 to 1546, when he resigned it. His Will is dated 1550.

1545.	In the Will of —— Bettenson, 1545, these words occur: "Per me Johannem Cardon Eucharisticœ Servum ac Curatum Ecclesiœ."
	Thomas Jenkynson, Will proved April, 1594. Robert Browne, Executor.
1619.	John Hayward. Administration 14 Jan., 1619. Relict Mary.
1619.	John Crooke, "Parson here." Will of Cornelius Fish, 1619.
1633.	Nathaniel Bernard, Preacher at St. Mary Woolchurch Sta. Pa. Dom. Ser.
1641.	"And for that some good part of my poore labours for many yeres hath byn bestowed in Woolchurch in London I will my body be buried in the Chancel there," Will of John Croke, "Professor of Divinitie and Bencher Grayes Inn," 1598.
1641.	William Fuller. Will 1641. His wife Mary, Executrix.
1684.	Richard Ball, see Will of J. Gosson, 1658; perhaps the same as Richard Ball, Master of the two Societies of the Temple, whose Will is dated 1684.

Chantry Certificates

MIDDLESEX ROLL 34 NO. 36.

Primo die Januarij anno Primo RR Edward vjti.

The paroche of St. Mary Woolchurchaw.

Sciz.

Anne Cawoode gave unto the parsonne and churche Wardens there to the fynginge of a prest to singe for her soule for ever all her Landes and tenements of the yerelie valew of viij*li.* whereof

In quiterentes yerelie	xx*s.*	
To Henrie Cockes prest	vj*li.* xvj*s.* viij*d.*	⎫
Spent at th obbit	ij*s.* viij*d.*	⎬ viij*li.* iij*s.* iiij*d.*
To the poore yerelie	iiij*s.*	⎭
And then Remayneth clere	*nil.*	

Roger Barlow gave unto the same parsonne and churche wardens to fynde a prest to singe for his soule for ever one tenement in the paroche of St. Mighelle in Cornhill by yere lxvj*s.* viij*d.*

Spent towards the findinge of Cawoods prest.

Walter Wenlock Bennet Cornewall Margaret Cornewall Willyam Wyken gave unto the same parsonne and churchwardens to the fyndenge of a prest one Annual rent goinge out of an entry in the paroche of St. Marye Wolnoth by yere lxvj*s.* viij*d.* one tenement in the paroche aforesaid liij*s.* iiij*d.* one shop within the paroche aforesaid lxvj*s.* viij*d.* one tenement in the paroche of St. Michell in Cornehill xlvj*s.* viij*d.* in all by yere xv*li.* viij*s.* iiij*d.* whereof

To Sir Lawrence Hay prest	vj*li.* xiij*s.* iij*d.*	⎫
Spent at th obbit	ij*s.* viij*d.*	⎬ vij*li.* vj*s.* viij*d.*
To the poore	x*s.* viij*d.*	⎭

And then Remaynethe clere viij*li.* vj*s.* viij*d.* towards the separation of the tenements.

Edwarde Culpeper gave unto the same parsonne and Churche wardens to the mayntennce of a Lampe there one Annual rent goinge out of dyvars tenementes in the paroche of St. Marye Wolchurche by yere ix*s.* not paid these viii yeres last past.

The Master of the bridgehouse paid yerelie to the parsonne and churche wardens aforesaid for the kepinge of an obite for Cristyan Manten and Sustenation of the poore by yere xij*s.* iiij*d.* inde to the poore x*s.* viij*d.*

William Swayne payethe yerelie to the same parsonne and churchewardens for the keping of an obite x*s.* inde to the poore vj*s.* viij*d.*

Memor^{D.}

There ys of howselinge people within the saide paroche the nombre of ccclx.

Sir Gryffyth Jones ys parsonne of the same Churche and the yerelie valew of same ys xviij*li.* xiij*s.* iiij*d.* and the same parsonne hathe hired one Nichas Audley to helpe to serve the Cure there with him and unto all the resydewe of Articles there ys nothinge to answere.

Extracts

From the CHURCHWARDENS' BOOKS OF
ST. MARY WOOLCHURCH HAWE.

The volume commences with the year 1560, Thomas Alen, Citizen and
Pewterer of London being Churchwarden.

1560

Item received for a Challis and Picks weying xxi oz at iiijs xd the oz sum	v*li*. xxiii*d*.
Item paid to Powell Myldred Conduct for his wage due at Christmas	v*li*. vis. viij*d*.
Item paid to William Comport Conduct for his wage due at Christmas	iij*li*. iij*d*.
Item paid to William Ryddell for ij bookes of Salmes	ijs.
Item paid for a Booke of the Articles	iiij*d*.
Item paid for the Commandments and another booke sent unto us by my Lorde of London	xvi*d*.
Item paid for a frame for the Commandments	ijs.
Item paid the xxix daye of March for making the Arber in the Churchyarde	xvi*d*.
Item paid to Richard Martyn Goldsmith for a Communyon Cuppe weinge xxix oz at vis ij*d* the oz sum	ix*li*. xxiij*d*.
Item paid for taking awaye the holy water stone and mending of the rose of the water in the Allye	viij*d*.
Item paid for carryinge of the Tymber of the Roodlofte into the churchyarde	viij*d*.
Item paid for Holy and Ivy against Christmas	iiij*d*.

[N.B.—The above charge occurs nearly every year.]

Item paid the xxv daye of January for vij ells of Holland cloth to make Mr. parsonne a surples of at xx*d* the ell	xis. viii*d*.
Item paid to Mr. Bullock the xxth day of Marche for wryting of the Scriptures and paynting of the church	iiij*li*. vijs.

1562

Item paid to the Sumner for the prayer that ys read after the Letany	ij*d*.
Item paid to the Sumnar for the bryngyng of the Comyssion for the vewe of strangers	iiij*d*.

1563

Item paid to Father Howe organ maker	is.
Item paid for the Booke of praier in the plage time the iij daye of Auguste	vi*d*.

Item paid for a Booke of the Omilies the v daye of
Auguste — iiij*s.* viij*d.*
Item for iij Bookes of Thankesgevynge after the plage — iij*d.*

1567

Item for the makinge of iiij greate Cowshins lyned with
Satten of Brydges — ii*s.* viij*d.*

1568

Item for articles from my Lord Byshopp for the Inquery
of Straungers — ij*d.*

1569

Item for a booke of Omelies against the rebells — viij*d.*

1570

Item paid for ringing the bells when the Queens Majestie
throughe the citie to the Royall Exchange — vii*d.*

1575

Item paid for a carpette for ye Communion Tabell — xvij*d.*

1576

Paid for viij lbs of corde for the Sayntus Bell the some of — xxi*d.*
Paid for ij new roopes for ij of the bells — v*s.* iiij*d.*
Paid for shootinge and mendinge the other iij roopes
the some of — xij*d.*

1580

Item to Mr. Kyrbie glasier for new scowring the olde
glasse and putting in new glasse for the paynted and
to furnish with newe wheare it lacketh and newe
leadinge wheare it needeth — viij*li.* x*s.*

1583

Paid for breade and drinke for the ringers the 17 of
November last — i*s.* iiij*d.*
Paid for a praier booke for that day — ij*d.*
Paid for ij sacks of greate coles for goodwife Newton — i*s.* vij*d.*
Paid to a freemason in recompence of stones caste of
the church walls — iiij*s.*

1585

Item for setting about the [newly cast] bell the yeare of
our Lord the parson and churchwardens names — iij*s.* iiij*d.*
Item for a coffyne for the churche — vi*s.*

1586

Paid to John Franklyn in Powles churchyard for xii lether buckites	i*li. xs.*
Paid for paynting of the buckites the name of the churche and the churchwardens names	ij*s. vid.*
Paid for xij wodden pines to hange the buckites on for naylles	i*s. iiijd.*
Paid to Thomas Addames dwellynge in the Duches place for cuttinge and bindinge upe of all the trees in the churchyard	viij*s.*
Paid to the ringers on the Daye after the Quen of Scotes was put to dethe	viij*d.*

1587

Item paide for carriage of an Irish woman into Fynsburie feildes who was delivered of a childe under the Stockes   allowed out of poors box.

1588

Item paid for tow servis bookes that came forth to be read in the church	viij*d.*

1590

Payd for a certificate from Doctor Stanhope of the devourcement of Shepard and his wyffe	vi*d.*
Item payd a certyficatt of pennance done by Sheppards wyfe and the powlter for openinge there wyndowes one the Sabathe daie	xvi*d.*

1591

Item payde for matts for the ladyes pewe	i*s. iijd.*
Item payde for vij certificates and one obligation of Thomas Crofte for the dischargement of the parishe of a childe called Elizabeth Venables which was borne in the howse of the sayde Thomas Crofte	iiij*s.*

1593

	£	s.	d.
More unto Doctor Stanhope because we did not present Mr. Jenkinson for that hee did not catechise upon ye Sabaoth daye	00	01	4

1594

	£	s.	d.
More for a Booke of Homelies	0	4	0
More for appearing before Doctor Stanhope about the presentment for opening of Shoppes upon St. Mathias Day	0	1	4
More unto the paratour and Doctor Stanhopes man for their favours	0	1	10

1595

	£	s.	d.
More for a key for Mr. Hamdenes pew doore	0	0	6

1599

	£	s.	d.
More unto Doctor Stanhope for the building of tow pewes without leave	0	3	0
More unto Benge [Benjamin] the Smith for 6 irons for the Queens arms &c.	0	4	0
More unto Daniell the painter for painting Jehovah over the Queens arms	0	2	6
More unto the carver for carving of two Cartoons for the Queens arms &c.	0	16	0
More unto Goodman Andrewes for punishing of vagran persones	0	2	0
More for the Communion Table	1	10	0
More unto Andrewes for carriing a poor bodie out of the parish	0	0	6

1601-2

Paid to Andrews for whipping the vagrants for one whole yeare	0	5	4

1603-4

More paid for a pare of Stokes Iron worke and paintinge and a locke	1	17	6
More payd for removing the Ladders from the Stocks side into the Stocks against the Kings coming by and setting them up agayne	0	2	4

1606-7

More paied for answering the 26 Articles and for a bill to certify whether all our parishoners received the Communion at Ester	0	3	0

1607-8

Paid Mr Godfrye for a doble hanging lock for the prison Stocks	0	1	0
Paid unto the searchers of deade bodies for the whole yeare allowed	0	10	0
Paid a warder for warding Mr. Clarkes house being infected ordered by the Mayor	0	4	0

[N.B.—This year the great bell seems to have been broken and have done some damage in its fall to the roof of the church and an adjoining house.]

1611-12

Paide to Robert Andrews for yiorne worke for the whiping poste	0	2	8

1612-13

Paide for the Booke of Cannons for the church	0	1	0
Received from the lottery for 50 lotts which was by order of the parish to be drawne in twelve penny lotts	0	10	0
Paid for Bishopp Jewells booke xxs and for a deske iiijs	1	4	0

[N.B.—After folio 114 there are leaves torn out, the next folio being 143. For the year 1628 apparently two leaves remain but after folio 144 other leaves are torn out and the next folio is 165.]

1637

	£	s.	d.
Paid for Rosemary and bayes at Christmas	00	05	00
Paid to Fish (the clerk) for strewing hearbes for the church against Easter	0	1	2

1639

Paid for Communion Cloth and Towell	01	00	03
Paid for a praier for the Kings happy successse	00	00	06

1642

Paid for ringing at the Kings return from Scotland and on the day of Thanksgiving	00	01	00
Paid for herbes and flowers to strew the church at Easter	00	03	02

1643

Received for an offering bason with the Image of a bull engraven in the middle of it which was taken of Mr George Haughton in lieu of a Fyne weighing 44 oz at 5s 4d per oz	11	17	4
Received more for a chalice cupp and cover and an old bread plate weighing together 40 oz at 5s 4d per oz	10	13	4
And of which somes so receaved for the generall parcells of plate aforesaid there is bought for the use of the church Two Communion cupps with covers and a bread plate all of silver suteable to the other plate as by the following account appears			
Paid Robert Miles free stonemason for scaffolding and use of boards and poles with his and other masons and labourers wages in taking away the superstitious Images of the Virgin Mary and the Angels attending her and framing them into another decent shape in all as by agreement and his acquittance is	09	00	00
Paid the carvers for worke done by them in the like kinde in altering of images	03	08	06
Paid the carver for taking up and laying down with brass pins the Monuments and defacing the superstitious inscriptions and cutting others in their stead that are not offensive the some of	04	09	06
Paid Robert Miles for filling up the places where the superstitious images of brass were taken up and not fit to be put downe againe	01	04	06
Paid for the care and reliefe of a workeman that was hurt with a fall from one of the Scaffolds	04	15	00
Allowed for 77 lb of old brass taken out of superstitious monuments		41	09

1644

Paid an officer which brought an order to demolish the cross and other superstitious things about or in the church	00	01	00
Paid and spent to have Mr. Rigby before the Committee being a dangerous man his house being searched for powder	00	02	06

	£	s.	d.

Paid the Scrivener for writing the names of those which would not take the League and Covenant ij*s* and going to Westminster to deliver it and back and spent iiij*s* — 00 06 00

Paid for strewings for the pews in the church — 00 02 06

Paid for Biskett and Cheese which was sent to the Souldiers in their marche to Gloucester more than was receaved in the Parish — 00 14 09

1646

Paid in the tyme when we had no Parson to several ministers for 44 sermons at *10s* per sermon — 22 00 00

1648

Paid for ringing on the Kings Coronation day — 00 05 00

1649

Paid for breade beere ale and sugar for the minister that preached the morning exercise in our church — 01 04 04

1650

Paid William Jellyman for conveying of children out of the parish *is* and carrying away a sick child ready to dye — 00 03 08

1651

Paid my Lord Maiors officer and clarke for a warrant he brought for the putting out of the church ye late Kings armes — 00 02 00

Paid for putting out the Kings armes according to the Lord Maiors order — 00 05 00

1653

Paid for 2 hower glasses for the church — 00 02 06

1654

Received for 18 sacks of coles being the guift of King James — 00 18 00

1656

Received for the charge of 2 flagons more than a new one came to — 0 2 4

Paid to Mr. Richardson for Naples bisquitt as by bil — 1 4 8

Paid for hearbes for the church at Easter — 0 5 6

1660

Paid Thomas Tempest (sexton) for holly ivy rosemary bay &c. — 1 06 09

Paid to the ringers the 5 Nov. — 0 05 00

	£	s.	d.
Paid to the ringers when my Lord Munc declared for a free parliament and after			
	0	07	00
Paid given to the ringers when King Charles the Second was proclaimed			
	0	05	0

1661

	£	s.	d.
Paid the ringers at the Kings return into London	00	05	00
Paid Mr. Walker for setting up and painting the Kings arms in the church	10	00	00
Paid for points for the children on Ascension day	00	05	00
Paid for a Thanksgiving booke	00	00	06
Paid for a Booke to Register the Kings Letters Patent	00	00	06
Paid for an Almanacke	00	00	02

1662

	£	s.	d.
Paid for Common Prayer bookes	0	2	0
Paid for new bindinge of a Common Prayer booke	0	1	2

1663

	£	s.	d.
Paid for points for the boys } [at perambulation] {	00	05	00
Paid for ribbons for the girls } {	00	08	00
Paid the Ringers for ringing the Kings birthday and at the landing of the Queene	00	03	06
Expended upon the ringers and other charges when the King and Queen came from Hampton Court	00	06	00
Paid Mr. Robert Freeston for the Stocks and whipping post and for mending and painting them	01	16	00
Paid for bringing home the Engine and buckets from Lothbury	00	01	06
Paid the ringers at the Kings Coronation day	00	02	00

[Here is given a list of benefactors.]

1. *Mr. Richard Petre* Brewer 1578. Coals &c.
2. *Sir Humphrey Handford Knt.* 1613. A cushion for the Pulpitt and a Pulpitt cloth both of greene velvett with a deepe silke fringe at the toppe and bottome imbroydered with the name of the church M.W. set of with six figures hand in hand and the date of the year 1613 and bewtifyed with foure small Garnets and eleaven faire Pearles besides small ones and several flowers embroidered.
Also left at his death £33 6s 8d for coal.
3. *Mr. George Scott* Grocer in 1616 gave the Clock to strike on the great bell and with two dyales one towards the streate the other within the church. Was made newe 1641.
4. *Sir Thomas Rich* Knt. and Baronet 1639. A pair of silver flagons and a silver plate for bread.
5. *Mr. George Hawton* Apothecary a silver bason about the value of £10 changed for other in 1642.
6. *Sir Nicholas Rainton* Knt. sometime Lord Mayor 1646 by will 40s for the poor.
7. *Mrs. Elizabeth Browneinge* the relict of the worshipful John Browneinge a white silver bason for the gathering of the oblations [no date] and in 1658 a crimson velvet cushcon with 4 tassels &c. for the pulpit.

8. *Mr. John Hamond* 1658 a crimson plush Communion cloth. This was stollen 1663 but was replaced in 1664 by ———— [*sic.*]
9. *Richard Ball D.D.* Rector 1658 £20 for repairing the church.

		£	s.	d.
10. *Sir Thomas Rich* Knt. and Baronet	Do.	£40	0	0
11. *Sir Hennage Smith*	Do.	20	0	0
12. *Sir George Smith*	Do.	20	0	0

13. *Mrs. Elizabeth Pinkney* in 1658 gave a Damask Tablecloth and 2 Damask Napkins for the Communion Table.
14. *Sir Thomas Chamberlain* 1658 a greene velvet cushion for the Pulpit.
15. *Mr. Richard Smith* Haberdasher 1662 at his death money for the poor.
16. *Mr. Edward Snoden* in 1625 a greene broade cloth carpete with a silke fringe imbroidered with the Kings armes in the middle with C.R.

1664

	£	s.	d.
Paid for the booke of Cannons and Table of Degree for marriage	00	01	02
Paid for two Prayer bookes for the fast for his Majesties Navy	00	02	00
Paid to watch a child endeavoured to be put on the parish by ye churchwardens of St. Mary Woollnoth	00	01	00

1665

	£	s.	d.
To Mr. Upton Master of the pest house for coming twice into Bearbinder Lane to view the bodies of two dead boys	00	10	00
Paid for 3 sent to the pest house and sedan to carry one	00	06	00
Paid for 2 bookes for the Fast in the visitation	00	02	00
Paid for 2 bookes of Thanksgiving for his Majestys victory against the dutch 2s and 6d given the officer	00	02	06
Paid for holly ivy rosemary and bays against Christmas	00	10	00

1666 to 1669 being 3 years accounts.

	£	s.	d.
Paid for removing the vest [ments] plate bookes and cushings in the tyme of the Fyre to severall places in the country and bringing them into London againe and then removing them to severall places to secure them and carriage about the same	005	06	00
Paid to severall watchmen to secure what was left unburnt about the church	009	18	00
Paid for repairing Rigbys shed the things being broken by taking down the stocks	002	11	00
Paid Mr. King Vintner since the Fire with the parishioners at severall meetings about parish business at the Rose Taverne and one at the Dog Taverne in all	008	02	06

NOTE.—Memorandum that this accomptant Thomas Langley having only the plate delivered to him before the fire by som of the parishioners and the vests for ministers pulpit and Communion Table with 2 embroidered beare clothes and vestry cushings the new great bible and some other small bookes and things belonging to the church brought out of the vestry to this accomptants house in the time of the fire by the Clarke and Sexton who could nott further preserve them being not able to doe more than to seeke the safty of there lives when this accomptant imployed all the help he had gotten to save his owne goods out of the fire and left his goods to be burnt all which goods have been carefully kept for the use of the church and are yet in the hands of the sayd Thomas Langley.

Thomas Langley Citizen and Upholder of London was Churchwarden 1667-1670.

MEMOR.—That after the fire 3 houses belonging to the parish of the aggregate rental of £70 were layd into the markett by vertue of an act of Parliament full value was paid for them viz. £350.

INVENTORY OF CHURCH PROPERTY.

1669

One great Bible one lesser bible one service booke Stows Survey one ground Book for Burialls one Salter and three little Bookes two noates of Dr. Masons one for the Rhenish Bible and another for a gowne and surplace and a service booke one crimson plush carpet with gold and silk fringe one crimson velvet pulpit cloth and cushion with gold and silk fringe one greene cloth carpet imbroydered fourteen cushions for the vestry one greene velvet pulpit cloth and cushion one Diaper Table Cloth and a napkin two baggs to putt the pulpit cushions in two large boxes with lockes and keyes one little old box without lock or hinges and two bearing clothes imbroydered with gold.

		oz.	p. weight
PLATE.	Two cupps with covers and one plate weighing	68	00
	Two flaggons weighing	86	00
	Another plate weighing all with cases	10	02
	One bason weighing	40	18

[The folio volume of 266 leaves bound in vellum ends 8th May 1673.]

Churchwardens
OF THE
PARISH of ST. MARY WOOLCHURCH HAW
BY THE STOCKS.

1560—1616.
1638—1673.

N.B.—From 1617–1637 the leaves have been torn out of the account book.

1560. Thomas Alen—Edmunde Ansell.
1561. Edmunde Ansell—John Lyche.
1562. John Lyche—Christopher Vahon.
1563. Cristopher Vawghan—William Shakelltown.
1564. William Shakelton—Lewis Sporyar.
1565. Lewis Sporyar—Richard Harison.
1566. Richard Harryson—John Jenynge.
1567. John Jennings—William Hanford.
1568. Willyam Handforde—John Spencer.
1569. John Spencer—Alexander Best (died 1570).
1570. Humfreye Fayrfaxe—William Massam.
1571. William Massam—Robarte Brooke.
1572. Robarte Brooke—John Smithe.
1573. John Smythe—Edward Holmden.
1574. Edward Holmden—Robert Whithand.
1575. Robart Whithand—John Newman.
1576. John Newman—William Sharlye.
1577. William Sharley—John Maskall.
1578. John Maskalle.
1579. John Maskall—Gylles Crouche.
1580. Gylles Crowche—Robert Parpoynte.
1581. Robert Pierrepoint—Nicholas Staines.
1582. Nicholas Staines—William Spencer.
1583. William Spencer—Henry Allington.
1584. Henry Alington—Peter Dewes.
1585. Peter Dewe—Daniel Andrewes.
1586. Daniel Andrews—John Haukyns.
1587. John Haukyns—Edward Nobell.
1588. Edward Noble—Richard Hunte.
1589. Richard Hunte—Robart Barnard.
1590. Robert Barnard—Luke Smythe.
1591. Luke Smythe—Cuthbert Boutch.
1592. Cuthbert Bouche—John Whetstone.
1593. John Whetstone—Cornelius Fish.
1594. Cornelius Fish—Thomas Chambers.
1595. Thomas Chambers—Edward Whorewood.
1596. Edward Whorewood—Robert Coxe.

1597. Robert Coxe—John Davies.
1598. John Davies—Robert Raynton.
1599-1600. Robert Raynton—Garett Warde.
1600-1. Garrett Warde—Christopher Scurrow.
1601-2. Christopher Scurrowe—John Stockliei.
1602-3. John Stockley—Martyn Smythe.
1603-4. Martin Smyth—John Chambers—Isaac Lilborne.
1604-5. John Chambers—Isaac Lilburne—Thomas Harwar.
1605-6. Isaac Lilborne—Thomas Harwar.
1609-7. Thomas Harwar—Humphry Handford.
1607-8. Humphry Handford—Robert Dodsoune.
1608-9. Robert Dodson—Peter Bevoier.
1609-10. Peter Beauvoir—Richard Trowte.
1610-11. Richard Trowte—Nicholas Rainton.
1611-12. Nicholas Rainton—George Scott.
1612-13. George Scott—Anthonie Crewe.
1613-14. Anthony Crewe—Thomas Ball.
1614-15. Thomas Ball—William Nichols.
1615-16. William Nichols—Edward Clarke.

Several pages torn out of Account Book. (See p. lii.)

1638. Leonard Bucknor—Thomas Arthington.
1639. Thomas Arthington—Mathew White, *Draper*.
1640. Mathew White—John Mayo.
1641. John Mayo—Samuell Small.
1642. Samuel Small—Michael Herring (? Herringhook).
1643. Michael Herring—Edward Salter.
1644. Edward Salter—Thomas Hocket.
1645. Thomas Hockett—Robert Thompson.
1646. Robert Thompson—John Seede.
1647. John Seede—Hogan Hovell.
1648. John Seede—John Grant—(N.B.—Mr. Hovell fined for the place of Church Warden).
1649. John Grant—Richard Finch.
1650. Richard Finch— N.B.—Thos. Gower, Esq., signs as minister.
1651. John Grant.
1652. John Freeston—Oswald Metcalfe.
1653. Oswald Metcalfe—Thomas Fawson.
1654. Thomas Fawson—William Medley.
1655. William Medley—Robert Grovesnor.
1656. Henry Radclyffe—Humphry Richardson.
1657. Humphry Richardson—John Sexton.
1659. John Sexton—John Vincent.
1660. John Vincent—Edward Pilkington.
1661. Edward Pilkington—Thomas Fitton.
1662. Thomas Fitton—William Aleyn.
1663. John Stead—Captain Giles Travers, *Citizen and Grocer*.
1664. Captain Giles Travers—Thomas Conye.
1665. Thomas Cony—Robert Morris.
1666. Thomas Cony—Thomas Langley.
1667. Thomas Langley—William King (for 3 years).
1671. Giles Blower—John Seed.
1672. John Seede—Jonathan Botham.
1673. Jonathan Botham—John Child.
1674. John Child—Samuell Putt.
1675. Samuell Putt—John Tempest.

1676. John Tempest—William Pigott.
1677. John Grosvenor—George Twyne.
1678. George Twyne—John Harling.
1679. John Harling—Edmond Adlard.
1680. John Harling—Moyes Edwards
1681. Robert Watkins—John Beaumant.
1682. Robert Watkins—John Cooke.
1683. John Beaumont—Thomas Nutt.
1684. Thomas Nutt—Henry Aynscombe.
1685. Henry Aynscombe—Thomas Sands.
1686. Thomas Sands—Richard Northon.
1687. Richard Northon—John Archer.
1688. John Archer—Jonathan Whalley.
1689. William Browne—Thomas Ward.
1690. Thomas Ward—Robert Baskett.
1691. Robert Baskett—Thomas Cockerill.
1692. James Sibley—William Wood.
1693. William Wood—Thomas Burford.
1694. Phillipp Dacres—Christopher Toms.
1695. John Knapp—Edward Ambrose.
1696. Edward Ambrose—Stephen Venables.
1697. Richard Gilbert—John Holmes.
1698. John Holmes—John Travell.
1699. John Travell—John Simpson.
1700. James Smith—James Taylor.
1701. James Taylor—Thomas Dakins.
1702. Thomas Dakins—Thomas Ferrall.
1703. Thomas Ferrall—William Bradbury.
1704. William Bradbury—David Gryle.
1705. David Gryle—Joseph Tovey.
1706. Joseph Tovey—Christopher Read.
1707. Christopher Read—John Silvester.
1708. John Winnd—Sam Bernard.
1709. Philip Dacres—James Sudall.
1710. Tim Rutter—Samuell Keynton.
1711. William Lawe—Phillip Waite.
1712. Phillip Waite—Joseph Forder.
1713. Joseph Forder—John Best.
1714. John Best—Timothy Roberts.
1715. Timoty Roberts—Hugh Tacknall.
1716. Hugh Tacknall—Bryan Robinson.
1717. Bryan Robinson—John Steger.
1718. John Steger—John Jeale.
1719. John Steger—George Hawkins.
1720. George Hawkins—Samuel Newey.
1721. Daniel Austin—Samuel Newey.
1722. Daniel Austin—Jonathan Woodley.
1723. Jonathan Woodley—Charles Cabrier.
1724. Richard Buller—John Veazey.
1725. Samuel Russell—Abraham Pinhorne.
1726. Abraham Pinhorne—James Allen.
1727, Robert Bishop—Thomas Ridge.
1728. Christopher Fowler—Richard Mainwaring.
1729. Richard Mainwaring—John Jackson.
1730. Thomas Knapp—Edm. Beck.
1731. Thomas Knapp—John Wood.

1732. John Wood—Thomas Pulkinhorn.
1733. Thomas Pulkinghorn—Thomas Stevenson.
1734. Thomas Stevenson—Mathew Fuller.
1735. Joseph Jefferys—Richard West.
1736. Richard West—Peter Budge.
1737. Peter Budge—Thomas Faickney.
1738. William Davis—Francis Randall.
1739. Francis Randall—David Dennison.
1740. William Davis—Francis Randal.
1741. David Dennison—Christopher Rose.
1742. Christopher Rose—Timothy Cooke.
1743. Timothy Cooke—William Saunderson.
1744. William Sanderson—John Cotterell.
1745. John Cotterell—Joseph Blandford.
1746. Joseph Blandford—John Shuttleworth.
1747. John Shuttleworth—John Wakefield.
1748. John Wakefield—Edward Wallington.
1749. Edward Wallington—Brough Maltby.
1750. Brough Maltby—George Hodges.
1751. George Hodges—Thomas Ransom.
1752. Thomas Ransom—John Wareing.
1743. John Wareing—John Bently.
1754. John Bently—Henry Jones.
1755. Henry Jones—Stephen Williams.
1756. William Shenton—John Town.
1757. John Pantree—Alex Mackintosh.
1758. Alex Mackintosh—Richard Moseley.
1759. Richard Moseley—Edmund Bick,
1760. Edmund Bick—John Burbank.
1761. John Burbank—Thomas Moidsley.
1762. Thomas Moidsley—William Palmer.
1763. William Palmer—Thomas Shuttleworth.
1764. Thomas Moseley—Thomas Shuttleworth.
1765. Edmund Bick—Thomas Moseley.
1766. Thomas Shuttleworth—Henry Looker.
1767. Henry Looker—Clement Bellamy.
1768. Clement Bellamy—William Robertson.
1769. William Robertson—Thomas Gladderer.
1770. Thomas Gladderer—Edmund Goldsmith.
1771. Edmund Goldsmith—John Tate.
1772. John Tate—Robert Gall.
1773. Robert Gall—John Pinckney.
1774. John Pinckney—James Orton.
1775. James Orton—John Smith.
1776. John Smith—Henry Cooke.
1777. Henry Cooke—David Lewis.
1778. William Cotterall—Charles Weatherley.
1779. Charles Weatherley—James Looker.
1780. James Looker—William Cotterell.
1781. William Cotterell—Edmund Bick.
1782. Edmund Bick—James Waters.
1783. James Waters—James Bolland.
1784. James Bolland—William Haughton.
1785. William Haughton—Edmond Slaughter.
1786. Edmond Slaughter—Charles Alsager.
1787. Charles Alsager—Robert Frost.

1788. Robert Frost—William Paul.
1789. William Paul—Robert Jones.
1790. Robert Jones—James Shenton.
1791. James Shenton—Francis Thwaites
1792. Francis Thaites—Thomas Mawdsley.
1793. Thomas Mawdsley—Joseph Ashford.
1794. Joseph Ashford—Richard Arnett.
1795. Richard Arnett—Edward Ledger.
1796. Edward Ledger—Henry Goddard.
1797. James Orton—James Bewley.
1798. James Bewley—Thomas Bish.
1799. Edmund Horsfall—John Williams.
1800. Edmund Horsfall—Joshua Bewley.

ABSTRACT OF AN·ORIGINAL DEED.

BACKWELL
AND
MELMOTH.
—

𝕴𝖓𝖉𝖊𝖓𝖙𝖚𝖗𝖊 dated 5th January, 1702 (3) BETWEEN John Backwell, of the Inner Temple, London, *Esquire*, son and heir of Edward Backwell, late of London, *Esquire*, deceased, Richard Backwell, Barnaby Backwell and Leigh Backwell, of London, *Gentlemen*, the three younger sons of the said Edward Backwell, deceased, Sir John Mordaunt, of London, *Knight*, Shem Bridges, of London, *Esquire*, Thomas Lofeild, of London, *Esquire*, Richard Mountney, of Kew, in the parish of Richmond, Surrey, *Gentleman*, and Anne his wife, sole daughter and heiresse of John Backwell, brother of the said Edward Backwell, late of Broughton, in the County of Bucks, deceased, surviving Trustee of the said Edward Backwell, of the first part; Nathaniell Syms, of London, *Gentleman*, of the second part; and William Melmoth, of Lincoln's Inn, County of Middlesex, *Esquire*, of the third part.

WITNESSETH that for and in consideration of the sum of £170 paid to Richard Snagg, Joseph Moore, Thomas Paine, Charles Shales, and William Atwill, of London, *Goldsmiths*, by said William Melmoth [pursuant to a decree in Chancery of the 9th March, 1698, between Sir Edward Turner, *Knight*, and others (Creditors of the said Edward Backwell) Plaintiffs, and the said John Backwell and others, Defendants], and also for 5s. each paid by said Melmoth to the others mentioned (in the first and second parts) the said John Backwell and others bargains, sells and confirms to the said Melmoth, his heirs and assigns for ever—

" All that messuage or tenement with the appurtenances situate
" and being in Lumbard Street, in the parish of St. Mary
" Woolnoth London comonly called or knowne by the
" name or signe of the Unicorne now or late in the tenure
" or occupation of Henry Lambe or his assigns, abutting on
" a messuage now in the possession of Andrew Stone called
" yᵉ Grasshopper in the East, another messuage late in the
" possession of James St. Johns called yᵉ White Horse in the
" West upon Lumbard Street aforesaid on the South and
" upon part of Garaway's Coffee House on the North, which
" said messuage or tenement mentioned to be hereby bar-
" gained or sold contains these several roomes following
" (that is to say) a cellar on the first story, a shopp and back
" shopp and with drawing roome on the second story, a
" dyneing roome, a little parlour and kitchen on the third
" story, two chambers on the fourth story, ffour garrett
" chambers on the fifth story and a little roome or turrett
" upon the leads over the same."

This ought to appear at end of S. Mary Woolnoth but was inadvertently omitted.

The Deed is signed by all of the persons mentioned in the three parts, eleven in number, and witnessed by Edward Mounteney and others. Also an endorsement receipt for the £170 signed by Rich. Snagg, Jos. Moore, Thos. Payne, Chas. Shales, and Wm. Atwill.

This is probably one of the most complete deeds descriptive of the transfer of a Lombard Street house in the reign of Queen Anne that is to be found.

Note.—In the collection of original documents from whence this has been kindly supplied, are also others relating to the old Goldsmiths and Bankers of London, and a very interesting deed dated 8th May, 1673, being a conveyance to Thomas Archer, of Tamworth, co. Warwick, of an extensive estate in the County of Huntingdon, signed by Edward Backwell, John Backwell, and Alderman Sir Robert Clayton. Attached to the deed are three of the most perfect seals possible to be met with.

Additional Extracts from Churchwardens' Books.

ST. MARY WOOLNOTH.

1577

Paid to gong farmer * for xv tonnes carriage out of the
vawte of Wm. Charleys house at xxii$d$ the tonne   xxvii$s$. vi$d$.
Item paid for foure pounds of candells for the gong
farmar for two nights

1578

A hundred of doble ten flemyshe xd nayles

1599

A flanders brick to scour the branches

1609

Frederick Frederigo "Merchant Stranger" is mentioned, also Martin Frederigo

1613

Mathew Glascock of St. Mary Woolnoth by will left £20 to buy "two potts of silver to serve at the communion table instead of the pewter potts now used there" and £30 "for the provision and maintenance of a lanthorne and candlelight to be sett out in due time every evening at the end of the said Church of St. Mary Woolnoth by the parsonage dore so that it may give light into Sherborne lane and towards St. Swithins lane and backward toward Lombard street."

1669

Sir John Frederick is mentioned

* Order by the Commissioners for Sewers, Pavements, &c., in London, 1671.
XXV. That no Goung fermer shall carry away ordure till after 10 o'clock in the winter and 11 o'clock in the summer at night, nor shall spill any ordure in the streets upon pain to forfeit and pay 13/4.
Stow Ed. 1720 vol. ii., app. p. 49.
The term Goldfinder was formerly used and perhaps is a corruption of gong farmer, but qy. as to the derivation of the old word.

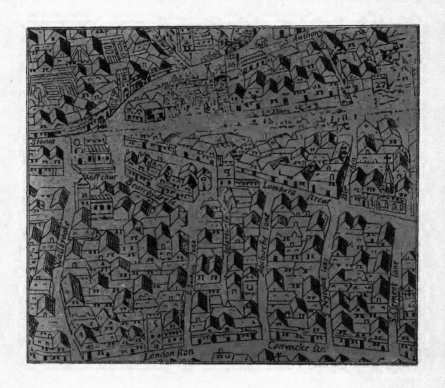

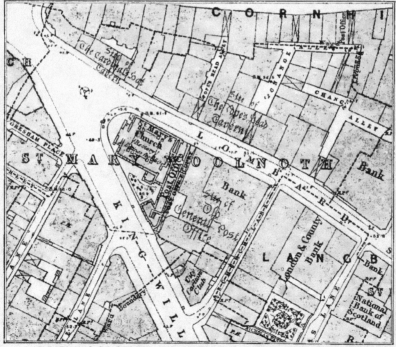

THE PARISHES OF ST MARY WOOLNOTH & ST MARY WOOLCHURCH HAW
IN 1560 & 1885.

A S CATTELL & CO, LITH

Baptisms

T HE Names of suche as be Christened in the Parishe of St. Marye
Wolnethe, in London, sythens the Sixtenthe daye of November, Anno Domini, 1538.

1538

Nov. 20.	Alice, daughter of Robert Percyvall.
Dec. 26.	Margaret, daughter of Robert Spycer, *Goldsmythe.*
Jan. 20.	Fraunces, daughter of John Alcytor, *Barbor.*
Feb. 21.	Xpofer, son of Henry Bossall, *Goldesmythe.*
Feb. 22.	Thomas, son of Thomas Boughton, *Goldesmythe.*

1539

April 3.	Anne, daughter of Richard Hall.
April 8.	Anne, daughter of William Humble, *Goldesmythe.*
April 21.	Maryon, daughter of John Keale, *Goldesmythe.*
May 5.	Thomas, son of Stephen Hawkyns, *Pewterer.*
May 14.	Stephen, son of John Segar.
May 29.	Katheren, daughter of John Gardener, *Goldesmythe.*
June 18.	Edmonde, son of Thomas Handcockke, *Vyntener.*
Aug. 2.	Johane, daughter of Thomas Marshall, *Gouldesmythe.*
Aug. 24.	Fabyan, son of Hughe Rooke, *Scryvener.*
Sep. 19.	Johan, daughter of Thomas Atkynson, *Citizen and Writer of the Courte Letter of the Cyttie of London.*
Oct. 2.	John, son of John Robson, *Citizen and Marchaunttaillor.*
Oct. 3.	Thomas, son of Bartholomew Canford.
Oct. 19.	Richard, son of Fabyan Wythers, *Goldesmythe.*
Nov. 10.	Edgare, son of George Webbe, *Goldesmythe.*
Dec. 8.	Marye, daughter of Rowlande Staunton, *Citizen and Goldesmythe.*
Dec. 15.	John, son of John Keale, *Goldsmythe.*
Feb. 6.	John, son of Thomas Erle.

1540

May 11.	Fabyan, son of Henry Bossall, *Goldesmythe.*
May 21.	John, son of Walter Lawndy.
May 31.	Elizabeth, daughter of Thomas Boughton, *Goldesmythe.*
June 18.	Annes, daughter of John Segar.
July 24.	Dorathy, daughter of Thomas Marshall, *Goldesmythe.*
July 26.	Gertrude, daughter of John Gyll.
July 26.	Anne, daughter of Thomas Handcokk, *Vyntener.*
July 31.	Franncis, son of Thomas Scryvener.

Aug. 11. Robert, son of John Wytherrby.
Sep. 6. Annes, daughter of Bastiane Bonyam.
Oct. 7. Johan, daughter of John Alcytor, *Barbor.*
Oct. 16. Marye, daughter of Nicholas Chester.
Oct. 24. Edward, son of Thomas Atkynson, *Citizen and Writer of the Courte Letter of London.*
Oct. 27. John, son of Fabyan Wythers, *Goldesmythe.*
Nov. 13. Richard de la Rose, the sonne of John Rose, *Barbor Surgeon.*
Nov. 19. Richard, son of Thomas Wetherell, *Goldesmythe.*
Nov. 19. Mary, daughter of John Massey.
Dec. 14. Nicholas, son of Bastian Byrde.
Dec. 14. Margarett, daughter of the said Bastian Byrde.
Jan. 4. Elizabeth, daughter of George Webbe, *Goldesmythe.*
Jan. 9. Johane, daughter of John Harte, *Goldesmythe.*
Feb. 1. Anne, daughter of John Barnes, *Goldesmythe.*
Feb. 24. Humfrey, son of William Humble, *Goldesmythe.*

1541

April 2. Richard, son of John Keale, *Goldesmythe.*
May 31. Myghell, son of Stephen Hawkins, *Pewterer.*
June 25. Edward, son of Rowland Staunton, *Goldesmythe.*
July 2. Anne, daughter of Thomas Glenton, *Goldesmythe.*
July 12. Nicholas, son of Walter Lawndy.
July 22. Johan, daughter of Sir Marten Bowes, *Knight and Alderman of London.*
July 23. Thomas, son of Henry Bossall, *Goldesmythe.*
Aug. 13. Margarett, daughter of Thomas Handcock, *Vyntener.*
Aug. 27. George, son of Thomas Marshall, *Goldesmythe.*
Aug. 29. Anne, daughter of Thomas Scryvener.
Sept. 9. John, son of John Alcytor, *Barbor.*
Oct. 8. Richard, son of Nicholas Caterley, *Grocer.*
Oct. 12. Richard, son of Hughe Rooke, *Scryvener.*
Oct. 24. Jeronymy, daughter of Thomas Atkynson, *Scryvener.*
Dec. 8. Katherin, daughter of Thomas Wytton, *Scryvener.*
Jan. 18. Nicholas, son of Nicholas Chester.
Feb. 8. Francis, son Xpofer Salmon, *Barbor.*
Feb. 9. Suzan, daughter, of George Webbe, *Goldesmythe.*
Feb. 15. Anne, daughter of Henry Crafte, *Merchaunttaillor.*

1542

May 1. Katheryn, daughter of Walter Blagge, *Cloth Worker.*
May 31. Elizabethe, daughter of Thomas Boughton, *Goldesmythe.*
June 3. Katheren, daughter of John Starcows.
June 24. Nicholas, son of Henry Bossall, *Goldsmythe.*
June 24. William, son of the said Henry Bossall, *Goldsmythe.*
June 25. Edward, son of Davye Rogers, *Merchaunttaillor.*
June 28. John, son of John Rokke, *Gentleman.*
July 8. Annes, daughter of Stephen Hawkyns, *Pewterer.*
July 31. Phillipp [*sic*] daughter of Albon Stylman.
Aug. 2. Margery, daughter of Anthony Moore.
Aug. 14. Amy, daughter of Rowland Stawnton, *Goldsmythe.*
Aug. 18. Annes, daughter of John Keale, *Goldsmythe.*
Sep. 24. Mary, daughter of Thomas Handcock, *Vyntener.*

Oct. 19.	Anne, daughter of Thomas Glenton, *Goldsmythe.*
Oct. 19.	Suzan, daughter of Fabyan Wethers, *Goldesmythe.*
Oct. 27.	Elizabeth, daughter of John Alcytor, *Barbor.*
Nov. 3.	Fanss, son of Sir Marten Bowes, *Knight and Alderman of London.*
Nov. 8.	Katherin, daughter of John Robson, *Merchaunttaillor.*
Nov. 12.	Suzan, daughter of Thomas Wytton, *Scryvener.*
Nov. 12.	William, son of William Marchaunt, of London, *Shomaker.*
Dec. 10.	Sens, daughter of Robert Ferman, of London, *Goldsmythe.*
Dec. 11.	Thomas, son of John Reynolde, *Goldesmythe.*
Dec. 15.	Zachary, son of William Robynson.
Dec. 25.	Matye, daughter of Thomas Marshall.
Feb. 25.	Xpofer, son of Thomas Wetherell, *Goldsmythe.*
Mar. 16.	Nicholas, son of John Segar.
Mar. 21.	John, son of Richard Wilson.
Mar. 22.	Thomas, son of James Johnson.

1543

Mar. 25.	Richard, son of Clement Wylde.
May 19.	Richard, son of George Webbe, *Goldsymthe.*
June 15.	Jane, daughter of Richard Tull, *Draper.*
July 2.	Richard, son of Thomas Atkynson, *Scryvener.*
Aug. 24.	Richard, son of Thomas Bowyer, *Grocer.*
Sep. 13.	Elles, son of Henry Crafte, *Taylor.*
Nov. 14.	Edward, son of Walter Blaygg, *Cloth Worker.*
Nov. 27.	Suzan, daughter of Thomas Boughton, *Goldsmythe.*
Nov. 29.	Alice, daughter of Thomas Glenton, *Goldsmythe.*
Dec. 3.	Edwarde, son of Thomas Wytton, *Scryvener.*
Dec. 15.	John, son of John Scryvener.
Feb. 15.	Alice, daughter of John Alcytor, *Barbor.*
Feb. 18.	Elizabeth, daughter of Henry Bossall, *Goldesmythe.*
Feb. 18.	Margarett, daughter of John Starkey.
Mar. 3.	Marye, daughter of John Sewer.
Mar. 4.	Cecyly, daughter of John Rocke, *Gentleman.*
Mar. 10.	William, son of Sir Martyn Bowes, *Knight and Alderman of the Cittie of London.*
Mar. 21.	Thomas, son of Thomas Marshall, *Goldesmythe.*

1544

April 3.	John, son of William Marchaunt, deceased.
April 3.	Richard, son of Nicholas Chester.
April 12.	Johan, daughter of John Segar.
April 18.	Johan, daughter of John Hobbes, *Syngyngman.*
April 29.	Fabian, son of Thomas Handcock, *Vyntener.*
June 1.	Christopher, son of John Keale, *Goldesmyth.*
June 2.	Salomon, son of Christopher Johnson, *Taylor.*
July 6.	Bennett, daughter of George Webbe, *Goldsmythe.*
July 31.	William, son of Stephen Hawkyns, *Pewterer.*
Oct. 24.	Tymothy, daughter [*sic*] of Thomas Atkynson, *Scryvener.*
Oct. 31.	Thomas, son of Thomas Wytton, *Scryvener.*
Nov. 2.	Johan, daughter of William Myrfynne, *Citizen and Vyntener of London.*
Nov. 5.	Marye, daughter of William Humble, *Goldsmythe.*
Nov. 9.	William, son of William Bowland, *Scryvener.*

Nov. 27.	Robert, son of Harman Whytpayne, *Haberdasher.*
Dec. 3.	Edward, son of John Robson, *Marchaunttaillor.*
Jan. 8.	Thomasyn, daughter of Thomas Glenton, *Goldsmyth.*
Jan. 10.	Suzan, daughter of Xpofer Salmon, *Barbor Surgeon.*
Jan. 12.	Thomasyn, daughter of Fabyan Wythers, *Goldsmythe.*
Feb. 13.	William, son of Anthony More.
March 13.	Johan, daughter of John Reynolds, of London, *Goldsmythe.*

1545

May 14.	Alyce, daughter of Henry Lector.
May 20.	Margarett, daughter of John Chamber, *Draper.*
June 8.	Frauncis, son of John Kele, *Goldsmythe.*
June 22.	Marye, daughter of Robert Smythe, *Merchaunttaillor.*
July 1.	Frauncis, son of Sir Martyn Bowes, *Knight and Alderman of London.*
July 3.	Thomas, son of Henry Bossall, *Goldsmythe.*
July 24.	Martyn, son of Martyn Bowes, *Goldsmythe.*
Aug. 6.	Esdras, son of Thomas Cotes.
Oct. 3.	Dorathy, daughter of George Webbe, *Goldsmith.*
Oct. 5.	Faith, daughter of Thomas Norton, *Grocer.*
Oct. 28.	Frauncis, daughter of Thomas Marshall, *Goldesmythe.*
Nov. 20.	Katheryn, daughter of Thomas Wytton, *Scryvener.*
Dec. 11.	Marten, son of Thomas Glenton, *Goldsmythe.*
Dec. 19.	Thomas, son of Walter Blaigge, *Clothworker.*
Jan. 10.	Elizabeth, daughter of Thomas Atkynson, *Citizen and Writer of the Court Letter of London.*
Jan. 20.	Thomas, son of William Bowland, *Scrivener ut Supra.*
Jan. 20.	Edward, son of John Beldon.
Jan. 20.	Josephe, son of Anthony More.

1546

May 4.	Elizabeth, daughter of John Chamber, *Draper.*
June 6.	Tymothy, son of William Myrfyn, *Vyntener.*
June 26.	Bridgett, daughter of Thomas Handcock, *Vyntener.*
June 29.	Richard, son of John Lewes.
July 7.	Alice, daughter of John Keale, *Goldsmythe.*
July 17.	Richard, son of James Johnson.
July 28.	Fabyan, son of George Appostelatt.
Aug. 4.	Thomas, son of Marten Bowes, *Citizen and Goldsmythe.*
Aug. 4.	Johan, daughter of William Humble, *Goldsmythe.*
Oct. 30.	Thomas, son of Thomas Kelynge, *Citizen and Goldsmythe of London.*
Nov. 13.	Dorathy, daughter of John Heryott.
Nov. 31.	Thomas, son of Robert Frew, of London, *Goldsmythe.*
Dec. 5.	Anne, daughter of Thomas Wytton, *Scryvener.*
Jan. 14.	Paule, son of George Webbe, *Goldsmythe.*
Jan. 20.	George, son of Henry Bossall, *Goldesmythe.*
Feb. 8.	Thomas, son of Xpofer Salmon, *Barbor Surgeon.*
Mar. 19.	Elizabeth, daughter of Thomas Norton, *Grocer.*

1547

June 26.	Thomas, son of John Keale, *Goldsmythe.*
June 30.	Tabytha, daughter of William Myrfyn, *Vyntener.*

July 2.	Johan, daughter of William Wright.
Aug. 4.	Phillippe, daughter of John Lewes.
Sep. 11.	Johane, daughter of Walter Blaygge, *Cloth Worker.*
Sep. 24.	Anthony, son of William Bowland, *Scryvener.*
Sep. 30.	Thomasyn, daughter of Henry Rushall, *Marchaunttaillor.*
Oct. 21.	Anne, daughter of Marten Bowes, the Younger, *Citizen & Goldsmythe of London.*
Oct. 26.	Thomas, son of Thomas Wytton, *Citizen and Writer of the Courte Letter of London.*
Nov. 30.	Margarett, daughter of Thomas Kelynge, *Citizen and Goldsmythe of London.*
Dec. 27.	Henry, son of Thomas Barnes.
Mar. 6.	Anne, daughter of Christopher More.

1548

April 12.	Thomas, son of Thomas Wetherell, *Goldsmythe.*
April 30.	Anne, daughter of Sir Percyvall Hartte, *Knight.*
July 3.	Anne, daughter of Thomas Bowyer, *Grocer.*
July 17.	Mary, daughter of John Chamber, *Draper.*
Aug. 27.	Alice, daugher of Robert Smythe.
Aug. 27.	Johan, daughter of George Webbe, *Goldsmythe.*
Aug. 27.	Mary, daughter of John Reynolds, *Goldsmythe.*
Sep. 19.	Sara, daughter of Thomas Handcock, *Vyntener.*
Sep. 22.	Sara, daughter of John Keall, *Goldsmythe.*
Nov. 6.	John, son of Clement Shelley.
Dec. 13.	Josephe, son of Josephe Boycke, *Person of St. Marye Bowe in London.*
Dec. 18.	Fabyan, son of George Appostellat, *Waterbearer.*
Dec. 25.	Charity, daughter of Sir Martyn Bowes, *Knight and Alderman of London.*
Jan. 18.	Pacyence, daughter of Martyn Bowes, son of the said Sir Martyn Bowes, *Citizen & Goldsmythe of London.*
Jan. 19.	Elizabeth, daughter of Henry Bysshopp.
Jan. 20.	Hamon, son of William Myrfyn, *Vyntener.*
Jan. 21.	Arthure, son of Thomas Kelynge, *Goldsmythe.*
Jan. 28.	Judeth, daughter of Gregory Johnson.
Mar. 21.	Humfrey, son of Thomas Barnes.

1549

April 19.	George, son of Walter Blaigge, *Clothworker.*
May 15.	John, son of Lawrence Smythe, *Vintener.*
July 1.	Sara, daughter of Roberte Stanbanke, *Baker.*
Aug. 24.	Bartholomewe, son of Robert Talboys, *Goldsmythe.*
Aug. 27.	Thomas, son of William Oldknowe, *Baker.*
Sep. 15.	Beysilla, daughter of Thomas Wytton, *Citizen & Writer of the Courte Letter of London.*
Oct. 18.	John, son of John Chamber, *Draper.*
Oct. 31.	Ambrose, son of John Blackburne.
Nov. 13.	Sara, daughter of Robert Brandon, *Goldsmythe.*
Nov. 24.	Thomas, son of Martyn Partryge, *Barbor Surgeon.*
Jan. 15.	Sara, daughter of John Kettelwood, *Goldsmythe.*
Jan. 23.	Thomas, son of John Granger.
Mar. 16.	Johan, daughter of Marten Bowes, *Citizen & Goldsmythe of London.*

1550

April 8.	Josua, son of John Keale, *Goldsmythe.*
April 17.	Francis, daughter of Derick Anthony, *Goldsmythe.*
April 24.	Alice, daughter of William Bowland, *Scryvener.*
May 1.	Henry, son of Sir Martyn Bowes, *Knight and Alderman of London.*
May 1.	Thomas, son of Thomas Handcock, *Vintener.*
Mar. 5.	Mary, daughter of George Webbe, *Goldsmythe.*
May 25.	Katheryn, daughter of Edwarde Addeson.
Sep. 17.	Marthey, daughter of Christopher More.
Sep. 27.	Hester, daughter of Gregorie Johnson.
Nov. 2.	William, son of Stephen Mollytubbe.
Nov. 24.	Thomas, son of Richard Parkyns.
Dec. 8.	Anne, daughter of Robert Frear, *Citizen and Goldsmythe of London.*
Dec. 26.	Edward, son of Thomas Kelinge, *Goldsmythe.*
Jan. 30.	Edwarde, son of Robert Brandon, *Goldsmythe.*
Mar. 1.	David, son of John Chamber, *Draper.*
Mar. 22.	John, son of Thomas Wytton, *Citizen and Writer of the Court Letter of London.*

1551

Mar. 25.	Thomas, son of Robert Smythe, *Marchaunttoitlour,*
April 14.	Christian, daughter of Thomas Whetherrell, *Goldsmythe.*
April 26.	Robert, son of George Apostelate, *Waterbearer.*
May 10.	Elizabeth, daughter of Humfrey Stephens, of London, *Goldsmythe.*
May 24.	Annes, daughter of Robert Addeson.
June 30.	Pawle, son of Derick Anthony, *Goldsmythe.*
Aug. 22.	John, son of John Reynoldes, *Goldsmythe.*
Aug. 24.	Amy, daughter of George Webbe, *Goldsmythe.*
Aug. 27.	Samuell, daughter [*sic*] of John Keale, *Goldsmythe.*
Aug. 31.	Sara, daughter of Marten Partrige, *Barbor Surgeon.*
Nov. 2.	John, son of Thomas Handcocke, *Vintener.*
Nov. 8.	Robert, son of Robert Taylboys, *Vintener.*
Nov. 8.	Andrewe, son of Cornelis Waters.
Nov. 24.	Thomas, son of Robert Stanbanke, *Baker.*
Nov. 24.	Walter, son of Thomas Parson.
Dec. 1.	Justice, son of William Myrfyn.
Feb. 8.	James, son of John Browne.
Feb. 18.	John, son of John Grannyer.
Mar. 11.	John, son of Thomas Kelinge, *Goldsmythe.*

1552

May 11.	Gabriell, son of Henry Rushall, *Merchanttaillor.*
May 28.	Elizabeth, daughter of Humfrey Stephens, *Goldsmythe.*
July 25.	Elizabeth, daughter of John Mathew, *Cooke.*
Aug. 13.	Brygett, daughter of John Pykkeringe, *Haberdasher.*
Sep. 20.	William, son of William Tracye, *Merchaunttaillor.*
Sep. 25.	Alice, daughter of Francis Barnarde, *Cooke.*
Oct. 12.	Thomas, son of Thomas Maxsell, *Prieste.*
Oct. 30.	Thomas, son of Thomas Atkynson, *Citizen and Writer of the Courte Letter of the Citie of London.*
Nov. 6.	Rauffe, son of Robert Taylboys, *Goldsmythe.*

Nov. 13. Margery, daughter of Richard Parkyns.
Nov. 28. Johan Stapulles.
Dec. 21. Rebecca, daughter of Robert Brandon, *Goldsmythe.*
Jan. 21. Abell, son of Martyn Partrige, *Barbor.*

1553

April 10. Mary, daughter of William Bowland.
May 11. Margarett, daughter of William Myrfyn.
July 13. Marye, daughter of Thomas Kelinge, *Goldsmythe.*
July 30. Katheryn, daughter of Humfrey Stephens.
Aug. 13. Olyver, son of Thomas Wytton, *Citizen and Writer of the Courte Letter of London.*
Aug. 19. Richard, son of Derick Anthony, *Goldsmythe.*
Sep. 3. Annes, daughter of John Pickeringe, *Haberdasher.*
Sep. 24. Richard, son of William Pynchester.
Sep. 28. Margaret, son [*sic*] of William Tracye.
Oct. 22. Alice, daughter of James Lynne, *Goldesmythe.*
Dec. 5. John, son of John Browne.
Jan. 28. Margarett, daughter of John Keale, *Goldsmythe.*
Feb. 3. Alice Clerke.
Feb. 8. Marye, daughter of Xpofer More.
Mar. 4. Anne, daughter of Francis Barnard, *Cooke.*
Mar. 14. Brigett, daughter of Thomas Atkynson, *Citizen and Writer of the Courte Letter of the Cytie of London.*

1554

April 28. Katheryn, daughter of William Abraham, *Vyntener.*
April 30. Thomas, son of Robte. Talboys, *Goldsmythe.*
May 29. Anne, daughter of Deryck Anthony, *Goldsmythe.*
May 20. Anne, daughter of John Cattell, *Salter.*
June 28. William, son of Nicholas Heys, *Grocer.*
July 1. Peter, son of John Adams.
Aug. 18. Suzan, daughter of John Denehyll.
Aug. 27. Anne, daughter of Richarde Payne, *Cooke.*
Sep. 9. James, son of Kenryckk Apryce.
Sep. 29. Margarett, daughter of Robert Stanbanke, *Baker.*
Oct. 15. Tobyas, son of Gregory Sylinge, *Straunger.*
Dec. 22. Richard, son of Richard Parkyns.
Dec. 23. Mary, daughter of Humfrey Stephens, *Goldsmythe.*
Jan. 22. Samuell, son of Richard Walton.
Jan. 30. Anthony, son of William Tracy, *Merchaunttaillour.*

1555

April 25. Thomas, son of Marke Norton, *Grocer.*
May 1. John, son of John Pickeringe, *Haberdasher.*
May 14. William, son of William Abraham, *Vintener.*
May 23. Jane, daughter of William Pynchester.
June 18. Jane, daughter of Thomas Atkynson, *Scryvener.*
July 28. Anne, daughter of John Cattell, *Salter.*
Aug. 13. Mary, daughter of Derick Anthony, *Goldsmythe.*
Aug. 15. Alice, daughter of John Reynolds, *Clothworker.*
Oct. 3. Hester, daughter of Gregory Selynge, *Straunger.*
Nov. 3. John, son of Marten Partryge, *Barbor and Surgeon, of London.*

Nov. 11. Gertrude, daughter of Stephen Spayman, *Citizen and Haberdasher of London.*

Nov. 12. Johane, daughter of Richard Payne, *Citizen and Cooke of London.*

Dec. 29. Margaret, daughter of James Lynne, *Citizen and Goldsmythe of London.*

Jan. 27. Dorathy, daughter of Thomas Wytton, *Citizen and Scrivener of London.*

Feb. 23. Thomas, son of Nicholas Hayes.

Mar. 21. Ellen, daughter of Frauncis Barnard, *Citizen and Cooke of London.*

1556

April 6. Elizabeth, daughter of William Tracye, *Citizen and Merchaunttaillour of London.*

April 13. Anne, daughter of Christopher More.

April 14. Robert, son of Thomas Kelynge, *Citizen and Goldsmythe of London.*

April 21. John, son of Richard Parkyns, *Citizen and Clothworker of London.*

May 20. Marye, daughter of William Sugden, *Citizen and Grocer of London.*

May 22. Isack, son of William Abraham, *Citizen and Vintener of London.*

June 15. Agnes, daughter of William Ingram, *Citizen and Baker of London.*

June 16. Richard, son of John Pikerynge, *Citizen and Haberdasher of London.*

June 26. George, son of Thomas Downton, *Citizen and Draper of London.*

July 18. Margarett, daughter of William Noble, *Citizen and Haberdasher of London.*

July 30. Jane, daughter of Kenryck Pryce, *Citizen and Clothworker of London.*

Aug. 10. William, son of Humfrey Stephens, *Citizen and Goldsmithe of London.*

Oct. 2. Benedicke, son of Thomas Atkynson, *Citizen and Scrivener of London.*

Oct. 4. Anne, daughter of John Cattell, *Citizen and Salter of London.*

Oct. 21. Nicholas, son of Thomas Corbett, *Citizen and Skynner of London.*

Dec. 8. William, son of Sir Martyn Bowes, *Knight and Alderman of London.*

Dec. 21. John, son of Robert Taylboys, *Citizen and Goldsmith of London.*

Feb. 14 Elizabeth, daughter of John Moyses, *Citizen and Haberdasher of London.*

Mar. 20. Edward, son of Hughe Redynge, *Citizen and Blacksmithe of London.*

1557

Mar. 28. Mary, daughter of John Kettellwood, *Citizen and Goldsmithe of London.*

June 3.	Aves, daughter of John Reynolds, *Citizen and Clothworker of London.*
June 8.	John Stephens and Johan Stephens, the daughters of Humfrey Stephens, *Citizen and Goldsmithe of London.*
July 18.	Mary, daughter of James Lynne, *Citizen and Goldsmithe of London.*
July 27.	Thomas, son of John Pekeringe, *Citizen and Goldsmithe of London.*
Sep. 15.	William, son of Thomas Harris, *Citizen and Mercer of London.*
Sep. 22.	Johan, daughter of Mark Norton, *Citizen and Grocer of London.*
Oct. 3.	Jesper, son of Thomas Kelynge, *Citizen and Goldsmith of London.*
Nov. 11.	Margarett, daughter of William Tracye, *Citizen and Merchant Taillour of London.*
Dec. 6.	Thomas, son of Edmonde Andrews, *Citizen and Mercer of London.*
Jan. 1.	Martyn, son of Martyn Partrige, *Citizen and Barbor and Surgeon of London.*
Jan. 10.	Richard, son of Thomas Corbett, *Citizen and Skynner of London.*
Feb. 1.	John, son of John Cattell, *Citizen and Salter of London.*
Feb. 6.	Penell, daughter of Thomas Atkynson, *Citizen and Scrivener of London.*
Mar. 15.	Martha, daughter of Thomas Wytton, *Citizen and Scrivener of London.*

1558

April 6.	Sara, daughter of Thomas Wattes, *Haberdasher.*
April 14.	Elizabeth, daughter of Nicholas Hayes, *Clothworker.*
April 18.	Frauncis, daughter of Frauncis Barnard, *Cooke.*
May 10.	William, son of John Moyses.
May 16.	Fortune, daughter of Richard Payne, late deceased.
May 30.	William, son of William Yngram, *Citizen and Baker of London.*
June 2.	Nicholas, son of Stephen Spayman, *Citizen and Haberdasher of London.*
June 14.	Edwarde, son of Edwarde Cortenall, *Citizen and Goldsmithe of London.*
July 14.	Elizabethe, daughter of Barnarde Carter, *Scrivener.*
July 27.	John, son of William Abraham, *Citizen and Vintener of London.*
July 31.	Alice, daughter of John Kettelwood, *Citizen and Goldsmythe of London.*
Sep. 12.	Elizabeth, daughter of John Pyckeringe, *Citizen and Haberdasher of London.*
Sep. 18.	Katheren, daughter of Adrian Tuball, *Straunger.*
Nov. 4.	Ellen, daughter of William Tracye, *Citizen and Merchaunt-taillor of London.*
Nov. 6.	Thomas, son of Francis Kidd, *Citizen and Writer of the Courte Letter of London.*
Nov. 16.	Elizabeth, daughter of Henrye Towers.
Dec. 17.	William, son of Thomas Giles, *Citizen and Haberdasher of London.*

Dec. 29.	Alice, daughter of Hughe Crooke, *Citizen and Goldsmythe of London.*
Dec. 31.	Thomas, son of Thomas Corbett, *Citizen and Skynner of London.*
Jan. 17.	Marten, son of John Robinson, *Gentleman.*
Jan. 18.	[*sic*] son of John Greye, *Straunger.*
Jan. 26.	Katherin, daughter of Thomas Kelinge, *Citizen and Goldsmythe of London.*
Feb. 3.	William, son of John Reynolde, *Citizen and Cloth Worker of London.*
Feb. 16.	Edward, son of Thomas Atkynson, *Citizen and Writer of the Courte Letter of London.*
Mar. 17.	Richard, son of Bowland Oker, *Citizen and Haberdasher of London.*

1559

June 18.	Dorathy, daughter of Nicholas Courtnall, *Citizen and Goldsmythe of London.*
July 14	Mary, daughter of Barnard Carter, *Scrivener.*
July 29.	Robert, son of Robert Taylboys, *Citizen and Goldsmythe of London.*
Aug. 14.	William, son of Nicholas Hayes, *Citizen and Draper of London.*
Sep. 24.	William, son of William Pickeringe, *Citizen and Haberdasher of London.*
Sep. 24.	Peter, son of Awdryan Tybauld, *Stranger.*
Sep. 27.	Julyan, daughter of Stephen Spayman, *Haberdasher.*
Dec. 17.	Margarett, daughter of John Wetherall.
Dec. 17.	Rose, daughter of Edwarde Sutton.
Jan. 7.	Thomasyn, daughter of Thomas Giles.
Jan. 10.	Suzan, daughter of Thomas Gylls.
Feb. 13.	Andrian, daughter of Thomas Wytton.
Feb. 17.	Elizabeth, daughter of Rowland Oker.

1560

May 12.	Joane, daughter of Thomas Kelinge, *Goldsmythe.*
July 14.	Elizabeth, daughter of John Robynson, *Gentleman.*
July 21.	John, son of John Nycolls, *Bedle.*
Aug. 11.	Thomas, son of Thomas Watte, *Haberdasher.*
Aug. 14.	John, son of Kyndrick Price, *Clothworker.*
Aug. 18.	Sysley, daughter of Marke Norton, *Grocer.*
Aug. 25.	Bartholomew, son of Xpofer More.
Sep. 15.	Thomas, son of Launcelott Bycars.
Nov. 1.	Sara, daughter of Adrian Tuball.
Nov. 3.	Robert, son of Nicholas Hayes.
Nov. 23.	Jane, daughter of John Pyckeringe.
Feb. 23.	Thomas, son of Francis Bernam.
Mar. 23.	Abraham, son of Thomas Corbett, *Skynner.*
Mar. 23.	Jasper, son of William Jones, *Goldsmythe.*

1561

Mar. 29.	Elizabeth, daughter of John Wetherall, *Goldsmythe.*
April 25.	William, son of Robert Taylboys.
June 5.	Mathewe, son of Rowland Oker.

June 10.	John, son of Edward Sutton.
June 18.	John, son of Thomas Kelinge.
Sep. 1.	Anne, daughter of Baptist Italyon.
Sep. 2.	John, son of Launcelot Bycaus.
Sep. 24.	Ann, daughter of Francis Kydd, *Scrivener.*
Oct. 28.	John, son of Thomas Short.
Jan. 4.	Stephen, son of John Kevall.
Jan. 8.	Francis, son of Adryan Tubull, *Straunger.*
Jan. 25.	George, son of John Pikeringe.
Feb. 8.	Thomas, son of Thomas Gyles
Feb. 12.	Hughe, son of Hughe Crokes.
Mar. 1.	Elizabeth, daughter of John Nutshaw.

1562

April 25.	William, son of Thomas Wytton.
April 30.	Suzan, daughter of John Wetherill.
May 17.	Henry, son of Edward Satton.
May 17.	Elynne, daughter of Robert Bromley.
May 27.	Anne, daughter of Robert Taylboys.
June 16.	Launcelott, son of George Taylor.
June 29.	Suzan, daughter of Francis Burnam.
June 29.	Anne, daughter of Hughe Keale, *Goldsmithe.*
Aug. 9.	Elizabeth, daughter of William Jonés, *Goldsmith.*
Aug. 22.	Suzan, daughter of Rowland Oker, *Merchaunttaillour.*
Sep. 5.	James, son of Xpofer More.
Sep. 15.	Thomas, son of John Mathewe, *Goldsmith.*
Sep. 29.	Alice, daughter of Grena Johnson.
Oct. 4.	Jane, daughter of Hughe Redinge, *Smythe.*
Oct. 4.	Edmunde, son of Robert Smythe, *Tallowchandler.*
Nov. 1.	William, son of Mr. Billingby.
Nov. 21.	Thomas, son of Kenrick Price, *Clothworker.*
Nov. 12.	John, son of William Robinson, *Merchaunt.*
Nov. 24.	William, son of John Stile, *Merchaunt.*
Nov. 27.	William, son Launcelot Vickers.
Dec. 26.	Stephan, son of Thomas Wattes, *Haberdasher.*
Jan. 24.	Thomas, son of Thomas Wylson, *Cooke.*
Feb. 14.	Rauffe, son of Thomas Gyles, *Haberdasher.*
Feb. 25.	Hughe, son of John Pickeringe, *Haberdasher.*
Feb. 25.	Jane, daughter of George Kevall, *Scrivener.*

1563

April 18.	Alyce, daughter of John Kettellwood, *Goldsmythe.*
June 13.	Humfrey, son of Humfrey Hayes, *Grocer.*
June 20.	Richard, son of Thomas Corbett, *Skynner.*
June 24.	Cicely, daughter of Mr. John Robinson.
June 24.	Rose, daughter of Katherine Wayman, *Straunger.*
July 4.	Rebecca, daughter of John Wetherhill, *Goldsmythe.*
July 11.	Cecily, daughter of Mr. Martyn Bowes, *Gentleman.*
Aug. 9.	Anne, daughter of Clement de Morunde, *Straunger.*
Sep. 12.	Thomas, son of Thomas Bromley, *Furyer.*
Sep. 29.	Mychaell, son of Francis Barnard, *Cooke.*
Oct. 10.	Rebecca, daughter of William Shorte, *Grocer.*
Oct. 17.	Rebecca, daughter of John Mathewe, *Goldsmythe.*

Nov. 9.	Jane, daughter of Edward Sutton, *Stacioner.*
Dec. 18.	Rauffe, son of Rowlande Oker, *Haberdasher.*
Mar. 1.	Francis, daughter of Robert Clark, *Grocer.*
Mar. 5.	John, son of Thomas Wylson, *Cooke.*

1564

April 2.	Margaret, daughter of George Taylor, late deceased.
April 18.	Alexander, son of Thomas Wytton, *Scryvener.*
April 23.	Thomasyn, daughter of Thomas Nutshawe, *Goldsmythe.*
July 8.	William, son of John Pickeringe, *Haberdasher.*
July 16.	Laurence, son of Thomas Corbet, *Skynner.*
July 30.	Thomas, son of Thomas Atkynson, *Scrivener.*
Aug. 13.	Thomas, son of M. John Robynson.
Aug. 27.	Jane, daughter of Grene Johnson, *Cobler.*
Sep. 17.	Rachell, daughter of John Wetherell, *Goldsmythe.*
Sep. 21.	Judeth, daughter of Thomas Gyles, *Haberdasher.*
Sep. 29.	Alice, daughter of Robert Tailboiz, *Goldsmythe.*
Nov. 26.	Mary, daughter of William Jones, *Goldsmythe.*
Dec. 3.	Suzan, daughter of Thomas Wattes, *Haberdasher.*
Dec. 28.	Christian, daughter of John Ferne, *Straunger.*
Feb. 2.	Mary, daughter of Edward Sutton, *Stacioner.*
Feb. 18.	Eliazer, daughter of William Shorte, *Grocer.*

1565

Mar. 25.	Cycely, daughter of Thomas Kelynge, *Goldsmythe.*
May 17.	Peter, son of Clement Morando, *Straunger.*
May 21.	Anne, daughter of Robert Clark, *Grocer.*
July 6.	Sara, daughter of Richard Bonde.
July 13.	Elizabeth, daughter of Thomas Wytton, *Scrivener.*
Sep. 2.	Alyce, daughter of Henry Lambert, *Straunger.*
Dec. 16.	Henry, son of Robert Tailboiz, *Goldsmythe.*
Dec. 28.	Robert, son of Thomas Atkyns, *Grocer.*
Feb. 1.	Jane, daughter of George Coomes.
Feb. 2.	Helyn, daughter of Henry Chalcome, *Cordwayner.*
Feb. 8.	James, son of Roger Spurstowe, *Vyntener,* Forthe of John Chamber's House.
Feb. 10.	Richard, son of John Pickeringe, *Haberdasher.*
Mar. 31.	David, son of William Jones, *Goldesmythe.*

1566

April 6.	Sarah, daughter of Rowlande Okeover, *Merchaunttaillor.*
April 11.	Thomas, son of Edward Sutton, *Stacioner.*
April 25.	Jane, daughter of John Wetherhill, *Goldesmythe.*
June 3.	Jane, daughter of Frauncis Barnarde, *Cooke.*
June 8.	Isaack and Annie, twynnes, son and daughter of Thomas Kelynge, *Goldsmythe.*
June 30.	Henry, son of Kenrick Price, *Clothworker.*
July 13.	Adryan, daughter of John Ferne, *Myllaner.*
July 26.	Ann, daughter of Richard Adams, *Stacioner,* dwellinge in the Rents of Frauncis Barnard.
Aug. 15.	Mary, daughter of George Kevall, *Notarie.*
Aug. 16.	Anne, daughter of John Mathewe, *Goldsmythe.*

Sep. 11.   Walter, son of Thomas Gyles, *Citizen and Haberdasher of London.*
Oct. 6.   William, son of Robert Clarke, *Citizen and Draper of London.*
Oct. 21.   Thomasyn, daughter of Richard Travell, *Citizen and Skynner of London.*
Nov. 16.   John, son of Hugh Keale, *Goldsmythe.*
Dec. 8.   Elizabethe, daughter of Thomas Atkynson, *Citizen and Scrivener of London.*
Dec. 16.   Thomas, son of Henry Gaynfford, *Goldsmythe.*
Jan. 19.   Anne, daughter of John Kettellwood, *Goldsmyth.*
Feb. 2.   Stephen, son of Marmaduke Hyggens, *Grocer.*

1567

Mar. 31.   William, son of Thomas Watte, *Haberdasher.*
April 6.   Jane, daughter of John Pickeringe, *Haberdasher.*
April 20.   Baptiste, son of William Fylian, *Sheregrynder.*
June 1.   Edward, son of Robert Taylboys, *Goldsmythe.*
June 15.   Jane, daughter of Roger Spurstow, *Vintner.*
June 22.   Anne, daughter of Thomas Wytton, *Scryvener.*
June 24.   John, son of Clement Morando, *Cutler.*
July 13.   Cuthbert, son of William Jones, *Goldsmythe.*
Aug. 24.   Dorathye, daughter of Thomas Kelynge, *Goldsmythe.*
Sep. 22.   Ruthe, daughter of Richard Grige, *Mynister.*
Oct. 28.   Thomas, son of John Shaw, *Clothworker.*
Nov. 16.   Anne, daughter of John Wetherhill, *Goldsmythe.*
Jan. 11.   Anne, daughter of Hughe Yemans.
Feb. 1.   Elen, daughter of John Tempest.
Mar. 5.   Walter, son of Thomas Gyles, *Haberdasher.*
Mar. 14.   John, son of Cuthbert Buckell, *Vyntener.*
Mar. 21.   John, son of Richard Robyns, *Goldsmythe.*

1568

April 17.   Richard, son of Richard Tonge, *Grocer.*
July 18.   John, son of Thomas Atkynson, *Citizen and Wryter of the Court Letter of London.*
Aug. 22.   Francis, son of Francis Barnarde, *Cooke.*
Aug. 22.   Lewes, son of Edward Sutton, *Stacioner.*
Aug. 28.   Jane, daughter of Robert Taylboys, *Goldsmythe.*
Sep. 12.   Thomas and John, sons of Humfrey Hayes, *Grocer,* beinge twoo twynnes.
Oct. 16.   Alice, daughter of John Shawe, *Clothworker.*
Nov. 14.   Elizabeth, daughter of John Ferne, *Myllaner.*
Nov. 28.   Barbara, daughter of Clement Morand, *Cutler.*
Dec. 15.   Marye, daughter of Henry Gayfforde, *Goldsmythe.*
Jan. 16.   Elyn, daughter of Arthur Chorismore, *Blacksmythe.*
Feb. 24.   Robert, son of Hughe Kell, *Goldsmythe.*

1569

April 12.   William, son of Xpofer Harrys, *Gentleman.*
May 19.   Bartholomew, son of John Pickeringe, *Haberdasher.*
Sep. 11.   John, son of Xpofer Cooke, *Tailor.*

Sep, 18.	Anne, daughter of Thomas Atkynson, *Scrivener.*
Sep. 25.	John, son of John Shawe, *Clothworker.*
Oct. 2.	Frauncis, daughter of John Lyon, *Pewterer.*
Nov. 27.	Alice, daughter of William Prestwood, *Lethersellar.*
Dec. 5.	Marye, daughter of Clement Morando, *Cutler.*
Dec. 17.	Julyan, daughter of William Jones, *Goldsmythe.*
Jan. 1.	Thomas, son of John Tempest, *Draper.*
Mar. 8.	Barsabay, daughter of Henry Gaynfford, *Goldsmythe.*

1570

Mar. 14.	John, son of John Day, *Clothworker.*
May 24.	John Andro, son of Thomas Totton, *Broker.*
June 29.	Elizabeth, daughter of Richard Robyns, *Goldsmythe.*
July 9.	Anne, daughter of John Pickeringe, *Haberdasher.*
Oct. 22.	Judeth, daughter of Thomas Perpoynt, *Draper.*
Nov. 5.	Thomas, son of Hugh Veal, *Goldsmythe.*
Nov. 10.	Richard, son of Gregorie Bonde, *Merchaunttaillor.*
Nov. 26.	Frauncis, son of Robert Taylboys, *Goldsmythe.*
Dec. 17.	John, son of John Ferne, *Myllaner.*
Dec. 17.	Cawood, son of Mark Norton, *Grocer.*
Feb. 17.	Edmund, son of Arthure Chesmore.
Mar. 14.	Alice, daughter of James Somner, *Clothworker.*
Mar. 17.	Jane, daughter of Humfrey Derycott, *Draper.*

1571

April 1.	Harman, daughter of John Geffrey, *Haberdasher.*
May 27.	William, son of Leonard Cooke, *Merchaunttaillor.*
June 10.	Rachell, daughter of Thomas Atkynson, *Scrivener.*
Sep. 4.	Richard, son of Thomas Hamond, *Mynstrell.*
Sep. 30.	Humfrey, son of Richard Robyns, *Goldsmythe.*
Oct. 7.	Thomas, son of Thomas Sympson, *Goldsmythe.*
Oct. 28.	Margaret, daughter of John Pickeringe, *Haberdasher.*
Dec. 14.	John, son of John Plomer, *Merchaunttaillor.*
Feb. 10.	Alice, daughter of Marke Norton, *Grocer.*
Feb. 10.	Edward, son of Richard Parker, *Mercer.*
Feb. 12.	Sara and Suzan, twoo twynes, dau'rs. of Bartholomew Beane, *Stranger, Goldsmythe.*

1572

April 6.	Johan, daughter of George Haynes, *Goldsmythe.*
April 27.	John, son of James Allyn, *Goldsmythe.*
May 11.	Richard, son of John Muns, *Draper.*
May 26.	Edmonde, son of Arthure Chesmore, *Blacksmyth.*
July 6.	Thomas, son of John Geffrey, *Haberdasher.*
Sep. 12.	Mary, daughter of Richard Saker, *Merchaunttaillor.*
Sep. 21.	William, son of William Jones, *Goldsmythe.*
Sep. 21.	Margaret, daughter of Richard Jones, *Carpenter.*
Nov. 2.	John, son of John Chaplen, *Grocer.*
Nov. 15.	Alyce, daughter of Thomas Hamond, *Mynstrell.*
Dec. 21.	George, son of Thomas Humble, *Stacioner.*
Jan. 25.	Mary, daughter of John Downes, *Haberdasher.*
Feb. 6.	Richard, son of Richard Parker, *Mercer.*
Mar. 8.	William, son of Thomas Davy, *Haberdasher.*

1573

April 12.	Francis, son of John Pickeringe, *Haberdasher.*
May 10.	Jane, daughter of James Sumner, *Clothworker.*
May 10.	Margaret, daughter of Humfrey Derycote, *Draper.*
July 19.	Sara, daughter of Bartholomew Beane, *Goldsmythe, Dutcheman.*
Oct. 4.	Sara, daughter of George Haynes, *Goldsmythe.*
Oct. 25.	William, son of John Geffrey, *Haberdasher.*
Nov. 8.	Elizabeth, daughter of James Stock, *Carpentar.*
Nov. 13.	Humfrey, son of Richard Saker, *Merchanttailor.*
Nov. 15.	Elizabeth, daughter of Cuthbert Crackplace, *Goldsmythe.*
Nov. 30.	Johan, daughter of John Monns, *Draper.*
Jan. 10.	Mathewe, son of Thomas Sympson, *Goldsmythe.*
Jan. 17.	William, son of John Chaplin, *Grocer.*
Feb. 5.	Sara, daughter of John Browne, *Gardyner.*

1574

April 25.	Elizabeth, daughter of Richard Parker, *Mercer.*
April 25.	Suzan, daughter of Thomas Humble, *Stacioner.*
May 16.	Dennys, daughter of Humfrey Derycote, *Draper.*
June 4.	Roberte, son of Richard Johnes, *Carpentar.*
July 6.	Charles, son of John Pickeringe, *Haberdasher.*
July 25.	John, son of Richard Robyns, *Goldsmythe.*
Sep. 12.	Margarett, daughter of James Somner, *Clothworker.*
Oct. 3.	John, son of John Fox, *Clothworker.*
Oct. 17.	Richard, son of Richard Cole, *Tapster* with Clement Webster, *Cooke.*
Nov. 11.	Blanche, daughter of Roger Tasker, *Goldsmythe.*
Nov. 14.	Jane, daughter of Thomas Stokes, *Carpentar.*
Nov. 21.	John, son of Thomas Davye, *Girdeler.*
Dec. 5.	Jane, daughter of John Bradley, *Merchaunttaillor.*
Jan. 8.	Robert, son of John Barker, *Draper.*
Jan. 9.	Suzan, daughter of Richard Sacre, *Merchaunttailler.*
Feb. 6.	Mary, daughter of Thomas Corbett, *Skynner.*
Feb. 14.	Margarett, daughter of Edward Williams, *Merchanttaller.*
Feb. 16.	Elizabeth, daughter of Thomas Knotte, *Mercer.*

1575

May 8.	Lucrecia, daughter of Clement Morando.
Sep. 22.	Mathew and Margarett, twynnes, son and daughter of Ferne, *Myllener*
Oct. 24.	Myldred, daughter of Thomas Humble, *Stacioner.*
Oct. 30:	John, son of John Mune, *Draper.*
Nov. 13.	Elizabeth, daughter of James Somner, *Clothworker.*
Jan. 1.	Elizabethe, daughter of Hughe Keyle, *Goldsmythe.*
Feb. 26.	Ann, daughter of William Judye, *Draper.*
Mar. 18.	Thomassen, daughter of Richard Robins, *Goldsmythe.*

1576

Mar. 29.	William, son of Mr. Edward Thorne, that married My Lady Harker.
April 3.	Christian, daughter of John Shorte, *Clothworker,* that was delyvered at the Church doore.

Sep. 21.	William, son of John Fox, *Clothworker*.
Oct. 7.	William, son of Emanuell Cole, *Goldsmythe*.
Oct. 7.	John, son of Xpofer Olde, *Draper*.
Nov. 11.	Frauncis, daughter of Humfrey Derycote, *Draper*.
Dec. 1.	Jerononny, son of Clement Morand, *Cutler* and *Straunger*.
Dec. 9.	Clement, son of Robert Bishop, *Taylor*.
Dec. 16.	Anne, daughter of John Wilkins, *Goldsmythe*.
Jan. 13.	Margaret, daughter of Thomas Humble, *Stacioner*.
Jan. 27.	Rowland, son of Thomas Sympson, *Goldsmythe*.
Feb. 12.	John, son of Richard Parker, *Merchaunte*.
Feb. 12.	Thomas, son of Roger Tasker, *Goldsmythe*.

1577

April 28.	Phillipp, son of Leonard Cooke, *Taylor*.
June 17.	William, son of Cuthbert Crachplace, *Goldsmythe*.
June 24.	Joane, daughter of William Judy, *Draper*.
Oct. 6.	Henrye, son of James Somner, *Clothworker*.
Nov. 2.	Hughe, son of Hughe Keale, *Goldsmythe*.
Nov. 22.	Octavian, son of Clement Morands, *Straunger* and *Cutler*.
Jan. 23.	Katherin, daughter of Edward Griffyn, *Bricklear*.

1578

April 4.	John, son of Richard Beard, *Mynister*.
July 7.	Ellyn, daughter of Thomas Payne, of Stamforde. She was Mr. Abraham's mayde.
July 8.	Blanche, daughter Roger Tasker, *Goldsmythe*.
July 13.	Marye, daughter of Humfrey Stevens, *Goldsmythe*.
July 27.	James, son of Thomas Humble, *Stacioner*.
Aug. 1.	Margarett, daughter of Emanuell Cole, *Goldsmythe*.
Aug. 3.	John, son of John Wilkyns, *Goldsmythe*.
Aug. 21.	Jone, daughter of William Judy, *Draper*.
Nov. 3.	Elizabeth, daughter of Thomas Simpson, *Goldsmythe*.
Jan. 27.	Sara, Watte, daughter of John Dayntry, in Mr. Warde's house."
Feb. 21.	John, son of John Wright, *Draper*.
Feb. 22.	Roger, son of James Somner, *Clothworker*.
Mar. 14.	George, son of Richard Parker, *Merchaunt*.
Mar. 15.	Thomas, son of William Powell.

1579

April 15.	John, son of William Warde, *Draper*.
May 10.	Richard, son of Nicholas Bradbanck, *Clothworker*.
July 1.	Elizabeth, daughter of Adam Beckinsall, *Glasier*.
July 4.	Abraham and Margaret, son and daughter of Roger Tasker, *Goldsmythe*.
July 13.	Selyna, daughter of John Chapman, *Letherseller*.
July 19.	Alice, daughter of Clement Morando, *Straunger*.
July 26.	Thomas, son of Humfrey Dethycote.
July 31.	William, son of Francis Kydd, *Scrivener*.
Sep. 11.	Edward, son of Edward Griffyn, *Bricklear*.
Sep. 23.	Launcelott, son of William Frank, *Goldsmythe*.
Oct. 4.	Robert, son of John Bawlderstan, *Sherman and Clothworker*.

Oct. 7.	Launcelott, son of Hughe Keale, *Goldsmythe.*
Oct. 11.	Francis and Marmaduke, sons of Marmaduke Higgins, *Grocer.*
Oct. 21.	Paule, son of Henry Kettellwood, *Goldsmythe.*
Nov. 15.	John, son of John Barker, *Draper.*
Feb. 5.	Marye, daughter of John Alderson, *Vintener.*
Mar. 19.	Marten, son of Richard Offley, *Merchaunte.*

1580

April 2.	Katherin, daughter of Edwarde Crosshawe.
April 24.	John, son of Edward Beldon.
May 8.	Thomas, son of William Warde, *Draper.*
June 26.	John, son of James Somner, *Clothworker.*
Aug. 12.	Roger, son of Roger Easton, *Goldsmyth.*
Aug. 31.	Anthony, son of Anthony Hayward, *Chaplen in the Queen's Majesties house.*
Oct. 5.	Mary, daughter of Thomas Simpson, *Goldsmythe.*
Oct. 22.	Henry, son of Thomas Turner, *Grocer.*
Dec. 4.	Henry, son of Henry Ketelwood, *Goldsmythe.*
Dec. 10.	Robert, son of Richard Baccus, *Haberdasher.*
Dec. 28.	Thomas, son of Richard Lory, *Goldsmythe.*
Jan. 21.	Israell, son of Thomas Newton.
Jan. 30.	William, son of Andrew Woodcock, *Butcher.*
Feb. 10.	Suzanna, daughter of Robert Bischope, *Taylor.*
Feb. 26.	Jane, daughter of John Aldersey, *Vintener.*
Feb. 26.	Bridgitt, daughter of John Collins, *Goldsmythe.*
Mar. 5.	Eliza, sone [*sic*] of Henry Knowsley.

1581

May 10.	Edmonde, son of Thomas Humble, *Stacioner.*
May 12.	Margaret, daughter of Edmond Grete, *Goldsmythe.*
May 21.	Francis, daughter of George Tompson, *Carpentar.*
May 29.	Thomas, son of Edward Beldon, *foryner Escholemaster.*
May 31.	Rowland, son of Walter Bolton, *Haberdasher.*
June 18.	John, son of Edward Crashawe, *Haberdasher.*
July 2.	Anne, daughter of John Wilkyns, *Goldsmythe.*
Aug. 8.	Jane, daughter of Anthony Hayward, *Chaplin, &c.*
Aug. 20.	Anne, daughter of Hugh Keale, *Goldsmythe.*
Sep. 20.	Easter, daughter of William Johnson, servant with Mr. Edward Bolton, in the parishe of Dunchurch, in Warwickshire.
Nov. 1.	Humfrey, son of Nicholas Style, *Grocer.*
Nov. 12.	John, son of Thomas, Walker, *Merchaunt.*
Dec. 10.	Martha, daughter of Edward Gryffin, *Merchaunt.*
Dec. 10.	Mary, daughter of Henry Kettillwood, *Goldsmyth.*
Dec. 24.	Jane, daughter of Arthur Cheesemore, *Blacksmythe.*
Dec. 26.	Jane, daughter of James Somner, *Clothworker.*
Dec. 30.	Cislye, daughter of Richard Lowrry, *Goldsmythe.*
Dec. 30.	Hughe, son of Richard Offley, *Merchaunt of the Staple.*
Jan. 28.	Anthony, son of John Aldersey, *Vintener*
Feb. 11.	Thomas, son of George Newbole, *Goldsmythe.*
Feb. 11.	Elizabeth, daughter of Thomas Simpson, *Goldsmythe.*
Feb. 11.	Anne, daughter of William Franck, *Goldsmythe.*

1582

April 1.	Margerye, daughter of William Huchinson, *Paynter*.
May 27.	Thomas, son of Thomas Clarke, *Haberdasher*.
June 3.	Zachary, son of Thomas Newton, *Mynister*.
June 24.	Elizabeth, daughter of Walter Bowlton, *Haberdasher*.
Aug. 12.	John, son of Richard Brooke, *Goldsmythe*.
Sep. 2.	John, son of Edmond Grete, *Goldsmythe*.
Sep. 12.	Cislye, daughter of Roger Tasker, *Goldsmythe*, Witnes by Roose Preest, Mydwief, that it was so weke that it coulde not tarry untill Sundaye.
Sep. 16.	Sybell, daughter of William Rawlinson, *Goldsmythe*.
Sep. 23.	Anne, daughter of William Warde, *Draper*.
Sep. 29.	Anthony, son of Anthony Hayward, *Chaplen, &c.*
Oct. 14.	Elizabeth, daughter of Robert Lyversage, *Draper*.
Dec. 26.	Elizabeth, daughter of George Tompson, *Carpentar*.
Jan. 13.	Rowland, son of Hugh Keale, *Goldsmythe*.
Jan. 27.	John, son of Robert Bisshopp, *Merchaunttaillor*.

1583

April 14.	Thomas, son of Edward Harwood, *Grocer*.
April 14.	Sara, daughter of Henry Knowslye.
May 12.	Margaret, daughter of William Hutchinson, *Paynter*.
June 2.	Christopher Lory.
June 7.	William, son of George Newbolde, *Goldsmythe*.
June 7.	William, son of William Jewdye, *Clothworker*.
July 25.	Jane, daughter of William Randall, *Haberdasher*.
Aug. 4.	Alice, daughter of George Savage, *Haberdasher*.
Sep. 1.	Francis, son of William Franck, *Goldsmythe*.
Sep. 22.	Hughe, son of Edmonde Greete, *Goldsmythe*.
Sep. 22.	William, son of John Wilkyns, *Goldsmythe*.
Oct. 6.	Elizabeth, daughter of John Aldersey, *Vyntener*.
Oct. 13.	Humfrey, son of Robert Mowldsworth, *Paynter Stayner*.
Oct. 15.	Rowlande, son of Richard Rogers, *Goldsmythe*.
Nov. 3.	Elizabeth, daughter of Thomas Francknell, *Goldsmythe*.
Dec. 15.	Adam, son of Adam Beckensaw, *Glasier*.
Dec. 21.	Agnes, daughter of Anthony Haywood, *Chaplin, &c.*
Jan. 26.	Helen, daughter of Walter Bowlton, *Haberdasher*.
Feb. 9.	Thomas, son of Humfrey Dutton, *Goldsmythe*.
Feb 9.	Margarett, daughter of Richard Brooke, *Goldsmythe*.
Feb. 23.	Robert, son of Henry Barne, *Skynner, also Scrivener and Clarke of this Parish.*
Mar. 1.	Margarett, daughter of Edward Hardinge, *Goldsmythe*.

1584

April 11.	William, son of William Rawlinson, *Goldsmythe*, at his owne house.
May 3.	Edward, son of Edward Griffith, *Merchaunt*.
May 10.	John, son of Arthur Chaesmore, *Blacksmythe*.
Aug. 9.	Richard, son of Thomas Clark, *Haberdasher*.
Aug. 16.	Sibell, daughter of Thomas Papworth.
Aug. 16.	Elizabeth, daughter of Roger Tasker, *Goldsmythe*.
Aug. 17.	At home. Samuel, son of Henry Butler, *Draper*.
Sep. 13.	William, son of William Jewdy, *Clothworker*.
Sep. 13.	Martha, daughter of Edmond Greete, *Goldsmythe*.

Sep. 29.	John, son of John Collyns, *Goldsmythe.*
Oct. 18.	Mary, daughter of William Franck, *Goldsmythe.*
Nov. 8.	Jane, daughter of Richard Rogers, *Goldsmythe.*
Nov. 20.	Elizabeth, daughter of Edward Phillips, *Upholster,* of the Parishe of St. Mighell upon Cornhill, London, whose wief lay in childbed of the same childe at her father Rowland Okeover his house by reason that the said Phillips house in Cornhill was a lyttle before that burnte by casualtie of Fyar.
Dec. 6.	Suzan, daughter of Thomas Francknell, *Goldsmythe.*
Dec. 20.	Elizabethe, daughter of Henrye Kettlewood, *Goldsmythe.*
Dec. 21.	Margarett, daughter of George Newbold, *Goldsmythe.*
Dec. 21.	Rowlande, son of Anthony Haywood, *Chaplen, &c.*
Jan. 3.	Elizabeth, daughter of Nicholas Style, *Grocer.*
Feb. 7.	Mary, daughter of William Dixon.
Feb. 14.	William, son of William Warde, *Draper.*
Feb. 14.	Margarett, daughter of Walter Bolton, *Haberdasher.*
Mar. 7.	Margarett, daughter of John Aldersey, *Vintener.*

1585

April 25.	Francis, daughter of Nicholas Cardwell, *Grocer.*
June 27.	Lea, daughter of Henry Barne, *Scrivener and Clarke of this Parishe Church.*
Sep. 12.	Nicholas, son of William Randall, *Haberdasher.*
Sep. 19.	Henrye, son of William Rawlinson, *Goldsmythe.*
Oct. 3.	Francis, daughter of John Lashley, *Merchaunttaillor.*
Oct. 17.	William, son of Edmond Greete, *Goldsmythe.*
Nov. 13.	Suzan, daughter of Richard Harrison, *Cowper.*
Nov. 14.	William, son of William Franck, *Goldsmythe.*
Nov. 14.	Helen, daughter of Francis Shute, *Goldsmythe.*
Nov. 14.	Dorathye, daughter of Xpofer Ivoryc.
Nov. 21.	Rachell, daughter of George Newbold, *Goldsmyth.*
Dec. 5.	Henry, son of Roger Easton, *Goldsmythe.*
Dec. 12.	Mary, daughter of Hughe Keall, *Goldsmythe.*
Dec. 12.	William, son of George Savage, *Haberdasher.*
Dec. 14.	Francis, son of Anthony Hawood, *Chaplen, &c.*
Jan. 2.	Suzan, daughter of Thomas Papworth.
Jan. 6.	William, son of John Morreys, *Goldsmythe.*
Jan. 9.	Judith, daughter of Leonard Gale, *Draper.*
Jan. 16.	William, son of William Dixon.

1586

April 3.	Mary, daughter of Nicholas Style, *Grocer.*
April 4.	Henry, son of Walter Bolton, *Haberdasher.*
April 7.	Edward, son of Thomas Cotton, at his dwellinge house.
April 29.	Elizabeth, daughter of William Dodd, *Clothworker.*
June 19.	Sibbell, daughter of Thomas Francknell, *Goldsmythe.*
July 4.	Elizabeth, daughter of Thomas Viccars, *Glasier.*
July 17.	Xpofer, son of Richard Dytch, *Clothworker.*
Aug. 14.	Sibble, daughter of Richard Brooke, *Goldsmythe.*
Sep. 21.	James, son of Edward Hardinge, *Goldsmythe.*
Oct. 9.	George, son of Edmond Greete, *Goldsmythe.*
Nov. 6.	Richard, son of John Alderson, *Vintener.*
Nov. 20.	Sara, daughter of Edward Greene, *Goldsmythe.*

Nov. 20.	Elizabeth, daughter of Anthony Hawood, *Chaplen, &c.*
Nov. 27.	Anna, daughter of Henry Butler, *Draper.*
Nov. 27.	Jeronamye, daughter of Richard Harrison, *Cooper.*
Dec. 6.	William, son of Francis Shute, *Goldsmyth.*
Jan. 29.	Jane, daughter of Justynia Spencer, *Goldsmythe.*
Mar. 19.	Elizabeth, daughter of George Newbold, *Goldsmythe.*
Mar. 19.	Elizabeth, daughter of Thomas Childe, *Armorer.*

1587

April 9.	Suzan, daughter of Peter Venables, *Shoemaker.*
April 24.	Roger, son of Walter Bowlton, *Haberdasher.*
April 24.	Jayne, daughter of Thomas Clark, *Haberdasher.*
April 24.	Peter, son of William Franck, *Goldsmythe.*
May 7.	True, daughter of Edward Brandon.
June 20.	Elizabeth, daughter of Adam Beckensall, *Glasier.*
Aug. 8.	Marye, daughter of James Allen, *Goldsmythe.*
Aug. 27.	Elizabeth, daughter of William Warde, *Draper.*
Sep. 3.	Robert, son of William Rawlinson, *Goldsmythe.*
Sep. 17.	Anne, daughter of William Randall.
Oct. 1.	Elizabeth, daughter of William Jewdy, *Clothworker.*
Nov. 8.	Charles, son of Anthony Hawood, *Chaplen, &c.*
Nov. 19.	Benedick, son of Edward Griffith, *Merchaunte.*
Dec. 17.	Prudence, daughter of Henry Butler, *Draper.*
Dec. 31.	Anna, daughter of Jasper Bossevyle, *Haberdasher.*
Jan. 1.	Katherin, daughter of Francis Shute, *Goldsmythe.*
Jan. 7.	Jane, daughter of Edward Delves, *Goldsmythe.*
Mar. 3.	In the house of Mr. Brandon, Rebecca, daughter of William Budder, *Gentleman.*

1588

Mar. 31.	George, son of George Newbold.
May 5.	Henry, son of Thomas Clark, *Haberdasher.*
May 26.	Elizabeth, daughter of Nicholas Style, *Grocer.*
May 27.	Dorothie, daughter of Thomas Francknell, *Goldsmyth.*
July 7.	Anna, daughter of John Alderson, *Vyntener.*
Aug. 4.	Elizabeth, daughter of Simon Sedgewyck, *Goldsmythe.*
Aug. 25.	John, son of William Dixon, *Paynter.*
Aug. 25.	Anne, daughter of Edward Greene, *Goldsmythe.*
Sep. 8.	Johan, daughter of Richard Dytch, *Clothworker.*
Sep. 15.	Katherin, daughter of [*sic*] Greenfeilde, who came out of the House of Xpofer Ivery.
Sep. 29.	Elizabeth, daughter of Richard Brooke, *Goldsmythe.*
Sep. 29.	Suzan, daughter of Walter Boughton, *Haberdasher.*
Oct. 6.	Sara, daughter of John Greene, *Tailor.*
Nov. 15.	Margaret, daughter of Anthony Hawood, late Clark, deceassed, within the house commonly called the Stone house.
Dec. 8.	Hellen, daughter of Thomas Viccars, *Glasier.*
*Dec. 15.	Elizabeth, daughter of George Samwell, *Notarie.*
Jan. 1.	Robert, son of Edward Delves, *Goldsmyth.*
Jan. 19.	Raphe, son of William Rawlinson, *Goldsmyth.*
Jan. 19.	John, son of Josua Hilliard, *Lyffetenaunte.*
Jan. 26.	Richard, son of Francis Shute, *Goldsmythe.*

* Mr. SAMWELL probably transcribed the registers : the entries concerning his own family are engrossed in large letters.

Feb. 23.   John, son of Leonard Gale, *Gilder*, also *Draper*.
Feb. 23.   Hellen, daughter of Thomas Dickenson, *Haberdasher*.
Mar. 16.   Joan and Elizabeth, daughters of Thomas Clark, *Haber-dasher*.
Mar. 23.   Richard, son of Richard Harrison, *Cooper*.

1589

April 13.   Anne, daughter of George Newbold, *Goldsmythe*.
June 1.   Elizabeth, daughter of Henry Butler, *Draper*.
July 6.   Alice, daughter of John Anderson.
Sep. 7.   Anne, daughter of William Dixson, *Peynter Steyner*.
Sep. 14.   Thomas, son of Nicholas Gryme, *Tailor*.
Sep. 29.   Elizabeth, daughter of William Franch, *Goldsmythe*.
Oct. 26.   Katheren, daughter of Thomas Francknell, *Goldsmythe*.
Nov. 2.   John, son of Walter Boughton, *Haberdasher*.
Nov. 2.   Mary, daughter of John Dobbes, *Haberdasher*.
Nov. 9.   Thomas, son of George Samwell, *Notarie*.
Nov. 30.   Dorothie, daughter of Edward Delves, *Goldsmythe*.
Feb. 1.   William, son of William Rawlinson, *Goldsmythe*.
Feb. 8.   Margarett, daughter of William Dutton, *Haberdasher*.
Mar. 6.   Marye, daughter of Thomas Williamson, *Laborer*, free of the Clothworkers.

1590

April 5.   Francis, son of Francis Longworth, *Goldsmythe*.
May 3.   Katherin, daughter of William Jewdye, *Clothworker*.
May 17.   Robert, son of William Warde, *Draper*.
May 17.   Richard, son of Richard Brooke, *Goldsmythe*.
May 10.   Cassandra, daughter of James Juce, *Mercer*.
May 24.   Scissely, daughter of Edward Raylton, *Draper*.
June 7.   Grace, daughter of Francis Shute, *Goldsmythe*.
June 14.   Robert, son of Hugh Peake, *Goldsmythe*.
Aug. 2.   Elizabeth, daughter of George Newbold, *Goldsmythe*.
Sep. 16.   Edeth, daughter of Richard Comyns, alias Williams, *Scrivener*.
Sep. 20.   Phillipp, son of William Randall, *Haberdasher*.
Oct. 4.   John, son of Walter Bowlton, *Haberdasher*
Oct. 11.   Thomas, son of William Franck, *Goldsmythe*.
Oct. 25.   Thomas, son of William Dickson, *Paynter*.
Jan. 1.   Richard, son of Edward Griffyn, *Haberdasher*.
Jan. 6.   Humfry, son of Henry Hargrave, *Goldsmythe*.
Jan. 17.   John, son of George Samwell, *Notarie*.
Feb. 2.   John, son of Henry Busshopp.
Feb. 11.   Anne, daughter of Thomas Francknell, *Goldsmythe*.
Mar. 14   Christian, daughter of Gyles Sympson, *Goldsmythe*.
Mar. 14.   Dorathie, daughter of William Dutton, *Haberdasher*.

1591

April 9.   Suzan, daughter of John Grene, *Taylor*.
April 18.   Prudence, daughter of John Skott, *Butcher*.
April 25.   Edward, son of Edward Delves, *Goldsmythe*.
June 2.   Katheren, daughter of Jeames Juce.
June 20.   Barnabye, son of Nicholas Wakefield, *Gentleman*.

June 20.	Allen, son of John Sothern, *Leatherseller*.
Aug. 4.	Alice, daughter of Walter Bolton, *Haberdasher*.
Sep. 19.	Marye, daughter of Francis Shute, *Goldsmythe*.
Feb. 2.	Bridgett, daughter of Henry Hargrave, *Goldsmythe*.
Feb. 27.	Anne, daughter of George Samwell, *Notarie*.
Mar. 19.	Edward, son of Richard Harrison, *Cooper*.

1592

April 8.	Mary, daughter of Thomas Evans, *Bricklear*.
April 16.	Anne, daughter of Gyles Sympson, *Goldsmythe*.
April 16.	Alice, daughter of Gyles Sympson, *Goldsmythe*.
April 16.	Scissely, daughter of Symon Siedgewick, *Goldsmythe*.
May 28.	Richard, son of Nicholas Gryme, *Merchaunt Taylor*.
June 4.	Thomas, son of Thomas Darby, *Merchaunt*.
June 4.	Elizabethe, daughter of Francis Longworthe, *Goldsmythe*.
Aug. 6.	Nicholas, son of Nicholas Wakefeilde, *Gentleman*.
Aug. 13.	Sara, daughter of William Hamore, *Scryvener*.
Sep. 24.	Martha, daughter of William Exton, *Pursemaker*.
Oct. 1.	James, son of John Sothern, *Leatherseller*.
Oct. 8.	John, son of George Bentley, *Cordwayner*.
Oct. 15.	Richard, son of John Alderson, *Vintener*.
Nov. 8.	William, son of Richard Cheaney, *Goldsmythe*.
Nov. 26.	Jane, daughter of William Dutton, *Haberdasher*.
Dec. 3.	William, son of Richard Brooke, *Goldsmythe*.
Dec. 17.	Francis, son of Francis Shute, *Goldsmythe*.
Jan. 21.	Peter, son of Edward Delves, *Goldsmythe*.
Feb. 4.	Joseph, son of Anthony Sownde, *Clothworker*.
Feb. 11.	Henry, son of John Bell, *Clothworker*.

1593

April 8.	John, son of Randall, Gravener.
May 6.	[*sic*] daughter of [*sic*] Hamden.
May 20.	Rebecca, daughter of George Samwell, *Notarye*.
June 30.	Jane, daughter of Henry Hargrave, *Goldsmythe*.
Aug. 5.	Elizabeth, daughter of Thomas Francknell, *Clothworker*.
Aug. 12.	Thomas, son of the aforesaid Thomas Francknell, *Clothworker*.
Aug. 12.	George, son of William Warde, *Draper*.
Aug. 15.	George, son of Nicholas Gryme, *Taylor*.
Aug. 26.	Elizabeth, daughter of John Williamson, *Labourer*.
Aug. 23.	Cisley, daughter of William Randall, *Haberdasher*.
Aug. 24.	Hellen, daughter of Henry Bisshopp.
Nov. 9.	Thomas, son of George Staynerod, *Grocer*.
Jan. 14.	Margarett, daughter of John Bell, *Clothworker*.
Jan. 17.	Sara, daughter of George Newbold, *Goldsmyth*, in his house.
Jan. 25.	James, son of Edward Delves, *Goldsmythe*.
Jan. 30.	Mary, daughter of Thomas Eagles, *Haberdasher*.
Feb. 24.	Reynold, son of John Sothern, *Leatherseller*.

1594

April 1.	Anne, daughter of John Dabb, *Haberdasher*.
April 14.	Thomas, son of Thomas Lawrence, *Goldsmythe*.

April 21.	Richard, son of James Traves, *Merchaunt*.
April 21.	Elizabeth, daughter of Edmond Brooke, *Goldsmythe*.
June 9.	John, son of Thomas Clark, *Haberdasher*.
June 30.	William, son of William Exton, *Purse Maker*.
July 7.	Margarett, daughter of John Lovejoye, *Goldsmythe*.
Aug. 25.	Francis, daughter of Francis Longworth, *Goldsmythe*.
Aug. 26.	William, son of Randall Gravener, *Dyer*.
Sep. 8.	Robert, son of John Burforde, *Silkweaver*.
Sep. 29.	Martha, daughter of Gyles Simpson, *Goldsmythe*.
Oct. 6.	Margarett, daughter of Francis Shute, *Goldsmythe*.
Oct. 6.	Margarett, daughter of Noye Farmer, *Goldsmythe*.
Oct. 20.	Mary, daughter of Richard Harrison, *Cowper*.
Dec. 1.	Margarett, daughter of John Carter, *Taylor*.
Dec. 15.	Elizabeth, daughter of John Barnabye, *Grocer*.
Dec. 22.	Suzan, daughter of Henry Busshopp.
Dec. 29.	John, son of John Cockenskell, *Taylor*.
Jan. 26.	Rowlande, son of Thomas Francknell, *Goldsmythe*.
Mar. 23.	Christian daughter of Thomas Robson, *Cordwayner*.

1595

April 20.	Thomas, son of Thomas Rudd, *Haberdasher*.
April 20.	Robert, son of Robert Brooke, *Goldsmythe*.
April 22.	George Woolnoth, a foundlinge.
April 27.	Martha, daughter of Thomas Whyte, *Grocer*.
May 18.	Charles, son of John Sothern, *Leatherseller*.
May 18.	John, son of John Mason, *Haberdasher*.
May 25.	James, son of James Traves, *Merchaunt*.
June 15.	William, son of Thomas Lawrence, *Goldsmythe*.
July 6.	Anne, daughter of Symon Sedgeweeke, *Goldsmyth*.
July 6.	Humfrey, son of Richard Hall, *Taylor*.
July 6.	Elizabeth, daughter of Richard Brooke, *Goldsmythe*.
July 27.	George, son of George Samwell, *Scryvener and Notarye*.
Aug. 10.	Elizabeth, daughter of John Twyne, *Vintener*.
Oct. 5.	Suzan, daughter of William Dutton, *Haberdasher*.
Nov. 2.	Richard, son of Randall Gravener, *Dyer*.
Nov. 23.	Judith, daughter of William Dixson, *Peynter Steyner*.
Nov. 31.	Rebecca, daughter of John Beeson, *Peynter Steyner*.
Dec. 3.	Robert, son of William Hamor.
Dec. 10.	Robert, son of Edward Hill, *Merchaunttaillor*.
Jan. 25.	Richard, son of Richard Cheany, *Goldsmyth*.
Feb. 1	Suzan, daughter of Francis Shute, *Goldsmythe*.
Feb. 24.	Hellen, daughter of Robert Blease, *Taylor*.
Mar. 21.	Alice, daughter of Edwarde Brooke, *Goldsmythe*.

1596

April 12.	John, son of Peter Powell, *Skynner*.
April 13.	Thomas, son of Edwarde Delves, *Goldsmythe*.
May 2.	William son of Richard Carter, *Clothworker*.
May 20.	Clement, son of Thomas Francknell, *Clothworker*.
May 30.	Anne, daughter of John Burfert, *Silkweaver*.
June 6.	Elizabeth, daughter of John Twyne, *Vyntener*.
June 20.	William, son of —— [*sic*] Hall, *Taylor*.
June 27.	Thomas, son of Robert Brooke, *Goldsmythe*.
July 18.	Anne, daughter of William Exton, *Purse Maker*.

Aug. 15.	Mary, daughter of George Nickson, *Taylor.*
Aug. 25.	John, son of Thomas Lawrence, *Goldsmythe.*
Sep. 6.	John, son of Christian Anthony.
Sep. 12.	John, son of ——— [*sic*] Newcombe, *Barber.*
Sep. 19.	Katherin, daughter of William Warde, *Draper.*
Sep. 29.	William, son of William Sales, *Hosiere.*
Oct. 17.	Gyles, son of Gyles Sympson, *Goldsmythe.*
Oct. 31.	Martyn, son of John Fludd, *Vintener.*
Nov. 7.	Elizabeth, daughter of William Dickson, *Paynter.*
Nov. 21.	Elizabeth, daughter of Noye Farmer, *Goldsmythe.*
Nov. 28.	John, son of Thomas Robson, *Blacksmythe.*

1597

April 7.	Rowlande, son of John Lovejoy, *Goldsmythe.*
June 12.	Thomas, son of Wydowe Francknell, the late wieff of Thomas Francknell, *Goldsmythe,* deceased.
July 3.	Judeth, daughter of Edward Delves, *Goldsmythe.*
July 10.	John, son of Thomas Lewes, *Haberdasher.*
July 30.	Robert, son of Robert Blease, *Taylor.*
Aug. 19.	George, son of Randall Gravener, *Dyer.*
Aug. 21.	Dorothie, daughter of Robert Brooke, *Goldsmythe.*
Sep. 4.	Thomasin, daughter of Francis Shute, *Goldsmythe.*
Sep. 11.	Arnold, son of Arnold Richardson, *Vintener.*
Sep. 21.	Thomas, son of Richard Cheanye, *Goldsmythe.*
Sep. 25.	Elizabeth, daughter of George Nickson, *Taylor.*
Oct. 4.	John, son of William Dickson, *Paynter.*
Oct. 30.	William, son of Gyles Sympson, *Goldsmythe.*
Nov. 2.	Gyles Woolnoth, a manchild, found layde at the gate of the Lady Ramsay.
Nov. 13.	John son of Edward Hyde, *Goldsmythe.*
Nov. 20.	William, son of Richard Brooke, *Goldsmithe.*
Nov. 26.	Andrew, son of Andrewe Fox, *Haberdasher.*
Dec. 4.	John, son of Francis Glanffeild, *Goldsmythe.*
Dec. 18.	Johane, daughter of John Carter, *Merchaunttaillor.*
Jan. 12.	Anna, daughter of Thomas White, *Grocer.*
Mar. 5.	Anna, daughter of John Beeson, *Gilder.*
Mar. 12.	Sara, daughter of Richard Carter, *Cloth Maker.*
Mar. 24.	Thomas, daughter of Stephen Taylor, *Girdler.*

1598

Mar. 30.	Margarett, daughter of Thomas Thrall, *Vyntener.*
	The same ——— [*sic*] day of May, Alice, daughter of Thomas Francknell, *Clothworker.*
June 25.	Jane, daughter of William Hams, *Scryvener.*
July 30.	Jane, daughter of John Bursett, *Silkweaver.*
Aug. 13.	John, son of Edward Delves, *Goldsmythe.*
Aug. 24.	Anne, daughter of William Cares, *Goldsmythe.*
Sep. 29.	Mary, daughter of George Woodward, *Merchaunttaillor.*
Oct. 9.	Anne, daughter of Gyles Sympson, *Goldsmythe.*
Dec. 10.	William, son of Francis Grenehaughe, *Iremonger.*
Dec. 14.	Ellis, son of Raphe Mynars, *Sileman.*
Dec. 24.	Rowland, son of John Lovejoy, *Goldsmythe.*
Jan. 7.	Edward, son of Roger Mountague, *White Baker.*
Jan. 14.	Henry, son of Daniell Binnell, *Goldsmythe.*

Jan. 28.	Suzan, daughter of Richard Cheney, *Goldsmythe.*
Mar. 4.	William, son of Thomas Lawrence, *Goldsmythe.*
Mar. 11.	John, son of Francis Shute, *Goldsmythe.*
Mar. 18.	Joane, daughter of Thomas Robson, *Cordwayner.*

1599

April 20.	William, son of James Robinson, *Gentleman.*
April 20.	Thomas, son of William Gallaway, *Haberdasher.*
April 22.	Henry, son of George Nixon, *Merchaunttaillor.*
April 29.	Steven, son of Samuell Buck, *Brown Baker.*
April 29.	Anne, daughter of Richard Carter, *Clothworker.*
May 6.	Edwarde, son of Andrew Foxe, *Haberdasher.*
May 17.	Joseph, son of John Gudburye, *Leatherseller.*
June 3.	Jane, daughter of James Travers, *Merchante.*
June 6.	Elizabeth, daughter of Francis Glanvill, *Goldsmythe.*
June 10.	Woolnoth, son of Robert Tompson, of the Parishe of Lambeth, in the County of Surrey, *Drayman,* the mother thereof is called Elizabeth, was delyvered in the Churchdore of the streate side of this Parishe.
July 22.	Ellis, son of Thomas Clayton, *Clothworker,* lying in the house of Thomas Viccars.
Aug. 5.	John, son of Thomas Westley, *Vintener.*
Sep. 9.	Thomas, son of Francis Greenehaugh, *Iremonger.*
Oct. 7.	John, son of John Carter, *Marchanttaillor.*
Dec. 9.	Richard, son of Gyles Sympson, *Goldsmythe.*
Dec. 9.	Elizabeth, daughter of John Lovejoy, *Goldsmythe.*
Dec. 16.	Judith, daughter of William Buntingdale, *Haberdasher.*
Jan. 27.	Judith, daughter of Robert Bleese, *Taylor.*
Feb. 3.	Beniomyn, son of Beniamyn Trewe, *Clothworker.*
Feb. 19.	John, son of John Burford, *Weaver.*
Mar. 9.	Henry, son of Edward Delves, *Goldsmythe.*

1600

May 18.	Elizabeth, daughter of Thomas White, *Grocer.*
June 15.	Jane, daughter of George Samwell, *Notary Publique.*
June 15.	Rowlande, son of William Sales.
June 10.	Nicolas, son of Samuel Buck, *Brown Baker.*
June 22.	Mary, daughter of William Terry, *Goldsmythe.*
Aug. 17.	George, son of William Galloway, *Haberdasher.*
Sep. 28.	Elizabeth, daughter of John Beeston, *Paynter Stayner.*
Oct. 5.	John, son of Robert Brooke, *Goldsmythe.*
Oct. 12.	Mary, daughter of Francis Shute, *Goldsmythe.*
Nov. 16.	John, son of George Humble, *Leatherseller.*
Nov. 23.	Francis, son of Francis Greenehaught, *Iremonger.*
Nov. 23.	Bartholomew, son of Thomas Wilford.
Nov. 30.	Jeremy, son of Gyles Sympson, *Goldsmith.*
Nov. 30.	Elizabeth, daughter of James Thorne, *Clothworker.*
Dec. 14.	Esther, daughter of William Ward, *Tailor.*
Dec. 18.	John, son of Thomas Lawrance, *Goldsmith.*
Jan. 25.	Anna, daughter of William Herring, *Haberdasher.*
Jan. 25.	Mary, daughter of George Nickson, *Taylor.*
Jan. 25.	Mary, daughter of Edmond Ballard.
Feb. 16.	Richard, son of George Cary.
Feb. 23.	Mary, daughter of William Hamore, *Scryvener.*

Mar 8.	Anne, daughter of Thomas Robson, *Cordwayner*.
Mar. 19.	John, son of Richard Carter, *Blacksmith*.

1601

April 20.	Hester, daughter of John Lovejoy, *Goldsmith*.
April 26.	Walter, son of Richard Brooke, *Goldsmith*.
June 14.	Elizabeth, daughter of Patrick Careck, *Vintener*.
July 19.	John, son of William Sales, *Tailor*.
July 26.	Posthumus son of John Savage, *Senr*.
July 29.	Phip, son of John Glasse.
Aug. 16.	John, son of John Acton, *Goldsmith*.
Aug. 23.	Mary, daughter of Fabyan Sympson, *Goldsmith*.
Sep. 13.	William, son of William Tirrey, *Goldsmith*.
Oct. 4.	Mary, daughter of Richard Phillipps.
Oct. 18.	John, son of John Pleydell, *Haberdasher*.
Nov. 22.	Elizabeth, daughter of William Galloway.
Nov. 22.	Elizabeth, daughter of John Carter, *Taylor*.
Dec. 6.	George, daughter [*sic*] of Andrew Tisdell, *Waterbearer*.
Jan. 7.	Henry, son of Abraham Sherifry, *Clark*.
Jan. 7.	Mary, daughter of Samuell Buck, *Baker*.
Feb. 8.	Daniell, son of Thomas Westley, *Vintener*.
Feb. 8.	George, son of John Colte, *Goldsmith*.
Mar. 21.	William, son of Thomas Franklyn.
Mar. 28.	William, son of Giles Sympson, *Goldsmith*.

1602

April 11.	John, son of John Sudbury, *Letherseller*.
July 18.	Dorathie, daughter of Francis Greenehaugh.
Aug. 1.	Richard, son of Edward Delves, *Goldsmith*.
Aug. 1.	Mary, daughter of Thomas Lawrence, *Goldsmith*.
Aug. 8.	Margaret, daughter of Robert Bleis, *Tailor*.
Sep. 5.	Cecill, daughter of George Samwell, of London, *Notarie Publique*.
Sep. 12.	William, son of George Cars, *Goldsmith*.
Oct. 30.	Nicholas, son of William Buntingale, *Haberdasher*.
Dec. 12.	Robert, son of William Terry, *Goldsmith*.
Jan. 23.	Mary, daughter of William Galloway.
Mar. 5.	Sara, daughter of Nicholas Goddard, *Stockingpresser*.
Mar. 20.	Arthur, son of John Keale, *a maker of Swete Balls*.

1603

April, 25.	Jane, daughter of John Beeston, *Gilder*.
May 1.	James, son of Francis Shute, *Goldsmith*.
May 8.	John, son of John Wollaston, *Box Maker*.
May 15.	William, son of John Pkydell.
May 22.	Francis, daughter of Giles Sympson, *Goldsmith*.
May 22.	Nathaniel, son of Thomas Westley, *Vintner*.
June 12.	William, son of Thomas Robson, *Cordwaynor*.
June 19.	Mary, daughter of Raphe Harison, *Merchaunt*.
July 10.	Thomas, son of John Colte, *Goldsmith*.
July —	John, son of Raphe Burfoot, *Silkweander*.
July 30.	Thomas, son of Thomas White, *Grocer*.
July 31.	Katherine, daughter of William Hamore.

Aug. 7.	George, son of George Humbee, *Leatherseller.*
Aug. 28.	Nicholas, son of Andrew Tisdall, *Waterbearer.*
Sep. 28.	George, son of George Nickson, *Taylor.*
Oct. 23.	Edmund, son of Robert Trigger, *Haberdasher.*
Nov. 6.	Judeth, daughter of Barnabye Gregory, *Goldsmith.*
Dec. 25.	James, son of John Carter, *Tailor.*
Jan. 21.	Samuell, son of Samuel Buck, *Baker.*
Jan. 28.	Mary, daughter of Edward Delves, *Goldsmith.*
Feb. 13.	Anne, daughter of Samuel Buck, *Baker.*
Feb. 20.	William, son of Thomas Lawrence, *Goldsmith.*
Feb. 23.	Katherin, daughter of William Galloway.
Feb. 27.	Nicholas and Richard, sonnes of Nicholas Halfpenny, in the County of Kent, and were borne in this Parish in Mr. Chesmore's house.
Feb. 28.	Anne, daughter of John Smith, *Comfit Maker.*
Mar. 24.	John, son of William Herringe, *Haberdasher.*

1604

April 1.	Thomas, son of Edward Annable, *Vintner.*
May 1.	Elizabeth, daughter of John Lovejoy, *Goldsmith.*
May 1.	John, son of Thomas Clay, was borne in the house of Mrs. Viccars, *Glasier.*
May 1.	William, son of William Wood, *Goldsmith.*
July 15.	Katherine, daughter of Richard Man, *Goldsmith.*
July 22.	Anna, daughter of John Beeston, *Painter Stayner.*
Aug. 5.	Dorathie, daughter of John Burford, *Silkweaver.*
Aug. 12.	Mary, daughter of Richard Harrison, *Cowper.*
Aug. 19.	Anne, daughter of George Samwell, *Notary.*
Sep. 3.	Katherine, daughter of Nicholas Goddard, *Stocking Presser.*
Oct. 14.	John, daughter of Hugh Gwilliam, *Haberdasher.*
Oct. 21.	Margret, daughter of William Jones, *Vintner.*
Oct. 21.	Elizabeth, daughter of George Caro, *Goldsmith.*
Oct. 28.	Isaac and Elizabeth, both children of William Hamore, *Scrivener.*
Nov. 4.	Rebecca, daughter of Francis Haddon, *Goldsmith.*
Nov. 12.	Mary, daughter of Richard Shacrofte, *Grocer.*
Nov. 18.	Elizabeth, daughter of John Acton, *Goldsmith.*
Dec. 2.	John, son of Richard Cheney, *Goldsmith.*
Dec. 11.	Thomas, son of William Salea, *Tailor.*
Dec. 16.	Margret, daughter of Giles Sympson, *Goldsmith.*
Dec. 30.	Daniell, son of William Dutton, *Haberdasher.*
Jan. 6.	Elizabeth, daughter of Raphe Harison, *Marchant.*
Feb. 24.	Mary, daughter of William Rolphe, *Goldsmith.*
Mar. 3.	Anne, daughter of Henry Butler, *Draper.*
Mar. 17.	John, son of George Nickson, *Tailor.*
Mar. 24.	William, son of Thomas Lawrence, *Goldsmith.*

1605

April 7.	William, son of Wilfred Spaldinge, *Cutler.*
April 7.	Easter, daughter of William Galloway, *Haberdasher.*
May 9.	Francis, son of George Humble, *Letherseller.*
July 8.	John, son of John Homewood, *Chandler.*
July 8.	Jane, daughter of Edward Annable, *Vintner.*
July 8.	Anne, daughter of Richard Man, *Goldsmith.*

Sep. 15.   Francis, son of John Colte, *Goldsmith.*
Sep. 15.   Elizabeth, daughter of William Wood, *Goldsmith.*
Sep. 22.   Anne, daughter of George Monnox, *Haberdasher.*
Sep. 22.   Sara, daughter of William Tirrey, *Goldsmith.*
Oct. 6.   Vincent, son of George Samwell, *Notarye.*
Nov. 2.   Mary, daughter of Francis Haddon, *Goldsmith.*
Nov. 3.   William, son of Barnabye Gregory, *Goldsmith.*
Nov. 25.   Anne, daughter of John Pickeringe, *Tailor.*
Dec. 18.   Anne, daughter of John Keale, *Sweetball Maker.*
Jan. 5.   John son of Valentyne Judd, *Goldsmith.*
Jan. 19.   William, son of William Rolf, *Goldsmith.*
Feb. 9.   Awdrey, daughter of Giles Sympson, *Goldsmith.*
Feb. 16.   Anne, daughter of William Dutton, *Haberdasher.*
Mar. 2.   John, son of John Carter, *Tailor.*
Mar. 9.   James, son of John Sudbury, *Stacioner.*
Mar. 9.   Elizabeth, daughter of William Jones, *Vintener.*
Mar. 12.   John, son of George Carol, *Silversmith.*

1606

June 29.   William, son of Fabyan Sympson, *Goldsmith.*
July 6.   Anne, daughter of Richard Man, *Goldsmith.*
July 11.   James, son of Jeames Stanford.
Aug. 24.   John, son of John Griffen, *Clothworker.*
Nov. 16.   Frances, son of Frances Bullock, *Merchant.*
Nov. 23.   Henry, son of William Sailes, *Tailor.*
Dec. 10.   John, son of Robert Offley, *Gentleman.*
Dec. 10.   John, son of William Herryng, *Trimmer of Hatts.*
Dec. 21.   Henry, son of Walter Amber, *Haberdasher.*
Dec. 27.   Frances, daughter of Valentyne Judde, *Goldsmith.*
Jan. 4.   Mary, daughter of George Monnox, *Haberdasher.*
Jan. 4.   Anne, daughter of George Nickson, *Tailor.*
Jan. 18.   William, son of William Haymore, *Notary.*
Jan. 18.   Anne, daughter of Francis Laurence, *Joyner.*
Feb. 8.   John, son of Francis Hadon, *Goldsmith.*
Mar. 1.   Richard, son of William Wood, *Goldsmith.*
Mar. 8.   Thomas, son of Richard Evans, *Grocer.*

1607

April 5.   William, son of John Burfert, *Silkweaver.*
April 17.   Richard, son of Richard Harrison, *Cooper.*
April 24.   Elizabeth, daughter of George Humble, *Leatherseller.*
May 3.   Suzanne, daughter of William Rolphe, *Goldsmith.*
May 24.   Thomas, son of George Carey, *Goldsmith.*
May 24.   Anne, daughter of Hugh Gdwillams, *Haberdasher.*
June 28.   Judith and Francis, daughters of John Beeson, *Paynter Styner.*
July 29.   Matthy, daughter of John Homewood, *Chandler.*
Aug. 2.   George, son of William Tirrey, *Goldsmith.*
Aug. 8.   Peter, son of John Carter, *Tailor.*
Oct. 4.   Elizabeth, daughter of Gabriell Barber, *Goldsmith.*
Oct. 25.   John, son of William Keale, *Goldsmith.*
Nov. 8.   Mary, daughter of William Jones, *Vintner.*
Dec. 7.   Richard, son of Richard Phillips, *Goldsmith.*
Dec. 25.   George, son of George Monnock, *Haberdasher.*

Dec. 31.	Loyce, daughter of William Wood, *Goldsmith*.
Jan. 3.	Elizabeth, daughter of Henry Butler, *Draper*.
Jan. 7.	Robert, son of Barnaby Gregory, *Goldsmith*.
Jan. 11.	Margaret, daughter of Robert Widmore, *Plasterer*.
Feb. 15.	Mary, daughter of Raphe Harrison, *Merchant*.
Feb. 29.	Mary, daughter of Nicholas Goddart, *Stocking Presser*.
Feb. 29.	Elizabeth, daughter of John Chasmore, out of the house of Arthure Chasmore.
Mar. 6.	Mary, daughter of William Rawlins, *Goldsmith*.

1608

Mar. 27.	William, son of William Dutton, *Haberdasher*.
Mar. 27.	Thomas, son of Thomas Colli, *Haberdasher*.
April 24.	Anne, daughter of Valentine Judd, *Goldsmith*.
May 1.	Frances, daughter of John Griffen, *Clothworker*.
May 8.	William, son of William Lewes, *Imbroitherer*.
May 29.	Sibbell, daughter of Fabyan Sympson, *Goldsmith*.
June 19.	Suzan, daughter of Henry Chessheire, *Goldsmith*.
June 26.	George, son of George Samwell, *Notary Publique*.
July 3.	Edward, son of William Rolphe.
July 10.	Anne, daughter of Nicholas Humfrey, of St. Swithen's Parishe.
July 17.	Anne, daughter of William Hamore, *Clothworker*.
July 25.	Elizabeth daughter of John Homewood, *Chandler*.
July 30.	Daniell, son of Daniell Harnickhook, in the french Church.
Sep. 12.	Mary, daughter of George Cary, *Goldsmith*.
Sep. 12.	Anne, daughter of Gabriell Barber, *Grocer*.
Sep. 25.	Edward, son of William Sailes, *Merchanttailor*.
Nov. 20.	Samuel, son of Phillip Allen, *Haberdasher*.
Nov. 20.	Clement, son of Barnaby Gregory, *Goldsmith*.
Feb. 5.	Thomas, son of William Wood, *Goldsmith*.
Feb. 12.	Jeane, daughter of William Rawlins, *Goldsmith*.
Mar. 23.	Honor, daughter of George Humble, *Leatherseller*.
Mar. 25.	Elizabeth, daughter of John Sudbury, *Leatherseller*.

1609

April 2.	William, son of George Nickson, *Merchanttailor*.
April 17.	Elizabeth, daughter of Thomas Cole, *Haberdasher*.
April 14.	William, son of William Jones, *Vintner*.
April 25.	Katherine, daughter of William Keale.
June 16.	Elizabeth, daughter of George Monnox, *Haberdasher*.
June 16.	Anne, daughter of Thomas Fewterer, *Pewterer*.
July 16.	Prcilla, daughter of Arthure Basset, *Goldsmith*.
July 30.	Peter, son of John Griffen, *Clothworker*.
Aug. 6.	Mary, daughter of Richard Man, *Goldsmith*.
Sep. 3.	Anthony, son of John Benn, servant in the Cardinals Hat.
Sep. 20.	Thomas, son of John Acton, *Goldsmith*.
Sep. 24.	Sarah, daughter of Edward Annable, *Vintner*.
Oct. 1.	Jeane, daughter of Thomas Tukeridge, *Grocer*.
Oct. 22.	Bennet, son of John Homewood, *Chandler*.
Nov. 10.	Raphe, son of William Dutton, *Haberdasher*.
Nov. 20.	Grace, daughter of John Addley, borne in George Nickson's house.

Nov. 25.   Charles, a childe taken up in this Parish.
Nov. 30.   Elizabeth, daughter of William Rolfe, *Goldsmith.*
Dec. 20.   Tobye, son of John Lande, *Gentleman.*
Dec. 21.   John, son of John Chasmore.
Dec. 21.   Margaret, daughter of Richard Harrison, *Cooper.*
Dec. 31.   Elizabeth, daughter of Henry Chessheire, *Goldsmith.*
Jan. 22.   Henry, son of Henry Butler, *Draper.*
Feb. 1.   Judeth, daughter of William Sailes, *Merchanttailor.*
Feb. 25.   John, son of Barnaby Gregory, *Goldsmith.*
Mar. 4.   John, son of Valentine Judd, *Goldsmith.*
Mar. 11.   John, son of William Wood, *Goldsmith.*
Mar. 18.   Margaret, daughter of Hugh Gwilliams, *Haberdasher.*

1610

June 22.   Frances, son of Francis Haddon, *Goldsmith.*
Aug. 30.   Johan, daughter of John Stanford, *Haberdasher.*
Sep. 30.   Ann, daughter of John Davyds, *Victualler.*
Oct. 7.   Symon, son of Thomas Price, *Cooke.*
Oct. 11.   John, son of William Rolfe, *Goldsmith.*
Nov 18.   Marthy, daughter of John Homewood, *Chaundler.*
Nov. 18.   Rebecca, daughter of George Nickson, *Taylor.*
Nov. 28.   Thomas, son of William Jones, *Vintner.*
Jan. 13.   George, son of William Dutton, *Haberdasher.*
Mar. 10.   William, son of Thomas Coles.

1611

May 8.   Priscilla, daughter of John Burfort, *Silkweaver.*
May 26.   Thomas, son of Thomas White, *Person of this Church.*
June 9.   William, son of George Humble, *Stacioner.*
June 9.   Joyce, daughter of William Wood, *Goldsmith.*
June 16.   Anthony, son of William Tirrey, *Goldsmith.*
Aug. 23.   Agnes, daughter of Nicholas Granger, *Haberdasher.*
Aug. 28.   Thomas and Bartholomew, sonnes of William Rolffe,
              Goldsmith.
Sep. 1.   John, son of John Stanford, *Haberdasher.*
Sep. 19.   Thomas, son of Bartholomew Pickering, *Haberdasher.*
Oct. 6.   Elizabeth, daughter of Godfrey Smith, *Vintener.*
Nov. 3.   Constance, daughter of William Rawlyns, *Goldsmith.*
Nov. 10.   Elizabeth, daughter of Thomas Price, *Cooke.*
Jan. 4.   Richard, son of John Griffyn, *Clothworker.*
Jan. 5.   Thomas, son of George Monnox, *Merchaunt.*
Jan. 12.   Richard, son of Richard Cheswright, *Silkman.*
Feb. 22.   Sara, daughter of Thomas Boyce, *Goldsmith.*
Mar. 8.   Thomas, son of John Jolly, borne in Mr. Butler his house.

1612

May 10.   Mary, daughter of William Wood, *Goldsmith.*
June 29.   Peter, son of Barnaby Gregory, *Goldsmith.*
July 26.   Mary, daughter of John Renton, *Haberdasher.*
Aug. 14.   James son of William Tirrey, *Goldsmith.*
Aug. 20.   Anne, daughter of Thomas Wigmore, *Playsterer.*
Aug. 20.   Ellin, daughter of George Nickson, *Taylor.*
Sep. 3.   Anne, daughter of William Rolffe, *Goldsmith.*

Sep. 6.	Elizabeth, daughter of John Stanford, *Haberdasher.*
Sep. 20.	Mary, daughter of Godfrey Smith, *Vintner.*
Oct. 20.	William, son of Thomas Evans, out of Mr. Cheswright his house.
Dec. 4.	Suzanna, daughter of Willyam Shorden, *Goldsmith.*
Dec. 6.	Willyam, son of Willyam Rawlyns, *Goldsmith.*
Dec. 28.	Martyn, son of Martyn Soames, *Scrivener.*
Mar. 7.	John, son of Ralphe Bennet, *Taylor.*
Mar. 21.	Barbary, daughter of William Dutton, *Haberdasher.*
Mar. 28.	John, son of Thomas Boysse, *Goldsmith.*

1613

April 6.	Elizabeth, daughter of William Cheney.
April 25.	John, son of Richard Mann, *Goldsmith.*
June 24.	John, son of William Feepond, *Ally keeper.*
Aug. 17.	Nicholas, son of Peter Wade, *Tailor.*
Sep. 12.	Obadias, son of Hughe Gwillyams, *Haberdasher.*
Sep. 12.	Ellen, daughter of George Bromley, *Grocer.*
Sep. 12.	Margaret, daughter of John Stanford, *Haberdasher.*
Sep. 19.	John, son of John Homewood, *Chandler.*
Sep. 19.	Mary, daughter of John Boswell, *Letherseller.*
Sep. 26.	Ann, daughter of Richard Numersly, *Taylor.*
Sep. 29.	Anne, daughter of Nicholas Grange, *Haberdasher.*
Oct. 12.	Elizabeth, daughter of Willyam Wood, *Goldsmith.*
Oct. 14.	Anthony, son of William Terry, *Goldsmith.*
Oct. 24.	George, son of George Monnox, *Marchanttailor.*
Oct. 31.	Anne, daughter of George Humble, *Leatherseller.*
Nov. 28.	Ann, daughter of John Griffen, *Clothworker.*
Dec. 5.	Bryan, son of Bartholomew Pickeringe, *Haberdasher.*
Jan. 1.	Elizabeth, daughter of Raphe King, *Vintner.*
Jan. 6.	John, son of Thomas Willis, *Victualer.*
Jan. 30.	Jane, daughter of William Woolsey.
Feb. 17.	Anne, daughter of Godefry Smith, *Vintner.*
Mar. 20.	Jane, daughter of John Acton, *Goldsmith.*

1614

May 1.	Esther, daughter of Hugh Armeson, *Joyner.*
May 8.	John, son of Richard Mann, *Goldsmith.*
June 8.	Mary, daughter of Richard Chesewright, *Silkman.*
June 29.	Ellen, daughter of Richard Harrison, *Cooper.*
Aug. 21.	Francis, son of Francis Chapman, *Goldsmith.*
Sep. 29.	Agnes, daughter of Lewes Bromhall.
Oct. 2.	Martha, daughter of John Renton, *Haberdasher.*
Nov. 18.	William, son of Raphe Bennet, *Taylor.*
Nov. 27.	Frances, daughter of Raphe Ving, *Vintner.*
Nov. 27.	Ann, daughter of Richard Nunnersley, *Tailor.*
Dec. 25.	Mary, daughter of John Pendry, *Clothworker.*
Dec. 27.	Katherine, daughter of Richard Keales.
Jan. 19.	Mary, daughter of Edward Phillips, out of Mr. Ockould his house,
Feb. 3.	Sara, daughter of Isaake Thomas, *Tailor.*
Feb. 26.	Anne, daughter of John Stanford, *Haberdasher.*
Mar. 12.	Henry, son of Henry Blackmore, *Goldsmith.*
Mar. 23.	Katherine, daughter of William Wood, *Goldsmith.*

1615

May 18.	Robert, son of William Rawlyns, *Goldsmith*.
May 20.	John, son of Edward Starkey, *Merchant*.
June 1.	Sara, daughter of Francis Chapman, *Goldsmith*.
July 25.	Richard, son of Richard Harrison, *Cooper*.
July 25.	William, son of Henry Balam, *Stationer*,
Aug. 3.	Peter, son of Peter Wade, *Taylor*.
Aug. 10.	Luigo, son of William Jones, *Vintener*.
Sep. 17.	Thomas, son of Richard Mann, *Goldsmith*.
Nov. 19.	Jeane, daughter of Richard Nunnersley, *Tailor*.
Nov. 26.	Blandyne, daughter of John Acton, *Goldsmith*.
Nov. 26.	Rebecca, daughter of Henry Annely, *Baker*.
Dec. 3.	Robert, son of John Moore, *Clothworker*.
Dec. 10.	Arthur, son of William Terry, *Goldsmith*,
Dec. 10.	Thomas, son of George Humble, *Letherseller*.
Feb. 4.	Steven, son of John Coale, *Haberdasher*.
Feb. 4.	Elizabeth, daughter of Thomas Burden, *Shoemaker*.
Feb. 11.	Henry, son of Ralph Kinge, *Vintner*.
Feb. 11.	William, son of Henry Blackmore, *Goldsmith*.
Mar. 3.	William, son of John Stanford, *Haberdasher*.

1616

April 10.	John, son of William Peacocke, *Goldsmith*.
April 13.	A childe founde in this Parish whose name was called Adam.
April 25.	John, son of Richard Margerison, *Tailor*.
July 14.	Edward, son of Edward Phillips.
July 14.	Sarah, daughter of William Wade, *Taylor*.
Aug. 1.	Mary, daughter of Richard Weld, *Goldsmith*.
Aug. 9.	James, son of Mark Caloone, *Stranger*.
Aug. 18.	Peeter, son of Peeter Sadler, *Stranger*.
Sep. 22.	John, son of John Hunter, *Bucher*.
Sep. 29.	Elizabeth, daughter of William Boddington, *Mercer*.
Oct. 20.	Anne, daughter of Christopher Fitz-jeffery, *Joyner*.
Oct. 27.	Richard, son of Richard Adam, *Goldsmith*.
Oct. 30.	Peeter, son of Danyell Heringhooke, *Merchant Strainger*.
Nov. 3.	David, son of William Ireland, *Goldsmith*.
Nov. 3.	Elyne, daughter of William Rawlence, *Goldsmith*.
Nov. 24.	Judith, daughter of Ralph Bennett, *Marchant Taylor*.
Dec. 1.	William, son of John Kempton, *Haberdasher*.
Jan. 19.	Paul, son of William Terry, *Goldsmith*.
Feb. 23.	Martha, daughter of Henry Balaam, *Stacioner*.
Mar. 11.	John, son of David Griffyn, *Clothworker*.
Mar. 15.	Rowland, son of Rowland Sadler, *Haberdasher*.

1617

May 20.	Katherine, daughter of William Rolfe, *Goldsmith*.
June 15.	Elizabeth, daughter of Edward Dexter, *Weaver*, our Parish Clerk.
July 16.	Parnell, daughter of Phillip Garland, *Haberdasher*.
Aug. 10.	Edmund, son of George Tapfield, *Carpenter*.
Aug. 24.	Elizabeth, daughter of Henry Blackmore, *Goldsmith*.
Aug. 28.	Thomas, son of John Acton, *Goldsmith*.

Aug. 31.	Elizabeth, daughter of Thomas Atkinson, *Goldsmith*.
Sep. 7.	Richard, son of Richard Weld, *Goldsmith*.
Sep. 7.	Katherine, daughter of John Coale, *Haberdasher*.
Oct. 26.	Jane, daughter of John Hill, *Goldsmith*.
Nov. 1.	Gabriell, son of Ralph Kinge, *Vintener*.
Nov. 2.	John, son of William Exton, *Merchant Taillor*.
Nov. 2.	Nicholas, son of Josua Walter, *Goldsmith*.
Nov. 23.	William, son of John Penry, *Clothworker*.
Jan. 11.	Anne, daughter of John Moore, *Clothworker*.
Jan. 13.	Margaret, daughter of Thomas Dent, *Merchant*.
Jan. 18.	Elizabeth, daughter of John Pecocke, *Goldsmith*.
Jan. 27.	Mary, daughter of George Humble, *Stacioner*.
Mar. 5.	George, son of William Wood, *Goldsmith*.
Mar. 15.	Jane, daughter of Thomas Burden, *Sexton*.
Mar. 18.	Anne, daughter of Richard Harryson, *Cooper*.

1618

Mar. 29.	Humfrey, son of Robert Brookes, *Pursemaker*.
Mar. 31.	John, son of William Ireland, *Goldsmith*.
April 19.	William, son of William Boddington, *Mercer*.
June 2.	Jane, daughter of Henry Feake, *Goldsmith*.
Aug. 2.	George, son of Richard Weld, *Goldsmith*.
Aug. 3.	Elizabeth, daughter of Clement Medley, *Gentleman*.
Sep. 10.	Anthony, son of Thomas Stevens, *Mercer*.
Sep. 29.	Anne, daughter of Henry Balam, *Stationer*.
Oct. 1.	Anne, daughter of George Binge, *Goldsmith*.
Oct. 11.	Thomas, son of William Rawlins, *Goldsmith*.
Oct. 25.	Edward, son of Henry Blackmore, *Goldsmith*.
Dec. 13.	Elizabeth, daughter of William Exstone, *Cutler*.
Jan. 6.	John, son of Robert Hamore, *Scrivener*.
Jan. 14.	Elizabeth, daughter of Samuel Dey, *Merchant*.
Jan. 24.	James, son of Peeter Sadler, *Merchant*, in the Dutch Church.
Mar. 1.	Dorithie, daughter of John Kenton, *Haberdasher*.
Mar. 21.	Thomas, son of Francis Chapman, *Goldsmith*.

1619

April 1.	Robert, son of William Rolfe, *Goldsmith*.
April 4	Simon, son of Thomas Willis, *Victualler*, free of the Tallowchandlers.
April 23.	Anne, daughter of Bartholomew Pickering, *Haberdasher*.
May 2.	Mary, daughter of Josua Waters, *Goldsmith*.
June 17.	Elizabeth, daughter of Thomas Tickeradge, *Merchant*.
July 22.	Edmund, son of Francis Baker, *Warehouseman*, and free of the Cutlers.
Aug. 1.	John, son of William Bodington, *Mercer*.
Aug. 29.	Anne, daughter of Henry Freeman, *Cobler*.
Sep. 12.	Ralphe, son of Ralphe Kinge, *Vintner*.
Sep. 12.	William, son of Edward Robinson, *Clothworker*.
Sep. 19.	Dorothie, daughter of Rowlande Sadler, *Haberdasher*.
Oct. 17.	Jane, daughter of George Tapsfield, *Carpenter*.
Nov. 4.	John, son of Thomas Dent, *Merchant*.
Nov. 30.	Edward, son of William Wood, *Goldsmith*.
Dec. 5.	William, son of William Rawlins, *Goldsmith*.

Dec. 19.	John, son of John Moore, *Clothworker*.
Jan. 1.	Mercy, daughter of Bartholomew Lame, *Drawer*.
Feb. 2.	Anne, daughter of William Sparrow, *Merchant Taylor*.
Feb. 7.	Daniel, son of Ralph Bennett, *Merchant Taylor*.
Feb. 20.	Alexander, son of Richard Weld, *Goldsmith*.
Mar. 5.	Stephen, son of John Cole, *Haberdashor*.
Mar. 14.	Sarah, daughter of Stephen Baker, *Merchant Grocer*.

1620

April 2.	Millicent, daughter of Roger Daniell, *Stationer*.
April 6.	Dorothie, daughter of John Peacock, *Goldsmith*.
April 19.	Phillis, daughter of Elias Carpentar, *Sheregrinder*.
April 23.	Anne, daughter of William Gibbins, *Merchant Tailor*.
May 25.	Anthony, son of Anthony Peniston, *Goldsmith*.
June 11.	Henry, son of Henry Balaam, *Stationer*.
June 26.	Elizabeth, daughter of Edward Dexter, *Clarke*.
June 30.	Thomas, son of Thomas Whitby, *Fishmonger* in St. Gyle's Parishe in the Fields, and cristened in this Parishe.
July 2.	Henry, son of Henry Blackmore, *Goldsmith*.
Aug. 7.	Suzan, daughter of Thomas Tickeridge, *Merchant Grocer*.
Aug. 9.	Angelett, daughter of Samuel Dey, *Merchant*.
Aug. 15.	Margarett, daughter of George Bromley, *Grocer*.
Aug. 31.	Anne, daughter of William Bodington, *Mercer*.
Sep. 29.	Thomas, son of Thomas Dent, *Merchant*.
Oct. 2.	Elizabeth, daughter of William Tirrey, *Goldsmith*.
Nov. 15.	Daniel, son of Peter Sadler, *Merchant*.
Dec. 14.	William, son of Thomas White, *Merchant*.
Jan. 19.	Thomas, son of Henry Freman, *Shoemaker*.
Feb. 14.	John Sherborne a foundling being found in Sherborne Lane.
Mar. 4.	Prudence, daughter of John Moore, *Clothworker*.

1621

Mar. 29.	Thomas, son of Francis Barker, *Mercer*.
April 8.	Abigall, daughter of Edward Robinson, *Clothworker*.
July 9.	James, son of Anthony Peniston, *Goldsmith*.
Aug. 8.	Jane, daughter of Robert Page, *Merchant Taylor*.
Aug. 12.	William, son of Raph King, *Vintner*.
Aug. 24.	Suzan, daughter of Francis Malbery, *Gouldsmith*.
Aug. 26.	Thomas, son of Francis Chapman, *Goldsmith*.
Aug. 30.	Anne, daughter of John Kempton, *Haberdasher*.
Sep. 2.	Elinor, daughter of Edward Chace, *Merchant Taylor*.
Sep. 9.	Suzan, daughter of Mark Caloune, *Merchant*.
Oct. 1.	Richard, son of James Chamberlaine, *Haberdasher*.
Oct. 16.	Ellen, daughter of Alexander Weld, *Druggester*.
Dec. 23.	Elizabeth, daughter of Roger Daniell, *Stacioner*.
Jan. 13.	In the Dutch Church, Daniell, son of Peter Sadler, *Merchant*.
Jan. 16.	Peter, son of Thomas Willis, *Chandler*.
Feb. 10.	Elizabeth, daughter of George Bing, *Goldsmith*.
Feb. 21.	Richard, son of William Rawlins, *Goldsmith*.
Mar 3.	Grace, daughter of Henry Balam, *Stacioner*.
Mar. 12.	Mary, daughter of Samuel Dey, *Merchant*.

1622

Mar. 25.	Bartholomew, son of Bartholomew Pickeringe, *Haberdasher.*
April 7.	Jane, daughter of Richard Weld, *Goldsmith*
April 17.	Josua, son of Mathew Holmes, *Playsterer.*
April 21.	Elizabeth, daughter of John Cole, *Haberdasher.*
April 28.	Peter Wolnoth, a foundling in our Parish.
May 20.	Jepha and Suzan, twins, son and daughter of Henry Bagley, *Shoemaker.*
June 29.	Christopher, son of Thomas Simpson, *Apothecary.*
July 21.	Martha, daughter of Anthony Penistone, *Goldsmith.*
July 22.	Frances, daughter of Thomas Tickeeridge, *Merchant Grocer.*
July 25.	Edward, son of William Timmins, *Merchant Tailor.*
Aug. 8.	Thomas, son of Henry Blackmore, *Goldsmith.*
Aug. 17.	Mary, daughter of Edward Ledger, *Bricklayer.*
Sep. 1.	Anne, daughter of Ellis Carpenter, *Shearegrinder.*
Sep. 15.	George, son of Thomas Rice, *Gent.,* in Mr. Webbe's house at the Tennis Courte.
Sep. 25.	Mary, daughter of Francis Baker, *Mercer.*
Oct. 20.	Martha, daughter of William Sparrowe, *Merchant Tailor.*
Oct. 25.	Millicent, daughter of Roger Tomson, *Curryer.*
Nov. 5.	Suzanna, daughter of Thomas White, *Merchant.*
Nov. 17.	Samuell, son of Thomas Whitby, *Chandler.*
Nov. 21.	Elizabeth, daughter of Arthur Fisher, *Merchant.*
Dec. 8.	Mary, daughter of Henry Freman, *Cobler.*
Dec. 26.	Elizabeth, daughter of George Bromley, *Grocer.*
Jan. 5.	John, son of Henry Fotherby, *Gentleman.*
Jan. 5.	Richard, son of Richard Brigginshaw, *Cutler.*
Feb. 2.	James, son of Thomas Cadle, *Comfett Maker.*
Feb. 6.	Francis, son of Francis Marbery, *Goldsmith.*
Feb. 7.	William, son of Thomas Vinor, *Goldsmith.*
Feb. 17.	William, daughter of Thomas Nevell, *Goldsmith.*
Mar 11.	Rebecca, daughter of John Linge, *Oyleman.*
Mar. 23.	Katherine, daughter of William Webb, *Clothworker.*
Mar. 29.	Elizabeth, daughter of John Morgan, *Haberdasher.*

1623

April 2.	Anthony, son of Anthony Baker, of the Parishe of Great St. Bartholomew, in Smithfield, borne in the Cardinal's Hatt Alley.
April 20.	Charles, son of Mark Calloone, *Merchant.*
June 15.	George, son of James Chamberlyn, *Haberdasher.*
June 29.	Barbara, daughter of John Peacocke, *Goldsmith.*
July 6.	Priscilla, daughter of Raphe Kinge, *Vintner.*
July 17.	James, son of Samuel Dey, *Merchant.*
July 18.	Elizabeth, daughter of Bartholomew Gilman, *Merchant.*
Aug. 8.	George, son of Thomas Holmes, *Haberdasher.*
Aug. 14.	Elizabeth, daughter of John Weld, *Goldsmith.*
Aug. 14.	Ellen, daughter of Alexander Weld, *Druggister.*
Aug. 24.	George, son of Anthony Penistone, *Goldsmith.*
Sep. 14.	John, son of William Rawlins, *Goldsmith.*
Sep. 21.	Richard, son of Francis Chapman, *Goldsmith.*
Oct. 5.	William, son of William Manley, *Scrivener.*
Oct. 7.	Suzan, daughter of John Cole, *Haberdasher.*

Oct. 19.	Simon, son of Henry Blackmore, *Goldsmith.*
Nov. 11.	Edward, son of William Webster, *Salter.*
Dec. 9.	Samuel, son of William Sute, *Playsterer.*
Dec. 14.	John, son of Richard Brigginshaw, *Cutler.*
Dec. 21.	Peter, son of Peter Sadler, *Merchant.*
Feb. 20.	John, found in our Parishe upon Mr. Sales his stall.
Feb. 23.	Margaret, daughter of George Bromley, *Grocer.*
Mar. 7.	John, son of John Myles, *Barbor Surgion.*
Mar. 14.	Alice, daughter of Thomas Nevett, *Goldsmith.*
Mar. 21.	George, son of George Tapeffeild, *Carpenter.*

1624

April 11.	Elizabeth, daughter of Thomas Webb, *Iremonger.*
April 11.	Sara, daughter of John Barter, *Clarke of St. Michaells in Cornhill.*
July 4.	William, son of Robert Daniell, *Stationer.*
July 23.	Mathew, son of Mathew Homes, *Playsterer.*
July 25.	John, son of John Weld, *Goldsmith.*
Aug. 4.	Anne, daughter of Thomas Vinor, *Goldsmith.*
Aug. 4.	Mary, daughter of John Beauchamp, *Gent.*
Aug. 14.	Richard, son of Richard Worrall, *Fishmonger.*
Aug. 29.	Margarett, daughter of Margarett Kempton, *Widow.*
Sep. 5.	Elizabeth, daughter of William Manley, *Scrivener.*
Sep. 6.	In the Dutch Church, Elizabeth, daughter of Abraham van Seldt, *Stranger.*
Oct. 3.	Jane, daughter of Richard Weld, *Goldsmith.*
Oct. 23.	John, son of George Cathman, *Fishmonger.*
Nov. 7.	Sara, daughter of Charles Bragge, *Scrivener.*
Nov. 12.	John, son of John Rogers, *Silkman.*
Nov. 14.	Luke, son of Luke Jackson, *Silkman.*
Nov. 17.	William, son of Francis Chapman, *Goldsmith.*
Nov. 29.	Thomas, son of Elinor Carpenter, *Widow.*
Dec. 5.	Anne, daughter of William Webster, *Salter.*
Dec. 12.	Anne, daughter of Thomas Fishlake.
Jan. 1.	Richard, son of Bartholomew Gilman, *Merchant.*
Feb. 20.	Anne, daughter of Anthony Peniston, *Goldsmith.*
Feb. 24.	Margaret, daughter of Thomas Tickeridge, *Grocer.*
Feb. 24.	Anne, daughter of James Chamberlyn, *Haberdasher.*
Mar. 1.	Barbara, daughter of John Goodwyn, *Chandler,*
Mar. 9.	Richard, son of Anne Surrt, *Widow.*

1625

Mar. 31.	Hanna, daughter of John Ling, *Oylman.*
April 6.	In the Dutch Church, James, son of Mark Coloune, *Merchant.*
April 8.	Samuell, son of Samuell Dye, *Merchant.*
April 17.	Thomas, son of Thomas Nevett, *Goldsmith.*
April 24.	Dorothie, daughter of Henry Freeman, *Cobler.*
April 28.	Katherine, daughter of Francis Marbury.
May 19.	George, son of Arthur Fisher, *Merchant.*
May 22.	Mathew, son of Thomas Cabble, *Comfitt Maker.*
July 22.	Rebecca, daughter of Thomas Baylie, *Hottpresser.*
Aug. 14.	Anne, daughter of Richard Briggenshaw.
Sep. 3.	Richard, son of Richard Weld, *Goldsmith.*

Sep. 16.	Elizabeth, daughter of Edward Phillipps.
Oct. 14.	Mary Wolnoth, a foundling which was found in the streete, over against the Church dore.
Jan. 11.	Rebecca, daughter of Luke Jackson, *Silkman*.
Jan. 25.	George, son of Widdowe Tappsffeilde.
Feb. 10.	George, son of William Manley, *Scrivener*.
Mar. 17.	Mary, daughter of John Goodwyn, *Chandler*.
Mar. 19.	Nicholas, son of Widdowe Whitby.
Mar. 21.	Charles, son of Charles Bragge, *Scrivener*.

1626

April 2.	In the Dutch Church, Anthony, son of Peter Sadler, *Merchant*.
April 14.	Richard, son of Thomas Nevett, *Goldsmith*.
May 21.	Elizabeth, daughter of Richard Childe.
June 11.	Anne, daughter of George Underwood, *Silkman*.
July 19.	Elizabeth, daughter of Roger Daniell, *Stationer*.
July 30.	Arthur, son of Arthur Fisher, *Merchant*.
Sep. 3.	John, son of Anthony Peniston, *Goldsmith*.
Sep. 10.	John, son of Henry Freman.
Sep. 10.	James, son of George Clidwell.
Sep. 13.	Mary, daughter of Thomas Vinor.
Sep. 24.	Elizabeth, daughter of Richard Briggenshawe, *Cutler*.
Oct. 8.	John, son of George Best, *Grocer*.
Oct. 12.	Edward, son of John Rogers.
Dec. 1.	Rose, daughter of Richard Weld.
Dec. 3.	Judith, daughter of Mark Coloune.
Dec. 10.	Andrew, son of Henry Blackmore.

[N.B.—There is gummed in in here half a sheet of old paper, on which is badly written, 1 Ockober, 1671, Ester Hill, daughter of John Hill, Goldsmith.]

Mar. 7.	Ann, daughter of Henry Pilkington, *Gent*.
Mar. 9.	Sara, daughter of Samuell Dey, *Merchant*.
Mar. 18.	Mary, daughter of James Chamberlin, *Haberdasher*.
Mar. 18.	Mary, daughter of Edward Ocklin, *Carpentar*.

1627

April 26.	Thomas, son of Francis Marbury, *Goldsmith*.
June 8.	Sara, daughter of Thomas Hodges, *Minister*.
June 28.	John, son of John Linge.
June 29.	Thomas, son of Thomas Denman, *Blacksmith*.
July 22.	Henry, son of Henry Sacheverell, *Vintner*.
July 25.	Thomas, son of William Wiles.
Aug. 12.	Anthony, son of Anthony Peniston, *Goldsmith*.
Aug. 14.	Suzan, daughter of Charles Latham, *Druggest*.
Aug. 15.	Thomas, son of Thomas Tickeridge, *Grocer*.
Aug. 19.	Henry, son of George Underwood, *Silkman*.
Aug. 20.	Gilbert, son of Martin Pollard, *Taylor*.
Sep. 2.	Mary, daughter of Richard Treate, *Goldsmith*.
Sep. 21.	George, son of George Best, *Grocer*.
Oct. 28.	Bartholomew, son of Bartholomew Gilman.
Nov. 8.	John, son of Thomas Nevett, *Goldsmith*.
Nov. 11.	Grace, daughter of Enock Porter.
Nov. 25.	Robert, son of Thomas Cawton, *Clothworker*.

Dec. 2.	Mary, daughter of Alexander Weld, *Druggest.*
Dec. 9.	Anne, daughter of William Sanckey, *Goldsmith.*
Dec. 13.	William, son of William White, *Haberdasher.*
Dec. 27.	Mary, daughter of Richard Briggenshawe, *Cutler.*
Jan. 6.	Ann, daughter of Gilbert Cornelius.
Jan. 27.	Stephen, son of Stephen Goodyear, *Merchant.*
Feb. 3.	William, son of Francis Bishopp, *Goldsmith.*
Feb. 10.	Hanna, daughter of Richard Child, *Merchant.*
Feb. 28.	Grace, daughter of Peter Sadler.
Mar. 23.	Elizabeth, daughter of James Chamberlin, *Haberdasher.*

1628

Mar. 25.	Richard, son of Thomas Willett, *Merchant.*
Mar. 25.	Peter, son of Mark Colonne, *Merchant.*
June 25.	Francis, daughter of Thomas Richardson, *Clothworker.*
July 1	Thomas, son of Thomas Vinor, *Goldsmith.*
July 2.	James, son of John Linge, *Oylman.*
July 27.	John, son of Thomas Hodges, *Minister.*
July 27.	William, son of Charles Bragge, *Scrivener.*
July 29.	Charles, son of John Rogers, *Silkman.*
Aug. 13.	Frances, daughter of Samuell Dey, *Merchant.*
Sep. 28.	John, son of George Clydwell.
Nov. 30.	Edward, son of Edward Chart, *Merchant Taylor.*
Dec. 5.	Thomas, son of John Weld, *Goldsmith.*
Dec. 5.	Thomas, son of Roger Daniell, *Stationer.*
Dec. 5.	William, son of Alexander Weld, *Druggest.*
Dec. 7.	Thomas, son of John Peacock, *Goldsmith.*
Dec. 7.	Mary, daughter of George Underwood, *Silkman.*
Dec. 18.	Elizabeth and Mary, daughters of Thomas Cawton, *Clothworker.*
Jan. 4.	Samuell, son of Robert Gravett.
Jan. 15.	Maudlin, daughter of Mr. Augier, *Gent.*
Jan. 15.	Francis, son of Francis Bishopp, *Goldsmith.*
Jan. 23.	Elizabeth, daughter of Charles Latham, *Druggist.*
Feb. 21.	Mary, a foundlinge, she was layd upon Mr. Daniell's stall.
Feb. 22.	Edward, son of Henry Sacheverell, *Vintner.*
Feb. 26.	Judith, daughter of Fancis Marbury, *Goldsmith.*
Mar. 1.	Suzan, daughter of Joseph Burden, *Silkweaver.*

1629

April 8.	Anne, daughter of John —— [*sic*] *White Silkdyer.*
April 12.	Honor, daughter of Humfrey Crouch, *Stationer.*
April 20.	Suzan, daughter of Christopher Branson, *Clothworker.*
May 2.	Henry, son of Richard Brinkinshaw, *Cutler.*
May 7.	William, son of George Best, *Grocer.*
May 14.	Timothy, a heathen Blackamoore.
May 17.	Gilbert, son of Gilbert Cornelius, of the Tokenhouse.
May —	Mary, daughter of John Hawes, *Merchant Tailor.*
June 28.	Margarett, daughter of Richard Trett, *Goldsmith.*
June 29.	Thomas, son of Thomas Denman, *Blacksmith.*
Aug. 2.	Anne, daughter of Francis Jackson, *Perfumer.*
Aug. 27.	Anne, daughter of John Lyng, *Oyleman.*
Aug. 30.	Elizabeth, daughter of Henry Freeman, *Cobler.*
Aug. 31.	Simon, son of Simon Kibble, *Gentleman.*

Sep. 6.	Abraham, son of Enock Porter, *Clothworker.*
Sep. 15.	Elizabeth, daughter of John Rogers, *Silkman.*
Oct. 4.	Thomas, son of Edward Okeley, *Carpenter.*
Oct. 5.	Sarah, daughter of Thomas Neve, *Goldsmith.*
Oct. 16.	John, son of Charles Bragge, *Scrivener.*
Oct. 16.	Sarah, daughter of John Smith.
Oct. 25.	Henry, son of James Chamberlaine, *Vintner.*
Nov. 9.	Thomas, son of David Jones, *Merchant Grocer.*
Nov. 16.	Thomas, son of Thomas Marichall, *Weaver.*
Jan. 10.	Abigail, daughter of Thomas Richardson.
Jan. 13.	William, son of Samuell Dey, *Merchant.*
Jan. 22.	Mary, daughter of Stephen Goodyear, *Merchant.*
Feb. 1.	Margaret, daughter of Henry Rowe, *Gentleman.*
Feb. 14.	Michell, son of William Sparrowe, *Merchant Taylor.*
Feb. 27.	William, son of Henry Sacheverell, *Vintner.*
Mar. 1.	William, a foundling in this Parish, layd upon Mr. Underlin's stall.
Mar. 7.	John, son of Thomas Calton, *Clothworker.*

1630

April 9.	Christopher, son of Christopher Branstone, *Clothworker.*
May 18.	Bridgett, daughter of John Lindsey, *Stationer.*
June 20.	Elizabeth, daughter of Mathew Paris, *Goldsmith.*
June 29.	Elizabeth, daughter of Thomas Vinor, *Goldsmith.*
July 18.	Elizabeth, daughter of William Manley, *Scrivener.*
July 25.	Richard, son of Richard Trett, *Goldsmith.*
Aug. 18.	Sara, daughter of John Rogers, *Silkman.*
Aug. 22.	Mary, daughter of Mark Callone, *Merchant.*
Aug. 27.	Richard, son of Richard Thoroton, *Apothecary.*
Aug. 30.	Elizabeth, daughter of Francis Malbury, *Goldsmith.*
Sept. 8.	Mary, daughter of Godfrey Plummer, *Draper.*
Sep. 26.	Rebecca, daughter of William Sanckey, *Goldsmith.*
Oct. 10.	William, son of Francis Jackson, *Paynter Steyner.*
Oct. 13.	John, son of John Smith, *Draper.*
Dec. 21.	Rebecka, daughter of Mathew Culliford, *Goldsmith.*
Jan. 1.	Samuell, son of Francis Bishopp, *Goldsmith.*
Mar. 8.	Raphe, son of Charles Latham, *Druggest.*

1631

April 3.	Richard, son of Anthony Penistone, *Goldsmith.*
April 12.	Elizabeth, daughter of Thomas Nevett, *Goldsmith.*
April 27.	Elizabeth, daughter of John Branthwaite, *Sitkdyer.*
May 29.	Christopher, son of Richard Brinkinshawe, *Cutler.*
May 29.	Elizabeth, daughter of Thomas Denman, *Blacksmith.*
June 2.	Stephen, son of Stephen Goodyeare, *Merchant.*
Aug. 2.	Bartholomew, son of Bartholomew Gilman, *Merchant.*
Aug. 3.	Abraham, son of Edward Chard, *Merchant.*
Aug. 3.	Frances, daughter of John Rogers, *Silkman.*
Aug. 5.	Sarah, daughter of James Chamberlain, *Haberdasher.*
Aug. 19.	John, son of George Underwood, *Merchant.*
Aug. 19.	Rebecka, daughter of Henry Zacheverell, *Vintner.*
Aug. 23.	Roger, son of Roger Daniell, *Stationer.*
Aug. 30.	Mary, daughter of John Acton, *Goldsmith.*
Aug. 31.	Anne, daughter of Edward Okeley, *Carpenter.*

Sep. 18.	Martha, daughter of Samuell Dey, *Merchant*.
Sep. 28.	Judith, daughter of Mathew Paris, *Goldsmith*.
Oct. 20.	Anne, daughter of George Best, *Grocer*.
Nov. 6.	John, son of Henry Freeman, *Cobler*.
Nov. 27.	Abraham, son of Henry Hovenor, *Merchant*.
Jan. 11.	Thomas, son of Thomas Willett, *Merchant*.
Jan. 19.	Josias, son of Francis Bishopp, *Goldsmith*.
Feb. 9.	Elizabeth, daughter of William Hubbard, *Haberdasher*.
Feb. 12.	Sarah, daughter of John Hawes, *Merchant Taylor*.
Feb. 24.	Hugh, son of Thomas Richardson, *Clothworker*.
Mar. 4.	Stephen, son of Susan Burden, *Widow*.
Mar. 8.	Joyce, daughter of Thomas Weld, *Drugster*.

1632

April 8.	Samuell, son of Samuell Moore, *Goldsmith*.
April 22.	Mary, daughter of Francis Jackson.
May 1.	Suzan, daughter of Thomas Vinor, *Goldsmith*.
June 5.	Edward, son of Thomas Nevett, *Goldsmith*.
Aug. 12.	Elizabeth, daughter of Anthony Penistone, *Goldsmith*.
Oct. 7.	Josias, son of David Jones, *Merchant*.
Oct. 7.	William, son of William Mantle, *Goldsmith*.
Nov. 9.	Elizabeth, daughter of Christopher Branson, *Clothworker*.
Nov. 13.	Michaell, son of Michaell Gardener, *Vintner*.
Nov. 14.	Richard, son of Stephen Phillipps, *Fishmonger*.
Nov. 18.	Elizabeth, daughter of Godfrey Plummer, *Fishmonger*.
Dec. 12.	Judith, daughter of Roger Peele, *Clothworker*.
Nov. 23.	Edward, son of Walter Shute, *Goldsmith*.
Jan. 3.	Thomas, son of Stephen Goodyear, *Merchant*.
June 13.	Elizabeth, daughter of John Acton, *Goldsmith*.
Jan. 15.	Anne, daughter of Peter Willett, *Draper*.
Jan. 29.	Mathew, son of Mathew Culliford, *Goldsmith*.
Feb. 24.	Charles, son of Charles Latham, *Druggest*.
Feb. 27.	Elizabeth, daughter of John Smith, *Draper*.
Feb. 28.	Hannah, daughter of Bartholomew Gilman, *Merchant*.

1633

Mar. 31.	John, son of John Steele, *Vintner*.
April 1.	Mary, daughter of Thomas Coxe, *Merchant*.
April 7.	Anne, daughter of William Brown, *Goldsmith*.
April 28.	William, son of Alexander Pollington, *Haberdasher*.
May 22.	Margaret, daughter of James Chamberlain, *Haberdasher*.
May 26.	Mary, daughter of John Branthwayte, *Silkdyer*.
May 30.	Abraham, son of Abraham Johnson, *Merchant*.
June 16.	Susan, daughter of William Sanckey, *Goldsmith*.
June 29.	Mary, daughter of Thomas Richardson, *Clothworker*.
July 25.	Martha, daughter of Richard Butler, *Hotpresser*.
July 27.	Carey, daughter of John Morgan, *Gentleman*.
Aug. 4.	Elizabeth, daughter of Edward Chare, *Merchant Tailor*.
Sep. 8.	Avys, daughter of Thomas Denman, *Blacksmith*.
Oct. 13.	Edmund, son of John Rolfe, *Scrivener*.
Oct. 27.	Joseph, son of Anthony Penistone, *Goldsmith*.
Nov. 17.	Mary, daughter of Francis Jackson, *Perfumer*.
Nov. 28.	John, son of Samuel Dey, *Merchant*.
Dec. 9.	Robert, son of David Jones, *Merchant*.

Dec. 21.	Anne, daughter of Mephibosheth Robbyns.
Dec. 27.	Ellen, daughter of Robert Petley, *Draper.*
Jan. 2.	Thomas, son of Henry Futter, *Goldsmith.*
Feb. 4.	Rebecka, daughter of Thomas Vinor, *Goldsmith.*
Mar. 16.	Izahel, daughter of Samuel Baylie, *Grocer.*

1634

April 3.	Andrewe, son of Stephen Goodyear, *Merchant.*
April 17.	John, son of John Johnson, *Gent.*
April 17.	Godfrey, son of Godfrey Plommer, *Draper.*
April 18.	Tymothy, a child found in this Parish at the dore of William Manley.
April 24.	Elizabeth, daughter of Peter Willett, *Silkman.*
May 11.	Thomas, son of Alexander Pollington, *Haberdasher.*
May 18.	Elizabeth, daughter of Edward Saltley, *Carpentar.*
June 17.	Thomas, son of Thomas Cork, *Merchant.*
June 26.	David, son of Henry Hovenor, *Merchant.*
July 15.	Ursula, daughter of George Best, *Grocer.*
July 24.	Mary Magdalend, daughter of Ralf Boys, *Hotpresser.*
July 27.	Mary, daughter of John Steell, *Vintner.*
Aug. 7.	Elizabeth, daughter of Abraham Johnson, *Merchant.*
Aug. 31.	John, son of John Skynner, *Carpentar.*
Sep. 19.	Elizabeth, daughter of George Underwood, *Silkman.*
Sep. 25.	Anne, daughter of George Latham, *Drugster.*
Oct. 5.	Richard, son of Jerman Honeyhurst, *Merchant.*
Oct. 6.	Thomas, son of Humphrey Brown, *Girdler.*
Oct. 10.	Richard, son of Samuel More, *Goldsmith.*
Oct. 10	Mary, daughter of Thomas Nevett, *Goldsmith.*
Oct. 24.	Mathew, son of Mathew Culliford, *Goldsmith.*
Nov. 1.	Dorothie, daughter of Francis Bishopp, *Goldsmith.*
Nov. 6.	Anthony, son of Richard Brinkinshaw, *Cutler.*
Nov. 19.	Anne, daughter of Roger Peele, *Clothworker.*
Dec. 4.	Elizabeth, daughter of Thomas Webb, *Drugster.*
Jan. 18.	Martha, daughter of Anthony Pennistone, *Goldsmith.*
Feb. 2.	Elizabeth, daughter of John Rolfe, *Scrivener.*
Feb. 22	Tobell, son of John Acton, *Goldsmith.*
Mar. 4.	Charles son of Richard Butler, *Hotpresser.*

1635

April 9.	Henry, son of William White, *Haberdasher.*
April 12.	Elizabeth, daughter of Richard Heyward, *Cooper.*
April 15.	Richard, son of Walter Shute, *Goldsmith.*
April 25.	James, son of James Chamberlin, *Vintner.*
May 10.	Richard, son of Richard Pepis, *Merchant.*
May 13.	Frances, daughter of Thomas King, *Merchant.*
May 19.	Suzan, daughter of Francis Jackson, *Perfumer.*
May 28.	Anne, daughter of Samuel Dey, *Merchant.*
June 7.	Elizabeth, daughter of Enock Porter, *Clothworker.*
June 28.	Robert, son of Robert Potley, *Draper.*
July 31.	Mary, daughter of Bartholomew Gilman, *Merchant.*
Aug. 16.	Edmond, son of John Branthait, *Silkedyer.*
Aug. 25.	Mary, daughter of David Jones, *Suger Merchant.*
Sep. 16.	Elizabeth, daughter of Jerman Honychurch, *Merchant.*
Oct. 18.	Richard, son of Thomas Collyer, *Goldsmith.*

Oct. 25.	Sara, daughter of John Steele, *Vintner.*
Nov. 8.	Elizabeth, daughter of James Beamount, *Goldsmith.*
Dec. 22.	Charles, son of Richard Briggenshaw, *Cutler.*
Dec. 22.	Mathew, son of Charles Latham, *Drugster.*
Dec. 31.	Joan, son of Hugh Morrell, *Merchant.*
Jan. 13.	Thomas, son of Thomas Vinor, *Goldsmith.*
Feb. 6.	Bartholomew, son of Lettic Chamberlyn, *Widow.*
Feb. 17.	Judith, daughter of Thomas Richardson, *Clothworker.*
Mar. 2.	Elizabeth, daughter of Eward [*sic*] Griffin, *Clothworker*, in the Parish of Abchurch, but was borne in this Parish.
Mar. 9.	Christian, daughter of Raphe Boyce, *Hotpresser.*

1636

Mar. 30.	Francis, son of Francis Bishopp, *Goldsmith.*
April 8.	Dorothy, son of Oliver Ridge, *Gent.*, borne in Mr. Daniell's house in this Parish.
April 10.	Sara, daughter of George Clydwell, *Imbroderer.*
April 14.	William, son of William Moorehead, *Merchant.*
April 17.	Katherine, daughter of Roger Peele, *Clothworker.*
April 18.	Mary, daughter of William Sankey.
July 1.	Thomas, son of Samuel Moore, *Goldsmith.*
July 24.	Edmond, son of Francis Jackson, *Perfumer.*
Aug. 14.	Robert, son of Anthony Peneston, *Goldsmith.*
Aug. 17.	George Wolnoth, (if not baptized before) being a child found in this Parish.
Oct. 30.	Ellin, daughter of William Merrick, *Glover*, borne in Thomas Denman his house in this Parish.
Nov. 10.	Samuell, son of Alexander Pollington, *Haberdasher.*
Dec. 9.	Mary, daughter of Francis Marbury, *Goldsmith.*
Dec. 16.	Mary, daughter of John Skinner, *Carpentar.*
Dec. 23.	Richard, son of Richard Harward, *Draper.*
Jan. 13.	Martha, daughter of William Dollin, *Blacksmith*, borne in Thomas Denman his house.
Jan. 25.	Mary, daughter of Obediah Guilyams, *Haberdasher.*
Feb. 26.	Margaret, daughter of Edward Oakley, *Carpenter.*

1637

Mar. 26.	Suzan, daughter of William Mantle, *Goldsmith.*
April 5.	James, son of James Fletcher, *Brown Baker.*
April 25.	Hannah, daughter of John Rolf, *Scrivener.*
May 3.	Thomas, son of John Steele, *Vintner.*
May 10.	Sara, daughter of Thomas Nevett, *Goldsmith.*
July 16.	Elizabeth, daughter of William Sankey, *Goldsmith.*
July 30.	Isabell, daughter of Samuell More, *Goldsmith.*
Sep. 14.	Nicholas, son of Hugh Morrell, *Merchant.*
Sep. 24.	Jane, daughter of Francis Jackson, *Perfumer.*
Oct. 1.	Mary, daughter of Charles Latham, *Drugster.*
Oct. 18.	Sara, daughter of George Underwood, *Merchant.*
Oct. 25.	Thomas, son of John Feake, *Goldsmith.*
Nov. 12.	Suzanna, daughter of Nicholas Collet, *Goldsmith.*
Nov. 15.	Hanna, daughter of Richard Butler, *Hotpresser.*
Dec. 13.	Ralph, son of Ralph Boyce, *Hotpresser.*
Dec. 17.	John, son of Anthony Pennistone, *Goldsmith.*
Feb. 1.	Thomas, son of Captain Thomas King.
Mar. 23.	Arthur, son of William Mainwearing, *Goldsmith.*

1638

Mar. 25.	Daniell, son of Abraham Johnson, *Merchant.*
April 4.	Stephen, son of Robert Fossett, *Millener.*
April 20.	Anne, daughter of Saunders Cheesman, of Lewis, in Sussex, borne in Mr. Bromhall's entry.
June 29.	Thomas, son of Thomas Wade, *Gent.*
July 29.	William, son of John Steele, *Vintner.*
Aug. 14.	William, son of William Hubbard, *Haberdasher.*
Aug. 15.	Bartholomew, son of Bartholomew Gilman, *Merchant.*
Aug. 24.	Roger, son of William Mantle, *Goldsmith.*
Aug. 31.	Mergaret, daughter of Thomas Nevett, *Goldsmith.*
Aug. 31.	Rebecca, daughter of Edward Cheare, *Merchanttaillor.*
Sep. 5.	William, son of Richard Pepis, *Merchant.*
Sep. 17.	Elizabeth, daughter of Richard Slydrest, a lodger in Mr. Jackson's house, Bearbinder Lane.
Sep. 21.	Maurice, son of Alexander Pollington, *Haberdasher.*
Sep. 28.	France, daughter of Thomas Cox, *Merchant.*
Oct. 18.	John, son of John Feake, *Goldsmith.*
Oct. 18.	Hannah, daughter of Robert Sweete, *Merchant.*
Oct. 24.	John, son of Richard Vance, *Goldsmith.*
Oct. 24.	Rebecca, daughter of Jerman Honnychurch, *Merchant.*
Nov. 1.	Clement, son of Clement Punge, *Goldsmith.*
Nov. 4.	Isabell, daughter of Francis Bishopp, *Goldsmith.*
Nov. 9.	Richard, son of John Shipman, *Bricklayer, a Strainger,* borne in Mr. Wolmer's house.
Nov. 14.	Abraham, son of Abraham Charke, *Merchant.*
Nov. 28.	Marie, daughter of Hugh Murrall, *Merchant.*
Dec. 12.	Elizabeth, daughter of George Best, *Grocer.*
Jan. 16.	Marie, daughter of Nicholas Collet, *Goldsmith.*
Jan. 23.	Anne, daughter of Francis Marbury, *Goldsmith.*
Jan. 26.	Frances, daughter of Thomas King.
Jan. 30.	Margaret, daughter of George Underwood, *Silkman.*
Feb. 10.	Richard, son of John Branthwaite, *Silkdier.*
Feb. 17.	William, son of William Sankey, *Goldsmith.*
Feb. 17.	Richard, son of Richard Butler, *Hotpresser.*
Feb. 20.	Mary, daughter of Samuell Moore, *Goldsmith.*
Feb. 20.	George, son of Thomas Viner, *Goldsmith.*
Feb. 24.	Elizabeth, daughter of Obediah Guilliams.
April 8.	Thomas, son of Thomas Baker, *Merchant.*
April 10.	Barbara, daughter of Robert Fosset, *Millenor.*
April 24.	Martha, daughter of Charles Latham, *Drugster.*
May 5.	Curtis, son of James Fletcher, *Browne Baker.*
May 8.	Dorothy, daughter of William Mannering, *Goldsmith.*
May 26.	Phebe, daughter of John Rolfe, *Scrivener,* [written large.]
June 7.	Thomas, son of Thomas Pratt, *Poyntagger.*
June 14.	Barthelmew, son of Barthelmew Layton, *Goldsmith.*
July 10.	Elin, daughter of Thomas Collier, *Goldsmith.*
July 14.	Anne, daughter of Anthony Pennistone, *Goldsmith.*
July 14.	Jane, daughter of Edmonde Walker, *Clasp Maker.*
Aug. 7.	Anne, daughter of Richard Hayward, *Cooper.*
Aug. 11.	Edward, son of William White, *Haberdasher.*
Oct. 2.	Marie, daughter of Griffin Hughes.
Oct. 6.	Thomas, son of Clement Pung, *Goldsmith.*
Oct. 16.	Thomas, son of Thomas Rednall, *Merchant.*
Oct. 16.	William, son of William Howson.

Nov. 12.	Sara, daughter of Stephen Goodyear, *Merchant.*
Nov. 14.	Elizabeth, daughter of Giles Pooley, *Merchant.*
Dec. 6.	Martha, daughter of Thomas Nevett, *Goldsmith.*
Dec. 11.	Elizabeth, daughter of Thomas Cox, *Merchant.*
Jan. 31.	Anne, daughter of Thomas Wade, *Merchant.*
Feb. 23.	Sara, daughter of Richard Pepis, *Merchant.*
Mar. 4.	Marie, daughter of Richard Garrad, *Merchant.*
Mar. 4.	Elizabeth, daughter of John Shipman, *Bricklayer.*
Mar. 22.	Robert, son of Robert Fossett, *Lynnendraper.*

1640

Mar. 25.	Thomas, son of George Underwood, *Silkman.*
Mar. 25.	Rebecca, daughter of Obediah Guilliams, *Haberdasher.*
Mar. 26.	Thomas, son of Thomas Weld, *Druggester.*
April 8.	Andrew, son of Samuell Moore, *Goldsmith.*
April 8.	Mary, daughter of William Moorhead, *Merchant.*
April 15.	Frances, daughter of Francis Jackson. *Perfumer.*
April 25.	Sarah, daughter of William Mantle, *Goldsmith.*
April 29.	Jane, daughter of Raph Boys.
May 6.	Hester, daughter of Richard Vause, *Goldsmith.*
July 16.	Nicholas, son of Nicholas Meade, *Druggester.*
July 22.	Thomas, son of Walter Morgan, *Haberdasher.*
Sep. 20.	John, son of Richard Butler, *Hotpresser.*
Sep. 26.	John, son of John Croumton, *Goldsmith.*
Nov. 4	Joseph, son of Bartholmew Layton, *Goldsmith.*
Jan. 3.	Prudence, daughter of William Toimsin, *Painter Stayner.*
Jan. 13.	Richard, son of John Feake, *Goldsmith.*
Jan. 19	Henry, son of Henry Futter, *Goldsmith.*
Jan. 26.	Sara, daughter of William Hubberd, *Haberdasher.*
Jan. 27.	Ann, daughter of William, Hughson, *Gent.*
Mar. 3.	Mary, daughter of Abraham Johnson, *Merchant.*
Mar. 11.	Elizabeth, daughter of William Mannering, *Goldsmith.*
Mar. 17.	Anne, daughter of William Humble, *Leatherseller.*
Mar. 17.	Alexander, son of Alexander Pollington, *Haberdasher.*
Mar. 17.	Benjamin, son of Anthony Penniston, *Goldsmith.*

1641

Mar. 26.	Hector, son of Samuell Moore, *Goldsmith.*
April 11.	Josias, son of Charles Latham, *Druggester.*
May 5.	Richard, son of George Best, *Grocer,*
June 10.	John, son of Nicholas Collett, *Goldsmith.*
July 14.	Abigale, daughter of Thomas Cox, *Merchant.*
Aug. 16.	David, son of Abraham Clarke, *Merchant.*
Aug. 24	Stephen, son of Walter Morgan.
Sep. 11.	Joseph, son of Richard Gerrad, *Merchant.*
Sep. 19.	Anne, daughter of Nicholas Mead, *Druggester.*
Oct. 10.	John, son of Nicholas Crosse, *Blacksmith.*
Oct. 21.	Hellen, daughter of Walter Smith, *Baker.*
Nov. 14.	William, son of Thomas Souden, *Box Maker.*

[*N.B.—This is the end of the Baptisms in the first volume.*]

[Vol. ij.]

THE Names of such as have bine christened in the Parishe of
St. Marye Wolnothe, in London, sythens the fourteenth day
of november, Ano Domini, 1641.

1641

Jan. 6.	Jane, daughter of John and Frances Neves, *Upholster.*
Jan. 9.	John, son of Francis and Anne Jackson.
Jan. 16.	Curtis, son of James and Mary Fletcher, *Browne Baker.*
Jan. 19.	Dorathy, daughter of Richard and Sislye Heaward, *Cooper.*
Jan. 23.	Abraham and Charles, sons of John and Marie Steele, *Vintner.*
Jan. 24.	Abigaile, daughter of Thomas and Alice Nevet, *Goldsmith.*
Jan. 28.	Abraham, son of Raphe and Anne Boyce, *Hotpresser.*
Feb. 2.	Anne, daughter of Richard and Ester Vase, *Goldsmith.*
Mar. 4.	Edward, son of Edward and Barbary Leavermore, *Tennis Court Keeper.*
Mar. 17.	Elizabeth, daughter of Richard and Elizabeth Whitaker, *Cook.*
Mar. 20.	Martha, daughter of James and Joane Loe, *Barber.*

1642

April 6.	John, son of William and Katherine Hoghson, *Attornie.*
April 20.	Thomas, son of Richard and Margerie Butler. *Hottpresser.*
May 12.	Roger, son of Roger and Elizabeth Wootton, *Merchant.*
May 13.	Samuell, son of William and Marie Hubbord, *Haberdasher.*
June 8.	Thomas, son of John and Elizabeth Crompton, *Goldsmith.*
June 12.	Sussana, daughter of Nicholas and Jane Collet, *Goldsmith.*
July 29.	James, son of Thomas and Thomasine Nevett.
Aug. 18.	John, son of John and Marie Westman, *Goldsmith.*
Aug. 23.	Elizabeth, daughter of James and Elinor Clarke, *Merchant.*
Aug. 28.	Marie, daughter of Anthony and Martha Peneston, *Goldsmith.*
Sep. 2.	John, son of William and Anne Sankey, *Goldsmith.*
Oct. 6.	Elizabeth, daughter of Thomas and Frances Cox, *Merchant.*
Oct. 11.	Katherine, daughter of William and Elizabeth Humble, *Leatherseller.*
Dec. 2.	Abraham, son of Abraham and Ellynn Smith, *Goldsmith.*
Jan. 1.	Sara, daughter of Edward and Prudence Orange, *Bricklayer.*
Jan. 18.	Daniell, son of John Fridswith Shipman, *Bricklayer.*
Jan. 27.	Elizabeth, daughter of Humfrie and Joan Bates, *Goldsmith.*
Feb. 6.	John, son of William and Rebecca Mantle, *Goldsmith.*
Feb. 17.	Rebccca, daughter of Abraham and Elizabeth Johnson, *Merchant.*

1643

Mar. 25.	Ester, daughter of Charles and Mary Latham, *Drugster.*
April 23.	Lovege, daughter of Francis and Anne Jackson, *Perfumer.*
April 26.	Raph, son of Raph and Lettis Hubbertson, *Mariner.*
Mar. 11.	William, son of George and Anne Best, *Grocer.*
June 4.	Anne, daughter of Ellin Bullock, *Widdow.*
June 10.	Thomas, son of William and Elizabeth Benly, *Leatherseller.*

June 21.	Abigail, daughter of Raph and Ann Boyce, *Hottpresser.*
June 30.	John, son of Thomas and Thomasin Nevet, *Merchant.*
July 9.	Mathew, son of Edward and Jane Stuthbery, *Joiner.*
July 19.	William, son of William and Katherin Hueson, *Lawyer.*
July 25.	Debora, daughter of William and Mary Hubbard, *Haberdasher,*
Aug. 4.	Elizabeth, daughter of Richard and Margerie Butler, *Hottpresser.*
Aug. 24.	Edward, son of Robert and Judith Bucher, *Drugster.*
Oct. 13.	Susan, daughter of John and Susan Hill, *Goldsmith.*
Oct. 16.	Hannah, daughter of Thomas and Hannah Billingly, *Gentleman.*
Oct. 30.	Thomas, son of Thomas and Joyce Weld, *Drugster.*
Nov. 7.	Elizabeth, daughter of John and Elizabeth Portman, *Goldsmith.*
Dec. 11.	Rebecca, daughter of Stephan and Rebecca Bouty, *Stationer.*
Feb. 13.	William, son of Thomas and Ellyn Collyer, *Goldsmith.*
Feb. 14.	Samuell, son of James and Mary Fletcher, *Brownbaker.*
Feb. 16.	William, son of Thomas and Joan Hogges, *Goldsmith.*
Feb. 21.	Joshua, son of Caleb Nicholas, *Barber Churugeon.*
Feb. 29.	Mary, daughter of William and Anne Sankey, *Goldsmith.*

1644

April 5.	Mary, daughter of Abraham and Mary Clarke, *Merchant.*
April 23.	Elizabeth, daughter of John and Elizabeth Crompton, *Goldsmith.*
April 30.	George, son of William and Elizabeth Humble, *Stationer.*
April 28.	A foundling, named John, if not before baptized.
June 27.	Edward, son of Edward and Jane Stuckbery, *Joiner.*
July 5.	Anne, daughter of Thomas and Elizabeth Humble, *Merchant.*
July 8.	William, son of William and Prudence Munday, *Tailor.*
July 11.	William, son of Abraham and Penelope Browne, *Vintner.*
July 26.	Samuel, son of Nicholas and Lucey Crosse, *Blacksmith.*
Aug. 29.	Thomas, son of Thomas and Tamasin Nevett, *Merchant.*
Sep. 10.	Christian, daughter of Robert and Jone Jones, *Confecioner.*
Sep. 13.	Josias, daughter of Thomas and Katherine Jarman, *Weaver.*
Sep. 18.	Joseph, son of Humfrey and Jone Batch, *Silversmith.*
Oct. 13.	Isaack, son of Raph Boyce, *Hottpresser.*
Oct. 20.	A foundling found in the Lady Ramsie's yard.
Oct. 23.	Elizabeth, daughter of Daniell and Ellen Bennett.
Nov. 6.	Josua, son of William and Mary Hubbard, *Habberdasher.*
Nov. 28.	Charles, son of Francis and Ann Jackson, *Perfumer.*
Dec. 4.	Edward, son of William and Elizabeth Bentley, *Bookseller.*
Jan. 17.	Mary, daughter of John and Mary Portman, *Goldsmith.*
Jan. 31.	James, son of William and Katherin Howson, *Atturney.*
Feb. 13.	Anne, daughter of Richard and Anne Middleton, *Translater.*
Feb. 24.	George, son of Robert and Judith Bowcher, *Grocer.*
Mar. 5.	John, son of Samuell and Judith White, *Haberdasher.*

1645

April 23.	Mary, daughter of Enoch and Rachell Porter, *Clothworker.*
June 5.	John, son of William and Elizabeth Humble, *Stacioner.*
July 13.	Mary, daughter of Charles and Mary Latham, *Drugster.*

July 16.	Mary, daughter of Clement and Margaret Pung, *Goldsmith*.
July 24.	John, son of Richard and Cicily Hayward, *Cooper*.
July 29.	Sara, daughter of Thomas and Sara Canham, *Merchant*.
Aug. 27.	Edward, son of Edward and Prudence Oringe, *Bricklayer*.
Sep. 21.	Sara, daughter of John and Margery Ceriton, *Tailor*.
Sep. 30.	George, son of James and Mary Fletcher, *Baker*.
Oct. 9.	Elizabeth, daughter of Isaack and Rebecca Allen, *Merchant*.
Oct. 19.	Israell, son of William and Anne Paybody, *Box Maker*.
Oct. 26.	Alice, daughter of Samuell and Isabel Moore, *Goldsmith*.
Oct. 29.	Edward, son of Edward and Jane Tuchbury, *Joiner*.
Nov. 3.	William, son of Matthew and Elizabeth Dexter, *Weaver*.
Dec. 7.	Mary, daughter of Abraham and Penelope Brown, *Vintner*.
Dec. 17.	Sarah, daughter of Stephen and Susan Bowtell.
Jan. 18.	Rebecca, daughter of William and Mary Hubbard, *Haberdasher*.
Jan. 21.	Anthony, son of John and Susan Hill, *Goldsmith*.
Jan. 27.	William, son of William and Katherine Hewson, *Attorney*.
Mar. 17.	Thomas, son of Thomas and Elizabeth Humble, *Merchant*.
Mar. 18.	Samuell, son of Abraham and Ellen Smith, *Goldsmith*.

1646

April 2.	William, son of Robert and Maud Mason, *Druggester*.
April 7.	Mary, daughter of Thomas and Joyce Wyld, *Grocer*.
April 9.	Jacob, son of Raph and Ellen Boys, *Hotpresser*.
May 9.	Elizabeth, daughter of Robert and Judith Bowcher, *Grocer*.
May 29.	John, son of John and Mary Portman, *Goldsmith*.
June 18.	Robert, son of Robert and Joanna Jones, *Confectioner*.
July 1.	Mary, daughter of John and Elizabeth Crompton, *Goldsmith*.
July 1.	Anne, daughter of Robert and Elizabeth Gale, *Merchant*.
July 19..	Martha, daughter of Nicholas and Jane Collet, *Goldsmith*.
Aug. 16.	Amy, daughter of John and Christian Willington, *Haberdasher*.
Aug. 23.	Hannah, daughter of George and Prudence Muntle, *Tailor*.
Sep. 3.	Martha, daughter of Robert and Martha House, *Bookbynder*.
Sep. 6.	Mary, daughter of Thomas and Mary Coxe, *Packer*.
Nov. 15.	Samuell, son of Humfrey and Joan Bates, *Goldsmith Workman*.
Nov. 25.	Francis, son of Francis and Ann Jackson, *Perfumer*.
Nov. 29.	Anne, daughter of John and Anne Exton, *Cutler*.
Dec. 4.	Isaack, son of Abraham and Mary Clarke, *Dutchman, Merchant*.
Dec. 9.	Thomas, son of Thomas and Katherine Jarman, *Weaver, and Clarke of this Parish*.
Jan. 6.	Jacob, son of Abraham and Elizabeth Johnson, *Merchant*.
Jan. 10.	Jane, daughter of Edward and Jane Tuckbury, *Joiner*.
Jan. 12.	Mary, daughter of Thomas and Sarah Canham, *Merchant*.
Jan. 17.	John, son of Edward and Sarah Alcock, inmate at Mr. Oakley's house.
Feb. 7.	Prudence, daughter of Edward and Prudence Oringe, *Bricklayer*.
Mar. 9.	Sarah, daughter of Samuell and Judith White, *Haberdasher*.
Mar. 10.	Susanna, daughter of Richard and Susanna Vahame, *Joiner*.
May 11.	Martha and Mary, twins, and daughters of William and Elizabeth Manneringe, *Goldsmith*.

1647

April 1. Anne, daughter of William and Anne Christopher, *Merchant*.
April 20. Rebecca, daughter of Richard and Anne Middleton, *Translator*.
April 30. George, son of William and Anne Sankey.
May 6. Isaack, son of Isaack and Rebecca Allen.
May 16. William. son of William and Mary Brickenshaw, *Gent*.
June 9. Elizabeth, daughter of Thomas and Elizabeth Humble, *Merchant*.
June 9. Hannah, daughter of Robert and Mary Gale, *Merchant*.
Aug. 12. Sarah, daughter of William and Sarah Ewester, *Carpenter*.
Aug. 10. Thomas, son of Thomas and Mary Brown, *Gent*.
Aug. 15. Abraham, son of Abraham and Penelope Brown, *Vintner*.
Aug. 31. Israel, son of William and Anne Paybody, *Box Maker*.
Sep. 10. Rebecca, daughter of Raph and Mary Robinson, *Minister of this Parish*.
Sep. 16. Mathias, son of Mathias and Mary Dackellon, *Duchman*.
Oct. 5. Clement, son of Clement and Margaret Pung, *Goldsmith*.
Nov. 10. Benjamin, son of Charles and Mary Latham, *Druggest*.
Jan. 10. Sarah, daughter of James and Mary Fletcher, *Brownbaker*.
Feb. 4. Elizabeth, daughter of John and Susan Hill, *Goldsmith*.
Feb. 13. Benjamin, son of Richard and Margerie Butler, *Hotpresser*.
Feb. 13. Mary, daughter of Stephen and Susan Bowtell, *Bookseller*.
Feb. 20. Judath, daughter of Robert and Judath Bowcher, *Grocer*.
Mar. 12. Samuel, son of Thomas and Joan Hodges, *Goldsmith*.
Mar. 28. George, son of John and Mary Portman, *Goldsmith*.

1648

April 18. Elizabeth, daughter of William and Elizabeth Humble *Leatherseller*.
May 14. Andrew, son of Thomas and Mary Kempe, of the Parish of St. Edmond, Lumbard Streete.
May 25. Martha, daughter of Robert and Joan Johns, *Grocer*.
May 26. Aron, son of Alexander and Dorothy Pollington, *Haberdasher*.
May 29. Sarah, daughter of Abraham and Penelope Browne, *Vintner*.
July 3. Nicholas, son of Nicholas and Jane Collett, *Goldsmith*.
July 8. Walter Woolnoth, a foundling.
July 25. Mary, daughter of Robert and Elizabeth Gale, *Merchant*.
Aug. 2. Sarah, daughter of Richard and Elizabeth Howard, *Cooper*.
Aug. 6. Elizabeth, daughter of George and Anneen Munry, *Tailor*.
Aug. 30. Mary, daughter of Robert and Mary Brian, *Tallowchandler*.
Oct. 10. James, son of Clement and Margaret Pung, *Goldsmith*.
Oct. 30. Thomas, son of John Willington, *Haberdasher*.
Nov. 12. William, son of William and Sarah Ewsten, *Carpentar*.
Nov. 26. George, a foundling in this Parish.
Dec. 12. William, son of William and Ann Christopher, *Merchant*.
Jan. 4. John, son of Humfrey and Joan Bates, *Goldsmith*.
Feb. 1. John, son of John and Dorothy Baber, *Merchanttailor*.
Feb. 2. Isaack, son of William Hubbard, *Haberdasher*.
Feb. 25. Rebecca, daughter of Isaack and Rebecca Allen, *Merchant*.
Feb. 28. Jabez, son of Richard and Susan Vahan, *Joyner*.
Mar. 13. Easter, daughter of William and Anne Sankey, *Goldsmith*.
Mar. 23. Mary, daughter of Daniell and Mary Morris, *Plaislerer*.

1649

Mar. 29. Annabella, daughter of William and Elizabeth Humble, *Leatherseller.*

April 1. Thomas, son of Thomas and Mary Kemp, *Silkman*, of the parish of St. Edmund the King.

April 8. Anne, daughter of William and Anne Paybody, *Box Maker.*

April 18. Lawrence, son of Lawrence and Hester Steele, *Merchant.*

April 24. Daniell, son of Thomas and Katherin Jerman, *Weaver, Clerk of this Parish.*

June 19. Thomas, son of Samuell and Judith White, *Haberdasher of Hatts.*

July 31. Anna, daughter of Anthony Markham, *Gentleman*, and Frances his wife, (daughter to Mr. Sweete.)

Aug. 9. Suzan, daughter of Nicholas and Jane Collett, *Goldsmith.*

Aug. 30. Richard, son of John and Susan Hill, *Goldsmith.*

Aug., 1649, the thirteenth day of this month was born Walter, the son of William and Elizabeth Manwaring, and baptized the 26 day following. [Written in the margin in a bad hand]

Sep. 3. Elizabeth, daughter of Abraham and Mary Clarke, *Merchant.*

Oct. 9. Rebeccah, daughter of John and Jane Runwell, *Glasier.*

Oct. 25. Robert, son of James and Mary Fletcher, *Brownbaker.*

Nov. 4. Arthur, son of Rowland and Jane Dee, *Merchant.*

Nov. 22. Clement, son of Clement and Margaret Pung, *Goldsmith.*

Dec. 6. Philip, son of John and Mary Portman, *Goldsmith.*

Dec. 20. Susannah, daughter of Robert and Joanna Joanes, *Comfitt Maker.*

Jan. 25. Mary, daughter of William and Mary Howson, *Attorney.*

Jan. 31. Anne, daughter of Robert and Audry Bowcher, *Grocer.*

Feb. 12. Elizabeth, daughter of Stephen and Susan Bowtell, *Bookseller.*

Feb. 3. John, son of Robert and Anne Lumpany, *Goldsmith*, an inmate.

Feb. 26. Ann, daughter of Robert and Elizabeth Gale, *Merchant.*

1650

Mar. 25. Obedias, of 5 year old, and Samuell, about 2 years old, both Foundlings put to nurse, Obediah att Langly, beyond Bramford, and Samuell att Ware, at one Mr. Boffs there.

Mar. 27. Daniel, son of John and Elizabeth Redman, *Haberdasher of Hatts.*

Mar. 31. Dorothy, daughter of Thomas and Mary Kempe, *Draper*, of St. Edmund the King in Lombard Streete.

April 8. Francis, son of Francis and Anna Bullfeilde. *Sadler.*

July 15. Isaack, son of Edward and Sarah Brush, *Glasier.*

July 25. William, son of William and Elizabeth Humble, *Leatherseller.*

Sep. 22. John, son of Abraham and Penelope Browne, *Vintner.*

Sep. 22. William, son of John and Jane Exton, *Cutler.*

Oct. 4. Robert, son of John and Susan Hill, *Goldsmith.*

Oct. 13. Mary, daughter of Thomas and Katherine Jarman, *Citizen and Weaver of London.*

Dec. 8. Hester, daughter of John and Katherine Mare, *Merchant.*

Dec. 17. Sarah, daughter of Isaac and Rebeccah Allein, *Merchant.*

Jan. 4. William, son of William and Elizabeth Ranson, *Goldsmith.*

E

Jan. 12.	Mary, daughter of Rowland and Jane Dee, *Merchant*.
Feb. 4.	Joseph, son of Humphrey and Johan Bath, *Goldsmith*.
Feb. 6.	Hannah, daughter of Robert and Elizabeth Gale, *Merchant*.
Feb. 12.	Sarah, daughter of Rowland and Margaret Knight, *Merchant*.
Feb. 16.	Katherin, daughter of Thomas and Mary Kempe, *Draper*, of St. Edmund the King in Lombard Streete.
Mar. 9.	Susannah, daughter of Francis and Hannah Bulified, *Sadler*.
Mar. 22.	Theobald, son of John and Elizabeth Hicks, in Mr. Morris's howse where he was borne.
Mar. 27.	John, son of Robert and Johan Jones.
	The tow and twenteith day of this month was born Ann Mannaring, daughter of William and Elizabeth Mannaring, and Baptized the 30th day following. [Written in the margin in a bad hand.]

1651

April 30.	Elizabeth, daughter of Clement and Margaret Punge, *Goldsmith*.
May 4.	Samuel, son of John and Jane Runwell, *Glasier*.
May 4.	Mary, daughter of Edward and Mary Stotbury.
May 18.	Mary, daughter of Richard and Margarett Butler.
May 18.	May, daughter of Samuel and Suzan Wright.
June 21.	Dorcas, daughter of George and Prudence Munle, *Taylor*.
June 22.	Richard, son of William and Katherine Howson, *Attorney-at-Law*.
June 24.	Stephen, son of Stephen and Suzanna Bowtell, *Bookseller*.
June 20.	Sarah, daughter of Theophilus and Elizabeth Joyner, *Merchant Taylor*.
July 8.	Joseph, son of William and Sarah Crofter.
July 31.	Honnour, daughter of William and Elizabeth Humble, *Leatherseller*.
Aug. 17.	Richard, son of Thomas and Mary Ashelor, *Shoomaker*.
Sep. 16.	John, son of John and Elizabeth Thompson, *Mercer*.
Oct. 1.	Michaell Woolnoth, a foundling, he was taken upp at Mr. Coxes his doore.
Oct. 30.	Mary, daughter of John and Mary Portman, *Goldsmith*.
Nov. 18.	Peter, son of Abraham and Mary Clarke, *Merchant*.
Nov. 22.	Samuell, son of William and Mary Hubbard, *Haberdasher*.
Feb. 17.	James, son of James and Mary Fletcher, *Baker*.
Feb. 29.	Izabell, daughter of Francis and Anna Ballfield.
Mar. 4.	Robert, son of Samuel and Judith White, *Haberdasher of Hatts*.
Mar. 4.	John, son of Isaack and Rebeckah Allen, *Merchant*.
Mar. 15.	Hugh, son of Hugh and Elizabeth Jones, *Grocer*.
Mar. 21.	Elizabeth, daughter of Thomas and Mary Kemp, *Draper*, of St. Edmund the King, in Lombard Street.

1652

April 8.	Elizabeth, daughter of Robert and Judith Bowcher, *Citizen and Grocer of London*.
April 27.	Suzan, daughter of John and Suzan Hill, *Goldsmith*.
June 22.	Thomas, son of William and Anne Paybody, *Boxmaker*, inmate at Mr. Jacksons, *Perfumers*, in Barebinder Lane.
June 23.	William, son of Robert and Joana Jones.

July 8.	James, son of Clement and Margaret Punge, *Goldsmith.*
Aug. 18.	Elizabeth, daughter of Francis and Elizabeth Jones, *Goldsmith.*
Sep. 9.	Margarett, daughter of Leonard and Mary Collard, *Goldsmith.*
Sep. 13.	Penelope, daughter of Abraham and Penelope Browne, *Vintner.*
Sep. 19.	John, son of Stephen and Susannah Bowtell, *Bookseller.*
Sep. 26.	Abigail, daughter of John and Katherine Mare, *Merchant.*
Oct. 14.	Richard, son of Richard and Bridgett Bulkley, *Merchant.*
Oct. 21.	John, son of John and Suzan Runwell, *Glasier.*
Dec. 30.	Francis, son of Francis and Sarah Meynell, *Goldsmith.*
Jan. 16.	John, son of Samuel and Suzan Wright, *Bookebinder.*
Jan. 29.	John, son of William and Anne Zimpany, inmates at the house of Mr. Mantell, in Lombard Streete.
Feb. 13.	Mary, daughter of John and Mary Eddon, *Bricklayer.*
Feb. 25.	John, son of John and Sarah Shacker, *Draper.*
Mar. 6.	Dorothy, daughter of Alexander and Anna Hoult, *Goldsmith.*

1653

Mar. 31.	Theophilus, son of Theophilus and Elizabeth Joyner, *Merchant Tailor.*
April 17.	Joseph, son of William and Suzanna Stringer, born April 13.
April 21.	William, son of John and Elizabeth Tompson, born April 12.
April 26.	Richard, son of Richard and Anne Pocock, born April 25.
May 5.	William, son of Hugh and Elizabeth Jones, *Grocer,* born May 5.
May 17.	Esther, daughter of Isaac and Rebecca Allen, *Merchant,* born May 17.
May, 1653,	the nine and twentieth day of May was borne John Manwaring, the son of William and Elizabeth Manwaring, and baptized the 6th of June following. [Written in the margin in a bad hand.]
————	Benjamine, son of Abraham and Elnor Smyth, born June 11, and is not baptized.
June 30.	Elizabeth, daughter of John and Suzannah Hill, *Goldsmith,* born June 21.
July 20.	Thomas, son of William and Elizabeth Browne, *Cordwainer,* born July 13.
July 26.	Isaac, son of William and Jane Paybody.
Sep. 6.	Nathaniell, son of William and Elizabeth Reason, *Goldsmith,* born Aug. 30.
Sep. 29.	John, son of John and Sarah Shaw, born Sep. 29.
Oct. 8.	Mary, daughter of Robert and Anne Coates, born Oct. 8.
Oct. 16.	Richard, son of Richard and Mary Jesse, born Oct. 16.
Dec. 8.	Alexander, son of Rowland and Jane Dee, *Merchant,* born Nov. 29.
Dec. 15.	Richard, son of Richard and Maudlin Crainsbie, born Dec. 7.
————	Deborah, daughter of John and Jane Runwell, *Glasier,* born Jan. 14, not baptized.
Jan. 26.	Sarah, daughter of Francis and Anna Bullfeilde, *Victualler,* born Jan. 26.
Mar. 14.	William, son of Robert and Johanna Jones, born Mar. 4.

Mar. 15.	William, son of Samuell and Judith White, *Haberdasher,* born Mar. 15.
Mar. 26.	Anne, daughter of John and Mary Edon, born Mar. 11.
Mar. 31.	Samuell, son of William and Sara Euster, born Mar. 31.

1654

May. 2.	Sarah, daughter of John and Sarah Hallsey,
May 13.	Benjamin, son of William and Suzanna Stringer, *Hottpresser,* born May 13.
May 25.	John, son of Edward and Sarah Backwell, *Goldsmith,* born April 20.
May 20.	Annabelle, daughter of William Humble, Esquire, and Elizabeth his wife, born May 11.
May 28.	Mary, daughter of Thomas and Katherine Jerman, *Citizen and Weaver of London and Clerke of this Parish,* born May 23.
July 9.	John, son of John and Sara Skather, *Draper,* born June 7.
June 11.	Anne, daughter of John and Jane Exton, born May 31.
July 7.	Martha, daughter of Thomas and Mary Canham, *Merchant,* born July 7.
July 9.	Judith, daughter of Robert and Judith Bowcher, born July 9.
July 10.	Phillipp, son of John and Mary Portman, *Goldsmith,* born July 10.
Aug. 20.	Mary, daughter of Henry and Prisca Ballowe, born Aug. 9.
Aug. 20.	Temperance, daughter of John and Ann Willington, born Aug. 13.
Aug. 26.	Edward, son of Francis and Sara Meynall, *Goldsmith,* born Aug. 17.
Sep. 12.	Rachell, daughter of Isaac and Rebecka Allen, born Sep. 12.
Sep. 17.	Hugh, son of Hugh and Elizabeth Jones, *Grocer,* born Sep. 16.
Oct. 12.	Martha, daughter of Nicholas and Jane Collett, born Oct. 1.
Nov. 13.	Samuell, son of Samuell and Mary Payne, *Merchantailor,* born Nov. 13.
Nov. 20.	Elizabeth, daughter of Samuel and Rhoda Toft, born Nov. 9,
Nov. 30.	Suzanna, daughter of Abraham and Mary Clarke, born Nov. 13.
Dec. 10.	Sara, daughter of Marmaduke and Sara Ferers, born Dec. 6.
Dec. 24.	Elizabeth, daughter of George and Elizabeth Cash, born Dec. 15.
Jan. 23.	Alexander, son of Alexander and Mary Holt, *Goldsmith,* born Jan. 22.
Jan. 28.	John, son of William and Elizabeth Browne, *Shoemaker,* born Jan. 28.
Feb. 20.	Charles, son of John and Suzan Hill, *Goldsmith,* born Feb. 13.
Mar. 11.	John, son of John and Katherine Maes, born Feb. 26.
Mar. 22.	Anne, daughter of Richard and Anne Turgis, *Grocer,* born Mar. 9.

1655

June 1.	Mary, daughter of Thomas and Ellen Seagood, *Bricklayer,* born May 29.

June 7.	Abraham, son of John and Frances Godfrey, born June 7.
June 20.	Sara, daughter of John and Sara Stacker, born June 14.
July 9.	Roberta, daughter of Benjamin and Roberta Cooke, born June 29.
July 1.	Nevill, son of Robert and Anne Coates, *Merchant*, born July 1.
July 1.	Daniell, son of William and Susan Stringer, *Hottpresser*, born July 1.
Aug. 29.	Thomas, son of Thomas and Mary Canham, born Aug. 29.
Sep. 27.	Godfrey, son of Francis and Sarah Meynell, born Sep. 14.
Sep. 27.	Joseph, son of George and Prudence Manly, born Sep. 27.
Dec. 2.	Sarah, daughter of Clement and Margaret Pung, born Nov. 29.
Nov. 12.	Rebeccah, daughter of Theophilus and Elizabeth Joyner, born Nov. 12.
Jan. 6.	Margarett, daughter of John and Sarah Halsey, born Dec. 28.
Jan. 25.	Anthony, son of William and Katherine Huson, born Jan. 25.
Feb. 10.	Susannah, daughter of Stephen and Susannah Boutell, born Feb. 4.
Feb. 17.	Sarah, daughter of John and Jane Exton, born Feb. 6.
Feb. 15	John, son of Robert and Joanna Jones, born Feb. 8.
Feb. 20.	John, son of Henry and Prisca Ballowe, born Feb. 8.
Feb. 13.	Elizabeth, daughter of Samuell and Elizabeth Gulyfor, born Feb. 13.
Feb. 19.	William, son of John and Susannah Hill, born Feb. 19.
Feb. 23.	Josias, son of John and Dorathye Colvile, born Feb. 21.
Mar. 9.	Thomas, son of John and Mary Eddon, born Feb. 27.
——	Sarah, daughter of John and Jane Runwell, *Glasier*, born Mar. 9. [Probably not baptized.]
Mar. 23.	Robert, son of Alexander and Mary Holt, born Mar. 11.
Mar. 15.	Thomas, son of Nicholas and Jane Collett, born Mar. 14.

1656

April 24.	Hannah, daughter of John and Mary Portman, born April 9.
April 22.	Jane, daughter of John and Jane Ellis, born April 21.
May 26.	Dorothy, daughter of Edward and Alice Coote, born May 5.
May 9.	Sarah, daughter of John and Sarah Moore, born May 9.
June 4.	Dinah, daughter of William Humble, Esquire, and Elizabeth his wife, born May 16.
May 30.	Rebekah, daughter of Richard and Maudling Crainsby, *Grocer*, born May 22.
June 8.	Elizabeth, daughter of Francis and Elizabeth Strandgridge, *Plaisterer*, born May 25.
June 13.	Elizabeth, daughter of William and Elizabeth Rawson, *Goldsmith*, born June 7.
June 22.	John, son of William and Sarah Euster, born June 10.
June 29.	Jasper, son of John and Sarah Sketcher, *Goldsmith*, born June 22.
Aug. 17.	Elizabeth, daughter of William and Elizabeth Browne, born Aug. 6.
Aug. 20.	Richard, son of Richard and Anne Turgis, born Aug. 7.
Aug. 20.	Thomas, son of John and Mary Waters, born Aug. 20.
Oct. 8.	Francis, son of Francis and Sarah Meynell, born Sep. 20.

Oct. 12.	Richard, son of Samuell and Roda Toft, born Sep. 30.
Oct. 20.	Sarah, daughter of Robert and Judeth Boucher, born Oct. 1.
Oct. 8.	Mary, daughter of Richard and Mary Jesse, born Oct. 8.
Oct. 14.	Samuell, son of Francis and Anna Bulfeilde, born Oct. 14.
Nov. 20.	Samuell, son of Samuell and Susannah Wright, born Nov. 9.
Dec. 12.	Martha, daughter of Thomas and Mary Canham, born Dec. 9.
Dec. 26.	John, son of John and Elizabeth Garfeilde, born Dec. 26.
Jan. 20.	Nathaniel, son of Samuell and Judeth White, born Jan. 19.
Feb 8.	Katherine, daughter of John and Frances Sayer, born Jan. 23.
Feb. 8.	Daniell, son of Thomas and Katherine Jerman, born Jan. 24.

1657

April 6.	Katherin, daughter of William and Katherine Hewson, born Mar. 27.
April 15.	Esther, daughter of Thomas and Abigail Mason, born Mar. 29,
April 24.	Sarah, daughter of Samuell and Sarah Dacker, born April 24.
May 12.	Martha, daughter of John and Abigail Randall, born April 30.
May 14.	Thomas, son of Samuell and Frances Baker, born April 30.
May 19.	Dorothy, daughter of John and Dorothy Colvile, born May 12.
June 14.	Mary, daughter of Robert and Johan Jones, born May 31.
July 5.	Margarett, daughter of Adam and Margaret Levingston, born June 29.
July 9.	William, son of William and Mary Smithier, *Goldsmith*, born June 29.
Aug. 27.	Sarah, daughter of John and Jane Ellis, *Merchant*, born Aug. 13.
Sep. 10.	Ellen, daughter of Richard and Anne Turgco, born Aug. 28.
Oct. 4.	Elizabeth, daughter of John and Jane Exton, born Sep. 25.
Oct. 9.	Mary, daughter of George and Elizabeth Gath, born Oct. 8.
Oct. 18.	Jasper, son of John and Sarah Skacher, *Goldsmith*, born Oct. 17.
Nov. 9.	Beniamen, son of Beniamen and Rebecca Cooke, born Oct. 26.
Nov. 15.	Duncomb, son of Rowland and Jane Dee, born Nov. 3.
Dec. 4.	Anne, daughter of Robert and Katherin Welsted, born Nov. 16.
Dec. 6.	Edward, son of Alexander and Mary Holt, born Nov. 18.
Dec. 18.	George, son of George and Rebecca Best, *Goldsmith*, born Dec. 9.
Dec. 24.	Sarah, daughter of Edward and Sarah Backwell, born Dec. 18.
Jan. 6.	Martha, daughter of Ralph and Martha Leeke, *Goldsmith*, born Jan. 6.
———	Not baptized, John, son of Hugh and Margarett Eccleston, born Jan. 26.
Feb. 14.	Isabella, daughter of Henry and Elizabeth Heath, *Bricklayer*, inmates at Mr. Runwells hous, born Feb. 7.

Mar. 14.	Francis, son of Francis and Elizabeth Strandgwidg, born Mar. 2.
———	Not baptized, John, son of John and Jane Runwell, Mar. 12.
Mar. 14.	Mary, daughter of John and Susannah Hill, born Mar. 14.

1658

Mar. 30.	Sarah, daughter of Francis and Sarah Meynell, born Mar. 14.
April 11.	Joshua, son of John and Frances Saywer, born Mar. 25.
April 28.	Elizabeth, daughter of Thomas and Susan Griffeth, born April 8.
April 26.	Elizabeth, daughter of John and Elizabeth Garfield, born April 11.
June 20.	Sarah, daughter of Samuel and Sarah Dorker, born June 13.
June 27.	Sarah, daughter of John and Dorothy Collivell, born June 27.
July 12.	Charles, son of Charles and Mary Everard, born June 30.
July 26.	Elizabeth, daughter of John and Marie Eddon, born July 25.
July —	Marie, daughter of John and Isabell Prichard, born July 4.
Aug. 25.	Elizabeth and Jane (twins), daughters of John and Jane Ellis, born Aug. 24.
Oct. 10.	William, son of William and Elizabeth Browne, born Oct. 4.
Dec. 7.	Mary, daughter of John and Mary Waters, born Nov. 26.
Nov. 30.	Humiliacon, son of John and Sarah Scacher, born Nov. 29.
Dec. 1.	Joseph, son of William and Sarah Ewser, born Dec. 1.
Dec. 25.	Edward, son of Richard and Maudlin Cransby, born Dec. 16.
Jan. 16.	Marie, daughter of John and Mary Portman, born Dec. 30.
Jan. 5.	Priscilla, daughter of Samuell and Roda Taft, born Jan. 5.
Feb. 4.	Elizabeth, daughter of Thomas and Abigail Mason, born Jan. 16.
Feb. 3.	Mary, daughter of Alexander and Mary Holt, born Jan. 21.

1659

April 14.	Elizabeth, daughter of William and Mary Smither, born April 2.
June 21.	Mary, daughter of Nicholas and Elizabeth Thurman, born June 10.
July 7.	John, son of Samuell and Judith White, born July 2.
July 4.	Margaret, daughter of John and Jane Eyton, born July 4.
July 24.	Adam, son of Adam and Margarett Levington, born July 12.
July 24.	John, son of Henry and Elizabeth Heath, born July 9.
July 24.	John, son of John and Dorothy Colvile, born July 21.
July 31.	Christopher son of Christoper and Susanna Bayles, born July 31.
Aug. 17.	Samuell, son of Samuell and Susannah Wright, born Aug. 2.
Aug. 10.	Mary, daughter of Henry and Suzan Cripps, born Aug. 10.
Aug. 10.	Mary, daughter of Charles and Mary Everard, born Sep. 9.
Sep. 2.	Susan, daughter of Marmaduke and Sarah Ferers, born Sep. 27.
Nov. 30.	Dorothy, daughter of Robert and Katherine Welsted, born Nov. 12.

Nov. 20.	John, son of John and Jane Ellis, born Nov. 14.
Nov. 30.	Sarah, daughter of John and Sarah Halsey, born Nov. 14.
Nov. 27.	James, son of Frances and Rebecca Taylor, born Nov. 20.
Nov. 27.	Martha, daughter of Francis and Mary Symons, born Nov. 26.
Dec. 15.	Judith, daughter of Thomas and Mary Canham, born Dec. 14.
Dec. —	Alice, daughter of Alexander and Susanna Tuttinmill, born Dec. 30, in Mr. Ellis' house.
Feb. 22.	Jane, daughter of Alexander and Mary Holt, born Feb. 5.
Feb. 6.	Anne, daughter of Clement and Anne Pung, born Feb. 6.
Mar. 12.	Sarah, daughter of Thomas and Abigail Mason, born Mar. 10.
Mar. 26.	Hannah, daughter of Richard and Mary Butler, born Mar. 11.
Mar. 14.	John, son of William and Elizabeth Brown, *Shoemaker*, born Mar. 14.
Mar. 29.	Elizabeth, daughter of Richard and Anne Turgis, born Mar. 18.

1660

April 24.	John, son of John and Abigail Randall, born April 13.
May 27.	Jane, daughter of John and Frances Sawyer, born May 12.
May 27.	Antonette, daughter of David and Antonette Legrill, of the french congregation.
June 5.	Vincent, son of Vincent and Jane Barrey, of Thame, Oxfordshire, at Mr. Robert Barrey's house in this Parish, born May 25.
July 4.	Rebecca, daughter of William and Anne Paybody, born July 4.
July 12.	Isaac, son of Benjamine and Rebecca Cooke, born July 11.
Aug. 15.	Mary, daughter of Thomas and Mary Gage, *Strangers*, at Mr. Bridges his house in Sherbourne lane, born Aug. 14.
Aug. 28.	Mary, daughter of George and Rebecca Best, born Aug. 19.
———	Not baptized. Benjamen, son of John and Jane Runwell, born Sep. 12.
Sep. 23.	Francis, son of John and Jane Eyton, born Aug. 23.
Oct. 20.	Jane, daughter of Thomas and Susan Griffeth, born Oct. 9.
Oct. 25.	William, son of William and Maudling Crainsby, born Oct. 11.
Nov. 30.	Ann, daughter of Charles and Mary Everard, *Goldsmith*, born Nov. 29.
Dec. 9.	Elizabeth, daughter of John and Isabella Prichard, born Dec. 7.
Dec. 16.	William, son of John and Jane Ellis, born Dec. 6.
Jan. 9.	Elizabeth, daughter of John and Katherin Scarlit, born Dec. 29.
Feb. 19.	Thomas, son of William and Elizabeth Huson, born Feb. 3.
Mar 3.	Susan, daughter of Samuel and Susan Wright.

1661

April 28.	Edward, son of Abraham and Frances Brown, born April 13.

May 29.	Stephen, son of Robert and Katherine Welsted, *Goldsmith*, born May 10.
June 9.	Elizabeth, daughter of Alexander and Mary Holt, born May 22.
June 14.	Judeth, daughter of Richard and Elizabeth Dudley, born May 26.
June 16.	Jane, daughter of Edward and Jane Price, born May 29.
June 20.	Mathew, son of John and Mary Portman, born June, 6.
June 19.	Isabella, daughter of John and Dorothea Colvell, born June 16.
July 9.	Thomas, son of Samuell and Rodea Toft, born June 28.
Aug. 11.	Francis, son of Francis and Elizabeth Strandwige, born July 13.
Aug. 22.	Mary, daughter of Michael and Mary Stamper, born July 27.
Sep. 1.	Elizabeth, daughter of William and Frances Bland, born Aug. 25.
Sep. 10.	Anne, daughter of John and Abigail Randall, born Aug. 27.
Sep. 17.	Charles, son of Michael and Mary Wearing, born Sep. 3.
Sep. 25.	Allexander, son of John and Ellinor Jesse, born Sep. 8.
Oct. 30.	Thomas, son of Sir Thomas Mercer, Knt., and —— [*sic*] his wife, borne in Chapel Streete, in Westminster, Oct. 27, baptized by Mr. William Outram.
Nov. 4.	Mary, daughter of Robert and Isabel Bowes, born Nov. 1, in Mr. Bishope's house.
Nov. 23.	Elizabeth, daughter of Richard and Margret Youdd, born Nov. 23, in widdow Wooldam's house.
Dec. 10.	Mary, daughter of Bassell and Anne More, born Dec. 9.
Dec. 22.	George, son of Henry and Anne Freeman, born Dec. 16.
Dec. 22.	Evan, son of John and Issabell Prichard, born Dec. 21.
Dec. 23.	William, son of John and Katherine Scarlett, born Dec. 22.
Jan. 1.	John, son of Henry and Susan Crippes, born Dec. 30.
Feb. 23.	Edward, son of Samuell and Susan Wright, born Feb. 11.
Feb. 23.	Henry, son of Paull and Mary Savage, born Feb. 14.
Mar. 2.	Alice, daughter of Adam and Margrett Livingstone, born Feb. 19.

1662

May 4.	Thomas, son of William and Pricilla Smith, born April 25.
June 1.	Isaac, son of Henry and Elizabeth Heath, inmates at Mr. Baker's, in Sherborne Alley, born May 31.
May 13.	Mary, daughter of Thomas and Mary Semore, born May 1.
June 9.	Luke, son of Richard and Elizabeth Turges, born June 8.
June 16.	Dorothy, daughter of John and Dorothy Tooker, *Straungers*, inmates at Mr. Ellis, in Sherborne Lane.
June 24.	Dulcibella, daughter of James and Alce Yardly, born June 13.
Aug. 29.	Alexander, son of Samuell and Mary Pollington.
Sep. 26.	Clliffe, daughter of William and Elizabeth Hewson.
Oct. 3.	Susan, daughter of John and Mary Smith, born Oct. 3.
Nov. —	Sarah, daughter of William and Anne Forrest, born Nov. 8.
Nov. 30.	Millicent, daughter of George and Jane Baker, born Nov. 17.
———	Elizabeth, daughter of Robert and Sarah Ridway, inmates in the Cock and Lyon, at Mr. Pritchard's house, born Dec. 6.

Jan. 29.	Edward, son of Abraham and Anne Johnson, born Jan. 16.
Feb. 3.	Katherine, daughter of Thomas Canham, Esq. and Katherine his wife.
Feb. 26.	Edward, son of Edward Backwell, Esq. and Mary his wife, born Feb. 6.
Feb. 26.	Hester, daughter of Clement and Lucy Manisty, born Feb. 24.
Mar. 8.	Mary, daughter of John and Jane Ellis, born Feb. 28.
Mar. 15.	Martha, daughter of John and Dorothy Colvill, born Mar. 11.

1663

April 21.	Sarah, daughter of Alexander and Mary Holt, born April 7.
April 23.	Jeremiah, son of Robert and Isabel Bowes, born April 23, Mr. Bishopp's house.
	[N.B.—The following entry is in a bad hand :—]
May 2, 1663, borne Joseph, the sonne of Richard and Mary Butler, and baptized the eleventh day following.
June 2.	John, son of James and Hester Berry, born May 26.
May 16.	Phillipp, son of Phillipp and Sarah Bayley, born May 14, in Mr. Savage's house.
July 11.	John, son of William and Sarah Blane, born June 20.
June 3.	Richard, son of Francis Meynell, *Alderman and Goldsmith*, and Sarah his wife, born June 3.
July 20.	Edward, son of Edward and Francis Price, born July 14.
Sep. 20.	Charles, son of William and Sarah Ewster, *Carpentar*,
Sep. 26.	Elizabeth, daughter of Henry and Elizabeth Heath, born Sep. 24.
Oct. 11.	Charles, son of Paul and Mary Savage, born Sep. 28.
Oct. 19.	Mary, daughter of Thomas and Mary Tindall, born Oct. 6.
Oct. 27.	Pricilla, daughter of Richard and Elizabeth Turges, *Drugest*, born Oct. 9.
Nov. 20.	Mary, daughter of Michael and Mary Wareing, born Nov. 5.
Jan. 3.	George, son of George and Jane Baker, born Dec. 23.
Feb. 14.	Elizabeth, daughter of Mathew and Anne Munday, born Feb. 9.
Feb. 23.	Dorothy, daughter of William and Katherine Welsted, born Feb. 14.
Mar. 2.	Mary, daughter of John and Mary Smith, born Feb. 21.
Mar. 7.	Amey, daughter of John and Jane Ellis, born Feb. 23.
Mar. 7.	Arthur, son of Arthur and Jane Standley, born Feb. 21.
Mar. 11.	Henry, son of Henry and Judith Jones, born Feb. 25.

1664

April 19.	Mary, daughter of John and Mary Portman, born Mar. 21.
May 1.	Daniell, son of Thomas and Mary Seymour, born April 29.
May 13.	Thomas, son of Thomas and Mary Pearce, born May 13.
May 29.	Ann, daughter of John Isable Prichard, born May 21.
June 24.	Jemima, daughter of Abraham and Ann Johnson, born June 23.
June 24.	Mary and Martha, daughters of Job and Mary Par, born June 24.
June 10.	Kathrine, daughter of James and Sarah Browne, born June 9.

July 8.   Thomas, son of Thomas and Abigall Samson, born June 24.
June 21.   Rebecca Woolnoth, a foundling.
July 17.   Elizabeth, daughter of George and Ann Shaw, born July 4.
Aug. 10.   Robert, son of Robert and Seball Carpenter, born July 26.
Aug. 28.   Ann, daughter of Alexander and Mary Holt, born Aug. 23.
Aug. 27.   Samuell, daughter of James and Mary Mallory, born Aug.
Aug. 25.   Jonothan Woolnoth, a foundling.
Nov. 20.   Richard, son of Thomas and Elizabeth Mottershed, born Nov. 20.
Nov. 22.   John, son of Thomas and Margrett Oliver, born Nov. 22.
Dec. 13.   Thomas, son of John and Dorothy Colvill, born Dec. 3.
Jan. 1.   Mary, daughter of Francis and Elizabeth Strandguidge, born Dec. 18.
Jan. 19.   Richard, son of Richard and Mary Butler, born Jan. 1.
Mar 26.   Petter, son of Petter and Susan Parker.

1665

Mar. 31.   Sarah, daughter of John and Sarah Blunt, born Mar. 17.
April 10.   Mary, daughter of Henry and Elizabeth Heath, born April 4.
May 7.   Margaret daughter of John and Jane Ellis, born May 14.
May 18.   William, son of Richard and Margaret Yrde, born May 16.
June 11.   Abigall, daughter of Thomas and Abigall Samson, born May 24.
June 20.   Sara, daughter of Adam and Margaret Livingstone, born June 6.
June 20.   Barbara, daughter of Walter and Anne Elford, born June 11.
June 25.   Thomas, son of Thomas and Christian Soames, born June 19.
June 30.   Elizabeth, daughter of Thomas and Mary Seymour, born June 19.
July 21.   Samuell, son of Phillip and Margerie Bosewell, born July 21.
July 2.   Elizabeth, daughter of David and Anthoniet le Griel, born June 18.
July 30.   Elizabeth, daughter of Thomas and Elizabeth Smith, born July 26.
Sep. 21.   John, son of Robert and Sebell Carpentar, born Sep. 20.
Nov. 26.   William, son of George and Jane Beaker, born Nov. 26.
Dec. 20.   Henry, son of Mary Savage, *Widdowe*, born Dec. 19.
Jan. 17.   George, son of John and Jane Hind.
Jan. 25.   Francis, son of John and Dorothe Colville, born Jan. 25.
Feb. 13.   Jane, daughter of Thomas and Jane Roggers, born Feb. 12.
Mar. 11.   Elizabeth, daughter of Abraham and Frances Browne, born Mar. 10.

1666

April 16.   Thomas, son of Godfrey and Elizabeth Beck, born April 16.
July 1.   Abraham, son of Ralph and Anne Lucas, born June 20.
July 3.   Abraham, son of Samuell and Anne Simonds, born June 22.
Sep. 7.   John, son of John and Mary Harleing, born Sep. 7, at Hanwell, in Mid.

1667

April 29. | Moses, son of Samuell and Sarah Jermyn, born April 27.
Oct. 5. | Rowland, son of George and Jane Baker, born Sep. 29, in Allgat parish.

1668

Dec. 13. | Eliz, daughter of George and Jane Beaker, born Dec. 13.

1669

Sep. 6. | Edmund, son of Edmund and Grace Rolphe, born Sep. 5.
Nov. 21. | Mary, daughter of Godfrey and Eliz Beck, born Nov. 14.
Jan. 9. | Mary, daughter of George and Jane Beaker, born Jan. 5.
Jan. 9. | Christian, daughter of James and Elizabeth Smith.
Feb. 10. | William, son of Edward and Joane Coales, born Jan. 29.
Feb. 10. | Benjamine, son of Walter and Ann Elford, by Mr. Guy, born Jan. 31.
Mar. 27. | Benjamin, son of John and Mary Harleing, born Mar. 12.

1670

May 5. | Margaret, daughter of Randolph and Mary Bolton, born April 30.
May 8. | Thomas, son of John and Kathrine Gravener, born May 6.
June 1. | Martin, son of Pauli Bowes, Esq. and Bridgett his wife, born May 24, in Chancery Lane.
July 30. | Suzanna, daughter of Peter and Suzanna Parkes, born July 19.
Sep. 23. | Thomas, son of William and Margaret Rutter, born Sep. 13.
Oct. 9. | Thomas, son of Thomas and Katherine Kirwood, born Sep. 24.
Oct. 21. | John, son of Thomas and Mary Williams, born Sep. 25.
Oct. 8. | Claude, daughter of David and Antoniette Griel, born Sep. 29.
Oct. 10. | George, son of Lawrence and Ann Bretland, born Oct. 10.
Oct. 18. | William, son of William and Mary Lovett, born Oct. 13.
Nov. 3. | Elizabeth, daughter of Mrs. Dorothea Colville, *Widow*, born Nov. 3.
Dec. 30. | Robert, son of Henry and Mary Lewis, born Dec. 29.
Jan. 4. | George, son of Robert and Sara Seignior, born Dec. 23.
Jan. 5. | Joseph and Benjamin, twins, sons of Robert and Elizabeth Watkins, born Dec. 25.
Jan. 8. | Rebecca, daughter of George and Jane Beaker, born Jan. 8.
Jan. 15. | Mary Woolnoth, a foundling, taken up Dec. 29, at Popes Head Alley gate.
Jan. 20. | William, son of William and Ann Stroude, born Jan. 8.
Feb. 2. | Richard, son of Thomas and Francis Foley, born Jan. 26.
Mar. 11. | George, son of John and Jane Inns, born Feb. 28.

1671

Mar. 31. | Joseph and Benjamine, sons of Thomas and Mary Seymour, born Feb. 22.
April 25. | George, son of George and Elizabeth Twine, born April 10

July 1.	Elizabeth, daughter of Richard and Ann Harbey, born July 1.
Aug. 1.	Richard, son of Francis and Margaret Fletcher, born July 3.
Aug. 1.	Was taken up a man child next the sign of the Cock in Sherborne Lane, and baptized the 8th day, Samuell Woolnoth.
Aug. 18.	By Dr. Mason, Thomas, son of Thomas and Elizabeth Butler, of the parish of St. Swithin's London Stone, born Aug. 13.
Aug. 24.	William, son of John and Alice Tempus, born Aug, 5.
Aug. 30.	Judith, daughter of John and Easter Bowcher, born Aug. 17.
May 14.	Martyn, son of John and Edith Beaumont, *Tallow Chandler*, born May 11. [Written at bottom of page.]
Sep. 12.	Elizabeth, daughter of Samuell and Ann Tirrick, born Sep. 12.
Sep. 13.	Thomas, son of Richard and Anne Neave, born Sep. 4.
Sep. 19.	Thomas, son of John Coleman, *Merchant*, born Sep. 19.
Oct. 8.	Francis, daughter of Thomas and Mary Williams, Sep. 22.
Oct. 12.	Ralph, son of Randolph and Mary Bolton, born Oct. 3.
Oct. 18.	Elizabeth, daughter of Samuell and Sara Jermyn, born Oct. 18.
Nov. 9.	Elizabeth, daughter of John and Elizabeth Morris, born Oct. 19.
Nov. 9.	Robert, son of Andrew and Meriell Crisp, born Oct. 31.
Nov. 12.	Elizabeth, daughter of Henry and Elizabeth Aynscomb, born Oct. 31.
Nov. 14.	Mary, daughter of Barnard and Mary Turner, born Oct. 31.
Nov. 17.	Elizabeth, daughter of John and Suzanna Tassell, born Nov. 9.
Nov. 20.	Katherine, daughter of John and Katherine Gravenor, born Nov. 12.
Dec. 30.	Elizabeth, daughter of William and Margaret Rutter, born Dec. 30.
Dec. 1.	Michaell, son of John and Elizabeth Hartshorne, born Nov. 23.
Jan. 24.	Hannah, daughter of John and Jane Cooke, born Jan. 24.
Jan. 31.	Mary, daughter of John and Mary Chambers, born Jan. 30.
Feb. 8.	Elizabeth, daughter of Robert and Elizabeth Bowman, born Jan. 26.
Feb. 8.	Godfrey, son of Godfrey and Elizabeth Beck, born Jan. 21.
Feb. 25.	Mary, daughter of Robert and Issable Bowes, born Feb. 21.
Mar. 6.	John, son of Moises and Hannah Edward, born Feb. 19.

1672

April 17.	Sarah, daughter of Mathew and Jemima Alleine, *Barbour*, born April 6.
May 5.	Anne, daughter of John and Margery Taylor, *Joyner*, born April 28.
May 15.	Margaret, daughter of Robert and Elizabeth Watkins, *Stationer*, born April 30.
June 26.	Francis, son of John and Margaret Farington, *Merchant*, born June 18.

July 7.	Katherine, daughter of George and Elizabeth Twine, *Vintner*, born June 22.
July 9.	Prisca, daughter of Austin and Elizabeth Ballow, *Norridg Merchant*, born June 25.
Aug. 28.	Anne, daughter of Timothy and Mary Taylor, *Merchant*, born Aug. 3.
Sep. 17.	Was taken up a manchild in Dow Court with a noate pinned to his breast of his name Thomas Williams.
Oct. 26.	Thomas, son of Robert and Margaret Fox, born Oct. 2.
Nov. 4.	Robert, son of William Rawlinson, born Oct. 9.
Nov. 27.	Sara, daughter of Godfrey Davis (Taylor) born Nov. 12.
Dec. 11.	Mary, daughter of Phillip and Dorothy Scarth, born Nov. 29.
Dec. 17.	John, son of Andrew Crisp, *Rector of this Church*, and Merriell his wife, born Dec. 17.
Nov. 29.	Suzann, daughter of David and Anthoniett Griell, born Nov. 16.
Dec. 22.	Henry, son of William Collins, *Goldsmith*, born Dec. 10.
———	Sarah, daughter of Samuell and Sara Jermyn, born Dec. 30.
Jan. 25.	Elizabeth, daughter of Peter White, born Jan. 25.
Feb. 2.	Mary, daughter of Davis Allmon, born Jan. 29.
Mar. 1.	George, son of Henry Payne, *Druggest*, born Feb. 27.

1673

April 6.	Thomas, son of John Bowcher, *Scrivener*, born Mar. 28.
May 4.	Daniell, son of George and Jane Baker, born April 29.
May 25.	Elizabeth, daughter of Thomas Woodlaw, *Barbour*, born May 9.
June 11.	Richard, son of Richard Hoare, *Goldsmith*, born May 24.
June 17.	Mary, daughter of Thomas Williams, *Goldsmith*, born May 31.
June 29.	John, son of John Colman, *Merchant*, born June 29.
June 9.	Mary, daughter of Austing Ballow, *Norridg Merchant*, born June 9.
June 24.	Martha, daughter of Thomas and Sara Morris, by Mr. Hunt, born June 20.
June 7.	Robert, son of John Gruvenor, *Upholster*, born June 7.
July 9.	Robert, son of John Morris, *Vintner*, born June 27.
July 10.	William, son of John Chambers, *Scrivener*, born July 9.
Aug. 31.	Jane, daughter of John Cooke, *Rasormaker*, born Aug. 12.
Sep. 29.	Barnard, son of Barnard and Mary Turner, *Goldsmith*, born Sep. 29.
Oct. 4.	Morris, son of John and Jane Inns, *Goldsmith*, born Oct. 4.
Oct. 30.	Mary, daughter of Joshua and Mary Haskyns, born Oct. 14.
Nov. 23.	Judith, daughter of Godfrey and Sara Woodward, *Attorney*, born Nov. 10.
Nov. 23.	Francis, daughter of Thomas and Frances Folie, *Packer*, born Nov. 23.
Nov. 30.	Nathaniell, son of William and Ann Frost, *Victualler*, born Nov. 13.
Dec. 2.	Isabella, daughter of Robert and Isabella Bowes, born Dec. 2.
Dec. 18.	Elizabeth, daughter of George Twine, *Vintner*, born Dec. 8.

Dec. 26.	Colvill, son of John and Dorotha Temple, *Goldsmith*, born Dec. 26.
Jan. 7.	Hester, daughter of John and Edith Beamount, *Tallow Chandler*, born Jan. 2.
Feb. 13.	William, son of Edward and Ann Gladin, *Goldsmith*, born Feb. 12.

1674

Mar. 29.	Abraham, son of John and Hester Vanhack, by Mr. Crisp, born March 14.
April 26.	Elizabeth, daughter of John and Easter Bowcher, born April 13.
May 12.	Thomas, son of Samuell and Sara Jermyn, born May 12.
May 24.	A male child, taken up in Cardinals Alley, named Morris Dixon.
May 24.	A male child, taken up at the great gates in Woolchurch Markett, named Broadgate.
June 2.	Sara, daughter of William and Margaret Foster, born May 17.
June 7.	A female child, named Jane Woolnoth.
June 11.	Thomas, son of Sir Thomas Markham, Knt., and of Mary his wife, born June 11.
June 26.	Elizabeth, daughter of Austin and Elizabeth Ballow, born June 25.
July 2.	Elizabeth, daughter of Thomas and Elizabeth Cooke, born June 29.
July 19.	Margaret, daughter of Robert and Margaret Fox, born July 2.
July 20.	Thomas, son of Godfrey and Elizabeth Beck, born July 20.
July 21.	Dorotha, daughter of Phillip and Dorotha Scarth, born July 16.
Aug. 2.	Mary, daughter of John and Elizabeth Morris, born July 17.
Aug. 2.	Elizabeth, daughter of Joseph and Elizabeth Boothe, born Aug. 2.
Sep. 6.	Robert, son of Robert and Joana Goldwell, born Aug. 23.
Sep. 20.	Thomas, son of Thomas and Rebecca Woodlaw, born Sep. 1.
Sep. 8.	Mary, daughter of John and Katherine Gravenor, born Sep. 1.
Sep. 26.	John, son of John and Susan Tapswell, born Sep. 14.
Oct. 1.	Ann, daughter of Ann Deury, born Oct. 1.
Nov. 19.	Humphrey, son of Thomas and Mary Seymour, born Nov. 5.
Nov. 21.	Hannah, daughters of Richard and Ann Harby, born Nov. 10.
Dec. 9.	John Woolnoth, taken up at Mr. Mingaye's, Sherborne Lane.
Jan. 22.	George Woolnoth, taken up next the church wall in Sherborne Lane.
Jan. 22.	Elizabeth, daughter of John and Hannah Archer, born Jan. 22.
Jan. 24.	Elizabeth, daughter of Paul and Elizabeth Ridley, born Jan. 21.
Jan. 31.	John, son of John and Mary Wirgen, born Jan. 24.
Jan. 30.	Jane, daughter of Thomas and Mary Williams, born Jan. 30.
Feb. 11.	Lettis Woolnoth, a female child taken at Mr. Mingay's doore.

Feb. 26.	Thomas, son of James and Elizabeth Windstandley, born Feb. 24.
Feb. 28.	Elizabeth, daughter of Godfrey and Elizabeth Davie, born Feb. 28.
Mar. 23.	John, son of Barnard and Mary Turner, born Mar. 14.

1675

April 29.	Thomas, son of Edward Howell, born April 13.
April 25.	Francis, daughter of Godfrey Woodward, *Attorney*, born April 14.
April 26.	William, son of Joseph Harvey, born April 25.
June 1.	James, son of Benjamen Comes Goldsmith, born May 30.
June 6.	Mary, daughter of Alexander and Elizabeth Pollington, born May 15.
June 4.	Elizabeth, daughter of John and Dorothe Temple, born June 4.
June 6.	Elizabeth, daughter of Thomas and Mary Price, born June 6.
June 5.	Ann, daughter of George and Elizabeth Twine, born June 5.
July 2.	John, son of Thomas Cooke, *Goldsmith*, born June 24.
July 13.	John, son of Samuel and Ann Simonds, born June 23.
July 15.	Ann, daughter of Peter and Elizabeth White, born July 15.
July 22.	Mary, daughter of Andrew Crisp, *Rector*, and of Merriall his Wife, born July 22.
July 29.	Thomas, son of William and Dorothy Thompson, born July 28.
Aug. 7.	Hannah, daughter of John and Easter Bowcher, born July 26.
Aug. 8.	Judith, daughter of Thomas and Frances Folie, born Aug. 7.
Aug. 13.	John, son of Joshua Haskins, born Aug. 10.
Sep. 17.	Baynard, son of Robert and Elizabeth Weilkins, born Sep. 3.
Oct. 17.	William, son of William and Suzan Collins, born Sept. 27.
Aug. 19.	Thomas, son of Austin Ballow, *Merchant*, and Elizabeth, born Aug. 10. [*sic*].
Nov. 7.	Jane, daughter of John and Jane Thursby, born Oct. 28.
Nov. 7.	William, son of Richard and John Harley, born Nov. 2.
Dec. 22.	Anne, daughter of Philip and Dorothe Scarth, born Dec. 22.
Jan. 10.	Elizabeth, daughter of Paul and Elizabeth Ridley, born Jan. 9.
Jan. 13.	Bridgett, daughter of John and Hannah Archer, born Jan. 10.
Jan. 4.	William, son of Thomas and Robena Woodlaw, born same day.
Mar. 17.	Thomas, son of Henry and Sarah Wybert, born Mar. 12.

1676

April 30.	Dorrothe daughter of John and Dorrothe Temple, *Goldsmith*, born April 30.
May 24.	Elizabeth and Martha, daughters of Robert Fox, *Boxmaker*, born May 24.

June 11. Loveday, daughter of Thomas and Mary Williams, born May 25.

Aug. 1. Hannah, daughter of Thomas and Hannah English, born July 31.

Aug. 27. Michaell, son of Hosea Walterer, born Aug. 17.

Sep. 7. Roberta, daughter of William Browne, *Merchant*, born Aug. 22.

Aug. 30. Robert, son of Robert and Elizabeth Hills, born Aug. 30.

Sep. 10. Constance, daughter of Peter and Elizabeth White, born Sep. 3.

Sep. 13. John, son of William Collins, *Goldsmith*, born Sep. 13.

Oct. 1. Mary, daughter of Thomas Price, *Goldsmith*, born Oct. 1.

Dec. 1. Amie Woolnoth, a female child, taken up in Sherborne Lane, at Mr. Inns his doore, Nov. 25.

Dec. 3. Robert, son of Barnard and Elizabeth Sirps, *Merchant*, born Dec. 2.

Jan. 5. Richard, son of John and Katherine Jones, *Oylman*, born Dec. 29.

Jan. 17. Elizabeth, daughter of Joshua and Elizabeth Bolt, *Drugest*, born Jan. 17.

Jan. 19. John Woolnoth, a male child, taken up in Lambe Alley, in Shoe Lane, Jan. 18.

Feb. 9. Anne, daughter of Austin and Elizabeth Ballow, *Merchant*, born Jan. 19.

Jan. 29. Fardinando son of John and Margarett Farington, born Jan. 29.

Feb. 3. Richard, son of Rebecca Nicoll, *Widdowe*, born Jan. 26. She was brought to bed in Mr. Pollington's house.

Feb. 14. Elizabeth, daughter of Phillip and Dorothe Scarth, born Jan. 14.

Feb. 11. Mary, daughter of George and Elizabeth Twine, born Jan. 26.

Feb. 7. Henry, son of Thomas and Rebecca Woodlaw, born Jan. 29.

Feb. 10 Hannah, daughter of Benjamin and Hannah Combs, born Feb. 10.

Feb. 17. Edward, son of Richard and Dorothe Thompson, born Feb. 17.

Feb. 10. Bridgett, daughter of John and Elizabeth Snell, *Goldsmith*, born, Feb. 10.

Feb. 19. Elizabeth, daughter of Alexander and Elizabeth Pollington, *Haberdasher of Hatts*, born, Feb. 19.

Mar. 4. Mary, daughter of Godfrey and Sarah Woodward, *Attorney*, born Mar. 2.

1677

Mar. 28. Hannah, daughter of Edmund and Grace Rolfe, *Scrivener*, born Mar. 22.

Mar. 17. Henry, son of Henry and Sara Wisbert, *Poulterer*, born

Mar. 17. Was taken up at the sign of the goate, near pope's head alley, a female childe named Anna Plained [?]

April 5. Anna, daughter of Thomas and Elizabeth Cooke, born Mar. 24.

April 7. Hannah, daughter of Thomas and Francis Folie, born April 7.

April 8.	Elizabeth, daughter of Godfrey and Elizabeth Beck, born April 8.
April 17.	John, son of Edward and Anne Gladwin, born April 10.
May 11.	Elizabeth, daughter of Bartholomew and Margarett Tombs, born May 11.
May 17.	Isaack Woolnoth, a male child taken at the fleece door next pope's head alley.
June 8.	———— a female child taken up.
June 6.	Francis, son of Francis and Mary Terruitt, born May 24.
June 18.	Sarah, a female child taken up at Mr. Gladwin's doore.
June 18.	Thomas Davis, was taken up in Lombard Streete in my Lord Mayor's entry and baptized Thomas Davis, my Lord Mayor's name.
July 1.	John, son of Michaell and Martha Whaley, born June 16.
July 14.	Elizabeth, daughter of Thomas and Elizabeth Sands, born July 10.
July 26.	Jacob, son of John and Jane Colman, born July 19.
July 29.	Was taken up in Little Lumbard Streete, Allein Clarke, he was 2 yeares old ye 21 of March last; ye letter was left in ye hands of Mr. Edmund Rolf.
Aug. 16.	Robert, son of Robert and Margarett Fox, born Aug. 5.
Aug. 22.	Jonathan, daughter of Robert and Ann Baskett, born Aug. 21.
Sep. 6.	Shorelott, daughter of Charles and Mary Letelle, born Aug. 25.
Aug. 29.	Suzanna, daughter of John and Jane Thursby, born Aug. 29.
Sep. 8.	Phoebe, daughter of William Taylor, Esq., and Martha, his wife, born Sep. 7.
Sep. 21.	John, son of Richard and Ann Harbey, born Sep. 18.
Sep. 25.	John, son of John and Issabell Browghton, born Sep. 25.
Oct. 19.	Edith, daughter of John and Dorothœ Temple, born Oct. 16.
Oct. 19.	Jane Woolnoth, a female child taken up.
Oct. 31.	Anne, daughter of William Browne, *Merchant*, born Oct. 31.
Nov. 26	Edward, son of Godfrey and Elizabeth Davis, born Nov. 26.
Dec. 20.	Samuell, ——— a male child taken up.
Dec. 19.	Jonathan, son of Jonathan Whaley, born Dec. 19.
———	A childe taken up, with a noate named Cooper Peircee, Dec. 29.
Jan. 1.	Thomas, son of Thomas and Mary Price, born Dec. 23.
Jan. 26.	Sara, daughter of Samuell and Sara Jermyn, born Jan. 26.
Feb. 7.	Elizabeth, daughter of George and Dorrothœ Sheepside, born Jan. 26.
Feb. 12.	Sara, daughter of Henry and Sara Wybert, born Feb. 12.
Feb. 25.	Margaret, daughter of Alexander and Elizabeth Pollington, born Feb. 25.

1678

Mar. 30.	Margarett Woolnoth, a female child taken up.
April 21.	Thomas, son of Thomas and Mary Williams, *Goldsmith*, born Mar. 29.
April 23.	John, son of John and Ann Bolitho, born April 23.
May 8.	Ann, daughter of Peter and Elizabeth White, *Goldsmith*, born April 19.

May 8.	Hannah, daughter of John and Mary Harleing, *Goldsmith*, born April 19.
May 26.	Kathrine, dughter of Austin and Elizabeth Ballow, *Merchant*, born May 15.
May 26.	John, son of Phillip Scarth, *Druggest*, born May 21.
June 14.	Mary, daughter of Thomas and Mary Flowerdew, *Merchant*, born June 14.
June 18.	Ann, daughter of Gabriell and Ann Smith, born June 18.
July 7.	Ann, daughter of Daniell and Suzan Lord, *Barbor*, born June 23.
July 11.	Robert, son of Joseph and Elizabeth Cozens, *Barbor*, born July 10.
July 22.	Thomas, son of Thomas and Rebecca Woodlaw, *Barber*, born July 22.
July 31.	Benjamen, son of Benjamen and Hannah Combe, *Goldsmith*, born July 31.
Aug. 9.	Bridgett, daughter of Barnard and Margarett Eales, *Goldsmith*, born Aug. 5.
Aug. 10.	Grace, daughter of Margaret Jones, bastard child by Robert Coxeter, born July 31.
Sep. 8.	John, son of Ambros and Mary Lightfoot, born Aug. 25.
Sep. —.	Phillip, son of Phillip Frewd, Esq., and Sarah his Wife, born Sep. 12.
Oct. 6.	Rebecca, daughter of John Tassell, *Goldsmith*, born Sep. 29.
Oct. 16.	Mary, daughter of William Browne, *Merchant*, born Oct. 16.
Nov. 7.	John, son of John and Alice Salendine, born Oct, 24.
Nov. 3.	Mary, daughter of Nicholas and Alice Love, born Nov. 3.
Nov. 10.	Martha, daughter of John and Dorothæ Temple, *Goldsmith*, born Nov. 17.
Nov. 17.	Martin, son of Edmund and Jane Halfcheid, *Vintener*, born Nov. 3.
Dec. 17.	Robert, son of John and Elizabeth Snell, *Goldsmith*, born Nov. 27.
Dec. 11.	Jane, daughter of John and Jane Thursby, *Goldsmith*, born Dec. 11.
Dec. 17.	John, son of Alexander Pollington, *Haberdasher*, born Dec. 10.
Jan. 7.	Mary, daughter of Michael and Martha Whaley, *Goldsmith*, born Jan. 6.
Jan. 21.	Elizabeth, daughter of John and Elizabeth Harison, *Coffeeman*, born Jan. 3.
Jan. 20.	Charles, son of Francis and Mary Terruitt.
Feb. 2.	Elizabeth, daughter of Edward Gladwin, *Goldsmith*.

1679

April 3.	Suzan, daughter of Nicholas and Suzan Carey, *Goldsmith*.
April 3.	Lucie, daughter of James and Martha Holliard, *Cheuirgeon*.
April 17.	Vreth, daughter of Robert and Ann Baskett, *Apothecary*.
April 20.	Joseph, son of Joseph Cozens, *Barber*.
May 11.	Charles, son of Hosea and Elizabeth Waterer, *Carpentar*.
May 18.	Nicholas, son of Austin and Elizabeth Ballow, *Merchant*.
May 20.	Edward, son of Peter Wade, *Merchant*.
June 25.	Daniel, son of John Browghton, *Victualler*.
July 28.	Margaret, daughter of Richard Burford.

Aug. 3.	Dorothœ, daughter of George Sheepsheid.
Aug. 10.	Margaret, daughter of Bartholomew and Margaret Tombs, *Upholder*.
Aug. 21.	Godfrey, son of Godfrey and Sarah Woodward, *Attorney*.
Sep. 23.	Martha, daughter of Barnard and Margaret Eels, *Goldsmith*.
Sep. 7.	Elizabeth, daughter of James and Elizabeth Thompson.
Sep. 18.	Hugh, son of Thomas Williams, *Goldsmith*.
Sep. 9.	Mary, daughter of Ambrose Lightfoote.
Sep. 11.	Rowland, son of Thomas and Mary Flowerdew, *Merchant*.
Sep. 17.	A female child, taken up ——— Woolnoth.
Sep. 28.	Phillip, son of Philip Frewd, Esq., *Master of the Post Office*, and of Sara, his wife.
Sep. 28.	Judith, daughter of John and Judith Wells, *Confectioner*.
Aug. 17.	Lewis, son of Joseph and Mary Munday, by a Minister of the Greek Church, the father a Grecian.
Oct. 8.	John, son of John and Alice Sallendine, *Clerk in the Post Office*.
Nov. 5.	Elizabeth, daughter of Thomas and Elizabeth Burford, *Factor*.
Nov. 8.	Suzanna, daughter of Daniell and Suzanna Lord, *Barber*.
Nov. 8.	Teringham, son of John Backwell, Esq., and Elizabeth his Wife.
Nov. 16.	Philip, son of Phillip and Dorothy Scarth, *Barber*.
Dec. 3.	John, son of Thomas and Elizabeth Cook, *Goldsmith*.
Dec. 7.	Alexand, son of Alexander and Elizabeth Pollington.
Dec. 23.	Sarah, daugter of Nicholas and Alice Love.
Jan. 8.	Thomas, son of William Brown, *Merchant*,
Jan. 31.	Mary, daughter of Henry and Ann Lamb, *Goldsmith*.
Feb. 5.	Grace, daughter of Gabriel and Ann Smith, *Druggest*.
Feb. 4.	Rebecca, daughter of Thomas and Rebecca Bowyer, at Mr. Belcher's house.
Feb. 8.	Peter, son of Peter and Elizabeth White, *Goldsmith*.
Feb. 15.	Elizabeth, daughter of Joseph Cozens, *Barbour*,
Feb. 29.	Samuel, son of Thomas and Rebecca Woodlaw, *Barber*.
Mar. 16.	Sarah, daughter of James and Elizabeth Nicholson.
Mar. 19.	Wild, son of John Clarke.

1680

April 13.	Samuel, son of John and Hannah Archer, *Poulterer*.
May 9.	Samuel, son of John Tassell, *Goldsmith*.
May 13.	A female child taken up at the Church doore.
May 14.	Marth and Mary, daughters of Benjamin Combs, *Goldsmith*.
May 16.	Mary, daughter of Edward and Ann Gladwin.
June 17.	Thomas ——— a male child taken up.
July 14.	Fortunata ——— a female childe taken up.
July 25.	Rebecca, daughter of John and Elizabeth Snell, *Goldsmith*.
Aug. 15.	Sarah, daughter of Mathew and Mary Coale, *Victualler*.
Aug. 30.	Bellingham, son of Phillip Frewd, Esq., *Master of the Post Office*, and of Sarah his Wife.
Sep. 3.	Christopher, son of John and Jane Thursby, *Goldsmith*.
Sep. 11.	A female child taken up.
Sep. 11.	Elizabeth ——— a female child taken up at the sign of the fox.
Sep. 11.	Jane, daughter of Nicholas and Suzan Carey, *Goldsmith*.
Sep. 24.	Alice, daughter of John and Alice Sallendine.

Oct. 6.	Elizabeth, daughter of Bernard and Margaret Eeles, *Goldsmith.*
Oct. 10.	Elizabeth, daughter of Richard and Hannah Burford, *Merchant.*
Oct. 10.	George, son of Jonathan and Jane Whaley, *Victualer.*
Oct. 10.	Henry, son of Augustine and Elizabeth Ballow, *Merchant.*
Oct. 19.	Edmunde, son of Nicholas Smith, *Goldsmith.*
Oct. 17.	George, son of Hosea and Elizabeth Waterer, *Carpentar.*
Nov. 14.	Elizabeth, daughter of George and Elizabeth Sheepsheid.
Dec. 6.	Jonathan, son of Jonathan and Dorothœ Miles.
Dec. 19.	Sara, daughter of Maurice and Sara Tepper, *Confectioner.*
Dec. 21.	Edmund, son of Edmund and Hannah Pike.
Dec. 30.	Thomas, son of Thomas and Mary Flowerdew, *Merchant.*
Jan. 2.	Sara, daughter of Robert and Mary King, *Silversmith.*
Jan. 9.	Elizabeth, daughter of Richard and Persus Franckling.
Jan. 8.	Mary, daughter of John and Dorothœ Temple, *Goldsmith.*
Jan. 16.	Jane, daughter of Henry and Ann Lamb, *Goldsmith.*
Jan. 31.	Staunton, son of James and Elizabeth Thompson.
Feb. 7.	George, son of Francis and Mary Terwhitt.
Mar. 9.	Suzannah, daughter of Nathaniel and Mary Deard.
Mar. 10.	Hannah, daughter of Richard and Hannah Burford.
Mar. 11.	Was the daughter of Widdow Thomas, baptized Sarah, in this Parish Church, at the age of 23, *Straunger,* by Mr. Andrew Crisp, *Rector.*
Mar. 13.	William, son of Alexander Ward, *Tailor.*

1681

April 16.	A male child taken up.
April 23.	George, son of Nicholas Love.
April 16.	William, son of Samuel and Sara Jermyn.
June 5.	John, son of John and Margaret Batch.
June 7.	James, son of John and Margaret Church.
June 26.	William, son of Phillip and Dorothœ Scarth, *Druggist.*
June 12.	Sarah, daughter of Daniel and Susan Lord, *Barber.*
June 23.	Joyce, daughter of John and Margaret Maurice, *French Merchant.*
Mar. 14.	Mary, daughter of Mr. John and Elizabeth Chambers.
July 17.	Honour, daughter of Elizabeth Rawlinson, Widow.
Aug. 2.	Mary, daughter of Peter and Rose Wade, *Goldsmith.*
Aug. 14.	Elizabeth, daughter of James and Mary Tombs.
Aug. 26.	Barnard, son of Barnard and Margaret Eeles, *Goldsmith.*
Aug. 30.	Katherine, daughter of John and Katherine Clark.
Sep. 18.	Elizabeth, daughter of John and Elizabeth Rigden.
Sep. 21.	William, son of John and Alice Sallendine.
Sep. 21.	Oliver, son of Jonathan Whaley, *Victualler.*
Sep. 9.	Thomas, son of Godfrey Woodward.
Sep. 20.	Elizabeth, daughter of John and Patience Belcher, *Packer.*
Oct. 9.	Harry, son of Richard and Sarah Guy, *Vintner.*
Oct. 14.	Hannah, daughter of Paule Ridley.
Oct. 19.	William, son of Thomas and Elizabeth Burford.
Oct. 30.	William and Joseph, two young men about 17 years of age.
Oct. 30.	Mary, daughter of Thomas Woodlaw.
Nov. 1.	Suzannah, daughter of Thomas and Elizabeth Sandis, *Merchant.*
Nov. 3.	Thomas, son of Nicholas Smith, *Goldsmith.*

Dec. 18.	Ann, daughter of Henry and Ann Lamb, *Goldsmith.*
Dec. 27.	Elizabeth, daughter of William Denne, *Silversmith.*
Jan. 19.	Hannah, daughter of Benjamin and Dorothy Crosley.
Jan. 22.	George, son of George Sheepsheid.
Feb. 7.	William, son of William and Mary Brown, *Merchant.*
Feb. 9.	Dorotha, daughter of Thomas and Sara Price, *Goldsmith.*
Feb. 21.	Elizabeth, daughter of John and Marian Golding.
Feb. 14.	Ebenezer, son of Abraham and Frances Whood.
Mar. 21.	Alice, daughter of Nicholas and Alice Love.

1682

April 3.	Jemima, daughter of John and Dorothœ Temple, *Goldsmith.*
April 11.	Jane, daughter of Morris and Sarah Tipper.
April 7.	William, son of Thomas and Hester Pashlen, *Clothmaker.*
April 17.	Elizabeth, daughter of Gray Lord, *Vintner.*
April 30.	Edward son of Edward Gladwin, *Goldsmith.*
May 7.	Vynor, son of Mr. John and Elizabeth Snell, *Goldsmith.*
May 21.	Martha, daughter of Mr. Augustine and Elizabeth Ballow, *Merchant.*
June 8.	Elizabeth, daughter of Richard and Hannah Burford.
June 11.	Henry, son of John and Margaret Smith.
June 21.	Ann, daughter of Robert and Ann Baskett, *Apothecary.*
June 30.	Gabriel, son of Mr. Gabriel and Ann Smith, *Drugist.*
July 8.	Thomas, son of John and Margaret Batho.
July 11.	Rebecca, daughter of William and Elizabeth Morden.
July 26.	Jane, daughter of Mr. Thomas and Mary Flowerdew, *Merchant.*
July 29.	Martha, daughter of James and Mary Tombs.
Aug. 23.	Frances, daughter of James and Mary Thonison.
Sep. 7.	William, son of William and Mary Stevenson, *Butcher.*
Sep. 6.	Elizabeth, daughter of Elizabeth and Mary Coopper.
Sep. 20.	Joseph, son of Mr. Charles and Ann Chapman, *Attorney-at-Law.*
Sep. 20.	Thomas, son of Mr. Phillip and Dorothy Scarth, *Druggist.*
Oct. 24.	Sara, daughter of George and Sara Capall.
Nov. 7.	Samuel, son of Mr. Alexander and Elizabeth Pollington, *Haberdasher of Hats.*
Nov. 21.	Mary and Grace, daughters of Richard and Sarah Guy, *Vintner.*
Nov. 23.	Suzan, daughter of Nicholas and Mary Smith, *Goldsmith.*
Dec. 21.	George, son of Thomas and Mary Macklin.
Dec. 22.	Browne, son of Mr. Thomas and Elizabeth Sandis, *Merchant.*
Dec. 31.	John, son of John Geard, *Victualler.*
Feb. 21.	Mary, daughter of John and Marian Golding, *Victualler.*
Feb. 13.	Peter, son of Peter and Anne Goodwin.
Feb. 18.	John, son of Henry and Ann Lamb, *Goldsmith.*
Feb. 25.	Peter, son of Christopher Pickard, *Jeweller.*
Mar. 13.	Robert, son of Robert and Elizabeth Amie, *Taylor.*
Mar. 4.	Richard, son of Richard and Persis Frankling, *Packer.*
Mar. 23.	William, son of William Whitehead.

1683

April 8.	Dorothœ daughter of George and Dorothœ Sheepsheid.

April 12.	Mary, daughter of Edward and Mary de Berg.
April 15.	Edward, son of Richard and Elizabeth Newell.
April 17.	John, son of John and Anne Sutton, by Mr. Calamie.
May 13.	Thomas, son of Thomas and Elizabeth Manwood.
May 24.	Jonathan, son of Jonathan and Elizabeth Whaley.
June 3.	Charles, son of Barnard and Margaret Eales, *Goldsmith.*
June 5.	Thomas, son of Thomas and Mary Browne.
June 10.	Samuel Darker, about the age of 24 years and William Ewers, about the age of 18.
June 12.	William, son of William Denne.
July 14.	Bellingham, son of Phillip Frowd, Esq., and Sara his wife.
July 13.	John, son of John and Alice Salendine.
July 9.	John, son of Thomas Pashlar, *Claspmaker.*
July 16.	Honour, daughter of George and Grace Beare, *Vintner.*
July 18.	John, son of John and Dorothœ Temple, *Goldsmith.*
Aug. 8.	Anna Maria, daughter of Mr. Peter and Elizabeth White, *Goldsmith.*
Aug. 21.	Jane, daughter of Mr. William and Mary Brown, *Merchant.*
Aug. 23.	Mary, daughter of James and Elizabeth Thompson.
Aug. 30.	Alice, daughter of Mr. Thomas Dorothy Price, *Goldsmith.*
Sep. 2.	Joseph, son of John Archer, *Poulterer.*
Sep. 10.	Frances, son of Thomas and Elizabeth Burford.
Oct. 3.	Elizabeth, daughter of Maurice and Sara Tipper, *Confectioner.*
Oct. 5.	Jonathan, daughter of James and Rebecca Sibley.
Oct. 14.	Charles and Elizabeth, son and daughter of Charles Tendring.
Oct. 9.	Sarah, daughter of Mr. John and Jane Thursby, *Goldsmith.*
Oct. 26.	Robert, son of Mr. John Maurice, *Goldsmith.*
Nov. 2.	Margaret, daughter of Mr. Phillips and Dorothy Scarth, *Druggest.*
Nov. 4.	Robert, son of Christopher and Ann Tomms.
Nov. 8.	Elizabeth, daughter of William and Elizabeth Gray, *Chirurgeon.*
Nov. 18.	William, son of Hosea Waterer, *Carpenter.*
Dec. 9.	Richard, son of Richard and Sara Guy, *Vintner.*
Dec. 5.	Henry and Richard, sons of Mr. Thomas and Mary Williams, *Goldsmith.*
Dec. 8.	Samuel, son of Samuel Gwinn, *Tailor.*
Jan. 3.	Melior, daughter of Richard and Melior Benskin.
Feb. 7.	Brown, daughter of William and Elizabeth Cooper.
Feb. 24.	Dorothy, daughter of John and Maijan Goldin.
Mar. 2.	Thomas, son of Phillip and Ellenor Rooker, *Silversmith.*
Mar. 20.	Thomas, son of William and Mary Greene.

1684

Mar. 30.	Thomas, son of Thomas and Rebecca Woodlaw, *Barber.*
April 21.	Thomas, son of Mr. Alexander and Elizabeth Pollington.
April 27.	George, son of John and Rebecca Geard, *Victualler.*
May 11.	Richard, son of Richard and Hannah Burford.
May 12.	Margaret, daughter of Mr. Peter Wade, *Goldsmith.*
May 18.	Elizabeth, daughter of Mr. John Snell, *Goldsmith.*
July 3.	Martha, daughter of John and Jane Cooke, *Rasormaker.*
July 13.	John, son of Mr. Edmund and Hannah Pike.
July 20.	Jonas, son of James and Mary Fletcher, *Baker.*

July —	[sic] William, son of Mr. Barnard Eales, *Goldsmith*.
Aug. 3.	Benjamin, son of Mr. Augustine and Elizabeth Ballow, *Merchant*.
Aug. 15.	Margaret, daughter of Mr. John and Margaret Smith, *Scrivener*.
Aug. 31.	Elizabeth, daughter of John and Elizabeth Catlett.
Aug. 31.	Joshua, son of John and Martha Taylor, *Washballmaker*.
Sep. 9.	Newton, son of Nicholas and Mary Smith.
Sep. 28.	Thomas, son of John and Ann Sutton, *Goldsmith*.
Oct. 7.	Charles and James, sons of Joseph and Ellenor Hindmarsh, *Bookseller*.
Oct. 16.	Ralph, son of Mr. Charles and Ann Chapman, *Attorney at Law*.
Oct. 26.	Katherine, daughter of Thomas and Elizabeth Burford.
Nov. 16.	John, son of Robert and Elizabeth Amie.
Dec. 11.	Mary, daughter of John and Suzan Batch, *Goldsmith*.
Dec. 18.	Charles, son of Thomas Brown, *Victualler*.
Jan. 4.	John, son of Mr. John and Elizabeth Chambers, *Scrivener*.
Jan. 18.	Henry, son of Richard and Sarah Guy, *Vintner*.
Jan. 18.	John, son of George and Elizabeth Merey.
Feb. 13.	Francis, daughter of John and Elizabeth Rennalls.
Feb. 22.	James, son of Mr. James and Elizabeth Thompson.
Feb. 22.	John, son of Mr. Phillip and Dorothœ Scarth, *Druggist*.
Feb. 22.	Suzanna, daughter of Thomas and Mary Manwood.
Mar. 1.	Ann, daughter of John and Marian Golding, *Victualler*.
Mar. 11.	Ann, daughter of Timothy and Joyce Williams.

1685

Mar. 25.	William, son of William and Elleanor Edmunds.
Mar. 28.	Melior, daughter of Melior, widow of late Richard Benskin.
May 8.	John, son of Christopher Smeeton, *Writing Master*.
June 20.	Katherin, daughter of William and Isabel Boswell.
June 26.	Judith, daughter of Mr. Thomas and Elizabeth Sandis, *Merchant*.
July 1.	Edward, son of Henry and Mary Robynson, *Goldsmith*.
July 19.	Peter, son of Mr. Peter and Rose Wade, *Goldsmith*.
July 14.	Thomas, son of Mr. Thomas and Dorothy Rice, *Goldsmith*.
July 20.	Benjamin, son of John Archer, *Poulterer*.
July 29.	Ann, daughter of Mr. John and Jane Thursby, *Goldsmith*.
Aug. 9.	Thomas, son of Mr. John and Dorothy Knap, *Merchant*.
Aug. 6.	Isaac, son of Mr. Thomas and Sarah Williams, *Goldsmith*.
Aug. 7.	Thomas, son of Mr. William and Mary Brown, *Merchant*.
Aug. 24.	Jane, daughter of Mr. John Colman, *Merchant*.
Aug. 14.	John, son of Mr. John Smith, *Scrivener*.
Sep. 6.	Ann, daughter of Capt. John Hillman.
Sep. 2.	Hellana, daughter of John and Hellena Hindmarsh, *Bookseller*.
Sep. 28.	John, son of Mr. John and Mary Flowerdew, *Merchant*.
Oct. 11.	Judith, daughter of Robert and Elizabeth Amey, *Taylor*.
Nov. 7.	Nicholas, son of Richard and Suzan Marriott.
Nov. 15.	John, son of John and Martha Taylor, *Washball Maker*.
Nov. 20.	Mary, daughter of John Campin.
Nov. 29.	Edward, son of Edward and Jane Chadcey, *Baker*.
Dec. 3.	William, son of Abraham and Sara Catlett.
Dec. 20.	William, son of Phillip and Elleanor Rooker, *Silversmith*.

Dec. 26.	Martha, daughter of James and Rebecca Sibley, *Glassman*.
Jan. 10.	Henry, son of Mr. Henry and Ann Lamb, *Goldsmith*.
Feb. 28.	Judith, daughter of Thomas and Ann Baskett, *Apothecary*.
Mar. 11.	Richard, son of Jeremie and Elizabeth Stoakes, *Coffeeman*.
Mar. 11.	John, son of Richard and Sarah Guy, *Vintner*.
Mar. 14.	Justinian, son of George Sheepsheid.
Mar. 21.	Lettis, daughter of Johathan and Joan Whaley.
Mar. 17.	Mary, daughter of John and Mary Knight.

1686

Mar. 28.	Charles, son of John and Rebecca Goare, *Victualler*.
April 4.	Arabella, daughter of Mr. Phillip and Dorothy Scarth, *Druggist*.
April 4.	John, son of John and Marian Goldinge, *Victualler*.
April 19.	William, son of Mr. Barnard Eales, *Goldsmith*.
May 2.	Judith, daughter of Robert and Sara Peck, *Hosier*.
May 18.	John, son of John and Suzan Batch, *Silversmith*.
June 9.	Saunders, son of John and Alice Underwood.
July 11.	Alice, daughter of Thomas and Rachell Gibbs.
July 11.	John, son of Robert and Elizabeth Wilson, *Vintner*.
July 17.	Blaney, son of Mr. Blaney and Jane Sandford, *Gentleman*.
July 18.	John, son of Maurice and Sarah Tipper, *Confectioner*.
July 25.	Thomas, son of James and Elizabeth Thompson, *Exchangeman*.
Aug. 16.	Anne, daughter of John and Jane Cooke, *Rasor Maker*.
Sep. 5.	Christopher, son of Christopher Tomms, *Barber*.
Sep. 26.	Jonathan, son of Thomas Manwood, *Bookbinder*.
Sep. 30.	Joseph, son of Mr. Joseph and Hellen Hindmarch, *Bookseller*.
Oct. 8.	Young, son of Daniel and Suzan Lord, *Barber*.
Oct. 12.	Charles, son of Mr. John Coleman, *Merchant*.
Oct. 31.	Willmore, son of Mr. Peter and Rose Wade, *Goldsmith*.
Nov. 8.	Ann, daughter of John and Mary Smith, *Packer*.
Nov. 8.	Hannah, daughter of Hannah Burford, *Widdow*.
Nov. 23. *Nov.* 30.	Thomas, William, } twin sons of Mr. Henry Lamb, *Goldsmith*.
Dec. 19.	Elizabeth, daughter of Isaack and Elizabeth Esson.
Jan. 11.	Henry, son of Henry and Mary Robinson.
Jan. 22.	Jane, daughter of Edward and Sarah Chadcey, *Baker*.
Feb. 26.	John, son of Mr. Augustine and Elizabeth Ballow.
Feb. 25.	Anne, daughter of Mr. Edward and Anne Ambrose, *Attorney at Law*.
Feb. 27.	Thomas, son of Phillip and Mary Cor de Roy, *Watch Maker*.
Mar. 20.	Margarett, daughter of Captain John and Ann Hillman, *Haberdasher*.
Mar. 21.	Jane, daughter of Mathew and Anne Shepherd, *Skynner*.

1687

April 18.	Elizabeth, daughter of John and Mary Jarvis.
May 10.	Elizabeth, daughter of Mr. John and Dorothœ Knap, *Merchant*.
May 10.	Sarah, daughter of Abraham and Sarah Catlett, *Ingraver*.
May 15.	Frampton, son of Mr. Richard and Mary Guy, *Vintner*.

May 22.	Martha, daughter of John Taylor.
May 26.	Katherine, daughter of James and Rebecca Sibley, *Glassman*.
June 8.	Anne, daughter of Mr. John and Jane Thursby, *Glassman*.
June 15.	Hazelelponie, [*sic*] daughter of David and Elleanor Howleing, *Coffeeman*.
June 26.	Sarah, daughter of Mr. Thomas and Elizabeth Sandis, *Merchant*.
July 8.	Sarah, daughter of John and Ann Sutton, *Goldsmith*.
July 24.	Elizabeth, daughter of Mr. Phillip and Anne Dacres, *Druggest*.
July 25.	Jane, daughter of Mr. John and Elizabeth Chambers, *Scrivener*.
July 30.	Suzanna, daughter of Mr. Barnard and Margaret Eales, *Goldsmith*.
Aug. 7.	Jeremie, son of Jeremie and Elizabeth Stoake, *Coffeeman*.
Aug. 7.	Richard, son of Mr. Phillip and Dorothy Scarth, *Druggest*.
Aug. 14.	Jonathan, son of Robert and Mary Mallinox, *Cutler*.
Sep. 17.	Samuel, son of Mr. James and Alice St. John, *Goldsmith*.
Sep. 11.	Thomas, son of Thomas and Hannah Tucker.
Sep. 20.	Rachell, daughter of Mr. James and Elizabeth Thompson, *Exchangeman*.
Sep. 29.	John, son of Mr. William Browne, *Merchant.*
Oct. 9.	Mary, daughter of Mr. Robert and Elizabeth Wilson, *Vintner*.
Oct. 23.	Sarah, daughter of Thomas Jarvis, *Coffeeman*.
Nov. 7.	Whitter, son of George and Dorotha Sheepside.
Dec. 14.	Henry, son of Mr. Thomas and Sarah Williams, *Goldsmith*.
Dec. 14.	Adam, son of Georg and Suzan Childrens.
Dec. 27.	Mary, daughter of Joseph and Martha Cozens, *Barber*.
Jan. 3.	Mary Tillard, of Reading, Co. Berks., aged about 26, lodges at Mr. Moores, *Goldbeater*.
Jan. 22.	Mary, daughter of Phillip and Eleanor Rooker, *Silversmith*.
Feb. 5.	Harry, son of Mr. Valentine and Elizabeth Maunder, *Vintner*.
Feb. 3.	Henry, son of Mathew and Anne Shephard, *Skinner*.
Mar. 13.	Andrew, Christopher, son of Mr. Peter and Dorothe Lauze, *French Merchant*.
Feb. 7.	George, son of Mr. John and Elizabeth Holmes, *Vintner*.
Feb. 12.	Richard, son of William and Mary James, *Washball Maker*.
Feb. 23.	Jane, son of James and Elizabeth Tedman, *Watchmaker*.
Mar. 4.	John, son of Mr. Edward and Ann Ambross, *Attorney-at-Law*.
Mar. 18.	Benjamin, son of Mr. John and Jane Coleman, *Merchant*.
Mar. 13.	Robert, son of Robert Wilkinson, *Taylor*.

1688

April 19.	Mary, daughter of Maurice and Sarah Tipper, *Confectioner*.
April 19.	Ann, daughter of Mr. John and Dorothy Knap, *Merchant*.
April 26.	Theophus, son of Mr. Thomas and Mary Flowerdew, *Merchant*.
April 29.	Martha, daughter of Mr. Robert and Sarah Peck, *Hosier*.
May 10.	Elizabeth, daughter of Abraham and Sarah Catlett, *Engraver*.

May 15.	(born) Elizabeth, daughter of John Moore, *Cook.*
June 3.	Mary, daughter of Edward and Rebecca Edwards, *Vintner.*
June 10.	Edward, son of Mr. Edward and Judith Dreyner, *Vintner.*
June 10.	Catherine, daughter of Henry and Anne Robinson, *Goldsmith.*
June 17.	Ann, daughter of Mr. Henry and Ann Lamb, *Goldsmith.*
July 8.	Lidia, daughter of Mr. Augustine and Elizabeth Ballow, *Merchant.*
July 8.	Sarah, daughter of Mr. Richard and Sarah Guy, *Vintner.*
Aug. 12.	Elizabeth, daughter of Mr. Robert and Jane Abbis, *Goldsmith.*
Aug. 19.	Thomas, son of Mr. Stephen and Elizabeth Venables, *Goldsmith.*
Aug. 26.	William, son of John and Dorotha Hebb, *Haberdasher of Smallwares.*
Sep. 6.	John son of Thomas and Elizabeth Sandis, *Merchant.*
Sep. 9.	Robert, son of Mr. Joseph and Hellena Hindmarsh.
Sep. 21.	William, son of Thomas and Elizabeth Cooper.
Nov. 11.	Rebecca, daughter of Mr. William Brown, *Merchant.*
Nov. 29.	John, son of Edward and Jane Chadsey, *Baker.*
Dec. 14.	Elizabeth, daughter of Mr. Edward and Ann Ambrose, *Attorney-at-Law.*
Jan. 6.	Elizabeth, daughter of Thomas and Elizabeth Martin, *Wine Cooper.*
Jan. 20.	Richard, son of William and Jane Wilkins, *Coffeeman.*
Feb. 17.	Thomas, son of John and Suzan Batch, *Silversmith.*
Feb. 19.	Ann, daughter of Nicholas and Suzan Marriott, *Packer.*
Mar. 9.	John, son of John and Hannah Holmes, *Vintner.*

1689

April 23.	Samuel, son of John and Ellinor Hawley, *Haberdasher of Hatts.*
May 11.	Hanna, daughter of Mr. Robert and Elizabeth Batho, *Confectioner.*
June 9.	Henry, son of Henry and Mary Robinson, *Goldsmith.*
June 9.	Charles, son of Thomas and Sarah Jarvis, *Coffeeman.*
June 3.	Thomas, son of William and Mary James, *Washball Maker.*
June 19.	Kenina, daughter of Thomas and Susannah Morgan, *Linendraper.*
June 28.	John, son of Phillip and Anne Parvis, *Drugist.*
June 30.	Lidia, daughter of John and Jane Coleman, *Merchant.*
June 23.	William, son of William and Jane Hooker.
Aug. 25.	Nathaniell, son of James and Sicilla Lawrence.
Sep. 1.	Thomas, son of Jeremiah and Elizabeth Stoakes.
Sep. 2.	Anne, daughter of William and Ann Browne.
Sep. 21.	Mary, daughter of Abraham and Sarah Catlett.
Oct. 11.	Sarah, daughter of William and Patience Jefferson.
Nov. 10.	Thomas, son of Christopher and Ann Tomms, *Barber.*
Nov. 8.	Stephen, son of Stephen and Elizabeth Venable, *Goldsmith.*
Nov. 15.	Robert, son of Thomas and Mary Booth, *Lodger.*
Nov. 15.	Ann, daughter of Joseph and Martha Cousens, *Barber.*
Nov. 21.	Ann, daughter of John and Ann Sutton, *Goldsmith.*
Dec. 1.	Charles, son of Richard and Sarah Guss.
Nov. 29.	Richard, son of John and Dorothy Knap, *Merchant.*

Jan. 19.	Mary, daughter of John and Mary Moore, *Paistreycooke.*
Jan. 26.	Ann, daughter of Robert and Elizabeth Willson, *Vintner.*
Feb. 2.	James, son of Robert and Jane Abbiss.
Feb. 2.	Elizabeth, daughter of James and Mary Smith.
Feb. 9.	John, son of Thomas and Judeth Martin.
Feb. 15.	Mary, daughter of William and Mary Browne.
Feb. 16.	Edward, son of Edward Edwards, *Victualler.*
Mar. 5.	John, son of Lord Edward Morley and Lady Katherine his wife.
Mar. 9.	Elizabeth, daughter of Edward and Elizabeth Paine.
Mar. 16.	Elizabeth, daughter of Edward and Ann Gladwin.
Jan. 21.	Benjamin, son of Bernard and Margaret Eeles, *Goldsmith.*
Mar. 23.	Samuell, son of George and Margaret Cooke, *Razor Grinder.*

1690

Mar. 30.	Gresilia, daughter of John and Martha Taylor, *Bookbinder.*
April 2.	Thomas, son of Thomas and Elizabeth Sands, *Merchant.*
April 6.	Benjamin, son of John and Hannah Holmes, *Vintner.*
April 6.	Elizabeth, daughter of Henry and Ann Lamb, *Goldsmith.*
April 30.	Jediael, son of Jediall and Sarah Turner.
June 15.	John, son of John and Elizabeth Roe, *Victualler.*
June 15.	Loyd, son of John and Mary Simpson, *Shoemaker.*
June 28.	Mihill, son of Robert and Elizabeth Batho, *Confectioner.*
Aug. 3.	Bazell, son of Jeremiah and Elizabeth Stoks, *Coffeeman.*
Aug. 24.	Barbara, daughter of Eustace and Judith Burgin, *Shoemaker.*
Sep. 8.	Heleana, daughter of Joseph and Heleana Hindmarsh.
Sep. 15.	Mary, daughter of John and Elner Hawley, *Haberdasher of Hatts.*
Oct. 9.	Adam, son of George and Susanna Children, *Ingraver.*
Oct. 23.	John, son of John and Dorothy Knap, *Merchant.*
Nov. 9.	Elizabeth, daughter of Robert and Sarah Peck, *Merchant.*
Nov. 19.	Susannah, daughter of Edward and Ann Ambrose.
Nov. 20.	Hannah, daughter of Dixey and Joane Kent, *Linnendraper.*
Dec. 4.	Seamor, son of Alexander and Mary Pile, *Woolendraper.*
Dec. 15.	Abigail Woolnoth, a foundling.
Dec. 25.	Abraham, son of Abraham and Sarah Catlett.
Jan. 23.	John North, a foundling.
Mar. 4.	Sarah, daughter of John and Susannah Beach.

1691

April 5.	John, son of Henry and Mary Robinson, *Goldsmith.*
May 7.	Elinor, daughter of Phillip and Elinor Booker, *Goldsmith.*
May 17.	Stephen, son of Stephen and Elizabeth Venables, *Goldsmith.*
May 25.	Elizabeth, daughter of John and Hannah Holms, *Vintner.*
May 26.	Jane, daughter of Richard and Mary Holdbrook.
May 29.	Phillip, son of Phillip and Anna Dakers, *Druggist.*
July 2.	Martha, daughter of Joseph and Martha Cozens, *Barber.*
July 12.	Susannah, daughter of John and Elizabeth Row, *Victualler.*
Aug. 26.	John, son of John and Elizabeth Dodwell.
Sep. 7.	Jeames, son of James and Sicilla Laurence, *Lodger.*
Sep. 12.	Mary, daughter of Edward and Elizabeth Paine, *Lodger.*
Oct. 21.	Susannah, daughter of Richard and Susannah Gilbert, *Norwitch Factor.*

Nov. 1.	Mary, daughter of John and Mary Moore, *Cooke.*
Nov. 4.	Mary, daughter of George and Elizabeth Cooke, *Rasor-maker.*
Nov. 8.	Richard, son of John and Mary Jarvis, *Lodger.*
Nov. 18.	Elizabeth, daughter of John and Elizabeth Smith, *Scrivener.*
Nov. 4.	Hannah, daughter of Samuel and Sarah White, *Norwitch Factor.*
Oct. 21.	Harman, son of William and Mary James, *Washball Maker.*
Nov. 10.	Mary, daughter of John and Mary Huggins, *Attorney.*
Nov. 6.	Mary, daughter of Thomas and Elizabeth Wickersham, *Lodger.*
Nov. 17.	Elizabeth, daughter of Thomas and Elizabeth Sands, *Merchant.*
Dec. 1.	William, son of John and Dorothy Knap, *Merchant.*
Dec. 27.	Francees, daughter of Joseph and Heleana Hindmarsh, *Bookseller.*
Jan. 15.	Mary, daughter of Thomas and Judith Martin, *Wine Cooper.*
Jan. 18.	James, son of Morris and Sarah Tipper.
Jan. 6.	Jane Woolnoth, a foundling.
Jan. 21.	Jean, daughter of Dixey and Jean Kent, *Draper.*
Feb. 7.	William, son of Richard and Sarah Guy, *Vintner.*
Feb. 14.	Rebecka, daughter of Alexander and Mary Pile, *Woollen-draper.*
Feb. 21.	Robert, son of Robert and Jane Abais, *Goldsmith.*
Mar. 16.	Margaret, daughter of William and Ann Aylworth, *Lodger.*

1692

April 6.	Sarah, daughter of Charles and Mary Lidgett, *Lodger.*
May 1.	George, son of Jeremie and Elizabeth Stoaks, *Coffeeman.*
May 20.	Jeptha Digby, a foundling.
April 29.	Elizabeth, daughter of John and Sarah Ladyman, *Silver-smith.*
July 7.	John, son of John and Ellenor Hawley, *Haberdasher of Hatts.*
July 17.	Jean, daughter of Abraham and Sarah Catlett, *Engraver.*
July 31.	Richard, son of Richard and Mary Holdbrooke.
Aug. 19.	Mary, daughter of Robert and Sarah Peck, *Hozier.*
Aug. 23.	Sarah, daughter of John and Elizabeth Holmes, *Vintner.*
Sep. 8.	Thomas, son of John and Susannah Batch, *Silversmith.*
Oct. 4.	William, son of Thomas and Rebecca Ferrall, *Lodger.*
Oct. 23.	Richard, son of Richard and Susannah Gilbert, *Norwitch Factor.*
Oct. 30.	Joseph, son of Joseph and Catherine Archer, *Victualler.*
Nov. 4.	Elizaman, daughter of John and Elizabeth Giles, *Hottpresser.*
Nov. 4.	Mary Buchworth, a foundling.
Nov. 3.	Thomas, son of John and Mary Huggins, *Attorney-at-Law.*
Nov. 30.	John, son of Henry and Mary Robinson, *Goldsmith.*
Dec. 14.	Ann, daughter of Edward and Rebekah Edwards, *Victualler.*
Dec. 23.	Robert, son of Robert and Elizabeth Bahdo, *Confectioner.*
Dec. 11.	Elizabeth Woolnoth, a foundling.
Dec. 27.	John, son of John and Mary Moor, *Cook.*
Jan. 2.	Richard, son of Thomas and Elizabeth Franklin, *Esquire.*

Jan. 2.	Jeans, son of John and Mary Ellit, *Sword Cutler.*
Jan. 5.	Penelope, daughter of John and Jean Thursbee, *Goldsmith.*
Jan. 29.	Handy, daughter of Edward and Abigall Loyd, *Coffeeman.*
Feb. 14.	Ann, daughter of John and Ann Sutton, *Goldsmith.*
Feb. 12.	Luke, son of John and Margrett Taylor, *Washball Maker.*
Feb. 5.	Thomas, son of Thomas and Elizabeth Blythe, *Norwitch Factor.*
Feb. 14.	Charles, son of William and Mary Browne, *Merchant.*
Feb. —	John Woolnoth, a foundling.
Mar. 7.	Thomas, son of Joseph and Heleana Hindmarsh, *Bookseller.*
Mar 6.	Mary, daughter of John and Dorothy Knap, *Merchant.*
Mar. 19.	John, son of Richard and Sarah Guy, *Vintner.*
Mar. 26.	Joseph, son of Nathaniel and Susanna Bayley, *Lodger.*

1693

Mar. 28.	Elizabeth Woolnoth, a foundling.
May 7.	Phillip, son of Phillip and Ellnor Booker, *Silversmith.*
May 5.	Anne, daughter of Dixey and Jean Kent, *Silversmith.*
June 14.	Mary, daughter of George and Rebecca Sims, *Haberdasher.*
June 25.	Henry, son of Henry and Ann Lamb, *Goldsmith.*
June 28.	Dove Woolnoth, a foundling.
July 15.	George Hands, a foundling.
July 17.	Richard, son of Stephen and Elizabeth Venables, *Goldsmith.*
Aug. 25.	Alexander, son of Alexander and Mary Pile, *Woolendraper.*
Sep. 1.	John, son of Jeams and Sicilla Lawrence, *Lodger.*
Sep. 7.	Abraham, son of Abraham and Ann Willcox, *Barber.*
Sep. 9.	Hester, daughter of Joseph and Martha Cozens, *Barber.*
Sep. 10.	Sarah, daughter of Robert and Jean Abbias, *Goldsmith.*
Sep. 24.	Elizabeth, daughter of John and Elizabeth Roe, *Victualler.*
Sep. 25.	John Woolnoth, a foundling.
Oct. 5.	John, son of John and Sarah Ruston, *Goldsmith.*
Oct. 15.	Jeames, son of Phillip and Ann Dacres, *Druggist.*
Oct. 25.	Abraham, son of Abraham and Sarah Cattlett, *Ingraver.*
Nov. 5.	John, son of John and Sarah Ladyman, *Silversmith.*
Dec. 3.	Mary, daughter of Jeams and Elizabeth Taylor, *Cheesemonger.*
Dec. 13.	Thomas, son of John and Mary Elliott, *Sword Cutler.*
Dec. 17.	Elizabeth, daughter of Robert and Mary Nicholson, *Lodger.*
Dec. 17.	Joseph, son of Joseph and Katherine Archer, *Victualler.*
Dec. 19.	John, son of Riehard and Suzannah Gilbert, *Norwitch Factor.*
Jan. 21.	Ann, daughter of Christopher and Ann Toms, *Barber.*
Jan. 19.	David, son of Thomas and Rebeckah Ferrall, *Fruiterer.*
Jan. 29.	Sherborne Woolnoth, a foundling.
Feb. 16.	Ann, daughter of George and Elizabeth Cooke, *Razormaker.*

[*The end of the Baptisms in the 2nd Volume of the Woolnoth Registers, with which are apparently entered the Woolchurch Haw Baptisms after the destruction of that Church by fire.*—Editor.]

[Vol. iij.]

THE Names of such as have been christened in the Parishe of St. Mary Woolnoth, in London, since the 28th day of February, Anno Domini, 1693.

1693

Mar. 14.   John, son of John and Elizabeth Giles, *Hotpresser*, born March 2.

Mar. 15.   Thomas, son of John and Hannah Holms, *Vintner*, born March 7.

1694

April 15.   Joshua, son of Edward and Judith Drayner, *Vintener*, born March 30.

April 15.   Sarah, daughter of John and Mary Moor, *Cooke*, borne April 8.

May 22.   Joan, daughter of Joseph and Hœlena Hindmarsh, *Bookseller*, born May 11.

June 23.   John, son of Stephen and Eliza Venables, *Goldsmith*, born June 23.

July 6.   Dorothy, daughter of Richard and Dorothy Laurance, *Apothecary*, born June 23.

July 15.   John, son of John and Mary Simpson, *Shoemaker*, born July 4.

Aug. 16.   Thomas, son of Thomas and Martha Nichols, *Lodger*.

Sep. 2.   John, son of Phillip and Ellin Booker, *Silversmith*, born Sep. 2.

Sep. 13.   Susanna, daughter of Henry and Mary Robinson, *Goldsmith*, born Sep. 13.

Oct. 14.   Sarah, daughter of William and Sarah Moor, *Cook*, born Oct. 7.

Oct. 25.   Martha, daughter of John and Dorothy Knapp, *Merchant*, born Oct. 10.

Nov. 2.   Thomas, son of Thomas and Mary Cleavely, *Exchangeman*, born Nov. 23.

Nov. 11.   Fredericke Manard, son of Thomas and Elizabeth Frankland, *Esquire*, born Oct. 21.

Nov. 27.   George, son of John and Elizabeth White, *Lodger*, born Nov. 27.

Dec. 13.   Thomas, son of Jeames and Ann Taylor, *Cheesemonger*, born Nov. 29.

Dec. 26.   Edward, son of Edward and Elizabeth Jones, *Goldsmith*.

Jan. 3.   By Mr. Shears, a Nonconformist Minister, Arraminta, daughter of Thomas and Elizabeth Blythe, *Norwich Factor*, born Dec. 28.

Jan. 5.   Cardinall Woolnoth, a male child, taken up in Cardinalls Cap Alley.

Jan. 11.   Mary Woolnoth, a female child, taken up in Dove Court, at Mr. Bates's dore.

Jan. 26.   Sedgwick, son of Richard and Susanna Gilbert, *Norwich Factor*, born Jan. 26.

Jan. 24.   John Woolnoth, a male foundling child, taken up at Mr. Colman's dore.

Feb. 9.	Ann, daughter of John and Elizabeth Roe, *Victualler*, born Feb. 9.
Feb. 19.	Ann, daughter of Robert and Ann Abias, *Goldsmith*, born Feb. 1.

1695

Mar. 28.	Elizabeth, daughter of Nicholas and Elizabeth Goodwin, born March 11.
Mar. 26.	Elizabeth, daughter of Robert and Elizabeth Westcott, *Vintner*, born March 26.
Mar. 27.	Thomas, daughter of Thomas and Elizabeth Wickershaw, *Lodger*, born March 26.
Mar. 19.	Dove Woolnoth, a female child taken up at Mr. Smith's dore in Dove Court.
Mar. 21.	Sarah Woolnoth, a female child taken up at Mr. Pollington's dore.
April 12.	Elizabeth, daughter of John and Shalletta Whitehorne, born April 11, son-in-law to the widdow Brindley.
April 19.	William, son of Thomas and Jeane Parr, born April 19, son-in-law to the widdow Cook.
April 21.	Was taken up under Mr. Munger's window a female child and a note left with it that it was named John Richardson [*sic*]
Aug. 15.	Richard, son of Richard and Elizabeth Haley of Chatham, Kent, *Gardner*, born Aug. 4 at Mr. Maddisons in Sherbourne Lane.
Oct. 2.	Charlett, daughter of Mr. Richard and Elizabeth Snagg, *Goldsmith*, born Sep. 12.
Oct. 9.	William, son of Richard and Dorothy Lawrence, *Apothecary*, born Sep. 26.
Oct. 17.	Sarah, daughter of John and Dorothy Knapp, *Merchant*, born Oct. 3.
Nov. 5.	George, son of George and Margrett Cooke, *Razor Maker*, born Nov. 4.
Nov. 19.	Mary, daughter of John and Sarah, Ladyman, *Silversmith*, born Nov. 19. S. M. W. N. * [In margin.]
Dec. 2.	George, son of George and Ann Evins, born Nov. 24. S. M. W. C. [In margin.]
Dec. 5.	Jeams, son James and Ann Taylor, *Cheesemonger*, born *Dec.* 5. S. M. W. C. [In margin.]
Jan. 1.	Katherine, daughter of Joseph and Katherine Archer, *Victualler*, born Dec. 26. S. M. W. N. [In margin.]
Jan. 9.	John, son of Richard and Mary Gilbert, St. Mary Woolchurch-haw, *Norwich Facter*, born Jan. 9.
Jan. 12.	Thomas Woolnoth, a male child taken up in Cardinall Capp Alley.
Jan. 26.	William, son of Mr. John and Elizabeth Giles, *Packer*, lodger at Mr. Margarett Evans, Sharborne Lane, born Jan. 14.
Jan. 24.	Phillip, son of Mr. Phillip and Ann Dawes, *Druggist*, born Jan. 21.
Jan. 26.	James Price, son of Mr. John and Mary Sebelle, *Merchant*, born Jan. 6.
Jan. 28.	Nicholas, son of Mary Nicholas and Elizabeth Goodwin, *Scrivener*, born Jan. 25.

* The initials which occasionally occur after A.D. 1666 indicate the two Parishes, S. M. W. N. St. Mary Woolnoth, S. M. W. C. St. Mary Woolchurch.

[No date of baptism.] Mary, daughter of John and Hannah Holmes, *Vintner*, of St. Mary Woolchurch-haw.

Feb. 9.   Nanny, daughter of Mr. Thomas and Damaris Manwood, *Bookebinder*, born Jan. 21.

Feb. 3.   Charity Woolnoth, a female child, taken up in Exchange Alley.

Feb. 4.   John Woolnoth, a male child, taken up at Mr. Shute's dore in Sherborne Lane.

Feb. 16.   Martha, daughter of Mr. Joseph and Martha Cozens, *Barber*, born Feb. 13.

Feb. 19.   Daniel, son of Mr. Daniel Puckle, *Gent.* and Ellinor, his wife, lodgers at Madam Platt's, in Bearbinder Lane, in the parish of St. Mary Woolchurch Haw, born Feb. 25.

Feb. 20.   Symon, son of Mr. Peter and Euphania Monger, *Gold-smith*, born Feb. 16.

Feb. 25.   John, son of John and Prudence Moore, *Goldbeater*, lodger of the parish of St. Mary Woolchurch-haw, born Feb. 25.

Mar. 1.   Robert, son of Mr. Robert and Elizabeth Westcott, of St. M. W. C. H., *Vintner*, born Feb. 29.

Mar. 3.   Prudence, a female child, taken up in Dove Court.

Mar. 5.   Rebecca, daughter of Thomas and Rebecca Farrer, of St. M. W. C. H., *Fruiterer*, born Feb. 17.

Mar. 8.   Judith, daughter of Mr. Edward and Judith Drayner, *Vintner*.

Mar. 11.   Elizabeth, a female child, taken up at Mrs. Evan's door.

1696

April 9.   John, son of Mr. John and Mary Allett, in Exchange Alley, *Sword Cutler*, born April 3.

April 30.   James, son of Mr. Richard and Mary Conyere, *Goldsmith.*

April 25.   Hester, a female child, taken up at Madam Lucye's door, in Sherborne Lane.

May 2.   John, son of John and Margaret Evans, *Porter*, lodge at Mrs. Evans, Hotpresser, in Sherborne Lane, born May 1.

May 6.   Dorothy, daughter of Mr. Mathew and Mary Blundall, *Custome House Officer*, lodgers at Mr. Sampson's, Barber, in Sherborne Lane, born April 15.

June 14.   Martha, daughter of Mr. Thomas and Martha Chippin, *Cooke*, born June 2.

July 3.   Penelope, a female child, taken up under the Cock ale-house, in Sherborne Lane.

June 30.   Priscilla, a female child, taken up in Six-bell Alley, in Dove Court.

July 26.   Thomas, son of Mr. Thomas and Jane Parr, of St. M. W. *Chirurgoins Instrument Maker*, born July 19.

Mrs. Hannah Gilling, lodger at Mr. Chadesy's, *Baker*, was delivered of a female still-born child as per certificate from midwife.

Sep. 3.   Adam, a male child taken up at Mr. Shute's door in Sherborne Lane.

Sep. 3.   Samuel and Sarah, twin children of Martina [*sic*] Beamond, of St. M. W. C., *Tallowchandler*, born Sep. 2.

Oct. 1.   Josias, son of Mr. Richard and Anne Cock, of St. M. W. C., *Linnendraper*, born Sep. 17.

Oct. 18.	Anne, daughter of Mr. John and Susanna Bach, *Goldsmith*, born Oct. 10.
Nov. 8.	Anna Maria, daughter of Mr. Richard and Anne Chapman, *Goldsmith*, born Oct. 19.
Oct. 22.	Jonathan, a male child taken up in Cardinall Capp alley.
Oct. 15.	Nathaniel, a male child taken up in Cardinall Capp alley.
Nov. 7.	Thomas, son of Richard and Mary Weldman, *Scrivener*, a lodger at Mr. Fryer's in Sherborne Lane, born Nov. 8.
Dec. 2.	Francis, son of Mr. Edward and Elizabeth Jones, of St. M. W. C. H., *Goldsmith*, born Dec. 2.
Dec. 20.	Samuel, son of Mr. Samuel and Mary Lynn, lodgers at Mr. Elliot's, in Exchange Alley, born Dec. 4.
Dec. 22.	Anne, daughter of Mr. Robert and ———— [*sic*] Wayfields, *Scrivener*, born Dec. 7.
Dec. 22.	Mary, daughter of Mr. John and Mary Sebelle, *Merchant*, born Dec. 22.
Dec. 29.	Thomas, a male child taken up in Exchange Alley.
Jan. 14.	Rebecca, daughter of Mr. John and Dorothy Knapp, of S. M. W. C. H., *Merchant*, born Dec. 24.
Jan. 19.	Daniel, son of Mr. Richard and Elizabeth Eames, *Pewterer*, lodgers at Mr. Beamond's, Tallowchandler in St. M. W. H.. born Jan. 9.
Jan. 15.	Ellinor, daughter of Mr. Phillip and Ellinor Roaker, *Goldsmith*, born Jan. 11.
Jan. 12.	Mary, daughter of John and Ann Taylor, of St. M. W. C. H., *Cheesemonger*, born Jan. 12.
Jan. 14.	Mary, daughter of Mr. Robert and Elizabeth Westcott, of St. M. W. C. H., *Vintner*, born Jan. 14.
Jan. 15.	Ellinor, daughter of Mr. Phillip and Ellinor Roaker, *Goldsmith*, born Jan. 11 [*sic*]
Jan. 18.	Anne, daughter of Mr. Charles and Elizabeth Jenning, of St. M. W. C. H., *Victualler*, born Jan. 22.
Jan. 31.	Anne, daughter of Mr. Joseph and Katherine Archer, *Victualler*, born Jan. 25.
Feb. 25.	William, son of Thomas and Damaris Manwood, born Feb. 25.
Mar. 21.	Richard, son of Mr. John and Elizabeth Giles, *Packer*, born Mar. 8.
Mar. 27.	Frances, daughter of Thomas and Elizabeth Frankland, *Esquire*, one of the *Postmasters General*, born March 18.

1697

April 11.	Mary, daughter of Mr. Anthony and Ann Hathway, of St. M. W. H., *Victualer*, born April 10.
May 25.	Anne, daughter of Abraham and Anne Wilcox, *Barber*.
June 10.	Thomas, son of John and Sarah Ladyman, *Goldsmith*, born June 10.
June 14.	John, son of George and Margarett Cooke, *Razor Makere*.
July 1.	Mary, daughter of Thomas Chippins, *Cooke*.
July 21.	Mary, daughter of John and Margarett Evans, *Lodger and Porter to the Post Office*, borne July 21.
July 22.	Thomas, son of Thomas and Elizabeth Kimberley, *Box-maker*, born July 22.

The four and twentieth day Hester Wilson the wife was delivered of an abortive female child as per certificate.

Aug. 25.	Elizabeth, daughter of Samuel Shipley, Lodger, *Fishmonger*, born Aug. 25. s. m. w. c.
Sep. 5.	Katherine, daughter of Mr. Joseph and Katherine Grosvenour, of St. M. W. C., *Scrivener.*
Sep. 7.	Jonas Woolnoth, a male child taken up at Mr. Foley's door. This child was taken away by Mr. May, the Grandfather. [In margin.]
Oct. 1.	Lucy, daughter of William and Elizabeth Horsepool, of St. M. W. C., *Merchant*, his wife daughter to Mr. Blythe.
Oct. 23.	Martha Woolnoth, a female child taken up under the house next to Anderson the Apothecaries in Dove Court.
Oct. 31.	Mary, daughter of Mr. Edward and Judith Drayner, *Vintner*, born Oct. 14.
Nov. 8.	Henry, a male child taken up in six bell alley, in Dove Court, near Lumbard Streete.
Nov. 27.	Robert, a male child taken up at Mr. Coleman's door.
Dec. 11.	William, son of Robert and Rebecca Louth, *Coffeeman*, born Dec. 11.
Dec. 14.	James, son of Richard and Ann Chapman, *Goldsmith*, born Dec. 14.
Dec. 27.	Ellinor, daughter of Daniel and Ellinor Puckle, *Gentleman*, lodger at widdow Platts, in St. M. W. C.
Jan. 9.	Windham, son of Robert and Elizabeth Westcott, of St. M. W. C., *Vintner.*
Jan. 12.	Elizabeth, daughter of John and Sarah Best, of St. M. W. C. *Razor Maker*, born Jan. 12.
Jan. 13.	John, son of Henry and Mary Robinson, *Goldsmith*, born Jan. 13.
Jan. 14.	Richard, son of Richard and Jane Baker, *Watchmaker*, in Exchange Alley.
Jan. 17.	Ellis, daughter of Mr. John and Tomazin Meynell, of St. M. W. C. *Draper.*
Jan. 21.	Gabriel, a male child, taken up in Dove Court, at Mr. Smith's back door. This child taken away by his mother. [In margin.]
Jan. 26.	Was taken up at the post-boy doore, a male child about two months old, and was baptized then, Richard, and exchanged for Gabriel; sent to nurse Dorokett.
Jan. 29.	Charity, a female child, taken up in Exchange Alley.
Feb. 12.	Mary, daughter of Mr. Joseph and Katherine Archer, *Victualler*, born Feb. 11.
Feb. 24.	Elias, son of John and Flora Malpass, of St. M. W. C., *Fishmonger*, born Feb. 24,
Mar. 20.	John, son of Martin Beaumond, of St. M. W. C., *Tallow-chandler*, born Feb. 25.
[No date.]	Tobijah Wynne, born March 19.
Mar. 22.	Charles, son of Mr. Edward Freeman, *Goldsmith*, lodger at Mr. Brown's, at the Spread Eagle, in St. M. W. C., born Mar. 22.
Mar. 22.	Audrey, daughter of Mr. Joseph and Martha Cozens, *Barber*, born Mar. 22.

1698

Mar. 30.	Richard, son of Mr. Thomas Farrall, of St. M. W. C., *Fruiterer*, born March 17.

April 1.   Richard, a female child [sic] of Mr. Thomas Parr, of St. M. W. C., *Chirurgeon Instrument Maker*, born Mar. 23.

May 1.   Symon, son of Symon and Margaret King, lodger at Mr. Best, born April 28.

June 12.   Christopher, son of Marke and Mary Stoddart, *Porter*, lodgers at Mr. Manwood's, *Bookbinder*, born May 17.

May 29.   Sarah, daughter of Edward and Sarah Richardson, son and daughter of Jediall Turner, letter-carrier to the post-office.

July 7.   Jasper Haw, a male child, taken up by the house of office in Stock-market.

July 8.   Margaret, daughter of John and Margarett Goodwin, *Apothecary*, born July 8.

July 20.   Thomas, son of George and Margaret Cooke, *Chirurgions Instrument Maker*, born July 20.

July 22.   Amie, daughter of Mr. Richard and Susanna Gilbert, of St. M. W. C., *Norwich Factor*, born July 22.

————   [sic] Richard, son of William and Mary Barwell, *Milliner*, born Aug. 5.

Aug. 16.   James, son of Samuel and Mary Lyon, lodgers at Mr. Elliott, Sword Cutler, in Exchange Alley, born Aug. 16.

Sep. 13.   Richardson, son of Thomas and Arabella Woolley, of St. M. W. C., *Draper*, born Sep. 12.

Sep. 30.   Hester, daughter of Michael and Hester Wilson, *Goldsmith*, of St. M. W. C., born Sep. 30.

Sep. 30.   Henry, son of Josiah and Katherine Grosvenour, *Scrivener*, of St. M. W. C., born Sep. 30.

Oct. 4.   Sarah, daughter of Mr. John and Mary Sebella, *Merchant*, born Oct. 4.

Oct. 13.   William, a male child taken up in Dove Court, in 6 Bell Alley.

Oct. 23.   Was taken up in the Church, Jeremy Jenkins, son of Anne Sims, the wife of Jeffery Sims, liveing in Catt Alley, Long Lane, which was put in the post boy the Friday following and taken away by the mother on Satterday.

Nov. 10.   Mary, daughter of Mr. William and Mary Jones, of St. M. W. C., *Apothecary*, born Nov. 3.

Nov. 13.   Susanna, daughter of Mr. John and Susan Bach, *Goldsmith*, born Nov. 13.

Nov. 16.   Ellzabeth, daughter of Mr. Mark and Elizabeth Gilbert, of St. M. W. C., *Norwich Factor*, born Nov. 16.

Nov. 24.   Rebecca, daughter of Robert and Rebecca Lowthe, *Coffeeman*, born Nov. 24.

Nov. 20.   Mary, daughter of Mr. John Giles, *Hottpresser*, born Nov. 16.

Dec. 7.   William, son of Mr. John and Jane Thursby, *Goldsmith*, born Dec. 6.

Dec. 22.   Thomas, son of Mr. James and Anne Taylor, of St. M.W.C. *Cheesemonger*.

Jan. 6.   Charles, son of the right hon. Sir Thomas Franckland, *baronett, one of his Majesty's Postmaster Generall*, and of Dame Elizabeth, his wife, born Dec. 19.

Jan. 1.   Elizabeth, daughter of Mr. George and Elizabeth Smith, of St. M. W. C., *Poulterer*, born Dec. 27.

Jan. 2.   Susanna, daughter of Mr. Robert and Elizabeth Westcott, of St. M. W. C., *Vintner*, born Jan. 2.

Jan. 6.   John, son of John and Sarah Ladyman, *Goldsmith*, born Jan. 6.

Jan. 19.   Anne, daughter of Mr. Andrew and Anne Stone, *Goldsmith, book-keeper* to Mr. Smith at the Grasshopper, born Jan. 9.

Mar. 4.   Rebecca, daughter of Mr. Charles and Elizabeth Jennings, of St. M. W. C., *Victualler*, born Mar. 4.

Mar. 5.   Elizabeth, daughter of John and Elizabeth Gough, of St. M. W. C., *Butcher*, lodging with his father at Globe Ale House, born March 5.

1699

Mar. 28.   Joseph, a male child, ¾ old, with a Blew Tamarett coat and English calico printed frock, was taken up at Mr. Manwood's door. Sent for away by the mother April 3. [In Margin.]

April 6.   Sarah, daughter of Gerrard and Sarah Roberts, of St. M. W. C., *Fishmonger*, born April 6.

April, 12.   John, son of Mr. William and Elizabeth Horsepoole, of St. M. W. C., *Merchant*, partner with Mr. Blyth, born April 1.

May. 4.   Elizabeth, daughter of Mr. Leonard and ———— [*sic*] Simpson, *Designer in Painting*, lodgers at Mr. Simpson, shoemaker, of St. M. W. C., born April 23.

April 27.   Samuel, son of Mr. Thomas and Damaris Manwood, *Bookbinder*, born April 26.

May 21.   Thomas, female child of Mr. Thomas and Martha Chippen, *Cook*, born May 14.

June 10.   Elizabeth, daughter of Mr. Phillip and ———— [*sic*] Roaker, *Goldsmith*, born May 14.

May 29.   John, son of Mr. John and Frances Travell, of St. M. W. C., *Linendraper*, born May 28.

June 18.   Thomas, son of Mr. John and Dorothy Stanton, *Jeweller*, born June 8.

June 18.   James, son of Mr. Joseph and Katherine Archer, *Victualer*, born June 18.

July 9.   Joseph, taken up under Mr. Wilcox, the Barber's window, put to Nurse Bramwood, near Wirehall, in Edmuntan parish

Aug. 6.   John, son of Mr. Edward and Judith Drayner, *Vintner*, born July 15.

July 30.   George, son of Mr. John and Dorothy Foster, of St. M. W. C., *Merchant*, born July 21.

Aug. 18.   Elizabeth, daughter of Mr. John and Anne Maple, *Scrivener*, born July 28.

Aug. 9.   Arthur, son of Mr. Thomas and Arabella Woolley, of St. M. W. C., *Linendraper*, born Aug. 7.

Aug. 28.   Jane, daughter of Thomas and Elizabeth Kimberley, *Boxmaker*, lodger at Mr. Giles, in Sherborne Lane, Packer, born Aug. 28.

Sep. 3.   Elizabeth, daughter of Thomas and Jane Parr, of St. M. W. C., *Chirurgion Instrument Maker*, born Aug. 24.

Sep. 28.	Michael, a child taken up between Deputy Moor and Mr. Mark Gilbert's house, with a striped white coate and painted frock, put to nurse Bramwood at Wirehall in Essex.
Nov. 12.	Mary, daughter of William Wollaston, lodger at Mr. Jediall Turners, born Nov. 5.
Dec. 3.	John, son of Mr. John and Mary Sebelle, *Merchant*, born Nov. 17.
Nov. 26.	Mary, daughter of Mr. John and Martha Taylor, *Washball Maker*, born Nov. 12.
Nov. 26.	Elizabeth, daughter of William and Mary Byrch, *Druggest*, born Nov. 26.
Nov. 30.	Robert, son of Mr. Robert and Rebecca Lowthe, *Coffeeman*, born Nov. 28.
Nov. 30.	Thomas, son of Mr. Richard and Susanna Gilbert, of St. M. W. C., *Factor*, born Nov. 30.
Dec. 8.	Elizabeth, daughter of Mr. Richard and Ann Cock, of St. M. W. C., *Linendraper*, born Dec. 8.
Dec. 18.	Elizabeth, daughter of Mr. Marke and Elizabeth Gilbert, of St. M. W. C., *Factor*, born Dec. 17.
Jan. 18.	Sarah, daughter of Abraham and Anne Wilcox, *Barbor*, born Jan. 18.
Jan. 24.	Susanna, taken up, nursed by Susan Towne, of Ware.
Jan. 30.	Sarah Woolnoth, taken up in Mr. Lloyd, the Coffeeman,
Feb. 17.	Mary, daughter of Mr. George and Dorothy Reed, *Bancker*.

1700

April 3.	William, son of William and Elizabeth Horsepoole, of St. M. W. C., *Merchant*, born Mar. 14.
April 8.	William, son of George and Elizabeth Tyler, *Watchmaker*, lodger at Waghern's Coffee House in Pope's Head Alley, born Mar. 29.
April 4.	Margarett, daughter of Mr. George and Margaret Cock, *Razor Maker*, born April 10.
April 10.	Elizabeth, daughter of John Moore the younger and Prudence, *Goldbeater*, lodgers at Deputy Moores in Dove Court, born April 10.
May 12.	John, son of Mr. Thomas and Damarie Manwood, *Bookbinder*, born April 21.
May 17.	Mary, daughter of Mr. Andrew and Ann Stone, *Goldsmith*, born May 9.
May 24.	Dorothy, daughter of Mr. John and Dorothy Stanton, *Jeweller*, born May 22.
May 27.	Mary, and Martha two twinns of Mr. John and Elizabeth Giles, *Packer*, born May 27.
July 4.	Benjamin, son of John and Elizabeth Gough, *Butcher*, of St. M. W. C., born July 4.
July 28.	Elizabeth, daughter of Martin and Dorothy Beamond, of St. M. W. C., *Tallowchandler*, born July 19.
Aug. 17.	Samuel, son of Mr. James and Ann Taylor, of St. M. W. C., *Cheesemonger*, born Aug. 17.
Sep. 18.	Anne, daughter of Mr. Charles and Anne Shales, *Goldsmith*, born Sep. 7.
Oct. 9.	Robert, son of Mr. Thomas and Rebecca Farrell, of St. M. W. C., *Fruiterer*, born Sep. 14.

Nov. 8.	Robert, son of Mr. Robert and Anne Waple, *Scrivener*, born October 18.
Oct. 23.	Ruth, a child taken up.
Nov. 11.	Rhoda, a child taken up.
Nov. 21.	Mary, daughter of Mr. Thomas and Jane Parr, of St. M. W. C., *Chirurgion Instrument Maker*, born Nov. 21.
Dec. 10.	Robert, son of the Right Worshipful Sir Thomas Franckland, *Knight* and *Baronett*, and *one of Her Majestie's Postmasters Generall*, and of Dame Elizabeth, his wife, born Nov. 30.
Dec. 4.	Thomas, son of Mr. Gerrard and Sarah Roberts, of St. M. W. C., *Fishmonger*, born Dec. 4.
Dec. 15.	Rachell, daughter of Mr. John and Dorothy Knapp, of St. M. W. C., *Merchant*, born Dec. 4.
Dec. 8.	Jane, daughter of Izaack Manley, of St. M. W. C., *Esquire*, and Ann, his wife, born Dec. 5.
Dec. 7.	Unisa, daughter of Mr. Richard and Susanna Gilbert, of St. M. W. C., *Norwich Factor*, born Dec. 6.
Dec. 18.	Elizabeth, daughter of Vincent and Elizabeth Williams, *Barber*, lodgers at the dary house in Sherborne Lane, born Dec. 18.
June 19.	Edward, son of John and Rachell Moore, *Apothecary*, born Jan. 11.
Feb. 16.	Grace, daughter of Phillip Roaker, *Goldsmith*, born Jan. 22.
Jan. 31.	Grace, daughter of Thomas and Elizabeth Kimberley, *Boxmaker*, lodgers at Giles the Hotpresser, born Jan. 31.
Feb. 26.	William, son of Mr. William and Mary Jones, *Apothecary*, of St. M. W. C., born Feb. 13.
Feb. 25.	Sarah, a child taken up.
Feb. 27.	William, one of two male children of Elizabeth, wife of Thomas Beare, of St. M. W. C. The other born dead.

1701

June 6.	John, son of Mr. Nathaniel and Anne Woolfrey, *Goldsmith*, born May 25.
July 10.	Borne Elizabeth, daughter of Mr. Thomas and Elizabeth Planck, of St. M. W. C., *Linendraper*.
July 3.	Elizabeth, daughter of Mr. John and Elizabeth Baldock, *Clerk to the Post Office*, born June 23.
July 20.	James, son of Edward and Judith Drayner, *Vintner*, born June 25.
July 20.	George, son of George and Elizabeth Tyler, *Watchmaker*, lodging at Waghorne's Coffee house, born July 4.
July 19.	Anne, daughter of John and Dorothy Stanton, *Jeweller*, born July 19.
July 22.	Was born Hanah, daughter of Thomas Falkenham, *Goldsmith*, baptized ——— [*sic*]
July 27.	Edward, son of William and Mary Byrch, *Druggest*, born July 27.
Sep. 15.	Katherine, daughter of Mr. George and Dorothy Reed, *Banker*, born Sep. 15.
Sep. 23.	James, son of Mr. John and Susan Bach, *Silversmith*,
Sep. 21.	Joshua, son of Mr. Thomas and Damaris Manwood, *Bookebinder*, born Sept. 21.

Oct. 5.	Elizabeth, daughter of Mr. Joseph Moore, *Goldsmith*, born Sep. 22.
Oct. 10.	Sarah, daughter of Mr. Richard and Ann Cock, of St. M. W. C., *Linnendraper*, born Oct. 9.
Oct. 24.	Elizabeth, daughter of Mr. Edmund and Elizabeth Bick, of St. M. W. C., *Waxchandler*, lodger at Mr. Tombs, Barber, next Mitre Tavern, born Oct. 24.
Oct. 31.	Hannah, daughter of Richard and Hannah Stacy, *Cabinet-maker*, lodgers at the Davy house, born Oct. 31.
Nov. 8.	Martha, daughter of Abraham and Ann Wilcox, *Barber*, born Nov. 8.
Nov. 16.	Stephen, son of George and Margaret Cooke, *Surgeons Instrument Maker*, born Nov. 16.
Dec. 20.	Elizabeth, daughter of Mr. Andrew and Anne Stone, *Goldsmith*, born Dec. 18.
Dec. 24.	William Chew, son of Mark and Elizabeth Gilbert, of St. M. W. C., *Norwich Factor*, born Dec. 24.
Jan. 18.	Thomas, son of Henry and Anne Lambe, *Goldsmith*, born Jan. 1.
Jan. 18.	John, son of Joseph and Katherine Moore, *Apothecary*, Jan. 2,
Jan. 18.	John, son of Joseph and Katherine Archer, *Victualler*, born Jan. 12.
Jan. 23.	Born a male child of Mr. John and Dorothy Knapp, of St. M. W. C., *Merchant*, died in a fit before baptized.
Feb. 5.	Mary daughter of Mr. Robert and Rebecca Lowth, *Coffeeman*, born Jan. 28.
Feb. 15.	Jane, daughter of Mr. John and Francis Travel, of St. M. W. C., *Draper*, born Feb. 6.

1702

April 6.	Born a female child, of Mr. Michael Wilcox, of St. M. W. C. *Engraver*, who dyed of the Culvisions before baptized.
April 19.	Elizabeth, daughter of Thomas and Elizabeth Beach, *Porter*, lodger at the Royal Oake Lottery, St. M. W. C., born April 8.
April 23.	Born Helena, daughter of John and Rebecca Walstead, *Book-keeper*, inmates at Mr. John Cole, in Sherborne Lane.
May 2.	Susannah, daughter of Martin and Dorothy Beaumond, of St. M. W. C., *Tallowchandler*, born May 2.
May 15.	Shaíto, son of Mr. Richard and Susannah Gilbert, of St. M. W. C., *Norwich Factor*, born May 10.
June 11.	Elizabeth, daughter of Mr. Gerrard and Barbara Roberts, of St. M. W. C., *Fishmonger*, born May 14.
June 17.	Nathaniel, Mathew, son of Mr. Nathaniel and Anne Woolfrey, *Goldsmith*, born June 7.
June 12.	Margarett, daughter of Mr. John and Sarah Bully, of St. M. W. C., *Vintner*, born June 12.
June 20.	Elizabeth, daughter of Mr. Cornelius and Elizabeth Herbert, of St. M. W. C., *Watchmaker*, born June 20.
July 6.	Thomas, son of Mr. Thomas Ashworth, *Butcher*, and lodger at the Globe Alehouse, in St. M. W. C., born June 25.
July 9.	Mary, daughter of Mr. Charles and Anne Shales, *Goldsmith*, born June 28.

July 4.   Denny, son of Mr. Thomas and Elizabeth Faulkeingham, of St. M. W. C., *Goldsmith*, born July 4.

Sep. 28.   Elizabeth, daughter of Mr. George and Elizabeth Tyler, *Watchmaker*, born Sep. 28.

Sep. 30.   Sarah, the wife of Mr. Thomas Martin, *Vintner*, of St. M. W. C., was delivered of a male still-born child.

Oct. 7.   Michaell, son of Michael and Mary Kent, of St. M. W. C., *Basketmaker*, lodgers at Mr. Sextons, Confectioner.

Oct. 25.   Sarah, daughter of Mr. Timothy and Sarah Butler, of St. M. W. C., *Upholster*, born Oct. 20.

Oct. 21.   Samuel, son of Henry and Thomazine Reeve, *Engraver*, lodgers at Godman's the Bakers, born Oct. 21.

Oct. 28.   Joseph, son of Edward and Elizabeth Bick, *Waxchaundler*, lodger at Mr. Some, Barber, St. M. W. C., born Oct. 25.

Nov. 5.   Gorgonis, daughter of Mr. George and Dorothy Reed, of St. M. W. C., *Goldsmith*, born Oct. 16.

Nov. 2.   Nathaniel, son of John and Damaris Manwood, *Bookbinder*, born Nov. 2.

Nov. 18.   Anne, wife of John Rogers, *Gentleman*, was delivered of a male still-borne child at Mr. Cozens, Barber.

Nov. 23.   Anne, daughter of Mr. Edmund and Mary Meekins, *Vintner*, born Nov. 23.

Dec. 20.   Mary, daughter of Joseph and Elizabeth Feilder, of St. M. W. C., lodgers at Mr. Sewell's, Victualler, born Dec. 5.

Dec. 18.   John and Mary, twins, son and daughter of John and Mary Boldock, *one of the Clerks at the Post Office*, lodgers at the Dary House, Sherborne Lane, born Dec. 18.

Dec. 17.   Rachell, daughter of William and Sarah Carter, *Vintner*, born Dec. 17.

Dec. 24.   Jane, wife of Mr. William Troope, of St. M. W. C., was delivered of a still borne childe.

Jan. 23.   William, son of Edward and Judith Drayner, *Vintner*, born Jan. 11.

Jan. 24.   Elizabeth, daughter of Mr. Robert and Mary Conant, of St. M. W. C., *Linendraper*, born Jan. 18.

Feb. —   [*sic*] Andrew, son of Mr. Andrew and Anne Stone, *Goldsmith*, born Feb. 4.

Feb. 14.   John, son of Charles and Elizabeth Kingman, *Cutler*, lodgers at Sampsons Barbers, born Feb. 5.

1703

Mar. 31.   Goddard, son of Mr. Richard and Philadelphia Nelthropp, *Goldsmith*, born Mar. 31.

April 22.   John, son of Mr. Richard and Anne Cock, of St. M. W. C., *Linendraper*, born April 21.

May. 28.   Hardie Moor, an iligitimate child, borne same day.

July 3.   Anne, daughter of Mr. Nathaniell and Anne Woolfrey, *Goldsmith*, born June 26th.

July 11.   James, son of Daniell and Elizabeth Stephen, *Coffeeman*, born June 26.

June 28.   Thomas Chew, son of Mark and Elizabeth Gilbert, of St. M. W. C., *Factor*, born June 28.

July 14.	John, son of Robert and Mary Nicholls, at Mr. Wilcox, *Barber*, born July 14.
July 2.	Moore Woolnoth, a male child taken up.
Aug. 8.	Ellinor, daughter of Mr. Joseph and Katherine Archer, *Victualer*, born July 30.
July 29.	William, son of Mr. William and Penelope Eaton, of St. M. W. C., *Linendraper*, born July 23.
Aug. 2.	Anne, daughter of Mr. George and Dorothy Read, *Banker*, born Aug. 2.
Aug. 22.	Katherine, daughter of Mr. Thomas and Jane Parr, of St. M. W. C., *Chirurgeons Instrument Maker*, born Aug. 2.
Aug. 31.	James, son of Mr. John and Rachell Moore, *Apothecary*, born Aug. 12.
Sep. 20.	Thomas, son of Mr. George and Margaret Cooke, *Chirurgeon Instrument Maker*, born Sep. 15.
Sep. 23.	Michael, son of Mr. Michael and Hester Wilson, of St. M. W. C., *Goldsmith*, born Sep. 18.
Sep. 21.	Timothy, son of Mr. Timothy and Sarah Rutter, of St. M. W. C., *Upholster*, born Sep. 19.
Nov. 7.	William, son of Mr. Edward and Mary Meekins, *Vintner*, born Oct. 20.
Oct. 27.	Mary, daughter of Mr. George and Elizabeth Tyler, *Watchmaker*, born Oct. 21.
Nov. 26.	George, son of Mr. Francis Jones, of Falmouth, Cornwall, *Gent.*, and Susanna, his wife, lodgers at Mr. Eaton's, Linendraper, born Nov. 26.
Jan. 3.	Elizabeth, daughter of William and Elizabeth Frowde, *Chandler*, lodgers with Mr. Haywood, Tillett Painter.
Jan. 31.	Rhoda Woolnoth, a female child taken up.
Feb. 10.	Cornelius, son of Mr. Cornelius and Elizabeth Herbert, of St. M. W. C., *Watchmaker*, born Feb. 10.
Feb. 16.	Elizabeth, daughter of Mr. John and Mary Baldock, *Clerk of the General Post Office*, born Feb. 10.
Feb. 13.	Benjamin, son of Mr. Benjamin and Katherine Gough, of St. M. W. C., *Victualler*, born Feb. 12.
Feb. 18.	Elizabeth, daughter of Mr. John and Mary Mathews, of St. M. W. C., *Merchant*, born Feb. 14.
Feb. 15.	John, son of Mr. John and Dorothy Stanton, *Jeweller*, born Feb. 15.
Mar. 26.	Lidia, daughter of Mr. Gerrard and Barbara Roberts, *Fishmonger*, born Feb. 24.
Mar. 1.	John, son of Mr. Richard and Susanna Gilbert, of St. M. W. C., *Merchant*, born Feb. 28.
Mar. 17.	Charles, son of Mr. Charles and Anne Shales, *Goldsmith*, born Feb. 29.
Mar. 15.	Philadelphia, daughter of Mr. Richard and Philadelphia Nelthropp, *Goldsmith*, born Mar. 8.
Mar. 27.	Arabella, daughter of Sir Thomas Franckland, *Knight Baronet, and one of the Commissioners of Her Majesties Post Office*, and Dame Elizabeth his wife, born Mar. 13.

1704

April 25.	Katherine, daughter of Mr. Edward and Judith Drayner, *Vintner*, born April 6.

April 19. Richard, son of Richard Stacey, *Philligreene Case Maker*, born April 8.

May 14. Mary, daughter of Mr. Robert and Mary Conant, of St. M. W. C., *Linendraper*, born May 6.

June 1. William, son of Mr. Henry and Thomazia Reeve, *Engraver*, born May 17.

May 28. Thomas, son of Mr. John and Anne Rogers, *Attorney*, born May 21.

July 4. Joseph, son of Mr. John and Katherine Foster, *Stationer*, born June 23.

July 9. Richard, son of Robert Gill, of St. M. W. C., Lodger, born July 9.

July 23. Thomas, son of Mr. Thomas and Hannah Pike, born July 18.

July 23. Caleb, son of Mr. Caleb and Jane Norgate, *Scrivener*, lodger at Mr. Bradbury, Millcnor, St. M. W. C., born July 22.

Aug. 17. John, son of Mr. John and Rachell Moore, *Apothecary*, born Aug. 17.

Aug. 18. Hannah Dove, a child taken up.

Aug. 23. Mary, daughter of Mr. William and Mary Byrch, *Drugster*, born Aug. 23.

Sep. 19. Was borne a female stillborne childe of Mr. Goodman, *Baker*.

Oct. 8. Samuell, son of Mr. Samuell and Mary Feild, of St. M. W. C., *Cheesemonger*, born Oct. 5.

Oct. 22. Joane, daughter of Mr. Edmund and Mary Meekins, *Vintner*, born Oct. 7.

Oct. 26. Edward, son of Mr. William and Penelope Eaton, of St, M. W. C., *Draper*, born Oct. 17.

Nov. 28. Anne, daughter of Mr. George and Elizabeth Tylor, *Watchmaker*, born Nov. 23.

Dec. 10. Thomas, son of Thomas and Jane Alcroft, *Cutler*, lodger at Waghorne's Coffee House, born Nov. 27.

Dec. 20. The wife of Mr. Abraham Wilcox was delivered of a male child stillborne.

Dec. 24. Sarah, daughter of Mr. John and Sarah Best, of St. M. W. C., *Instrument Maker*, born Dec. 24.

Dec. 27. John, son of Mr. Robert and Mary Pattison, *Norwich Factor*, born Dec. 24.

Dec. 26. Thomas, son of Mr. Edmund and Elizabeth Bick, *Waxchandler*, of St. M. W. C., born Dec. 26.

Feb. 18. Susanna, daughter of John and Dorothy Stanton, *Jeweller*, born Feb. 12.

Mar. 8. Mary, daughter of William and Mary Fellowes, *Esquire*, of St. M. W. C., born Mar. 3.

Mar. 13. Elizabeth, daughter of Mr. Joseph and Elizabeth Feilder, St. M. W. C., *Poulterer*, born Mar. 11.

Mar. 13. Borne Garthrude, daughter of Samuel Trefusis, *Esquire*, and Alice his wife, living with the Right Hon. Sir Robert Cotton, Knt., one of the Commissioners of Her Majesties Post Office Generall.

1705

April 1. Elizabeth, daughter of Mr. Thomas and Elizabeth Faulkenigham, *Goldsmith*, born Mar. 28.

April 19.   Peter, son of Mr. Roger and Emma Susanna Hudson, *Goldsmith*, born Mar. 30.

April 22.   John, son of Mr. Timothy and Sarah Rutter, of St. M. W. C., *Upholster*, born April 11.

May 2.   Richard, son of Mr. Richard and Anne Stone, *Goldsmith*, born April 19.

April 29.   Anne, daughter of Mr. William and Elizabeth Law, of St. M. W. C., *Confectioner*, born April 17.

April 30.   Jane, daughter of Mr. Thomas and Jane Parr, of St. M.W.C., *Chirurgeon Instrument Maker*, born April 30.

May 3.   Margarett, wife of Mr. Stephen Child, *Goldsmith*, was delivered of a male stillborn infant.

May 29.   Elizabeth, daughter of Mr. Robert and Mary Conant, of St. M. W. C., *Linnendraper*, born May 25.

June 19.   Rebecca, daughter of Mr. Richard and Philadelphia Nellthrop, *Goldsmith*, born June 8.

Aug. 8.   Charles, son of Mr. Thomas and Frances Webb, *Mariner*, born Aug. 7.

Sep. 14.   Rachell, daughter of Mr. John and Rachell Moor, *Apothecary*, born Aug. 17.

Sep. 3.   John, son of Mr. John and Elizabeth Sergeant, lodger at Mr. Reed's, Tinplate Worker, St. M. W. C., born Sep. 3.

Sep. 29.   Dorothy, daughter of Mr. George and Dorothy Reed, *Banker*, born Sep. 7.

Sep. 23.   William, son of Mr. John Moore, Junr., *Goldbeater*, lodging at Mr. Wynns, St. M. W. C., born Sep. 22.

Oct. 14.   Griffith, son of Mr. Thomas and Mary Chippin, *Cooke*, born Oct. 2.

Oct. 18.   Rich, son of Mr. Charles and Ann Shales, *Goldsmith*, born Oct. 4.

Nov. 15.   William, son of William and Isabella Frowde, *Porter*, born Oct. 26.

Oct. 30.   Susanna and Dorothy, two twin daughters of Mr. Richard and Anne Cock, of St. M. W. C., *Linendraper*, born Oct. 29.

Nov. 16.   Elizabeth, daughter of Mr. George and Margaret Cooke, *Chirurgion Instrument Maker*, born Oct. 30.

Nov. 4.   Abigail, daughter of Mr. William and Mary Jones, of St. M. W. C., *Apothecary*, born Nov. 3.

Dec. 7.   Marian, daughter of Mr. William and Dorcas Bennett, *Blacksmith*, born Nov. 10.

Nov. 30.   Jemima, daughter of Mr. Nathaniel and Anne Woolfrey, *Goldsmith*, born Nov. 15.

Dec. 13.   John, son of Mr. John and Katherine Foster, *Stationer*, born Nov. 29.

Nov. 18.   Anne, daughter of Mr. James and Rebecca Wilbraham, of St. M. W. C., *Fruiterer*, born Nov. 17.

Dec. 14.   Purlino, daughter of Mr. John and Mary Baldock, *Clerk of the General Post Office*, born Dec. 3.

Dec. 23.   Mathew, son of Mr. Edmund and Mary Meekins, *Vintner*, born Dec. 10.

Dec. 26.   Elizabeth, daughter of Mr. George and Elizabeth Tyler, *Watchmaker*, lodger at Waghorne's Coffee House, born Dec. 11.

Jan. 3.   Alice, daughter of Mr. Robert and Mary Pattison, *Factor*.

Jan. 14.	Margaret, daughter of Richard and Anne Baker, *Butcher*, lodgers at the Dolphin Cookes in Little Lombard Street, St. M. W. C., born Jan. 2.
Jan. 6.	Anne, daughter of Thomas and Ann Crawford, *Taylor*, born Jan. 4.
Feb. 4.	Robert, son of Mr. Samuell and Mary Feild, of St. M. W. C., *Cheesemonger*, born Jan. 31.
Feb. 28.	Benjamin, son of Mr. John and Dorothy Knapp, of St. M. W. C., *Merchant*, born Feb. 16.
Feb. 20.	Daniel, son of Mr. Gerard and Barbara Roberts, of St. M. W. C., *Fishmonger*, born Feb. 19.
Mar. 14.	Anna, daughter of Mr. Thomas and Anna Chadwell, *Jeweller*, born Mar. 1.
Mar. 17.	John, son of Mr. William and Ann Mooring, of St. M. W. C., *Cooke,* born Mar. 3.
Mar. 9.	Was borne Edward son of Edward and Sarah Richardson, *Tanner*, lodger at Jediael Turner's, letter carrier.
Mar. 18.	Mrs. Susannah, wife of Mr. Richard Gilbert, of St. M. W. C. *Merchant*, was delivered of two twins, the one a female child still borne, the other a male baptized then Edmund.

1706

April 2.	Anne, daughter of Mr. Joseph and Martha Cozens, *Barber*, born April 1.
June 2.	John, son of Mr. Robert and Mary Conaut, of St. M. W. C. *Linnendraper*, born May 18.
June 7.	Samuel, son of Mr. Stephen and Margarett Child, of St. M. W. C., *Goldsmith*, born June 5.
June 17.	Olive [*sic*] son of John and Sarah Best, of St. M. W. C., *Chirurgion Instrument Maker*, born June 3.
July 5.	Elizabeth, daughter of William and Elizabeth Laws, of St. M. W. C., *Confectioner*, born July 5.
Aug. 2.	Henry, son of Mr. Richard and Philadelphia Nelthropp, *Goldsmith*, born July 26.
Aug. 2.	William, son of William and Mary Fellows, *Esquire*, of St. M. W. C., born July 28.
July 29.	Sarah, daughter of Samuel and Sarah Gibson, *Drugster*, lodgers of Mr. Chippins, Cooke, born July 29, and exp. 31 July. [In margin.]
Aug. 1.	Elizabeth, daughter of Timothy and Sarah Rutter, of St. M. W. C., *Upholster*, born Aug. 1.
Sep. 1.	Jane, daughter of Daniell and Margarett Cahowne, of St. M. W. C., *Mariner*, lodgers at Mr. Gerrard Roberts, Fishmonger, born Aug. 12.
Sep. 5.	John, son of Thomas and Elizabeth Freeman, *Packer*, lodgers at Mrs. Herringmans, widdow.
Oct. 6.	Robert, son of Mr. William and Penelope Eaton, of St. M. W. C., *Draper*, born Oct. 4.
Oct. 16.	Clare Elizabeth, daughter of Mr. Peter and Elizabeth Sargeant, *Book-keeper*, lodgers at Mr. Reed, Tinplate-worker, St. M. W. C., born Oct. 16.
Nov. 10.	Lucretia, daughter of John and Rachel Moore, *Apothecary*, born Oct. 24.

Nov. 13.	Susanna, daughter of James and Susanna Thomasson, *Goldsmith*, born Nov. 13.
Dec. 1.	George, son of Thomas and Jane Alcroft, *Cutler*, lodgers at Waghorne's Coffeehouse, born Nov. 15.
Dec. 6.	Rebecca, daughter of Mr. Richard and Anne Cock, of St. M. W. C., *Linnendraper*, born Nov. 17.
Dec. 15.	Edmund, son of Mr. Edmund and Mary Meekins, *Vintner*, born Dec. 10.
Dec. 15.	Sarah, daughter of Mr. John Pinkethman, *Cutler*, born Dec. 6.
Dec. 27.	John, son of Mr. John and Mary Baldock, one of the *Clerks of the Post Office*, born Dec. 16.
Jan. 26.	Hester, daughter of Mr. William and Mary Byrch, *Drugster*, born Jan. 26.
Jan. 26.	Mary, daughter of Mr. John and Elizabeth Lumley, *Pastry Cooke*, lodgers at Mr. Mooring, at the Dolphin, Cooke, St. M. W. C.
Jan. 29.	Elizabeth, daughter of Samuel and Alice Trefusis, *Esquire*, living with the Right Hon. Sir Robert Cotton, Knt., one of the Commissioners of Her Majesties Post Office Generall, born Jan. 19.
Feb. 12.	George, son of William and Isabella Frowde, *Porter*.
Feb. 23.	William, son of Mr. John and Katherine Foster, *Stationer*, born Feb. 23.
Mar. 12.	Israel, son of Mr. Samuel and Mary Keynton, of St. M. W. C. *Citizen and Haberdasher of London*, born Mar. 12.
Mar 23.	Francis, son of Thomas and Anna Chadwell, *Jeweller*, born Mar. 12.

1707

April 13.	Daniel, son of Daniel and Elizabeth Woodcock, of St. M. W. C., *Poulterer*, and lodger at the Cheshire Cheese, born Mar. 31.
May 21.	Mary, daughter of Mr. Richard and Susanna Gildert, of St. M. W. C., *Merchant*, born May 21.
June 22.	Thomas, son of Bryan and Hannah Robinson, of St. M. W. C., *Turner*, born June 22.
July 1.	Susanna, daughter of Martin and Dorothy Beamond, of St. M. W. C., *Tallowchandler*, born July 1.
Aug. 17.	Elizabeth, daughter of Mr. John and Sarah Best, of St. M. W. C., *Chirurgion Instrument Maker*, born Aug. 22.
Sep. 26.	Ellinor, daughter of Mr. Samuel and Mary Chase, in Exchange Alley, *Sword Cutler*, born Sep. 25.
Sep. 28.	Samuel, son of Joseph and Ellinor Feilder, of St. M. W. C., *Poulterer*, born Sep. 19.
Oct. 15.	Benjamin, son of Mr. Stephen and Margarett Childs, of St. M. W. C., *Goldsmith*, born Oct. 12.
Nov. 6.	Essex, daughter of Mr. Charles and Anne Shales, *Goldsmith*, born Oct. 18.
Dec. 7.	Penelope, daughter of Mr. William and Penelope Eaten, of St. M. W. C., *Linendraper*, born Nov. 27.
Dec. 14.	Isabella, daughter of Mr. John and Elizabeth Lumley, *Pastrycook*, inmates of Mr. William Mooring, of St. M. W. C., Cooke, born Dec. 10.

Dec. 17. Martha, daughter of Mr. Richard and Anne Cock, of St. M. W. C., *Linnendraper*, born Dec. 1.

Dec. 17. Thomas, son of Mr. Samuel and Sarah Gibson, *Drugster*, living at Mr. Perkins, Drugster, born Dec. 11.

Dec. 18. Robert, son of Mr. Robert and Mary Conant, of St. M. W. C., *Linnendraper*, born Dec. 11.

Jan. 2. Rachell, daughter of James and Rachell Alport, *Taylor*, lodger at Mr. Coles.

Jan. 18. Hannah, daughter of Mr. James and Susannah Thomasson, *Goldsmith.*

Feb. 11. George, son of Mr. Andrews and Ann Stone, *Goldsmith*, born Jan. 7.

Feb. 26. Dorothea Leonora, daughter of Peter and Elizabeth Sergeant, *Bookeeper*, lodger at Mr. Redd, Tinplate Worker, of St. M. W. C.

Mar. 8. John, son of Mr. John and Rachell Moore, *Apothecarry.*

Mar 8. Lidia, daughter of Mr. George and Dorothy Reid, *Bancker*, born Feb. 27.

Mar. 21. Was borne, Robert, the son of Samuel Trefusis, *Esquire*, and Alice his wife, living with The Right Hon. Sir Robert Cotton, Knight, one of the Commissioners of Her Majesties Post Office Generall, and was baptized the first day of April following, by the Right Rev. Father in God Sir Jonathan Trelawney, Knight and Bishop of Winchester, by the permission and assistance of Mr. Samuel Angier, Rector.

1708

April 2. Mary, taken up at Mr. Broomfield's doore.

April 15. George, son of Mr. George and Mary Hawkins, of St. M. W. C., *Perriwigmaker*, born April 7.

May 17. Maynard and Alice, female twins of Mr. William and Alice Spencer, of St. M. W. C., *Victualer*, born May 16.

May 25. Robert, son of Mr. Bryan and Hannah Robinson, of St. M. W. C., *Turner*, born May 14.

May 25. Michael, son of Michael and Mary Kent, of St. M. W. C., *Basketmaker*, born May 24.

June 7. Anne, daughter of John and Anne Cheltenham, *Joyner*, lodgers with Jane Brown, Daryhouse, born June 7.

July 4. Timothy, son of Mr. Timothy and Mary Rutter, of St. M. W. C., *Upholder*, born June 31.

Oct. 24. Elizabeth, daughter of Robert and Jane Hurst, *Barber*, in one part of Mr. Bowles house in Lombard Street, born Oct. 8.

Nov. 1. Pegge, daughter of Stephen and Pegge Child, partner with Mr. Benjamin Tudman, of this parish, *Banker*, born Oct. 27.

Nov. 16. Thomas, son of Mr. Thomas and Margaret Bromfield, *Drugster*, born Nov. 12.

Dec. 25. Jeremiah Hilton, son of Samuel and Mary Keynton, in Stock Market, born Dec. 22.

Jan. 4. Was born Edward, son of Richard and Philadelphia Nelthorp, a *Banker*, in Exchange Alley.

Jan. 24. —— [sic] daughter of Richard and Susanna Gilbert, *Norwich Merchant*, born Jan. 24.

Jan. 25.	Was born Charles, son of John Evelyn, *Esquire, Postmaster General* and Ann his wife.
Jan. 26.	Was born Anne, daughter of Richard and Anne Cock, *Linnendraper* in Stock Market.
Mar. 4.	Peter, son of Peter and Elizabeth Buck, lodger at Mr. Wyns in Stock Market, born March 3.

1709

May 20.	Michael, son of Michael and Mary Kent in Stock Market, born May 13.
Aug. 28.	Elizabeth, daughter of William and Anne Lawes, *Instrument Maker*, born Aug. 14.
Sep. 30.	Elizabeth, daughter of Robert and Elizabeth Lowthe, *Coffeeman* in Exchange Alley, born Sep. 17.
Nov. 24.	Anne, daughter of William and Mary Byrch, *Druggist* in Little Lombard Street, born Nov. 18.
Nov. 21.	Jane, daughter of John and Elizabeth Blinkhorne in Stock Market, born Nov. 14.
Dec. 11.	Richard, son of John and Sarah Best, *Instrument Maker* in Little Lombard Street, born Dec. 8.
Dec. 10.	Was born Katherine, daughter of Timothy and Sarah Rutter, *Upholsterer* in Cornhill.
Jan. 10.	Joseph, son of Joseph and Elinor Fielder, *Poulterer* in Stock Market, born Jan. 8.
Feb. 16.	Phillip, son of William and Isabella Frowde, *Chandler*, born Feb. 8.

1710

April 24.	Judith, daughter of Richard and Cock, *Linnendraper* in Stock Market, born March 26.
June 8.	William, son of Peter and Elizabeth Buck, lodger at Mr. Wynn, Stock Market, born June 4.
Sep. 12.	John, son of Charles and Anne Shales, *Goldsmith* in Lombard street, born Sep. 1.
Sep. 11.	Katherine, daughter of Samuel and Mary Keynton, in Stock Market, *Norwich Factor*, born Sep. 11.
Sep. 30.	Anne, daughter of John Evelyn, *Esq., Commissioner of the Post Office*, and Anne his wife, born Sep. 18.
Dec. 8.	———— [*sic*] of John Alcroft, *Cutler*, born Dec. 5.
Dec. 10.	Henrietta Maria, daughter of George Tiler, *Watchmaker*, in Popes Head Alley, born Dec. 6.
Dec. 12.	James, son of William and Anne Browne, *Merchant* in Lombard Street, born Dec. 6.
Dec. 14.	Charles, son of Robert and Mary Abbot, *Barber in* Bucklersbury, born Dec. 4.
Dec. 12.	Mary, daughter of Richard and Philadelphia Nelthorp, *Goldsmith* in Exchange Alley, born Dec. 8.
Jan. 12.	Joseph, son of Joseph and Eliner Fielder, *Poulterer*, Bearbinder Lane, born Jan. 6.
Jan. 21.	Ann, daughter of ————[*sic*] and Frances Rogers, at the Fountaine Taverne in Stocks Market, born Jan. 21.
Feb. 2.	Christian, daughter of John and Christian Harrison, *Shoemaker*, under the Globe Alehouse, in Stocks Market, born Jan. 23.

Feb. 21.   Charles, son of Walter and Sarah Robotham, *Cutler* in Pope's-head Alley, born Feb. 9.

May 7.   William, son of William Hudson, *Razor Maker* in Lombard Street, born March 6.

Mar. 13.   Hester, daughter of Stephen and Elizabeth Geree, *Musician* at Mr. Abbot's in Bucklersbury, born Mar. 13.

Mar. 20.   Mary, daughter of Michael and Mary Kent, in Stocks Market, born Mar. 17.

1711

April 4.   Thomas, son of Robert Yeates, Mr. Penkethman's son-in-law, born Mar. 18.

April 30.   Theodosia, daughter of Robert Jones, at the Globe Alehouse in Stock Market, born April 16.

April 25.   William, son of William and Mary Byrch, *Drugist.*

April 8.   William, son of William and Anne Lawes, *Confectioner* in Lombard Streete, born April 8.

April 21.   Peter, son of Peter and Elizabeth Serjant, at Mr. Read in Walbrooke, borne April 16.

June 7.   Mary, daughter of Stephen and Pegge Child, *Goldsmith* in Lombard Street, born May 25.

June 12.   Thomas, son of Thomas and Ann Blaney, born June 11. [In margin.]

Aug. 3.   Frances, daughter of John and Hannah North, *Jeweller*, lodger at Mr Robert Hurst, in Lombard Street, born July 12.

Aug. 12.   Elizabeth, daughter of ———— [*sic*] and Elizabeth Simons, *Victualer* at the Crown in Exchange Alley, born Aug. 8.

Aug. 31.   Theophilus, son of William and Issabella Frowde, *Porter and Chandler* in part of Mr. Deard's house, born Aug. 5.

Sep. 19.   Esther, daughter of Richard and Esther Brookes, *Razor Maker* in part of Mr. Hurst's house, born Aug. 25

Sep. 21.   Cornelius, son of Michael and Jane Cheltenham, *Watchmaker*, born Sep. 20.

Oct. 7.   Lydia, daughter of James and Rebecka Willbraham, *Fruiterer* in Stocks Market, born Sep. 17.

Oct. 7.   Henry, son of John and Susannah Lloyd, *Linnendraper* in Stocks Market, born Oct. 4.

Oct. 14.   Mary, daughter of Bryan and Hannah Robinson, *Turner* in Bearbinder Lane, born Oct. 12.

Oct. 15.   Penelope, daughter of William and Penelope Eaton, *Linnendraper* in Stocks Market, born Sep. 29.

1712

May 27.   Thomas, son of Samuel and Sarah Gibson, born May 24.

Aug. 7.   At Mr. Nelthorps, Richard son of Richard and Mary Cordell, of Elford in Barkin Parish in Essex, born July 31.

Aug. 10.   Elizabeth, daughter of Peter and Elizabeth Buck, born Aug. 1.

Aug. 10.   James, son of Edmond and Mary Meekins, born Aug. 1.

Aug. 31.   Mary, daughter of John and Hannah North, born Aug. 10.

Aug. 20.   William, son of William and Mary Lawe.

Oct. 26.   Susannah, daughter of Thomas and Elizabeth Chadwell.

Oct. 28.	James, son of James and Rachell Alport.
Oct. 27.	Jane, daughter of Samuel and Mary Keynton.
Nov. 6.	Phillip, son of Thomas and Margaret Bromfield, born Oct. 22.
Nov. 2.	Christopher, son of John and Mary Blinkhorn.
Nov. 7.	Son of John Boddicot.
Nov. 16.	Elizabeth, daughter of James and Susannah Thomason, *Goldsmith.*
Nov. 9.	Frances, daughter of Thomas and Martha Menes.
Dec. 25.	John, son of William and Mary Collins, born Dec. 9.
Jan. 26.	John, son of John and Elizabeth Morris, born Jan. 9.
Feb. 21.	Elizabeth, daughter of William and Sarah Pennell, born Jan. 21.
Feb. 9.	Philladpher, daughter of Richard and Philladelpher Nelthorp, born Feb. 5.
Mar. 4.	Sarah, daughter of Walter and Sarah Robatham, born Mar. 2.

1713

Mar. 15.	Martha, daughter of John Aller, of Cutleris [*sic*]. [In margin in rather darker ink the word "try" or "qry."]
April 24.	William, son of William and Martha Webster, born April 13.
May 9.	Richard, son of Richard and Esther Brooke-Brooke [*sic*].
May 14.	Benjamin, son of Champion and Mary Brainfill, born May 11.
June 7.	John, son of Thomas and Elizabeth Robinson, born May 12.
June 14.	James (a Postumus) of James [blot] [Jame Jonk in margin] born June 10.
July 31.	Ann, daughter of Thomas and Mary Stretfield, born July 17.
July 30.	Susana, daughter of Stephen and Peggy Child, born July 19
Aug. 2.	George, son of Sir John Evelyn and Ann his lady, born July 25.
Aug. 9.	Sarah, daughter of Richard Guy, born Aug. 9.
Aug. 19.	Jonathan, son of Jonathan and Sarah Woodley.
Aug. 22.	Katherine, daughter of Timothy and Sarah his wife, born Aug. 22. [*sic*]
Sep. 13.	Thomas, son of William and Mary Lawe.
Oct. 2.	Thomas, son of Thomas and Marth Mence.
Dec. 27.	Bridget, daughter of William and Mary Byrch.
Jan. 3.	John, son of John and Christian Harrison.
Jan. 29.	Elizabeth, daughter of John Herringe, of Uxbridge, at Mrs. Scotsons.
Dec. 27.	1713 [*sic*] was born and baptized John, son of Richard and Philadelphia Nelthrop.
Jan. 31.	Hannah, daughter of Bryan and Hannah Robinson.

1714

Mar. 24.	Charles, son of Charles and Mary Cabriere, born Mar. 7.
Mar. 7.	John, son of Peter and Elizabeth Buck, born Mar. 7.
Mar. 19.	Elizabeth, daughter of Daniell Austen.
Mar. 25.	Thomas, son of Andrew and Suzan North.

Mar. 28.	Anne, daughter of Thomas and Mary Catline, born Mar. 28.
May 18.	Robert, son of Robert and Mary Hayes.
June 6.	Anne, daughter of John and Anne Maylard, born May 16.
June 16.	Hugh, son of Hugh and Elizabeth Powle.
June 7.	Robert, son of Gersen
June 14.	———— [*sic*] daughter of Amos Hatton.
June 27.	Mary, daughter of Samuell and Mary Keynton, born June 27.
July 6.	John, son of Thomas Bromfield, born July 6.
July 28.	Ann, daughter of Thomas and Anne Chadwell, born July 22.
Oct. 3.	Martha, daughter of Thomas and Elizabeth Falkingham, born Oct. 1.
Nov. 3.	Sarah, daughter of Samuell and Sarah Gibson, born Oct. 28.
Nov. 2.	John, son of John Herring, born Nov. 2.
Nov. 4.	George, son of Richard Brookes, born Oct. 8.
Jan. 27.	Dickson or Dixon [*sic*] son of Walter and Sarah Robsthorn, born Jan. 16.
Mar. 1.	Robert and Thomas, twins, and sons of William and Mary Collins, born Feb. 28.

1716

Aug. 7.	William, son of William and Laura Martin, born Aug. 5.
Jan. 2.	John, son of John and Mary Dingley, born Dec. 30.
Jan. 24.	Mary, daughter of Nathaniel and Bilhiah Brassey, born Jan. 24.

* 1718

Aug. 12.	Mary, daughter of Thomas and Ann Potter, born July 30.
Oct. 16.	Rebecca, daughter of Charles Cabriere, born Oct. 5.
Oct. 24.	Was born, Elizabeth, daughter of Samuell and Sarah Russell.

1720 [*sic* ‡ *probably a mistake for* 1721.]

Jan. 6.	Was born, John, son of Samuell and Sarah Gibson. [In margin.]
April 28.	Susannah, daughter of William and Rebecca Stephens, born April 16.
May 1.	John and Samuell, sons and twins of Samuel and Mary Keynton, born April 30.
May 13.	John, son of Champion and Mary Branfill, born May 13.
May 18.	Mary, daughter of Robert and Elizabeth Berney, born May 18.
May 26.	Elizabeth, daughter of George Dawson, born May 7.
June 12.	Nehemiah, son of William and Ann Davis, born June 6.
July 24.	John, son of John and Mary Jackson, born July 16.
Aug. 7.	Roger and Sarah, twins of John and Elizabeth Middleton, born Aug. 6.

1721 [*sic*]

Aug. 18.	William, son of William and Mary Watkins, born Aug. 2.
Aug. 18.	Dorothy, daughter of Walter and Sarah Robotham, born Aug. 10.

* 1717 is crossed out.   ‡ In a different and much better hand.

Aug. 31.	William, son of William Stevenson, born Aug. 4.
Sep. 20.	William, son of Robert and Elizabeth Berney, born Sep. 20.
Sep. 21.	Michaell, son of Michael and Jane Cheltenham.
Dec. 7.	Ann, daughter of James Tomlins, born Nov. 30.

1722

Mar. 27.	Mary, daughter of John and Mary Martendall, born Mar. 1.
April 28.	John, son of John Kidgell.
July 14.	Mary Wind.
Oct. 30.	Sarah, daughter of William and Rebecca Stephens, born Oct. 17.
Nov. 11.	Easter, daughter of John and Rebecca Holden, born Oct. 24.
Nov. 6.	Catherine, daughter of John and Susannah Bodicoat, born Oct. 17.
Nov. 25.	Elizabeth, daughter of Robert and Elizabeth Berney, born Nov. 18.
Dec. 10.	Isabella, daughter of William and Ann Davis, born Dec. 4.
Jan. 9.	William, son of Jonathan and Sarah Woodley.
Jan. 20.	Sarah, daughter of John and Sarah Wood.

1723

May 9.	Sarah, daughter of John and Elizabeth Vesey, born April 30.
June 23.	James, son of James and Susanna Thomason, born June 1.
July 6.	John, son of John and Elizabeth Nash, born June 27.
July 10.	Mary, daughter of Samuell and Mary Kenton, born July 10.
July 25.	Samuell, the posthumous son of the late William Watkins, deceased, and Mary his widdow, born July 23.
July 31.	Samuell, son of Champion and Mary Branfield, born July 27.
Sep. 5.	Rebecka, daughter of Ralph and Elizabeth Willson, born Aug. 17.
Sep. 29.	Jame, son of James and Elizabeth Anderton, born Sep. 18.
Oct. 20.	Thomas, son of Thomas and Sarah Pulkinhorn, born Oct. 14.
Nov. 3.	Mary, daughter of Walter and Sarah Robotham
Nov. 17.	William, son of William and Sarah Wrag.
Dec. 20.	Catherine, daughter of Joh and Susan Boddicote, born Nov. 24.
Dec. 30.	Thomas, son of John and Mary Rowley, born Dec. 22.
Jan. 12.	Mary, daughter of Richard and Mary Manwaring, born Dec. 26.
Jan. 26.	Ann, daughter of Robert and Elizabeth Berney, born Jan. 6.
Jan. 29.	Sarah, daughter of Thomas and Rebecca Stephens.

1724

July 7.	Charlott, daughter of Champion and Mary Branfield, born June 20.
Aug. 23.	Benjamins, son of Thomas and Ann Blany, born Aug. 14.
Oct. 16.	Samuell, son of Samuell and Mary Kenton, born Oct. 16.

Sep. 24.	John, son of John and Amey Borowes, born Oct. 24.
Dec. 14.	William, son of John Kidgell, born Dec. 4.
Dec. 14.	Mary, daughter of William and Elizabeth Kirby, born Nov. 20.
Dec. 20.	Catherine, daughter of Richard and Catherine Dickerson, born Dec. 8.
Jan. 3.	Ann, daughter of Thomas and Sarah Wrag, born Dec. 26.
Jan. 6.	William, son of Daniel and Elizabeth Austin, born Dec. 26.
Jan. 8.	Elizabeth, daughter of Thomas and Elizabeth Boulton.
Jan. 25.	Ann, daughter of Walter and Sarah Robotham, born Jan. 9.
Feb. 25.	Joseph, son of Thomas and Sarah Pulckinhorn, born Feb. 15.
Mar. 19.	Mary, daughter of William and Mary Treagose, born Mar. 7.

1725

April 12.	Elizabeth, daughter of Ralph and Elizabeth Willson, born Mar. 22.
April 25.	Charles, son of William and Ann Davis, born April 20.
May 9.	Jane, daughter of Robert and Elizabeth Berney, born April 15.
May 5.	Richard, son of John and Elizabeth Nash, born April 18.
Aug. 11.	Thomas, son of Jonathan and Elizabeth Woodley, born Aug. 11.
Aug. 24.	Mary, daughter of Samuell Roode, born Aug. 24.
Sep. 15.	Catherine, daughter of William and Rebecka Stephens, born Aug. 28.
Oct. 10.	Catherine, daughter of John and Mary Vesey, born Sep. 29.
Nov. 7.	Mary, daughter of John and Sarah Wood, born Nov. 4.
Nov. 26.	Benjamins, son of Champion and Mary Branfield, born Nov. 23.
Nov. 26.	Raby, son of Lewes and Bridget Williams, born Oct. 28.
Dec. 15.	Martha, daughter of Peter and Elizabeth Griffis, born Dec. 4.
Dec. 12.	Thomas, son of Thomas and Sarah Wrag, born Dec. 1.
Jan. 17.	George Coper, born Jan. 11.
Feb. 27.	John, son of John Stanton, born Feb. 11.
Mar. 12.	George, son of John and Amy Barrows, born Mar. 2.

1726

June 2.	Henry, son of Henry and Sarah Wittridge, born May 24.
April 8.	John, son of Thomas and Sarah Pulkinhorn, born April 7.
June 7.	John, son of Samuel and Mary Kenton, born June 6.
June 18.	John Posthumus, son of the late John Nash and Elizabeth his widdow, born June 13.
July 3.	Mary, daughter of James and Ursula Eldridge, in Exchange Alley, born June 15.
Aug. 15.	Robert, son of Robert and Elizabeth Berney, born July 23.
Aug. 16.	Elizabeth, daughter of Jeremah and Mercy Garrard, born July 23.
Aug. 17.	Samuell, son of Richard and Mary Manwaring, born July 31.
Aug. 31.	Gulielma, daughter of John and Mary Lefebure, born Aug. 13.
Sep. 14.	Joseph, son of Joseph and Ann Barrow, born Sep. 12.

Oct. 9.	Mary, daughter of Franses and Lucy Thomkins, born Oct. 6.
Oct. 18.	Mary Posthumus, daughter of the late Daniell Bankes and Mary his widdow, born Sep. 28.
Oct. 20.	John, son of Anthony and Catherine Peek, born Oct. 3.
Nov. 16.	Richard, son of William and Ann Turner, born Nov. 9.
Nov. 28.	Edward, son of Edward and Ann Wallington, born Nov. 21.
Nov. 29.	John, son of John and Mary Martindale, born Nov. 1.
Mar. 6.	Ester, daughter of Richard and Catherine Dickerson, born Mar. 5.
Mar. 23.	Ann, the Posthumus daughter of the late Phillip Boys and Mary his widdow, born Mar. 6.

1727

May 15.	John, son of Ralph and Elizabeth Wilson, born April 26.
June 6.	Rebecka, daughter of John and Mary Rowley, born May 25.
June 11.	Jesmond, son of Richard and Margrett Davis, born June 1.
June 19.	Elisabeth, daughter of John and Sarah Bowen, born June 13.
June 28.	John, son of Thomas and Alice Ayscough, born June 26.

End of Christenings in the 3rd Volume of the Registers.

[Vol. iiij.]

THE Names of such as have been Christened in the united Parishes of St. Mary Woolnoth and St. Mary Woolchurch-Haw, London, since the 29th of July, Anno Domini 1727.

SAMUELL ANGIER, *Rector.*

JOSEPH LOWE, } *Churchwardens of*
WILLIAM LAWE, } *St. Mary Woolnoth.*

CHRISTOPHER FOWLER, } *Churchwardens of St.*
RICHARD MAINWARING, } *Mary Woolchurch-Haw.*

1727

July 31.	William, son of Daniell and Mary Andrews, born July 31. S. M. W. N. *
Sep. 17.	Millesent, posthumus daughter of the late Jeremiah Garrad and Mary his widdow, born Aug. 19. S. M. W. N.
Sep. 24.	Elizabeth, daughter of William and Rebecca Stevens, born Sep. 6. S. M. W. N.
Oct. 15.	Sarah, daughter of Thomas and Sarah Wragg, born Sep. 22. S. M. W. C.
Nov. 21.	Patience, daughter of Benjamin and Elizabeth Ash, born Nov. 7.

* In this, and some other cases, the Initials are given in the original in the outside margin.

Nov. 26.	Susanna, daughter of Jonathan and Elizabeth Woodley, born Nov. 22.
Dec. 6.	Lavinia, daughter of William and Elizabeth Kerby, born Nov. 10.
Dec. 11.	Mary, daughter of Edward and Ann Wallington, lodging at John Woods, inhabitant of St. Mary Woolchurch Hawe, born Nov. 27.
Dec. 24.	Elizabeth, daughter of John and Hannah Tyson, born Dec. 23.
Jan. 8.	Anne, daughter of William and Anne Davis, born Dec. 27.
Feb. 11.	John, son of John and Elleanor Justin, born Feb. 11.
Feb. 15.	Sarah, daughter of John and Ellianor Vaughan, born Jan. 28.
Mar. 18.	Anne, daughter of Thomas and Anne Blaney, born Feb. 29.

1728

April 1.	Joseph, son of Edward and Elizabeth Hughes, born Mar. 10.
May 2.	Thomas, son of Thomas and Sarah Saunders, a pensioner of St. Mary Woolchurch parish.
May 23.	Nathaniell, son of John and Elizabeth Edwards, born May 4. The first baptized in the new Font.
May 30.	George, son of John and Amy Burrows, born May 8. S. M. W. C.
June 21.	Joseph, son of Richard and Catherine Dickerson, born June 21.
June 26.	Elizabeth, daughter of John and Sarah Wood, born June 20. S. M. W. C.
Aug. 18.	Hannah, daughter of Ralph and Elizabeth Willson, born July 27. S. M. W. C.
Aug. 23.	Isaac, son of James and Ann Tomlyns, born July 31. S. M. W. C.
Sep. 10.	Katherine, daughter of Anthony and Katherine Peek, born Sep. 4. S. M. W. N.
Sep. 22.	Elisabeth, daughter of Thomas and Martha Welsted, (lodger at Mr. Scotsons) born Sep. 7. S. M. W. C.
Sep. 29.	Morris, son of Thomas and Elizabeth Starkey, born Sep. 5. S. M. W. N.
Oct. 2.	Elisabeth, daughter of Daniell and Mary Andrews, born Oct. 30. S. M. W. N.
Oct. 8.	Elisabeth, daughter of Hatch and Mary Underwood, born Oct. 12. S. M. W. C.
Oct. 27.	James, son of John and Elizabeth Jaques, born Oct. 21. S. M. W. N.
Nov. 6.	Story, son of Benjamin and Elizabeth Ash, born Nov. 5. S. M. W. N.
Nov. 12.	Mary Woolnoth, a foundling supposed to be 6 months old.
Feb. 20.	Anne, daughter of Edward and Anne Hasted, born Feb. 6. S. M. W. N.
Mar. 9.	Anne, daughter of William and Margaret Searle, born Feb. 15. S. M. W. N.
Mar. 8.	Joseph, son of Thomas and Sarah Wrag, born Mar. 8. S. M. W. C.
Mar. 10.	Anne, daughter of John and Mary Martindale, born Feb 2. S. M. W. N.

1729

April 10. Elizabeth Margret, daughter of John and Diana Davies, at the George in Stock Market.

April 11. Mary, a female child taken up at Mr. Lefebure's doore.

April The 23 of last month was born Thomas, the son of Thomas Glegg *(Banker)* and Jane his wife, and was baptized privately the 24th, and received into the Church this 15th day of this month, April.

June 20. Charlotte, daughter of William and Rebecca Stevens, born June 15.

Aug. 4. Elizabeth, daughter of Richard and Katherine Dickerson, born Aug. 4.

Aug. 29. Henry, son of Thomas and Elizabeth Hilton, born Aug. 24.

Sep. 2. Thomas, son of James and Ann Tomlyn, born Aug. 10.

Sep. 9. Elizabeth, daughter of Peter and Elizabeth Budge, born Aug. 17.

Sep. 17. Mary, daughter of John and Ann Burrows, born Aug. 24.

Sep. 24. Peter, son of Peter and Mary Martin, born Sep. 17.

Oct. 8. Susanna, daughter of John and Mary Lefebure, born Sep. 17.

Nov. 28. Mathew, son of Mathew and Elizabeth Read, born Oct. 4.

Dec. 2. Elizabeth, daughter of John and Elizabeth Edwards, born Nov. 19.

Dec. 15. Anthony, son of Thomas and Sarah Pulkinhorn, born Nov. 11. S. M. W. C.

Jan. 13. Thomas, son of Daniel and Mary Andrews, born Dec. 18. S. M. W. N.

Feb. 11. Thomas Watson, of the parish of St. Mary Woolchurch, Mr. Blancy and his son, godfathers.

Feb. 27. Mary, daughter of Richard and Anne Caswell, born Feb. 8. S. M. W. N.

Mar. 1. Thomas, son of William and Anne Davis, born Feb. 19. S. M. W. N.

1730

May 18. Eliza Maria, daughter of Robert and Mary Evans, born April 26. S. M, W. N.

May 22. Elizabeth, daughter of Benjamin and Elizabeth Ash, born May 20. S. M. W. N.

June 7. Charles, son of Richard and Mary Maddockes, born May 18. S. M. W. C.

July 21. Mary, daughter of Thomas and Rebecca Price, born July 2.

Aug. 23. John, son of John and Frances Thompson, born July 25. S. M. W. N.

Sep. 3. William, son of John and Elizabeth Jaques, born Aug. 11. S. M. W. N.

Sep. 20. Robert, son of Peter and Mary Martin, born Sep. 15.

Oct. 16. Susan, daughter of Richard and Mary Elmes, born Sep. 24.

Oct. 21. John, son of John and Mary Lefebure, born Sep. 30.

Oct. 29. Katherine, daughter of Robinson and Sarah Knight, born Oct. 13.

Nov. 8. William, son of William and Mary Searle, born Oct. 18. S. M. W. N.

Nov. 13.   Elizabeth, daughter of Thomas and Mary Beech, born
        Nov. 11.   S. M. W. C.

Dec. 4.   Amy, daughter of John and Amy Burrows, born Nov. 17.
        S. M. W. N.

Nov. 8.   Was borne Edward, the son of Thomas Clegg and Jane
        his wife, and was baptized the 9th day of the same,
        and received into the Church the thirtieth day.

Dec. 10.   John, son of John and Elizabeth Edwards, born Dec. 8.

Jan. 1.   Henry, son of William and Mary St. Leger, born Dec. 4.

Jan. 8.   Joseph, son of Edward and Anne Hasted (of Dove Court,
        in Lombard Street), *Gent.*, born Dec. 19, at half an
        hour past 12 this morning.

Jan. 10.   Joseph, son of James and Anne Tomlyns, born Jan. 1.

Jan. 13.   Susanna Maria, daughter of Isaac Lewes Giborne and
        Catherine his wife, born Jan. 1.

Feb. 28.   Mary Longbridge, aged 22 years, was baptized.

Mar. 11.   John, son of Peter and Elizabeth Budge, born Feb. 15.

Mar. 7.   A foundling male child, named Moses.

1731

April 16.   Lydia, daughter of William and Mary Bache, born Mar. 19.

April 25.   Jenny, daughter of John and Sarah Wood, born Mar. 31.

April 3.   John, son of William and Barbara Hawkins, born April 2.

June 6.   Ambrose, son of William and Mary Sparrow, born May 23.

July 8.   Judith, daughter of Richard and Judith Mainwaring,
        born July 4.   S. M. W. C.

Aug. 29.   William, son of William and Rebecca Stevens, born
        Aug. 27.   S. M. W. N.

Oct. 24.   Anne, daughter of Benjamin and Hannah Wilding, born
        Sep. 29.

Oct. 31.   Richard, son of John and Francis Thompson, born Oct. 9.

Nov. 7.   David, son of John and Rebeccah Carmichael, born
        Oct. 30.

Nov. 21.   William, son of William and Mary Searle, born Nov. 9.

Nov. 30.   Major, son of Major and Anne Smith, born Nov. 11.

Dec. 3.   Joseph, son of Ralph and Elizabeth Wilson, born Nov. 15.

Dec. 16.   Elizabeth, daughter of John and Amy Borrows, born
        Dec. 5.

Jan. 12.   Martha, daughter of Thomas and Rebecca Price, born
        Dec. 26.

Feb. 5.   Peter, son of Michael and Abigail Cheltenham, born
        Jan. 23.

Feb. 6.   Hewer Elisabeth, daughter of David and Elisabeth Den-
        nison, born Jan. 20.

Mar. 13.   Peter, son of Peter and Elizabeth Budge, born Feb. 27.

1732

May 9.   Cordelia, daughter of Isaac and Catherine Giborne, born
        April 9.   S. M. W. C.

June 8.   Mary, daughter of Mathew and Elizabeth Read, born
        May 21.   S. M. W. C.

July 16.   Sarah, daughter of Samuel and Anne Walker, *Fishmonger*,
        born June 26.   S. M. W. C.

July 20.   Sarah, daughter of John and Elizabeth Jaques, born
        July 19.   S. M. W. N.

Aug. 27.   Thomas, son of William and Mary St. Leger, born Aug. 2.
Sep. 10.   Anne, daughter of Thomas and Mary Beach, born Aug. 31.
Sep. 21.   Mary, daughter of Edward and Sarah Neale, born Sep. 14.

1733

July 27.   John Godfrey, son of John and Mary Dand, born July 26.
Aug. 21.   Thomas, son of Thomas and Mary Geary, born Aug. 7.
Sep. 16.   Benjamin, son of Benjamin and Hannah Wilding, born Aug. 22.

> [The next page is blank, save that on the top of it in very bad writing, is the following :—]
>
> Mem The Follow Affidavit was made to testify the age of Michael Kent.
>
> Sarah, the mother of Michael Kent, maketh oath that he was born on the 17 February, 173¾ in the Parish of St. Mary Woolchurch. Hannah Tyler maketh oath he was baptized the 10 of March following at the Parish Church of St. Mary Woolnoth and St. Mary Woolchurch, she standing godmother for the said Michael Kent.

Sworn the 29 *May* 1744, } *By* SARAH KENT,
before WALTER BERNARD, } HANNAH TYLER.

1734

Mar. 24.   Hannah, daughter of Thomas and Frances Raynolds, born March 2.
Mar. 21.   Ester, daughter of Robinson and Sarah Knight, born Mar. 3.
July 16.   Charles, son of Peter and Elizabeth Budge, born June 24.

1735

June 21.   Susana, daughter of Timothy and Susana Cook, *Poulterer*, born May 21.
June 10.   John, son of Joseph and Elizabeth Browne, born June 1.
July 21.   Robert, son of Robert Evans, born July 3.
Aug. 30.   Hannah, daughter of John and Grace Mould, born Aug. 16.
Oct. 12.   Elizabeth, daughter of Benjamin and Ruth Jackson.
Nov. 14.   ——— [*sic*] son of Peter and Elizabeth Budge, born Oct. 17.
Jan. 14.   John, son of John and Martha Heaton, born Jan. 3.
Jan. 16.   Mary, daughter of Benjamen and Hannah Wilding, born Dec. 25.
Jan. 31.   John, son of John and Sarah Cotterell, born Jan. 21.
Feb. 22.   Margret, daughter of John and Mary Croome, born Feb. 9.
Mar. 14.   Samuell, son of Castle and Rebecka Thorpe, born Feb. 27.

1736

April 11.   Ann, daughter of John and Mary Vaughan, born Mar. 28.
June 12.   Catherine, daughter of Timothy and Susana Cook, born May 25.
June 6.   George, son of Robert and Anna Thompson, born May 18.

Aug. 29.	Mary, daughter of Zachary and Mary Grove, born Aug. 3.
May 14.	1735 [*sic*] George, son of Thomas and Mary Geary, born May 2.
Aug. 12.	Elizabeth, daughter of Thomas and Hester Chesley.
Sep. 3.	David, son of David and Elizabeth Dennison, born Aug. 27.
Nov. 4.	Elizabeth, daughter of Peter and Elizabeth Budge, born Oct. 9.
Nov. 11.	William, son of William and Susanna Pepys, born Oct. 10.
Mar. 3.	Elizabeth, daughter of Edward and Sarah Neale, born Feb. 18.
	Anne, daughter of Benjamin Wilding and Hannah his wife, was privately baptized, and was received into the Church according to the form appointed, Jan. 23; born Dec. 30 before.
Jan. 23.	Thomas, son of John and Mary Dand, born Jan. 1.

1737

April 4.	George, son of Benjamin and Hannah Wilding, born March 16 [*sic*].
	[The next page of the register has no entries on it.]
May 15.	William, son of Thomas and Martha Jackson.
May 21.	Thamizin, posthumus daughter of the late Nathaniell Lancaster, *Barber*, and Thamizin, his wife, born May 18.
June 28.	Christopher, son of James and Jane Weston, born June 14.
Sep. 5.	Hester, daughter of Thomas and Hester Chesley, born Aug. 2.
Aug. 31.	Ann, daughter of Thomas and Mary Minors, born Aug. 7.
Sep. 20.	Elizabeth, daughter of William and Elizabeth Cook, *Blacksmith.*
Oct. 2.	Castle, son of Castle and Rebecca Thorp, born Oct. 1.
Dec. 18.	Catherine, daughter of Peter and Elizabeth Budg, born Nov. 26.
Dec. 13.	George, son of Edmund and Barbara Newland, born Nov. 30.
Dec. 5.	William, son of John and Ellinor Justin, born Dec. 5.
Jan. 2.	Ann, daughter of Stephen Anthony and Agness English, born Dec. 11.
Jan. 22.	Sarah, daughter of Timothy and Susanna Cook, born Dec. 23.
Feb. 4.	Elizabeth, daughter of Robert and Anna Thompson, a lodger at Mr. Hasle.
Feb. 14.	Joseph, son of Joseph and Hermon Blandford.
Mar. 20.	Susanna, daughter of Castle and Rebecca Thorp, born Mar. 18.

1738

April 13.	Mary, daughter of John and Rachell Burghall.
April 28.	John, son of John and Rebecka Knight, born April 14.
June 4.	William, son of Christopher and Hannah Rose, born May 13.
Aug. 31.	John, son of John and Mary Croom, born Aug. 7.

Oct. 13.   Elizabeth, daughter of Samuel and Hannah Haynes, born Oct. 4.

Nov. 4.   Richard, son of John and Martha Heaton, born Oct. 21.

Jan. 12.   Elizabeth, daughter of Joseph and Elizabeth Brown, born Jan. 12.

Jan. 12, and admitted Feb. 14 following, Mary, daughter of John and Sarah Best, born Jan. 12.

1739

April 29.   Mary, daughter of John and Mary Hasell, born April 6.

June 1.   Thomas, son of Timothy and Susanna Cooke, born May 7.

June 11.   Mary, daughter of William and Elizabeth Cook, *Blacksmith*, born June 1.

July 15.   Maria, daughter of Christopher and Hannah Rose, born June 23.

Sep. 2.   Jane, daughter of Robert and Mary Cope, born Aug. 15.

Sep. 13.   Henreta, daughter of John and Rebecca Knight.

Oct. 7.   Ann, daughter of Richard and Mary Stone, born Sep. 26.

Nov. 1.   Joseph, son of Ralph and Elizabeth Willson, *Drugest*, born Oct. 11.

Dec. 14.   Thomas, son of Peter and Elizabeth Budg, born Nov. 16.

Jan. 24.   John, son of John and Martha Heaton, born Jan. 4.

Feb. 27.   Catherine, daughter of Robinson and Sarah Knight, born Feb. 4.

1740

April 3.   Susannah, daughter of Job and Susannah Archer, born April 3.

April 10.   Jane, daughter of William and Maria Martin, born Mar. 15.

April 17.   Rachel, daughter of John and Rachel Burghall, born April 3.

May 18.   Edmund Bick, son of Edward and Elizabeth Wallington, born May 2.

June 10.   John, son of Robert and Mary Garrard.

July 17.   Ann, daughter of Joseph and Alice Lee, born July 3.

Aug. 3.   John, son of Castle and Rebecca Thorp, born July 30.

Aug. 19.   Sarah, daughter of Robert and Elizabeth Collings, born Aug. 4.

Aug. 31.   Anthony Bartholomew, son of Stephen Anthony and Agness English.

Oct. 12.   William, son of William and Elizabeth Baker, *Stationer*, born Sep. 21.

Nov. 19.   Ann, daughter of William and Elizabeth Cook, *Blacksmith*.

1741

May 15.   John, son of Francis Hasking Eyles Stiles and Sibilla, his wife, born April 16.

[After the above the following is inserted in small writing :—]

The 20 day of June was born, Elizabeth, daughter of John Best and Sarah his wife, and was baptized the same day. Witness my hand, JOHN BEST.

July 2.   Andrew, son of Richard and Mary Stone, born July 1.

July 21.   Timothy, son of Timothy and Susanna Cooke.

Aug. 9.   William, son of John and Sarah Cotterell.

Aug. 23.	William, son of William and Sarah Webster, born Aug. 15.
Sep. 20.	John, son of Jeremiah and Catherine Thompson, born Sep. 7.
Sep. 24.	Thomas, son of Peter and Elizabeth Budge, born Sep. 12.
Oct. 2.	Sarah Horton, daughter of Griffith Loyd.
Oct. 18.	Ann, daughter of Benjamin and Elizabeth Badilly, born Oct. 15.
Dec. 20.	Hannah, daughter of Benjamin and Hannah Wilding, born Dec. 15.
Dec. 26.	William, son of William and Elizabeth Cook, *Blacksmith.*
Jan. 24.	Ann, daughter of Robert and Ann Cager, jun. born Jan. 22.
Feb. 11.	Mary Margrett, daughter of John and Margrett Harris, born Jan. 9.

1742

April 27.	Ann, daughter of Ralph and Elizabeth Willson, born April 11.
April 13,	was born Elizabeth, daughter of Joseph Brooke, *Esquire*, of Rochester, in Kent, and Elizabeth his wife, and was baptized the same day privately, and was received into the Church according to form appointed, May 10 following.
May 21.	George, son of William and Elizabeth Baker, *Stationer*, born May 16.
June 6.	Charlotte, daughter of Robert and Anna Thompson, born May 11.
June 8.	Lucas, son of William and Hannah Pepys, born May 24.
July 20.	Elizabeth, daughter of Richard and Mary Stone, born July 11.
Sep. 26.	John, son of John and Jane Wakefield, born Sep. 9.
Oct. 31.	Castle, son of Castle and Rebecka Thorp, born Oct. 28.
Nov. 10.	Sasanna, daughter of Timothy and Susanna Cooke, born Oct. 22.
Jan. 16.	Margaret, daughter of Joseph and Elizabeth Brown, born Dec. 31.
Feb. 2.	Mary, daughter of Joseph and Elizabeth Wilson, *Coffeeman*, born Feb. 22.
Mar. 15.	Mary, daughter of Francis and Frances Griesdale, born Feb. 15.
Mar. 27.	Charles, son of John and Sarah Cotterell, born Mar. 14.

1743

June 21.	Benjamin, son of Benjamin and Elizabeth Baddily, born June 12.
June 22.	Timothy, a male child, was dropt in St. Mary Woolchurch.
July 4.	Anna Maria, daughter of Edward and Margaret Ann Grace Highmoor, born June 12.
July 20.	Elizabeth, daughter of Edward and Elizabeth Philpot, born June 24.
Sep. 19.	Rebecca, daughter of Richard and Mather Baker, *Coffeeman*, born Aug. 24.
Oct. 2.	Richard, son of Benjamin and Hannah Wilding, born Sep. 21.
Oct. 26.	Sarah, daughter of Richard and Mary Stone, born Oct. 22.

Oct. 28.	Henry, son of Timothy and Susanna Cook, born Oct. 13.
Nov. 2.	William, son of William and Elizabeth Baker, *Stationer*, born Oct. 22, baptized privately, and died Nov. 4.
Nov. 21.	George, son of Robert and Anna Thompson, born Oct. 25.
Jan. 12.	William, son of William and Sarah Noyes, born Dec. 31.
Jan. 27.	Richard, son of Richard and Elizabeth Woodruff, born Jan. 5.
Feb. 29.	Richard, son of William and Sarah Webster, born Feb. 19.
Mar. 5,	was born Thomas, son of Thomas and Mary Davis, and was privately baptized Mar. 12, and died Mar. 13.
Mar. 18.	Sarah, daughter of John and Sarah Cotterell, born Mar. 2.

1744

June 20.	Peter, son of John and Amelia Langley, born June 16.
July 18.	Henry, son of William and Hannah Manning, born July 12.
July 31.	Edward, son of Edward and Elizabeth Philpot, born July 4.
Aug. 8.	Mary Woolnoth, a female child, was dropt neare at Mr. Keale's doore.
Oct. 30.	Frances, daughter of Francis and Frances Grisdell, born Oct. 28.
Nov. 14.	Samuel, son of William and Elizabeth Baker, born Nov. 8.

[*End of Christenings in Vol.* 4.]

[Vol. b.]

THE REGISTER of such Persons as have been Christened in the Parish of St. Mary Woolnoth, Lombard Street, London, and the United Parish of St. Mary Woolchurch Haw, since December the First, 1744. (One Thousand Seven Hundred Forty and Four.)

1744

Dec. 9.	Rebecca, daughter of Benjamin and Hannah Wilding, born Dec. 6.
Dec. 16.	Catherine, daughter of Jeremiah and Catherine Thompson, born Nov. 23.
Feb. 9.	John, son of John and Catherine Healy, lodger at Mr. Edwards, Silversmith, in the parish of St. Mary Woolnoth, born Feb. 1.
Mar. 10.	Benjamin, son of Robert and Elizabeth Prince, born Feb. 19.
Mar. 14.	George, son of Richard and Mary Stone, born Feb. 24.
Mar. 15.	James, son of Thomas and Elizabeth Hannah (a casualty child), born Feb. 19.
Mar. 24.	Ann, daughter of John and Sarah Cotterell, born Mar. 5.

1745

Aug. 17.   Miriam, daughter of Jacob and Elizabeth Marsh, born Aug. 17.

Sept. 19.   Elizabeth, daughter of Joseph and Elizabeth Alderson, born Aug. 27.

Dec. 8.   Mary, daughter of Thomas and Jane Wartring, born Nov. 17.

Dec. 12.   Thomas Tooley, son of Joseph and Hermon Blandford, born Dec. 2.

Dec. 15.   Joseph, son of Joseph and Elizabeth Wilson, born Dec. 1.

1746

April 6.   William, son of James and Mary Painter, born April 2.

April 15.   William, son of John and Frances Waring, born Mar. 23.

May 4.   Jane, daughter of John and Sarah Cotterell, born April 18.

May 23.   Frances, daughter of Richard and Mary Stone, born May 20.

May 27.   Jane, daughter of Richard and Mary Bridges, lodgers at Mr. Waring's, born May 12.

June 12.   Hannah, daughter of William and Hannah Manning, born June 1.

June 22.   William, son of Joseph and Ann Brown, born May 30.

July 11.   Joseph, son of Stephen and Sarah Wilson, born July 4.

Aug. 3.   John, son of William and Sarah Olifer, born July 21.

Sep. 19.   James, son of George and Mary Hodges, born Sep. 16.

Sep. 23.   Miriam, daughter of Jacob and Betty Marsh, born Sep. 4.

Nov. 4.   William, son of Samuell and Mary Chase, born Oct. 23.

Nov. 9.   Thomas, son of Timothy and Susannah Cooke, born Oct. 17.

Nov. 11.   Elizabeth, daughter of Michael and Judith Juckes, born Nov. 9.

[The above is entered on the opposite and otherwise blank page.]

Feb. 1.   John, son of John and Hannah Bently, born Jan. 11.

Feb. 25. received into the Church, Daniell Miles, son of William and Sarah Webster, born Jan. 10, baptized Jan. 20.

Mar. 16.   Samuel Robert, son of Edward and Margaret Ann Grace Highmoor, born Feb. 17.

Mar. 18.   Thomas Tooley, son of Joseph and Hermon Blandford, born Mar. 4.

1747

May 27.   Sarah and Dinah, twin daughters of Stephen and Sarah Willson, lodgers at Mr. Edwards, the Silversmith, born May 23.

June 4.   Elizabeth Ann, daughter of William and Elizabeth Baker, born May 21.

June 25.   Elizabeth, daughter of Joseph and Ann Brown, born June 3.

July 21.   Mary, daughter of Thomas and Mary Minors, born July 3.

Aug. 7.   Isaac Schomberg, *Student in Physic* of Trinity College, in Cambridge.

Aug. 11.   William, son of William and Elizabeth Philpot, born July 27.

Sep. 1.   Samuell, son of John and Frances Wareing, born Aug. 17.

Oct. 1.	Sarah, daughter of George and Mary Hodges, born Sep. 15.
Oct. 21.	Ann, daughter of Richard and Ann Barnard, born Oct. 3.
Nov. 20.	Mary, daughter of James and Susannah Reade, born Oct. 26.
Nov. 29.	John, son of John and Sarah Cotterell, born Nov. 6.
Dec. 27.	Samuell Egglestone, a foundling, born Dec. 1.
Dec. 27.	Elizabeth, daughter of John and Elizabeth Potter, born Dec. 17.
Jan. 15.	Susannah Powers, a child from the Workhouse, born Jan. 2.

[The above is entered on the opposite and otherwise blank page.]

Feb. 9.	Mary, daughter of John and Mary Town, lodgers at Mr. Pinhorn's, born Feb. 6.
Feb. 28.	William, son of Nicholas and Winifred Farnborough.
Mar. 16.	William, a foundling.

1748

May 18.	John, son of John and Mary Hodgson, lodgers in Bearbinder Lane, born April 28.
July 7.	Richard, son of Richard and Martha Baker, born July 2.
July 10.	Hannah, daughter of John and Hannah Bentley, born June 18.
Aug. 2.	Andrew, son of Richard and Mary Stone, born July —
Aug. 9.	Ann, daughter of Joseph and Ann Brown, born Aug. 9.
Oct. 19.	Lætitia, daughter of Thomas and Esther Chesley, born Oct. 12.
Oct. 27.	Elizabeth, daughter of Joseph and Hermon Blandford, born Oct. 18.
Nov. 4.	Sarah, daughter of Richard and Ann Barnard, born Oct. 18.
Nov. 27.	Frances, daughter of Charles and Mary Lilly, born Nov. 5.
Dec. 1.	John, son of George and Mary Hodges, born Nov. 18.
Dec. 11.	George, son of Robert and Elizabeth Prince, born Nov. 27.
Jan. 25.	Godfrey, son of William and Sarah Webster, born Jan. 3.
Feb. 13.	Mary, daughter of John and Elizabeth Webb, born Feb. 12.
Feb. 13.	Susanna, daughter of Mary Cornish, born Feb. 82.

1749

April 2.	John, son of William and Jane Best, born Mar. 29.
April 9.	Elizabeth, daughter of William and Matilda Collins, born Mar. 25.
May 18.	Joseph, son of John and Elizabeth Potter, born May 12.
July 13.	Elizabeth, daughter of John and Elizabeth Beecroft, *Bookseller*, Lombard Street, born July 20. s. m. w. n.
July 31.	Thomas, son of William and Mary Hornblower, of Little Lombard Street, born July 20. s. m. w. c.
Aug. 4.	Anne, daughter of Henry and Anne Jones, opposite the Mansion House, born Aug. 2. s. m. w. c.
Sep. 5.	Maria, daughter of William and Elizabeth Baker, the corner of the Post Office, Lombard Street, born Aug. 28. s. m. w. n.
Sep. 17.	Elizabeth, daughter of David and Elizabeth Thomas, in Sherborne Lane, born Aug. 27. s. m. w. n.
Sep. 27.	Thomas, son of Mary Cimilow by Thomas Holmes, gone to sea, was born in the Workhouse, Sep. 14.

Sep. 29.   William, son of Samuel and Catherine Wiseham, in Walbrook, born Aug. 30.

July 4.   John Lumbard, brought from the Workhouse. s. m. w. n.
[The above is entered at the bottom of the opposite and otherwise blank page, in a different hand.   After this the entries are made on both pages.]

Oct. 18.   Elizabeth, daughter of Mary Price, by John Bradbury, gone to sea, was born in the Workhouse, Oct. 14. s. m. w. n.

Oct. 22.   William, son of Benjamin and Hannah Wilding, in Pope's head Alley, born Oct. 9.   s. m. w. n.

Dec. 20.   Privately, John, son of John and Mary Griffiths, in Lombard Street, born Dec. 15.   s. m. w. n.

Dec. 21.   Thomas, son of Thomas and Martha Roberts, in Sherborne Lane, born Dec. 15.   s. m. w. n.

Jan. 7.   Thomas, son of Joseph and Eleanor Martin, in Lombard Street, born Dec. 12.   s. m. w. n.

Jan. 7.   Elizabeth, daughter of Timothy and Susannah Cook, in Walbrook, born Dec. 29.   s. m. w. c.

Jan. 18.   Daniel, son of William and Sarah Webster, in Change Alley, born Dec. 30.   s. m. w. n.

Jan. 29.   Joseph, son of Joseph and Herman Blandford, in Little Lombard Street, born Jan. 10.   s. m. w. c.

Feb. 26.   William Tolme, son of John and Hannah Bentley, near the Mansion House, born Feb. 22.   s. m. w. c.

Mar. 13.   John, son of John and Anne Bunn, in the the Workhouse, born Mar. 9.   s. m. w. n.

1750

Mar. 28.   Sarah, daughter of Joseph and Anne Brown, in Sherborne Lane, born Mar. 23.   s. m. w. n.

Mar. 30.   Elizabeth, the wife [*sic*] of Thomas Hewitt, in Sherborne Lane.   s. m. w. n.

June 10.   Mary, daughter of William and Dorothy Shenton, in Cornhill, born May 19.   s. m. w. c.

June 21.   Mary, daughter of Thomas and Mary Paste (casual poor), born June 5.   s. m. w. n.

June 27.   Joseph, son of John and Elizabeth Potter, born June 22.   s. m. w. n.

Aug. 11.   John, son of Stephen and Catherine Williams, in the Poultry, born Aug. 9.   s. m. w. c.

Aug. 24.   Susanna, daughter of Isaac and Margaret Sewsel, from the Workhouse, born Aug. 18.   s. m. w. n.

Aug. 26.   Martha, daughter of William and Matilda Collins, in Sherborne Lane, born Aug. 5.   s. m. w. n.

Aug. 29.   John, son of Henry and Anne Jones, opposite the Mansion House, born Aug. 26.   s. m. w. c.

Sep. 18.   John Tisoe, son of James and Susanna Reade, in Lombard street, born Sep. 6.   s. m. w. n.

Oct. 9.   Henry, son of Henry and Elizabeth Haskey, in Lombard Street, born Sep. 11.   s. m. w. n.

Nov. 9.   John Woolnoth, a foundling.   s. m. w. n.

Dec. 5.   John, son of John and Elizabeth Beecroft, in Lombard Street, born Nov. 23.   s. m. w. n.

Dec. 8.   Anne, daughter of William and Anne Gamon, born in the Workhouse, Nov. 28.   s. m. w. n.

Dec. 21.	John, son of Hannah Shaw, base born in the Workhouse, Dec, 7. S. M. W. C.
Jan. 4.	Mary, daughter of John and Mary Griffiths, in Lombard Street, born Dec. 12. S. M. W. N.
Jan. 19.	Samuel, son of Samuel and Catherine Wiseham, in Wallbrook, born Dec. 26. S. M. W. C.
Jan. 27.	Anne, daughter of Timothy and Susanna Cook, in Wallbrook, born Jan. 10. S. M. W. C.
Feb. 3.	Alexander, son of Alexander and Anne Smith, in Lombard Street, born Jan. 12. S. M. W. N.
Feb. 7.	Penelope, daughter of George and Mary Hodges, in Bucklersbury, born Jan. 25. S. M. W. C.

1751

April 21.	Charlotte, daughter of John and Sarah Cotterell, in the Poultry, born Mar. 28. S. M. W. C.
April 27.	Robert, son of Hannah Webb, *Widow*, born April 18. S. M. W. N.
May. 24.	Elizabeth, daughter of Thomas and Elizabeth Howitt, of Sherborne Lane, born May 21. S. M. W. N.
July 11.	Hester, daughter of William and Elizabeth Baker, the corner of the Post Office, born June 29. S. M. W. N.
Aug. 3.	Thomas, son of Henry and Anne Jones, opposite the Mansion House, born Aug. 2. S. M. W. C.
Sep. 1.	Thomas, son of John and Elizabeth Seymour, in Pope's-head Alley, born Aug. 17. S. M. W. N.
Sep. 1.	Mary, daughter of David and Elizabeth Thomas, in Sherbone Lane, born Aug. 20. S. M. W. N.
Sep. 10.	John, son of John and Elizabeth Pantree, in Bearbinder Lane, born Aug. 14. S. M. W. C.
Sep. 26.	Privately, Thomas, son of George and Martha Truelock, in Little Lombard Street, born Sep. 4. S. M. W. C.
Oct. 8.	Privately, Catherine, daughter of Joseph and Eleanor Martin, in Lombard Street, born Oct. 7. S. M. W. N.
Oct. 20.	James, son of Andrew and Catherine Moffatt, born Oct. 16. S. M. W. N.
Oct. 22.	John, son of John and Mary Hornblower, born Oct. 21. S. M. W. C.
Oct. 31.	Joseph, son of Joseph and Anne Brown, born Oct. 14. S. M. W. N.
Dec. 5.	Beata, daughter of Joseph and Herman Blandford, born Nov. 15. S. M. W. C.
Dec. 11.	Anne Isabella Elizabeth, daughter of Samuel and Anne Wood, born Nov. 3. S. M. W. N.

1752

Jan. 26.	Edward, son of Joseph and Ann Newcombe, (lodger at the Sexton's) born Jan. 22. S. M. W. N.
Feb. 13.	Sarah, daughter of Thomas and Mary Hisbon, (lodger at Rymer's, Sherbourne Lane), born Jan. 19. S. M. W. N.
Mar. 13.	Anne, daughter of Stephen and Catherine Williams, in the Poultry, born March 5. S. M. W. C.
April 23.	James, son of Samuel and Catherine Wiseham, in Walbrook born Mar. 13. S. M. W. C.

June 3.   Margaret, daughter of John and Anne Oakley (lodgers at Mr. Princes) born May 13. S. M. W. N.

June 9.   Mary, daughter of Thomas and Elizabeth Howitt, born June 9. S. M. W. N.

June 14.   Was received into Church, William, son of John and Hannah Bentley (in Bearbinder Lane) born May 19, and baptized May 29. S. M. W. C.

June 18.   Elizabeth, daughter of Thomas and Penelope Rawson, in Bucklersbury, born May 30. S. M. W C.

July 14.   Henry, son of John and Elizabeth Beecroft, in Lombard Street, born June 30. S. M. W. N.

July 19.   Richard Hollingworth, son of John and Anne Wilding, in Abchurch Lane, born June 28. S. M. W. N.

Aug. 10.   Sarah, daughter of Henry and Anne Jones, opposite the Mansion House, born Aug. 9. S. M. W. C.

Aug. 14.   Mary, daughter of John and Sarah Cotterell, in the Poultry, born July 22. S.. M. W. C..

Sep. 24.   Robert, son of William and Dorothy Shenton, born Aug. 13. S. M. W. C.

Oct. 22.   John, son of John and Elizabeth Seymour, of Pope's-head Alley, born Sep. 30. S. M. W. N.

Oct. 27.   Jacob, son of Isaac and Catherine Dolston, from the Workhouse, born Oct. 24. S. M. W. N.

Oct. 31.   John, son of Jonathan and Isabella Brideoake, born Oct. 4. S. M. W. C.

Nov. 7.   Jhoseph, son of Jhoseph and Eleanor Martin, in Lombard Street, born Nov. 5. S. M. W. N.

Dec. 7.   Richard, son of Thomas and Mary Hudson, born Nov. 20. S. M. W. C.

Dec. 29.   Timothy, son of Timothy and Susanna Cook, near the Mansion House, born Dec. 12. S. M. W. C.

1753

Mar. 13, privately, John, son of Paston and Judith Cartwright, born Feb. 23. S. M. W. C.

Mar. 14.   John, son of James and Sarah Arnold, born Feb. 26. S. M. W. C.

Mar. 18.   Jane, daughter of James and Mary Townley, born Feb. 21. S. M. W. C.

        N.B.—James Townley is a Parishioner of St. Andrew's, Holborn, and a Lodger here.

April 4.   Elizabeth, daughter of John and Mary Griffiths, in Lombard Street, born Mar. 18. S. M. W. N.

April 15.   Susanna, daughter of Stephen and Catherine Williams, born April 10. S. M. W. C.

June 1.   Mary, daughter of John and Sarah Sevell, from the Workhouse, born May 25.

June 3.   Mary, daughter of William and Mary White, in Little Lombard Street, born May 12. S. M. W. N.

July 6, privately, Thomas, son of Thomas and Elizabeth Howitt, in Sherborne Lane, born July 3. S. M. W. N.

July 15.   Mary, daughter of Henry and Elizabeth Gretton, in Change Alley, born June 21. S. M. W. N.

Aug. 23.   William, son of William and Jamima Manning, born July 10. S. M. W. N.

Sep. 25.	William, son of Henry and Anne Jones, born Sep. 21. S. M. W. C.
Oct. 14.	James, son of Charles and Elizabeth Holmes, born Sep. 3. S. M. W. N.
Oct. 29.	William, son of John and Elizabeth Pantree, born Oct. 4. S. M. W. C.
Nov. 1.	Joseph, son of Joseph and Eleanor Martin, born Oct. 24. S. M. W. N.
Nov. 18.	Thomas, son of Thomas and Mary Hudson, born Oct. 31. S. M. W. C.
Dec. 10.	Thomas, son of Thomas and Mary Brown, born Nov. 16. S. M. W. N.
Dec. 16.	Mary, daughter of Isaac and Mary Pack, born Nov. 27. S. M. W. N.
Dec. 19.	Mary Woolnoth, a foundling.

1754

Jan. 10.	Elizabeth, daughter of Jonathan and Isabella Brideoake, born Dec. 15. S. M. W. C.
Jan. 16.	Thomas, son of John and Elizabeth Beecroft, born Jan. 2. S. M. W. N.
Jan. 30.	Joseph, son of John and Hannah Bentley, born Jan. 1.
Jan. 6.	Mary, a foundling. S. M. W. N.
Feb. 8.	Charles, son of Samuel and Letitia Tucker, born Jan. 2. S. M. W. N.
Feb. 24.	Mary, daughter of Thomas and Ann Godley, born Feb. 2. S. M. W. C.
Mar. 3.	Thomas, son of James and Mary Townley, born Feb. 19. S. M. W. N.
Mar. 7.	John, son of Peter and Eleanor Snee, born Feb. 5. S. M. W. C.
Mar. 10.	William, son of William and Matilda Collins, born Feb. 27. S. M. W. N.
Mar. 15.	Alphonsus, son of William and Sarah Webster, born Mar. 1. S. M. W. N.
Mar. 14.	Privately, Hannah, daughter of Thomas and Mary Parsons, born Mar. J. S. M. W. N.
April 5.	Jhoseph Chance, a foundling.
April 25.	Henry, son of Henry and Elizabeth Haskey, born April 18. S. M. W. N.
May 5.	Mary, daughter of John and Hannah Chapman, born April 19. S. M. W. N.
May 16.	Privately, Charlotte, daughter of Alexander and Ann Smith. S. M. W. N.
May 26.	Josias, son of John and Elizabeth Seymour, born May 10. S. M. W. N.
Aug. 1.	Elizabeth, daughter of Henry and Elizabeth Boldero, born July 31. S. M. W. N.
Aug. 12.	Ann, daughter of John and Ann Wilding, born July 17. S. M. W. N.
Aug. 18.	Charles Davis, a Negro servant to Mr. Perrcneau. S. M. W. N.
Sep. 6.	John, son of William and Mary Hornblower, born Aug. 12. S. M. W. C.
Oct. 2.	Jamima, daughter of William and Jamima Manning, born Sep. 3. S. M. W. N.
Oct. 14.	David, son of Sarah Leget, born Sep. 30.

Dec. 15. William, son of William and Dorothy Shenton, born Nov. 15. S. M. W. C.

Dec. 19. John, son of John and Mary Griffiths, born Nov. 22. S. M. W. N.

Dec. 20. Mary, daughter of Samuel and Elizabeth Hall, born Nov. S. M.. W. C.

Dec. 23. John, son of Andrew and Catherine Moffat, born Dec. 4. S. M. W. N.

1755

Jan. 24. Thomas Swan, a foundling.

Feb. 6. Elizabeth, daughter of John and Elizabeth Pantree, born Jan. 9. S. M. W. C.

Feb. 12. James, son of William and Mary Palmer, born Jan. 20. S. M. W. C.

Feb. 12. Henry, son of Henry and Ann Jones, born Feb. 21. S. M. W. C.

Mar. 17. Mary Deneven, daughter of Thomas and Mary Brown, born Mar. 3. S. M. W. N.

April 3. Mary, daughter of Thomas and Mary Hudson, born Mar. 18. S. M. W. C.

April 4. Thomas, son of Thomas and Elizabeth Howit, born Mar. 22. S. M. W. N.

April 11. John, son of Thomas and Elizabeth Shuttleworth, born April 6. S. M. W. C.

April 29. Elizabeth, daughter of John and Hannah Bentley, born April 2. S. M. W. C.

May 21. Thomas, son of Peter and Susanna Botham, born May 1. S. M. W. C.

May 4. Nathan, son of Nathan and Dorothy Davis, born April 30. S. M. W. N.

June 17. Thomas Woolley, son of John and Frances Kentish, born April 23. S. M. W. N.

June 24. Eleanor, daughter of Joseph and Eleanor Martin, born June 4. S. M. W. N.

June 24. John, son of Pastorn and Judith Cartwright, born June 1. S. M. W. C.

July 4. Blisset, son of Blisset and Elizabeth Woodeson, born June 7. S. M. W. N.

July 15. Thomas, son of Jonathan and Isabella Brideoake, born June 17. S. M. W. C.

Aug. 19. Godfrey, son of William and Sarah Webster, born Aug. 7. S. M. W. N.

Aug. 28. Henry, son of John and Elizabeth Beecroft, born Aug. 22.

Sep. 8, 1754. Privately, and had the baptism completed Nov. 5, 1755, John Benjamin, son of Moses and Mary Depaiba, born Aug. 11, 1754. S. M. W. N.

Nov. 5. Mary, daughter of Moses and Mary Depaiba, born Oct. 19. S. M. W. N.

Nov. 18. Hannah, daughter of William and Jemima Manning, born Oct. 22. S. M. W. N.

Dec. 14. Rebecca, daughter of Joseph and Ann Brown, born Nov. 18. S. M. W. N.

Dec. 29. Robert Corby, son of James and Ann Peto, born Dec. 27. S. M. W. N.

1756

Jan. 17. Randall, son of Henry and Elizabeth Bolders, born Jan. 13. s. m w. n.

Memorandum [In the Margin.] Thomas Martin, a negro lad, was baptized in this Church on the 6th day of this month.

Jan. 29. Elizabeth, daughter of Andrew and Katherine Moffat, born Jan. 2. s. m. w. n.

April 15. James, son of James and Ann Arnold, born Mar. 29. s. m. w. c.

April 7. Mary, daughter of Edward and Mary Doody, born Jan. 18.

May 13. Eleanor, daughter of Timothy and Sarah Cook, born April 13. s. m. w. c.

May 24. George Connell, son of George and Ann Wilding, born April 19. s. m. w. n.

June 2. Rebecca, daughter of Blissett and Mary Woodeson, born May 22. s. m. w. n.

Aug. 3. Sarah, daughter of Thomas and Elizabeth Shuttleworth, born July 31. s. m. w. c.

Aug. 15. George, son of John and Frances Kentish, born July 23. s. m. w. n.

Oct. 3. Joseph, son of Stephen and Catherine Williams, born Sep. 22. s. m. w. c.

Sep. 1. Catherine, daughter of Gabriel and Elizabeth Nichols, born Aug. 16.

Nov. 16. Catherine Ann, daughter of Robert and Ann Jones, of Change Alley, born Nov. 5. s. m. w. n.

1757

Jan. 23. Frances, daughter of George and Mary Manser, born Jan. 5. s. m. w. c.

John, son of John and Elizabeth Pantree, was born Jan. 13. s. m. w. c.

Feb. 10. John, son of John and Elizabeth Pantree, was baptized.

Feb. 16. Joseph, son of Joseph and Eleanor Martin, born Feb. 2. s. m. w. n.

Mar. 10. Catherine, daughter of John and Sarah Bowditch, born Mar. 1. s. m. w. c.

April 26. Richard, son of William and Sarah Webster, born April 17. s. m. w. c.

May 15. Jane, daughter of Timothy and Sarah Cook, born April 24. s. m. w. c.

June 8. James, son of Jonathan and Isabella Brideoake, born May 22. s. m. w. c.

June 14. Arundel, daughter of John and Mary Griffiths, born May 18. s. m. w. n.

July 3. Frederick, son of Blissett and Elizabeth Woodeson, born May 1. s. m. w. n.

Aug. 7. Elizabeth, daughter of William and Dorothy Shenton, born July 13. s. m. w. c.

Aug. 12. Rebecca Keeling, daughter of John and Hannah Bentley, born Aug. 4. s. m. w. c.

Aug. 28. Edward Gale, son of Henry and Elizabeth Boldero, born Aug. 16. s. m. w. n.

Oct. 30.	David, son of David and Elizabeth Thomas, born Sep. 27.
Nov. 2.	Judith, daughter of William and Jemima Manning, born Oct. 8. s. m. w. n.
Nov. 4.	James, son of Thomas and Mary Brown, born Nov. 2. s. m. w. n.
Dec. 23.	John, son of William and Mary Palmer, born Dec. 7. s. m. w. c.
Dec. 23.	Martha and Elizabeth, daughters of Pharaoh and Elizabeth Kirby, from the Workhouse, born Dec. 2.

1758

Jan. 4.	Privately, Elizabeth Mary, daughter of John and Elizabeth Mary Tomlinson, born Dec. 16. s. m. w. c.
Jan. 31.	Elizabeth Corbey, daughter of James and Ann Peto, born Jan. 26. s. m. w. n.
Feb. 19.	Benjamin, son of John and Ann Wilding, born Jan. 23. s. m. w. n.
Feb. 23.	Henry Lendrick, son of Peter and Susanna Botham, born Feb. 13. s. m. w. c.
Mar. 10.	Robert, son of Henry and Ann Jones, born Mar. 2. s. m. w. c.
Mar. 10.	William, son of Samuel and Mary Moore, born Feb. 9. s. m. w. c.
Mar. 27.	John, son of John and Sarah Bowditch, born Mar. 11. s. m. w. c.
April 1.	Robert, son of Robert and Ann Jones, born May 14. s. w. m. n.
May 26.	Edward, son of John and Esther Jones, born May 4. s. m. w. n.
June 20.	Jane Temariah, daughter of Robert and Jane Smith, born May 23. s. m. w. n.
July 7.	William, son of Henry and Elizabeth Haskey, born June 12. s. m. w. n.
July 13.	Mary, daughter of John and Elizabeth Pantree, born June 17. s. m. w. c.
July 30.	Francis, daughter of Timothy and Sarah Cook, born July 9. s. m. w. c.
July 30.	Sarah, daughter of John and Rebecca Simister, born July 14. s. m. w. n.
Aug. 20.	Leonard, son of Blissett and Elizabeth Woodeson, born July 24. s. m. w. n.
Oct. 1.	John and Ann, son and daughter of James and Ann Arnold, born Sep. 16. s. m. w. c.
Oct. 11.	Elizabeth Margaret, daughter of Benjamin and Elizabeth Tennit, born Sep. 3. s. m. w. n.
Oct. 17.	Weames, son of Job and Elizabeth Peachy, born Oct. 5. s. m. w. n.
Oct. 9.	Privately, Richard son of John and Hannah Bentley, born Sep. 17. s. m. w. c.
Nov. 3.	Jane, son of William and Grace Copeland, born Oct. 4. s. m. w. c.
Dec. 1.	William, son of William and Jemima Manning, born Nov. 3. s. m. w. n.

1759

Jan. 14. Grace, daughter of John and Elizabeth Townley, born Dec. 31. S. M. W. N.

Jan. 18. Mary Ann, daughter of William and Mary Palmer, born Dec. 29.

Feb. 19. John Palmer, son of Thomas and Bridget Holloway, born Jan. 21. S. M. W. N.

April 20. William, son of Alexander and Martha How, born April 4. S. M. W. C.

May. 4. William, son of William and Ann Winchester, born April 6. S. M. W. N.

May 3. Sarah Esther, daughter of William and Sarah Webster, born April 19. S. M. W. N.

May 3. John, son of Richard and Katherine Allsager, born April 6. S. M. W. N.

May 15. Edward, son of Rowland and Elizabeth Stephenson, born April 22. S. M. W. N.

May 16. Sarah, daughter of Samuel and Mary Hodgkin, born April 27. S. M. W. N.

May 24. Susanna, daughter of Peter and Susanna Botham, born May 7. S. M. W. C.

June 27. Samuel, son of John and Sarah Bowditch, born July 19. S. M. W. C.

June 25. Joseph Deneven, son of Thomas and Mary Brown, born July 25. S. M. W. C.

Aug. 17. Mary, daughter of Simon and Jane Halliday, born Aug. 8. S. M. W. N.

Dec. 26. Catherine Mary, daughter of John and Rebecca Satchel, born Nov. 30.

1760

Jan. 7. Robert, son of John and Elizabeth Pantree, born Dec. 7. S. M. W. C.

Feb. 24. Jonathan, son of Jonathan and Lucinda Parsons, born Feb. 4. S. M. W. C.

Feb. 24. James, son of William and Dorothy Shenton, born Jan. 26. S. M. W. N.

May 15. Sarah, daughter of William and Ann Winchester, born May 5. S. M. W. N.

July 18. Murdoch, son of William and Mary James, born June 23. S. M. W. N.

July 21. Anthony, son of William and Mary Palmer, born July 16. S. M. W. C.

Aug. 10. Elizabeth, daughter of Thomas and Elizabeth Green, born Aug. 5. S. M. W. C.

Aug. 30. Christopher, son of Christopher and Sarah Clarke, born July, 26.

Nov. 9. John, son of John and Hannah Jaques, born Oct. 12.

Dec. 10. Mary Matilda, daughter of Joseph and Ann Moorhouse, born Nov. 21. S. M. W. N.

[*The Registers of Baptisms from this date are well kept.*]

Mariages

1538

Imprimis Nov. 27. Thomas Scryven and Margerye Raye.
Jan. 19. Thomas Atkynson and Parnell Bowyer.
Jan. 26. Herman Godfry and Margarett Starlynge.

1539

June 19. John Machym and Katherin Goodwyn.
June 22. Jasper Borton and Edithe Younge.
July 20. Willyam Ogle and Margarett Gybson.
Sep. 16. John Barnes and Joane Bowes.
Oct. 26. John Calverley and Olave Lewys.

1540

April 20. Thomas Roydon and Jone Hubberd.
Aug. 8. Robert Ashehurst and Elizabeth Atcombe.
Aug. 29. Thomas Glenton and Alice Johnson.
Sep. 21. Robert Grevys and Isabel Rawlens.
Feb. 6. Walter Blake and Annes Wynstanle.

1541

May 15. Thomas Wytton and Jone Bentley.
Aug. 28. John York and Joane Barnes.

1542

April 23. John Wytton and Joan Lynnett.
Aug. 24. Lawrence Snowe and Beteryce Prety.
Oct. 2. John Clonell and Elizabeth Clerk.
Oct. 5. John Chamber and Joane Mershall.
Nov. 19. William Smythe and Joane Hyggyns.

1543

May 20. Thomas Bayly and Malyan Oterygham.
Oct. 7. Galfridus Pound and Phillip Johnson.
Nov. 4. Richard Hawworth and Margarett Gutter.
Nov. 18. John Bell and Rose Galamore.
Jan. 21. Thomas Upryse and Dorothy Vachan.
Feb. 3. William Murfyn and Annes Tawdle.

1544

Sep. 1.	Thomas Bowes and Thomasyn Wylkinson.
Sep. 1.	Martyn Bowes and Francis Strope.
Sep. —.	[*sic*] William Browne and Elizabethe Alwyn.
Sep. —.	[*sic*] Thomas Benson and Joan Carter.
Sep. 21.	John Parker and Anne Ryse.
Oct. 17.	Nicholas Oksee and Alice Marshe.
Jan. 25.	William Hedyngton and Alice Sutton.

1545

June 7.	Nicholas Hills and Margaret Hamans.
June 15.	Anthony Browne and Elizabeth Whitkirtle.
July 26.	William Franklyn and Em Frauncis.
Oct. 7.	Beniomyne Wyllowes and Agnes Basse.
Nov. 30.	Thomas Kelinge and Alice Robinson.
Feb. 9.	Richard Grigg and Francis Spicer.
Feb. 15.	John Wright and Joane Styan.

1546

May 9.	John Woodroff and Elizabeth Jentyll.
May 10.	John Watson and Margery Bolseworthe.
May 16.	John Chamley and Elizabeth Carr.
May 24.	James Stanely and Joane Taylor.
June 20.	John Rashe and Katherin Morris.
Aug. 1.	Lawrance Semencia and Elizabeth Todlawe.
Aug. 8.	William Hawson and Margaret Yonger.
Sep. 10.	John Paver and Em Bull.
Oct. 25.	John Brombrough and Christabel Mase.
Oct. 25.	Henry Russell and Barbara Johnson.
Nov. 13.	Thomas Barnes and Margaret Bawdwyn.
Nov. 27.	Thomas Gilbard and Margare Fowle.
Feb. 5.	Thomas Northarp and Alice Sympson.

1547

June 12.	Thomas Goodan and Alice Wilkynson.
Sep. 18.	Humfrey Daye and Letys Wylson.
Oct. 22.	John Chambers and Katherin Hill.
Nov. 23.	Robert Sely and Elizabethe Calcolte.
Dec. 7.	Robert Sutton and Joane Grayn.
Jan. 22.	Edward Clapoll and Jone Byderdyn.

1548

April 29.	Richard Sympson and Mary Begrave.
May 17.	John Bernard and Jone Polleyn.
May 27.	Lawrance Smyth and Agnes Polleyne.
June 3.	Standbank and Margaret Marchaunt.
June 10.	Robert Taylebousse and Agnes Handbury.
June 11.	John Morgan and Agnes Roothe.
June 13.	Robert Brandon and Katherin Barber.
July 1.	Thomas Atkyns and Agnes Wydders.
July 17.	Nicholas Skyres and Alice Grene.
July 30.	William Dawkes and Mary Rosse.
Sep. 2.	John Deyne and Cycely Francklyn.

Oct. 23.	Nicholas Skeele and Catherine Selbe.
Jan. 13.	James Lynne and Elizabeth Tubl.
Feb. 3.	John Kellillwoode and Margerye Kelinge.
Feb. 10.	Richard Ambrose and Elizabeth Snowdam.
Feb. 25.	Richard Perkyns and Elizabeth Selye.
Feb. 26.	Jasper Fysher and Alice Wethers.

1549

May 5.	Robert Egles and Alice Whethers.
May 12.	George Hunter and Elizabeth Brockbank.
May 20.	Richard Makynge and Margaret ———— [*sic*]
— [*sic*] 21.	Patrick Colley and Margaret Buck.
July 20.	John Mynylco and Margaret Stanley.
Sep. 1.	Roger Nycoles and Anne Boston.
Nov. 17.	Nicholas Wylliams and Elizabeth Burford.
Jan. 23.	William Banester and Elizabeth Robson.

1550

April 15.	John Mathew and Elizabeth Chester.
April 20.	Robert Gwery and Margaret Johnys.
April 27.	Henry Sharpe and Christian Arnall.
May 17.	Cornelis Haven and Marye Morys.
May 29.	Augustin Bawden and Agnes Sympson.
July 31.	Edwarde Cage and Adryan Grygge.
Oct. 26.	Richard Colmore and Cysely Wythers.
Nov. 13.	Bartholomewe Osmonde and Garter Polle.
Nov. 30.	Marmaduke Constable and Alice Spaulden.
Dec. 8.	John Thomas and Joan Renbruge.
Jan. 7.	John Staveley and Winefrede Jake.
Jan. 12.	William Yonge and Agnes Chomley.
Jan. 25.	Robert Taylboys and Margaret Spycer.
Feb. 1.	John Lark and Joan Olyver.
Feb. 3.	William More and Julyan Pollen.

1551

April 26.	John Browne and Joane Good.
April 26.	Xrofer Laurance and Margaret Brakebank
May 24.	Xrofer Becke and Jone Sympson.
May 24.	Adam Spencer and Julyan Mylles.
Dec. 12.	Frauncis Bernard and Alice Habry.
Jan. 21.	John Tull and Dorothe Webb.
Jan. 31.	Robert Brownley and Margaret Dowsse.
Feb. 13.	Edmund Smythe and Agnes Postlat.

1552

May 16.	William Crumpton and Elizabeth Pore.
Aug. 14.	Richard Botr and Barbara Todlon.
Jan. 29, 1553 [*sic*]	John Henbery and Margerye Tedley
Feb. 2.	Humfrey Brooke and Josyan Blockley.
Feb. 12.	Richard Peyms and Hellen Mathewe.

1553

June 29.	William Barnslay and Joane Roodes.

1554

Jan. 21.	John Essex and Katherin Barber.
Jan. 21.	John Wyes and Elizabeth Meryweder.
April 15.	Robert Kaye and Elizabeth Bredley.
May 23.	Edward Slatter and Alice Rooke.
July 1.	Xrofer Kyldyne and Anne Fulmer.
July 16.	William Ynchorem and Margarett Wetherall.
Sep. 9.	John Reynold and Elizabeth Key.
Jan. 27.	Thomas Hyotto and Anne Armestronge.

1555

April 28.	John Homes and Joane Lovette.
April 6.	Stephen Bargen and Hellen Brackbanke.
Oct. 20.	Roger Patterton and Margaret Longe.
Nov. 17.	Humfrey Adams and Emme Harryson.

1556

May 31.	John Kelsey and Elizabeth Warren.
Aug. 2.	Leonarde Smythe and Johan Atkynson.
Aug. 13.	Henry Warcop and Katherin Rawlyns.
Oct. 5.	John Rowlles and Johan Kinge.
Oct. 18.	Henry Kinge and Alice Rogers.
Feb. 13.	Edmunde Andrewe and Elizabethe Lowe.

1557

June 27.	Robert Kelk and Alice James.
July 4.	Nicholas Pollyn and Elynor Darby.
Oct. 31.	Richard Johnson and Margaret Homes.
Feb. 5.	Thomas Wylloughby, *Esquier*, and Katherin Harte.
Feb. 20.	Robert Hawse and Jane Petyngar, *Wydow* of this Parishe, by *lycence* of my Lord Cardinalle.

1558

June 19.	Thomas Basse and Alice Stewarde.
June 26.	Thomas Basse and Ellin Payne.
July 2.	Xrofer Johnson and Elizabeth Smythe.
Nov. 26.	John Mylles and Margarett Francklin.

1558 [*sic*]

Jan. 30.	Raffe Davys and Johan Goldinge.

1559

April 18.	William Seman and Joan Atkynson, *Wydowe, by lycence.*
May 22.	William Busterd and Johan Markes.
June 18.	Thomas Charles and Denys Dicker.
Aug. 15.	Robert ap Rice and Katherin Roberts.
Aug. 31.	William Knight and Agnes Castell.
Oct. 26.	John Murfyn and Cycely Ventres, *Wydowe.*
Nov. 11.	Owyn Wylson and Margarett Letter, *Wydowe.*
Dec. 19.	Thomas Shawe and Anne Muscham, daughter of William Muschamp, of Peckham, *Esquier.*

1560

April 22.	John Collmar and Suzan Wythtro.
April 28.	Richard Hanbery and Alice Fysher.
May 5.	Olyver Walker and Anne Hubberd.
May 12.	William Cater and Joyce Humble.
May 19.	William Jones and Elizabethe Nuporte.
July 14.	Was married three daughters of Thomas Atkynson Scrivener and Parvell his wieff, their father and mother beinge both at that presente day of marriage there presente. That is to saye William Handford, was married to Jeronyme Atkynson, George Lee was married unto Tymothie Atkynson, and Thomas Nicholls was married unto Elizabeth Atkynson.
Aug. 18.	Richard Sympson and Marye Jarratt.

1561 [*sic*]

Dec. 4.	John Allen and Bridgett Allcyter, *Wydowe*.
Aug. 5.	William Robinson and Barbara Hayes.
Sep. 21.	John Mathewe and Elizabeth Lynne.
Nov. 19.	Frauncis Gaynesforth and Joan Wymark.
Dec. 21.	Bartholomew Dawbeny and Frauncis Allciter.
Jan. 18.	William Mayhhew and Anne Davye.
Jan. 20.	William Byrchley and Pascal Raynoldes.
Feb. 3.	John Dawlinge and Katherin Barker, of St. Clements without Temple barr.

1562

April 12.	Christopher Fletcher and Elizabeth Ratcliffe.
April 27.	William Mure and Cicely Billingsley.
May 25.	Hughe Ingram and Anne Goldthropp.
May 7.	Nicholas Sunderlande and Alice Jenkynson.
Sep. 28.	John Lowbere and Thomasyn, daughter of Fabyan Wythers, *Goldsmythe*.
Sep. 28.	Arnolde Lowbere and Cicely, daughter of John Rocke, *Gentleman*.
Oct. 6.	Robert Browne and Alice Wulfride.
Jan. 31.	Thomas Armorer and Dorothy Mundye.
Feb. 7.	Robert Wright and Mary Nutshawe, *by lycence*.
Feb. 22.	Robert Lewknor and Isabell Gylpyn, *by lycence*.
Feb. 22.	Thomas Hesterby and Thomasyn Dawes, *by lycence*.

1563

June 20.	William Sharpe and Emery Collyns.
June 28.	William Walker and Jane Dickenson.
July 18.	William Cooke and Marye Jakelyn.
Aug. 3.	Launcellott Wytton and Alice Ryder.
Sep. 29.	William Parmenter and Margarett Patter.
Jan. 23.	Thomas Shorte and Elizabeth Rydley.
Jan. 24.	Cutbert Buckle and Johan Davye.
Jan. 28.	Henry Shalacum and Godlyf Garland.
Jan. 29.	Was maried our Curat, Mr. Thomas Buckmaister, beinge our Mynister, to a wydowe.

1564

April 30.	Thomas Humble and Agnes Johnson.
Nov. 12.	William Feeke and Marye Wetherhyll.
Nov. 20.	Richard Powell and Katherin Redinge.
Dec. 10.	Randall Rightle and Joise Stewarde.
Jan. 14.	Thomas Dunell and Agnes Norton.
Jan. 18.	Roger Yemanse and Grace Kerke.
Feb. 25.	Richard Dyconson and Margarett Corbett.
Mar. 4.	John Warrener and Katherin Robson.
	[N.B.—The date 1565 is not inserted here.]
May 20.	Robert Crippes and Anne Wytton.

1565

July 8.	Thomas Davys and Mary Bickers.
July 22.	Tronnyon Shorte and Anne Okeover.
July 31.	William Bonde and Margarett Welche.
Aug. 19.	William Swifte and Margarett Bennett.
Sep. 30.	Richard Dennolle and Agnes Machym.
Dec. 13.	Nicholas Gaynesforde, of Darlinge, and Elinor Sackside, *by lycence*.
Feb. 17.	Marmaduke Higgens, *Grocer*, and Aves Noble, *by lycence*.
Feb. 25.	Roger Spurstowe and Margarett Foden, *by lycence*.
	[N.B —The date 1566 is not inserted here.]
May 26.	Richard Tonge, *Grocer*, and Elizabeth Norton.

1566

July 8.	Thomas Crymes and Jane Muschampe.
Nov. 17.	Thomas Brytwell and Agnes Jordayn.
Jan. 19.	Nicholas Poore and Johan Wytton.
Jan. 25.	Xrofer Armestronge and Margery Staple.
Jan. 21.	William Gestlye and Myllesent Blackburne.
Feb. 5.	Thomas Sackforde and the Lady Elizabeth Bowes.

1567

April 27.	John Francklin and Elyn Phillippes.
April 7.	Edward Martyn and Marye Warde, *with lycence*.
April 29.	William Matreves and Elyn Uprande.
July 6.	John Chuner and Joane Blese.
July 6.	William Smythe and Cycely Ynse.
July 20.	Hughe Heywarde and Margarett Richardson.
Nov. 9.	John Prestwood and Isabell Mathewe.
Jan. 13.	Rauffe Kynge and Phillippe Asshefeilde.
Feb. 15.	William Lanam and Anne Reneyer.

1568

May 1.	Arthure Charismore and Isabell Redynge, *Wyddowe*.
May 23.	Robert Eden and Katherin Buddell, *by lycence*.
June 8.	John Rayne and Johan Parker, *by lycence*.
Oct. 31.	William Gardyner and Elizabeth Johnson.
Feb. 13.	William Allen and Margarett Stanbanck.

1569

July 10.	Gregorie Bonde and Alice Peeke.
Aug. 21.	James Jobson and Saba Snowe, *by lycence.*
Oct. 2.	Henry Kyndelmarsh and Audrey Collyns.
Nov. 6.	Thomas Pole and Agnes Rigge.
Dec. 4.	Thomas Spragge and Margerye Whytehedd.

1570

May 30.	John Roots, *Gentleman*, and Johan Turke, *by lycence.*
June 18.	James Somner and Elizabeth Shawe.
Aug. 26.	Robert Spark, *Gentleman of the Savoy*, and Elizabeth Ley, of this parishe.
Sep. 17.	Thomas Gelderson and Ellen Bowyer.
Dec. 3.	Robert Robson and Elizabeth Norton.
Feb. 25.	John Etheridge and Elizabeth Feild, *by lycence.*
	[N.B.—No date of year here.]
April 29.	John Armorer and Alice Hamond.

1571

May 28.	George Haynes and Agnes Perpoynt, *by lycence.*
June 12.	Eleachim Wall and Katherin Wytton.
June 14.	Dunston Waplod and Joan Sutton, *by lycense.*
July 29.	William Cowper and Margaret Leche.
Oct. 14.	Richard Johnes and Margery Lyon, *Wydowe.*
Dec. 10.	Nicholas Martyn and Jane Poynet.

1572

April 21.	George Gifford and Agnes Leonarde.
June 2.	Henry Trussell and Sara Ketlewood.
June 2.	Edward Holmeden and Elizabeth Taylor, *by lycence.*
July 13.	John Kyng and Jone Clark.
Aug. 14.	Clynten Atkynson and John Lyster, *by lycence.*
Sep. 7.	Richard Hadley and Anne Barnard, *by lycence.*
Oct. 19.	Arthure Norton and Dorothie Cocknedge.
Nov. 9.	Richard Evans and Rose Fellowes.
Nov. 13.	Richard Lomley, *Gentleman*, and Mary Wynterfall, *by lycence*

1573

April 30.	Clement Webster and Ellyn Wilson, *Wydowe, by lycence.*
May 14.	James Stokes and Elizabeth Forrest.
May 14.	Richard Richardson and Mary Ede.
Aug. 2.	William Corbett and Katherine Parke.
Aug. 17.	John Fowle and Elizabeth Stevens.
Aug. 30.	Nicholas Marshall and Awdrye Bargena.
Nov. 10.	John Wye, Ducheman, and Magdalen van Hove, Duchewoman.
Jan. 3.	Richard Cole and Ellys Hodgeskyn.
Feb. 14.	John Bradley and Alice Chace.

1574

April 25.	Thomas Byllam and Anne Watts.
May 11.	Thomas Knells and Katherin Jacobb, *Wyddowe.*
June 6.	Rice Reede and Johan Curtise.

June 6.	Peter Sedgewick and Margerye Somersarte.
June 27.	William Gurton and Jane Dixson.
Aug. 29.	Nicholas Abram and Ann Bostock.
Sep. 12.	Robert Ferkyngham and Sara Stanbank.
Sep. 23.	John Bever, *Gent.*, and Fraunces Moyes, *Wydowe*.
Nov. 21.	John Smythe and Jane Mason.
Dec. 6.	Richard Glascock and Elizabeth Taylor, *by licence.*
Dec. 19.	Joseph Gye and Johan Jaxson.

1575

May 15.	John Alderson and Cicily Gallaway.
May 15.	John Bennett and Katherin Buckle.
May 29.	Symon Curtys and Anne Arlande.

1576

April 15.	Henry Colley and Joan Humberston.

1577

April 21.	Edward Griffyn and Margerye Joanes.
April 22.	Thomas Held and Katherin Stevens, *by lycence.*
May 27.	John Nashe and Margarett Foster.
June 23.	John Murton and Thomasyn Barnard.
Sep. 23.	Humfrey Streetc and Lea Wetherhill.
Jan. 19.	Richard Johnson and Annes Hedrington.
Jan. 20.	William Warde and Marye Watts.
Jan. 20.	Randall Horton and Anne Lodeseman.
Jan. 21.	Henry Tapsfeilde and Suzan Muschampe.

1578

Aug. 3.	Hugh Sponer and Mary Cooke, of this Parish.
Aug. 31.	Robert Bowyar, of Helston, in Cornewell, and Suzanna Kettlewood, of this Parish.
Oct. 20.	John Garrat, of St. Margarett's, in Lothbery, and Mary Chapman, of this Parish.
Nov. 30.	William Frank and Thomasen Robins, of this Parish.
Feb. 23.	Richard Williams, *Grocer*, and Margaret Tasker, out of Robert Tasker's howse, *by lycence.*

1579

April, 30.	Anthony Hayward, *Chaplin*, and Frances Kitson, of this Parish.
May 10.	Beniamyn Holdstock and Elizabeth Sparcke, of this Parish.
May 4.	Edward Croshawe and Mary Stevens, *Widowe* of this Parish.
May 31.	Henry Barnc and Sara Weatherhill, of this Parish.
June 9.	William Gryffin and Elizabeth Elton, of this Parish.
June 9.	Thomas Wells and Margery Mann, of this Parish.
Nov. 9.	Edmond Pearson, *Merchant*, and Elizabeth Pickeringe, of this Parish, *by lycence.*
Jan. 17.	Frauncis Lodge, *Haberdasher*, and Bridgett Pott, out of Edward Crowshawe's howse, his Mayde, *by lycence.*
Jan. 31.	David Akson, *Haberdasher*, and Marye Ramond, of this Parish, out of Robert Eastfeild's howse.

1580

April 24. Henry Knowsly and Suzanna Bayles.
July 17. Nicholas Hudson and Luce Patcell, of this Parish.
Aug. 12. A *Stranger*, Andrewe Baptist Decorano and Janét Balay-myne, *by lycence.*

Nov. 29. Richard Rogers, *Goldsmyth*, and Anne Beswick, *by lycence.*
Nov. 29. Thomas Hopkyns, *Draper*, and Anne Rawlyns, the daughter of John Rawlyns, of the Parish of Morten-henmarsh, Glo'stershire, *by lycence.*

1581

April 2. Jarvys Woordsworth and Judith Sawyer, of this Parish.
May 30. William Judy and Katherin Harrison, of this Parish.
July 9. John Cawldwell, *parson* of the Parish Church of Maw-berley, Cheshire, and Margaret Hylde, of this Parish, *by lycence.*

Oct. 1. Robert Leversage, *Draper*, and Katherin Helde, *Wydowe, by licence.*

Nov. 5. Thomas Garthe, *Clothworker*, and Ellyn Harrison, of this Parish.

Dec. 7. Thomas Standbanke, *Curryar*, and Hellen Hunte, out of Mr. Rowlande Ockover's house.

1582

June 17. William Randall and Joane Johnson, of this Parish.
Sep. 3. Thomas Barefoote and Jane Revall [or Kevall], *by lycence.*
Sep. 24. Arkyn Fessar and Alice Rop, of this Parish.
Oct 21. George Savage, *Haberdasher*, and Suzan Barnard, of this Parish.
Dec. 18. Thomas Lodge, *Gentleman*, and Annes Wetherhill, daughter of Elizabeth Wetherell, *Wydowe, by lycence.*
Dec. 18. The same morninge, Robert Molsworth, *Haberdasher*, and Margaret Wetherhill, her sister, *by lycence.*
Jan. 28. Thomas Francknell, *Goldsmythe*, and Suzan Okeover, daughter of Rowland Okeover, *Merchanttaillor, by lycence.*

1583

May 27. Edwarde Phillipps, of the Parish of St. Michaell Uppon Cornehill, and Elizabeth Okeover, daughter of the above named Rowland Okeover, *by lycence.*

Aug. 5. John Tyler, of the Parish of St. Michaell's, near Quenehith, London, and Alice Standon, a *mayden*, of this parish, and daughter of John Standon, *Gent.*, deceased, while he lived, of Micham, Co. Surrey, *by lycence.*

Sep. 9. Thomas Goffe, of the Parish of St. Olaves, in Southwark, and Johan Whaplett, *Wydow*, of this Parish, *by lycence.*

1584

May 10. Henry Heyborne, of the Parish of St. Albons, in Hart-fordshire, and Isabell Kevell (or Revell), of this Parish.

May 24. William Saunders, of the Parish of St. Botolph without Algate, and Margerye Johnson, of this Parish.

June 28.	Christopher Every, of the Parish of St. James, nere Garlickhith, and Mary Harryson, of this Parish, *by lycence.*
June 29.	John Kirby, of the Parish of St. Fayth's under Powles, *Goldsmith*, and Ose Burton, of this Parish, *Wydowe*, by lycence.
Oct. 15.	Richard Crawley, of Luton Co. Bed. *Yoman*, and Elizabeth Preston, of St. Michaell's, near St. Albons, Co. of Herts, daughter of William Preston, *by lycence.*

1585

April 18.	John Paers, of the Parish of St. Edmonde the kinge, and Margaret Turky, of this Parish.
Sep. 8.	Richard Readinge, of the Parish of St. Andrewe's, in Holborne, and Reynes Wilshier, of this Parish.
Sep. 27.	Thomas Childe, of this Parish, and Rebecca Weatherhill, also of the same Parish.
Nov. 23.	William Pullen, of the Parish of Edmunton, Co. of Mid., *Gent.*, and Anne Tayleboyes, *mayden*, of this Parish, *by lycence.*
Jan. 9.	Chidiock Roe, of this Parish, and Anne Vermvers, of the same Parish.
Jan. 13.	Tymothie Shotten, of the Parish of St. Dunston's in the East, *Merchanttaillor*, and Ursula Bartlett, of the Parish of St. Gabriell Fenchurch, *by lycence.*
Jan. 30.	William Pickeringe, of the Parish of St. Gabriell Fenchurch, and Anne Kinge, of this Parish.

1586

May 12.	Thurston Croxston, of the Parish of Chaldwell, in Essex, and Johan Tasker, of this Parish.
June 8.	James Thomas, of this Parish, and Elizabeth Somner, *Wydowe*, also of this Parish.
Sep. 9.	William Johnson, of the Parish of St. Andrewe Undershaft, in London, and Cissely Smyth, of this Parish.
Sep. 18.	Symon Wood, of the Parish of St. Anne and Agnes within Aldersgate, and Margaret Grene, of this Parish.
Oct. 23.	Richard Lane, of the Parish of St. Pulcres, and Joane Normecoote, of this Parish.
Dec. 4.	William Betterley, of the Parish of St. Catherine's, nr. the Tower of London, and Prudence Smyth, of this Parish.

1587

Oct. 2.	George Samwell, of this Parish, and Anne Lovejoye, of the same Parish, *by lycence.*
Nov. 9.	Gyles Keys, of the Parish of St. Peter ad vincula within the Tower of London, and Elizabeth Astley, *Wydow* of this Parish, *by lycence.*
Nov. 26.	Peter Wayman, of the Parish of St. Gabriell Fanchurch, and Christian Weatherhill, of this Parish.
Jan. 28.	George Barne, of the Parish of All Hallows, in Lombard Streete, and Margery Manby, of this Parish.
Feb. 11.	William Dutton, of the Parish of St. Marye Woolchurche, and Margerye Dunnedge, of this Parish.

Mar. 4.   John Johnson, of the Parish of St. Ann and Agnes, Alders-gate, *Barbor-Surgeon,* and Margarell Askew, of this Parish, *by Abp's lycence.*

Mar. 13.   John Dudley, of the Parish of Hackney, Middlesex, *Gent.* and Marye Mosley, of the same Parish, *by Abp's lycence.*

1588

April 21.   John Blakestone, of the Parish of St. Marye Abchurch, and Betteresse Stockton, of this Parish.

May 12.   John Keyle, of this Parish, and Anne Slowes, of the Parish of Hackney, Midx.

May 13.   Thomas Hampton, of the Parish of St. Sepulchre's with-out Newgate, and Anne Betinson, *by lycence.*

May 19.   Henry Whaplod, of the Parish of St. Bridgett in Flete Street, and Dorothie Lutton, of this Parish, *by lycence.*

May 20.   John Phillippes, of the Parish of St. Buttolphe without Algate, and Elizabeth Phenick, of this Parish, *Wydowe.*

Oct. 22.   Thomas Evans, of this Parish, and Marye Jones, also of this Parish.

Nov. 11.   John Billingforde, of the Parish of St. Christofer's, nere the Stocks, and Elizabeth Robins, of this Parish.

Nov. 18.   Henry Barne, of this Parish, and Katherin Padmore, of the Parish of St. Edmunde the Kinge, *by Abp's lycence.*

Feb. 8.   Edwarde Davys, of Ludlowe, Co. Salop, and Hellenor Handbury, of this Parish.

Feb. 23.   Walter Dorrell, of Farneboroughe, Co. Warwick, *Gent.* and Dorothie Lane, of Chadwell, Co. Essex, *Wydowe,* *by Abp's lycence.*

1589

April 13.   Humfrey Baker, of the Parish of St. Bartholomew the lesse, near the Exchange, and Phillis Batchelor, of this Parish.

April 14.   William Presgrave, of the Parish of St. Margarett, in Lothbury, and Samuell [*sic*] Wakefeilde of this Parish.

May 4.   Mathew Salisburye, of the Parish of St. Mary Matfellon alias Whitechappell, and Johan Kirby of this Parish.

May 18.   Thomas Rippon, of the Parish of St. Andrewe Under-shafte, and Mary Ratcliffe, of this Parish.

May 19.   Francis Johnson, of the Parish of Laighton, Co. Essex, *Gent.*, and Mary Baker, of this Parish, *by Abp's lycence.*

June 22.   John Dunnydge, of the Parish of St. Margarett, in Lothbury, and Alice Sleighe, of this Parish, *by Abp's lycence.*

July 3.   Edward Nicholas of the Parish of St. Sepulchres without Newgate, and Margarett Offley, of this Parish.

Sep. 7.   Robert Randall, of St. Leonardes in Shoreditch, and Agnes Bradborne, of this Parish.

Jan. 27.   Gyles Sympson, of this Parish, and Christian Ferne, of the same Parish.

Feb. 26.   John Lancashier, of Highe Arcall, Co. Salopp, *Yoman,* and Johan Crosse, of the Parish of Eastethorneden, Co. Essex, *Wydowe, by lycence.*

1590

May 10.	James Powell, of the Parish of St. Clements, near Eastcheape, and Elizabeth Forrest, of this Parish.
Aug. 9.	Xpofer Wylkes, of the Parish of All Hallowes, Barkinge, in Tower Streete, and Jane Hall, of this Parish.
Sep. 3.	Nicholas Wakefeilde, of the Parish of St. Clement Danes without the barres, of the new Temple, *Gentleman*, and Hellen Chaesmore, of this Parish, *by lycence*.
Oct. 11.	Henrye Williams, of the Parish of Saviours, in Southwark, and Ursula Ridley, of this Parish.
Jan. 18.	William Swinborne, of the Parish of St. Andrewe's, in Holborne, and Sarah Cooke, of this Parish.
Feb. 14.	Maurice Evans, of the Parish of St. Anne in the blackfriers, and Betterice Roberte, of this Parish.

1591

Nov. 14.	Francis Hobbes, *Gentleman*, and Hellen Hamonde, of London, *Wydowe, by lycence*.
Jan. 10.	Francis Clark, of Stock Newington, Co. Midx., and Mary Bright, of Southwylde, in Essex, *Wydowe, by lycence*.
Feb. 6.	Richard Cheange, of this parish, and Elizabeth Offley, of the same Parish, *by lycence*.

1592

June 26.	Randall Gravener, of this Parish, and Elizabeth Woode, of the same Parish.
Oct. 1.	John Banberrye, of the Parish of Alhallows the Great, and Agnes Sympson, of this Parish.
Sep. 26.	John Gye, of Clifford's Inne, *Gentleman*, and Julian Sheeres, of this Parish, *by lycence*.
Jan. 30.	George Staynerodd, of the Parish of St. Vedast, in Foster Lane, and Mary Corbett, of this Parish.
Feb. 11.	Thomas Peare, of the Parish of S. Botulpe without Algate, and Suzan Clifford, of this Parish.

1593

Aug. 26.	Henry Parrey and Betteres Prestwoode, of the same Parish.
Sep. 3.	Henrye Dunne, of Modburrye, Co. Devon, and Dorothie Allen, of this Parish, *by lycence*.
Sep. 10.	Samuel Gee, of London, *Merchant*, and Cisley Alderson, of this Parish, *by lycence*.
Sep. 30.	William Evans, of the Parish of St. Lawrence Powntney, and Elizabeth Powell, of this Parish.
Nov. 7.	Samuell Boothe, of this Parish and Margarey Lowes, *Wydow*, late the wief of Cornelius Lowes, of the Parish of St. Saviour's, in Southwark, *Skynner, by lycence*.
Nov. 12.	John Cornishe, of the Parish of St. Mary Abchurch, and Cisley Wylner, of this Parish.
Dec. 9.	John Ivatt, of the Parish of St. Olaves, Silver Street, and Elizabeth Phillipps, of the Parish of St. Michaell's, London, *by lycence*.
Feb. 10.	Thomas Robson, of the Parish of St. Marie Abchurch, and Marye Heywarde, of this Parish, *by lycence*.

1594

April 21. Samuell Parker, of Ludlowe, Co. Salop, *Mercer*, and Hellen Barnard, of this Parish, *by lycence.*

June 23. Roger Mason, of the Parish of St. Martin's in the vintery, and Agnes Lews, of this Parish.

Oct. 6. Roberte Heardson, of the Parish of St. Augustine by Paule's gate, and Alice Thomas, of this Parish.

Sep. 15. William Ledesham, *Scrivener*, of London, and Elizabeth Wilson, of this Parish, daughter of Hughe Wylson, late Cityzen of London, deceased, *by lycence.*

Nov. 18. Raphe Burnett, *Draper*, and Magdalen Clark, of this Parish, *by lycence.*

Dec. 1. William Grafton and Frances Lyon, of this Parish.

Jan. 19. Richard Bowdeler, of this Parish, and Katherin Palmer, of the same Parish.

Feb. 16. Christian Anthonye, of this Parish, and Elizabeth Willamson, *Wydowe*, also of this Parish.

1595

May 18. John Morgan, of the Parish of St. Hellins, and Jane Parry, of this Parish, *Wydowe.*

June 29. Abraham Moore, of the Parish of St. Clement Dane without Temple Barr, and Elizabeth Smythe, of this Parish.

Aug. 31. John Cowper, of the Parish of St. Nicholas Acon, *Merchanttaillor*, and Agnes Hadley, of this Parish, *by lycence.*

Oct. 14. Thomas Harware, of the Parish of St. Mary Woolchurch, *Merchanttaillor*, and Katherin Averill, of Hatton, Co. Warwick, *Yeoman, by lycence.*

Feb. 22. George Nickson, of the Parish of St. Swithin, neare London Stone, *Merchanttaillor*, and Jane Grymes, *Wydowe*, of this Parish, *by lycence.*

1596

June 7. Xpofer Walker, of Hunsdon, Co. Herts, *Yoman*, and Grace Laneham, of the same Towne and Parish of Hunsdon, *by lycence.*

Oct. 3. Thomas Elinge, of the Parish of St. Botulphs without Algate, and Marye Jarveys, of this Parish.

Jan. 23. John Nicolles, of this Parish, and Elizabeth Tanner, also of this Parish.

1597

April 17. Richard Rudd, of the Parish of St. Milrede in the Powltrye, *Haberdasher*, and Anne, daughter of Thomas Clarke, of this Parish, *Haberdasher, by lycence.*

April 22. John Woold, *Yeoman*, and Adrye, daughter of Roger Keymer, of East Grenewich, Co. Kent, *Gent., by lycence.*

April 24. Richard Brigge and Elizabeth Bulvand, both of this Parish.

May 8. Melchizadeck Fraunce, of the Parish of All St. Stayninge, and Johan Myll, of this Parish.

Sep. 21.	Mathewe Lownes, of the Parish of St. Dunstan's in the West, *Stacioner*, and Ann, daughter of Thomas Halwood, of the Cittie of Westminster, deceased, *Yeoman, by lycence.*
Oct. 3.	William Talent, of the Parish of St. Nicholas Acon, *Pewterer*, and Hellen Weld, of London, *Wydowe, by lycence.*
Feb. 26.	Francis, Grenehaughe, of the Parish of St. Mary Botchawe, of London, *Iremonger*, and Jane Offley, of this Parish, *by lycence.*

1598

July 26.	George Humble, of this Parish, and Agnes Moodye, also of this Parish.
July 10.	Richard Baylie, of the Parish of Beckenfeild, Co. Bucks, and Alice Brothers, of this Parish.
Nov. 30.	Richard Phillippes, of the Parish of St. John Zacharie, and Suzan Hutchins, of this Parish.
Dec. 10.	Roberte Olde, of the Parish of St. Nicholas Acon, and Thomazin Robins, of this Parish.

1599

July 23.	Edmund Parker and Elizabeth Bayllie.
Sep. 23.	William Herring, of the Parish of St. Lawrence Pountney, and Suzan Hargrave, of this Parish.
Oct. 31.	James Pemmerton, *Goldsmith*, of the Parish of St. Foster, in Foster Lane, and Mistress Anne Hadley, *Widdowe*, of this Parish, *by licence.*
Dec. 20.	John Nobbs, of Stanstead, Co. Herts, and Martha Bothell, of the same place, *by lycence.*
Jan. 20.	Stephen Blanck, of Barkinge Parish, in Tower Streete, and Anne Hammerton, of this Parish.

1600

April 26.	Frauncis Fisher, of the Parish of St. Martine's Ludgate, and Katherin, daughter of Thomas Clark, *Haberdasher*, of this Parish, *by lycence.*
May 18.	Edward Jones, of the Parish of St. Sepulchre's, and Jane, daughter of Anthony Sounde, *Clothworker*, of this Parish.
July 20.	Richard Shertoune and Christian Massey, both of the Parish of St. Andrewe Hubbard, *by licence.*
Aug. 17.	William Doughtie, of the Parish of St. Bartholomew the great, and Joan Watte, of this Parish, out of the house of William Jones.
Sep. 28.	Barnabye Turvill and Anne Alloway, both of this Parish, out of the house of William Alloway
Nov. 26.	Robert Sachis, of Stepney Parish, and Martha Holand, of this Parish.
Jan. 19.	James Dod, of the Parish of Barking in Tower Streete, and Elizabeth Conyes, of the Parish of St. Bartholomew, near the Exchange, *by lycence.*

1601

April 26.	George Bronkard, of the Parish of St. Buttolpps, near near Billingsgate, and Joane Backhouse, of this Parish.

May 10.   John Bramley, of Totnam high Crosse, and Joane Haword, of this Parish.

June 29.   William Rainecock, of the Parish of St. Sepulchre, and Margery Wood, of this Parish, *by lycence.*

Nov. 1.   Nicholas Urben and Joane Rocrofte, of the Parish of St. Olaves, in Hart Streete, *by lycence.*

Feb. 8.   Barnabas Gregory and Elizabeth Feake, both of this Parish.

1602

April 5.   Richard Harison, of this Parish, and Mary Chambers, of Heese, in the Co. Mid., *by lycence.*

May 2.   Henry Wilson, of this Parish, and Margery Mallett, of the Parish of St. Leonard, in Shorditch.

May 16.   Edward Monny and Barbary Sagrose, both of this Parish.

May 30.   George Harding, of the Parish of St. John uppon Wal-brook, and Alice Lowe, of this Parish.

July 18.   Daniell Cooper, of St. Mary Hills, and Mary Coates, of St. Martin Outwich, *by lycence.*

Aug. 8.   Robert Trigger and Jane Kenton, of this Parish, *by licence.*

Oct. 30.   Richard Francklyn and Jane Busbye, both of this Parish.

Dec. 9.   William Ritch, *Gentleman*, of the Parish of St. John Zachary, in Foster Lane, and Cicely Patchin, of Camberwell, in Surry, *by lycence.*

Dec. 16.   George Baynard, *Gentleman of the Savoy*, and Tibatha Rawlins, of the Parish of St. Auntlins, *by lycence.*

Feb. 14.   William Herringe, of St. Swithen's, and Katherin Childerley, of this Parish.

1603

May 1.   Roger Trapells, of the Parish of St. Michaell, near Queenehith, and Elizabeth Phippes, of this Parish.

June 13.   Thomas Letthall, of the Parish of St. Peter, in Cornehill, and Margrett Sympson, of this Parish.

June 21.   John Meredeth and Prudence Butler, *by lycence.*

June 21.   William Ellis and Rose Rosse, *by lycence.*

Dec. 22.   Charles Harney, of the Parish of St. Margrette, in new Fishe Strete, and Margreat Marlow, of this Parish, *by licence.*

Dec. 26.   William Jones, of this Parish, and Jane Westley, of this Parish, *by licence.*

Jan. 2.   Thomas Sone, of the Parish of St. Mary Wolchurch, and Hester Robynson, of this Parish, *by licence.*

Feb. 16.   Peter Waters and Anne Cobb, both of the Parish of Grenewich, *by licence.*

Mar. 11.   Symon Brome, of the Parish of St. Sepulchre's, and Isabell Copley, of this Parish, *by licence.*

1604

April 22.   John Bull, of St. Faithe's Parish, and Elizabeth Hen, of this Parish.

May 14.   John Porter, of the Parish of Mary, Whitechappell, and Joane Ardway, of this Parish.

June 21.   William Chetwick, of Suffolk, *Gentleman*, and Katherin Slaney, of St. Dunston's in the Easte.

Aug. 12.   Morgan Guillam, of St. Steven's, in Colman Strete, and Marye Robson, of this Parish.

Aug. 16.   Ambrose Greene, of St. Mary, Aldermanbury, *Curryer*, and Edith Anthonye, of this Parish, *by licence.*

Sep. 10.   David Lewes, of the Parish of St. Swithen, and Katherin Connus, of the Parish of St. Lawrence Poultney, *by licence.*

Nov. 4.   Edward Clarke, of the parish of St. John's, in Walbrook, and Beatrice Norbery, of this Parish.

Nov. 7.   William Louis and Denis Sadler, both of this Parish.

Jan. 21.   Lewes Thomas, of St. Bride's Parish, and Anne Vicars, of this Parish, *by licence.*

Feb. 10.   John Hill, of the Parish of St. Edmund, in Lombard Strete, and Anne Swinton, of this Parish, *by licence.*

1605

April 1.   William Stragge, *Butcher*, of St. Sepulchre's Parish, and Margery Batman, of this Parish, *by licence.*

May 5.   John Danger and Anne Spencer, both of this Parish.

July 7.   John Pickeringe, of the Parish of St. Edmond the kinge, and Ellen Blees, of this Parish.

Dec. 1.   Thomas Burbage, of the Parish of St. Buttolph without Bishopsgate, and Allis Stockdon, of this Parish.

Jan. 9.   Thomas Bowen and Blanch Noble, both of this Parish.

Feb. 16.   William Jones, of St. Buttolphe without Bishopsgate, and Joane Hopper, of this Parish.

1606

May 22.   George Melton, of the Parish of Bushy, Co. Herts., *Gentleman*, and Bridget Rishby, of the Parish of Thorpe Mortaux, Co. Suffolk.

June 24.   Thomas Addy, of the Parish of St. Michaell, in Cornehill, and Mildred Umble, of this Parish.

July 4.   Edward Reeve, of the Parish of Alhollowes the great, in Thames strete, and Margerye, daughter of William Kirkman, of Bristow, *Marchant.*

Aug. 2.   Abraham Peeter, of the Parish of St. Leonard, in Shorditch, and Jane Tadinclowe, of the same Parish, *by licence.*

Aug. 24.   Richard Ratcliffe, of the Parish of Henden, Co. Midx., and Elizabeth Silvestre, of this Parish.

Sep. 7.   Thomas Clarke, of the Parish of St. Margrett's, in Lothbury, and Elizabeth Tisdell, of this Parish.

Jan. 25.   George Bate, *Minister* of the Parish of Maids Norton, Co. Bucks., and Mary Willkes, of Layton Bussard, Co. Beds.

Feb. 17.   Francis Taverner, of St. Christopher's, and Agnes Duns, of St. Fayth's, *by licence.*

1607

April 2.   Edmund West, of Maresmorth, Co. Bucks., *Esquier*, and Theodosia, daughter of Edward Terrill, in the same Co., *Gent.*, *by licence.*

June 14.   Leonard Hattly, of this Parish, and Joan Michener, of the same, *by licence.*

June 28.   James Skipp, of the Parish of Hackney, and Anne Davides, of this Parish.

Dec. 26.   William Allet, *Marchanttaillor*, of the Parish of St. Marye, Abchurch, and Anne Dixon, of this Parish, *by licence.*

Feb. 7.   Robert Easte, of the Parish of St. Gyles, and Alice Easte, of this Parish.

1608

May 10.   John Illingworth, of the Parish of St. Leonard, in Foster Lane, and Ellin Goodman, of this Parish.

Oct. 15.   William Carter, of the Parish of St. Mary Magdalen, and Agnes Tailor, of this Parish.

Nov. 15.   Thomas Hughes, of the Parish of Christchurch, and Joan Francklin, of this Parish.

Nov. —[*sic*] John Neweman, of the Parish of St. Margaret, in Lothbury, and Margaret Hall, of this Parish, *by licence.*

Dec. 11.   Thomas Westley, *Vintner*, and Elizabeth Chessheire, *by licence.*

Jan. 2.   Edward Andrewe, of the Parish of St. Andrewe, in Holborn, and Easter Smith, of Allhallowes, Barking, *by licence.*

Feb. 9.   Thomas Ferrars, of the Parish of St. Andrew Undershaft, and Joane Clarke, of this Parish.

Feb. 26.   William Wade, of St. Buttolphs without Bishopsgate, and Margery Courny, of this Parish.

Feb. 28.   Henry Annly, of the Parish of St. John Zachary, Foster Lane, and Suzan Lowell, of St. Mary Abchurch Parish.

1609

Aug. 3.   William Selby, of Lambeth, *Gentleman*, and Jeane Wilkinson, of Essex, *by licence.*

Oct. 22.   Robert Nunne, of the Parish of St. Lawrence Poultny, and Jeane Crones, of this Parish.

1610

April 9.   Nathaniel Bucocke and Katherin Shuter, *by licence.*

April 17.   Robert Osborne and Frizell Jackson, of Westminster, *by licence.*

May 6.   John Greenehocke, of St. Margaret, New Fish Strete, and Johan Rolfe, of this Parish, servant to Mr. Herringhooke.

Jan. 12.   Sir Robert Douglas and Nicholas Murrey, *by licence.*

Sep. 17.   Henry Goldinge, of the Parish of Great Allhallowes, in Thames Strete, and Allis Bury, of this Parish.

Oct. 8.   Thomas Chapman, and Anne Harding, both of this Parish, *by licence.*

Oct. 22.   Thomas Atkinson and Lettis Hamore, both of this Parish, *by licence.*

Jan. 7.   Richard Wright, of Essex, *Gentleman*, and Dorathye Dutton, of this Parish, *by licence.*

Jan. 31.   Gilbert Picket, of Witham, in Essex, and Grace Nokes, of Essex also, *by licence.*

1611

April 8.	John Hayes and Elizabeth Dunne, both of Bennet Grace-church, *by licence.*
Sep. 29.	Hugh Davyds and Anne Chesmore, *Widdowe*, of this Parish, *by licence.*
Oct. 8.	William Benbow, of St. Margaret on New Fish Strete, and Marye Meane, of this Parish.
Oct. 12.	John Frances and Clement, daughter of Thomas Waferer, of Sandwich, *by licence.*
Dec. 1.	John Murfey, of St. Albons Parish, and Clary East, of this Parish.
Jan. 1.	George Chambers and Debora Tangby, both of this Parish.
Jan. 9.	Christopher Thwayte and Mary Allyson, both of St. Sepulcre's, *by licence.*
Feb. 6.	Jasper Cressey, of the Parish of Stratford bowe, Co. Middx., and Johan, daughter of Edward Poole.

1612

May 3.	Richard Prosser, of the Parish of Katherine Creechurch, and Agnes Griffen, of this Parish.
June 29.	John Hubbard, of St. Mychaell in the Querne, *Stationer*, and Elizabeth Hawkes, of Itcham, Co. Kent, *by licence.*
July 8.	Thomas Hunter and Margaret Kent, both of this Parish.
Aug. 2.	Robert Mann, of Mattellon, alias Whitechappell, and Effen Weden, of this parish.
Aug. 9.	Robert Winne, of Margaret, Lothbury, and Ellen Fasset, of this Parish.
Aug. 9.	William Hutchinson, of Alford, Co. Lincoln, *Mercer*, and Anne, daughter of Francis Marbury, *Minister, by licence.*
Sep. 10.	James Bowes, of St. Alphege, *Currier*, and Jone Horne, of St. Stephen's, Colman Street, *by licence.*
Sep. 27.	Robert Button, of St. Bennett Finck, and Elizabeth Clarke, of this Parish, *by licence.*
Nov. 1.	William Clarke, of St. Clement Dane, and Venis Swifte, of this Parish.
Nov. 18.	George Stevenson, of Fullam, Co. Middlesex, and Anne Newman, of the same Parish, *by licence.*
Jan. 21.	Thomas Issot, of St. Ganors Parish, and Margaret Batersby, of this Parish.
Feb. 14.	Richard Colethurst, of St. Bride's Parish, London, and Margaret, daughter of Robert Millington, of Rutford, in Chesshire, *Esquier.*

1613

April 22.	Richard Henson, of Barnard's Inn, *Gent.*, and Margaret Howard, of the Co. of Norfolk, *by licence.*
May 4.	Jarvis Haughton, of St. Magnus, and Jane Vutton, of this Parish, *by licence.*
May 25.	William Tompson, of St. Martin's in the feildes, and Ellen Fisher, of this Parish.
July 24.	Willyam Greene and Anne Leake, both of St. Savor's Parish, *by licence.*
Oct. 15.	Anthony Hayward and Susan, daughter of Willyam Lancaster, of Bexsley, in Kent.

Nov. 11.	Robert Jeames, of Whetstone, Co. Middlesex, *Butcher*, and Anne, daughter of Richard Voue, *Tanner*, by *licence*.
Feb. 16.	Richard Baker, of Low Layton, in Essex, and Marget Aburne, of Christchurch, in London, *by licence*.

1614

April 25.	Mr. Josias Shute, *Parson*, and Elizabeth Glanvild, of this Parish, *by licence*.
June 5.	Thomas Hopswood and Mary Nicols, both of this Parish.
June 13.	Thomas Young and Mary Bradley, both of this Parish.
Nov. 17.	Thomas Bownest, of St. Nycholos Acons, and Mary Gynne, of this Parish, *by licence*.
Nov. 30.	James Archer, *Mynister*, and Anne Legat, *by licence*.
Dec. 29.	Francis Browne, of Mary Woolchurch, *Haberdasher*, and Susan Newman, of Mychaell, Cornehill, *by licence*.

1615

May 4.	Willyam Packwood, of Katherine Colman, and Agnes Smith, of this Parish.
May 16.	Thomas Willyams, of Broxbourne, Co. Hartford, and Elizabeth, daughter of Edward Myles, of the same Co., Yoman.
June 11.	John Creswell, of St. Gyles, Cripplegate, and Lettis Jones, of this Parish.
June 26.	Richard Watlington, *Marchanttaylor*, of the Parish of Margret Moyses, and Elizabeth Browne, of this Parish.
Aug. 3.	John Osborne and Cornelia Dorper, both of this Parish.
Sep. 26.	Thomas Willson and Katherine White, of Wood Street, *by licence*.
Oct. 23.	Robert Chaplin, of St. Bride's, and Rose Bettes, of this Parish, *by licence*.
Nov. 7.	William Boddington and Elizabeth Kelsy, both of this Parish, *by licence*.
Jan. 31.	Francis Cullumbre, *Merchant*, and Chrystyon Vinchowe, *Wyddowe*, *by licence*.

1616

Aug. 14.	Sir Nicholas Carewe, alias Throckmorton, and Suzan Butler, of this Parish, *Widdowe*, *by licence*.
Oct. 20.	Henry Avens, of St. Swethen, and Anne Thackam, of this Parish.
Oct. 24.	John Falkener, of Baldon, in Sussex, and Thimothia —— [*sic*] *by licence*.
Nov. 24.	Nicholas Mules, of St. Katherine Creechurch, and Jane Temple, of this Parish.
Jan. 24.	Aearome Crue, of St. Katherin Colmans, and Mandlyn Buckett, of St. Saviour's, in Southwark, *by licence*.
Feb. 27.	John Ketch, of St. Olaves, in Southwark, and Sara Weldinge, of the same Parish, *by licence*.
Mar. 3.	Edward Wynerd, of St. Martin, Ludgate, *Taylor*, and Elizabeth, daughter of Thomas Duffield, of Bridgwell, in Buckinghamsheir, *by licence*.

1617

April 21. Thomas Johnson, of Stepney, in Middx., *Marryner*, and
            Elizabeth Bugebery, of this Parish.
April 22. George Segar, of Lewes, Co. Sussex, and Suzan, daughter
            of one Bennett, late of the County of Devonshire,
            Clarke, deceased, *by licence*.
April 29. Thomas Allen and Judith Rydge, both of this Parish.
Oct. 7.   Samuell Kinge, of St. Michael's in the Querne, *Haber-
            dasher*, and Katherin Peeterson, of Albany, Co.
            Hereford [*sic*].
Nov. 30.   Gilbert Wood and Margaret Terrey, both of this Parish.
Dec. 8.   Ellys Carpentar, *Sheeregrynder*, of this Parish, and Helene
            Person, of St. Clement without Temple Barre.

1618

May 17.   Nathaniel Gestford, of St. Buttolph's without Bishopsgate,
            and Elizabeth Crippes, of this Parish.
June 18. Richard Harris, of Studley, Co. Warwick, *Butcher*, and
            Anne, daughter of one Kerby, of Henly, Co. Warwick,
            Baker, *by licence*.
July 13. Walter Farr, of Buttesbury, Co. Essex, and Katherine,
            daughter of John Cliff, of Ingerstone, Co. Essex, *by
            licence*.
Sep. 23. Michael Boone, of Great St. Helens, and Bridgett
            Ampleford, of this Parish.
Oct. 22. Robert Goff, of Blachington, Co. Sussex, and Martha
            Barber, of Camberwell, Co. Surrey, *Widowe, by licence*.
Dec. 15. Richard Lowcock, of St. Michaell Basingshaw, and
            Dorothy Lanly, of this Parish.
Dec. 18. Anthony Turner and Dorithie Buckingham, of Higate,
            Co. Middlesex, *by licence*.
Dec. 21. Thomas Fisher, of St. Katherine, neare the Tower, and
            Mary Lumber, of this Parish.
Dec. 21. Richard Sharpe, of the Inner Temple, London, *Gentleman*,
            and Mary Terry, of this Parish, *by licence*.
Jan. 27. Peeter Early, of St. Clements without Temple Barre, and
            Venice Walker, of Wotton Underwood, Co. Bucking-
            ham, *by licence*.
Feb. 8.   John Battell and Dennys Mansworth, of Stamford
            Byuers, Co. Essex, *by licence*.

1619

May 2.   Thomas Woodlowe, of St. Michaell, Basingshall, and
            Alice Jordan, of this Parish.
May 9.   Thomas Whitby, *Fishmonger*, of St. Gyles in the Feildes,
            and Susan Wilson, of this Parish, *by licence*.
June 13. Repentance Hatch, *Pavier*, of St. Olave, Southwark, and
            Mary Wenne, of this Parish.
June 24. Roger Danyell and Dorithie Ridge, both of this Parish.
June 26. Leonard Baxtrey, *Serjeant of law*, of the towne of Boston,
            in Lyncolnsheire, and Mary, late wife of Robert Tigh,
            Doctor of Divinitie, of Barkinge, London, *by licence*.
July 15. Henry Croane, of the parish of Trinity, in Trinity Lane,
            and Anne Hillar, of this Parish, *by licence*.

Aug. 8.	Nicholas Keyes, of St. George, Southwark, and Elizabeth Elders, of this Parish.
Nov. 28.	Francis Wright, of St. Saviour's, Southwark, and Elizabeth Cheven, of this Parish.
Dec. 2.	Thomas Burles, of Chelmsford, Co. Essex, *Gent.*, and Penelope Brampton, of St. Michaell the Querne, *by licence.*
Dec. 8.	William Johnson, of St. Stevens in Walbrook, and Mary Staples, of this Parish, *by licence.*
Feb. 24.	John Benbowe, of St. Martins in the ffeildes, and Elizabeth, daughter of William Hodges, of Ilchester, Co. Somerset, *by licence.*

1620

May 16.	Francis Browne, of St. Mary Woolchurch, and Anne Lee, *Widdow*, of St. Peter in Cornhill, *by licence.*
June 29.	Samuel Pritchard, of St. Buttolphe without Algate, and Michol, daughter of Henry Rhodes, of Dover, *by licence.*
July 6.	Lewis Malapart, of Whitechappell, and Dorathy, daughter of Nichas Keys, of Eaton Bridg, Co. Kent, *by licence.*
Oct. 3.	Marke Coloune and Marye Glascock, both of this Parish, *by licence.*
Oct. 12.	William Starling, of Gillingham, in Kent, and Anne Troughton, of this Parish, *by licence.*
Oct. 18.	John Rapley, of St. Buttolphe without Bishopsgate, and Margarett Hill, of St. Giles without Cripplegate, *by licence.*
Oct. 18.	Henry Richarson, *Haberdasher*, and Elizabeth Cooke, *Widdowe*, both of this Parish, *by licence.*
Oct. 26.	Henry Wilkinson, of the pish gate, Burton in Lincolneshire, and Jone Wright, of Westmynster, *by licence.*
Oct. 29.	Richard Huswhat, of Ware, and Helen Bristow, of this Parish.
Nov. 8.	Xpofer Rose, of East Derham, Co. Norff, and Mary, daughter of John Neve, of the same Parish, *by licence.*
Nov. 9.	Thomas Morton and Margaret Banes, *Widdowe*, both of Alhallowes in the Wall, *by licence.*
Nov. 12.	Edward Chave and Ellen Bellison, both of this Parish.
Dec. 26.	Andrew Glascock, of St. Xpofers by the Stocks, *Haberdasher*, and Siceley Sedgwick, of this Parish, *by licence.*
Jan. 29.	Thomas Smithsby, *Saddler*, and Martha, daughter of John Smith, *Cordwayner*, of St. Dunston's in West, *by licence.*

1621

Mar. 25.	Mathew Hart, *Cooke*, of Stepney, and Cristian Hawes, of St. Foster's, in Foster Lane, *by licence.*
May 1.	John White, of Alhallowes in the Wall, and Elizabeth Beeston, of this Parish.
May 24.	Gresham Hincks, of St. Vedast, in Foster Lane, *Goldsmith*, and Hellen, daughter of Peter Potter, of St. John, Walbrooke, Haberdasher, *by licence.*
July 11.	William Everly, *Goldsmith*, and Anne Shevery, both of this Parish, *by banes.*

July 11.   George Glidwell, *Milliner*, and Sara Jeckins, both of this Parish, *by banes.*

Aug. 29.   John Richardson and Anne Deakins, both of this Parish, *by licence.*

Oct. 21.   William Gardiner, of Aldermanbury, and Elizabeth Lugg, of this Parish, *by licence.*

Dec. 9.   George Suger, of Little Alhallowes, in Thames Strete, and Mary Sanders, of this Parish, *by licence.*

Jan. 6.   John Fossey, of Great Alhallowes, and Christian Blowe, of this Parish, *by banes.*

Feb. 5.   William Sute, of St. Alphage, and Margery Holdes, of this Parish.

Feb. 10.   John Morgan, of St. Ethelbergh, and Elizabeth Guilliams, of this Parish, *by banes.*

Mar. 3.   Andrew Holford, of St. Leonard's, in Eastcheap, and Hellen Webster, of Christe Church, *by licence.*

Mar. 4.   Robert Bradshawe and Elizabeth Bedford, *Widdowe*, both of Stepney.

1622

Sep. 26.   Thomas Wharton, of Gillingwood, Co. York, and Susan Hayes, of Aldermanbury, *by licence.*

Nov. 4.   John Weld, and Elizabeth Glanfield, both of this Parish, *by licence.*

Dec. 10.   James Dickinson, of St. Olaves, Southwark, and Rachaell Tomlins, of this Parish, *by licence.*

Dec. 26.   William Manley and Elizabeth Samwell, both of this Parish, *by licence.*

Feb. 11.   Thomas Gold, of St. Mary Maudlin, Southwark, and Anne Wilkinson, of this Parish, *by banes.*

Feb. 23.   John Mayfeilde, of St. Gyles without Cripplegate, and Rose Waring, of this Parish, *by licence.*

1623

April 20.   Henry Stone, of St. Thomas Apostle, London, and Anne Lammas, of this Parish, *by banes.*

July 21.   John Foster, of Stepney, Co. Middlesex, and Ginnifer Foster, of this Parish, *by licence.*

July 24.   William White, of Colchester, in Essex, and Thomasine, Harsenet, of this Parish, *by banes.*

July 30.   Henry Semer, of Westend, and Mary Wellsted, of Riselipp, in Co. Middlesex, *by licence.*

Aug. 3.   Robert Hamore and Mary Hill, both of this Parish, *by licence.*

Sep. 25.   Thomas Godfree, of St. Leonard's, Brumley, Co. Middlesex, and Joahne Muddle, of the same Parish, *by licence.*

Sep. 29.   Thomas Grove, *Letherseller*, of St. Mildred, in the Poultrey, and Susan Gilbert, of St. John, Walbrook, *by licence.*

Oct. 2.   Walter Carpenter, of St. Clement's without Temple barre, and Dorothy Blandy, of St. Mary Bothawe, *Widdowe*, *by licence.*

Oct. 13.   Jeremy Jones, of St. Bartholomew, and Dorothy Seyliard, of Delaware, in Kent, *by licence.*

Oct. 29.   John Power and Jane Jenings, of St. Steven's, Colman Street, *by licence.*

Nov. 9.   Gabriell Ellis, of St. Sepulchres without Newgate, and Elizabeth Bowes, of this Parish, *by banes.*

Jan. 20.   Sir John Andrewes, of Longden, Co. Worcester, *Knight,* and the Lady Mary Prince, of Longden, in the Co. of Salop, *Widdowe, by licence.*

1624

Mar. 26.   William Watkins, of St. Christopher behind the Exchange, *Merchant Grocer,* and Mary, daughter of William Rolfe, *Goldsmith,* of this Parish, *by licence.*

July 5.   Nicholas Hussey, of St. Olaves Stayning in Marke Lane, and Anne Tilton, of this Parish, *by banes.*

Aug. 22.   Mathew Kinaston and Judith Lonewell, both of this Parish, *by licence.*

Nov. 7.   Valentine Smith, of St. Dunstans in the West, *Taylor,* and Mary Babham, of this Parish, *by licence.*

Nov. 18.   Edward Dexter, *Clerk of this Parish,* and Thomasyn Jennings, of St. Swythens, *by banes.*

Nov. 21.   Ambrose Brunskell, of St. Edmund, Lumbard Street, and Elizabeth Humble, of this Parish, *by licence.*

Nov. 30.   Thomas Onslowe, of St. Brides, and Judith Addison, of St. James' Parish, in Duke's Place, *by licence.*

Dec. 27.   Joseph Skynner, of Abchurch, and Mary Layton, *Widow,* of St. Edmund the King, Lombard Street, *by licence.*

Feb. 2.   Henry Washborne, of St. Antholins, and Ann Tukeridge, of this Parish, *by licence.*

Mar. 31.   John Davis, *Barber Surgeon,* of St. Gregorie, Paules-churchyard, and Mary Briggenshaw, of Aston, Co. Bucks, *by licence.*

1625

Feb. 13.   John Hobson, of Islington, *Yeoman,* and Alice Deacon, of Worcester, *by licence.*

Feb. 17.   Richard Raper, of St. Dunstans in the West, and Margaret Hall, of St. Clements without Temple Barr.

Mar. 11.   Robert Bagley, of Ffurnifalls Inne, *Gent.,* and Ellen Hall, of St. Clements without Temple Barr, *by licence.*

Mar. 23.   John Peirce, of Isleworth, in Middlesex, and Rebecca Sheffeild, of St. Michaells in the Querne, *by licence.*

1626

April 25.   John Heape, *Grocer,* of St. Laurence in the Jury, and Ann, daughter of Thomas White, of this Parish, *by licence.*

May 26.   Henry Clow, of Tunbridge, in Kent, and Martha Stanton, in Essex, *by licence.*

June 18.   John Fooke, *Merchant,* of Barkinge, and Katherine Brigges, of this Parishe, *by licence.*

Sep. 21.   John Ling, *Oylman,* and Elizabeth Hill, both of this Parish, *by licence.*

Sep. 21.   John Willughby, of Penshur, in Kent, *Gent.,* and Anne Lested, of Snigfield, in Surrey, *by licence.*

Oct. 29.	Thomas Warde, of St. Dunstan's in the East, and Mary Turkey, of this Parish, *by banes.*
Oct. 30.	James Crips, of Northflete, in Kent, and Mary Sharpe, *Widdowe,* of Chart Magna, in Kent, *by licence.*
Jan. 9.	James Turner, of Christchurch, and Ellen Taylor, *Widdowe,* of Abchurch, *by licence.*
Jan. 10.	Enock Porter, of Alhallowes, in Thames Streete, and Margarett Fishley, of this Parish, *by licence.*
Feb. 4.	William Sanckey and Anne Farfeild, both of this Parish, *by licence.*

1627

Mar. 26.	Hezekiah Hardinge, of Clifford's Inne, and Judith Billingsley, of St. Dunstan's in the East, *by licence.*
Mar. 26.	Israell Scarlett, of Wapping, and Julian Theobalds, *Widdowe,* both of the Parish of Whitechappell [*sic*] *by licence.*
April 22.	Richard Dixson, of St. Mary Whitechappell, and Suzan Nicholls, of this Parish, *by banes.*
May 6.	John Staples, of St. Giles without Cripplegate, and Joane Thorpe, of Alphage, *by licence.*
July 8.	Edward Porter, *Carman,* of St. Martin's in the Vintree, and Francis Tapp, *Widdowe,* of St. Olaves, Hart Street, *by licence.*
Dec. 27.	Robert Lewis, of St. Buttolphes without Bishopsgate, and Anne Smith, of this Parish, *by licence.*
Feb. 3.	Francis Johnson, of St. Buttolph's, Aldersgate, and Mary Walford, of the same Parish, *by licence.*
Feb. 5.	John Hawkins, of St. Edmund the King, in Lumbard Streete, and Mary Hill, of this Parish, *by licence.*

1628

April 24.	Thomas Weld, of this Parish, *Grocer,* and Anne Kempton, of Ware, *by licence.*
May 20.	William Boswell, of St. Saviours, and Jane Gimlett, of this Parish, *by banes.*
June 5.	Thomas Woodward, *Esquier,* of St. Bartholomew, near the Exchange, and Jane Haynes, *by licence.*
June 15.	William Hawkins, of St. Margarett's, in Westminster, and Mary, daughter of Francis Mills, of Hampshire, *by licence.*
June 22.	Humfrey Crouch, of St. Edmond, in Lombard Streete, and Winifride Worshipp, of this Parish, *by banes.*
June 26.	Robert Meacin, *Parson,* of Yeldam Magna, in Essex, and Sara Shorter, *Widdowe,* of St. John, in Wolbrook, *by licence.*
July 3.	Francis Jackson, of St. Xpofer's, and Anne Nixon, of this Parish, *by licence.*
Sep. 24.	Thomas Dobbs, of St. Clement Danes, and Margarett Day, of Midd, at Drayton, *by licence.*
Nov. 3.	Edward Tuffin, of Isleworth, *Baker,* and Jone Tomes, of this Parish, *by licence.*
Nov. 25.	John Dranstile, of St. Magnus, *Grocer,* and Anne Leigh, of this Parish, *by licence.*

Nov. 27.	Walter Costerloe, of St. Katherine, Colman, and Anne Ashe, of Yorkshire, *by licence.*
Dec. 14.	Edward Ragdale, of Abchurch, and Bridgett Lawson, of this Parish, *by licence.*
Dec. 18.	John Smith, of Abchurch, and Sara Sherman, of this Parish, *by licence.*
Dec. 28.	Andrewe Dansey, of Abchurch, and Anne Rudd, of this Parish, *by licence.*
Feb. 16.	Thomas Battersby, of St. Martin's in the Feilds, and Judith Rushford, of the same Parish, *by licence.*

1629

April 19.	Thomas Goodman, of St. Butholphs, Aldersgate, and Johan Turner, of this Parish, *by banes*
May 18.	Henry Kempton, of Mepershall, Co. Bedford, and Annie Parratt, of Shillington, same Co., *by licence.*
May 18.	John Tighe, of Kirby, in Co. Lincolne, *Esquire*, and Anne Lister, of Rippingale, same Co., *by licence.*
Aug. 18.	John Dearsley, of Whitechappell, and Mary Harris, of Deptford, in Kent, *by licence.*
Aug. 24.	Richard Nevell, of St. Clements in Eastcheap, and Mary Harris, of this Parish, *by licence.*
Sep. 2.	Richard Cooke, of St. Mary Mounthawe, and Elizabeth Daudley, of St. Giles Without Cripplegate, *by licence.*
Sep. 14.	Edwin Rich, of Luccoly, Co. Middlesex, *Esquire*, and the Lady Jane Suckling, of St. Brides, *Widowe.*
Oct. 29.	Thomas Riske, of Aldermary, *Haberdasher*, and Anne Harrison, of this Parish, *by banes.*
Nov. 8.	Thomas Hudson, of St. Mary Bothawe, *Haberdasher*, and Honor Humble, of this Parish, *by licence.*
Nov. 23.	William Goddard, *Doctor of Phisik*, and Mary Mathewes, both of St. Brides in Fleete Streete, *by licence.*
Dec. 15.	Richard Withip, of St. Dunstans in the West, and Thomazin Mason, of St. Leonards, Shoreditch, *by licence.*
Feb. 2.	Edward Greene, of St. Martins in the Feilds, and Mary Bancroft, of Wilsden, Middlesex, *by licence.*
Feb. 9.	Frauncis Malbery, of this Parish, and Elizabeth Burton, of Epping, Co. Essex, *by licence.*

1630

Mar. 29.	Robert Wood, of St. Peters at the Tower, and Elizabeth Wilde, *Widowe*, of this Parish, *by licence.*
April 11.	Thomas Burton, of St. Leonards, Shoreditch, and Florence Gulston, of this Parish, *by licence.*
April 20.	Henry Bengie, of St. Bartholomews, near the Royal Exchange, *by licence* [*sic*]
April 25.	Nicholas Henton, of St. Mary, Somersett, and Katherine Turnor, of this Parish, *by banes.*
May 10.	Thomas Cooper, of St. Nicholas Acons, and Johan Bisse, of this Parish, *by licence.*
May 18.	Henry Blackmeere, *Goldsmith*, and Mary Magdalene Kinge, *Widowe*, both of this Parish, *by licence.*
May 18.	Arthur Wakefield, of Creechurch, and Elizabeth Leake, of Costack, Co. Leicester, *by licence.*

June 2.	John Stone, of St. Dunstan in the West, and Margarett Stithe, of this Parish, *by licence*.
July 15.	James Woodcott, of Stepney, and Ellen Frith, of the same Parish, *by licence*.
Oct. 14.	Thomas Parne, of St. Butolph, Aldgate, and Mary Price, of this Parish, *by licence*.
Oct. 28.	William Porter, of Creechurch, and Elizabeth Chappell, of this Parish, *by licence*.
Oct. 28.	John Coxe and Martha Standish, both of this Parish, *by licence*.
Oct. 31.	Isaack Walker, of St. Mary Maudlins, in Bermondsey Streete, and Johan Leighard, of this Parish, *by licence*.
Nov. 25.	William Wigg, of St. Bennett, Sherehogg, and Cecely Kinge, of this Parish, *by licence*.
Dec. 5.	William Worthington, of this Parish, and Bridgett Gill, of St. Olaves, Southwark, *by licence*.
Dec. 9.	William Faldo, of St. Mathewe, in Fryday Streete, and Barbara Evans, of this Parish, *by licence*.
Dec. 9.	Robert Dewhurt, of Graye's Inne, and Anne, daughter of Roger Dye, deceased, *by licence*.
Dec. 12.	Anthony March, of St. Swithin's, by London Stone, and Elizabeth Rolphe, of this Parish, *by licence*.

1631

April 12.	John Adams and Alice Badston, both of this Parish, *by licence*.
April 19.	Reginald Forster, of the Inner Temple, and Blandina Acton, of St. Mathewe, in Friday Streete, *by licence*.
May 12.	Thomas Nevett, of St. Allhallowes, Lombard Streete, and Thomazin Evans, of this Parish, *by licence*.
Aug. 25.	George Snell, of St. Allhallows, in Lombard Street, and Mary Viner, of this Parish, *by licence*.
Nov. 12.	Daniell Powerr, of St. Andrewe's, in Holborne, and Mary Wright, of St. Mary, Aldermanbury, *by licence*.
Nov. 4.	Edward Marson, of St. Stephen, in Colman Streete, and Grace Ezard, of the same Parish, *by licence*.
May 20.	Elias Walker, of St. Mary Maudlin, in Southwark, and Alice Beven, of this Parish, *by banes*.
Jan. 5.	Samuell Parker, of Barden, in Kent, and Joyce Grant, *Widow* of Radmortham, in Kent, *by licence*.
Jan. 5.	Thomas Lord, of Radmortham, in Kent, and Elizabeth Reyson, of the same Parish, *by licence*.
Feb. 20.	Richard Kinsman, of Stockwell,, and Anne Bancroft, of Wilsden, Middlesex, *by licence*.

1632

April 3.	John Johnson, of the Inner Temple, and Anne Bromhall, of this Parish, *by licence*.
April 22.	James Hill, of St. Mary Whitechapel, and Avys Collyer, of this Parish, *by banes*.
June 7.	John Steele, of Foster Lane, and Mary Almors, *Widowe*, of this Parish, *by licence*.
July 3.	Sir John Dreydon, of Northamptonshire, *Knight*, and Honour, daughter of Sir Robert Bevill, *by licence*.

Dec. 13   Samuell Ravenscroft, of St. Michaell, in Cornhill, and Anne Goodfellowe, of St. Laurence, in the Ould Jewry, *by licence.*

1633

Mar. 26.   William Hunt, of Tisehurst, Surrey. and Anne Baylie, of the same Parish, *by licence.*

May 12.   Edward Cooke, of St. Buttolph's without Bishopsgate, and Minifride Lade, of this Parish, *by banes.*

May 16.   Limning Dickenson, of St. Martin in the Fields, and Frances Greatwick, of St. Peters the poore, *by licence.*

June 24.   Thomas Kinge, of Stepney, and Fraunces Kinge, of this Parish, *by licence.*

Aug. 22.   Roger Greene, of Hatfeild Broadoke, Essex, and Margarett Man, *Widowe,* of the same Parish, *by licence.*

Dec. 8.   Peter Sparre, of St. Andrews in the Wardrobe, and Johan Martin, of Marleborough, Wilts, *by licence.*

Dec. 11.   Thomas, the son of Sir Edward Hussey, of Hunnington, in Lincolneshire, and Rhoda, daughter of Thomas Chapman, in Soper Lane, *by licence.*

Feb. 9.   Clement Nicholl, of St. Butholph without Aldgate, and Katherine Man, of this Parish, *by licence.*

Feb. 18.   Thomas Symcock, of St. Margarett, at Westminster, and Sarah Wannerton, of the same Parish, *by licence.*

1634

May 18.   Thomas Rosse, of St. Leonard, in Shoreditch, and Rebecca Phenix, of this Parish, *by licence.*

June 8.   John Cleaver, of St. Olave, Southwark, and Eseldred——— [*sic*] of this Parish, *by banes.*

June 8.   Richard Johnson, of St. Leonard, in Foster Lane, and Suzan White, of this Parish, *by banes.*

June 12.   Thomas Cranaway, of St. Sepulchre's, and Elizabeth Gorrell, of this Parish, *by licence.*

July 10.   Richard Smith, of St. Buttolph without Aldersgate, and Mary Ive, of Hornsey, *Widowe, by licence.*

July 15.   John Runwell and Margarett Dange, *Widowe,* both of this Parish, *by licence.*

Sep. 2.   Edward Croftner, of St. Faith, and Margarett Hebbe, of this Parish, *by licence.*

Sep. 14.   William Rowe, of St. Leonard, Shoreditch, and Grace Freeman, of this Parish, *by licence.*

Oct. 19.   William Townsend, of St. Mary Abchurch, and Elizabeth Scott, of this Parish, *by licence.*

Nov. 16.   John Baker, of St. Thomas, Southwark, and Anne Adlovin, of this Parish, *by banes.*

Dec. 7.   William Rowe, *Leatherseller,* of St. Swithin, and Anne Humble, of this Parish, *by licence.*

Feb. 8.   Humfrey Webb, of St. Swithin, and Jane Curtis, of this Parish, *by banes.*

1635

April 7.   Thomas Smith, of Stock Newington, and Elizabeth Brittaine, of this Parish, *by licence.*

April 12.   Thomas Webb, of St. George, Southwark, and Anne Evins, of this Parish, *by banes.*

May 19.   Edward Trussell, of St. Faith, and Mary Humble, of this Parish, *by licence.*

June 29.   James Crosfeilde, of St. Clement's, in Eastcheap, and Sara Sankey, of this Parish, *by licence.*

July 2.   Sir Gorde Southcott, of Shillington, Devonshire, and Martha Sucking, of St. Dunstan, in the West, *by licence.*

Sep. 12.   Andrew Saunders, of Eysham, Co. Northampton, and Dame Sara Brett. *Widdowe, by licence.*

Sep. 29.   Thomas Audley, *Minister*, and Jane Rawlins, *by licence.*

Dec. 1.   Thomas Forbensh, of Hunsdon, Herts, and Mary Earth, of the same place, *by licence.*

Dec. 10.   William Claxton, of Kirton, Co. Nottingham, and Elizabeth Williamson, of Markham, in the same County, *by licence.*

1636

May 1.   William Whitewood, of Woodford, Essex, and Mary Fryerson, of this Parish, *by banes.*

May 24.   Joseph Chafey, of St. Sepulchres, and Elizabeth Read, of St. George, Southwark, *by licence.*

June 3.   Sir John Garrat, *Knight*, of Lammor, Herts., and Dame Jane Lambert, of Greenwich, Kent, *by licence.*

Feb. 13.   Guy Holland, of St. Michaell, in Cornhill, and Mary Plomeare, of this Parish, *by licence.*

1637

July 10.   Samuell Boardman and Elizabeth Mason, *by licence.*

Aug. 2.   John Thelwall, of Graye's Inne, *Esquire*, and Dame Elizabeth Bodwell, *by licence.*

Aug. 17.   Hamond Hawkes, of St. John Baptist, London, and Katherine Ward, of this Parish, *by licence.*

Oct. 19.   John Vincent, *Shearegrinder*, of this Parish, and Joan Hill, of this Parish, *by licence.*

Oct. 22.   Thomas Greene, of St. Leonard's, Shordich, and Alice Felps, of this Parish, *by banes.*

Oct. 28.   Sir Thomas Surmfeld, of Stayning, Sussex, *Knight*, and Elizabeth Cudmore, of Keldon, Essex, *Widdow, by licence.*

Dec. 5.   Richard Vase, *Goldsmith*, and Hester Hill, both of this Parish, *by licence.*

Jan. 22.   Thomas Vyner and Honor Hudson, *Widow*, both of this Parish, *by licence.*

1638

Mar. 27.   John Tanner, of St. Saviour, Southwark, *Merchant*, and Suzan Spycer, of this Parish, *by licence.*

April 24.   William Wilks, of Arcoll, Shropshire, and Elizabeth Plum, of St. Giles without Cripplegate, *by licence.*

July 10.   John Hall, of St. Olave, in Southwark, and Mary Skinner, of the same place.

Oct. 18.	William Grove, of St. Bride's, and Margaret Atkinson, of this Parish, *by licence.*
Oct. 23.	John Man, of High Unger, Essex, and Mary Crosier, of Abbas Redding, in the same County, *by licence.*
Nov. 1.	Walter Smith, of St. Bennet, Paules Wharfe, and Elizabeth Holding, of this Parish, *by banes.*
Nov. 19.	Thomas Niccols, *Stationer,* and Suzan Hancock, both of this Parish, *by licence.*
Dec. 4.	John King, of St. Sepulchers, and Alice Faucett, of the same place, *by licence.*
Dec. 4.	John Cockshutt, of Grayes Inne, and Elizabeth Robinson, of Westin, *by licence.*
Feb. 3.	Richard Fetterby, of St. Michaell Wood Streete, and Suzan Hayward, of St. Edmunds in Lombard Streete, *by licence.*
Feb. 21.	James Stanneir, of Allhallows in the Wall, and Thomasine Meade, of St. Andrewes Undershaft, *by licence.*

1639

May 2.	Sir Henry Skipwith, of Coats, Leicestershire, *Knight and Baronett,* and Blandina Acton, of St. Mathew, Friday Streete, *Widdow, by licence.*
May 21.	Edward Conder, of Stepney, and Francis Carpentar, of this Parish, *by licence.*
May 29.	Rich Gerrard, of St. Mary Abchurch, and Mary Leighton, of this Parish, *by licence.*
June 3.	William Bolton, of St. Christophers, and Elizabeth Willett, *Widdow,* of this Parish, *by licence.*
June 3.	Jeremy Saltmarsh, of St. Leonards, Bromley, and Mary Woodcock, of this Parish, *by licence.*
June 13.	Richard Hooper, of Lincolnes Inn, *Esquire,* and Grissell Ware, of Rayley, in Essex, *Widdow, by licence.*
Oct. 16.	Sir John Cotton, of Eltham, Kent, *Knight,* and Mary Offley, *by licence.*
Dec. 8.	John Cromton and Elizabeth Vyner, both of this Parish, *by licence.*

1640

April 14.	John Styles, of Staple Inn, and Frances Hughes, of St. Giles Without Cripplegate, *by licence.*
May 26.	Daniell Downes, of St. Clements Dane, and Phœbe Lambert, of St. Margarett in Westminster, *by licence.*
Feb. 2.	William Cogges, of St. Buttolph Aldgate, and Elizabeth Staples, of this Parish, *by licence.*
Feb. 16.	Robert Halton, of Bishop Stratford, Hertfordshire, and Anne Shute, of St. Mildreds in the Poultney, *Widdow, by licence.*
Mar. 4.	Samuell Hedge, of St. Peters the Poor, and Elizabeth Weld, of this Parish. *by licence.*
Mar. 4.	John Botley, of Allhallows in the Wall, and Sislie Harris, of this Parish, *by licence.*
Mar. 4.	Thomas Blackstone, of St. James', Clerkenwell, and Annie Gardner, of St. Giles without Cripplegate, *by licence.*

1641

May 9.   Nicholas Fearer, of St. Martins in the Vinterie, and Martha Davis, of this Parish, *by banes.*

July 15.   George Sligh, of Little St. Bartholomew, and Anne Aston, of Long Ditton, Surrey, *by licence of the Archbishop.*

Aug. 5.   John Madox, of St. Saviour, Southwark, and Alice Russell, of St. Helen, *by licence.*

Aug. 31.   William Bright and Elizabeth Yates, both of this Parish, *by licence.*

Sep. 2.   Richard Sharpe and Katherin Hanmer, both of St. Marie Matfellon alias Whitechapple, *by licence.*

Oct. 24.   Nicholas Wood, of Battersey, and Hellen Greene, of Enfield.

End of Marriages in the first Volume of Registers of St. Mary Woolnoth.

[Vol. ij.]

THE Names of such as were Maryed in the parishe church of St. Marye Wolnoth, London, sithence the foure and twentieth day of October, Anno Domini 1641.

1641

Mar. 17.   Humfrie Bath and Joan Cox, both of this Parish, *by licence.*

1642

June 27.   Nicholas Southcott, of St. Martin's in the Feildes, and Dorothy Forth, of Suffolk, *by licence.*

July 24.   Edward Tuchbery, of St. Michaell, in Wood Streete, and Jane Miller, of this Parish, *by banes.*

Sep. 18.   George Swanley, of Stepney, and Elizabeth Browne, of the same place, *by licence.*

Oct. 10.   William Booby, of St. Clement's Danes, and Frances Jury, of Malmesbury, Wilts, *by licence.*

Nov. 15.   Walter Powell, of St. Laurence Pountneys, and Frances Deyes, of this Parsh, *by licence.*

Jan. 1.   Henry Cooke, of St. Thomas, in Southwark, and Marie Reyner, of this Parish, *by licence.*

Feb. 7.   Robert Jones, of Wansworth, and Patrinella Smith, of Micham, *by licence.*

1643

April 4.   Humfrey Heath, of St. Michaell, in Crooked Lane, and Betterice Blackson, of this Parish, *by licence.*

April 4.   Nicholas Serth, of St. Michaell, in Cornhill, and Elizabeth Charleton, of St. Dunstan's in the East, *by licence.*

April 11.   Nicholas Jackson, of St. Giles without Cripplegate, and Abigaill Wicke, of St. Laurence, in the Jury, *by licence*.

April 25.   Symon Vegelman, of St. Dunstan's in the East, and Margaret Lewes, of this Parish, *by banes*.

Oct. 23.   John Leasnet, of West Ham, Essex, and Anne Graunt, of the same place.

Oct. 31.   Raphe Boyce, *Hottpresser*, and Ellyn Bollock, both of this Parish.

Nov. 13.   Gregorie Dye and Jane Procter, both of St. Bothell's without Bishopsgate.

Jan. 2.   Thomas Griffie and Gillian Shipman, both of Stepney, Middx.

Jan. 4.   William Douncar, of St. Martin's, and Mary Moore, of this Parish.

1644

June 25.   Thomas Bignall and Margaret Minos, of Stepney.

July 4.   John Townsend and Elizabeth Ayers, both of St. Olaves, Southwark.

July 15.   Hercules Billings, of Wansteed, and Elizabeth Robins, of Hackney, *without licence*.

July 21.   John Hood, of St. Sepulchre's, and Madder —— [*sic*] of this Parish, *without licence*.

Nov. 31.   John Banks, *Upholsterer* in Greate Estcheape, and Anne Crafts, of this Parish.

Dec. 3.   William Palmer, of Albon's, Wood Streete, and Elisabeth Hutton, of Andrewe's, Holborne.

Feb. 4.   Thomas Butler, of Nicholas Cole Abbey, and Mary Birdsey, of Mathew's, Friday Streete.

Mar. 8.   Thomas Briscoe, of Olaves Jury, and Margarett Bailey, of Marleborough, Wiltshire.

1645

June 2.   Robert Mason and Maudlin Hawkings, both of this Parish.

Sep. 16.   Theophilus Fitts, of Margarett, Westminster, and Elizabeth Markes, of St. Mary Olave, in Southwark.

Oct. 2.   William Brinkinshaw, of this Parish, and Mary Randall, of Little Metstone, Bucks.

Nov. 27.   Thomas Day, of Austins, London, and Elizabeth Tanner, *Widowe*, of Backway, Herts.

Jan. 29.   Robert Tennbe, of Mary, Whitechappell, and Mary Choster, of this Parish.

Feb. 15.   James Hockley, of Andrew's, Holborn, and Jane Beverley, of the same Parish.

1646

April 30.   Thomas Corbett and Elizabeth Therston, both of Michaell, Cornhill.

May 7.   Cuthbard Hackett, of Mildred, Poultry, and Anne Briggishaw, of this Parish.

July 2.   Corbett Cheety and Elizabeth Stanley, both of this Parish.

Aug. 24.   John Lawford, of Margarett, New Fish Streete, and Susan Hoare, of this Parish.

Sep. 4.	Timothy Drake and Sarah Gifferd, both of Mary Abchurch.
Sep. 7.	Thomas Martin and Mary Fletcher, of Dunstan in the East.
Oct. 1.	William Crofter and Susan How, of Catherine Creedchurch.
Oct. 5.	John Johnson, of Lingfeild, Surrey, and Hester Vaus, of this Parish.
Oct. 2.	Nicholas Wooldam, of Southwark, and Jane Dexter, of this Parish, *Widowe*.

1647

Sep. 13.	Roberte Brookshead and Anne Drue, both of Stepney.
Sep. 21.	Richard Hudson, of Michaell, Queenhith, and Anne Blunt, of Shepartom, Middlesex.
Nov. 26.	Edmund Widdowes, of Brooked, and Margarett Cockain.
Jan. 6.	Mr. Thomas Bellin and Mrs. Sarah Greene, of Olave, Old Jury.
Feb. 10.	Richard Bissel, of St. Martin in the feilds, and Sarah Martin, of Mary Abchurch.
Feb. 15.	John Jelson, of St. Giles', Criplegate, and Martha Watts, Mr. Jurious' servant.
Mar. 23.	William Piggott, of St. Steven's, Walbrook, and Anne Sankey, of this Parish.

1648

June 21.	Richard Maund, of St. Martin's in the feilds, and Anna Goodlad, of Shadwell, in Stepney.
Sep. 2.	Dancer Hancock, of St. Botulph, Aldersgate, and Elizabeth Ottley, of St. Faith's, *Widowe*.
Dec. 25.	John Chamberlaine, of St. Thomas, Southwark, and Mary, daughter of Thomas Cox.

1649

April 12.	William Heard and Johan Smith, both of Rumford, Essex.
May 23.	James Anselm, of Stepney, Middlesex, and Mary Wills, of Christofer's, London.
Sep. 20.	Richard Taylor, of St. Katherine Creechurch, and Jane Fisher, of this Parish.
Nov. 20.	John Ward, of St. Dunstan's in the East, and Hester Payne, of Downe, Kent.
Feb. 14.	Thomas Mason, of St. Ollaves, in Hart Streete, and Alice Shipman, of this Parish.
Mar. 6.	John Palmer, of Farnham, Surrey, and Mary Dampard, of Hampton Wick, Middlesex.

1650

July 29.	John Herbert and Sarah Bridgin, both of Chattam, Kent.
Aug. 1.	William Bancks, of St. Giles, Cripplegate, and Anne Goodringe, of St. John Zacharies, London.
Aug. 7.	Gilbert East and Sarah Browne, *Widdow*, both of St. Botulph, Aldersgate.
Oct. 12.	Albertus Warren and Dorothy Barton, both of Epping, Essex.

Nov. 7.	Peter Gerrard, of Olaves, Southwark, and Hannah Van Horton, *Widdow*, of Peters the poore.
Jan. 7.	Thomas Dexter and Sybill Hodgkis, both of St. Mary Somerset, London.
Jan. 23.	Gabriell Marden and Thomasin Watts, both of Mildred, in the Poultry.

1651

April 29.	Thomas Baker and Anne Stedman, of Great St. Bartholomews.
Aug. 8.	Daniell Price and Anne Podney, both of Elmsted, Essex.
Jan. 6.	William Davies, of St. Swithin's, London Stone, and Lucretia Palmer, of Magnus, London.
Jan. 15.	William Stringer and Obedience Waters, both of Michael's. Crooked Lane.
Feb. 5.	Nicholas Pindlebury, of Dunstan's in the West, *Gentleman*, and Mrs. Bridgett, daughther of John Watkin, of Morton, Essex, *Gentleman*.
Feb. 24.	Mr. Peter Jurian, of Pancras, Soper Lane, and Mrs. Anne Pickeringe, of Allhallows in the Wall.
Mar. 18.	William Emmett, of Nicholas Olaves, and Sarah Barnham, of Swithins, London Stone.

1652

June 14.	James Rymon, of Carlile, in the County of Northumberland, and Ann Knowles, of Mary Islington.
Sep. 6.	William Howell, of Bartholomew the Lesse, and Francis Vicars, of the same place.
Dec. 30.	Samuell Harbert, of All Saints, in Northampton, and Frances, daughter of Frances Brome, *Widdowe*, of Magnus, London.
Feb. 9.	James Patchinge, of Bennet fynk, and Judith Howell, of the same Parish.
Feb. 22.	Henry Sutton, of St. Christopher's, London, and Susannah French, of Allhallows Staynings.
Mar. 10.	Humphrey Towne, of Mary Woolchurch, and Martha Balam, of Michaell, Queenhithe.
Mar. 22.	Henry Sibry, of Magdalene, Bermondsey, Surrey, and Anne Early, of Lawrence Jury.

1653

April 10.	Anthony Robinson, of Mary le Bowe, and Hannah Coleman, of Magdalen, Bermondsey, Surrey.
July 3.	John Halsey and Sarah Chamberline, both of this Parish.
July 10.	John Eustar, of St. Margarets by Rochester, Kent, and Elizabeth Thomas, of Rochester, Kent.
Aug. 4.	Richard Tubervile, of Margarets, Lothbury, and Elizabeth Pewsy, late servant to Mr. Lawrence Steele, of this Parish.
Sep. 27.	James Brickill, of Kensington, Middlesex, and Mary Starkey, *Widdowe*, of Martin's Ludgate.
Sep. 28.	George Jenkin, of Twittenham, Middlesex, and Mary Hewet, of the same Parish.

Sep. 28.	Thomas Woodfen, of Low Layton, Essex, and Elizabeth Clayward, of Allhallows, Lombard Streete.
Sep. 29.	John Goode, of Greenwich, Kent, and Jennett Loud, of the same Parish.
Sep. 29.	Daniell Benfeild, of Walthamstowe, Essex, and Anne Dauncer, of Fulham, Middlesex.
Jan. 12.	Edward Wilmer, of Mildred, Bred Streete, and Elizabeth Stone, of Margarett, Westminster.
Jan. 31.	William Boswell and Elizabeth Chamberline, both of this Parish.
Feb. 6.	Henry Moone and Katherine Bucston, both of Giles', Cripplegate.

1654

May 9.	Francis Harris, of St. Katherine's near the Tower, and Alice Walker, of Walthamstow, Essex.
Oct. 4.	William Sallowes, of St. Dunstans in the East, and Frances, daughter of Mr. William White, *Haberdasher*, of this Parish.
Oct. 5.	Stephen Hooke, of Walthamstowe, Essex, and Margarett Harwood, of the same Parish.
Oct. 24.	Robert Bayley, of St. Buttolph without Aldgate, and Elizabeth Thomas of the same Parish.
Jan. 3.	Mathew Meade, of Solber, Bucks., and Elizabeth Walton, of Allhallows, Lombard Streete.
Feb. 13.	William Elliott, of Aldenham, Herts., and Mary Yeates, of Christchurch, London.
Feb. 14.	Hugh Lay, of St. Saviour's, Southwark, and Jane Carter, of the same Parish.

1655

Mar. 31.	John Hoare, of Christ Church, London, and Elizabeth, daughter of Arthur Jackson, *Minister* of St. Faith's under Pauls.
April 3.	John Tipping and Elizabeth Webb, both of Bennett Fink.
April 19.	Francis Strangcridge, of this Parish, and Elizabeth Colles, of St. Thomas, Southwark.
April 22.	Robert Bacon and Katherine Rugles, of this Parish.
June 26.	"Lawfully married by the Justice" John Ellis, of this Parish, *Taylor*, and Ann Harris, of Giles', Cripplegate, *Widdowe*.
July 24.	John Huxley, of Edmonton, Essex, *Esquire*, and Sarah Hadley, of Lawrence in the Jewry.
July 24.	"Lawfully married by the Justice" Edward Webster, of Bennet Grace Church, and Sarah Head, of this Parish.
Aug. 20.	"Lawfully married by the Justice" John Waters, of this Parish, and Mary Dakins, of Katherine's, Tower.
Sep. 14.	"By the Justice" Giles Hussee and Martha Booker, both of this Parish.
Nov. 16.	"By the Justice and the Minister" William Greene, of Albans, Wood Streete, and Mary Ellmore, of this Parish.
Nov. 26.	Thomas Jolland, of St. Mary Abchurch, and Sarah Greene, of St. Peter's Poore in Broad Streete.

1656

May 13.   Francis Leeke, of St. John Zacharie, and Mary Temple, of this Parish, "by Mr. Jaccombe, Minister, and Sir Thomas Vyner, Alderman, and one of the Justices of this City."

Aug. 21.   John Penington, of Chigwell, Essex, *Esquire*, and Katherine Pennington, of the same place, *Widdowe*.

1657

Mar. 31.   Thomas Lambert, of Gregories, London, and Johan Clewells, of Mile End in the Quern.

May 18.   Thomas Mottershed, of this Parish, and Elizabeth Foster, of Allhallowes the less, Thames Streete.

Oct. 15.   Thomas Goldsmith, of Marten's, Vintry, *Fruiterer*, and Anne Trevell, Mr. Charles Everard's *servant*.

Nov. 19.   Richard Person, of St. Olave in Southwark, and Elizabeth Coxson.

Jan. 28.   William Grosvenor, *Goldsmith*, and Hester Marr, both of this Parish.

Feb. 4.   William Shepheard, *Clarke and Pastor of the Parish Church of Tilbrook*, Bedfordshire, and Hannah Parsons, of Leonard, Eastcheape.

1658

April 6.   James Maden, of Alphage, London, and Elizabeth Light, of Allhallows the less, Thames Streete.

Feb. 4.   Richard Franklyn, of Broomeham, Wilts., *Esquire*, and Mrs. Mellisent Hodison, of Diones Backchurch.

Mar. 13.   Robert Paine and Bridgett Keepe, of Trinity, London, Bow Lane.

1659

April, 4.   John, son of John Shipman and Anne England, both of this Parish.

July 21.   William Lapp, of Great St. Bartholomew's, and Elizabeth, daughter of Allexander Fermer, of Rotherfeild, Sussex.

Dec. 22.   Nicholas Jackson, of St. Antholius, *Cittizen and Mercer*, and Anne Burridge, of Allhallowes, Stayning, *Widowe*.

1660

Nov. 19.   Robert Carpentar, of St. Pulcher's, and Sybbell Farrington, of this Parish.

Jan. 1.   John Winchfield, of Creechurch, and Margaret Cugsley, of St. Mary, Somerset.

Jan. 22.   Richard Yedd, *Cutler*, and Margaret Johnson, both of this Parish.

Jan. 26.   Francis Pring, of St. Martin's in the Fields, and Jane Morgan, *Widdowe*, of Isleworth, Middlesex.

Feb. 21.   William Nutt and Elizabeth Brunskin, of St. Alhallows, Stayning.

Mar. 17.   Edward Hudson and Elizabeth Clarke, both of St. Mary, Magdalen, Bermondsey.

Mar. 24. Richard Jenkins and Elizabeth Bayles, both of St. Giles, Cripplegate.

Mar. 26. John Roberts, of St. Mary, Whitechapple, and Ruth Clarkson, of St. Giles, Cripplegate.

1661

April 7. Edward Robinson and Anne Dormer, both of St. Gregory, London.

April 16. Richard Biskion and Elizabeth Haines, both of Abchurch.

April 25. Mr. Roland Saml. John, of St. Buttolph, Bishopsgate, and Mrs. Mary Parkhurst, of Purford, Surrey, *by licence of Abp. of Canterbury.*

May 1. Henry Taylor, of Downeham, Co. Derby, and Anne Newbold, of St. Olave, Old Jewry, *by Abp.'s licence.*

Sep. 5. William Godfrey and Mrs. Sarah Clarke, both of Buggles, Essex.

Oct. 9. Thomas Bare, of St. Peter's the Apostell, London, and Mary Gott, of St. Battell, Sussex, *by Abp.'s licence.*

Nov. 3. John Oxford, of Lenard, in Shoreditch, and Anne Fiell, of St. Andrewe's Undershaft, *by licence.*

Dec. 12. Philip Ward, of the Inner Temple, London, and Penelope Edmonds, of St. Andrewe's, Holborne, *by Abp.'s licence.*

Jan. 23. Nicholas Smith, of St. Magnus, and Mary Bridges, of St. Michaell, Cornehill, *by Abp.'s licence.*

Feb. 4. Abraham Hill, *Widower*, of Dionis, Backchurch, and Elizabeth Prast, of Stepney, *by Abp.'s licence.*

Feb. 4. Thomas Harrison and Elizabeth Bathe, both of St. Swe-thing's, *by Abp.'s licence.*

1662

Aug. 14. Daniell Gifford, of Bassingshaw, London, and Susanna Woodford, of St. Leonard's, Foster Lane, *by Abp.'s licence.*

Nov. 11. Henry Jones and Judeth White, both of this Parish, *by Abp.'s licence.*

Nov. 19. Edward Good and Elizabeth Wriexagg, both of Steeven, Coleman Streete, *by Abp.'s licence.*

Nov. 18. Thomas Tindell, of St. Andrewe's, Holbourne, and Mary Smithier, *Widow*, of this Parish, *by Abp.'s licence.*

Jan. 11. *Young Bull, of Stepney, and Mary Highfield, of Beavers Market, London, *by Abp.'s licence.*

Jan. 15. Thomas Fuller, "*person of the Parish of Nansbey, in the County of Lincolne,*" and Mrs. Elizabeth Perkins, of St. Mary le Bow, *by Abp.'s licence.*

Feb. 24. Richard Morley, of Hatfield, Herts., and Mrs. Anne Bradbourne, of St. Allhallowes Barkin, *by Abp.'s licence.*

Mar. 2. Thomas Whitlsey, of St. Edmund the King, and Elizabeth Lowe, of St. Michaell in the Querne, *by Abp.'s licence.*

1663

April 14. Joseph Avory, of St. Steven's, in Walbrooke, and Anna Moore, of St. Buttolph without Bishopsgate, *by Abp.'s licence.*

May 19. John Elton, of St. Mary Woolchurch, and Mary Streete, of this Parish.

---

* The word "young" is in slightly paler ink.

Aug. 11.	Thomas Smith, of Broaksted, Essex, and Katherine Hone, of Wicken, Essex, *by licence.*
Sep. 3.	Robert Leath, of Allhallowes, Bread Street, and Anne Leigh, of St. Clement's, Eastcheape, *by Abp. licence.*
Nov. 12.	Thomas Wadsworth, *Widdower*, of St. Lawrence Pountney, and Margarett Shayve, of St. Olave's, Southwark, *Widdow*, *by Abp. licence.*
Nov. 30.	Hugh Robinson, of Stepney, and Francis Slade, of St. Katherine Tower, *by Abp.'s licence.*
Dec. 24.	George Butterfeilde, of Stepney, Middlesex, and Sarah Westwood, "of the Parish of ——" [*sic*], *by Abp. licence.*
Dec. 24.	Mihih Gardnier, of the Inner Temple, *Esquire*, and Mrs. Anne Keele, of St. James', Clerkenwell, *by Abp.'s licence.*
Jan. 3.	John Elvyn, of St. Mary, Whitechappell, and Jane Azlewell, of this Parish, *by banes.*
Jan. 23.	Robert Watson, of Freindesbury, Kent, *Widdower*, and Mrs. Isabel Rednall, of St. Mary Abchurch, *by Abp.'s licence.*
Feb. 23.	Thomas Firmin, of St. Edmonde, in Lombard Street, and Margaret Dent, of St. Steven, in Colman Street, *by Abp.'s licence.*
Mar. 23.	Ralph Ingram, of St. Dionis Backchurch, and Mrs. Sara Edwards, of the Town of Huntington, *by Abp.'s licence.*

1664

April 17.	Robert Lay, of Bishop's Stratford, Herts., and Dorothy Lane, of the same place, *by Abp.'s licence.*
April 11.	Edward Evans, of St. Bride's, and Mary Smith, of Lambeth, Surrey, *by Abp.'s licence.*
April 12.	John Innes, of St. Mary Abchurch, and Jane Morris, of this Parish, *by Abp.'s licence.*
May 28.	Jonathan Buck, of St. Saviour's, Southwark, and Mrs. Anne Doggett, of St. Albans, Herts, *by Abp.'s licence.*
June 19.	Jonas Barrett, of St. Annes, Blackfriers, and Jane Jones, of this Parish, *by banns.*
June 30.	John Newman, of St. James', Garlickhith, and Mrs. Elizabeth Gregory, of St. Michaell, Royall, *by Abp.'s licence.*
Sep. 22.	Thomas Pearce, of Allhallows, honilane, and Mrs. Jane Lee, of St. Clements, Eastcheape, *by Abp.'s licence.*

1665

May. 11.	Richard Hobson, of this Parish, and Elizabeth Clarke, of St. Andrews, Holborne, *by Abp.'s licence.*
June 27.	Mr. Blair White, of St. Margarettes, Westminster, and Mrs. Anne Burges, of the same place, *by Abp.'s licence.*

1666

May 17.	Thomas Wood and Elizabeth Deane, both of Westerham, Kent, *by Abp.'s licence.*

June 1. John Goodwin, *Widdower*, of Stepney, and Ann Timbrill, of Portsmouth, Co. of Southampton, *Spinster*, by *Abp.'s licence.*

Aug. 7. Samuel Jermyn, *Clark of this Parish*, and Sara Topley, of this Parish, *by Abp.'s licence.*

1671

Nov. 26. Joseph Watts, of St. Edmund the King, in Lombard Street, and Grace Bennet, of this Parish, *by Abp.'s licence.*

Dec. 7. William Spinnag, of St. Mary Abchurch, and Catherine Major, of the Tower Libertie, *by Abp.'s licence.*

Jan. 11. Samuell Langley, of Brumbley, Salop, *Gent.*, and Elizabeth Hammon, of St. Peter le Poore, *by Abp.s licence.*

1672

Oct. 2. Zacharia Browne, of Stepney, *Widdower*, and Sarah Barnes, *Widdowe*, of St. Ollaves, Hart Streete, *by Abp.'s licence.*

Dec. 24. Edward Evans, of St. Gabriell Fenchurch, and Ann Child, of St. Martin's in the Feilds, *by Abp'.s licence.*

Jan. 9. James Knivin, of St. Andrew, Holborne, and Ann Harris, of St. Mary Abchurch, *by Abp.'s licence.*

Feb. 4. Richard Chaplaine, of St. Stevens in Coleman Streete, and Margaret Smith, of St. Pancras, Soper Lane, *by Abp.'s licence.*

Feb. 5. John Temple and Dorrothie Colvill, *Spinster*, both of this Parish, *by Abp.'s licence.*

Feb. 11. Caleb Westbrook, of St. Steven in Coleman Street, and Judith Bowcher, of this Parish, *Spinster, by Abp.'s licence.*

1673

Mar. 31. Mathew Gibbs, of St. Leonard, Foster Lane, and Sara Palmer, of St. Sepulcher's, *by Abp.'s licence.*

May 1. William Goode, *Widdower*, and Rebecca Prichett, *Widdowe*, both of St. Giles Cripplegate, *by licence.*

July 20. Phillip Williams, of St. Dunston's in the West, in Cursitors Alley, and Ann Mills, of St. Bridgett's, *Spinster*, by *Abp'.s licence.*

Oct. 16. Thomas Edwards, of St. Margarett's Westminster, and Elizabeth Barringer, of St. Dunstan's in the East, *by Abp.'s licence.*

Nov. 4. John Blake, of Redrif, Surrey, and Grace Cramer, of St. Saviour's, Southwark, *Spinster by Abp.'s licence.*

Nov. 20. Thomas Jermy, of St. James, Clerkenwell, and Mary Allen, of St. Bartholomew the Great, *by Abp.'s licence.*

Dec. 3. John Eden, of Bathdon, Essex, *Esquire, Widdower*, and Ann Laurance, of Theobalds, Co. Herts, *Widdow, by Abp.'s licence.*

Feb. 13. John Barrow, *Minister*, of Micham, Surrey, *Widdower*, and Mary Bowton, of the same place, *Spinster*, by *Abp.'s licence.*

Feb. 18. Hector Moor, of Wood Street, *Mariner*, and Elleanor Woodrich, of Hackney, *Widdow, by Abp.'s licence.*

1674

Aug. 27. Martin Watson, of St. Gregorie's by St. Paule's, *Widdower*, and Margarett Reade, *Widdow*, of Allhallowes the Great, in Thames Street, *by licence.*

Oct. 8. Edward Rodorne, of Furnival's Inn, *Gent.*, and Mary Southwells, of the Savoy Parish, *by licence.*

Nov. 24. Delabar Winston, of St. John Leicharie, and Mary Leeke, of St. Giles without Cripplegate, *by licence.*

Jan. 14. John Rolfe, of St. Steephen in Walbrook, *Skynner*, and Ann Hicks, of St. John Baptist, *Widdow, by licence.*

1675

Aug. 2. Thomas Burton, of St. Stephen's in Coleman Street, *Plaisterer*, and Elizabeth Clayton, of St. Olaves, Old Jury.

1676

May 11. Henry Reeve, of Stepney, and Judeth Giles, *Spinster*, of Magnus, *by licence Cant.*

July 20. William Andrews, of Lambeth, *Gent.*, and Sarah Boilstone, *Widdow*, of St. Gabriel, Fenchurch, *marryed by the Lord Bishop of Rochester.*

Oct. 19. Edmund Lloide, of St. Bennett, Gracechurch, and Katherine Philpott, of this Parish, *by licence.*

Oct. 30. Richard Beecher, of St. Bennett Sherehogg, and Lidia Marston, of this Parish, *by Abp.'s licence.*

Nov. 9. John Fisher, of St. Leonard's, Eastcheap, and Elizabeth Smith, of St. Gregorie's, *by licence.*

Dec. 27. Thomas Bonham, of Vallance, Essex, and Elizabeth Jones, *Spinster*, of St. Swithin, *by Bishop of London's licence.*

Feb. 6. William Sarson, of St. Laurence Jurie, and Anne Simonds, of St. Swithin's, *by Abp.'s licence.*

Feb. 14. Jonathan Dodsworth, of Deptford, Kent, and Jane Dowthwaite, of Wells, Somersetshire, *Spinster*, *by Abp.'s licence.*

Mar. 18. William Bland, of this Parish, and Suzanna Halfhead, of St. Christopher's, *by Abp.'s licence.*

1677

April 26. Daniell Heath, of Much Hollingbury, Essex, and Rebecca Dayles, of East Hanningfield, Essex, *by licence.*

May 13. Richard Phipps and Suzanna Morgan, both of St. Sepulchres, London, *by Abp. licence.*

July 11. Thomas Woodstock, of St. Clement Danes, and Sara Creston, of St. Andrews, Holborn, *by licence.*

Oct. 5. Henry Gold, of Trenchard Leite, Devon, and Elizabeth Leggott, of St. Swithins, *by Bishop of London's licence.*

Dec. 9. Arnold de Bowthery, of Canterbury, *Minister of the French Church there*, and Sara Mathews, of St. Mary Bothaw, *by Abp's licence.*

Feb. 14. Richard Patten and Elizabeth Pott, both of Woollwich, [*sic*] Kent.

1678

Aug. [*sic*] Alldrig Roffee, of St. Andrew, Holborn, and Mary Groves, of Greenwich, Kent, *by licence.*

Jan. 2. Thomas Burdikin and Mary Groves, *Widow*, both of St. Sepulchres, *by licence.*

1679

June 26. Benjemine Watson, of St. Katherine Coleman, and Mary Still, of St. Bottolphs, Bishopsgate, *by licence.*

July 21. Caleb Smith, of St. Andrews, Holbourn, and Mary Carpentar, of the same Parish, *by licence.*

Dec. 21. Thomas Price, of this Parish, and Dorrotha Price, of St. Sweethins, *by Abp's licence.*

Feb. 26. Edmund Pike, of Margarett, New Fish Streete, and Hannah Hopkinson, of St. Mary Woolchurch Haw, *by licence.*

1680

May 6. Joseph Ballard, of St. Martin's in the fields, and Elizabeth Price, of the same Parish, *by licence.*

May 26. Elisha Bennent, *Mariner*, of St. Mary Whitechapple, alias Matfelson, and Dorothe Ellis, of St. Lawrence Jury, *by licence.*

Sep. 14. John Wagstaff, of St. Mary lee Bow, *Silkman*, and Jane Hatt, of St. Sepulchers, *by licence.*

Feb. 10. Charles Middleton, of Crouched Fryers, and Ann Samford, of St. Michaells in Cornhill.

Feb. 10. Thomas Arne, of St. Paul's, Covent Garden, and Mary Thursfield, of St. Martin's in the fields, *by licence.*

1681

Oct. 13. John Browne, *Cooper*, of St. Mary Whitechapel, and Joan Whitehall, of the same place, *by licence.*

Dec. 15. Thomas Page, of St. Giles, Cripplegate, and Mary Moore, of St. Michael, Wood Street, *by Abp.'s licence.*

Feb. 14. Francis Minshall, of Bottolph's, Billingsgate, and Elizabeth Slaney of Stretham Surrey, *by Abp. licence.*

Feb. 27. William Eaton, of Dover, *Merchant*, and Mary Prentice, of Canterbury, *by Abp. licence.*

1682

May. 29. John Phelps, of St. Albans, Wood Street, *Jeweller*, and Suzan Ragdale, of St. Mary Magdalene, Milk Street, *by Abp's licence.*

Aug. 17. Thomas Spane, of St. Giles without Cripplegate, *Carver*, and Mary Boyles, of the same Parish, *by Abp. licence.*

Oct. 19. Thomas Langley, of Spittlefeilds, Stepney, alias Stebbenheath, *Carpentar*, and Elizabeth Holt, of the same Parish, *Spinster*, *by banns.*

Jan. 2. Robert Siderfin, of the Middle Temple, *Esquire*, and Mrs. Katharine Groves, of St. James', Clerkenwell, *by Abp's licence.*

Feb. 19.   Mr. William Hill, of St. Mary in Guildford, Surrey, and
             Mrs. Ann Crosswell, of the same Parish, *by Bishop of
             London's licence.*
Feb. 20.   Adam Kimpton, of Stepney, and Dorrothe Bayly, of St.
             Margaret, Lothbury, *by Abp. licence.*

1683

Mar. 25.   Mr. Thomas Leighton, of Waterborough, Salop, and Mrs.
             Suzanna Nott, of Richmond, Surrey, *Spinster, by Abp.
             licence.*
June 5.   Mr. Thomas Leister, of Colbey, Lincolnshire, and Mrs.
             Jane Hawtrey, of Pinner, Middlesex, *by Bishop of
             London's licence.*
June 28.   John Batch, *Silversmith,* and Suzanna Moore, *Spinster,*
             both of this Parish.
July 17.   Thomas Heard, of St. Dunstan's the East, and Marthe
             Little, of St. Bartholomew Exchange, *by Abp.'s licence.*
Aug. 26.   Thomas Ackerman, of St. Ann's by Aldersgate, and
             Elleanor Prickett, of St. Lawrence Jury, *by Bishop of
             London's licence.*
Sep. 6.   Jacob Rayner, of St. Olave's, Southwark, and Mary Smith,
             of Stepney, *by Abp. licence.*
Sept. 21.   Thomas Wheldale, of St. Paul's, Convent Garden, and
             Mary Brandon, of St. Sepulchers, *by licence.*

1684

June 2.   John Knowles, of St. Martin's in the Fields, and Elleanour
             Buggins, of this Parish, *by Abp. licence.*
Dec. 27.   Newdygate Owsley, of St. Martin's in the Fields, *Gent.,*
             and Mrs. Elizabeth Jones, of the Parish of ——[*sic*]
             Thames Streete, *by licence.*
Dec. 18.   Mathew Grissell, of this Parish, and Katherine Blinkinsop,
             of Fulham, *by Abp. licence.*
Jan. 29.   Mr. Robert Wilson, of this Parish, *Vintner,* and Mrs.
             Elizabeth Buggins, of Hampstead, *by Bishop of
             London's licence.*
Feb. 5.   Benjamine Giles, of Hackney, and Sara Leigh, of Lambeth,
             Surrey, *by Abp. licence.*

1685

June 9.   John Dellamere, of St. Giles without Cripplegate, *Dyer,*
             and Ellizebeth Gardner, of the same Parish, *by licence.*
Oct. 8.   Nathaniel Neech, of St. James, Clerkenwell, *Gent.,* and
             Ann James, of the Parish of St. Mary Woolnoth, *by
             licence.*

1686

Oct. 19.   Richard Hobbard, of Staines, *Yeoman,* and Jane Wheldale,
             of St. Sepulchres, *by Abp.'s licence.*
Mar. 10.   William Busbey, of St. Bride's, and Judith Ward, of St.
             George's by Billingsgate, *by Abp. licence.*

1687

May 16. Robert Walker, of St. Clement Danes, Westminster, and Elizebeth Brazier, *Spinster*, of this Parish, *by banns.*

June 5. Edward Edwards, of St. Ollaves in Southwark, and Rebecca Goare, of this Parish, *Widdow, by licence.*

Aug. 19. William Mascall, of St. Ollaves in Southwark, and Katherine Beares, of St. Mary at Hill.

Oct. 31. Mr. David Nicholas, *Gent.*, and Kathrine Marwin, *Spinster*, both of New Windsor, Bucks, *by Abp's licence.*

Nov. 15. Mr. Richard Paggett, of St. Margaret, Westminster, *Gent.*, and Elizabeth Sandis, of St. James' in the feildes, Westminster, *Spinster, by licence London.*

Dec. 29. Georg Lawson, of St. Saviour's, Southwark, *Widdower*, and Ellizabeth Roding, of St. Leonard's, Shoreditch, *Widdow, by licence Cant.* *

Feb. 23. Thomas Jennings, of St. Margarett, Westminster, *Gent.*, and Ellizabeth Loton, of the same Parish, *by licence.*

1688

Sep. 6. Henry Allein, of St. Dunstan's in the East, and Johanna Pennie, of St. Mary, Whitechappell, alias Matfellon, *by licence Cant.*

Feb. 2. Charles Mason, of this Parish, and Elizabeth Gould, of the same Parish, *by licence Cant.*

1689

April 7. Thomas Taylor, *Widower*, of St. Margaret's, Westminster, and Sarah Stanbrook, of St. Mary le Bow, *Widow, by licence Cant.*

1691

April 7. Sir John Roberts, *Knight*, of Bromley by Bow, Middlesex, and Deborah Boffitt, of St. Austine by Pauls, *Widow, by licence.*

May 4. Thomas Munday, of St. Ann, Blackfryers, *Batchellor*, and Dorothy Tayes, of St. Mary Woolchurch Haw, *by licence.*

July 2. William Butler, *Batchellor*, and Katherine Sparks, *Spinster*, both of St. Katherine Colman, *by licence.*

Dec. 19. Robert Hancock, *Batchellor*, and Mary Beyford, *Widdow*, both of Stepney, *by licence.*

1692

Nov. 3. Jacob Broughton, *Batchelor*, of St. Clement Danes, and Susan Lord, *Widdow*, of this Parish, *by licence.*

Nov. 6. Seth Jeremies, *Batchellor*, and Mary Pickett, *Widdow*, both of St. Antholins, *by licence.*

Dec. 1. Clement Boehm, *Bachelor*, of St. Margaret Pattons Parish, and Anne Dilke, of this Parish, *Single Woman, by licence London.*

Jan. 12. Benjamin Brown, of Willingham, Lincolnshire, *Batchelor*, and Ursula Michell, of Broxbourne, Herts., *Spinster*, *by licence.*

* *i.e.* Archbishop of Canterbury.

Feb. 12.   Richard Eales, of St. Giles without Cripplegate, *Widdower*, and Ann Ashley, of St. James, Westminster, *Spinster*, *by licence.*

1693

May 1.   Richard Abney, *Batchelor*, and Margaret Fill, *Spinster*, both of St. Michaell Bassishaw, *by licence.*
Oct. 31.   Thomas Wilson, of Gosfield, Essex, *Batchellor*, and Elizabeth Byatt, of Felsted Essex, *by licence Cant.*
Jan. 1.   Richard Fryer, *Batchelor*, and Elizabeth Hanley, *Spinster*, both of this Parish, *by licence Cant.*

1694

May 22.   Marco Boutley Browne, of St. Mildred's, Bread Streete, *Batchellor*, and Mary Skinner, *Spinster*, of St. Vedast alias Foster, London, *by licence Cant.*
Sep. 4.   William Woodgate, of Chidingstone, Kent, *Bachelor*, and Sarah Cony, of Sevenoaks, Kent, *Spinster*, *by licence Cant.*
Nov. 17.   Thomas Swanton, of Chatham, Kent, *Batchellor*, and Elizabeth Robinson, of the same place, *Spinster*, *by licence Cant.*
Dec. 4.   John Choate, of Ipswitch, Co. Suffolk, *Batchellor*, and Francis Foley, of this Parish, *Spinster*, *by licence.*
Mar. 10.   John Brown, *Widdower*, and Mary Serjeant, *Widdow*, both of this Parish, *by licence.*

1695

Sep. 1.   Thomas Sone, of this Parish, *Batchellor*, and Mary Jefferyes, of St. Mary Woolchurch, *Spinster, by licence.*
Nov. 7.   John Heath, of St. Vedast, *Batchelor*, and Dorothy Perkins, of St. Botolph Aldersgate, *Spinster, by licence.*
Nov. 14.   Thomas Gardiner, of St. Bartholomew Exchange, *Batchelor*, and Jane Jubb, of St. John, Wapping, *Widdow*, *by licence London.*
Jan. 5.   John Boltey, of Allhallows, Thames Streete, *Batchelor*, and Hannah Mosse, of St. Martin Orgars, *Spinster*, *by licence Cant.*
Feb. 20.   Daniel Lucas, of Chelmsford, Essex, *Bachellor*, and Deborah Adams, of the same Parish, *Spinster*, *by licence Cant.*

1696

May 3.   Thomas Mason, of St. Michaell's Querne, *Batchellor*, and Elizabeth Davis, of St. Mary Woolchurch Haw, *by licence London.*
Aug. 27.   Edward Glenn, of St. Gregories, London, *Batchellor*, and Jane Berdin, of St. Martin in the feilds, *Widdowe, by licence London.*
Aug. 27.   William Armestrong, of St. Andrew, Holborne, *Gent.*, and Elizabeth Plummer, Barton in le Clay, Co. Beds., *Widdow, by licence Cant.*

Nov. 29.   Leonard Phillips, of St. Saviour, Southwark, *Batchellor*, and Ann Shrewsbury, of Newington Butts, Surrey, *Spinster, by licence Cant.*

Dec. 27.   Edward Richardson, of Luisham, Kent, *Batchelor*, and Sarah Turner, of this Parish, *Spinster, by licence London.*

1697

April 16.   John Bowyer, of Deptford, Kent, *Batchellor*, and Anne Smith, of Mottringham, Surrey, *Spinster, by licence Cant.*

Mar. 4.   Hogen Swanson, of Putney, Surrey, *Batchellor*, and Deborah Bramley, of the same place, *Widdow, by licence Cant.*

July 15.   John Breakstone, of St. Antholins, London, *Batchellor*, and Jane Curtis, of Guildford, Surrey, *Widdow, by licence Cant.*

Oct. 30.   Thomas King, of Chatham, Kent, *Batchellour*, and Isabella Jordan, of Stepney, *Spinster, by licence London.*

Nov. 25.   John Bartholomew, of St. Margarett, Westminster, *Widdower*, and Sarah Soule, of the same Parish, *Widdow, by licence London.*

Dec. 16.   John January, of St. Sepulchres, *Batchellor*, and Mary Woodhouse, of St. Mary Woolchurch Haw, *Spinster, by banns.*

Feb. 17.   Samuel Strickland, of St. Mary le Savoy, *Widdower*, and Ann Good, of St. Martin in the feilds, *Spinster, by licence Cant.*

Mar. 3.   John Stoaks, of Chislett, alias Chislehurst, Kent, *Bachelor*, and Anne Hasell, of Elton, Kent, *Spinster, by licence Cant.*

1698

April 24.   Thomas Sivedale, *Batchelor*, and Mary Loyd, *Spinster*, both of this Parish, *by licence London.*

May 5.   Eliazer Bownd, of the Temple, *Batchellor*, and Hannah Maplesden, of Bishop Starford, Herts., *Spinster, by licence Cant.*

May 13.   Edward Persevell, of St. Giles, Cripplegate, *Batchellor*, and Mary Walker, of St. Michaell, Cornhill, *Spinster, by licence London.*

June 12.   James Mumford, of St. Giles, Cripplegate, *Batchellor*, and Margery Thompson, of St. Mary Woolnoth, *Widdow, by banns.*

June 26.   Edmund Gibbon, of Cranbrooke, Kent, and Sarah Browne, of Beningden, Kent, *Spinster, by licence Cant.*

Sep. 1.   Henry Carter, of St. Giles without Cripplegate, *Widdower*, and Elizabeth Ford, of St. John, Hackney, *Spinster, by licence London.*

Sep. 6.   Charles Draper, of St. Giles without Cripplegate, *Batchellor*, and Elizabeth Hooper, of the same Parish, *Spinster, by licence Cant.*

Oct. 6.   George Wormley, of Allhallows in the Wall, *Widdower*, and Elizabeth Smith, of the same Parish, *by licence London.*

Oct. 9.   Thomas Hampson, of St. Clements Danes, *Batchellor*, and Elizabeth Mardeth, of St. James, Westminster, *by licence Cant.*

Jan. 12.   John Blake, of St. Mary Magdalen, Bermondsey, *Widdower*, and Mary Smith, of this Parish, *Widdow*, *by licence London.*

Feb. 14.   Thomas Harrington, of Acton, Middlesex, *Batchellor*, and Elizabeth Andrews, of this Parish, *Spinster, by banns.*

Feb. 16.   John Sollers, of Finsbury, in the County of Kent [*sic*], *Batchellor*, and Rachell Edwards, of the same place, *Widdow, by licence Cant.*

Feb. 19.   Adam Jellicoe, of St. Leonard's, Shoreditch, *Widdower*, and Katherine Holloway, of this Parish, *Widdow, by banns.*

1699

June 20.   Robert Murray, of St. Martin in the feilds, *Batchellor*, and Letitia Young, of the same place, *Widdow, by licence London.*

Sep. 21.   John Troughton, of Maidstone, Kent, *Batchellor*, and Ellinor Hooker, *Spinster, by licence Cant.*

Jan. 30.   Edward Spurling, of St. Faith's, *Batchellor*, and Elizabeth Roberts, of Christchurch, London, *Spinster, by licence Cant.*

Feb. 25.   Samuel Joyce, of St. John, Wapping, *Batchellor*, and Elizabeth Bellamy, of St. Dunstan, Stepney, *Spinster, by licence Cant.*

1700

April 1.   Thomas Alcroft, *Batchellor*, and Jane Crecy, *Spinster*, both of this Parish, *by licence London.*

April 2.   Edward Lewis, of St. Bennett's, Paul's wharfe, *Batchellor*, and Mary Reed, of this Parish, *Spinster, by banns published three times in this Parish Church, viz., Good Friday, Easter Sunday and Munday.*

April 2.   William Harding, of St. Mary, Whitechapple, *Batchellor*, and Isabella Barker, of the same Parish, *Spinster, by licence London.*

April 7.   William Gregory, of Lambeth, *Batchellor*, and Mary Harper, of this Parish, *Spinster, by banns.*

April 14.   Mr. Jonathan Whalley, of St. Mary Woolchurch Haw, *Widdower*, and Alice Shrimpton, of St. James, Clerkenwell, *Spinster, by licence London.*

May 12.   Joshua Gosslin, of the Island of Guernsey, *Batchellor*, and Judith Tomes, of the same place, *Widdow, by licence Cant.*

June 4.   Thomas Okenden, of Carrenden, Essex, *Farmer*, and Mary Crisp —— [*sic*], *by licence London.*

June 24.   Edward Browne, of St. Mary Athill, London, *Widdower*, and Elizabeth Roberts, of St. Swithin's, *Widdow, by licence London.*

Aug. 13.   John Crooke, of Eltham, Kent, *Batchellor*, and Sarah Cooke, of Edmonton, Middlesex, *Spinster, by licence Cant.*

Sep. 24.	John Little, of St. Sepulchres, *Widdower*, and Susanna Bryan, of St. Austin, London, *Widdow*, *by licence Cant.*
Sep. 29.	John Whitty, of St. Swithin's, London, *Batchellor*, and Mary Fox, of the same Parish, *Spinster*, *by licence London.*
Oct. 18.	Mr. Henry Bickerton, of Micham, Surry, *Batchellor*, and Anne Rolfe, of Harwich, Essex, *Spinster*, *by licence Cant.*
Dec. 3.	John Wilkins, of St. Margaret, Westminster, *Widdower*, and Mary Drake, of St. Martin's in the feilds, *Spinster*, *by licence London.*
Mar. 25.	William Selden, of Rotherhith, Surrey, *Batchellour*, and Judith Clements, of the same Parish, *Widdow*, *by licence Cant.*

1701

April 12.	John Bishopp, of St. Buttolph, Bishopsgate, *Batchellor*, and Mary Hilliard, of the same Parish, *Spinster*, *by licence Cant.*
May 29.	William Scarlett, of St. Leonards, Foster Lane, and Mary Flaskett, of St. Olaves, Silver Streete, *Widdow*, *by licence London.*
June 8.	Robert Gunthrop, of St. Martin in the feilds, *Widdower*, and Mary Andrews, of St. Bartholomew Exchange, *Spinster*, *by licence Cant.*
July 15.	Randolph Hopley, of St. Margarett, Westminster, and Dorcas Davis, of St. Olaves, Southwark, *Widdow*, *by licence Cant*
July 31.	William Proutening, of St. Giles without Bishopsgate, *Batchellor*, and Rebecca Wodsworth, of this Parish, *Spinster*, *by licence Cant.*
Oct. 1.	William Warren, of Ethelburgh, London, *Widdower*, and Mary Simpson, of Stepney, *Widdow*, *by licence Cant.*
Oct. 7.	John Storey, of Stepney, *Batchellor*, and Mary Hartshorne, of the same Parish, *Spinster*, *by licence Cant.*
Nov. 4.	Robert Harris, of St. James', Westminster, *Batchellor*, and Ruth Stanton, of the same Parish, *Spinster*, *by licence Cant.*
Feb. 12.	John Browne, of this Parish, *Clerke*, and Mary Parker, of St. Mary Abchurch, *Widdow*, *by licence Cant.*

1702

April 9.	Thomas Coleman, *Batchellor*, and Dorothy Munday, *Widdow*, both of this Parish, *by licence Cant.*
April 23.	Thomas Morey, of St. Mary, Whitechappell *Widdower*, and Elizabeth Bishopp, of this Parish, *Widdow*, *after banns published on Sunday, March 29th, on Good Friday, the 3rd inst., and on Easter Sunday.*
July 2.	Thomas Farrow, of St. Mary Woolchurch Haw, *Bachellor*, and Mary Sexton, of the same, *Widdow*, *by banns.*
July 30.	Gabriel Plumbe, of St. Olaves, Harte Streete, *Gent. and Batchellor*, and Annie Winchhurst, of the Liberty of the Tower, *Spinster*, *by licence Cant.*
Aug. 13.	Thomas Rochfort, of St. John, Wapping, *Batchellor*, aud Martha Sleigh, of St. Katherine, near the Tower, *Spinster*, *by licence London.*

Aug. 26.   William Fletcher, of St. Giles in the Fields, *Batchellor,* and Mary Fletcher, of St. Mary Woolchurch Haw, *Spinster, by banns.*

Sep. 21.   James Mawbert, of St. Martin in the feilds, *Batchellor,* and Mary Hawley, of the same Parish, *Spinster, by licence Cant.*

Oct. 25.   Charles Heath, of Vedast, alias Fosters, *Batchellor,* and Mary Morfen, of this Parish, *Spinster, by licence London.*

Nov. 8.   Thomas Farrell, of Bucklersbury, *Batchellor,* and Jane Haydon, of St. Buttolph, Aldgate, *Spinster, by licence Cant.*

Dec. 15.   Richard Draper, of St. Martin in the feilds, *Batchellor,* and Sarah Hooper, of St. Giles without Cripplegate, *Spinster, by licence Cant.*

Jan. 1.   George Franck, of Christchurch, London, *Batchellor,* and Elizabeth Wicks, of St. Vedast, alias Foster, *Widowe, by licence Cant.*

Jan. 1.   Anthony Pouch, of St. Anne, Westminster, *Batchellor,* and Suzannah Grimand, of Lumbard Street, *Widdow, by licence Cant.*

Jan. 12.   William Clever, of St. Andrew, Holborne, *Batchellor,* and Anne Hooper, of the same Parish, *Spinster, by licence Cant.*

Jan. 24.   Henry Bland, of St. Dunstan in the West, *Batchellor,* and Anne Hudson, of the same Parish, *Spinster, by licence Cant.*

Feb. 4.   William Elsley, of Mortlock, Surrey, *Batchellor,* and Rose Styles, of the same Parish, *Spinster, by licence Cant.*

Mar. 18.   Thomas Willis, of St. James', Westminster, *Batchellor,* and Elizabeth Combes, of the same Parish, *Spinster, by licence London.*

1703

Mar. 30.   William Langbridge, of St. Giles without, Cripplegate, *Batchellor,* and Elizabeth Greene, of this Parish, *Spinster, by licence London.*

April 10.   Edward Mathew, of St. Paul's, Shadwell, *Widdower,* and Priscilla Hardy, of the same Parish, *Widdow, by licence Cant.*

May 13.   Ward Rich, of St. Leonard, Shoreditch, *Bachelor,* and Joane Slader, of the same Parish, *Widdow, by licence Cant.*

June 1.   George Langrake, of St. Dunstan in the West, *Batchellor,* and Mary Clever, of St. Bridgett, alias Bride, *Spinster, by licence Cant.*

June 6.   Edward Harris, of St. Dunstan's the East, *Widdower,* and Hannah Yeane, of St. Buttolph, Aldgate, *Spinster, by licence of Cant.*

July 19.   William Wright, of Finchley, Middlesex, *Batchellor,* and Alice Rowland, of the same Parish, *Spinster, by licence London.*

Nov. 18.   Samuell Feild, of this Parish, *Batchellor,* and Mary Smith, of St. Mary Woolchurch Haw, *Spinster, by licence Cant.*

Dec. 3.   Joseph Creemer, of St. Dunstan's, Stepney, *Widdower,* and Elizabeth Grant, of this Parish, *by banns.*

Dec. 4. Joseph Southerne, of Mary at Hill, London, *Batchellor*, and Suzanna Wood, of the same Parish, *by licence London.*

Dec. 25. Jeremy Gregory, of Lambeth, Surrey, *Batchellor*, and Elizabeth Walker, of the same Parish, *Spinster, by licence London.*

Feb. 3. John Corbison, of St. Giles without Cripplegate, *Batchellor*, and Mary Thynne, of St. John's, Hackney, *Spinster, by licence Cant.*

Mar. 13. Peter Temple, of Woolwich, Kent, *Widdower*, and Sara Crow, of Deptford, Kent, *Widdow, by licence Cant.*

1704

June 8. Edward Potter, of Coone-Genne, Essex, *Batchellor*, and Mary Mason, of Mitcham, Kent, *Spinster, by licence London.*

June 8. George Perkins, of St. Giles without Cripplegate, *Batchellor*, and Ann Mason, of St. Bartholomew, near Exchange, *Spinster, by licence London.*

June 13. Thomas Geering, of St. Olaves, Southwark, *Batchellor*, and Katherine Stow, of the same Parish, *Widdow, by licence Cant.*

1705

April 8. Mr. Brandon Goddard, of St. Michaell, Crooked Lane, *Batchellor*, and Sarah Goade, of Allhallows the less, *Spinster, by licence Cant.*

April 17. Thomas Chubb, of St. Buttolph's without Bishopsgate, *Widdower*, and Mary Sprangdrell, of St. Mary Woolchurch Haw, *Spinster, by banns.*

April 22. John Steelefax, of the United Parish of St. Mary Woolchurch-haw, *Batchellor*, and Mary Clarke, of the same Parish, *Spinster, by banns.*

April 28. James Angillis, of St. Mary at Hill, London, *Batchellor*, and Frances Babbington, of St. Peter's, Cornehill, *Widdow, by licence Cant.*

May 19. Richard Ford, of St. Austin, London, *Batchellor*, and Elizabeth Adams, of the same Parish, *Spinster, by licence Cant.*

July 17. Mr. Thomas Baily, of St. Leonard's, Shoreditch, *Batchellor*, and Sarah Ashwood, of the same Parish, *Spinster, by licence Cant.*

Sep. 4. Mr. Peter Leonard, of St. Buttolph, Aldersgate, *Batchellor*, and Sarah Waldron, of St. Sepulchres, *Spinster, by licence Cant.*

Sep. 6. Mr. Christopher Roffey, of Woolwich, *Batchellor*, and Sarah Greenhill, of the same Parish, *Spinster, by licence Cant.*

Oct. 2. Mr. Robert Leaver, of St. Michaell, Cornhill, *Batchellor*, and Barbara Filkes, of St. Mary, Whitechappell, *Spinster, by licence Cant.*

Oct. 21. Mr. Henry Grevile, of St. Nicholas Acons, *Batchellor*, and Katherine Browne, of this Parish, *Spinster, by licence Cant.*

Nov. 7.   William Garner, of Stepney, *Batchellor*, and Anne Willis, of St. Marylebow, *by licence London*.

Mar. 24.   William Allen, of St. Dunstan, Stepney, *Widdower*, and Isabella ——* [*sic*], of the same Parish, *Widdow, by licence Cant*.

1706

April 2.   William Thacker, of St. Margarett Pattents, *Batchellor*, and Elizabeth Westall, of the same Parish, *Widdow, by licence Cant*.

April 25.   William Holden, of St. Clement Danes, *Batchellor*, and Mary Macwright, of the United Parish of St. Mary Woolchurch-haw, *Spinster, by banns*.

May 17.   Alexander Harding, of Goosener, Co. Lancaster, *Batchellor*, and Agnes Holmes, of the same, *Spinster, by licence Cant*.

Aug. 8.   Thomas Power, of this Parish, and Mary Cawdle, of St. Mary, Whitechappell, *Widdow, by licence Cant*.

Nov. 14.   Robert Lynum, of St. Giles without Cripplegate, *Bachelor*, and Mary Hooper, of the same Parish, *Spinster, by licence London*.

Dec. 12.   Robert London, of Grayes Inn, *Widdower*, and Sarah Hobdey, of the same Parish, *Widdow, by licence Cant*.

Feb. 7.   Rowland Kent, *Batchellor*, and Mary Harding, *Spinster*, both of this Parish, *by banns*.

1707

April 13.   Samuel Curson, of St. Dunstan in the West, *Batchellour*, and Rebecca Clarke, of the same Parish, *Spinster, by licence Cant*.

June 21.   Walter Hamond, of St. Mary at Hill, *Batchellor*, and Margaret Longlands, of the same Parish, *Widdow, by licence Cant*.

Sep. 4.   Thomas Graine, of St. Mary Magdalen, Bermondsey, *Batchellor*, and Mary Brockford, of St. Paul's, Shadwell, *Widdow, by licence Cant*.

Oct. 8.   James Clarke, of Stoake Newington, in the Parish of Hackney, *Widdower*, and Sisley Allen, of the Parish of Newington, *Spinster, by licence Cant*.

Oct. 16.   John Turner, of Whitechappell, *Widdower*, and Elianor Day, of the Parish aforesaid, *Single woman, by licence London*.

Oct. 22.   John Browne, of St. Giles' in the feilds, *Batchellor*, and Mary Broughton, of this Parish, *Spinster, by banns*.

Dec. 23.   James Litchman, of St. Buttolph without Aldgate, *Batchellor*, and Mary Copping, of St. Magnus the Martyr, *Spinster, by licence London*.

Jan. 27.   John Scutt, of Petworth, Sussex, *Batchellor*, and Elizabeth Minshall, of St. Buttolph, Bishopsgate, *Spinster, by licence Cant*.

Feb. 12.   Robert Eaton, of Edmunton, Co. Middlesex, *Batchellor*, and Sarah Wilkinson, of St. Mary Woolchurch-haw, *Spinster, by licence London*.

April 29.   Barwell Smith, of Swithins, London, *Batchellor*, and Jane Turney, of St. Mary Abchurch, *Spinster, by licence Cant*.

---

* "King" is supplied in a small volume, which apparently was the Clerk's Memorandum Book.

1708

June 17. The Honble. Henry Bertie, of the Inner Temple, *Batchellor*, and the Right Honoble. Suzanna, Countess of Dungannon, of St. Martins in the feilds, *Widdow*, *by licence Cant.*

July 8. John Cheeseman, of Greenwich, *Batchellor*, and Suzanna Walker, of the same place, *Spinster, by licence Cant.*

July 15. William Rycroft, of Woolwich, Kent, *Batchellor*, and Mary Davie, of Dartford, Kent, *Spinster, by licence Cant.*

Aug. 22. William Carpenter, of St. Michael, Queenhithe, *Batchellor*, and Jane Clarke, of Mortclack, Surrey, *Spinster, by licence Cant.*

Nov. 4. Thomas Allcroft, of St. Michaell, Cornhill, *Widdower*, and Martha Garbrand, of St. Stephen's Wallbrook, *Spinster, by licence London.*

Nov. 4. Christopher Clipperton, of Yarmouth, Co. Norfolk, *Widdower*, and Elianor Hickets, of St. Martin's L'Grand, *Widdow, by licence Cant.*

Mar. 5. Edward Troward, of St. John, Wapping, *Batchellor*, and Frampton Hooke, of the same, *Spinster, by licence Cant.*

Mar. 6. Arthur Harrison, of St. Leonard, Shorditch, *Batchellor*, and Rachell Gutteridge, of St. Giles', Criplegate, *Spinster, by licence London.*

1709

May 19. George Watemouth, of St. Mary Woolnoth, and Elizabeth Dukes, of the same, *by licence Cant.*

Aug. 9. William Wakefield, of St. James', Garlic-hithe, *Batchellor*, and Mary Packer, of St. Mary Woolchurch, *Spinster, by banns.*

Sep. 22. Edward Falkener, of this Parish, *Batchellor*, and Abigall Loyde, of this Parish, *Spinster, by licence Cant.*

Oct. 25. Edward Greep, of St. Ann, Blackfryers, *Widdower*, and Martha Barrington, of St. Bartholomew the Great, *Widdow, by licence London.*

1710

Mar. 25. John Herbert, *Batchellor*, of St. Bennet Sherehog, and Tabritha Healy, of the same Parish, *Widdow, by licence Cant.*

June 4. Thomas Buller, *Batchellor*, of St. James, Westminster, and Mary Clerke, of the same Parish, *Widdow, by licence Cant.*

June 16. Thomas Hacthet, of St. Nicholas Acons, and Alice Cowper, of this Parish, *Spinster, by licence Cant.*

May 18. John Bush, of Hertford, *Batchellor*, and Sara Honour, of the same, *Spinster, by licence London.*

May 28. Thomas Chappell, *Widdower*, of St. Leonard, Shoreditch, and Mary Arkelstall, of St. Dionis, Backchurch, *Spinster, by licence Cant.*

June 24. William Corderoy, of Henley upon Thames, *Batchellor*, and Anne Baldwin, of the same, *Spinster, by licence Cant.*

July 11.   Samuel Chandler, of St. Giles in the Fields, *Batchellor*, and Elizabeth Paine, of St. Dunstan in the East, *Spinster, by licence Cant.*

Aug. 20.   Nathaniell Lilly, of St. Buttolph without Aldgate, *Batchellor*, and Mary Hargrave, of this Parish, *by licence London.*

Nov. 6.   James Willson, of Whitechappell, *Widdower*, and Margery Naylder, of the same, *Widow, by licence London.*

Nov. 10.   Benjamin Jordan, of St. Antholin's, *Batchellor*, and Sarah Tailler, of Westham, Essex, *Spinster, by licence Cant.*

Nov. 16.   Daniell Guy, of Clapham, *Widdower*, and Anne Lane, of this Parish, *Spinster, by licence Cant.*

Nov. 24.   Joshua Barnes, of St. Olaves, Southwark, *Batchellor*, and Elizabeth Collier, of St. Edmonds the King, *Spinster, by licence Cant.*

Dec. 3.   David Edwards, of St. Mary, Whitechappell, *Batchellor*, and Elizabeth Cranell, alias —— [*sic*] of the Parish aforesaid, *Spinster, by licence Cant.*

Dec. 9.   Edward Edwards, of St. Bartholomew the Great, *Batchellor*, and Mary Crompt, of St. Giles, Cripplegate, *Spinster, by licence Cant.*

July 16.   Thomas Williams, of St. Sepulchre's, Cambridge, *Batchelor*, and Sarah Huske, of Cambridge, *Spinster, by licence Cant.*

Dec. 21.   Richard Maddocks, of St. Buttolph, Aldersgate, *Widdower*, and Elizabeth Avery, of the Parish aforesaid, *Widdow, by licence Cant.*

1711

April 22.   Hugh Powell, of St. Benedict Fink, *Batchelor*, and Elizabeth Blackborn, of this Parish, *Spinster, by licence London.*

April 28.   Joseph Wright, of Allhallows, Lombard Streete, *Batchelor*, and Elizabeth Savage, of this Parish, *Spinster, by licence London.*

May 21.   George Bryan, of Stepney, *Widower*, and Mary Browne, of St. Mary Woolnoth, *Widdow, by licence Cant.*

June 27.   James Mackay, of St. Martin's in the Fields, and Mary Abbot, of St. Mary Woolchurch, *Widdow, by licence Cant.*

Aug. 15.   John Low, of St. John, Wappin, *Batchelor*, and Alice Carr, of Chelsea, *Spinster, by licence Cant.*

Sep. 15.   Daniell Martin, of the Parish of Wapping, Stepney, in Middlesex, *Widdower*, and Esther Coleman, of St. Buttolp, Aldgate, *Spinster, by licence Cant.*

Sep. 30.   Peter Mince, alias Minse, of Stepney, *Batchelor*, and Sarah White, of St. Edmund the King, *Spinster, by licence Cant.*

Oct. 1.   William Sarjent, of Stepney, *Batchelor*, and Ann Hooke, of St. John, Wapping, *by licence Cant.*

Nov. 10.   John Brewer, of Stoake Newington, *Batchelor*, and Martha Wright, of Hackney, *Spinster, by licence Cant.*

Jan. 15.   Lloyd Simpson, of St. Peter's Cheape, and Palestine Higgins, of St. Andrew's, Holborne, *Spinster, by licence Cant.*

1712

May 14. William Stead, of St. Buttolph without Algate, *Bachelor*, and Hanna Wattson, of St. Giles, *Spinster, by licence Cant.*

May 22. William Brideforth, of Tottenham, Middlesex, *Widdower*, and Mary Dickson, of St. Dionis Backchurch, *Widdowe*, *by licence Cant.*

Aug. 16. Richard Powey, of St. Mary le Bow, *Bachelor*, and Anne Chadwick, of St. Paul's, Covent Garden, *Spinster*, *by licence Cant.*

Sep. 21. William Read, of Richmond, Surry, *Batchelor*, and Elizabeth Saunders, of the Parish aforesaid, *Spinster*, *by ticence Cant.*

Nov. 14. John Chamberlaine, of Broughton, in Hertfordshire, and Elizabeth Houlgate, of St. Mary Woolnoth, *Spinster*, *by licence Cant.*

Dec. 6. George Webb, of St. Giles' without Cripplegate, *Bachellor*, and Anne Saunders, of St. James' Clerkenwell, *Widdow*, *by licence Cant.*

Jan. 2. William Rogers, of St. Sepulchre, *Bachelor*, and Elizabeth Lane, of Hatfield, Herts, *Spinster, by licenee Cant.*

Jan. 30. William Newton, of St. Mary Woolnoth, *Bachelor*, and Handy Lloyd, of the same Parish, *Spinster, by licence Cant.*

1713

June 26. John Mitchell, of St. John, Wapping, *Widdower*, and Rebecca Farrant, of St. Mary Woolchurch Haw, *Spinster, by banns.*

July 13. John Bloss, of Tower Hamlett, *Bachelor*, and Susannah Curtis, of St. Dionis Backchurch, *Spinster, by licence Cant.*

July 20. Robert Hayes, of St. Mary Woolnoth, *Bachelor*, and Mary Cooke, of the same Parish, *Spinster, by licence Cant.*

July 24. William Smith, of St. Dunstan in the East, *Bachelor*, and Mary Alton, of the same Parish, *Spinster, by licence Cant.*

Aug. 13. Joseph Ruttar and Elizabeth Hemings, both of this Parish, *by banns.*

Sep. 29. William Prat, of St. Olave, Jewry, *Bachelor*, and Elizabeth Martin, of St. John, Hackney, *Spinster, by licence Cant.*

Dec. 26. John Morrice, of St. Olave, Silver Street, *Batchelor*, and Mary Farrell, of St. Mary Woolnoth, *Spinster, by licence Cant.*

1714

April 17. John Shaw, of Clapham, Surrey, *Batchelor*, and Mary Gurney, of the same Parish, *Spinster, by licence Cant.*

May 19. Russell Gatliffe, of St. Catherine Cree Church, *Batchelor*, and Charity Lee, of the same Parish, *Spinster, by licence Cant.*

Aug. 6. Jonathan Shipperd, of St. Saviour, Southwark, *Bachelor*, and Mary Hawkins, of the same Parish, *Spinster, by licence London.*

Aug. 17. Charles Round, of St. John Zachary, *Batchelor*, and Elizabeth Ilsley, of the same Parish, *Spinster*, *by licence Cant.*

1715

Aug. 10. Richard Hewlet, of St. Andrew under shaft, *Widdower*, and Sarah Cooley, of St. Peter, Cornhill, *Widdow*, *by licence Cant.*

Aug. 14. Solomon Staple, of Stepney, *Batchelor*, and Sarah Ward, of St. Mary Woolnoth, *by licence London.*

Aug. 18. Thomas Miller, of St. Giles', Cripplegate, *Batchellor*, and Mary Prissick, of St. Mary Woolnoth, *Spinster*, *by licence Cant.*

1727*

April 23. Benjamin Harsee, of St. John, Hackney, *Batchelor*, and Mary Rootherass, of St. Mary Woolnoth, *Spinster*, *by licence London.*

July 13. Peirce Francis, of St. Hellen's, London, *Bachelor*, and Elizabeth Stillgo, of the same Parish, *Spinster*, *by licence London.*

End of the Marriages in the 2nd Volume of the Registers.

[Vol. iv.]

THE Names of such as were Married in the Parish Church of St. Mary Woolnoth, London, since the Twenty-fifth day of August, Anno Domini 1715, when the Church was begun to be taken downe in order to be rebuilt, and was finished and opened on Easterday Anno Domini 1727.

Joseph Lowe,	}	*Churchwardens of*
William Lawe,	}	*St. Mary Woolnoth.*
Richard Mainwaring,	}	*Churchwardens of St.*
Christopher Fowler,	}	*Mary Woolchurch Haw.*

April 23. Benjamin Harsee, of St. John Hackney, *Bachelor* [*sic*[, and Mary Rootheross [*sic*], of St. Mary Woolnoth, *Spinster*, *by licence London.*

July 13. Peirce Francis, of St. Hellen's, London, *Batchellor* [*sic*], and Elisabeth Stillgo, of the same Parish, *Spinster*, *by licence London.*

Aug. 22. Robert Lamb, of Haither, Lincolnshire, *Bachelor*, and Elizabeth Shrawley, of Aram, Nottinghamshire, *Spinster*, *by licence Cant.*

Sep. 21. Edward Cutburd, of St. Dunstan, Stepney, *Batchelor*, and Sarah Sparvall, of the same Parish, *Widdow*, *by licence Cant.*

* The two entries of April 23rd and July 13th, 1727, are entered in this Volume and also in the Fourth Volume of Registers. The Third Volume does not contain any Marriages.

1728

April 21.   William Bird, of St. Sepulchres, *Widdower*, and Elizabeth Holland, of Stepney, *Widdow, by licence Cant.*

June 14.   Robert Porter, of St. Leonard, Shoreditch, *Bachelor*, and Sarah Herbert, of the same Parish, *Spinster, by licence London.*

Nov. 14.   Peter Budge, of St. Mary Woolchurch, *Batchelor*, and Elizabeth Fogg, of Allhallows, Lombard Street, *Spinster, by licence London.*

Feb. 18.   Joseph Berry, of Kingston, Surrey, *Batchelor*, and Sarah Snape, of the same Parish, *Spinster, by licence Cant.*

1729

April 21.   Charles Dixon, of St. Giles Cripplegate, *Batchelor*, and Mary Smith, of this Parish, *by banns.*

Oct. 29.   Benjamin Baxter, of St. Thomas the Apostle, *Batchelor*, and Anne Colebatch, of St. Mary Woolnoth, *Spinster, by licence London.*

Jan. 22.   Robert Jennings, of St. Andrew Undershaft, *Batchelor*, and Sarah Coxhead, of the Tower Liberty, *Spinster, by licence Cant.*

1730

Nov. 12.   William Wheate, of St. Michael, Wood Street, *Bachelor*, Elizabeth Marshall, of Barnet, Hertfordshire, *Spinster, by licence London.*

Dec. 31.   Thomas Aspinall, of St. Clement Danes, *Bachelor*, and Frances Pluckent, of Christopher's, London, *Spinster, by licence Cant.*

1731

April 22.   Benjamin Whiteing, of St. Buttolph, Bishopsgate, *Widdower*, and Mary Priddy, of the same Parish, *Spinster, by licence Cant.*

May —[*sic*] Thomas Clutterbuck, *Esquire*, of St. George, Hanover Square, *Bachelor*, and the Honorable Henrietta Tolmache, of Westbury, in the Parish of Eastmead, Co. Southampton, *Spinster, by licence Abp.* Dated 29 April, 1730 [*sic*].

Aug. 5.   John Moore, of Bridgewater, Somersetshire, *Widdower*, and Mary Taylor, of Christchurch, London, *Widdow, by licence Cant.*

Sep. 26.   John Biss, of Christchurch, in Surrey, *Bachelor*, and Elizabeth Finnimore, of the same Parish, *Spinster, by licence Cant.*

Nov. 16.   Michael Wilson, of St. Dunstan's in the East, *Batchelor*, and Elizabeth Wilson, of Allhallows Barking, *Spinster, by licence London.*

Jan. 12.   William Davison, of Woolwich, in Kent, *Widdower*, and Catherine Bennet, of the Tower Liberty, *Spinster, by licence London.*

Feb. 16.   John Valentine Heckert, of Christchurch, Spittlefields, *Batchelor*, and Mary Peirson, of St. Antholine, London, *Spinster, by licence Cant.*

Feb. 17.   Thomas Wells, of St. Antholin's, London, *Batchelor*, and Mary Hoe, of St. Mary Woolnoth, *Spinster, by licence Cant.*

1732

April 27.   William Hodges, of St. Mary Magdalene, Bermondsey, *Widdower*, and Susannah Hall, of St. Buttolph, Bishopsgate, *Spinster, by licence Cant.*

April 29.   William Jephson, *Clerk*, Vicar of Hormead, Hertford-shire, *Batchelor*, and Mary Cheshire, of Hornchurch, Essex, *Spinster, by licence London.*

Aug. 3.   Hasden Young, of Stoke Damarell, Devonshire, *Batchelor*, and Sarah Adams, of St. Mary Axe, London, *Spinster, by licence London.*

Aug. 19.   Thomas Cox, of Kingston upon Thames, Surrey, *Batchelor*, and Susanna Brownrigg, of St. Saviour's, Southwark, *Widdow, by licence Cant.*

Nov. 16.   [The rest of the line, which is near the top of the page, and the rest of the page is blank, the next leaf is cut out, and four blank leaves remain.]

End of Marriages in 4th Volume of the Register.

[Vol. b.]

[There is no record of any Marriages from 1732 to 1745, although the Baptisms and Burials are complete between these dates.]

1745

June 27.   George Eckersall, of Lincoln's Inn, and Catharine Malthus, of St. Andrew's, Holbourn.

Aug. 22.   Joshua Margary, of St. Dionis, Backchurch, and Elizabeth Beardin, of Highgate.

Sep. 24.   Thomas Somner, of St. Saviour, Southwark, and Elizabeth Hague, of St. Olave's, Southwark.

Nov. 3.   William Smith, of Christchurch, London, and Mary Matthews, of St. Swithin, London.

1746

Mar. 2.   Thomas Blaney, of St. Mary Woolnoth, and Ann Faulkner, of St. Alphege, London.

Mar. 3.   Josiah Swindell, of St. Leonard, Eastcheap, and Elizabeth Gallopin, of the same Parish.

Mar. 30.   John Bentley and Hannah Keeling, both of St. Mary Woolchurch Haw.

April 19.   Daniel How, of St. John's Southwark, and Elizabeth Van Deuren, of St. Mary, Whitechapel.

April 24.   John Staples, of St. Dunstan in the East, and Martha Van Deuren, of St. Mary, Whitechapel.

Dec. 9.	John Sheppard, of St. Paul, Shadwell, and Elizabeth Wharham, of the same.
Dec. 10.	Robert Sutton, of St. Saviour's, Southwark, and Sarah Wrister, of the same Parish.

1747

April 12.	Alexander Cushirie, of the Parish of St. Saviour, Southwark, and Ann Horn, of Stonefield, in the County of Oxford.
July 26.	James Castle, of the Parish of St. Matthew, Bethnal Green, and Martha Miller, of the Parish of St. Mary Woolnoth.
Dec. 31.	James Herring, of the Parish of St. John, Southwark, and Eleanor Gregory, of the Parish of St. Dunstan, Stepney.
Mar. 16.	James Godwin, of St. Margaret, Westminster, and Joanna Fulbrooke, of Hammersmith, in the Parish of Fulham.

1748

Feb. 1.	William Smith, of St. George the Martyr, Southwark, and Ann Knight, of St. Leonard, Shoreditch.
Sep. 10.	William Hill, of the Parish of St. Saviour, Southwark, and Hannah Powell, of Christ Church, in the same.
Dec. 18.	William Palmer and Mary Strologer, both of the Parish of St. Mary Woolnoth.

1749

Feb. 6.	Charles West, of the Parish of Great Stanmore, in the County of Middlesex, and Susanna Derby, of St. Mary Woolnoth.
Dec. 2.	Herbert Thomas, of Tottenham High Cross, Middlesex, and Sarah Smith, of the same.

1750

April 28.	Robert Hankins, of the Tower of London, and Jane Barbaroux, of the Parish of St. Bennet Finck, London.
May 29.	Benjamin Tasker, of the Parish of St. Vedast, otherwise Foster, London, and Anne Kingdom, of the Parish of St. Mary le bone, Middlesex.
June 9.	The Rev. Mr. John Blyth, of the Parish of Colshill, in the County of Warwick, and Mary Alden, of the same Parish.
June 21.	William Fox, of the Parish of St. Mary Abchurch, London, and Elizabeth Wilkes, of Great St. Helen, London.
June 23.	Kenton Couse, of the Parish of St. Martin in the Fields, Middlesex, and Sarah Hamilton of the same Parish.
Aug. 12.	Robert Hyett, of the Parish of St. Swithin, London, and Sarah Jones, of the Parish of St. George, Bloomsbury.
Oct. 30.	John Phillips, of the Parish of St. Mary Magdalen, in Oxford, and Mary Binfied, of the Parish of St. Michael, in Oxford.
Dec. 10.	John Bates, of the Parish of Endfield, in the County of Middlesex, and Elizabeth Scale, of the Parish of St. Olave, Hart Street.

1751

July 4.   William Simpson, of the Parish of St. Clement Danes, in the County of Middlesex, and Mary Robinson, of the same.

Sep. 13.   Loomworth Dane, of Enfield, Middlesex, and Grace Foxcroft, of the same.

Dec. 7.   Henry Jones, of St. Bartholomew, behind the Royal Exchange, London, and Mary Ware, of St. John Baptist, London.

1752

June 11.   Thomas Blaney and Elizabeth Page, of St. Mary Woolnoth.

July 6.   William Watts, of St. Dunstan, Stepney, and Jane Matthews, of the same.

Aug. 27.   Robert Smith, of Kew, Surrey, and Ann Collinson, of the same.

Dec. 6.   Christopher Clifft, of St. Gabriel, Fenchurch, London, and Elizabeth Ping, of St. Clement Danes, Middlesex.

1753

Mar. 1.   Thomas Coates, of St. Botolph's, Aldgate, and Mary Burch, of All Hallow's, Barking.

1754

April 9.   Samuel Saunders and Martha Baker, both of St. Mary Woolnoth.

July 5.   Thomas Phipps, of St. Katharine Coleman, and Mary Brister, of St. Mary Woolnoth.

Aug. 22.   John Preston, of St. Sepulchre's, and Ann Shepherd, of St. Mary Woolnoth.

Nov. 4.   John Peach and Margaret Edwards, both of St. Mary Woolnoth.

Nov. 10.   James Brackstone and Mary Hall, both of St. Mary Woolnoth.

End of Marriages in 5th Volume of the Registers.

Burials

THE names of such as are buried in the Parishe of Sainte Marye Woolnoth, of London, sythence the Sixteenth daye of November, 1538.

1538

Im primis. Jan. 26. Thomas Parker.
Mar. 1.   Thomas Boughton.

1539

April 10.   William Goodwyn.
Dec. 3.   Margarett Morton, *Wydowe.*
Dec. 15.   John, son of John Kele.
Jan. 11.   Jane Rufford.

1540

Mar. 27.   William, son of Robert Marten.
July 10.   Katheren, daughter of John Gardener.
July 15.   Hellina, wife of Walter Blake.
July 16.   Margaret, wife of Robert Grevis.
Sep. 7.   John, son of Walter Lawndye.
Sep. 10.   Annes, daughter of Bastian Boma.
Sep. 17.   Elizabethe Donington, *Wydowe.*
Oct. 4.   Marten, son of George Weld.
Oct. 12.   John Barnys, *Goldesmythe.*
Oct. 13.   Xpofer Rayne, *Draper.*
Oct. 20.   Marye, daughter of Robert Emerye.
Oct. 20.   Sir William Tobye, *Preste.*
Oct. 30.   Fabian, son of Fabian Wethers.
Nov. 12.   William Harrison, *servant* to Thomas Taylor.
Nov. 13.   Hughe, son of Robert Warde.
Nov. 30.   Richard, son of Thomas Wetherall.
Dec. 3.   Ralfe Brabyn, *servant* to Thomas Taylor.
Dec. 3.   John Paxton, *servant* to James Michell.
Dec. 7.   John Gardener, *Goldsmythe.*
Dec. 8.   Thomas Backhouse, *servant* to James Michell.
Dec. 15.   Nicholas, son of Bastian Birde.
Dec. 24.   Elizabeth, daughter of Bastian Birde.
Jan. 5.   Elizabeth, daughter of George Webb.
Jan. 24.   Oswald Deggis, *Straunger.*
Feb. 26.   Annis Paxston, *servant* with Mr. Michell.

1541

Jan. 13.	John Bare, *estraunger.*
Jan. 26.	Thomas Selbe, *servant* with James Stevens.
Sep. 30.	Thomas and Ellen, grandchildren of John Gardener.
Oct. 8.	Henry Herdman, *servant* to Mr. Mathew Coke.
Oct. 11.	Thomas, son of Mr. Hancock.
Oct. 20.	Maude, *servant* to Mr. Trill.
Oct. 24.	Robert Boughton, *servant* to Mr. Boughton.
Oct. 25.	Elizabeth, daughter of Sir Martyn Bowes, *Knight.*
Oct. 30.	Margarett, daughter to Mr. Hancock.
Dec. 11.	Henry, son of Thomas Wetherall.
Dec. 23.	William, *servant* to John Mathewe.
Jan. 7.	John Browne, *servant* to Mr. Atkinson.
Feb. 2.	William, son of Thomas Bowyer.
Feb. 23.	Margarett, *servant* to Goodman Fowlene.
Mar. 10.	Grafter, *an estranger.*
Mar. 6.	Nicholas Pollen, *servant* to Mr. Pollen.
Mar. 14.	Elizabeth Leighe, *servant* with John Keyle.
Mar. 19.	A daughter of Henry Crafte.
Mar. 20.	Eiizabeth Stevens, *servant* to Mr. Henry Foule.

1542

April 7.	William Whelly, *servant* to Mr. Foule.
July 19.	Annis, daughter of John Hankins.
Aug. 16.	Robert Shethe.
Sep. 4.	Anne, daughter of Mr. Thomas Glinton.
Oct. 18.	James Michaell.
Nov. 22.	Annis, daughter of Thomas Taylor.
Dec. 4.	Susan, daughter of Thomas Witton.
Jan. 18.	John Oteringham, *Baker.*
Feb. 12.	John, son of John Harte.
Mar. 17.	Alyce Brigge.

1543

April 1.	Mr. John Brigge.
Mar. 16.	Katherin, daughter of Thomas Witton.
May 10.	William Loye, *servant* to Thomas Wytton.
May 10.	Richard, son of George Webbe.
June 1.	Elizabeth Bowyer, *servant* to Thomas Atkynson.
June 1.	Timothy, daughter of Walter Landy.
June 1.	Annis, daughter of George Webbe.
Aug. 1.	Katheren, daughter of Walter Blake.
June 7.	Annis, wife of " one Clemente."
Aug. 2.	Gilliam Cary, otherwise Martyn, *Goldsmythe* and *servant* to Thomas Stevens, *Goldsmythe.*
Aug. 8.	Richard Boreman, *servant* to Thomas Stevens, *Goldsmythe.*
Aug. 18.	Raffe, son of Reginalde Wage.
Aug. 18.	Elizabeth Stronge, *Gentlewoman*, warde to Sir Martyn Bowes, *Knyght.*
Aug. 18.	Margarett Soryll, *servant* to John Robson.
Aug. 21.	John Kinge, *servant* to John Robson.
Aug. 24.	Maryan, daughter of ——— [*sic*]
Aug. 24.	Alice and Hellen, daughters of Reginalde Watha [*sic*]
Aug. 24.	Richard Uprice, *servant* to Reginalde Warham.

Sep. 1.	Elizabeth Gull, *servant* to Mr. Thomas Marshall.
Sep. 6.	Richard Jookes, *servant* to Mr. Warham.
Sep. 10.	Reynolde Warham, *Householder and Baker.*
Sep. 10.	Benet, daughter of Stephen Hodson.
Sep. 18.	Grace, daughter of William Tyndall.
Sep. 23.	Elizabeth Batterton.
Oct. 2.	Hellen, daughter of William Robinson.
Oct. 17.	Elizabeth Balere, *servant* to William Robinson.
Oct. 7.	John Wryte, *servant* to Stephen Hawkyns, *Goldsmyth.*
Oct. 9.	Nicholas, son of Walter Landy.
Oct. 15.	Suzan and Zachri, son and daughter of William Robinson.
Oct. 16.	Ursula, daughter of John Hugynes.
Oct. 18.	Alita Colman, *servant* of Xpofer Salmon.
Oct. 18.	Thomas, son of Thomas Wetherall.
Oct. 21.	Katherin Zeskyns, *servant* to Mr. Bowyer.
Oct. 26.	Annes Wele, *servant* to John Scrivener.
Oct. 26.	Annes Dawe, *servant* to Stephen Hawkyns.
Nov. 8.	Richard Scrivener, *servant* to John Scrivener.
Nov. 12.	Jane, daughter of Anthony More.
Nov. 13.	Bryan Wilson, *servant* to Henry Crafte.
Nov. 13.	William Merchaunt.
Nov. 19.	Henry Tynemaker, *servant* to John Scrivener.
Dec. 7.	Anne, daughter of John Scrivener.
Jan. 9.	Rose, wife of ———— [*sic*] Rogers.
Jan. 15.	Richard, *servant* to John Scrivener.

1544

April 22.	Joane, daughter of John Segar.
April 28.	Stephan, son of William Hull.
May 15.	John Lyttenburye.
May 15.	Anne, daughter of Henry Crafte.
May 19.	Davie Rogers, *Householder.*
July 13.	William, son of Stephen Hawkins.
Aug. 6.	Racomen, wife of Mr. Norton.
Sep. 19.	Joan, daughter of John Hobbes.
Sep. 24.	Hellen, daughter of John Harte.
Oct. 16.	John, daughter [*sic*] of William Murfene.
Nov. 2.	George Salmone, *servant* to Xpofer Salmon.
Nov. 5.	Elizabeth Gisby, *servant* to Robert Emerye.
Dec. 3.	Mary, daughter of Thomas Hancocke.
Dec. 6.	Nicholas Crede, *servant* to John Crede.
Jan. 2.	Thomas, son of Robert Spicer.
Jan. 6.	Richard Wadsworth, *servant* to Richard Kele.
Feb. 1.	William Bowes, *servant* to Thomas Uprichard.
Mar. 1.	Margaret, daughter of Robert Spicer.
Mar. 7.	Thomas Wellman, *servant* to Henry Boswell.
Mar 19.	William, son of Anthony More.
Mar. 24.	Edward Gargill, *servant* to Mr. Pollen.
Mar. 18.	Thomas Jones, *servant* to Mr. Uprichard.

1545

Mar. 31.	Nicholas Pollen.
April 4.	John Brigborne, of Feversham.
April 10.	Thomas, son of Henry Boswell.

April 10.	John ———-[*sic*] *servant* to Henry Boswell.
April 10.	Nicholas, *servant* of Henry Bowwell.
Mar. [*sic*] 4.	Humffrey Stenly, *Stranger.*
May 26.	Alice, daughter of Henry Lector.
June 25.	William Tadlowe.
July 1.	Francis, son of Sir Martyn Bowes, *Knight.*
July 10.	Richard, *servant* to Thomas Norton.
Aug. 8.	Anne Bowdry, *servant* to Fabyan Wethers.
Aug. 13.	Phillip, *servant* to Mr. Wetherill.
Aug. 13.	Elizabeth, wife of Mr. John Hobbes.
Sep. 1.	William Botsone.
Sep. 21.	William Jones, bachelor and *servant* to Mr. Martyn Bowes.
Sep. 25.	Elizabeth Bradhowst, *Wydowe.*
Oct. 14.	Robert Marshall, *servant* to Thomas Marshall.
Oct. 23.	Henry Keye, apprentice to Henry Boswell.
Nov. 20.	Elizabeth, daughter of Mr. Henry Boswell.
Nov. 26.	Katheren Elveden, *servant* to George Ladlowe [*sic*].
Dec. 9.	Margarett, daughter of Stephen Berye.
Dec. 12.	Marye, daughter of William Humble.
Dec. 19.	Stephen Hawkyns.
Jan. 4.	John, son of William Francklyn.
Jan. 17.	Katherin Mason, *servant* to William Francklyn.
Feb. 15.	George, son of Thomas Marshall.
Feb. 18.	William Reste.
Mar. 19.	Thomas Fowle.

1546

April 14.	Thomas Taylor.
April 7.	Hellen Ellyot, *estranger.*
April 19.	"A strange woman."
May 23.	Joane, wife of John Chambers.
July 3.	Edwarde, son of Walter Blake.
July 19.	Elizabeth Spender.
Aug. 16.	Thomas, son of Martyn Bowes.
Sep. 9.	Thomas, son of Henry Boswell.
Sep. 25.	James Johnson.
Sep. 30.	John Byoma, *Grocer and Straunger.*
Oct. 25.	Joane Jervis.
Oct. 25.	Margerye, daughter of Anthony More.
Nov. 21.	Annis Gutter.
Nov. 3.	Margarett, daughter of Thomas Stevens.
Dec. 5.	"Dyed with childe," Alice, wife of John Morgayne.
Jan. 7.	Thomas, son of Robert Fryer.

1547

Aug. 19.	Phillipp, daughter of John Lewes.
Sep. 15.	Joane, daughter of Walter Blake.
Sep. 22.	Ellyn Piningtorye.
Oct. 21.	William Crewe, *servant* to Hughe Roke.
Oct. 29.	Anne, daughter of Mr. Martyn Bowes (the younger).
Nov. 10.	John Backhouse, otherwise called John of Callys.
Nov. 22.	Jane Aberye, *servant* to Hughe Rooke.
Oct. 29.	Elizabeth Alebrye, *servant* to Hughe Rooke.
Jan. 14.	Baptist Rote, *Italyon.*

Jan. 22. Humfrey Rogers, *servant* to Henry Rushall.
Jan. 27. Elizabeth Richardson, *Wydowe.*
Feb. — [*sic*] Thomas Adderton, *servant* to Walter Blace.
Mar. 8. Richard Tull, *servant* to Walter Blake.
Mar. 25. Emme Francklyn, *servant* to Thomas Wetherall.
Mar. 25. Fabyan Apostlett.
Mar. 12. Christopher, son of Thomas Wetherall.
April 1. Richard Pollyn Taylor.
April 2. Thomas Taylor, "dicd sodenly in the streete."
April 14. Thomas, son of William Oldhall.
— [*sic*] 22. Richard Belkc, *servant* to John Browne.

1548

July 20. Thomas Grigis, *servant* to Lawrance Smythe.
July 21. William Ebdon, *Grocer.*
July 22. William Seltworthe, Randall Chedley and Steven Rowe, *servants* to Thomas Bowten.
July 31. John Kelinge, *servant* to Thomas Kelinge.
Sep. 11. Richard Bristo, *servant* to George Webbe.
Sep. 10. William Johnson, *servant* to James Staneley.
Sep. 11. "Charles, a frenche boye, *servant* unto George Tadlowe."
Sep. 15. Joane, daughter of Stephen Hawkyns.
Sep. 6. Suzan, daughter of Thomas Bowton.
Sep. 28. "Anno 1547" [*sic*] Margarett Streat, *servant* to Fabyan Wethers.
Sep. 29. Charitye West, *servant* to John Tyndall.
Oct. 13. John Robson.
Oct. 19. Hance Kovley, *servant* to Thomas Kelynge.
Oct. 19. Raffe Bayes, *servant* to Marten Bowes.
Oct. 20. Ciser Dowchman, *servant* to Thomas Kelynge.
Nov. 10. George Pinchester.
Oct. 11. John, son of Clement Shelley.
Dec. 24. William, son of Thomas Boycr.
Dec. 28. Elizabethe, wife of Clement Shelley.
Dec. 31. Susan, daughter of Mr. Sympson.
Jan. 16. Elizabeth, daughter of Mr. Simpson.
Jan. 18. Walter Cocks.
Jan. 24. Fabyan Wethers.
Feb. 15. William Brayton, *servant* to John Crede.
Mar. 26. Margarett Wyer.
April 24. 1548 [*sic*] Baptist, son of Thomas Cleyton.
April 24. 1548 [*sic*] George, son of Walter Clark.

1549

Aug. 14. Hellen, daughter of John Sherley.
Aug. 16. Jane, *servant* to William Ventres.
Aug. 28. Agnes, wife of Robert Taylboys.
Sep. 24. Edmond Hyde, *servant* to Mr. Tadloe.
Sep. 28. Agnes, wife of Xpofer Johnson.
Nov. 21. Robert More.
Dec. 14. John Myddelton, prentice with William Hubte.
Jan. 10. Joyce Hegges.
Feb. 13. Thomas Stevens, *Goldsmythe.*
Mar. 25. Anne, daughter of Thomas Storye.

[N.B.—The date 1549 is continued through the year 1550, by mistake in the original.]

1550

Mar. 30.	Katherin, wife of John Mathewe.
April 24.	Jane, daughter of Henry Rushall.
June 16.	——— [*sic*] daughter of William Murfeilde.
Nov. 8.	John Elmere, Prentice with John Alcetor.
Nov. 26.	Myles Newton, of York.
Nov. 29.	Elizabeth Stevyns, *Wydowe.*
Jan. 27.	Edmunde, son of Thomas Hancock, *Vintener.*
Mar. 14.	Reynold Payne, *servant* to Sir Martyn Bowes.
Mar. 23.	Joane, wife of Thomas Wytton.

1551

Mar. 27.	Denys Boreman, *servant* to Humfrey Stevens.
April 1.	Marye Donec, *servant* to Martyn Bowes.
April 4.	George Apostelett, *Waterbearer.*
May 1.	Robert, son of George Apostelett.
July 10.	Edmonde More.
July 10.	Agnes, wife of Laurence Smythe.
July 12.	Laurence Smythe, *Vintener.*
July 12.	Edmunde Tricklande.
Aug. 28.	George Webbe, *Goldsmith.*
Sep. 1.	Elizabeth Dawson.
Sep. 1.	Paule, son of Derick Anthony.
Sep. 16.	Alice Style.
Nov. 11.	James Staveley, *Vintner.*
Dec. 12.	Agnes Notor, *servant* to John Morgan.
Dec. 24.	Edwarde Barboure, *Scrivener.*
Jan. 1.	Justus Merphen.
Jan. 11.	Brycilla, daughter of Thomas Wytton.
Jan. 25.	Jane Scrivener.
Jan. 30.	Thomas Deane, *servant* of with Mr. Fisher.
Feb. 6.	Katheren, daughter of Edward Addesson.
Feb. 28.	Katheren Willoughby.
Mar. 12.	Elizabeth, wife of William Humble.
Mar. 24.	Sara, daughter of Martyn Partrige.

[N.B.—The following 21 entries are all, save two, dated 1553, no entry for the year 1552 is to be met with.

May 15.	Gabriell, son of Henry Rushall.
May 23.	Katherin, daughter of Thomas Maxtell.
May 28.	Jane Robynson, *servant* to Roger Nicolles.
Aug. 21.	Robert Emerye.
Oct. 28.	Isabell Kyddley, *servant* to Mr. Benson.
Oct. 31, 1551 [*sic*].	John Matthewe.
Dec. 16.	James Browne.
Jan. 10.	Margarete Chester.
Jan. 28.	William, one Sir Marten Bowes' men.
Feb. 26.	William Humble.
Mar. 19.	John, *servant* to Mr. Hancock.
April 4.	Abell Parterige.
June 20.	Noy Chanye.
Aug. 18.	John Spagman.
Sep. 25.	Richard Pinchester.
Oct. 22.	Lady Anne Bowes.
Dec. 1.	Hughe Roke.
Dec. 11.	Mr. Partrige childe.

Dec. 3.	Joys Slater.
April 27.	1554. Thomas Wetherall.
April 14.	Fymmore [query Fynimore].

1554

July 25.	William, son of William Tracye.
Oct. 27.	Bridget and Mary, daughters of Mr. John Kettlewoode.
Nov. 7.	Alice, wife of Thomas Kelinge.
Feb. 7.	John Browne.
Feb. 23.	Richard, son of William Penchester.
Mar. 6.	Edward Robsonne.

1555

April 20.	Julyan, daughter of John Robson.
May 28.	Thomas Stevens, *Skynner*.
June 16, 1551 [*sic*].	Robert Smyth, *Laberer*.
July 2.	John, son of Francis Hunte.
Aug. 14.	Agnes, daughter of Richard Gravenor.
Aug. 31.	William, *servant* to William Laten, *Haberdasher*.
Sep. 1.	Francis, daughter of Derick Maxselton.
Sep. 7.	Elizabeth, wife of Thomas Stevens.
Sep. 16.	Thomas, son of Edward Sutton.
Nov. 24	Hester, daughter of Gregorie Selinge, *Straunger*.
Feb. 21.	Mr. Gilbert, *Citizen and Pewterer of London*.
Mar. 21.	Robert, son of Robert Taylboys, *Goldsmythe*.
Mar. 28.	Katherin, wife of William Smythe, of the Towne of Callis.

1556

June 3.	Jane, daughter of Thomas Atkynson, *Scrivener*.
June 15.	William, son of Marten Patrige, *Barbor Surgeon*.
July 15.	Richard Parkyns, *Citizen and Clothworker of London*.
Aug. 1.	William, son of Nicholas Hayes, *Clothworker*.
Oct. 29.	Nicholas, son of Thomas Corbett, *Skynner*.
Nov. 11.	Anthony Richardson, *Parson of St. Sythe Shorhogge, in the Cytie of London*.
Nov. 26.	Alice, wife of Thomas Foster, *Grocer of London*.
Dec. 6.	Robert Yerland, *servant* to John Reynoldes, *Citizen and Goldsmythe of London*.
Jan. 7.	Richard Lege, *servant* to Stephen Spagman, *Haberdasher of London*.
Feb. 15.	Christopher Johnson, *Haberdasher of London*.
Feb. 18.	Thomasyne, wife of Robert Handford, *Merchauttaillor*.
Feb. 26.	Noye Fagott, *estranger*, which died in the house of John Moria, *estranger*, in Abchurch Lane.
Mar. 22.	Edward, son of Hughe Redinge, *Citizen and Blacksmith of London*.
April 20.	Thomas, son of William Nobell, *Haberdasher*.
April 29.	Lucres, wife of Francis Patten, of Abchurch Lane.

1557

May 12.	George Tadlowe, *Haberdasher*, burd. in St. Magnus, near London Bridge.
May 23.	Gartherd Spagman, daughter to (one*) Stephen, *Citizen and Haberdasher of London*.

* The word "one" is written above the line.

June 8. Johan and Johan [*sic*] daughters of Humfrey Stevens, *Goldsmith.*

June 16. Clement Ryder.

July 14. Annes, daughter of William Aligat, *Haberdasher.*

Aug. 1. Anne, wife of John Kele, *Goldsmith.*

Aug. 24. Robert Fancrin, late merchant of Irelande, died in the house of Robert Goldinge, *Vintener.*

Oct. 17. Henry Boswell, *Cityzen and Goldsmith.*

Oct. 30. John Siddell, *Clerk, Chaplen of* Sir Martyn Bowes, *Knight and Alderman of London.*

Oct. 26. Richard Payne, *Pasteler.*

Nov. 1. Margerie Nevill, *servant* of Innocent Locattell, *Straunger*, she died in the house of Elizabeth Smyth, *Widowe.*

Jan. 4. George, son of William Noble, *Haberdasher.*

Feb. 15. Margarett, wife of Thomas Gilbert, *Pewterer.*

1558

July 25. Martyn, son of Martyn Partridge, *Barbor Surgeon.*

July 30. William Franklyn, *Goldsmith.*

Aug. 22. Robert Goldinge, *Vintener.*

Sep. 16. Henry Letter, of London, *Yoman.*

The 19 and 20 day of the same monthe was kept the monethes mynde of Robert Goldinge, *Vintener.*

Sep. 23. Sir John Morys, then being *Parson of St. Marye Woolnothe's Churche.*

Oct. 26. Edward Acerod, *one of the Yomen of the Queen's Majesties Garde.*

Oct. 24. Katherin, daughter of Adrian Tuball, *Stranger.*

Oct. 30. Sabia Cowman, Mother-in-Law to Mr. Muschamp, *Goldsmith.*

Nov. 14. Margaret Babington, *servant* to Wydowe Franklen.

Nov. 18. John, son of Xpofer More, was christened by the midwife in his house.

Nov. 19. John Alceter, *Barbor Surgeon.*

Dec. 17. John, son of Hugh Redinge, christened in his house.

Jan. 1. Richard, son of Thomas Corbett, *Skynner.*

Jan. 19. Alice, daughter of John Alceter, deceased.

Mar. 4. Christopher Marke, *Citizen and Draper of London.*

Mar. 10. Wele, *servant* of Robert Stanbank, *Baker.*

Mar. 11. John Tyndall.

Mar. 14. George Tadlow, the younger, of London, *Yoman.*

1559

May 15. James Lyne, *Goldsmith.*

May 25. John, son of Thomas Wytton, *Scrivener.*

May 29. Thomas, son of William Tracy, *Merchanttaillor.*

July 1. Barbara Emery, died in the house of Robert Stanbank.

July 6. John Medcalf, *servant* to Robert Stanbank.

Aug. 6. —— [*sic*] wife of —— [*sic*] Crasswell, *Pewterer*, which died in the Parish of Little Bartholomew, and lieth with her father, Nicholas Warley.

Nov. 5. Peter, son of Awdrian Tybaulde, *estraunger.*

Nov. 6. John Medowes, of Fange, in Essex, died at Water Blake's house in this Parish.

Jan. 18. Elizabeth, wife of John Caveyllare.
Feb. 4. Mr. John Fysher, father of Mr. Jasper Fisher.
April 11. Lawnce Rycle, *Goldsmith and estranger.*
Aug. 11. Elizabeth Hygat, *Mayde,* which died in Alderman Marten's house.
Aug. 27. Julian Story, *Wydowe,* of St. Dunston in the Este.
Oct. 23. Elizabeth Blundell, *servant* to William Abraham.
Oct. 24. Elizabeth, the daughter of Moyses ———— [*sic*]
Oct. 31. Robert, *servant* of Nicholas Hayes.
Nov. 4. Hughe Risbeke, *Citizen and Pewterer of London.*
Jan. 27. Katheryn, *servant* of Sir Martyn Bowes, *Knyght.*
Feb. 30. Elizabeth Billingsley, the daughter-in-Lawe of Sir Martyn Bowes.
Mar 1. Margaret More, *servant* to Gabriel Braunger, *estraunger.*

1561

April 8. Jasper, son of William Johnes, *Citizen and Goldsmith of London.*

1562 [*sic*]

July 2. Anne, daughter of William Tracye.
Oct. 4, 1562. [*sic*]. Anne, daughter of Baptist Italian.
Dec. 4, 1561. [*sic*]. Parnell, wife of Thomas Atkinson, *Scrivener.*
Jan. 4, 1562. [*sic*]. Anne, daughter of William Yngram, *Baker.*
Feb. 10, 1562- [*sic*]. Marye Puggett, *servant* to John Nutshaw.

[1562]

April 6, 1562. Alice, daughter of John Kettlewoode.
Aug. 1. John Phillips, *servant* to Frauncis Barnard.
Aug. 1. Francis, son of Awdrian Tyballe, *Straunger.*
May 6, 1562. Garrett Gilbarth, *servant* of Cornelius Becher.
Mar. 26, 1562. John, son of Rowland Oker.
June 14, 1562. Robert Randall, *servant* with Mr. Gabriell, *Stranger.*
Aug. 3, 1562, A child of John Sindertons.
Aug. 6. William, son of John Pickeringe.
Sep. 1, 1562. Cicely, *servant* with John Synderton.
Nov. 23, 1562. Alice Godford, *servant* with Launcelott Vicares,
Nov. 24, 1562. William, son of John Stile.
Dec. 7, 1562. Marten Partrige, *Barbor.*
Dec. 9. Hughe, son of Hughe Cokes, *Goldsmythe.*
Dec. 10. Gabrell, son of Robert Danyell, *Curat.*
Mar. 5, 1562. Elizabeth, daughter of Nicholas Hayes, *Clothworker.*

1563

May 8. Bartholomew, son of Xpofer More.
June 12. Christopher More.
June 20. James, son of Xpofer More.
June 27. Katherin Wayman, *a straunge woman.*
June 29. Elizabeth, daughter of Owen Wilson, *Labourer.*
July 2. Agnes Reyner, *servant* with Alexander Penyx.
July 9. Richard and Thomas, sonnes of John Pickeringe, *Haberdasher.*

July 20.   Isabell, *servant* of Thomas Bromley, *Laborer*.
Aug. 3.   Richard Garlande, *Shoemaker*.
Aug. 3.   Elizabeth Joseph, a childe out of the house of Mrs. Tyndall.
Aug. 4.   Robert Ap Thomas, *servant* to Richard Garlande, late deceased.
Aug. 4.   Agnes, daughter of Thomas Bromley, *Laborer*.
Aug. 5.   Marye, daughter of William Tracy, *Merchaunttaillor*.
Aug. 6.   Thomas, son of Thomas Stanbanck, *Baker*.
Aug. 10.   Johan Reve, *servant* with John Mylls.
Aug. 21.   John Mardendell, *servant* with Robert Stanbank, *Baker*.
Aug. 27.   Margerye Brooke, *servant* with William Johnes.
Sep. 1.   John, son of Laurence Smythe, and *servant* with Mrs. Raynwick.
Sep. 2.   Prudence Cooke, *servant* with Francis Kydd, *Scrivener*.
Sep. 2.   John Jefferson, *servant* with Robert Clarke, *Grocer*.
Sep. 3.   Margaret, daughter of John Allen.
Sep. 4.   William Bannesley, *Merchant Tailor*.
Sep. 4.   James Carran, *servant* with Rauff Davye, *Vintener*.
Sep. 10.   Jane, daughter of Hughe Readinge.
Sep. 11.   George Bostock, *servant* with William Abram, *Vintener*.
Sep. 11.   Raynolde Butler, *Estranger*, out of the house of Kenrick Price.
Sep. 11.   John Madame, out of the house of Rauffe Davey, *Vintner*.
Sep. 15.   Richard, son of William Tracye, *Merchanttaillor*.
Sep. 16.   George Taylor, *Merchanttaillor*.
Sep. 19.   Thomas, son of Thomas Wetherhill, *Goldsmythe*.
Sep. 19.   Marye Allen.
Sep. 20.   Thomas Kelinge, *servant* with Henry Naylor.
Sep. 21.   John, son of Thomas Smythe, *Draper*.
Sep. 22.   Joyse, wife of Thomas Smythe.
Sep. 22.   Thomas Casye, *servant* of Thomas Wylson, *Cooke*.
Sep. 23.   Richard, son of Cornelis Bynam, *Butcher*.
Sep. 23.   Thomasyn, wife of Thomas Esterbye, *Coke*.
Sep. 23.   Annes Eggington, *servant* with William Shorte, *Grocer*.
Sep. 25.   Thomasyn daughter of William Noble, *Haberdasher*.
Sep. 26.   Peter Pyke, *servant* with Henry Gaynsford, *Goldsmith*.
Sep. 26.   Xpofer Blackston, *servant* with William Abrams, *Vintener*.
Sep. 26.   John Cartmell, *servant* with Rauff Davye, *Vintener*.
Sep. 27.   Eustes Madan, sister of Mr. Davye.
Sep. 28.   Anthonye, son of William Tracye.
Sep. 29.   William Fearefeilde, *servant* with William Abram, *Vintener*.
Sep. 29.   Alice, sister of John Pickeringe.
Sep. 30.   Rose, daughter of Edward Sutton, *Stacioner*.
Oct. 4.   Christian, daughter of Thomas Wetherhill, *Goldsmith*.
Oct. 5.   Henry Furthawe, *servant* with Marke Norton, *Grocer*.
Oct. 6.   Edward Pemerton, *servant* with Mr. Francis Barnarde, *Cooke*.
Oct. 7.   Eliezer, son of William Shorte, *Grocer*.
Oct. 8.   Rauff Davye, *Vintener*.
Oct. 8.   Margarett Conwey, *servant* with Lancelot Bickers, *Haberdasher*.
Oct. 10.   John, son of William Shorte, *Grocer*.
Oct. 12.   Ellen Highed, *servant* with William Yngram.
Oct. 13.   Thomas Smythe, *Hosiar* in Abchurch Lane.
Oct. 15.   Marye Pynson, *servant* with William Robynson.
Oct. 15.   Arthure, son of Thomas Kelinge, *Goldsmyth*.

Oct. 15.	William, son of William Moyses.
Oct. 17.	Francis, daughter of Francis Barnard, *Cooke.*
Oct. 20.	William Noble, *Haberdasher.*
Oct. 20.	Alice, daughter of Francis Barnard, *Cooke.*
Oct. 22.	George Gaynsforde, *servant* with Mr. Henry Gaynsforde, *Goldsmyth.*
Oct. 22.	Stephen, son of George Kevall, *Scrivener.*
Oct. 24.	Francis, wife of Bartholomew Dawbney, *Skynner*, dwelling in Aldermarye.
Oct. 24.	John Alsopp, *Citizen and Goldsmith* of London.
Oct. 26.	Sara Keall, *servant* with Thomas Benson.
Oct. 27.	Edward Whitethorne, *servant* with Walter Lynche, *Barbor.*
Oct. 28.	Nicholas Atkinzon, *servant* with Thomas Benson, *Goldsmith.*
Oct. 30.	Alice, daughter of James Lynne, *Goldsmithe.*
Nov. 10.	Robert Conyworth, *servant* with Francis Barnard, *Cooke.*
Nov. 10.	Maryan, daughter of Owen Wilson, *Waterbearer.*
Nov. 11.	Launcellott Bickers, *Haberdasher.*
Nov. 14.	Alice More, *servant* with William Robinson.
Nov. 17.	Anne, daughter of John Pickeringe, *Haberdasher.*
Nov. 17.	Marye Bullock, *servant* with George Kevall, *Scrivener.*
Nov. 18.	Was the Remembrance of Sir Martyn Bowes, *Knyghte.*
Nov. 20.	John, son of Edward Sutton.
Nov. 20.	John Calley, *servant* with Richard Brusley, *Haberdasher.*
Nov. 20.	Thomas, son of Francis Barnard, *Cooke.*
Nov. 26.	George Harding, a *servant* out of the house of Owen Wilson, *Waterbearer.*
Dec. 7.	William Robinson, a *Marchantman.*
Dec. 8.	Johan, daughter of Thomas Kelinge, *Goldsmith.*
Dec. 11.	Stephan, son of Thomas Watts, *Haberdasher.*
Dec. 17.	William, son of William Abram, *Vintener.*
Dec. 19.	Isaac, son of William Abram, *Vintener.*
Jan. 18.	Myldred, daughter of William Moyses.

1564

June 9.	Robert Stanbanck, *Joyner, our Parish Clark.*
Aug. 21.	Nicholas, son of Xpofer Muschamp, brother of Thomas Muschamp, *Goldsmith.*
Aug. 22.	Mathew, son of Thomas Muschampe, *Goldsmith.*
Oct. 23.	Awdrye, daughter of Thomas Wytton, *Citizen and Writer of the Court Letter of London.*
Nov. 13.	Was the remembrance of the Worshipful Sir Martyn Bowes, according to his devyse, yerelye.
Dec. 17.	Cicely Morfyn.
Jan. 24.	Michaell, son of Francis Barnard, *Cooke.*
Feb. 1.	Jane Johnson.

1565

June 22.	Edward, son of John Hosyar.
July 22.	Launcellott Wytton, *Citizen and Girdler of London.*
July 31.	John, son of Thomas Kelinge, *Goldsmythe.*
Sep. 9.	Alice, daughter of Hughe Crookes, *Goldsmith.*
Sep. 29.	Suzanna, wief of William Shorte, *Grocer*, and daughter to Mr. Rogers, late burned in Smithfield.

Oct. 4.   William Hawkesworth, *servant* with Thomas Wilson, *Cooke*.

Oct. 4.   Ciceley Brian, *a Wydowe, a straunger*, not of the Parishe.

Oct. 29.   William Smythe, *servant* with Mr. Robert Cannon, *Gentleman*.

Nov. 6.   Joane, wief of Thomas Corbett, *Skynner*.

Nov. 12.   Was the remembrance of Sir Martyn Bowes, *Knight*, accordinge to his devise yerelye.

Nov. 17.   Mr. Thomas Mylls, *Gent.*, of Southampton, which departed at the Bushopp heade.

Nov. 21.   Parnell, daughter of Thomas Atkinson, *Scrivener*.

Dec. 28.   Metkyn Gosson, a *Dutche Mayde*, fourthe of Frauncis Barnarde's rents.

Jan. 4.   Margarett Gosoin, a *Dutche Mayde*, fourthe of Frauncis Barnarde's rents.

Mar. 2.   John Webbere, *Taylor*, and *servant* to Mr. Martyn Bowes.

1566

April 26.   Agnes Gosoin, a *Dutche Mayde*, forthe of Frauncis Barnarde's rents.

June 12.   Alice, *Wydowe* of Launcellott Wytton, *Girdler*.

July 23.   Ellin, daughter of William Fyllian, *Sheregrinder*.

July 30.   Rose Tyndall, *Wydowe*.

Aug. 19.   Was buried the Right Worshipfull Sir Martyn Bowes, *Knyght*, in the vault in the highe quere, and the mouthe of the vault is a foote within the ende of the marble stone or tombe straighte downe closed up with bricke, and the bricke to be broken downe with a pickaxe before you can see the coffyn.

Nov. 16.   Gregorye Bacon.

Jan. 17.   Hugh Croke, *Goldsmithe*.

1567

June 4.   Hughe Readinge, *Blacksmythe*.

June 22.   Margarett Porter, *servant* to Thomas Keelinge.

June 23.   Agnes Raynyke, *Wydowe*.

July 4.   George Hygatt, *servant* to Roger Spurstowe, *Vintner*.

Aug. 15.   Margarett Wylson.

Feb. 6.   Agnes, wief of Roger Nycholls, *Pulter*.

Feb. 9.   Margarett Lyon, *Wydowe*.

Feb. 26.   Jane, daughter of Frauncis Barnarde, *Cooke*.

Mar. 10.   Walter, son of Thomas Gyles, *Haberdasher*.

1568

Aug. 17.   Henry, son of Kenrick Prise, *Clothworker*.

Aug. 22.   Katherin Averell, daughter to Mrs. Okover.

Aug. 25.   Sara, daughter of Roulande Okeover, *Merchaunttaillor*.

Sep. 16.   Thomas, son of Humfrey Hayes, *Grocer*.

Sep. 26,   Anne, wife of John Lyon, *Taylor*.

Oct. 26.   Elizabethe, wife of Xpofer Johnson, *Haberdasher*.

Oct. 19.   Roger Lorymer, *servant* to Nicholas Lawrence.

Dec. 19.   John Cholmely, *Waterbearer*.

Jan. 19.   John Maria, son of Clement Morando, *Cutler*.

Jan. 30.   Edwarde Sutton, *Stacioner*.

Jan. 30.	Katherin Uphy, *Stranger,* out of Cocknedge's house in Abchurch Lane.
Feb. 2.	John, son of Hughe Keale, *Goldsmithe.*
Feb. 21.	Humfrey Loo, *Draper.*
Feb. 25.	Marye Tubbs, *servant* with William Cocknedge.
Mar. 15.	Ellyn, daughter of Henry Chalacom, *Cordwayner.*
Mar. 15.	John Loyea, *Straunger,* out of Cocknedge's house.

1569

April 25.	Thomas Barnarde.
May 2.	Joan, wief of John Man, *Waterbearer.*
May 20.	Anne, daughter of Leonarde Barners, of Tobye [Tollesbury ?] *Gent.*
June 1.	Nicholas Turke, *Grocer.*
Aug. 8.	Thomasyn, sister of Xpofer Johnson.
Aug. 10.	Margarett, wief of John Mylls, *Sadler.*
Sep. 13.	John Lyon, *Pewterer.*
Oct. 15.	Dame Alice Harper, wief of Sir William Harper, *Knight and Alderman of London.*
Oct. 19.	Marke Norton, *Grocer.*
Nov. 2.	Garrard Bowdans, *Stranger,* out of Mr. Barnarde's rents.
Nov. 3.	Marye Noble, *Wydowe.*
Nov. 9.	Anthony Copanoll, *Zelzere stranger,* out of Mr. Barnarde's rents.
Nov. 29.	Owen Wylson, *Waterbearer.*
Dec. 6.	Margarie Rigge, out of goodwief Stanbank's house.
Dec. 19.	Adryan, daughter of John Ferne, *Myloner.*
Jan. 16.	Hughe Yeomans, *Haberdasher.*
Feb. 2.	Johan Delastat, *Straunger.*
Jan. 25.	John, son of Leonarde Cooke, *Merchaunttaillor.*
Feb. 28.	Monakyn Monge, *Straunger.*
Mar. 18.	John Howgatt, out of John Shawe his house.
Mar. 26.	Thomas, son of John Shawe, *Clothworker.*
Mar. 31.	Thomas Wytton, *Scrivener.*
Mar. 31.	Alice, daughter of John Shawe, *Clothworker.*

1570

April 6.	David Lloyd, *servant* of Arthure Charismore, *Blacksmythe.*
April 12.	Mary, daughter of Humfrey Stevens *Goldsmythe.*
April 13.	John Shawe, *Clothworker.*
May 5.	Emery, daughter of Humfrey Derycot, *Draper.*
May 18.	Alice Hedge, *servant* with Henry Chalacum, *Shomaker.*
July 15.	Thomas Hudson, out of Goodwief Stanbank's house.
July 15.	Dorothy, wief of John Plomer, *Sexton.*
Aug. 18.	Margarett ——— [*sic*] *servant* with John Bolton.
Aug. 18.	Henrye Bennynge, out of the house of the said John Bolton.
Aug. 26.	John Moyses, *Haberdasher.*
Sep. 11.	Johan Clark, out of John Moyes house.
Sep. 16.	Margarett Selby, out of John Moyses house.
Sep. 20.	Anne Mathewe, out of John Moyses house.
Oct. 27.	Hellen Hill, out of the house of John Archer.
Oct. 31.	Oryente Paves, *Straunger,*
Dec. 23.	Thomas Perpoynte, *Draper.*
Feb. 24.	Edmonde, son of Arthure Chesmore.

1571

May 27.	Nicholas Fropp, *Frenchman*.
July 18.	Thomasyn, daughter of John Wetherall, *Goldsmythe*.
July 19.	Elizabeth Cholmley, *Wydowe*.
Aug. 11.	Agnes Wyllett, *servant* of Xpofer Olde, *Draper*.
Sep. 8.	Richard, son of Thomas Hamonde, *Mynstrell*.
Sep. 30.	Mabell, daughter of John Worme.
Oct. 6.	William Marchaunt, out of William Allyn's house.
Oct 8.	William, son of Humfrey Stevens, *Goldsmythe*.
Nov. 3.	William Catlyn, out of the howse of Thomas Hawkyns, *Clothworker*.
Nov. 10.	Margaret —— [*sic*] *servant* of John Geffrey, *Haberdasher*.
Dec. 21.	Margaret, daughter of John Geffrey, *Haberdasher*.
Dec. 27.	Christopher, son of Xpofer Harris, *Gentleman*.

1572

Mar. 26.	Brigett, wief of Thomas Francknell, was brought out of Sethinge Lane.
April 22.	Ellyn Dixson, out of Goodman London's house.
May 2.	Johan, daughter of James Somner, *Clothworker*.
May 12.	John, son of John Day, *Clothworker*.
May 13.	John Castell, *Goldsmythe*, *servant* of James Allyn, *Goldsmith*.
May 27.	Edward ap Price, out of Goodman Daye's house.
June 16.	Marye, daughter of Edwarde Sutton, *Stacioner*.
Sep. 11.	Henry van Hove, *Duchman*.
Sep. 27.	Adryan Cokytt, *Frenchman*, out of Mr. Mill's house.
Oct. 15.	Katherin van Cullen, out of Henry van Hove's house.
Oct. 22.	Joan Stamford, of Kent, out of John Myll's house.
Nov. 15.	Cawood, son of Marke Norton, *Grocer*.
Dec. 1.	Thomas Atkinson, *Citizen and Writer of the Court Letter of London, and Notarie Publique*.
Dec. 1.	Sara, daughter of Henry van Hove, *Duchman*.
Dec. 5.	Magdalen, daughter of Henry van Hove.
Jan. 4.	Alice, daughter of Thomas Hamond, *Mynstrell*.
Feb. 3.	Thomas Wilson, *Cook*.
Feb. 5.	John, son of Henry van Hove, *Duchman*.

1573

April 14.	Randolph Barnard, out of Francis Barnard's house.
April 21.	Anne Averey, daughter of Sibell Okeover.
May 25.	Edward Hawley, *Stacioner*, out of Richard Adams' house.
June 2.	Edmond Parkyns, *servant* of William Redshaw, *Haberdasher*, out of Whitehorse Alley.
June 27.	John Gill, *Salter*.
July 4.	Margarett, daughter of Humfrey Derycote, *Draper*.
July 25.	William Leighton, *Goldsmithe*.
Oct. 9.	Roger Nycolls.
Jan. 1.	Johan, daughter of Edward Williams, *Merchaunttailor*, out of Francis Barnarde's Alley.
Jan. 2.	Richard Grevell, *Sergeante*.
Jan. 15.	Elizabeth Walker, out of Goodwief Dyer's house.
Mar. 13.	Cornelius Beynam, out of Francis Barnarde's rents.
Mar. 23.	Margaret More, out of Mr. Sherington's house.

1574

May 4. Sara Jackson, out of Thomas Hawkyns' house, *Clothworker*.
May 7. Judeth, daughter of Thomas Perpoynt, *Draper*.
May 17. Thomas, son of John Geffrey, *Haberdasher*.
May 22. William Rawlinson, *servant* to Thomas Hawkyns, *Clothworker*.
May 22. Humfrey Dericott, *Draper*, out of John Daye's house, *Clothworker*.
June 4. Robert, son of Richard Johnes, *Carpenter*.
June 4. Jane Tytinge, out of Goodman Hawkyns' house.
June 8. John Smythe, *Merchanttaillor*, out of Goodwiefs Wilson's house, *Wydowe*.
June 19. Agnes Smythe, out of Goodwief Wilson's house.
July 10. Elizabethe Grevell, *Wydowe*.
Oct. 11. Alice Richardson.
Nov. 1. William Gorton, *Draper*.
Nov. 1. John Keyle, *Goldsmythe*, out of Hughe Keyle's house,
Dec. 16. Edward Williams, *Merchaunt*.

1575

April 9. Anne Osborne, out of Marmaduke Higgens' house,
April 9. Thomas Sparke, out of Richard Johnes' house, *Carpenter*.
May 14. Margarett Synne, out of Richard Johnes' house.
May. 29. Richard Johnes.
June 2. Margarett, daughter of the said Richard Johnes.
June 4. Ellys Evans, out of John Barker's house.
June 7. Beltram Myller, out of Anthonye Fetherick's house.
June 26. Martyn Shelton, out of John Barker's house.
Aug. 17. Nicholas Farrior, out of William Warde's house.
Aug. 19. Thomas Ayiers, out of William Warde's house.
Aug. 21. Elizabeth Blondon, *servant* with Goodwief Wood, *Wydowe*.
Sep. 5. Richard Greene, *servant* with William Warde.
Sep. 27. Katherin, daughter of Humfrey Dethycote, *Draper*.
Oct. 3. William Fuller, *servant* with Thomas Hamonde, *Goldsmith*.
Oct. 3. Margarett, daughter of John Ferne, *Millener*.
Oct. 14. John, son of Thomas Davye, *Girdler*.
Nov. 15. Anne, daughter of Richard Crompton, *Pewterer*.
Nov. 16. Elizabeth, daughter of Cuthbert Crackplace, *Goldsmithe*.

1576

Mar. 28. Eme Martyn, *servant* with Thomas Morgan.
Mar. 30. William, son of Mr. Edward Thorne.
June 9. Robert, son of Cuthbert Crackplace, *Goldsmithe*.
Nov. 1. Theophila, wyfe of William Bugardte, *Straunger*, dwelling in Mr. Harris' great house.
Jan. 13. Clement, son of Robert Bishopp, *Taylor*.
Mar. 12. Thomas, son of Thomas Jenkynson, *Goldsmythe*.
Mar. 15. Elizabethe, the wyfe of Humfrey Stevens, *Goldsmythe*.

1577

April 31. The daughter of Nicholas Style, *Marchaunt*, dead borne, not christened.
May 17. Richard Robins, *Goldsmithe*.

June 3.	Joane, wief of Gilbert Buckle, *Vintner.*
June 28.	John Baker, the olderman.
Sep. 4.	Elizabeth Prise, William Judye's *Mayde.*
Oct. 5.	Margaret Mosley, Robert Eastefeilde's *Mayde.*
Oct. 12.	Jane, daughter of John Pickeringe, *Haberdasher.*
Oct. 20.	Richard Smythe, *servant* with Richard Harrison, *Goldsmythe.*
Oct. 20.	Blaunche, daughter of Roger Tasker, *Goldsmith.*
Nov. 20.	Ellyn Foule, wief of Robert Eastefeilde, *Notarie.*
Dec. 12.	John London, dwelling in the Tennys Court.
Jan. 23.	Katherin, daughter of Edward Griffyn, *Bricklear.*
Jan. 28.	Dame Alice Ramsey, the same yeare beinge *Ladye Mayris.*
Feb. 20.	Phillip Patrick, *servant* with William Abraham, *Vintner.*

1578

Mar. 31.	Margarett, wief of Thomas Muschamp, *Goldsmythe,*
April 6.	John, son of Richard Beard, *Minister.*
April 28.	Margarett, daughter of John Bemonde, *Gentleman,* in Dorsetshier, brought out from Robert Bishopp's house, *Taylor.*
May 13.	Anne, wieff of Robert Bishopp, *Taylor.*
May 15.	Gabriell, son of John Wells, of Berkeshier, out of Robert Bishope's house, and *servant* with his partener Thomas Quarrington.
May 26.	Thomas Muschamp, *Goldsmythe.*
June 5.	John Wetherhill, *Goldsmythe.*
June 28.	Mychaell, son of Michaell Garratt.
July 6.	Suzanna, daughter of Thomas Walls, *Haberdasher.*
Aug. 11.	John Stacie, *servant* with Thomas Hawkins, *Clothworker.*
Aug. 13.	Myles Armsted, *servant* with John Wright, *Draper.*
Aug. 15.	Henry Challacome, *Shoemaker.*
Aug. 18.	Margarett, wieff of Emmanuell Cole, *Goldsmith.*
Aug. 19.	Jonathas Linnes, *servant* with John Wright, *Draper.*
Aug. 20.	Thomas Winder, *servant* with John Wright, *Draper.*
Aug. 21.	Joane, daughter of William Judy, *Draper.*
Aug. 25.	Katherine, wief of William Judy, *Draper.*
Aug. 26.	Anne Greene, *servant* with Thomas Hawkins, *Clothworker.*
Aug. 30.	Anne Churkes, *servant* with Alice Baker, *Wydow.*
Aug. 31.	Katherin Collins, *servant* with John Bradley, *Taylor.*
Sep. 8.	John, son of Richard Robins, *Goldsmythe.*
Sep. 9.	John Norris, *servant* with Edward Griffyn, *Bricklear.*
Sep. 14.	Edmunde, son of Arthur Chesmore, *Blacksmithe.*
Sep. 15.	Alice Baker, *Wydowe.*
Sep. 16.	Robert Cutler, borne at Boston, a *servant* with John Wright, *Draper.*
Sep. 19.	Joane Daye, dwelling with the wief of Gabriell Brayngyre.
Sep. 20.	John Bayles, *Draper.*
Sep. 21.	Elizabeth Turney, *servant* with Edward Griffyn, *Bricklear.*
Sep. 21.	Hester Towle, *servant* with Marmaduke Higgins, *Grocer.*
Sep. 29.	Margaret Messenger, *servant* with William Judy, *Draper.*
Oct. 6.	Marye Garton, dwellinge with Richard Crumpton, *Pewterer.*
Oct. 6.	Margarett Murton, *servant* with Marmaduke Higgins, *Grocer.*
Oct. 8.	Jane and Margarett, daughters of James Sumner, *Clothworker,* they lye bothe in one Pitt.

Oct. 8.   Mathewe Seggore, *Merchauntstraunger*, out of Mr.
             Anthony Fetherigoe's howse, *Straunger*.
             [In the margin is written in same hand]—
             his father duke in Italie.
Oct. 9.   John Apowell, *Haberdasher*.
Oct. 21.   Katherin Morrey, daughter-in-lawe to John Perry, *Haber-
             dasher*.
Oct. 24.   Bryan Wyatt, *servant* with James Sumner, *Clothworker*.*
Oct. 27.   Annes, wief of Thomas Walls, *Haberdasher*.
Oct. 27.   Richard Crumpton, *Pewterer*.
Oct. 28.   Jonas, son of William Boggarde.
Oct. 28.   Robert, son of Bartholomew Dawbney, *Skynner*.
Oct. 31.   Richard, son of Cuthbert Crackplace, *Goldsmith*.
Nov. 1.   Hellen, daughter of John Ludlowe, *Skynner*.
Nov. 2.   Thomas, son of John Syce, *servant* with Cuthbert
             Crackplace, *Goldsmythe*.
Nov. 8.   John Perry, *Haberdasher*.
Nov. 17.   Elizabeth Clarke, dwellinge with Mr. John Wilkins, *Gold-
             smythe*.
Nov. 22.   William Ratford, *servant* with Mr. Thomas Watts,
             Haberdasher.
Nov. 23.   Marye, daughter of Cuthbert Crackplace, *Goldsmythe*.
Nov. 26.   John Dayntry, *servant* with Mr. Thomas Watts, *Haberdasher*.
Nov. 28.   William, son of William Taylboyes, *Goldsmythe*.
Dec. 8.   John Fresbye, *servant* to Mr. William Dowgle, *Haberdasher*,
             dwelling in Cheapside.
Dec. 19.   Edward, son of Robert Taylboyes, *Goldsmythe*.
Jan. 1.   Katherin Lawrance, *servant* to with Mr. John Mawldon,
             Haberdasher.
Jan. 28.   John, son of John Mawldon, *Haberdasher*.
Jan. 31.   Richarde Stronge, *servant* with John Wilkyns, *Goldsmythe*.
Feb. 5.   Humfrey Stevens, *Goldsmythe*.
Feb. 15.   A man child which was dead borne the childe of Suzan
             Bayles, *Wydowe*.
Mar. 6.   Anthony Fisher, *servant* with James Sumner, *Clothworker*.
Mar. 19.   Francis, daughter of Humfrey Dethycote.

1579

April 5.   John Grene, *servant* with Clement Webster, *Cooke*.
April 6.   Dennis, daughter of Humfrey Dethycote.
April 7.   Joan Pearson, *servant* with Humfrey Dethycoth.
April 19. James Sutton, *servant* with Cutebert Buckle, *Vintener*.
April 19. Another of his men, John Gibson.
July 6.   Margarett, daughter of Roger Tasker, *Goldsmith*.
Oct. 13.   John Chapman, *Leatherseller*.
Oct. 14.   Marmaduke, son of Marmaduke Higgins, *Grocer*.
Nov. 19.   Eme, wief of Humfrey Dethycote, *Merchant*.
Jan. 6.   Thomas Held, *Haberdasher*.
Jan. 23.   Margarett, wief of William Allen, otherwise called
             Goodwief Stanbanck.
Mar. 14.   Katherin Healdes childe, *Wydowe*, which was stillborne.

1580

Mar. 29.   James, son of Thomas Humble, *Stacioner*.

* This entry is repeated by mistake.

May 9.	Rebecca Clint, *Wydowe*, out of Mrs. Atkinson's house.
May 26.	Rachell, daughter of Mrs. Atkinson, *Wydowe*.
June 14.	Hellen Witton, *Wydowe*, the wief of Thomas Witton, *Notarie*.
July 2.	Robert Taylboys.
July 14.	Godly Shallycomb, *Wydowe*.
July 18.	Charles, son of John Pickeringe, *Haberdasher*.
July 21.	Dyed in this Parishe, in Mr. Gabriell's house, one Rowlande Beswicke, *Gentleman*, and was buried at St. Lawrence Poultney.
July 25.	Robert, son of John Barker, *Taylor*.
July 30.	Mr. John Pickeringe, *Haberdasher*.
Aug. 3.	George, son of George Tompson, *Carpenter*.
Aug. 10.	Francis, son of Marmaduke Higgins, *Grocer*.
Aug. 14.	Was Margaret Buckmaster caried to be buried from this Parish to Allhallowes in the Wall.
Aug. 28.	Isbell, wief of Arthur Chadsmore, *Smythe*.
Oct. 23.	Henry, son of Thomas Turner, *Grocer*.
Oct. 30.	Danyell Loyght, *servant* with William Dawkes, *Merchant*.
Mar. 1.	Robert Planckney, *Goldsmythe*.

1581

April 7.	John Clark, *Goldsmythe*.
May 10.	Annes, wief of Thomas Humble, *Stacioner*.
May 29.	Thomas, son of Edward Belden, *Scholemaster and Forrener*.
Aug. 15.	Francis, son of Richard Offley, *Merchant*.
Sep. 15.	Edward, son of Edward Griffyn, *Bricklayer*.
Sep. 15.	In the same pitt was buried Margarett, wief of James Johnson, *Dutchman*.
Sep. 21.	Pawle, son of Henry Kettellwoode, *Goldsmythe*.
Nov. 10.	Margery Hawkyns, *Wydowe*.
Dec. 2.	Elizabeth Wakefeild, *servant* with Arthure Chesmore, *Smythe*.
Jan. 17.	Joane, daughter of William Judy, *Draper*.
Feb. 1.	Hughe, son of Richard Offley, *Merchant*.

1582

Mar. 28.	Anthony Federygoe.
April 1.	Jasper, son of Edward Newton, *Yoman*, dwelling in Butley in Cheshier.
April 22.	Thomas, son of Humfrey Dethycote.
July 18.	John, son of Thomas Walker, *Haberdasher*.
Aug. 16.	Elizabeth Sawyer, James Godstall's wyve's mother.
Aug. 29.	David Firminger, *Gentleman*, of the Isle of Sheppey, Kent, which laye in Mrs. Allin's howse, *Wydowe*.
Oct. 8.	Nicholas Alderson, *servant* with Roger Tasker, *Goldsmythe*.
Oct. 12.	A man childe, stillborne, of Henry Kettellwood, *Goldsmyth*.
Nov. 20.	Edmunde Frayne, *Irishman*, dwelling with Robert Blisse, *Fishmonger*, and kept a fence scoole.
Dec. 23.	Richard Hollond, *servant* with Emmanuell Cole, *Goldsmyth*.
Dec. 24.	John Tanner, *servant* with Emmanuell Cole, *Goldsmythe*.
Jan. 7.	John Yeomantz, *servant* with Henry Kettillwood, *Goldsmythe*.

Jan. 16. John Burton, *Salter, and Clarke of this Parish Church*, who was slaine at the Parris garden.

Feb. 11. Henry, son of Henry Taylboys, deceased.

Feb. 25. Rawfe Eaton, *servant* to John Evans, *Taylor*.

1583

April 3. Mary Kettelwood, wife of John Kettelwood, *Goldsmith*.

April 18. Anne Kernell, *servant* to Mrs. Gabriell, alias Brangier.

April 25. William Leache, *servaunte* to Mrs. Ofley, *Widowe*.

May 2. Elizabeth Boode, *servaunte* to Edmunde Griffyn, *Bricklayer*.

May 14. Suzan, daughter of Mrs. Offley, *Widdowe*.

July 9. A Chrysom named William, son of William Jewdy, *Clothworker*.

July 24. William Hutchinson, *Painter*.

Sep. 2. Jeffery Hitchcocke, *servaunte* to Arthure Cheasemore, *Smith*.

Sep. 4. Francis, son of William Franke, *Goldsmith*.

Sep. 17. Michaell Clarke, *servant* with George Tompson, *Carpenter*.

Sep. 17. Jeane, daughter of Arthur Cheasemore, *Smith*.

Sep. 19. John Boode, *servant* to Clement Webster, *Cooke*.

Jan. 1. Roger, son of Roger Tasker, *Goldsmith*.

Jan. 24. Adam, son of Adam Beckersawe, *Glasier*.

1584

May 25. Katherin, late *Mayde servaunte* with John Barrett.

July 26. Margret, daughter of Edward Harding, *Goldsmith*.

Aug. 19. Samuell, son of Henry Butler, *Draper*.

Aug. 23. Emma Young, *Maiden, servant* with Mrs. Allin, *Widdowe*.

Sep. 2. Peeter Coppin, *servaunt* with William Warde.

Oct. 7. John, son of John Collins, *Goldsmith*.

1585

April 8. Isabell Abram, *servant* with Mr. William Abram, *Vintener*.

April 16. Anne, daughter of Anthony Haywood, *Chaplin in the Queenes Majesties house*.

April 21. Agnes, wife of John Barker.

May 5. Julyan Brize, *Wydowe*.

May 20. Elizabeth Weatherhill, *Widdowe*.

May 26. Margreat, daughter of Richard Brooke, *Goldsmith*.

June 9. A man child of Thomas Viccars, *Glasier*, which was stillborne.

June 30. Bridget Mouldesworth, sister unto Robert Mouldesworth, *Painter Stayner*, and daughter to ——— [*sic*] Mouldesworth, deceased, *late one of the Knights of Windsor*.

July 3. Alexander Penix, *Drommer to the Quenne's Majestye that now is*.

July 7. Alice Woare, *servaunte* to Leonard Gaite.

July 20. Thomas Biffin, *servaunte* to Sir Thomas Ramsey, *Knight*.

July 20. William Smith, *Taylor*.

Aug. 13. A man childe of Richard Dytches, *Clothworker*, which was still borne.

Oct. 21. Blaunche, daughter of Roger Tasker, *Goldsmith*.

Nov. 19. Suzan, daughter of Richard Harryson, *Cowper*.

Nov. 27.	Anthony Abram, *servaunte* to Mr. William Abram, *Vintner.*
Jan. 4.	Thomas Rawlyns, *Gentleman*, out of the house of Mrs. Brangier.
Jan. 28.	William, son of George Sanadye, *Haberdasher.*
Feb. 13.	Elizabeth, wife of Thomas Papworth, was buried in the upper end of the Cloyster, near unto the house or place wheare Mr. Parsons drincke lyeth.
Feb. 18.	Marie, wife of David Evans, *Merchaunt Taylor*, who dyed out of Mr. Papworth's house.
Feb. 18.	John, son of Jeames Somner, *Clothworker.*
Feb. 23.	Thomas Papworth.
Mar. 18.	James Somner, *Clothworker.*

1586

April 8.	Edward, son of Thomas Cotton.
June 26.	Bridget Allyn, *Widdowe.*
Aug. 4.	Ann Atkinson, *Widdowe.*
Aug. 5.	Kendricke Pryce, *Clothworker.*
Oct. 5.	Edward, son of Edward Griffith, *Merchaunte.*
Oct. 8.	Dame Elizabeth Bowes, wife of ——[sic] Sackford, *one of her Majestie's Maisters of her Courte of Requestes and Surveyor of her Courte of Wardes*, and lyeth within the tombe of her late husband, Sir Martin Bowes, *Knight*, diceased.
Jan. 1.	Peter Domieolo, *Stranger.*
Feb. 23.	Margery Morley, *Widdow.*
Feb. 25.	Alice Hargrave, only sister of Henry Hargrave, *Goldsmith.*
Mar. 12.	A poore boy, named Thomas, who was taken up in the streete and placed by Mr. Hugge Kayll, *Goldsmith, Deputy,* with Widdowe Price at his owne proper cost and charges.

1587

April 15.	Henry Hetherington, *servaunte* to Nicholas Bradley, *Clothworker.*
June 22.	William Hartford, of Cella, in Worcestershire, *Gentleman*, out of Mr. Brangier's house.
July 4.	Thomas Watts, *Haberdasher.*
Aug. 28.	Joan, the wife of George Samwell, *Notary.*
Sep. 12.	Robart, son of William Rawlinson, *Goldsmith.*
Sep. 26.	Martha, wife of Edmunde Greete, *Goldsmith.*
Oct. 11.	Xpofer, son of Richard Ditche, *Clothworker.*
Oct. 16.	Elizabeth, daughter of Nicholas Stile, *Grocer.*
Oct. 26.	John Aman, *Waterbearer.*
Nov. 6.	Elizabeth Basse, *Widdowe*, out of Mr. Francis' howse, *Goldsmith.*
Nov. 6.	James Widley, *servaunte* to ——— [sic], *Carpenter* in the Church yare, who fell of of a scaffall made one the outside of Mr. Lake's new house now a building.
Dec. 10.	Elizabeth, wife of John Blackmore, *Goldsmith.*
Feb. 16.	Adam Berkonsall, *Glasier.*
Mar. 4.	Rebecca, daughter of William Budder, *Gent.*, out of Mr. Brandon's house.
Mar. 16.	Jane, daughter of John Pickering, *Haberdasher*, deceased.
Mar. 23.	Margreat, daughter of Walter ——— [sic] *Haberdasher.*

1588

Mar. 31.   John Reynolds, *servaunte* with Sir Thomas Ramsey, *Knight.*
May 12.   Thomas Wilson, of Rochester, *free of the Cookes of London*, out of the house of Clement Webster, *Cooke*, his father in law.
July 16.   Sarah, wife of Henry Barne, *Clarke of this Parish Church.*
Aug. 23.   Anthony Hawood, *Confessor of Her Majestie's househoulde.*
Oct. 6.   Elizabeth, daughter of Richard Brooke, *Goldsmith.*
Oct. 9.   Thomas Lacy, out of the house of John Dabbe, *Haberdasher.*
Jan. 5.   William Hussey, *servant* of Francis Barnard.

1589

May 25.   John, son of James Allen, *Goldsmith.*
Sep. 27.   The Daughter of Henry Butler, *Draper.*

1590

May 5.   Elizabeth, daughter of George Nebolde, *Goldsmith.*
June 1.   Sir Thomas Ramsey, *Knight, and Alderman of the City of London*, who deceased the 9th day of May last past.
June 23.   Judeth, daughter of Bartholomew Johnson, *a stranger.*
July 7.   Hellen, daughter of Thomas Viccars, *Glasier.*
Aug. 5.   Elizabeth, wife of John Blackmore, *Goldsmith.*
Nov. 9.   John, soun and heire of John Weatherhill, late of this Parish, *Goldsmith*, deceased.
Feb. 11.   Benedict, son of Edward Griffin, *Merchant.*

1591

Mar. 30.   Adam Samforde, of the Parish of Childe Arcall, in Shropshire, *Gent.*, out of the house of William Francke, *Goldsmith.*
April 29.   John Robinson, *Goldsmith, servaunt* with Mr. Hugge Kayll, *Goldsmith.*
April 30.   Richard Bonner, *servaunte* with Richard Harrison, *Cooper.*
May 2.   Richard, son of Francis Smith, *Goldsmith.*
June 14.   Thomas Bowes, *Goldsmith*, son and heire to Sir Martin Bowes, *Knight*, deceased.
Aug. 5.   Hellen, wyfe of Walter Bolton, *Haberdasher.*
Aug. 6.   Alice, daughter of Walter Bolton aforesaide.
Aug. 16.   William Benton, *servant* with Henry Butler, *Marchaunt.*
Aug. 21.   —— [sic] daughter of Bartholomew Johnson, *Stranger, Taylor.*
Oct. 4.   —— [sic] daughter of Edward Griffith, *Marchaunt.*
Oct. 11.   Edward Griffen, *Mercer*, free of the Company of the Haberdashers.
Oct. 26.   Thomas French, *servaunte* of John Blachmore, *Goldsmith.*
Jan. 20.   Richard, son of John Alderson, *Vintener.*
Feb. 10.   John, son of Widdowe Price.
Mar. 11.   Thomas Corbett, *Skinner.*
Mar. 17.   Thomas, son of William Exton, *Haberdasher.*
Mar. 25.   —— [sic] Brisley, *Widdowe.*

1592

April 9.   Mary, daughter of Thomas Evans, *Bricklayer.*

April 10.	John Hole, of Yorkshire, *Clothier*.
May 9.	Richard Rabone, *Vintener*.
May 9.	Edmunde Brooke, of Otherfield [Huddersfield?] in Yorkshire, *Clothier*.
May 20.	Susan, daughter of John Greene, *Taylor*.
May 24.	Hugge Price, *servaunt* of Edward Mathew, *Pursemaker*, and free of the Company of the Silkeweavers.
July 7.	John Fludd, *servaunt* of Timothy Elkin, *Vintener*.
Aug. 1.	Thomas Williamson, *Laborour*.
Aug. 6.	Margery London, *Widdow*.
Aug. 8.	Edward Ceelies.
Aug. 13.	Johan, daughter of Richard Ditch, *Clothworker*.
Aug. 13.	George Chibnall, *Goldsmith*.
Sep. 11.	William Shade, *servaunt* with Richard Ditch, *Clothworker*.
Nov. 20.	John Sheade, *servant* to Henry Hargrave, *Goldsmith*.
Dec. 13.	John, son of Nicholas Grimes, *Taylor*.
Feb. 16.	Nicholas Ashley, *Clothworker*.
Mar. 15.	Anne, daughter of Gyles Simpson, *Goldsmith*.

1593

April, 4.	Thomas Evans, *Bryckelayer*.
May 26.	Margreate, wyfe of John Greene, *Taylor*.
July 5.	Anne Foote, alias Williamson, *Widdow*, out of Jewdye's house.
July 28.	Richard Wood, *servaunte* with Samwell Chamberlayne, *Haberdasher*.
Aug. 6.	Isabel Dickinson, *servaunt* with George Bentley, *Cordwayner*.
Aug. 17.	Thomas Parrey, *Clothworker*.
Aug. 19.	Judeth, daughter of Leonard Gale, *Gilder*.
Aug. 22.	Anne, daughter of George Samwell, *Notary*.
Aug. 24.	John Stocken, *Tailor*.
Aug. 25.	Jaques Fearne, *Stranger*.
Aug. 26.	Elizabeth, daughter of Thomas Viccars, *Glasier*.
Aug. 26.	Susan Woodcocke, *servaunt* with the aforesaide Thomas Viccars.
Aug. 31.	Samuell, son of Samuell Chamberleyne, *Haberdasher*.
Aug. 31.	Bridget Gee, *servaunte* Ralph Coniers, *Goldsmith*.
Sep. 1.	Thomas Chare, *servaunte* with Tymothie Elken, *Vintener*.
Sep. 2.	John Browne, *servaunte* with the aforesaide Tymothie Elken, *Vintener*.
Sep. 4.	John Williamson, *Laborer*, out of Widdow Evans' house.
Sep. 5.	Jaque Mysken, *Waynarth stranger*, *servaunte* with John Kirkworth.
Sep. 11.	John, son of Leonard Gale, *Gilder*.
Sep. 12.	John Fearne, *Millener*, *Stranger*.
Sep. 15.	Samuell Chamberleyne, *Haberdasher*.
Sep. 18.	Ellyn Williscroft, *servaunte* with John Dutton, *Haberdasher*
Sep. 20.	Charles Rogers, *servaunte* to Samwell Gee, *Marchan Tailor*.
Sep. 23.	Elizabeth Grimes, *servaunte* to Nicholas Grimes, *Merchan Tailor*.
Sep. 27.	Marye, daughter of John Williamson, *Laborer*, deceased.
Sep. 28.	John, son of Samwell Chamberleyne, *Haberdasher*.
Oct. 7.	Marke Hartewell, *servaunte* with Nicholas Grimes, *Taylor*.

Oct. 17.   The aforesaide Nicholas Grimes.
Oct. 24.   Alice, daughter of Anthony Sounde, *Clothworker.*
Oct. 25.   George, son of the above Nicholas Grimes.
Oct. 26.   Margreat, wyfe of William Dutton, *Haberdasher.*
Oct. 26.   William Lewes, *servaunte* with the said John Dutton.
Oct. 26.   Alice Harrys, *Widdowe,* out of Widdow Grimes' house.
Nov. 11.   Kathrin, daughter of Anthony Sounde, *Clothworker.*
Dec. 21.   Allen Hayes, *Cobler.*
Jan. 4.   John Ley, *servaunte* with Anthony Sounde, *Clothworker.*
Jan. 25.   A woman childe of William Cares, *Goldsmith,* stillborne.
Feb. 23.   Lawrence Nickson, *servaunte* with Anthony Sound, *Clothworker.*
Mar. 5.   Francis Barnard, *Cooke,* Senior.

1594

June 2.   Hellen, daughter of Francis Shewte, *Goldsmith.*
Aug. 20.   Mariy, daughter of Francis Shewte aforesaid, *Goldsmith.*
Sep. 10.   Robert, son of John Burforde, *Silkweaver.*
Sep. 17.   John, son of John Bickworth, *Marchaunte.*
Nov. 1.   Charles, son of Anthony Hawood, *late Confessor to her Majesties househoulde.*
Dec. 14.   Mary, wyfe of Richard Ditche, *Clothworker.*

1595

April 16.   Richard Murton, *Goldsmith,* [buried] in the Parish Church of St. Michaell Bassinghaw, who died in this Parishe.
May 6.   Margreat Price.
May 15.   Grisley, wife of Francis Longworth, *Goldsmith.*
June 1.   Robart Bourne, *servaunte* of Richard Crosshaw, *Goldsmith.*
July 5.   Peter, son of Edward Delves, *Goldsmith.*
Oct. 10.   A man childe of Giles Simpsons, *Goldsmith,* stillborne.
Oct. 31.   Martha, daughter of Edward Griffeth, *Clothworker.*
Jan. 5.   William Backe, *one of Her Majesty's servauntes of the garde,* who was slaine in the Taverne called by the name of the Bishopp's Head.
Feb. 12.   Adrian Thomas, alias Kerbye, out of the house of John Kerby, *Trompett Maker,* who dyed of a hurte in fight.

1596

April 29.   Joan, wyfe of Arnold Richardson, *Vintener.*
July 7.   Frances, wyfe of ———— [*sic*] Grafton, *Grocer.*
Aug. 22.   Anne Crosshaw, *Maiden,* and sister of Richard Crosshaw, *Goldsmith.*
Aug. 28.   John, son of Thomas Lawrence.
Aug. 29.   Jane, wyfe of George Nickson, *Marchantailor.*
Sep. 8.   Alice, daughter of Edwarde Brook, *Goldsmith.*
Sep. 12.   John, son of Christian Anthony ———— [*sic*].
Oct. 14.   Avies, wife of Marmaduke Higgens, *Grocer.*
Nov. 10.   Hughe, brother and *servaunte* of Richard Harrison, *Cooper.*
Jan. 21.   Henry Hargrave, *Goldsmith.*
Jan. 21.   Anne, daughter of John Burford, *Silkweaver.*
Jan. 23.   William, son of Richard Carter, *Clothworker.*
Mar. 12.   Thomas Franckwell, *Goldsmith.*

1597

Mar. 27.	John Broad, *servaunte* unto John Kerby, *Trompet Maker.*
April 3.	Thomas Kayll, *Master of Art and Fellowe of Jhesus Colledge, in Cambridge,* the son of Mr. Hughe Kayll, *Goldsmith, the Alderman Deputy of Langeborne Warde.*
May 2.	—— [*sic*] *Maiden, servaunte* with John Flud, *Vintener.*
May 4.	Em. Uttoy, *Maiden, servaunte* to Marmaduke Higgons, *Grocer.*
Sep. 5.	Thomas Rudd, *Haberdasher.*
Sep. 15.	Elizabeth, daughter of Edward Brook, *Goldsmith.*
Sept. 18.	James, son of Robert Hutchins, *Goldsmith,* deceased.
Sep. 19.	Clare Hammerton, *Widdow,* of Mr. Brewes' house
Dec. 7.	Sarah, daughter of John Greene, *Tailor.*
Mar. 21.	John Seaverns, *Haberdasher.*

1598

May 1.	Frances Longworth, *Goldsmith,* his daughter cauled by the name of Frances.
May 15.	Thomas Cramor, *Virgenall Maker.*
June 13.	Francis Longworth, *Goldsmith.*
July 8.	Richard Hadley, *Haberdasher.*
July 11.	Hamonde Upton, of Lincolnesheire, *Esquier.*
July 31.	Mrs. Anne Brangier.
Aug. 30.	William Francke, *Goldsmith*
Sep. 20.	Elizabeth, wife of William Thorne, and Elizabeth Wood, *Widdow,* both in one grave.
Sept. 25.	Jane Blanchard.
Dec. 20.	—— [*sic*] Hall, wife of —— [*sic*] Hall.
Mar. 15.	Henry, son of Daniell Binnell, *Goldsmith.*
Mar. 23.	William, son of Gyles Simpson, *Goldsmith.*

1599

Mar. 26.	Mr. Thomas Buckminster, *Person of this Parrish.*
May 16.	Stephen, son of Samuell Buck.
May 24.	Anne, wife of William Cares, *Goldsmith.*
June 3.	Margrett, wife of Hughe Udall, *Haberdasher.*
July 3.	Elizabeth, wife of Noy Farmer, *Goldsmith.*
July 13.	Agnes, daughter of William Ashton, of Shidlington, Co. Bedford, *Gentleman,* and *servaunte* with William Sallaway, of this Parrishe, *Haberdasher.*
July 15.	—— [*sic*], son of Richard Brooke, *Goldsmith.*
July 24.	Ellis, son of Thomas Clayton, inmate in Viccars' house.
July 30.	Ot—— [*sic*], childe of Robert Brooke, *Goldsmith.*
Aug. 15.	Suzan, daughter of Francis Shute, *Goldsmith.*
Aug. 16.	Grace, daughter of the said Francis Shute.
Aug. 22.	Mary, daughter of John Sudbury.
Sep. 24.	Mrs. Dixson, wife of William Dixson.
Sep. 25.	Sarah Bere, *maid servaunte* of Edward Delves, *Goldsmith.*
Sep. 31.	Judith, daughter of Edward Delves, *Goldsmith.*
Oct. 21.	Easter, daughter of William Marishaw, *Stranger.*
Nov. 19.	Jane, daughter of Richard Cheny, *Goldsmith.*
Nov. 21.	Elizabeth, daughter of George Humble, *Letherseller.*
Dec. 21.	John, son of William Salloway.
Feb. 7.	John Wilkins, *Goldsmith.*

1600

Feb. 5.	Noy Farmer.
Feb. 9.	Richard Ford, *servaunte* to Lady Dame Mary Ramsay.
Feb. 19.	John, son of Richard Carter, *Blacksmith*.

1601

April 18.	Alice Buckminster.
May 20.	John Savage, *Scrivener*.
June 1.	Jane, daughter of George Samwell, *Notary Publique*.
June 19.	Hester, daughter of William Ward, *Tayler*.
July 27,	Poshumus Savage, son of John Savage, *Scrivener*, in his father's grave.
Aug. 18.	Rachell, daughter of Richard Fletcher, died in the house of Mr. Cary.
Sep. 21.	A maiden child that was taken up in the Parishe.
Sep. 26.	Richard Longeworth, *servaunte* with Mr. Hampton.
Oct. 22.	Agnes, wife of Thomas Barret, *Shomaker*.
Nov. 12.	Dame Mary Ramsey.
Nov. 29.	Margret, wife of Richard Harison, *Cooper*.
Dec. 28.	John, son of John Pleydell.
Feb. 11.	Mrs. Butler.

1602

Mar. 26.	Utor Parishe, *servant* of Thomas Barret, *Shomaker*.
April 15.	Mrs. Cocknage, wife of William Cocknage.
April 30.	Joane, daughter of Thomas Robson.
July 18.	Henry Battell, *servaunt* of John Lovejoy, *Goldsmith*.
July 28.	Elizabeth, daughter of John Acton, *Goldsmith*.
July 30.	Thomos Viccars, *Glasier*.
July 30.	Anthony Sound, *Clothworker*.
Aug. 19.	A child of William Sailes, *Taylor*.
Oct. 1.	Mrs. Dutton, wife of William Dutton.
Oct. 20.	George, son of Andrew Tisdell.
Nov. 1.	Father Udall.
Nov. 7.	One of George Nickson's children.
Nov. 19.	A Crisom childe of Barnaby Gregories.
Dec. 16.	Thomas Rudd, *servaunt* unto Mr. Bartholomew Pickeringe
Dec. 31	Margaret, daughter of Robert Bleeze, *Tailor*.
Jan. 27.	Mary, daughter of William Salloway.
Feb. 5.	Agnes Hutchin, *servaunte* unto Mr. Richard Brooke.
Feb. 11.	Mary, daughter of William Hamore.
Mar. 23.	Walter, son of Richard Brooke, *Goldsmith*.

1603

April 20.	Daniell, son of Thomas Westley, *Vintener*.
May 7.	Giles Bultell, *Marchantstranger*.
May 15.	Robert Westley, *servaunt* unto Edward Annable, *Vintener* in the Cardinall's hatt.
May 17.	John, son of John Wollaston.
May 24.	Mrs. Alexander, wife of Michaell Allexander, *Tailor*.
June 13.	Thomas, son of Edward Delves, *Goldsmith*.
June 24.	A Crizom child of William Marloe, *Baker*.
July 4.	Richard Danger, *Trumpeter*, out of Mr. Kirbye's house.

July 7.	Anne, wife of John Younge, out of the house of Mr. Richard Brooke.
July 11.	Martha, daughter of Thomas White, *Grocer.*
July 30.	George Thornell, *servaunt* to Mr. Sound.
Aug. 6.	George, son of William Salloway.
Aug. 7.	Followes, *servant* of William Marlow, *Baker.*
Aug. 7.	Mrs. White, wife of Thomas White, *Grocer.*
Aug. 16.	Judith Blancke, a childe out of the house of Mr. Brew, *Goldsmith.*
Aug. 17.	William Shacroste, *Grocer.*
Aug. 18.	Edward Parker, out of the house of Mr. Glasse.
Aug. 18.	Judith, daughter of Robert Bleize, *Tailor.*
Aug. 19.	Robert, son of Robert Bleize, *Tailor.*
Aug. 20.	John Astley, *servaunte* to John Burfoote, *Silkeweaver.*
Aug. 22.	Nicholas, son of Samuell Buck, *Baker.*
Aug. 23.	Mrs. Pleydell, wife of John Pleydell, *Stocking Seller.*
Aug. 28.	William Marlow, *Baker.*
Aug. 29.	William Doughtie, *servaunte* unto Mr. Westley, *Vintener.*
Aug. 29.	Edwarde Bedle, *servaunt* unto Mr. Sudbery.
Aug. 30.	John, son of John Burfoote.
Aug. 30.	Jane, daughter of John Burfoote, *Silkwever.*
Aug. 30.	Nicholas, son of Andrew Tisdell, *Waterbearer.*
Aug. 30.	John, son of John Carter.
Aug. 30.	Andrew Tisdell, *Waterbearer.*
Aug. 30.	Evans, *servant* unto John Burfert, *Silkweaver.*
Sep. 1.	Raphe, son of John Burfoote, *Silkweaver.*
Sep. 1.	Mrs. Barker, wife of Stephen Barker, *Haberdasher.*
Sep. 4.	Thomas Robson, *Cordwayner.*
Sep. 4.	Sara, daughter of Abram Sherifrye, *Clarke of this Church.*
Sep. 5.	Joane, daughter of Richard Thomas. The mother of it was the keeper in Thomas Robson his house.
Sep. 6.	Anne, wife of Stephen Blanck, out of Mr. Brew his house.
Sep. 6.	Alice Richardson, *servant* unto Mr. Richard Brooke.
Sep. 6.	Abraham, son of Abraham Sherifrye, *Clarke of this Church.*
Sep. 7.	Robert Phillipps, *servant* unto Mr. George Fludd.
Sep. 7.	Thomas Shely, out of Mr. Fludd his house.
Sep. 7.	Edwarde Jordaine, *servaunt* unto Mr. Harison, *Cowper.*
Sep. 8.	Samuel Buck, *Baker.*
Sep. 8.	Briget Ridley, *servant* unto Mrs. Offley.
Sep. 8.	Jane, wife of Marke Coulon, *Stranger.*
Sep. 8.	Alexander Weeldon, *servant* unto Mr. Hamore.
Sep. 9.	Elizabeth Handmor, *servant* unto Mr. Barker.
Sep. 9.	Ellene Traton, *servant* unto Mr. Barker.
Sep. 9.	William, son of William Keate.
Sep. 9.	Anna, daughter of William Exton.
Sep. 10.	Elizabeth Boulton, *servant* unto Mr. Lovejoy.
Sep. 11.	Margarett Manlie, out of Mr. Fludd his house.
Sep. 12.	Roger Procter, *servant* unto Mr. Fludd.
Sep. 13.	Francis Boston, Mr. Cotton his *servant.*
Sep. 13.	Anna, daughter of Thomas Robson.
Sep. 13.	Margaret Lampley, *servant* unto goodman Carter.
Sep. 14.	Richard Fursland, *servant* to Mr. Butler.
Sep. 15.	Anna, daughter of John Beeston, *Gilder.*
Sep. 15.	Mr. William Burtingale, *Haberdasher.*
Sep. 17.	Edward Phillipp, *servant* to Mr. Humfrey Flood.
Sep. 18.	John, son of Thomas Robson, *Shomaker.*

Sep. 18.   Maynard, son of William Wakefeild, out of Mr. Chesmore his house.
Sep. 18.   Rebecca, daughter of Thomas Robson, *Shomaker.*
Sep. 20.   Richard, son of Richard Brooke, *Goldsmith.*
Sep. 20.   Anne Vaughan, *servaunte* unto Mr. Salloway.
Sep. 22.   Richard Cotten, *servant* unto Mr. Cotten, *Silkeman.*
Sep. 22.   Richard, son of Nicholas Goddart, *Stocking Presser.*
Sep. 22.   Mrs. Buntingale, wife of William Buntingale, *Haberdasher.*
Sep. 22.   Jane Browne, *servant* unto Doctor Childerley.
Sep. 22.   Raphe Todd, *servant* to Mr. Buck, *Baker.*
Sep. 23.   Mathew, daughter [*sic*] of goodman Exton.
Sep. 24.   John Smith, *Joyner.*
Sep. 24.   Nathaniell, son of Nicholas Goddart, *Stocking Presser.*
Sep. 26.   William, son of Thomas Robson, *Cordwayner.*
Sep. 26.   John Bynion, *servant* unto Mr. Goddard, *Stocking Presser.*
Sep. 27.   Jeronomy, daughter [*sic*] of Mr. Harison, *Cowper.*
Sep. 28.   Mr. Edward Cotten, *Silkeman.*
Sep. 28.   Awdrey Wakefield, *servant* unto Mr. Dutton.
Sep. 29.   Anthony Stevens, Mr. Buntingale's *man.*
Sep. 29.   Robert Hamond, Mr. Trigger's *servant.*
Sep. 30.   Mr. Stephen Barker.
Sep. 30.   Jane, daughter of Mr. Beeston, *Gilder.*
Sep. 30.   Robert Porter, *servant* unto Mr. Harison, *Cooper.*
Oct. 1.   Mr. William Walker, *Lynendraper.*
Oct. 1.   Marye, wife of Mr. Richard Harison.
Oct. 2.   Elizabeth, daughter of Noah Farmer.
Oct. 3.   Charles, son of Mr. William Ward.
Oct. 3.   Agnes Ellwin, *servant* to Mr. Glascock.
Oct. 3.   Barbara Conyers.
Oct. 5.   Thomas Westley.
Oct. 7.   William Axton, *Glover.*
Oct. 9.   Edward, son of Richard Harison, *Cowper.*
Oct. 10.   Thomas, son of Thomas Bowdler.
Oct. 11.   Mary, daughter of Richard Harison, *Cooper.*
Oct. 17.   Nicholas, son of Nicholas Wakefield, out of Mr. Chasmore's house.
Oct. 17.   Agnes Barley, *servant* unto Mr. Raphe Harison.
Oct. 19.   Mr. William Ward, and his daughter Katherine.
Oct. 19.   Marye, daughter of Mr. Raphe Harison.
Oct. 19.   John Lewen, *servant* to Mr. Laurence.
Oct. 22.   Thomas Richman, *servant* unto Richard Harison.
Oct. 22.   Sara, daughter of Nicholas Goddard, *Stocking Presser.*
Oct. 23.   Agnes, daughter of William Ward.
Oct. 27.   Richard Cobbet, *servant* unto Goodman Francklyn.
Oct. 29.   Richard, son of Richard Harison, *Cowper.*
Nov. 3.   Robert, son of William Warde.
Nov. 3.   Anne, daughter of Thomas Bowdler.
Nov. 7.   Mr. James Robinson.
Nov. 22.   Alice, daughter of Thomas Francknell.
Dec. 4.   John Smith, *Tailor.*
Jan. 2.   John Kirbye, *Trumpet Maker.*
Jan. 14.   Mr. Hughe Kayll.
Jan. 16.   Richard Francklyn.
Jan. 20.   Henry Tailor, *servant* unto Thomas Francklyn.
Jan. 25.   Arthur, son of Richard Keale, *Sweeteball Maker.*
Feb. 20.   William, son of Thomas Lawrence, *Goldsmith.*

1604

April 17.	Jacomo Devielmo, *an Italian*, out of Mr. Frederigo his house.
May 4.	John, son of Thomas Claye.
Aug. 31.	Edward Wigley, *servant* unto Mr. William Sailes, *Tailor*.
Nov. 13.	George, son of George Nickson, *Tailor*.
Nov. 13.	Elizabeth, daughter of William Hamore, *Scrivener*.
Nov. 16.	Marye, daughter of Richard Shawcrosse, *Grocer*.
Dec. 19.	Thomas, son of William Sales, *Tailor*.

1605

April 18.	William Sauvage.
April 20.	Henry Farnaby.
May 14.	Katherin, daughter of Humfrey Knevit.
May 19.	Joane Tanner, the mother of Mr. Beeston.
June 16.	Mother Clarke.
June 29.	Henry Twiford, *servant* with Mr. Lacye.
July 7.	Thomas, son of William Salloway.
July 16.	Marye Soones, *servant* unto Mr. Dauper.
July 17.	William, son of Giles Sympson, *Goldsmith*.
Aug. 1.	William, Cade, *servant* to Mr. Mildemay.
Aug. 5.	Richard Dolman, *Scolemaster*.
Sep. 15.	Henry Chesshiere.
Nov. 6.	Marye, daughter of Francis Haddon, *Goldsmith*.
Nov. 11.	Mrs. Griffen, wife of Mr. Edward Griffen, *Bricklayer*.
Nov. 19.	William, son of Barnaby Gregorye.
Dec. 8.	Marye, daughter of Richard Harison, *Cowper*.
Dec. 22.	William, son of Thomas Lawrence, *Goldsmith*.
Dec. 25.	Jane, daughter of Edward Annable, *Vintener*.
Jan. 3.	Isaac, son of William Hamore, *Scrivener*.
Feb. 16.	Thomas, son of John Woodward.
Mar. 22.	John, son of George Caro, *Goldsmith*.

1606

June 13.	Anne, daughter of John Smith, *Comfit Maker*.
Sep. 11.	Elizabeth Hammon, *servant* to Mrs. Kerby.
Sep. 14.	Dorothy, daughter of Edward Delues, *Goldsmith*.
Sep. 26.	Frances Hyam, daughter of Widdowe Chamberlaine.
Sep. 27.	Mary Johnsowne.
Sep. 30.	John Bracknet, *servant* to Mr. Rawlins, *Silversmith*.
Oct. 2.	Robert Prudent, *Trumpeter*.
Oct. 7.	Edward, son of George Savage.
Oct. 9.	Alice, daughter of George Savage.
Oct. 18.	John, son of John Carter.
Oct. 20.	Thomas Germain, *servant* unto Mr. Savadge.
Oct. 26.	Christian Conniers, kinswoman unto Mr. Raphe Conniers, *Goldsmith*.
Oct. 29.	Jacob, son of Raphe Harison, *Merchant*.
Jan. 6.	Anne Fend, *servant* to Mr. Butler.
Feb. 3.	Katherin Pendrin, out of Mr. Annable his house.
Mar. 15.	Anne Chamberlaine, *Widdowe*.

1607

April 24.	Richard, son of Richard Harrison, *Cooper*.

May 7.	John, son of George Nickson, *Merchantailor.*
May 21.	Anne, daughter of Richard Man, *Goldsmith.*
June 19.	Elizabeth, daughter of Humfrey Knevett.
July 6.	Henry, son of George Nyckson, *Tailor.*
Aug. 2.	Matthy, daughter of John Homewood, *Chaundler.*
Aug. 13.	Mrs. —— [*sic*] Kerby.
Aug. 16.	John, son of John Homewood, *Chaundler.*
Aug. 29.	Judith, daughter of John Beson, *Painter Stainer.*
Sep. 10.	Stephen Boyse.
Sep. 25.	Elizabeth, daughter of John Loveioye, *Goldsmith.*
Oct. 4.	Roger Chattock, *servant* to Mr. George Humble.
Oct. 23.	William Hall, out of Mr. Ambler's house.
Jan. 4.	Joyce, daughter of William Wood, *Goldsmith.*
Jan. 8.	Barbary, daughter of Richard Evans, *Grocer.*
Jan. 18.	Margaret Kinge.
Jan. 20.	Mr. Richard Brooke.
Feb. 12.	Margaret, daughter of Giles Sympson.
Feb. 22.	Elizabeth, daughter of George Caro, *Goldsmith.*
Feb. 29.	William Petison, *servant* unto Mr. Francklyn.

1608

Mar. 30.	A Crizom childe of Francis Hadon, *Goldsmith.*
April 15.	Martin Frederigo, *an Italian.*
April 19.	John, son of John Giffen, [*sic*] *Clothworker.*
April 22.	Elizabeth, daughter of Thomas Francknell, *Fustian Dresser.*
May 9.	Giles Sympson, *Goldsmith.*
May 14.	Mr. Francis Shute.
June 4.	Francis Udall.
June 9.	Mary, daughter of William Jones, *Vintner.*
June 12.	Thomas Francknell, *Clothworker.*
Aug. 8.	Thomas Ward.
Aug. 15.	Margaret Wade, *servant* unto Mr. Phillips.
Aug. 23.	Margaret Wigmore.
Aug. 30.	John Romball, son in lawe to Walter Ambler.
Aug. 31.	Henry, son of Walter Ambler.
Oct. 17.	Elizabeth, daughter of John Carter.
Nov. 22.	Elizabeth, daughter of William Wood, *Goldsmith.*
Nov. 25.	Phillipp Allen, *Haberdasher.*
Jan. 10.	Mary —— [*sic*] *servant* unto Mr. Chasmore.
Jan. 12.	Anne, daughter of Francis Lawrence, *Joyner.*
Jan. 13.	Margaret Gibson.
Jan. 15.	Mrs. Beeston, wife of John Beeston, *Painter Stainer.*
Feb. 12.	William Ardway.
Feb. 24.	James Holme, *servant* unto Mr. Acton.

1609

May 14.	Richard Cray.
June 2.	John Ardway, *servant* with Mr. Chesmore.
June 28.	Anne, daughter of Francis Fewtrer.
July 12.	John Chasmore.
July 24.	Jeane Francklin.
Sep. 18.	Henry, son of Thomas Cole.
Jan. 6.	Frances, daughter of John Griffen.
Jan. 3.	Mary, daughter of Nicholas Goddard, *Stocking Presser.*
Feb. 1.	Mary, wife of William Sailes, *Marchantailor.*

1610

April 9.	Anne, daughter of William Hamore, *Stacioner*.
May 10.	Mary, daughter of William Rawlyns, *Goldesmith*.
May 29.	Jacob Lucas, Lucas Jacob his father.
June 3.	Thomas, the son of George [*sic*]
June 23.	Francis, son of Francis Haddon, *Goldsmith*.
Aug. 2.	Edward Winckfeilde.
Aug. 4.	Susanna, daughter of William Tirrey.
Aug. 13.	Alice, wife of Francis Barnard.
Aug. 14.	Elizabeth, wife of George Cary, *Goldsmith*.
Aug. 30.	A Crysome childe of Mr. *Bolstone's.
Sep. 18.	Leonard Conyers, *servant* to Mr. Raphe Conyers.
Sep. 20.	Francis Haddon, father unto Francis Haddon.
Sep. 25.	Thomas Mody, *servant* unto Mr. Humble.
Oct. 8.	Anthony, son of Abraham Sherifry, *Clarke of this Church*.
Oct. 14.	William Stockes, out of Mr. Sudbury his house.
Oct. 15.	John, son of William Rolppe.
Oct. 17.	Thomas, son of John Acton, *Goldesmith*.
Oct. 21.	Durdyn Bathy, out of Mr. Chasmore his house.
Oct. 27.	Meldred Godfrey.
Nov. 3.	Parnell, wife of John Sudbury, *Letherseller*.
Nov. 28.	Raphe Conyers.
Dec. 1.	Thomas, son of William Jones, *Vintener*.
Dec. 30.	Robert Offley.
Jan. 21.	Dorothy, daughter of John Burfert.
Feb. 8.	Mrs. Mann, wife of Richard Mann, *Goldsmith*.
Mar. 9.	Elizabeth, daughter of John Cowper.

1611

April 4.	Mrs. Goddard, wiffe of Nicholas Goddard.
April 12.	Willyam, son of William Rolffe, *Goldsmith*.
April 25.	Thomas Johnson, *servant* to Mr. Haddon.
May 20.	Thomas, son of Richard Evans, *Grocer*.
June 24.	Anthony, son of William Terry, *Goldsmith*.
June 24.	Lydya Lewen, out of Mr. Lawrence his house.
June 26.	Emme, wife of John Acton, *Goldsmith*.
Aug. 25.	Agnes, daughter of Nicholas Grange.
Sep. 1.	Elizabeth, daughter of George Monnox.
Sep. 27.	John, son of Jhon Chesmore.
Nov. 13.	Oliver Jones, *Victualer*.
Nov. 20.	Katherine, daughter of Richard Keales.
Nov. 20.	Mr. Thomas White, *Parson of this Parish*.
Dec. 6.	Peter Malory, of East Haddon, in Northamptonshire.
Dec. 7.	John Conyers.
Jan. 1.	Elizabeth, daughter of John Chesmore.
Jan. 21.	Marye, wiffe of Richard Harryson, *Cowper*.
Feb. 15.	Alse Hartrup.
Feb. 19.	Mr. Gossen Vanderbecke, *Chaundeler*.
Feb. 19.	Anne Kent.
Feb. 20.	Thomas Offley.
Feb. 29.	Jane Offley, of the Parish of St. Edmund the King, in Lumbard Streete.
Feb. 29.	A childe of Mr. Dutton.
Mar. 7.	Mrs. Margaret Pickering.

* "Thomas Boylstone" in the Churchwarden's accounts for the fee for the "laystall" of his child.

Mar. 12.   Mrs. Anne Dutton.
Mar. 16.   Edmund Batchelor, of Buckinghamshire.
Mar. 20.   Katherine, daughter of Willyam Hamore, *Scrivener.*

1612

April 7.   Constance, wife of Mr. Chapman, *Merchant.*
April 16.   John Bever, *Gentleman.*
May 17.   Elizabeth Blunt, *Scholemistress.*
June 17.   Teodore, son of Raphe Bennet, *Taylor.*
July 10.   Mary, daughter of Willyam Wood, *Goldsmith.*
July 12.   Peter, son of John Carter.
Aug. 2.   John Loveioye.
Aug. 8.   Valentine Judde.
Aug. 15.   James, son of Willyam Terrey, *Goldsmith.*
Aug. 20.   Anthony, son of Willyam Hartley.
Nov. 16.   Alice Axton, *Widdowe.*
Nov. 23.   Willyam, son of Thomas Cooke.
Dec. 2.   Richard, son of John Griffen, *Clothworker.*
Dec. 4.   Joane, wife of Willyam Shorden, *Goldsmith.*
Jan. 1.   Martin, son of Martine Swone.
Jan. 22.   Mrs. Brewe, wife of Partrick Brewe.

1613

April 20.   John, son of Richard Man, *Goldsmith.*
April 26.   A Crism of Mr. Sadler.
June 18.   Richard, son of Richard Chesewright.
July 3.   Mr. Charles Glascock, *Grocer.*
July 8.   Anne, daughter of Willyam Jones, *Vintner.*
July 10.   Margaret Bristowe, *servant* of Thomas Man.
July 27.   Willyam, son of George Nickson.
July 31.   Frances, wiffe of John Beaver, *Gent.*
Aug. 6.   John Mouldesworth.
Sept. 18.   Willyam Keale, *Joyner.*
Sept. 23.   John, son of Marke Calone.
Oct. 7.   John Bouthby, *Goldsmith.*
Oct. 12.   Anne, daughter of Richard Nunnersley, *Taylor.*
Oct. 24.   Jane Cotes.
Nov. 28.   John Boswell, *Letherseller.*
Dec. 20.   Mary, daughter of Francis Shute, *Goldsmith.*
Dec. 24.   Anne Sowndes, *Widdowe.*
Dec. 29.   Willyam, son of Willyam Rawlyns.
Dec. 31.   Thomas Davies.

1614

Mar. 28.   Francis, wiffe of John Acton, *Goldsmith.*
Mar. 29.   John, son of Raphe Bennet, *Taylor.*
May 2.   George Morgan.
May 21.   John Pryce, *Gentelman.*
May 26.   Mary, daughter of John Boswell, *Letherseller.*
June 5.   Willyam Warde, *Taylor.*
June 10.   Elizabeth, daughter of Raphe King, *Vintener.*
Aug. 23.   Anne, daughter of Symion Sedgewicke, *Goldsmith.*
Oct. 21.   Edward Gryffen.
Nov. 17.   Nicholas, son of Peter Wade, *Taylor.*

Nov. 19.	John, son of George Binge, *Goldsmith*.
Nov. 29.	Anne, daughter of Richard Nunnesley, *Taylor*.
Dec. 3.	Willyam Lewes, *Imbrotherer*.
Dec. 31.	Bridget, wife of Willyam Garland.
Jan. 4.	Abraham, son of Lucas Jacob.
Feb. 4.	John, son of Richard Keale, *Swetebalmaker*.
Feb. 9.	Sara, daughter of Isaacke Thomas.
Feb. 13.	A Crizoming child of Richard Weldes, *Goldsmith*.
Mar. 18.	Anne, wife of John Gryffen.
Mar. 22.	John Gryffen, *Clothworker*.

1615

April 13.	Katherine Cheney.
May 11.	John Homewood.
May 16.	Mr. Henry Butler, *Draper*.
May 28.	Docter John White, who was *Docter of Divinitie*.
June 10.	Sara, daughter of Francis Chapman, *Goldsmith*.
June 11.	Godfrey Smith.
June 21.	Joane, wife of Francis Haddon, *Goldsmith*.
July 31.	Robert Underwood.
Aug. 1.	Phillipp, son of Edward Starkey.
Aug. 20.	Mrs. Elizabeth Cheney, wife of Richard Cheney, *Goldsmith*.
Oct. 22.	John Colt, *Goldsmith*.
Nov. 6.	Anne, daughter of Christopher fitzgeofrey, *Joyner*.
Nov. 26.	Pricilla, daughter of Raphe Kinge, *Vintner*.
Dec. 10.	Robart, son of William Terrey, *Goldsmith*.
Jan. 4.	Thomas, son of Richard Mann, *Goldsmith*.
Jan. 7.	Joane, wife of Jeremy Clerke, *Gentleman*, out of Mr. Wollestone's house.
Jan. 30.	Jeane, daughter of Richard Nunnersley, *Taylor*.
Feb. 13.	John Elliot.
Feb. 23.	Richard Hodges.
Feb. 28.	Mary, wife of George Bromley.
Mar. 3.	Monsieur Patton,* *a Scotch gentleman*, in the body of the church, under the three peeced stone.

1616

April 15.	A foundlinge, whose name was called Aodam [*sic*].
April 28.	William, son of Henry Balaam.
May 3.	Abraham Shrivery, *Clarke of this Parish*.
May 21.	Peter Torrentine, *Duchman*.
June 3.	George, son of George Monnox.
June 24.	John, son of Hugh Gwilliams.
July 1.	Margaret, wife of John Carter, *Merchantaylor*.
July 23.	Edward, son of Edward Phillippes.
Aug. 2.	A childe of William Butlers, *Poticary*.
Aug. 10.	James, son of Marke Caloone, *Weaver, stranger*.
Sep. 20.	Elener, wife of Thomas Tickerage, *Grocer*.
Oct. 15.	Marie Shute, *Widdowe*.
Oct. 17.	Anne, daughter of John Tapeffeild, *Carpenter*.
Oct. 28.	Henry Reanoles, *servant* to Hugh Gwilliams, *Haberdasher*.
Oct. 28.	Steven, son of John Cole, *Haberdasher*.
Dec. 27.	Thomas Sheereman, *Clothworker*.

* "Monsiur Patten, a Scot, who died at John de Dorper's house," Ch. Acc.

1617

May 1.	John, son of George Humble, *Stacioner.*
June 15.	A Crisome childe of Henry Feake, *Goldsmith.*
July 17.	A Crisome childe of George Binge, *Goldsmith.*
Sep. 1.	A Crisome childe of Marke Calone, *Weaver, stranger.*
Sep. 10.	Rebecca, daughter of Thomas Stevens, *Mercer.*
Sep. 18.	Angell Weldon, *servant* to Michaell Gardener, *Vintener.*
Oct. 30.	Elizabeth, wife of Symon Sedgewick.
Nov. 14.	William, son of William Terrey, *Goldsmith.*
Nov. 24.	Christian, wife of Hugh Gwilliams, *Haberdasher.*
Dec. 22.	Ellen, daughter of George Brumley, *Grocer.*
Jan. 2.	Peter, son of Peter Sadler, *Marchant.*
Mar. 9.	Arthur Cheesemore, *Blacksmith.*

1618

Mar. 26.	Francis, son of George Humble, *Stacioner.*
Mar. 26.	John, son of John Hunter, *Butcher.*
April 8.	John Middleton, *Goldsmith.*
April 16.	Mary Bowers, *servant* unto George Nickson.
April 25.	Katheryn, daughter of William Wood, *Goldsmith.*
May 11.	David Lascony, *Weaver.*
June 6.	Edward Chappell, *servant* unto Walter Furler, *Goldsmith.*
June 10.	Christopher Phillippes, *servant* to Raphe King, *Vintener.*
June 16.	Anne, wife of Robert Myldmay, *Grocer.*
June 16.	Charles, son of Marke Caloone, *Weaver, Stranger.*
June 20.	Margaret, daughter of Hugh Gwilliams, *Haberdasher.*
Aug. 24.	Richard Slany, *Stranger*, dyed in Mr. Lucas his house.
Sep. 6.	Henry, son of Widdowe Shrevy.
Oct. 22.	A Crisome childe of Mr. Thomas Dentes.
Dec. 30.	Jane, daughter of Henry Feake, *Goldsmith.*
Jan. 9.	John Casselman.
Jan. 31.	Elizabeth, daughter of Clement Medley, *Gentleman.*
Feb. 13.	Elizabeth, daughter of Edward Dexter, *Clarke of this Parishe.*
Feb. 19.	John Lucas, *Marchant.*
Feb. 23.	Dyed in this Parishe, Sir William Swanne, and was carried into Kent to be buried.

1619

Mar. 30.	A Crisome child of John Acton's, *Goldsmith.*
April 1.	Elizabeth, daughter of Thomas Burden, *Sexton.*
April 16.	Jone Cheesemore, *Widdowe.*
May 12.	Anne, daughter of Bartholome Pickeringe, *Haberdasher.*
June 2.	Gabriell Sewell, *Haberdasher.*
July 14.	Anne, wife of George Samwell, *Notary.*
Aug. 25.	Elizabeth Wall, *servant* unto Mr. King, *Vintener.*
Sep. 1.	George Samwell, *Scrivener and Notary Publique.*
Sep. 25.	Martin, son of Thomas Garrett, *Goldsmith.*
Oct. 2.	Mary, wife of Marke Gallone, [*sic*] *Stranger.*
Oct. 23.	Mary, wife of John Hunter, *Butcher.*
Oct. 30.	William, son of Edward Robinson, *Clothworker.*
Nov. 27.	Barnaby Simborne, *Fishmonger.*
Dec. 29.	Symon Sedgwick, *Goldsmith.*
Mar. 11.	Xpofer Roberts, *Brewer.*

1620

April 2.   Sara Bagger, *servant* to Walter Furlo, *Goldsmith*.
May 16.   Thomas, brother to John Kompton, *Haberdasher*.
June 19.   Anne Keale, *Pentioner*.
June 29.   Elizabeth, wife of Edward Dexter, *Clark*, and Elizabeth, his daughter.
July 8.   Anthony, son of Anthony Peniston, *Goldsmith*.
Aug. 6.   William, son of John Babham, *Draper, Stranger*.
Aug. 19.   Margarett, daughter of George Bromley, *Grocer*.
Aug. 20.   Owen Cooke, *Schoolmaster*.
Oct. 4.   Thomas, son of Francis Chapman, *Goldsmith*.
Nov. 24.   Daniel, son of Peter Sadler, *Merchant*.
Nov. 28.   Sara, daughter of Richard Ockold, *Goldsmith*.
Dec. 18.   William, son of Thomas White, *Merchant*.
Feb. 15.   James Sixty, out of Mr. Furrey's house, being a *Stranger* and borne at Hagh in the low Countries.
Feb. 24.   Elizabeth, daughter of John Coate, *Haberdasher*.

1621

May 4.   Mary Moodey.
May 9.   Ann, wife of William Everley, *Goldsmith*.
June 14.   Barbara Mallett, grandchild of John Beeston.
June 21.   John Jousy, *Merchant*. Plene [Written in the margin.]
June 27.   A Crisome child of William Wood, *Goldsmith*.
July 5.   Thomas Hunter, *Merchanttailor*. Plene [Written in the margin.]
July 16.   Henry Lacy, *servant* with William Lacy.
Aug. 8.   James, son of Anthony Peniston, *Goldsmith*.
Aug. 10.   Anne, daughter of Richard Harrison, *Carrer*.
Sep. 14.   Elizabeth, daughter of John Peacock, *Goldsmith*.
Sep. 26.   Symon, son of Thomas Willis, *Vitler*.
Sep. 28.   George Humble, *servant* unto Mr. Sherman, *Vintner at the Cardinall's Hatt*.
Oct. 27.   Ellen, daughter of Alexander Weld, *Druggester*.
Nov. 26.   Margarett, wife of Edward White, *Grocer*.
Dec. 13.   Ellen, wife of Lewis Roberts, *Clothworker*.
Dec. 20.   Anne, daughter of Hugh Gwilliams, *Haberdasher*.
Jan. 14.   Maudlin, daughter of Rowland Sadler. Plene [Written in the margin.]
Jan. 15.   John, son of Robert Hamore, *Scrivener*.
Mar. 4.   Elizabeth Browne, *servant* unto Mr. Mildmay.

1622

April 4.   Henry Balaam, *Stationer*.
May 20.   Susan, wife of Henry Bagley, *Shoemaker*.
Aug. 7.   Peter, son of Thomas Willis, *Vitular*.
Aug. 13.   Elizabeth, daughter of William Terry, *Goldsmith*.
Aug. 18.   Mary, daughter of Edward Ledger, *Bricklayer*.
Oct. 4.   John, son of Henry Freeman, *Cobler*.
Nov. 26.   Margarett, wife of Gilbert Rigby, *Merchanttailor*.
Jan. 0.   Thomas, son of Thomas Cadwell, *Confettmaker*.
Jan. 12.   Par Molde-worth, *Stranger, servant* unto Mr. Garrett, *the Farthinge Maker*.
Feb. 6.   Prudence, daughter of John Moore.
Feb. 9.   William, son of Thomas Vinor, *Goldsmith*.

Mar. 14.   Edward Legard, *Bricklayer.*
Mar. 19.   Thomas, son of Thomas Whitby, out of Mr. Taylor's house.

1623

April 5.   Susan, daughter of Thomas White, *Merchant.*
April 5.   Katherine, daughter of William Webb, *Clothworker.*
May 1.   William Hamore, *Scrivener.*
May 9.   Martyn Grapes, *servant* unto William Sparrow.
May 13.   George, son of Richard Weld, *Goldsmith.* Plene [Written in the margin.]
May 23.   Margery, daughter of Thomas White, *Merchant.*
May 21.   George Nickson, *Merchantailor.*
June 5.   Hanna, daughter of Henry Lillye, of St. Buttolph without Aldersgate, buried out of Mr. Simpson's house, *the Apothecary.*
June 23.   Jane, daughter of John Hill, *Goldsmith.*
June 23.   Elizabeth, daughter of John Cole, *Haberdasher.*
July 4.   Alice, wife of William Hamore, *Scrivener,* deceased.
July 24.   Barbara, daughter of John Peacock.
Aug. 3.   George, son of Arthur Fisher, *Merchant.* Plene [Written in the margin.]
Aug. 5.   Jane, wife of Edward Dexter, *Clarke.*
Sep. 27.   John Sherman, a foundling.
Sep. 29.   Richard, son of James Chamberlin, *Haberdasher.*
Oct. 7.   William, son of William Manley, *Scrivener.*
Oct. 22.   George, son of Anthony Peniston, *Goldsmith.*
Nov. 23.   Ellen, wife of William Woodward, of St. Olaves in Southwark, *Brewer.*
Dec. 10.   Emanuell, son of William Oute, *Plaisterer, Stranger.*
Jan. 6.   John Kempton, *Haberdasher.*
Feb. 8.   A crisom child of Marke Colonne, *Stranger.*
Mar. 7.   Susan, daughter of John Cole, *Haberdasher.*

1624

April 13.   Susan, daughter of Marke Colonne, *Stranger.*
June 18.   George, son of George Catchmay, *Fishmonger.*
June 19.   Damaris, daughter of George Tapsfeild.
Aug. 4.   Jone, wife of John Beauchamp, *Gent.*
Aug. 14.   Richard, son of Richard Worrall.
Sep. 1.   George, son of George Humble, *Stacioner.*
Sep. 1.   Phillis, daughter of Elias Carpentar.
Sep. 3.   Marcy, daughter of Henry Freeman.
Sep. 10.   Dorothie, *servant* unto William Axton.
Sep. 19.   Elizabeth, wife of John Billingford.
Sep. 22.   A younge childe that was found in the Parishe.
Sep. 30.   Elias Carpenter, *Sheeregrinder.*
Oct. 7.   Thomas Fishlake, *Clothworker.*
Oct. 7.   Margarett Collins.
Oct. 8.   Daniel, son of Peter Sadler.
Oct. 23.   Edward Hurt, *Ymbrotherer.* Plene [Written in the margin.]
Nov. 4.   Richard Harrison, *Cowper.*
Nov. 4.   Precilla, daughter of Raphe Kinge.
Nov. 20.   Henry, son of Humfrey Webb, *Coachman.*
Dec. 1.   William, son of Francis Chapman, *Goldsmith.*
Jan. 4.   Edward, son of Abraham Brand, *Merchantaylor.*

Jan. 5.	A Crisome child of Edward Hole, *Goldsmith.*
Feb. 3.	Margrett, wife of Thomas Clarke.
Feb. 23.	James, son of Samuell Dey, *Merchant.*
Mar. 2.	Anne, daughter of Anthony Peniston.
Mar. 4.	A Crisome child of William Rawlins, *Goldsmith.*
Mar. 18.	Richard, son of Richard Briggs, *Mercer*, buried in Aldermanbury Church, but died in Mr. Gilman's house in this Parish.

1625

April 2.	George, son of William Wood, *Goldsmith.*
April 19.	Margarett, daughter of George Bromley, *Grocer.*
April 19.	Margarett, wife of John Carter.
April 29.	Hanna, daughter of John Linge, *Oylman.*
April 30.	Frances, daughter of Thomas Tickeridge, *Grocer.*
May 1.	William Wood, *Goldsmith.* Plene [Written in the margin.]
May 1.	Margarett Kempton, daughter of Margarett Kempton, *Widow.* Plene [Written in the margin.]
June 3.	Hugh Guilliams.
June. 16.	John, *servant* to Widdowe Fishlake, *Clothworker.*
June 25.	Katherine, daughter of William Rolfe, *Goldsmith.*
June 30.	Josua Homes, Katherine Brode, and Rebecca Williams.
July 2.	Constance, daughter of William Rawlins, *Goldsmith.*
July 3.	William Cary, the *servant* of William Rawlins.
July 4.	James Kenedy, *servant* to John Peacocke, *Goldsmith.*
July 4.	Edward, son of Henry Blackmore, *Goldsmith.*
July 6.	Erasmus, son of Edward Dexter, *Clarke.*
July 6.	A stillborne child of Elizabeth Wood.
July 10.	Elizabeth Wood, *Widdowe.*
July 10.	Thomas Cade, *Comfittmaker.*
July 13.	Elizabeth Cloun, *servant* unto Mathew Homes.
July 14.	Thomas Whitby.
July 18.	Thomasin, wife of Edward Dexter, *Clarke.*
July 22.	Mathew Homes, *Laysterer.*
July 23.	Richard, son of Richard Ockold, *Goldsmith.*
Aug. 1.	Thomas, son of John Cole, *Haberdasher.*
Aug. 6.	Thomas, son of Thomas Ferrers, buryed in Paule's Churchyard.
Aug. 6.	Elizabeth Cadewell, *Widdowe*, and her son Mathewe.
Aug. 8.	George, son of George Tabfeild, *Carpenter.*
Aug. 13.	Katherine Bethell, *servant* unto John Cole, *Haberdasher.*
Aug. 14.	Edward, son of George Tapfeild, *Carpenter.*
Aug. 14.	Jane, daughter of the said George.
Aug. 15.	Stevenand William, son of John Cole, *Haberdasher.*
Aug. 15.	A Crisome of William Gibbons.
Aug. 19.	George Tapfeild, *Carpenter.*
Aug. 20.	Rebecca, wife of John Ling, *Oyleman.*
Aug. 24.	Thomas Martin, *Taylor*, his wife and child, and also Anne Keale.
Aug. 26.	Katherine, daughter of Edward Delves, *Goldsmith*, buried in Pawles Churchyard.
Aug. 28.	William Gibbons, *Merchantaylor.*
Aug. 31.	Samuell, son of Suzan Whitby, *Widdow.*
Sep. 1.	Anne, daughter of John Beeston, *Paynter Stayner*, and Andrew Mallett, both of them buried out of Mr. Beeston's house.

Sep. 3.	Thomas Burden, *Sexton of this Parish.*
Sep. 9.	Jane Burden, *Widdowe.*
Sep. 10.	Thomas Flud, *servant* unto John Beeston.
Sep. 13.	William, son of William Freeman, *Cobler.*
Sep. 13.	Anne, daughter of Raphe Kinge.
Sep. 14.	Sara, daughter of Barbara Bowes, *Widdowe.*
Sep. 16.	Nathaniell, son of Henry Coolinge, and Rebecca his daughter.
Sep. 19.	Anne, daughter of Suzan Gibbons, *Widdowe.*
Sep. 20.	Joke, wife of Henry Coolinge, *Hottpresser.*
Sep. 20.	John Jarfeild, son-in-law to Henry Blackmore, *Goldsmith.*
Sep. 22.	Cicely Lovejoy, *Widdowe.*
Sep. 22.	Katherine, daughter of John Cole, *Haberdasher.*
Sep. 23.	Judith, daughter of Widdowe Sales.
Sep. 25.	Henry Thetford, and likewise Mr. Nevett's man, *Goldsmith.*
Sep. 25.	Jane, daughter of Thomas Burden.
Sep. 28.	Nicholas Hassellwood, *Shoomaker.*
Sep. 29.	Dorothie, daughter of Henry Freeman, *Cobler.*
Oct. 8.	Rebecca, daughter of Raph Baylie, *Hotpresser.*
Oct. 10.	Mabell Waker, *servant* unto Mrs. Sales.
Oct. 15.	John Hampton, *Shoemaker.*
Oct. 19.	Elizabeth, daughter of Edward Leathermore, *Tennis Court Keeper.*
Oct. 28.	Anthony Joblin, a *Lynnenman.*
Nov. 6.	Jane Waker, out of Smithfield, *Stranger.*
Nov. 12.	Bettris, wife of John Downes, *Haberdasher.*
Nov. 15.	Sara, daughter of John Peacock, *Goldsmith.*
Nov. 18.	Robert Downes, *Apothecarry.* Plene [Written in the margin.]
Dec. 24.	Judith Feake, buried in St. Edmund's Church, in Lombard Streete, *Stranger*, but died in this Parish.
Jan. 3.	Ellen, daughter of Alexander Weld, *Druggest.*
Jan. 10.	Humfrey Tulley, *servant* unto William Sparrowe, *Merchantaylor.*
Jan. 20.	Rebecca, daughter of Luke Jackson.
Jan. 31.	Monsieur de Golay, buried in the Chappell of St. James, but died in the house of Paule Foorey, of this Parish.
Mar. 1.	Jane Turner, *Schoolemistress.*

1626

April 4.	Edward Stiles, *servant* unto Samuell Taylor.
April 25.	Anna, daughter of Henry Freeman, *Cobler.*
May 20.	Elizabeth, daughter of William Manley, *Scrivener.*
June 29.	Alexander, son of Richard Weld, *Cobler.*
Aug. 1.	Barbara, of John Gooding.
Sep. 11.	William Guy, *servant* to Raphe Kinge, *Vintner.*
Oct. 5.	Jone, wife of Samuell Taylor, *Chirurgeon.*
Oct. 20.	John, son of George Beast, *Grocer.*
Nov. 28.	Thomas Clarke, *Deputy.*
Dec. 11.	William Wolfall, *Merchantaylor.*
Dec. 12.	William, son of Henry Blackmere, *Goldsmith.*
Jan. 26.	A stillborne child of John Weld, *Goldsmith.*
Feb. 1.	Joane Farfield, daughter of Henry Blackmere, *Goldsmith,* Plene [Written in the margin.]
Mar. 1.	John Bagnall, *a stranger.* Plene [Written in the margin.]

1627

May 28.	Thomas Ticheridge, *Grocer*.
June 27.	George, son of Anne Tapfield.
July 7.	Elizabeth, daughter of Richard Childs.
Aug. 18.	Hanna, daughter of Martin Pollard, *Taylor*.
Aug. 23.	Henry, son of George Underwood, *Silkeman*.
Nov. 9.	Edward Dexter, *servant* to Mr. Gilman.
Dec. 26.	John Carter, *Merchantaylor*.
Jan. 4.	William, son of Francis Bishopp.
Feb. 19.	Hanna, daughter of Robert Sweete, *Merchant*.
Feb. 25.	Stephen, son of Stephen Goodyeare.
Mar. 2.	Anne, daughter of Gilbert Cornelius.
Mar. 12.	Edward, son of John Rogers, *Silkman*.

1628

April 15.	Jane Seares, *Widdowe*.
May 16.	Edmond, son of Edmond Ockley, *Carpenter*.
May 20.	Robert, son of Thomas Cawton, *Clothworker*.
June 18.	Bartholomew, son of Bartholome Gilman, *Merchant*.
July 18.	Richard Briggenshawe, *Cutler*.
July 20.	Henry, son of Henry Sacheverell, *Vintner*.
Aug. 5.	William Lewin.
Aug. 31.	Thomas Manning, *servant* unto Mr. Bromhall.
Sep. 24.	A stillborne child of Thomas Nevetts.
Oct. 3.	Anne, the wife of Thomas Weld, *Grocer*.
Oct. 4.	Bartholomew Pickeringe.
Oct. 4.	Thomas, son of Thomas Willett.
Oct. 26.	Grace, daughter of Enock Porter.
Nov. 7.	Edward White, *Merchant*.
Nov. 23.	Alexander Jesup, *servant* unto Mr. Hawes, *Merchant*.
Dec. 19.	Thomas, daughter of John Weld, *Goldsmith*.
Dec. 26.	Elizabeth and Mary, the daughters of Thomas Cawton.
Dec. 30.	Henry Rowse, *servant* to John Branthwaite.
Feb. 10.	John, son of Martin Pollard, *Merchant Taylor*.
Feb. 13.	John, son of Henry Freeman, *Cobler*.
Feb. 26.	Anne, wife of Henry Blackmere, *Goldsmith*.
Feb. 26.	Judith, wife of Francis Marbury.
Mar. 16.	Thomas, son of Thomas Denman.

1629

April 1.	Richard, son of Thomas Willett, *Merchant*.
April 20.	Susan, daughter of Christopher Branson, *Clothworker*.
April 30.	Elizabeth, daughter of Edward Share, *Merchantaylor*.
May 31.	A Chrisome childe of Stephen Burden, *Haberdasher*.
July 5.	Grisagon, wife of Edward Dexter.
July 27.	Anne, wife of Edward Levermore, *Tennis Court Keeper*.
Aug. 3.	Thomas Robinson, *servant* with Nicholas Brigginshaw, *Cutler*.
Aug. 8.	Margarett, daughter of Richard Treate, *Goldsmith*.
Sep. 4.	Robert Meakin, *Parson*, of Yealdpledum, in Essex.
Oct. 2.	William Terry, *Goldsmith*.
Oct. 17.	William Weld, *Clothworker*.
Nov. 13.	William, son of Thomas Cocks, *Merchant Grocer*.
Dec. 10.	A Chrisome child of Widdowe Weld.

Jan. 25.   Mary Stone, *servant* with Mr. Sweete, *Merchant.*
Mar. 17.   A stillborne childe of John Welde, *Goldsmith.*

1630

April 20.   Abraham, son of Enock Porter, *Clothworker.*
May 2.   William, son of Henry Zacheverell, *Vintner.*
May 10.   Martha Whitfeilds, *Stranger.*
May 19.   Thomas Baylie, *servant* unto Raphe Kinge, *Vintner.*
June 18.   John, son of Anne Fotherby, *Widowe.*
July 28.   Deborah, daughter of William Hubbard, *Habberdasher.*
July 30.   Richard, son of Richard Treate, *Goldsmith.*
Aug. 31.   Elizabeth, daughter of Francis Malberry, *Goldsmith.*
Sep. 18.   Robert, son of Thomas Hudson, *Habberdasher.*
Oct. 16.   Thomas Calton, *Clothworker.*
Oct. 30.   Francis, son of Francis Bishop, *Goldsmith.*
Nov. 9.   John, son of Thomas Calton, *Clothworker.*
Nov. 11.   David Lewes, *servant* unto Thomas Calton.
Dec. 24.   Thomas, son of Edmond Okeley, *Carpenter.*
Jan. 3.   Annie, daughter of Henry Starkey, *Goldsmith.*
Jan. 13.   Edward Nucum, of Lester.
Feb. 1.   John Shalts, *Gentleman, a Stranger*, out of Mr. Paul
           Furres house.
Mar. 1.   Paul Furre, of the Dutch Ordinary.
Mar. 28.   Lydia, daughter of William Mantle, *Goldsmith.*

1631

Mar. 30.   Suzan, daughter of Stephen Burden, *Hottpresser.*
April 16.   Elizabeth, wife of Edward Dexter.
May 30.   Elizabeth, daughter of Henry Blackmere, *Goldsmith.*
July 23.   A stillborne childe of John Rogers, *Silkman.*
Aug. 24.   Roger, the childe of Roger Daniell, *Stacioner.*
Sep. 23.   A stillborne childe of Francis Malberry, *Goldsmith.*
Oct. 28.   Stephen Burden, *Hottpresser.*
Oct. 31.   Robert North, *Dyer.*
Nov. 20.   A stillborne childe of Christopher Branston, *Clothworker.*
Jan. 9.   Barbara Boyse, *Widowe.*
Feb. 25.   Mrs. Alice Bissack, a *Stranger.*
Mar. 14.   William Almons, *Vintner.*
Mar. 13.   Mary, daughter of John Acton, *Goldsmith.*
Mar. 15.   Johan, wife of Richard Ockoles, *Stationer.*
Mar. 29.   Walter Furser, *Goldsmith.*

1632

May 4.   A stillborne child of George Underwood, *Silkeman.*
June 23.   Hughe, son of Thomas Richardson, *Clothworker.*
July 28.   James, son of James Sparrowe, *Habberdasher, Stranger.*
Aug. 14.   Daniell, son of Henry Hovenor, *Merchant.*
Sep. 18.   Richard, son of Anne Fotherby, *Widowe.*
Sep. 27.   Frances, wife of William White, *Habberdasher.*
Nov. 1.   Samuell, son of Anthony Penistone, *Goldsmith.*
Nov. 10.   Elizabeth, daughter of Christopher Branston, *Clothworker.*
Nov. 20.   Thomas, son of Thomas Vinor, *Goldsmith.*
Nov. 20.   James, son of John Linge, *Oyleman.*
Nov. 24.   Lydia, wife of William Mantle, *Goldsmith.*

Jan. 5.	John Gridges, *servant* unto Thomas Cock, *Tobacko Merchant.*
Jan. 24.	Mary, daughter of Godfrey Plummer, *Fishmonger.*
Jan. 28.	A stillborne child of John Johnson, *Gentleman.*
Jan. 30.	Mathew, the son of Mathew, the son of Mathew [*sic*] Gulliford, *Goldsmith.*
Feb. 11.	Ellen, wife of Edward Bisse, *Watchmaker.*

1633

Mar. 25.	William, son of Raphe Boyce, *Habberdasher.*
April 29.	John Hawes, *Merchantaylor.*
May 2.	Rebecka, daughter of William Bodington, *Stranger.*
June 7.	William Manley, *Scrivener.*
July 12.	A stillborne child of George Underwood, *Silkeman.*
Aug. 6.	Sarah, daughter of Mary Hawes, *Widdowe.*
Aug. 30.	Susanna, daughter of Thomas Vinor, *Goldsmith.*
Oct. 1.	Two stillborne children of Samuell Moore, *Goldsmith.*
Oct. 1.	John, son of Henry Freeman, *Cobler.*
Oct. 24.	Rebecka, daughter of William Sanckey, *Goldsmith.*
Nov. 4.	Katherine, wife of George Tench, *Myllener.*
Nov. 18.	Mary, daughter of Francis Jackson, *Perfumer.*
Nov. 28.	Samuell, son of Samuell Moore, *Goldsmith.*
Dec. 17.	Anne Sheveleare, a *Stranger* who came out of Mrs. Furre's house.
Dec. 31.	Angelett, daughter of Samuell Dey, *Merchant.*
Jan. 11.	Margarett, wife of Enock Porter, *Clothworker.*
Jan. 24.	John Morgan, a *Boxemaker*, a *Stranger.*
Jan. 28.	Prudence Walton, *Widow*, a *Stranger* who came out of Mr. Pollington's house.

1634

Mar. 28.	Jane Hacke, *servant* unto Thomas Richardson, *Clothworker.*
April 4.	Emanuell Castleman, *Glasier.*
April 23.	Margery, wife of Thomas Willis, *Chandler.*
Aug. 26.	Ellen, daughter of Thomas Collier, *Goldsmith.*
Sep. 12.	Samuel, son of Samuel Bayley, *Comfittmaker.*
Sep. 17.	Elizabeth, daughter of John Branthwaite, *Silkedier.*
Oct. 8.	Thomas, son of Humfrey Browne, *Girdler, stranger.*
Oct. 11.	Anne, daughter of George Beast, *Grocer.*
Oct. 12.	Dorothy, wife of Humfrey Browne, *Girdler and stranger.*
Oct. 25.	Katherine, wife of Daniel Roberts, *Tallowchandler.*
Oct. 27.	Millesent, daughter of Roger Daniel, *Stationer.*
Nov. 25.	Richard Ocall, *Goldsmith.*
Dec. 16.	William, son of George Best, *Grocer.*
Jan. 21.	Elizabeth, daughter of Godfrey Plummer, *Fishmonger.*
Mar. 6.	Suzan, wife of John Beeston, *Paintersteyner.*
Mar. 13.	Martha, daughter of Richard Butler, *Hotpresser.*
Mar. 20.	Alice, wife of Robert Sweete, *Merchant.*
Mar. 24.	A stillborne child of John Smith, *Draper.*

1635

April 4.	Lovede, daughter of Henry Ware, *Merchant*
May 15.	Frances, daughter of Thomas King, *Merchant.*

May 20.	Anne Davis, *servant* unto William Hubbard, *Haberdasher*.
June 4.	Elizabeth, wife of William Hubbard, *Haberdasher*.
July 3.	Mathew, son of Mathew Gulliford, *Goldsmith*.
Aug. 25.	Bartholomew, son of Bartholomew Gilman, *Merchant*.
Sep. 8.	A crisom of Stephen Goodyeare, *Merchant*.
Sep. 26.	Elizabeth, daughter of Edward Oakeley, *Carpenter*.
Sep. 30.	John, son of John Skinner, *Carpenter*.
Nov. 2.	Lewis Bromall, *Attorney*.
Nov. 10.	Richard Blachford, *Merchantstrainger*.
Nov. 22.	Peter White, *Goldsmith, a strainger*.
Nov. 25.	Elizabeth Rothwell, *servant* unto Mr. Charles Latham, *Drugester*.
Dec. 1.	Thomas, son of Thomas Coxe, *Merchant*.
Dec. 3.	Anne, daughter of Thomas Vynor, *Goldsmith*.
Jan. 18.	James Chamberlin, *Sexton*.
Feb. 7.	Bartholomew, son of Lettis Chamberlin, *Widow*.
Feb. 8.	John Lewis, *Baker*.
Feb. 18.	Francis Chapman, *Goldsmith*.
Mar. 12.	John, son of William Hubbard, *Haberdasher*.

1636

Mar. 25.	William, son of Roger Daniell, *Stacioner*.
Mar. 29.	Lea, wife of Samuell Hovenor, *Merchantstrainger*.
April 24.	William Wilmore, *Shearegrinder*.
May 16.	Ursula Cassellman, *Widow*.
May 26.	Richard, son of Richard Pepis.
June 11.	Martin Cock, *servant* to Mr. Richard Briggenshaw, *Cutler*.
July 11.	Joseph Stockwell, *servant* to Mr. Humble.
July 18.	John Beeston, *Paynterstayner*.
July 22.	William Butcher, *servant* to Mr. Humble.
July 29.	Grace, wife of John Lynly.
Aug. 6.	Stephen Jones, *servant* to Mr. David Jones, *Merchant*.
Aug. 8.	Edmond, son of Francis Jackson, *Perfumer*.
Sep. 5.	Thomas Latham, *servant* to Henry Champney.
Sep. 10.	Dorothy, wife of William White, *Haberdasher*.
Sep. 20.	Thomas Fox, *servant* to Mr. Porter.
Oct. 7.	Anne, wife of Thomas Vinor, *Goldsmith*.
Oct. 13.	Alice Woodson, *servant* to Mr. Morall, *Merchant*.
Oct. 24.	Hugh Richardson, *Draper*.
Jan. 3.	Judith Ronkesby, *Widdow, a strainger* who came out of Cheapside, in the Parish of St. Madlin's, Milk Streete.
Feb. 9.	Phillis Sherman, *Widdow*.*
Mar. 18.	Alice Lewis, *Widdow*.
Mar. 29.	John, son of Samuell Dey, *Merchant*.

1637

April 16.	William, son of William Mantle, *Goldsmith*.
April 22.	Robert Stockdell, *servant* to Michael Gardner, *Vintner*.
May 1.	Jonathan Tille, *servant* unto William Mantle, *Goldsmith*.
July 6.	William Rawlins, *Goldsmith*.
July 17.	Thomas, son of Thomas Vynor, *Goldsmith*.
Sep. 1.	Nathaniell Moone, *a strainger*, buried in the Quire, close to Sir Martin Bowes his stone.
Oct. 9.	Suzan, daughter of William Mantle, *Goldsmith*.

* "Mrs. Seaman, Stranger." Ch Acc.

Nov. 12.	Mathew Whitefield, kinswoman of Mr. Willis.
Nov. 16.	John, son of Anthony Peningston, *Goldsmith.*
Nov. 25.	Suzanna, daughter of Nicholas Collett, *Goldsmith.*
Dec. 2.	Elizabeth, wife of William Exton.
Dec. 13.	Rowland, son of John Feake, *Goldsmith.*
Dec. 27.	William Eversley, *Goldsmith*, being a Pensioner.
Jan. 15.	Roger Hill, *Merchantaylor, a strainger.*
Mar. 1.	Anne, daughter of Robert Sweete, *Merchant.*
Mar. 14.	Jane Beesan, kinswoman of Hector du Mount, *Merchant-strainger.*

1638

April 11.	Stephen Morton, *servant* to Richard Butler, *Hotpresser.*
April 20.	Thomas, son of Thomas Weld, *Druggester.*
May 14.	Amy, daughter of Thomasin King, *Widdow, a strainger.*
June 25.	Mary, daughter of Obediah Guilliams, *Haberdasher.*
July 3.	William Breeres, *Goldsmith, a strainger*, brought out of the Parish of St. Leonard, Shoreditch.
Sep. 5.	Jane, daughter of Francis Jackson, *Perfumer.*
Sep. 13.	William Lowen, *servant* to Nicholas Meade, *Druggester.*
Sep. 15.	Mary Ward, *Widdow.*
Sep. 18.	Sara Meakyns, *Widdow, a strainger.*
Sep. 20.	William, son of Richard Popis, *Merchant.*
Oct. 4.	Edward Delves, *Goldsmith.*
Oct. 5.	John, son of John Feake, *Goldsmith.*
Oct. 12.	Anne, daughter of William Manwaring, *Goldsmith.*
Oct. 26.	Thomas Willett, *Merchant.*
Nov. 10.	Richard, son of John Shipman, *Bricklayer.*
Nov. 17.	Hannah, daughter of John Rolfe, *Scrivener.*
Nov. 23.	Walter Gill, a lodger in Mr. Gill's house.
Nov. 27.	Bridgett, daughter of Thomas Weld, *Druggester.*
Dec. 21.	A stillborne child of Raphe Boyce, *Hotpresser.*
Dec. 22.	Thomasin, daughter of Hugh Morrall, *Marchant.*
Jan. 8.	Mary, daughter of John Martin, *Grocer.*
Feb. 2.	Rebecca, daughter of Josuah Saunders, *Gentleman.*
Mar. 9.	Wayman, son of ———— Smith, of ————, in the County of Essex, *Gent.* [*sic*]
Mar 18.	Francis Marbury, *Goldsmith.*
Mar. 23.	James Collard, *Merchant, a Strainger.*
Mar. 23.	A stillborne child of Walter Smith, *Baker.*
Mar. 28.	Anne Ball, *Widdow.*

1639

April 10.	Anne, wife of Hector du Mount.
April 13.	John Tailor, *Gent., a Strainger.*
Sep. 6.	Stephen, son of Robert Fossett, *Millener.*
Sep. 24.	John Goodwin, *Goldsmith.*
Oct. 2.	Edward, son of William White, *Haberdasher.*
Oct. 10.	Thomas, son of Richard Rednal, *Merchant.*
Nov. 14.	Sara, daughter of Stephen Goodyear, *Merchant.*
Dec. 2.	Daniel, son of Abraham Johnson.
Dec. 18.	Thomas, son of Captain Thomas King.
Dec. 27.	Margarett, daughter of Thomas Collyer, *Goldsmith.*
Jan. 18.	John Ward, *Draper.*
Jan. 22.	Thomas, son of Thomas Baker, *Merchant.*

Feb. 6.	A stillborne child of John Steele, *Vintner.*
Feb. 26.	Edward Gills, *Plasterer, Strainger.*

1640

April 1.	Thomas, son of Thomas Weld, *Druggester.*
April 20.	Anne, daughter of Thomas Wade, *Merchant.*
July 1.	Henry, the Kinsman of Symon Baker.
July 15.	Elizabeth, daughter of Obedia Guilliams, *Merchant.*
July 22.	Nicholas, son of Nicholas Meade, *Druggester.*
Aug. 21.	Adrian Evans, *Merchant.*
Aug. 27.	James West, *servant* to William Woodcock, *Stranger.*
Sep. 2.	Anne Rothwell, *servant* to Mr. Charles Latham, *Druggester.*
Sep. 4.	John, son of John Feake, *Goldsmith.*
Sep. 6.	A stillborne child of Giles Pooley, *Merchant.*
Nov. 2.	Elizabeth Moone, *Widdow.**
Nov. 7.	John Cole, *Haberdasher.*
Nov. 11.	Thomas Rabones, *servant* to Mr. King, *Vintner.*
Nov. 24.	Thomas Willis, *Chandler.*
Dec. 15.	Elizabeth, daughter of William Townsin, *Gilder.*
Dec. 17.	Mr. George Humble, *Leatherseller,* Deputie of this Ward.
Jan. 2.	Bartholomew, son of Bartholomew Layton, *Merchant.*
Jan. 3.	Elizabeth, wife of William Townsin, *Painterstainer.*
Jan. 7.	David, son of William Morehead, *Merchant.*
Jan. 8.	Anne Everley, *Widdow.*
Jan. 14.	Prudence, daughter of William Townsin, *Painterstainer.*
Jan. 14.	Curtis, son of James Fletcher, *Baker.*
Jan. 23.	Elizabeth, daughter of John Shipman, *Bricklayer.*
Jan. 28.	Anne, wife of John Johnson, *stranger.*
Jan. 29.	William, son of William Hughson, *Gent.*
Feb. 9.	Mary, daughter of Thomas Nevett, *Goldsmith.*
Feb. 18.	Elizabeth, wife of Ambrose Brunskell, *Silkman,* being a stranger.
Mar. 9.	Mathew Smith, *servant* to James Fletcher, *Baker.*
Mar. 13.	Thomas Hollowell, *servant* to Mr. Holt, *Goldsmith.*
Mar. 20.	Benjamin, son of Anthony Penniston, *Goldsmith.*

1641

April 20.	Mr. Collier's child.
May 2.	William Barton, *servant* to Clement Pung, *Goldsmith.*
May 21.	Thomas Gardner, *Merchant, a stranger.*
May 21.	Christian, daughter of Raph Boys, *Hotpresser.*
May 30.	Thomas, son of John Feake, *Goldsmith.*
June 19.	Richard Vance, *Goldsmith.*
June 23.	Robert Carter, *servant* to Mr. Butler, *Hottpresser.*
July 3.	Joane, daughter of Thomas Hodges, *Goldsmith.*
July 4.	John, son of Nicholas Collett, *Goldsmith.*
July 6.	Elizabeth, daughter of William Manwaring, *Goldsmith.*
Sep. 8.	Sara, daughter of William Mantle, *Goldsmith.*
Sep. 13.	A stillborne child of Mr. Giles Pooley, *Merchant.*
Sep. 14.	Joseph, son of Richard Gerrad, *Merchant.*
Sep. 19.	Deborah, wife of Giles Pooley, *Merchant.*
Sep. 29.	John Crawley, a *Stranger.*
Oct. 15.	Robert Turnor, *servant* to Mr. Willis.
Oct. 18.	Ellen, wife of Edward Cheare, *Merchantaylor.*
Oct. 27.	Mr. Allexander Reade, *Doctor of Phisicke.*

* "Mrs. Moone, a Stranger." Ch. Acc.

End of Burials in Vol. I of Registers.

Vol. ij.

THE names of such as have bine buried in the Parishe of St. Mary Wolnothe in London Sithence the Seven and Twentieth day of October Anno Domini 1641.

1641

Jan. 11.	John, son of Francis Jacksonn, *Perfumer*.
Jan. 26.	Jane Huswife, daughter of Mr. Cox, *Merchant*.
Feb. 4.	Katherine Styler, *servant* unto William Manweringe, *Goldsmith*.
Feb. 17.	A stillborne childe of Samuell Mores, *Goldsmith*.
Feb. 18.	Abraham, son of John Steele, *Vintener*.
Feb. 19.	Uceseday, wife of Mr. William Cheney, *Esquire*, a *Strainger*.
Feb. 20.	Mary Roberts, which came from Mr. Coxe's house.
Feb. 21.	Sara, wife of John Smith, *Merchantstranger*.
Mar. 16.	Anthony Dengalam, a *Norwich Merchant*.

1642

April 7.	Nicholas Meade, *Drugster*.
April 26.	Edmond Oakely, *Carpenter*.
May 8.	Jane Jevans, *servant* to Mr. Danyell.
June 6.	Thomas Potter, *Haberdasher*.
June 9.	Sara, daughter of George Glydewell.
June 23.	Margarett Evans, *Widow*.
Aug. 17.	Elizabeth, daughter of Anne Gower, *Widow*.
Sep. 2.	John, son of John Portman, *Goldsmith*.
Sep. 17.	Elizabeth, daughter of Thomas Cox, *Merchant*.
Sep. 18.	John, son of Robert Bullard, *Merchantaylor*.
Nov. 8.	Rogger, son of Rogger Wotton, *Merchant*.
Nov. 8.	Mary, daughter of Thomas Richardson, *Clothworker*.
Dec. 17.	Martha Care, *servant* unto Thomas Richardson.
Dec. 27.	William, son of William Hubberd, *Haberdasher*.
Jan. 12.	Elizabeth, daughter of Mr. Thomas Cox, *Merchant*.
Jan. 14.	Mary, daughter of Abraham Johnson, *Merchant*.
Feb. 2.	Mary, daughter of Samuell More, *Goldsmith*.
Feb. 3.	Bartholomew Gilman, *Scrivener*.
Feb. 9.	Mary, daughter of Richard Garret, *Merchant*.
Feb. 17.	Isabell, daughter of Samuell More, *Goldsmith*.
Feb. 18.	William, son of Captaine Marshe.
Feb. 20.	Martha, wife of Captaine Marshe.
Mar. 15.	Frances, daughter of Francis Jackson.

1643

April 11.	Mathew Edwards, *Grocer*.
April 18.	Joseph Skinner, *Merchant*.
April 19.	Anne Harrod, *servant* unto Mr. Saunders, *Drugester*.
April 22.	Marie, daughter of Charles Latham.
May 1.	John, son of William Hughsonne, *Attornie*.
May 1.	Sarah, daughter of Edward Grange, *Bricklayer*.
May 14.	Robert Bullock, *Merchantaylor*.
May 29.	Josias, son of Charles Latham, *Drugster*.
June 6.	William, son of George Best, *Grocer*.

June 9.	John, son of William Mantle, *Goldsmith*.
June 13.	Thomas, son of John Crumpton, *Goldsmith*.
June 14.	Mr. Josias Shute, *Parson of this Parish*.
June 17.	Sara, daughter of William Manweringe.
Aug. 2.	Captaine Soloman Richardson.
Sep. 20.	Anne, wife of Raphe Boyse, *Hottpresser*.
Oct. 6.	A stillborne child of Thomas Cox, *Merchant*.
Oct. 14.	Suzanna, grandchild unto Mr. Furlo.
Oct. 20.	Jane Whichchurch.
Oct. 22.	Elizabeth Manly, *servant* unto Mrs. Manly.
Nov. 6.	Judith, daughter of Thomas Richardson, *Clothworker*.
Nov. 16.	Elizabeth, wife of Nicholas Gardner, *Gent.*, *a stranger*.
Jan. 8.	Anthonie, son of Richard Brigenshaw, *Cutler*.
Jan. 15.	Margaret, wife of Enock Porter, *Clothworker*.
Jan. 15.	Marie, wife of Thomas Richardson, *Clothworker*.
Mar. 4.	Josua, son of Caleb Nicholas.
Mar. 14.	Mathew, son of Charles Latham, *Drugster*.

1644

May 3.	Mr. Thomas Witham, *Parson of this Parish*.
May 13.	Edward Dexter, *Clarke of this Church*.
July 3.	Edward, son of Christopher Anio, *Victualler*, and of Mary his wife.
June 20.	Henry, son of Raph Kinge, *Vintner*.
July 28.	Thomas, son of Thomas Wild, *Druggister*.
Aug. 26.	A child of Edward Gringe.
Aug. 28.	John Sanders, *Druggister*.
Sep. 26.	Elizabeth, daughter of Anthony Penniston, *Goldsmith*.
Oct. 28.	Allen, son of Raph Boice, *Hottpresser*.
Oct. 29.	Joseph, son of Anthony Penniston, *Goldsmith*.
Nov. 1.	Abigall, daughter of Thomas Coxe.
Nov. 2.	George Phenix, *Upholster*.
Nov. 7.	The wife of Richard Knite, *Porter*.
Nov. 19.	Mary Pellinge, *servant* to Mr. Mannering.
Nov. 22.	Daniell Buller and Anne Boyce.
Nov. 23.	Raph Boyce and Magdalen Boice.
Nov. 25.	Peter and Jane Boyce, in one grave, children of Raph Boice.
Dec. 2.	William, son of William Huson, *Attorney*.
Dec. 13.	John, son of Anthony Penniston.
Feb. 10.	Mrs. Denloo.
Mar. 12.	Elizabeth Greaves, *servant* to Mr. Mannering.
Mar. 12.	Daniell, son of John Shipman.

1645

May 18.	Widow Manly.
July 17.	A stillborne childe of Mr. Willington.
Aug. 1.	Hester, daughter of Hester Vanse, *Widow*.
Aug. 20.	Bridgett, daughter of Thomas Fenix.
Aug. 26.	William, son of William Monday, *Tailor*.
Sep. 14.	A stillborne child of Mr. William Manneringe.
Oct. 17.	Mathew Dexter, *Clarke of this Parish Church*.
Oct. 21.	Mrs. Ann, wife of Mr. George Humble.
Oct. 30.	Edward, son of Edward Tuckberry [Stuchbury, written in margin], *Joiner*.

Nov. 12.	Mary, daughter of John Portman, *Goldsmith.*
Dec. 7.	Edward, son of Edward Gringe, *Bricklayer.*
Dec. 11.	John, son of Richard Rednall, *Merchant.*
Dec. 7.	[inserted here] Mary Arnett, *servant* to Mr. Fenix.
Dec. 16.	Joane, daughter of John Exton, *Cutler.*
Dec. 25.	James, son of James Baker.
Jan. 2.	Anne, daughter of William Rolfe.
Jan. 2.	Samuel, son of Nicolas Crosse.
Jan. 6.	Lettice, daughter of Richard Joy, of Bedford, *Gent.*
Jan. 17.	Charles, son of Francis Jackson, *Perfumer.*
Jan. 20.	Thomas Mounteney, *servant* to Mr. Brinkinshaw, *Cutler.*
Jan. 27.	William, son of Mathew Dexter.
Feb. 11.	Daniell Roberts, *Tallowchandler.*
Feb. 18.	Edward Roman, *servant* to Mr. Bishopp, *Goldsmith.*

1646

April 13.	John Hill, *Goldsmith.*
May 7.	William, son of Richard Vaughan, *Joyner.*
June 17.	James Loe.
June 26.	Thomas, son of Edward Lleeds, of Griston, in the County of Cambridge, *Esquire*, buried out of Samuell White's house, Haberdasher.
July 8.	Ann, daughter of Robert Saile, *Merchant.*
July 23.	Mary, daughter of Daniell Morris, *Plasterer.*
July 26.	Josias, son of Thomas Jarman, *Clarke.*
July 31.	Andrew Quash, *Merchant*, of Exiter.
Aug. 1.	Thomas, son of Clement Ponge, *Goldsmith.*
Aug. 5.	A crisome of Mr. Jacob Jurion, of the French Congregacion, *Merchant.*
Aug. 12.	Elizabeth, daughter of Robert Boucher, *Grocer.*
Aug. 11.	John Bease, *Clothworker.*
Aug. 18.	Amey, daughter of John Willington, *Haberdasher.*
Sep. 12.	Walter Smith, *Baker.*
Oct 1.	Frances Brambrick, *servant* to Mr. Willis, *Victualler.*
Oct. 24.	Elizabeth Algate, Widow.
Jan. 5.	George, son of Lettice Chamberlin.
Jan. 8.	Elizabeth, wife of Abraham Johnson, *Merchant.*
Feb. 29.	Jerman Honychurch, *Merchant.*
Mar. 4.	Thomas Humble, *Draper*, out of Mr. William Humble's house.
Mar. 22.	Israell, son of William Paybody, *Boxmaker.*

1647

April 25.	Rebecca, daughter of Richard Middleton, *Translater.*
May 10.	Mary, daughter of Robert Gall.
May. 31.	Mary, wife of Richard Bancks, *Merchant.*
June 1.	Elizabeth, wife of Symon Baker.
July 13.	Thomas, son of Mr. Thomas Humble, *Merchant*, and of Elizabeth, his wife.
Aug. 5.	A female child, a foundling in Sherborne Lane.
Aug. 7.	Anne, wife of John Exoll, *Cutler.*
Aug. 31.	Abraham, son of Abraham Browne, *Vintner.*
Aug. 31.	William Greene, *stranger.*
Sep. 7.	Samuell Hiron, *servant* to Mr. Howe, *Bookebynder.*

Sep. 13.	Sarah, daughter of John Crumpton, *Goldsmith.*
Sep. 14.	Mrs. Frances Keighteley.
Sep. 16.	William, son of Thomas Coller, *Goldsmith.*
Oct. 2.	Ellen, daughter of William Mantle, *Tayler.*
Nov. 8.	Margarett, wife of John Runwell.
Nov. 10.	Love, daughter of Francis Jackson, *Perfumer.*
Nov. 13.	Susan, daughter of Charles Latham, *Druggester.*
Nov. 22.	Elizabeth, daughter of Charles Latham.
Dec. 28.	Mary, daughter of Abraham Clark, *Merchant.*
Dec. 31.	Mrs. Anne Bromwall, *Gent.*
Jan. 18.	John Branthwayte, *Silkdyer.*
Feb. 4.	Martha, daughter of Nicholas Collett, *Goldsmith.*
Feb. 10.	Mr. William Rolfe, *Goldsmith.*
Feb. 16.	Jane, wife of Daniell Morris, *Playsterer.*
Mar. 3.	A stillborne child of Mr. Alderman Viner.
Mar. 15.	Sarah, daughter of Thomas Ganhans.
Mar. 31.	Judeth, daughter of Robert Bowcher, *Grocer.*

1648

April 7.	Thomas Richardson.
April 8.	Hannah, daughter of Robert Gale, *Merchant.*
April 8.	Jacob, son of Raph Boyce.
May 11.	Elizabeth, wife of Mr. John Crumpton, *Goldsmith.*
May 11.	Roger, son of William Mantle.
May 12.	A stillborne child of Edward Tuchbury, *Joyner.*
June 29.	A stillborne child of Abraham Browns, *Vintner.*
July 11.	William Exton, *Cutler.*
July 29.	Aron, son of Alexander Pollington.
Sep. 18.	Dorothy, wife of Roger Daniell, *Leatherseller.*
Oct. 2.	Anne Rolfe, *Widow.*
Nov. 6.	Elizabeth Raphle, *Widow.*
Nov. 27.	Thomas Clark, *servant* to Richard Midleton.
Dec. 11.	Martha Walker, *Widow.*
Dec. 15.	Martha Foster, *Widow.*
Jan. 14.	Laurence, son of John Bramble.
Feb. 7.	John, son of John Baber, *Taylor.*
Feb. 18.	Two Chrisoms, children of Stephen Bowtell, *Bookseller.*
Mar. 19.	Isaack, son of Abraham Johnson.

1649

May 17.	William Sturgiss, *Merchantaylor*, who lived in the house of Mr. Cross, *Blacksmith,* in Abchurch Lane.
May 18.	Mary, daughter of Jacob Jurion, *Merchant.*
May 30.	James Ferne, *servant* to Mr. Portman, *Goldsmith.*
June 26.	Eling, wife of Mr. ——— [*sic*] Petres.
July 15.	A fondling.
July —— [*sic*]	Richard Vahan, *Joyner.*
Aug. 19.	James Persy, *servant* to Mr. Chubb, *Cook.*
Sep. 1.	Mary, wife of Charles Lathum, *Grocer.*
Sep. 2.	William Worth, *servant* to Captain Hubbard, *Haberdasher.*
Sep. 20.	Phebe Knell, the *servant* to Mr. Brush.
Oct. 2.	Daniel, son of Thomas Jarman, *Clerke of this Parish.*
Oct. 5.	Samuel Curtis, of Myldred in the Poultry.
Oct. 12.	Barnabie, son of Thomas Coates.

Nov. 9.	Jane, wife of Edward Tuchbory, *Joyner*.
Dec. 19.	Thomas, son of John Willington, *Haberdasher*.
Dec. 16.	William, son of John Steele, *Vintner*, and of Mary, his wife.
Dec. 20.	Marie, daughter of Enoch Porter, *Clothworker*.
Jan. 2.	Arthur, son of Rowland Dee, *Merchant*, and of Jane, his wife.
Feb. 2.	Suzan, wife of Alexander Holt, *Citizen and Leatherseller*, of London. Buried in the vault of Sir Thomas Ramsey.
Feb. 11.	Phillip, son of John Portman and Mary his wife.
Mar. 4.	Mary, daughter of Abraham Browne, *Vintner*.

1650

April 13.	Richard Knight, *Porter*.
April 19.	Sarah, daughter of John Smith, *Merchant*.
May 13.	John, son of John Phipps, *Merchant*.
May 26.	Rebeccah, daughter of Steven Bowtell, *Bookseller*.
June 4.	Rebeccah, daughter of John Runwell, *Glasier*.
July 17.	Katherin, daughter of William Huson, *Gentleman*.
Aug. 19.	Joyce Peerks, *servant* to Mr. Daniell Morris, *Plasterer*.
Sep. 25.	Anne Willmore, a maid that lived in the Parish of St. Bartholomew, behind the Exchange.
Oct. 20.	Suzan, wife of Richard Vahan.
Nov 6.	Sarah, wife of Thomas Canham, *Merchant*.
Dec. 28.	Elizabeth, daughter of John Crumpton, *Goldsmith*.
Mar. 6.	John, son of Richard Bunckle, by Bridget his wife.
Mar. 22.	Edward Vavasour, *Grocer*.

1651

Mar. 27.	Anne, daughter of Robert Bowcher, *Grocer*, by Judith, his wife.
April 10.	David Clarke, *Merchant and stranger*, was buried in the vault of Sir Thomas Ramsey. He was brought out Bennett Fynch Parish.
June 24.	Francis Cole, apprentice to Mr. Isaac Allen, *Merchant*.
July 15.	Mistress Mary Monnox, *Widdow*, who died in the Parish of St. Giles', Criplegate, London.
Aug. 21.	James Armstead, *servant* to Mr. Moyses Browne, *Milliner*.
Sep. 10.	Stephen Scaresbrook, who died at Mr. Mantles, *Goldsmith*.
Sep. 15.	Michaell Gardner, *Citizen and Vintner of London*.
Sep. 19.	Mary, daughter of Thomas Jerman, *Weaver and Clark of this Parish*.
Sep. 29.	Raph, son of Charles Lathum.
Oct. 5.	Elizabeth, daughter of Theophilus Joyner, *Taylor*.
Oct. 10.	Stephen, son of Stephen Bowtell, *Bookseller*, by Suzan his wife.
Oct. 21.	Henry Blackmore, *Citizen and Goldsmith of London*.
Nov. 11.	Margarett Beck, *Widdowe*, mother of Mr. John Willington.
Nov. 28.	Samuell, son of John Runwell, by Jane his wife.
Jan. 1.	Towe abortive children of Mr. Lawrence Steele, *Merchant*.
Jan. 8.	Joseph, son of William Ewstes, by Sarah his wife.
Jan. 9.	Mary, daughter of Widdowe Ponn, living in Mr. Morgan's house in Abchurch Lane.
Jan. 22.	Charles, son of Charles Lathum.

Feb. 4   William son of John Exton, by Jane his wife.
Feb. 24.   Elizabeth, daughter of Mr. John Hill, *Goldsmith*, by
              Suzana his wife.
Mar. 20.   Elizabeth Jones, the sister of Hugh Jones, *Grocer*.
Mar. 23.   Hugh, son of Hugh Jones, *Grocer*, by Elizabeth his wife.

1652

April 12.   A small child that was taken upp dead, under the stall
              Mr. W. Hills, *Druggester* his shop, was buried in the
              Churchyard, by the order of the Crowner of London.
June 21.   Francis, wife of Thomas Coxe, *Tobaccoe-cutter*.
July 4.   Mary, daughter of Samuell Wright, *Bookebinder*, and of
              Suzan his wife.
July 7.   Sarah, daughter of Theophilus Joyner, *Taylor*, and of
              Elizabeth his wife.
July 30.   Thomas Watson, *Citizen and Goldsmith of London*.
Aug. 2.   Thomas, son of William Paybody, *Boxemaker*.
Aug. 10.   William, son of Robert Jones, by Joanna his wife.
Aug. 14.   Robert Downer, who was an inmate, and died at the house
              of Mr. Crosse, *Blacksmith*, in Abchurch Lane, London.
July 17.   Suzan Judd, the mother of Mrs. Watson, of this Parish,
              died at her house.
Sep. 11.   Margarett, daughter of Leonard Collard, *Gouldsmith*.
Sep. 11.   James Wattes, *servant* to Mr. Chubb, *Cooke*, *in* Abchurch
              Lane
Sep. 13.   Penelope, wife of Abraham Browne, *Vintener*.
Sep. 20.   Israell, son of William Paybody, *Boxemaker*.
Oct. 25.   James Fletcher, *Baker*.
Oct. 27.   Gabriell Dowsc, *servant* to Mr. William Godbed, *Watch-
              maker*.
Dec. 13.   Edmond, son of Richard Butler.
Dec. 18.   Lidia, wife of Thomas Wilcox, *Citizen ond Turner of
              London*, and sister to Mr. Nathaniell Cock, of this
              Parish.
Dec. 20.   John, son of John Runwell, and of Suzan his wife.
Jan. 6.   Anne Exton, *Widdowe*, by trade a *Cutler of Knives*.
Jan. 20.   William Hubbard, *Citizen and Merchantaylor of London*.
Feb. 28.   Died, Isabell Turner, *Widdowe*, sister-in-lawe to Mr.
              Whitehead, *Goldsmith*, and was buryed the 1st Mar.
              following.

1653

May 29.   Died, Christian, the wife of John Willington, and was bur.
              May 31.
May 30.   Died, Lawrence Cockine, at Mr. Orenges, the *Bricklayer*
              in Beerebinder Lane, and was bur. May 31.
June 21.   Henry Henshawe, sonne-in-law to Widdowe Ockley, was
              bur.
June 26.   William, son of William Paybody, inmate at Mr. Jackson's,
              in Beerbinder Lane, was bur.
July 4.   A chrisom child of Edward and Sarah Backwell.
July 15.   A stillborne childe of Richard Sturgis.
Sep. 26.   Died, Elizabeth, daughter of George and Prudence Manley,
              Taylor, bur. Sep. 27.

Oct. 28.	Died, Elizabeth, daughter of Robert and Judeth Bowcher, *Citizen and Grocer of London*, bur. Oct. 31.
Nov. 2.	Died, Thomas Humble, *Merchant and Citizen of London*, bur. Nov. 4, under the stone in the quier, where his father, George Humble, *Esquier*, lieth.
Nov. 11	Died, Phillip Tesdelie, *servant* to Thomas Vyner, nowe Lord Mayor of London, buried Nov. 14.
Nov. 24.	Died, Mary Maudlin Blackmore, *Widdowe*, bur. Nov. 25.
Nov. 24.	Died, Mary Allen, bur. Nov. 28.
Dec. 3.	Died, John Holmes, father to Martin Holmes, *Barber*, bur. Dec. 4.
Dec. 4.	Died, Margarett Hewes, *maidservant* to Mr. John Steele, bur. Dec. 5.
Dec. 6.	Died, Nathaniell, son of William and Elizabeth Rason, bur. Dec. 8.
Dec. 10.	Died, Mary Skelton, bur. Dec. 11.
Dec. 20.	Died, Mary Hambleton, *Widdowe*, she came out of Mr. Wollestone's house.
Dec. 31.	Died, Margery Colle, *Widdowe*, *Burnisher* by trade, bur. Jan. 1.
Jan. 9.	Bur., Nicholas Wooldham, *Feltmaker*.
Mar. 8.	Died, Robert Jones, father of Robert Jones, *Confectioner*, whoe came from Malborowe, bur. Mar. 14.
Mar. 9.	Died, Allexander, son of Rowland and Jane Dee, bur. Mar. 10.

1654

April 6.	Died, William, son of John and Elizabeth Thompson, bur. April 7.
April 16.	Died, Peter White, *Citizen and Haberdasher* of London (sonne of Doctor John White), of the Parish of St. Antholins, London.
May 14.	Died, Benjamin, son of William and Susanna Stringer, bur. May 14.
July 9.	Died, Thomas Cox, *Citizen and Salter*, of London, bur. July 12.
July 19.	Died, Phillipp, son of John Portman.
Aug. 13.	Bur., a crisome child of Richard Jesse.
Sep. 18.	Died, Jane, daughter of Rowland Dee.
Sep. 22.	Died, Mary, daughter of Henry Ballowe, bur. Sep. 23.
Oct. 8.	Dyed, Edward Leathermore, a penconer of this Parish, bur. Oct. 9.
Nov. 2.	Bur., an abortive child of Mr. Richerd Bunckley, *Merchant*.
Nov. 8.	Bur., Elizabeth, daughter of Francis Joanes.
Nov. 17.	Died, Randell Weld, *servant* to Samuell White, *Haberdasher*, bur. Nov. 18.
Dec. 27.	Died, William Barwicke, *servant* to William Hewson, bur. Dec. 29.
Feb. 19.	Died, Margarett Burden, *Widdowe*, bur. Feb. 20.
Feb. 25.	Died, John, son of William and Elizabeth Browne, bur. Feb. 25.
Feb. 25.	Died, Temperance, daughter of John and Anne Willington, bur. Feb. 26.
Mar. 13.	Bur., a stillborne child of Mr. Joell Coxe.
Mar. 14.	Died, William Munns, *Stranger*, bur. Mar. 15.

1655

April 8.	Died, Joyce, daughter of Thomas and Joyce Weld, *Grocer*, bur. April, 11.
April 22.	Died, Hester, daughter of Isaac and Rebecca Allen, *Merchant*, bur. April
May 17.	Died, Henry, son Mary Henshawe, *Widdowe*.
May 29.	Bur., an abortive child of Mr. Charles Everard.
June 15.	Died, Mr. Ralph Robinson, the *Minister of this Parish*, bur. June 18.
June 20.	Died, Sarah, daughter of John and Sarah Halsey, bur. June 21.
Aug. 11.	Died, Benjamine, son of Abraham Smith, bur. Aug. 13.
Aug. 20.	Died, Samuell, son of William Ewster, bur. Aug. 21.
Oct. 3.	Died, Francis, son of Francis Meynell, *Goldsmith*.
Nov. 20.	Died, John Perrott, *Scrivener*, bur. Nov.
Nov. 23.	Died, Thomas Nevett, *Goldsmith*, bur. Nov. 29.
Dec. 10.	Died, Susan Clarke, of London, *Widdowe*, she was brought out of St. Bennett Finck's Parish and bur. Dec. 21 in a vault called Sir Thomas Ramsey's vault, lyeth by her husband and daughter.
Dec. 21.	Died, Elizabeth, wife of Henry Woolaston, *Haberdasher*, bur. Dec. 27.
Dec. 29.	Died, Elizabeth, wife of Thomas Chubb, *Cooke*, bur. Dec. 30.
Jan. 15.	Died, Abraham Smith, *Goldsmith*, bur. Jan. 16.
Feb. 16.	Bur., John, son of Robert and Joana Jones.
Feb. 19.	Died, Frances, daughter of James Whitehead, *Goldsmith*, bur. Feb. 21.

1656

April 1.	Died, Samuell Brocke, *servant* to the Worshipfull William Humble, *Esquire*, bur. April 2.
April 8.	Died, Sarah, daughter of John and Sarah Skacher, bur. April 9.
April 12.	Died, at Grinsted, in Sussex, Mrs. Anne Hill, *Widdowe*, bur. in the body of the Church.
April 14.	Died, Daniell, son of William and Suzan Stringer.
April 21.	Died, Robert Fletcher, *a serving man* unto the Worshipfull Sir Thomas Vyner, bur. April 22.
April 27.	Bur., Alexander Johnson, *Blacksmith*, Pentioner of this Parish.
May 10.	Bur., Jane, daughter of John and Jane Ellis.
May 18.	Died, Margery, wife of Richard Butler, of Abschurch Lane, bur. May 21.
May 22.	Died, Henry Freeman, bur. May 24.
June 12.	Bur., Francis Chapman, hee came out of St. Giles, Cripplegate Parish, *a stranger*.
June 26.	Died, the Lady Honor Vyner, the wife of the Worshipfull Sir Thomas Vyner, *Knight and Alderman of this City*, bur. July 10.
July 13.	Died, Thomas, son of Nicholas and Jane Collett, *Goldsmith*, bur. July 14.
July 30	Died, Anne, daughter of John and Jane Exton, *Cutler*, bur. June 31.

Aug. 3.   Died, Samuell, son of Samuell and Rhoda Toft, *Merchant*, bur. Aug. 4.

Aug. 3.   Died, Sarah, daughter of Stephen and Susanna Bowtell, *Bookeseller*, bur. Aug. 4.

Sep. 4.   Died, Annabella, daughter of William Humble, *Esquire*, and of Elizabeth, his wife.

Sep. 11.   Died, Thomas, son of John and Mary Waters, bur. Sep. 12.

Sep. 27.   Died, Francis Collier, *servant* unto Richard Jesse, *Cooke*, bur. Sep. 28.

Oct. 2.   Died, Jesper, son of John and Sarah Sketcher, bur. Oct. 3.

Oct. 9.   Died, Robert Hall, *Esquire*, bur. Oct. 14.

Jan. 1.   Died, Mary Carpenter, wife of — [*sic*] Carpenter, of Newington, Middlesex, bur. Jan. 30. She was daughter to Lettis Chamberlaine, of this Parish, *Widdowe*.

Jan. 27.   Died, Mary, daughter of the deceased William Hubbard, *Habberdasher of Hatts*, bur. Jan. 30.

1657

April 20.   Died, Elizabeth, wife of Hugh Jones, of Queenhithe, bur. April 22.

April 20.   Died, John Eies, *Minister, a stranger*, at Mr. John Rason's house, of this Parish, bur. April 24.

April 28.   Died, Alexander Holt, *Esquire*, bur. May 8. in the vault called Sir Thomas Ramsey's vault.

June 24.   Elizabeth, daughter of Owen and Marie Win.

July 17.   Bur., Margaret, daughter of John and Sarah Halsey.

Aug. 2.   Died, Joh Dove, at Mr. Firmin.

Aug. 7.   Bur., — [*sic*] daughter of William Paybody.

Aug. 22.   Died, Sarah, daughter of Robert and Judeth Bowcher, *Grocer*, bur. Aug. 25.

Aug. 25.   Bur., Ellen Johnson, a pensioner to this Parish, at the charges of the Parish.

Sep. 5.   Died, Katherin, wife of William Huson, bur. Sept. 9.

Oct. 8.   Died, William Manwaring.

Oct. 17.   Died, Richard, son of Samuell and Rodea Best, bur. Oct. 18.

Oct. 17.   Died, Marie, daughter of John and Marie Portman, bur. Oct. 21.

Oct. 20.   Died, Elizabeth, wife of William Humble, *Esquire*, bur. Oct. 27, in the quier under the great stone of Georg Humble, *Esquire*, which has his armes cutt upon the stone.

Oct. 26.   Bur., Anthony, son of William and Katherine Huson.

Nov. 5.   Died, Elizabeth, daughter of William and Elizabeth Browne. bur. Nov. 8.

Nov. 9.   Bur., Beniamine, son of Beniamine and Rebecca Cooke.

Dec. 8.   Died, Hugh Clough, bur. Dec. 12.

Jan. 2.   Bur., John, son of John and Marie Waters.

Jan. 9.   Died, John Crumpton, *Goldsmith*, bur. Jan. 13.

Jan. 17.   Died, —— [*sic*] wife of Francis Bishopp.

Jan. 28.   Bur., Francis, son of Francis Jackson.

Feb. 23.   Died, Susan Capps, *Widdow*, a lodger at Mr. Tuchburie's house, *Dyer*, in Sherburne Lane, bur. Feb. 24.

Mar. 3.   Died, Martha, daughter of Thomas and Marie Canham, bur. Mar. 5.

1658

Mar. 26. Died, Frances, wife of Samuell Baker, of St. Gregories by Paules, buried in the middle ile, against the first of the women's greene pews.

April 6. Died, Samuell, son of Samuell and Suzan Wright.

April 12. Died, Thomas, son of Samuell Baker.

April 15. Died, Nathaniell, son of Samuell and Judith White, *Haberdasher of Hatts.*

May 2. Died, Richard Howard, *Cooper*, bur. May 5.

May 18. Died, Elizabeth Bolton, *Widdow*, bur. May 27.

May 24. Died, Anne, wife of Francis Bulfield.

June 18. Died, Alce Phillipson, *a maidservant* of Mr. Richard Brinkinshaw, bur. June 19.

July 14. Died, Elizabeth, daughter of John and Elizabeth Garfield, *Bookseller*, bur. July 16.

July 26. Died, Thomas, son of John and Eddon [*sic*] bur. July 29.

Aug. 9. Bur., Josling, son of Hugh and Mary Jones, at Michaell, Queenhithe.

Aug. 14. Died, Mary, wife of John Eddon, bur. Aug. 16.

Aug. 28. Died, Henry, son of Henry and Susan Crips.

Sep. 11. Died, Elizabeth, daughter of Richard Butler.

Oct. 2. Bur., a crisom daughter of Robert and Judith Bowcher.

Oct. 14. Died, Katherine Barton, sister unto Mr. Abraham Browne.

Nov. 2. Died, Thomas, son of Thomas Mason.

Nov. 20. Died, Mary, wife of Abraham Chambers, *Esquire*, and was buried in the quier close to the vault of Sir Martin Bowes.

Dec. 12. Died, Alice Phenix, *Widdowe and Penconer to this Parish.*

Dec. 21. Died, Katherine Buckock, daughter of Francis Shute, *Goldsmith.*

Dec. 23. Died, Richard Barr, *Apprentice* unto Mr. Daniell Morrice.

Dec. 30. Died, Samuell Shirman, *Minister*, and was buried in the Quier of the Church.

Dec. 30. Died, Mary, daughter of Richard and Maudlin Cransby.

Mar. 2. Died, John, son of Samuell White.

Mar. 4. Died, Ellen Gressam, a *servant maid* unto Mr. John Field, *Vintner.*

Mar. 21. Died, John, son of John Randall.

1659

May 3. Mr. —— [*sic*] daughter of Francis and Sarah Meynell.

May 20. Bur., John, son of William and Sarah Ewster.

June 12. Died, Samuell Jacomb, *Parson and Rector of this Parish*, bur. in the quier of the church.

June 27. Died, Charles Brinkingshaw.

Aug. 2. Died, George Humble, sonne to the deceased Merchant, and *Apprentice* to William Humble, *Esquire*.

Aug. 4. Died, Prudent, wife of Edward Orange.

Aug. 13. Died, Mary, daughter of John and Isabell Pritchard.

Aug. 14. Died, Jane, daughter of John and Jane Ellis.

Aug. 19. Died, Mary, daughter of Robert Jones.

Aug. 22. Henry Taylor.

Sep. 14. Dorothy, daughter of Thomas and Dorothy Peart, *Goldsmith.*

Sep. 20.	John Garrett, *Goldsmith.*
Sep. 30.	A Chrisom male child of John Pritchard.
Oct. 6.	Abraham Clerk, *Merchant*, buried in Sir Thomas Rawney's vault
Oct. 6.	Died, Sarah, wife of Edward Brackwell, *Goldsmith*, bur. Oct. 13.
Oct. 27.	Abraham Boyce, *Hotpresser.*
Nov. 4.	The daughter of Robert Jones, *Confectioner.*
————	In this month was bur. Annie Rudde, *Widowe.*
Nov. 22.	Margaret, daughter of John Jane Exton.
Dec. 29.	Dorothy, daughter of Robert and Katherin Welsted.
Feb. 1.	William Mainwaring, *Goldsmith.*
Feb. 25.	Elizabeth Packe, a *maidservant* to Esquire Humble.
Mar. 30.	Francis Gower, an *apprentice* unto Mr. Daniell Morrice, *Plasterer.*

1660

April 29.	A stillborne child of Nicholas Crosse, Junr.
May 21.	An abortive child of John Smith, *Watchmaker.*
Aug. 17.	Died, Robert Bowcher, *a Citizen and Grocer*, of London, bur. Aug. 23.
Aug. 19.	Died, Ellen wife of Thomas Collier, *Goldsmith*, bur. Aug. 21.
Aug. 21.	Abraham, son of Abraham Johnson, Junr.
Oct. 16.	Samuell —— [*sic*] *apprentice* to John Ellis, *Merchant.*
Oct. 22.	Died, Stephen Bowtell, bur. Oct. 20 [*sic*].
Nov. 1.	Died, John Exton, *Cutler*, bur. Nov. 3.
Nov. 17.	Mary, daughter of John and Mary Portman, *Goldsmith.*
Nov. 27.	Adom, son of Adam and Margaret Livingston, *Fruiterer.*
Dec. 29.	———— [*sic*] Aunt to Mr. Hotton, *Cloathdrawer.*
Jan. 1.	Mary, daughter of William and Mary Smyther.
Jan. 5.	Jane Chapman, *Widdow.*
Jan. 11.	Samuell, son of Samuell Baker, from St. Gregories, by Pawles.
Jan. 13.	Edward, son of Francis Meynall, *Aldran* (?) *
Feb. 18.	Stephen, son of William and Sarah Euster.
Feb. 23.	Richard, son of Richard and Maudlin Crainsby.
Feb. 25.	Elizabeth, daughter of John and Isabella Prichard.
Mar. 1.	Marmaduke Ferrers, who dyed suddenly, with the Coroner's order for his buriall.
Mar. 3.	Samuell, son of Samuell Wright.
Mar. 27.	———— [*sic*] of John and Jane Runwell.

1661

April 16.	Anne, wife of Joell Cox, and daughter to Widdow Oakley.
May 1.	Mary, daughter of Henry and Susanna Cripps, *Bookseller.*
May 13.	Anne, wife of Francis Jackson.
June 14.	Christian, daughter of Robert Jones.
June 15.	Isaac, son of Benjamine Cooke.
July 14.	Elizabeth, daughter of Alexander Holt.
Aug. 11.	Joane Cooke, a *servant maid*, she came out of the Parrish of St. Nicholas Olave, in Bred Streete.
Sep. 19.	Rodger Bradley, an *apprentice* of Sir William Humble, *Knight.*

* "*Aldran*" perhaps is an abreviation for "*Alderman.*"

Sep. 20.	Rebeccah, wife of William Mantell.
Sep. 30	The Lady Margaret, the wife of the Right Honorable Sir John Clobery, *Knight,* in the Quier of this Church neere to Sir John Percevell's monument stone.
Oct. 1.	Elizabeth, daughter of William Whalie.
Oct. 8.	John Randall, an *aprentice* to Mr. John Randall.
Nov. 21.	Benjamine Swanne, an *aprentice* to Mr. Robert Wealstead
Nov. 24.	Thomas Love, an *aprentice* of George Best.
Dec. 2.	Elizabeth, daughter of William Euster.
Dec. 5.	John Izod, an *aprentice* of Mr. Dixon.
Dec. 5.	Hester, daughter of Clement Manistey.
Dec. 8.	Dorothy, daughter of Thomas Peirce.
Jan. 9.	John Sweething.
Jan. 28.	Mary, wife of Abraham Chaire.
Feb. 11.	Francis, daughter of John Exton.
Mar. 20.	Dyed, Robert Lant, *Strainger,* he was brought from St. Lawrence Parrish by Guildhall, and bur. Mar. 24.
Mar. 25.	A Parrish child at Waltham Abbey.

1662

April 5.	Charles, son of Michael Waring.
April 11.	Elizabeth, daughter of Henry Heath, dyed in Mr. George Baker's house, in Shirbon Lane.
April 13.	Judeth, daughter of William Godbed.
April 22.	John, son of John Ellis.
April 23.	Dyed, Mrs. Anne Hoane, the wife of Mr. John Hoane, of the Parrish of Beconsfield, in Buckinghamshiere, and was bur. April 25.
May 6.	Ellina, wife of John Harding.
May 13.	Antonyet, daughter of David Legrill, of the French Congregacon.
July 23.	Elizabeth Exton, daughter of Jane Baker.
Aug. 30.	Allexander, son of Samnell Pollington.
Sep. 2.	Susan, the wife of John Hill, brought from Horseshow Alley, just towards Shoredich Parrish.
Sep. 15.	Edward Hall, of the Parrish of Dorchester, *stranger,* bur. in the Cloisters.
Sep. 18.	John, son of Henry Jones, of the Parrish of St. Michaell, Queenhithe.
Oct. 7.	Suzan, daughter of John Smith.
Nov. 10.	Mr. Robert Rolph.
Nov. 15.	Henry, son of Paull Savage and his wife.
Nov. 16.	Died, Katharine, a *servantmaid* to Mary Fletcher, *Widow.*
Nov. 20.	Richard Crainsby, *Grocer.*
Nov. 28.	Jane, daughter of Allexander and Mary Holt.
Dec. 14.	Millisent, daughter of George and Jane Baker.
Dec. 16.	Died, Mary, wife of Major Charles Everard, bur. Dec. 23, in the middle Isle.
Dec. 20.	John Hill, brought from Mr. Mantle's house in Lombard Street.
Feb. 3.	Died, ———— [*sic*] daughter of Thomas and Mary Saimour.
Feb. 14.	Died, Jane Weldam.
Feb. 23.	Died, Francis Jackson.
Mar. 4.	Died, Henry Cripps, *Stationer,* bur. Mar. 7.
Mar. 14.	Died, a chrisom child of Mr. Wealsted.

Mar. 22.　Was bur. ——— [*sic*] daughter of Samuell and Susan Bright.
Mar. 23.　Died, Thomas Jermyn, *Clerke and Sexton of this Parrish*.
Mar. 25.　Died, Edward Rolph.

1663

April 26.　Died, Mary, daughter of John and Jane Ellis, *Merchantaylor*,
　　　　　bur. April 27.
April 24.　Dyed, Dorothy, wife of Thomas Pearse, *Goldsmith*, bur.
　　　　　April 29.
April 27.　Dyed, Edward, son of Edward Backwell, *Esquire, Gold-
　　　　　smith*, bur. April 29.
June 9.　Dyed, Elizabeth, wife of Richard Tanner, *Cutler*, bur.
　　　　　June 10.
June 24.　Dyed, Anne, daughter of Thomas Wilde, *Esquire*, and
　　　　　Jane his wife, bur. June 26.
July 12.　——— [*sic*] late wife of ——— [*sic*] Branthwaite, *Silk-
　　　　　dyer*, deceased, bur. July 14 (poore).
July 22.　Dyed, Thomas Thatcher, *apprentice* unto Francis Lucye,
　　　　　Druggest, bur. July 24.
Aug. 29.　Dyed, Robert Jones, *Confectioner*.
Sep. 16.　Dyed, Bridgett Walker, *servant* unto Mr. Rawson, bur.
　　　　　Sep. 17.
Oct. 12.　Dyed, Sarah, wife of George Glidwell, bur. Oct. 18.
Oct. 22.　Dyed, Dorothy Misle, *servant* unto Mr. Rawson, bur.
　　　　　Oct. 23.
Nov. 31.　Dyed, William Hewson, *Attorney-at-Law*, bur. Dec. 1.
Dec. 10.　Dyed, Phillipp, son of Phillipp and Sarah Bayley, bur.
　　　　　Dec. 11.
Jan. 7.　Dyed, George Glidwell, *Pentioner*, bur. Jan. 8.
Mar. 7.　Dyed, Cornelius, son of John Bonus, bur. Mar. 8.
Mar. 15.　Dyed, Anne, daughter of Richard and Anne Collier,
　　　　　bur. Mar. 16.
Mar. 21.　Dyed, Mary, daughter of John and Mary Smith, bur.
　　　　　Mar. 24.
Mar. 23.　William, son of William and Susanna Stringer, bur. Mar. 24.

1664

April 20.　Dyed, Honor, daughter of Thomas Vyner, *Minister* of
　　　　　——— [*sic*] County of Glocester, bur. April 22.
May 29.　Died, Joseph, son of Walter and Anne Elford, bur. June 1.
June 17.　Died, John, son of John and Mary Walters, bur. June 19.
June 27.　Died, John Adtherton, *Goldsmith*, bur. June 29.
July 3.　Died, Jemima, daughter of Abraham and Ann Johnson,
　　　　　bur. July 4.
July 7.　Died, Thomas, son of Thomas and Abigal Samson, bur.
　　　　　July 8.
Aug. 1.　Died, Thomas Platt, bur. Aug. 2.
Aug. 1.　Died, Edward, son of Edward Stockbury, *Joyner*.
Aug. 11.　Died, Robert, son of Robert and Seball Carpenter, bur.
Aug. 23.　Died, Mr. Samuell White, *Haberdasher of Hatts*, bur.
　　　　　Aug. 26.
Sep. 3.　Died, Jonathan Woollnoth, a foundling, bur. Sep. 26.
Oct. 4.　Died, Rebecca, daughter to Mr. Ralph Robbingson, late
　　　　　Parson of this Parish, bur. Oct. 6 in the chancel by
　　　　　Ministers pue ; she came from Harro on the Hill.

Oct. 5. Died, John, son of Henry and Elizabeth Heath, bur. Oct. 8.

Oct. 11. Died, William Godbed, *Watchmaker*, bur. Oct. 21.

Jan. 16. Died, Mrs. ——— [sic] Whitehead, wife of Mr. James Whitehead, bur. Jan. 19.

Feb. 6. Mr. Juhn Cleyton, bur. Feb. 15.

Mar. 3. Bur., a stillborne childe of Mr. Richard Tirgis.

Mar. 26. Died, Rebecca, daughter of William and Ann Paybody, bur. Mar. 30.

Mar. 5. Bur., John Bonus.

1665

April 30. Dyed, Clement Punge, *Goldsmith*, bur. May 3.

May 11. Dyed, Sir Thomas Vyner, *Knight and Baronett*, at his mansion house at Hackney, in the 77th yeare of his life, and brought to this church and interred in the chancel at the east end of the communion table, the first of June following.

June 4. Dyed, ——— [sic] daughter of Thomas and Abigail Mason, bur. June 6.

June 4. Dyed, Elizabeth, wife of Isaack Meynell, *Goldsmith*, bur. June 13.

June 13. Dyed, Rebecca, wife of James Taylor, *Goldsmith*, of the Parish of St. Edmund in Lombarde Streete, bur. June 15.

July 1. Dyed, Charles, son of Abraham and Anne Johnson, bur. July 3.

July 19. Dyed, and was bur. Robert Pauley, *aprentice* to Mr. Richard Tirges, *Drugest*.

July 25. Dyed, Robert Shaw, *servant* to Edward Backwell, *Esquire*, *Goldsmith*, bur. July 26.

Aug. 11. Dyed, Mr. Nicholas Clobury, *Goldsmith*, bur. same day.

Aug. 21. Dyed, Thomas Reading, *servant* to Thomas Futter.

Aug. 23. Bur. Anne Standley.

Aug. 27. Bur. Elizabeth, daughter of Thomas and Elizabeth Smith.

Aug. 29. Hannah, daughter of George Munday.

Aug. 31. John Shipman, Senior.

Sep. 2. Sara, daughter of William and Sara Euster.

Sep. 7. Bur., Mrs. Judith Ratlif, alias Boucher.

Sep. 7. William Miles, *aprentice* to William Paybody.

Sept. 7. Richard, son of Richard and Margarett Yrde.

Sep. 12. William Euster.

Sep. 12. Widdew Bonus.

Sep. 13. Mary, wife of Alexander Daniell.

Sep. 15. William Paybody, *Boxemaker*.

Sep. 15. James ——— [sic] *aprentice* to Mr. Briggs.

Sep. 15. Andrew Woolnoth, a foundling.

Sep. 16. Barbar, daughter of Walter and Anne Elford.

Sept. 18. ——— [sic] wife of William Mantill.

Sep. 20. Mary, a foundling.

Sep. 20. John Shipman, Junior.

Sep. 21. Elizabeth, daughter of Richard and Margaret Yrde.

Sep. 21. John Porter.

Sep. 22. George, son of Mary Fletcher, *Widdow*.

Sep. 22. William, son of Richard and Margaret Yrde.

Sep. 23.	Seball, wife of Robert Carpenter, and John, his son.
Sep. 23.	Thomas Day and Mary Hatt, both *servants* to Mr. Abraham Browne.
Sep. 24.	Anne Paybody, *Widdow.*
Sep. 27.	William Davies, *aprentice* to William Paybody, late dead.
Sep. 28.	Ann Shipman.
Sep. 30.	John Meynell, late *aprentice*, and nephew to Mr. Mcynell.
Sep. 30.	Mary Exton, daughter of Mr. Beaker, alias Axton.
Sep. 30.	John Halsey.
Sep. 30.	Thomas Langley, *Fishmonger.*
Sep. 30.	Samuell ——— [*sic*] *aprentice* to Richard Yrde, at the new ground.
Oct. 3.	Elizabeth Plummer, *servant* to Mr. Rowe.
Oct. 6.	Thomas, son of Widdow Jermyn.
Oct. 8.	Margeret, wife of Thomas Olliver.
Oct. 8.	Sara Axton, daughter of Jane Beaker, alias Axton.
Oct. 9.	——— [*sic*] son of Thomas Olliver.
Oct. 9.	Charles, son of Widdow Ewster.
Oct. 9.	Anne Elizabeth, daughter of George Shawe.
Oct. 9.	——— [*sic*] son of John Shipman, Junior, deceased.
Oct. 9.	William Mantill, *Goldsmith.*
Oct. 10.	——— [*sic*] *servant maid* to Mr. Isaack Meynell.
Oct. 10.	The wife of Edward Orringe.
Oct. 14.	Anne Barker, *servant* to All Holt.
Oct. 20.	Judith, daughter of Robert Carpenter.
Oct. 26.	Anne, wife of George Shawe.
Oct. 27.	Herbert Longley, *aprentice* to George Beaker.
Oct. 27.	George Munday, *Taylor.*
Oct. 28.	Charles Everrard, *Goldsmith.*
Oct. 28.	Joane, wife of Edward Stuchburo.
Nov. 9.	Anne, daughter of John and Isabell Prichard.
Nov. 16.	William Browne, *Cordwainer.*
Nov. 16.	Edward Stuchbury, *Joiner.*
Nov. 27.	Thomas, son of Francis Bulfell.
Dec. —[*sic*]	Henry, son of Widdow Savage.
Jan. 10.	Joane Ferris, *Widdow.*
Jan. 25.	Amey Wills.
Mar. 5.	Bridget Capon, *servant* to Mr. Peart.
Mar. 7.	A stillborne male childe of Mr. William Foster.
Mar. 12.	Mary, daughter of Francis and Elizabeth Strandginge.
Mar. 24.	Thomas Willmore.

1666

April 13.	Elizabeth Manwaring, *Widdow.*
April 24.	Died, Mrs. Joyce Young, *Widdow*, at Mr. Jones, in Sherburne Lane, bur. April 26,
May 2.	Died, Evan, son of John and Isabell Pritchard, bur. May 3.
July 3.	Died, Abigal, daughter of Thomas and Abigal Sampson, bur. July 26 [*sic*].
July 21.	Male stillborne child of Mr. Richard Tirges.
July 29.	Died, Elizabeth, wife of Richard Turges, *Druggest*, bur. July 31.
Oct. 18.	Richard Yrde, late of this Parish, being stifled in a house of office on the back side of deputie Canham's house, after the Cittie was burnt.

1667

April 8. John, son of John and Isabell Prichard.
July 26. Dyed, Suzanna, daughter to Robert Jones, deceased.
July 29. Died, Abigall, the wife of Thomas Sampson, bur. July 31.
Feb. 6. Lettis Chamberlaine, *Widdow*.

1668

Mar. 27. Died, Richard Tirges, *Druggest*, bur. Mar. 29.
April 10. Died, Margaret, daughter of William and Margaret Foster, April 11.
May 11. Died, Martha, daughter of Thomas and Mary Seymour, bur. May 13.
July 8. Dyed, Mistris Hannah Street, *Widdow*, bur. July 11.
Sep. 24. Dyed, John, son of John and Jane Hind, bur. Sep. 25.
Nov. 4. Dyed, ——— [*sic*] son of John and Isable Prichard, bur Nov. 5.
Mar. 12. Dyed, Abraham Chambers, *Esquire*, bur. Mar. 16.
Mar. 23. Dyed, Thomas Sampson, bur. Mar. 25.

1669

Sep. 29. Dyed, Dorothy, daughter of Richard and Dorothy Tompson, bur. Aug. 2.
Oct. 5. Dyed, Henry, son of John and Alice Tempest, bur. Oct. 6.
Oct. 23. Dyed, Elizabeth Masters, *servant* to Mr. Nathaniel Cock, *Merchant*, bur. Oct. 25.
Oct. 31. Dyed, Friswell Shipman, *Widdow*, bur. Nov. 1.
Nov. 7. Dyed, Mr. Mathew Randall, *Merchant*, bur. Nov. 9.
Nov. 8. Dyed, Adam, son of Adam and Margaret Livingstone, bur. Nov. 9.
Nov. 6. Dyed, Mr. Abraham Johnson, Junior, bur. Nov. 12.
Nov. 29. Dyed, Anne, daughter of Giles Bloomer, bur. Nov. 30.
Jan. 21. Dyed, Isabell, wife of John Prichard, bur. Jan. 25.
Feb. 27. Dyed, Edward Ball, *servant* to Mr. John Sayer, *Vintner*, bur. Feb. 28.

1670

Mar. 30. Dyed, Hugh Jones, *Grocer*, bur. April 1.
April 10. Dyed, Mary, wife of John Waters, bur. April 14.
May 12. Dyed, Alice Oakley, *Widdow*, bur. May 13.
May 19. Dyed, William Smithies, *apprentice* to Mr. Watkin, bur. May 20.
June 8. Dyed, Daniell, son of John and Jane Juns, bur. June 9.
June 11. Dyed, Elizabeth Shute, *Widdow*, bur. June 14 at the east end of the chancel by her late husband.
July 28. Dyed, Elizabeth, daughter of Godfrey and Anne Davis, bur. July 30.
Aug. 11. A male bastard child of Abigail Web, *servant* to Mr. John Sayer, *Vintner*, murthered by the mother.
Aug. 20. Dyed, Josiah Lowdain, *servant* to Theophilus Dorrington, bur. Aug. 21.
Sep. 22. A male stillborne child of Mr. Giles Blomer.
Sep. 20. Died, Mrs. Susan Rolfe, *Spinster*, from Ealing, Middlesex, bur. Sep. 27.
Oct. 10. Dyed, Alice, daughter of Katherine Welstead, bur. Oct. 12

Nov. 11.	Dyed, Hannah, daughter of John and Easter Boucher, *Scrivener*, bur. Nov. 14.
Nov. 15.	Dyed, Elizabeth Gorton, *Widdow*, bur. Nov. 17.
Nov. 24.	A female Chrisom child of Mr. Samuell Hartlif, *Gent.*
Nov. 25.	Dyed, John, son of ——— [*sic*] Welding, *Gent.*, of the Parrish of St. Olaves in Hartt Streete, bur. Nov. 27.
Dec. 7.	Dyed, Robert Coale, *Plummer*, bur. Dec. 10.
Dec. 29.	An abortive female child of Rogger Livingtone.
Dec. 26.	Died, Mary, wife of Samuell Hartliff, *Gent.*, bur. Dec. 29.
Jan. 10.	Dyed, Anne, daughter of John and Elizabeth Maidwell, bur. Jan. 13.
Jan. 18.	Dyed, John, son of Thomas and Mary Williams, bur. Jan. 19.
Feb. 14.	Dyed, Joseph, son of Joseph and Judith Hornby, of the Parish of St. Nicholas Acon, London, bur. Feb. 15.
Mar. 1.	Dyed, Elizabeth, daughter of Elizabeth and Ahashuerus Burcher, bur. Mar. 2.
Mar. 30.	Dyed, Joseph, son of Thomas and Mary Seymour, bur. April 1.

1671

April 21.	Dyed, Robert, son of Henry and Mary Lewis, bur. April 22.
July 22.	Dyed, John Walters, *Cutler*, late of the Parish of St. Michaell Cornhill, bur. July 24.
July 26.	Dyed, Elizabeth, daughter of Clement and Mary Browne, bur. July 27.
Aug. 7.	Dyed, Ann Jenkins, *Widdow*, of the Parish of St. Peters le poore, bur. Aug. 10.
Aug. 27.	Dyed, Thomas, son of Mrs. Dorothoe Colvill, *Widdow*, bur. Aug. 30,
Sep. 22.	Dyed, William Browne, of the Parish of St. Dionis, Backchurch, bur. Sep. 24.
Sep. 25.	Dyed, Thomas Tabour, *servant* to Mr. Jeremie Snow, *Goldsmith*, of the Parish of St. Edmund the King, in Lombard Strecte, bur. Sep. 28.
Oct. 7.	Dyed, Francis, son of John and Margeret Farrington, bur. Oct. 12.
Oct. 31.	Dyed, Elizabeth, daughter of Samuell and Sarah Jermyn, bur. Nov. 1.
Nov. 30.	An abortive child of Mr. Edward Taylor.
Dec. 11.	Dyed, Mr. Clement Browne, *Grocer*, bur. Dec. 13.
Dec. 14.	Dyed, Robert, son of Robert and Sarah King, bur. Dec. 16
Dec. 15.	Mary Kent, *servant maid* to Mr. Scarth, bur. Dec. 16.
Jan. 25.	A male child of Mr. Moyse Lowman.
Feb. 8.	Dyed, Ralph, son of Randolph and Mary Bolton, bur. Feb. 9.
Mar. 10.	Dyed, Joseph, son of Robert and Elizabeth Watkins, bur. Mar. 13.
Mar. 22.	Dyed, Elizabeth Care, *servant* to Margaret Cock, bur. Mar. 23.

1672

Mar. 26.	Dyed, Robert Payne, *servant* to Mr. Farrington, bur. Mar. 27.
April 5.	Dyed, Elizabeth, daughter of Francis and Ann Hayes, bur. April 6.

April 3.	Dyed, Ann, daughter of Robert and Katherine Welstead, of the Parish of St. Nicholas Acons, bur. April 10.
May 26.	Dyed, Berklay, son of John Sayer, *Gent.*, bur. May 28.
June 5.	A foundling.
June 5.	Dyed, Benjamine, son of Robert and Elizabeth Walkin, bur. June 7.
June 8.	Dyed, Ellenor, daughter of Ellenor Smith, *Widdow*, bur. June 9.
June 27.	Bur., a male stillborne child of Ahashuerus Bircher.
June 28.	Dyed, Joseph Taylor, bur. June 29.
July 9.	Dyed, Abraham Browne, *Vintner*, at Chartlon, Kent, bur. July 10.
July 21.	Dyed, William, son of Godfrey Davis Taylor, bur. July 23.
July 20.	Dyed, George Portman, *Goldsmith*, bur. July 25.
Aug. 3.	Dyed, Suzanna, daughter of Robert . . ige, *Goldsmith*, bur. Aug. 6.
Aug. 9.	Dyed, Margaret Payne, *Widdow*, bur. Aug. 12.
Aug. 29.	Dyed, Charitie, daughter of Henry Younge, *Goldsmith*, of St. Mary Abchurch, bur. Aug. 31.
Sep. 2.	Dyed, Robert, son of Andrew Crisp, *Rector of this Church*, bur. Sep. 4.
Sep. 9.	Silvanus, son of Henry Wyburne, bur. Sep. 10.
Sep. 12.	A female abortive child of Mr. John Bullens, *Goldsmith*.
Sep. 13.	Dyed, Katherine, wife of Mr. George Dixson, *Goldsmith*, bur. Sep. 15.
Sep. 22.	Dyed, Daniell East, *Watchmaker*, bur. Sep. 24.
Sep. 28.	Dyed, Suzan Smith, *servant* to Mr. Garroway, bur. Sep. 29.
Oct. 8.	A male stillborne child of Mr. John Moores.
Oct. 8.	Dyed, Mr. Nicholas Carey, bur. Oct. 9.
Oct. 12.	Dyed, Christopher Coke, *Esquire*, of Tregose, in the Parrish of St. Ewe, in the County of Cornwall, bur. Oct. 17.
Nov. 1.	Dyed, Benjamine, son of Thomas Seymour, *Goldsmith*, bur. Nov. 2.
Nov. 28.	Dyed, Hannah, daughter of John Cooke, bur. Nov. 30.
Nov. 30.	Dyed, Thomas Willett, *Esquire*, of Fulham, Middlesex, bur. Dec. 11.
Dec. 23.	Dyed, John Stables, *Hosier*, bur. Dec. 26.
Dec. 26.	Dyed, Mary Peake, bur. Dec. 28.
Jan. 4.	Dyed, Sara, daughter of Samuell and Sara Jermyn, bur. Jan. 5.
Jan. 31.	Dyed, Laurance, son of Laurance Weld, *Druggest*, bur. Feb. 3.
Feb. 1.	Dyed, Mary Crome, *servant* to Mr. Northame, bur. Feb. 2.
Feb. 4.	Dyed, Elizabeth, daughter of Peter White, *Goldsmith*, bur. the same day.
Feb. 21.	Dyed, John, son of Adam and Margareti Livingston, bur. Feb. 23.
Mar. 10.	Dyed, Humphrey, son of Humphrey Willett, *Merchant*, of the Parish of St. Sweethins, London, bur. Mar. 12.
Mar. 14.	Dyed, Dorothe, daughter of Phillip Scarth, *Drugest*, bur. Mar. 16.

1673

April 2.	Dyed, William Skapes, *aprentice* to Mr. Woodland, *Barbour*, bur. April 3.

April 10.	Dyed, May Gold, *servant* to Deputy Sexton, bur. April 11.
April 11.	A female abortive child of Mr. Bowmans.
April 11.	Judith, daughter of John Bowcher, bur. April 13.
April 22.	Dyed, Elizabeth, wife of Robert Bowman, bur. April 24.
April 24.	Dyed, Samuell, son of Richard Northame, bur. April 26.
April 29.	Dyed, Elizabeth, daughter of George Bloomer, bur. May 1.
June 6.	Dyed, Richard Horkey, *aprentice* to Mr. Thomas Williams, *Goldsmith*, bur. June 7.
July 15.	Dyed, Mary, wife of John Chambers, *Scrivener*, bur. July 19.
Aug. 1.	Thomas Vyner, *Esquire*, who dyed the 14th day of Feb., 1666, and was interred at Cree Church, by reason the Church was not built then since the dredfull fier.
Aug. 7.	A male stillborne child of Thomas Eles.
July 5.	Dyed, Sir George Vyner, *Knight and Barronett*, and the twenty-fifth died Dame Abygall, his wife, and were both buryed from there Mansion house att Hackney, the 18th of August foll : in the Chancell, under the Communion table.
Aug. 21.	Dyed, Robert, son of John Gravenor, bur. Aug. 22.
Aug. 26.	Mrs. Prisca Ballow, *Widdow*, bur. Aug. 29.
Sep. 1.	Dyed, Meriall Marshall, servant to Mr. Rawlinson, bur. Sep. 2.
Sep. 2.	Dyed, Mary, the wife of Edward Howell, bur. Sep. 4, by the Artillery in the new ground.
Sep. 15.	Dyed, Samuell, son of Samuell Corke, *Stationer*, bur. Sep. 17, att New Church by Bethlehem.
Oct. 14.	Dyed, Elizabeth Witham, *Widdow*, bur. Oct. 17, att St. Ollavs, Hart Streete.
Oct. 20.	Dyed, William, son of John Chambers, *Scrivener*, bur. Oct. 21.
Nov. 3.	A male abortive child of Mr. Peter White, *Goldsmith*.
Nov. 3.	Dyed, Peter Lumbard, bur. Nov. 4.
Nov. 27.	Dyed, Robert, son of Isaack Meynell, *Goldsmith*, bur. Nov. 28.
Dec. 23.	Dyed, James Gibbs, *Carpenter*, bur. Dec. 24.
Jan. 1.	Dyed, Colvill, son of John and Dorothe Temple, bur. same day.
Jan. 16.	Dyed, Dorothe, daughter of Isaack and Elizabeth Meynell, bur. Jan. 17.
Jan. 20.	Dyed, Edmund, son of Edmund and Grace Rolph, bur. Jan. 23.
Feb. 2.	Dyed, John Layton, *servant* to Edward Backwell, *Esqr.*, bur. Feb. 4.
Feb. 9.	Dyed, Ann, the wife of Edward Hill, *Victualler*, bur. Feb. 12.
May 6.	A male stillborne child of Samuel Tuttey.
Mar. 7.	Dyed, Richard, son of Thomas and Frances Folie, bur. Mar. 8.
Mar. 7.	Dyed, Isabella, daughter of Mrs. Dorothe Colvill, *Widdow*, bur. Mar. 12.
Mar. 8.	Dyed, Charles Butler, *servant* to Mr. Strot, *Victualler*, bur. Mar. 11.
Mar. 12.	Dyed, Ann, daughter of John Taylor, *Joyner*, bur. Mar. 14.
Mar. 13.	Dyed, Elizabeth, daughter of David Poiegg, bur. Mar. 14.
Mar. 15.	Dyed, Isaack Boyes, *Upholster*, late of St. Buttolphs, Bishopsgate, bur. May 17.

Mar. 17.   Dyed, Joseph, son of Robert and Sarah Kinge, *Goldsmith*, bur. Mar. 19.

Mar. 20.   Robert, son of William Rawlinson, bur. Mar. 22.

Mar. 23.   Dyed, Amye, daughter of Thomas and Mary Seymour, bur. Mar. 24.

Mar. 24.   Dyed, Elizabeth Tutty, bur. Mar. 25.

Mar. 25.   Dyed, George, son of Mrs. Margaret Portman, *Widdow*, bur. Mar. 26.

1674

April 4.   Elizabeth Graunt, at Mr. Garrowaye's, bur. April 5.

April 4.   Dyed, Elizabeth, daughter of Richard Thompson, bur. April 5.

April 13.   Dyed, Morris, son of John and Jane June, bur. April 16.

April 20.   Dyed, Joseph Wyar, bur. April 21.

April 29.   Dyed, William Godbey, *Victualler*, bur. May 1.

May 3.   Dyed, Thomas Hambleton, *servant* to Mr. Wills, *Victualler*, bur. May 5.

May 7.   Dyed, William, son of Elizabeth Browne, *Widdow*, bur. May 10.

May 20.   A male stillborne child of Mr. William Rutters.

May 22.   Dyed, John Stenwick *servant* to Mr. Edward Stenwick, bur. May 23.

May 28.   Dyed, Dorothe, wife of Charles Mell [or Moll] *Goldsmith*, of St. Mary Abchurch, bur. 22 [*sic*]

June 15.   Dyed, Eve, daughter of Adam Livingston, bur. June 17.

June 19.   A female foundling taken up 3 weeks before in Pope's Head Alley.

July 2.   Dyed, ——— [*sic*] *servant* to Mr. Standly, bur. July 3.

July 23.   Dyed, Doratha, daughter of Phillip Scarth, *Drugest*, bur. July 24.

Aug. 30.   Dyed, Katherine Mitchell, *Widdow*, Mr. Foster's house, bur. Sep. 1.

Sep. 2.   Dyed, Elizabeth Hancks, *servant* to Mr. Peter White, bur. Sep. 3.

Sep. 7.   Dyed, Dorothe, daughter of Michael Wearing, bur. Sep. 8.

Oct. 3.   Dyed, Ann Martin, *servant* to Major Wallis, bur. Oct 4.

Oct. 30.   Dyed, Anne Berrey, at Mr. Baker's house, and bur. Nov. 1.

Nov. 8.   Dyed, Mrs. Mary Portman, wife to John Portman, *Deputy of Ward of Lamborne*, bur. Nov. 13.

Nov. 13.   A female chrisome child of Mr. Henry Young, (Abchurch Church).

Nov. 26.   Did through himself from the top of his masters house, Thomas Browne, *aprentice* to Mr. Peter White, *Goldsmith*, the corner house next Exchange Alley, against Abchurch Lane.

Nov. 26.   Dyed, John, son of Mrs. Dorotha Colvill, *Widdow*, bur. Nov. 27.

Dec. 1.   Dyed, David Griell, *Merchant*, bur. Dec. 5.

Dec. 9.   Dyed, Arthur Standley, *Vintner*.

Dec. 15.   Dyed, Nathaniell, son of Joseph Horneby, bur. Dec. 17 (St. Nicholas Acons Parish).

Dec. 18.   An abortive child of Mores Edwards.

Dec. 31.   Dyed, Henry Van Dunyseller, *Dutchman*, bur. Jan. 1.

Jan. 7.   Dyed, Richard Abraham, *aprentice* to Mr. Casey, *Goldsmith*, bur. same day.

Jan. 1.	Dyed, Dame Mary Vyner, late Lady Maiores, wife to the Right Honorable Sir Robert Vynor, *Knight and Barronett, Lord Maior of the City of London,* and bur. 19th following in his vault in the South Chapple.
Feb. 26.	Dyed, George Baker, *Sexton of this Parish,* bur. Feb. 27.
Feb. 22.	Dyed, John Seed, *Oylman,* bur. Mar. 2, in the Chancell.
Mar. 31.	A female chrisome child of Henry Wybert.
Mar. 29.	Dyed, Mary, daughter of Isaac and Ellizabeth Meynell, bur. Mar. 31.
Mar. 29.	Dyed, James Whitehead, *Goldsmith,* bur. April 1.

1675

April 12.	Dyed, Robert, son of Robert Welstead, *Goldsmith,* bur. April 14.
May 7.	Dyed, Abraham, son of Paul Ridley, *Goldringe Maker,* May 9.
May 8.	Dyed, Ann, daughter of William Collins, *Goldsmith,* bur. May 12.
May 20.	A male stillborne child of John Richard, *Norridge Merchant.*
May 20.	Dyed, Elizabeth, daughter of Robert Bowes, of St. Lawrence Poultney.
June 19.	Dyed, Mr. Francis Bishop, bur. June 21.
June 26.	A Blackamore boy of Mr. John Temple, *Goldsmith.*
June 26.	Dyed, Mr. William White, Senior, late of this Parish, of the Parish Allhollowes, Staining, bur. July 2, *Haberdasher.*
July 1.	Dyed, William, son of John Child, *Grocer,* bur. July 2.
July 2.	Richard Ride, *apprentice* to Samuel Kempe, bur. July 3, at New Churchyard, by Bethlehem.
July 12.	Dyed, Ruth, daughter of John White, *Goldsmith,* bur. at New Churchyard, by the Artillery.
July 13.	Dyed, Richard Canning, *apprentice* to James Yeardley, *Victualer,* bur. July 14.
July 18.	Dyed, Ann, daughter of Peter White, *Goldsmith,* bur. July 18.
July 22.	Dyed, Mary, daughter of Andrew Crisp, *Rector of this Church,* bur. July 23.
Aug. 6.	Dyed, Mary, wife of John Huxley, *Gent.,* bur. Aug. 10.
Aug. 10.	Dyed, Elizabeth, daughter of Paule Ridley, *Goldring Maker,* bur. Aug. 11.
Aug. 13.	Dyed, John, son of Joshua Haskyns, bur. Aug. 14.
Aug. 21.	Dyed, Cebella, daughter of Adam Tinley, *Taylor,* bur. Aug. 22.
Sep. 7.	Dyed, Elizabeth, daughter of John and Katherine Jones, bur. Sep. 9, *Oylman.*
Sep. 10.	Dyed, Elizabeth, wife of Abraham Hind, of St. Swithin's, London, *Silversmith,* bur. Sep. 13.
Sep. 14.	Rebecca, daughter of Abraham Hind, of St. Swithin's London.
Sep. 26.	Dyed, Mary, wife of James Bloomer, *Upholster,* bur. Sep. 29.
Sep. 29.	Dyed, Barnard, son of Robert and Elizabeth Watkins, bur. Oct. 1.
Oct. 3.	A male stillborne child of Jonathan Whale.

Nov. 3.	Dyed, Elizabeth Bircher, *Widdow*, bur. Nov. 5.
Nov. 4.	Dyed, Isaack Meynell, *Goldsmith*, bur. Nov. 6.
Nov. 11.	Dyed, John Spencer, *apprentice* to John Cooke, *Razor-maker*, bur. Nov. 12.
Nov. 17.	Dyed, Ellis Boyes, *Widdow*, bur. Dec. 2.
Nov. 24.	Dyed, John Weeden, *servant* to Sir Robert Vyner, *Knight and Baronett*, bur. Nov. 25.
Dec. 1.	Dyed, Thomas Stockton, *Gent.*, bur. Dec. 2.
Dec. 3.	A male abortive child of Mr. Nicholas Carey, *Goldsmith*.
Jan. 8.	Dyed, Ann, daughter of Phillip and Dorothe Scarth, bur. Jan. 9.
Jan. 31.	Dyed, Elizabeth, wife of Paule Ridley, bur. Feb. 2.
Feb. 19.	Dyed, John Feake, *Noridge Factor*, bur. Feb. 20.
Feb. 24.	Dyed, Hannah, daughter of Richard Harbey, *Silversmith*, bur. Feb. 25.
Feb. 24.	An abortive child of Ahashuerus Bircher.
Mar. 1.	William Godbey, and an abortive child of John Harding, at the new churchyard by Bethlehem.
Mar. 22.	Dyed, Mary, daughter of Mrs. Elizabeth Meynell, *Widdow*, bur. Mar. 28.

1676

Mar. 28.	Dyed, Ruth, daughter of John and Ruthe White, bur. Mar. 30, in the new churchyard by Finsbury.
April 25.	Dyed, Martha, daughter of Robert Fox, *Boxmaker*, bur. April 27.
May 10.	Dyed, Cassandria, daughter of Thomas English, *Barbour*, bur. May 11.
June 23.	Dyed, Abraham Johnson, Esq., at his mansion att Hackney, bur. July 3.
July 5.	Dyed, Adam, son of Adam Timnall, bur. July 6.
July 10.	Dyed, Richard, son of Daniell Lord, *Barbour*, bur. July 12
July 30.	Dyed, Elizabeth, daughter of Robert Kinge, *Goldsmith*, bur. Aug. 1.
July 29.	Phillip Harris, *servant* to John Hardin, *Cooke*, hanged himself, and bur. at new churchyard by Bethlehem, July 30th.
Aug. 15.	Dyed, John, son of Richard Hayes, *Packer*, bu. Aug. 17.
Aug. 29.	A male chrisome child of Jonathan Whaley's, *Victualler*.
Aug. 30.	Dyed, Mary, daughter of John Archier, *Poulterer*, bur. Sep. 1.
Sep. 1.	Dyed, Ann Adams, *servantmaid* to Deputy Portman, bur. Sep. 2.
Sep. 1.	Robert Stone, a foundling of Woolchurch Parish.
Sep. 13.	Dyed, Robert, son of Robert Hills, *Gent.*, bur. Sep. 14.
Sep. 15.	Dyed, Henry Eversden, *Stacioner*, bur. Sep. 17.
Sep. 26.	Dyed, John Eaton, bur. Sep. 28.
Oct. 6.	Dyed, Judith, daughter of Thomas Folie, *Packer*, bur. Oct. 8.
Nov. 22.	Dyed, Rogger Pottinger, bur. Nov. 23,
Nov. 26.	Dyed, Francis, wife of Mr. John Sayer, *Victualler*, bur. Nov. 30.
Dec. 2.	Dyed, Ann, daughter of Edward Fenwick, bur. Dec. 4.
Dec. 3.	A male stillborne child of Thomas Cobb, at New Church by B . . . [*sic*].

Dec. 6.	Dyed, Humphrey Bridges, *Bricklayer*, bur. Dec. 9.
Dec. 7.	Dyed, Elizabeth, wife of Mr. Barnard Sirps, *Merchantt*, bur. Dec. 9.
Dec. 13.	Mary, wife of Thomas Cobb, at the New Churchyard by Bethlehem.
Dec. 21.	Dyed, Thomas, son of Samuell and Sara Jermyn, bur. Dec. 22.
Jan. 15.	Dyed, John Richards, *Norridg Factor*, bur. Jan. 17.
Jan. 18.	Dyed, Abigail Edwards, *servant* to Mr. John Jones.
Jan. 19.	Dyed, Ann, daughter of Mr. John Hillman, *Merchant-taylor.* bur. Jan. 20.
Mar. 8.	———— [*sic*] *maidservant* to Mr. Austin Ballow.
Mar 13.	Dyed, Sara Pledger, *maidservant* to Henry Wybert.
Mar. 20.	Dyed, John, son of John Cooke, *Rasormaker*, bur. Mar. 21.

1677

April 5.	Dyed, Elizabeth, daughter of George Sheepside, bur. April 8.
April 5.	Dyed, Mrs. Jane Johnson, *Widdow*, at her house in Hackney, bur. April 9.
April, 18.	Dyed, James Hughes, *groome* to Sir Robert Vyner, *Knight and Barronett*, bur. April 19.
April 22.	Dyed, Loveday, daughter of Thomas Williams, *Goldsmith*, bur. April 24.
June 1.	Dyed, Mary daughter of John Archer, *Poulterer*, bur. June 3.
June —.	[*sic*] Dyed, Honour, wife of Sidney Pickering, *Merchant*, bur. June 7, in the chancell the south side of the Communion table.
June 7.	Dyed, Edward Page, suddenly in Woolchurch Market, and bur. June 8.
June 30.	Dyed, William, son of Henry Aynscombe, bur. July 1.
June 21.	Dyed, John Scotson, *Turner*, bur. July 22.
Aug. 2.	Dyed, Thomas, son of Edward and Mary Howell, bur. Aug. 3, at New Churchyard by Bunhill.
Aug. 14.	Dyed, Elizabeth, wife of Godfrey Beck, *Goldsmith*, bur. Aug. 16.
Aug. 21.	Dyed, Margerret Halfheid, *Spinster*, bur. Aug. 23.
Sep. 8.	Dyed, Ann, daughter of Francis and Ann Hughes, bur. Sep. 9.
Sep. 21.	Dyed, Thomas Addis, *apprentice* to John Moore, *Goldbeater*, bur. Sep. 23.
Sep. 26.	Dyed, John, son of John Broughton, *Victualler*, bur. Sep. 26.
Sep. 28.	Dyed, Henry, son of Henry Wybert, *Poulterer*.
Oct. 2.	Dyed, Rebecca, daughter of John Hillman, by an accidental fall from a window, bur. Oct. 4.
Oct. 2.	Rebecca, daughter of Robert King, *Silversmith*.
Sep. 19.	Dyed, Christopher Northan, *Gent.*, bur. Nov. 11.
Oct. 22.	Dyed, John Pattenham, kinsman to Alld [? Alderman] Backwell, bur. Oct. 24.
Oct. 27.	Dyed, Thomas, son of John Heard, bur. Oct. 27.
Nov. 11.	———— [*sic*] Atherton, *Widdow*.
Nov. 11.	Dyed, Benjamine, son of John Harleing, *Goldsmith*, bur. Nov. 13.

Nov, 20.	Dyed, John Grimes, *Goldsmith*, bur. Nov. 22.
Dec. 28.	Dyed, Hugh North, *apprentice* to Mary Fletcher, *Widdow*, bur. Dec. 30.
Jan. 10.	Dyed, Samuell Moore, *Goldsmith*, bur. Jan. 13.
Jan. 20.	Dyed, William Holsworth, *Porter*, bur. Jan. 21.
Jan. 21.	Dyed, Thomas, son of Thomas Price, *Goldsmith*, bur. Jan. 23.
Jan. 31.	Dyed, Richard, son of Richard Northan, bur. Feb. 1.
Feb. 2.	Edmund Hiller, *Coffeeman*, at New Churchyard, by Bethlehem.
Feb. 5.	Dyed, Jane, daughter of John Thursbey, *Goldsmith*, bur. Feb. 7.
Feb. 17.	Dyed, Sara, daughter of Henry Wybert, *Poulterer*, bur. Feb. 18.
Mar. 18.	Dyed, Dorothe, daughter of George Sheepshied, *Collourmon*, bur. Mar. 20.
Mar. 19.	Dyed, William Nelme, *Packer*, bur. Mar. 22.
Mar. 25.	Dyed, Francis Shephard, bur. Mar. 26.

1678

April 8.	Margarett Woolnoth, a foundling.
April 3.	Dyed, John, son of John Bolitho, *Goldsmith*, bur. April 4.
April 19.	Dyed, Humphrey Towne, *Scrivener*, bur. April 23.
May 12.	Dyed, Rebecca Eversden, *Widdow*, bur. May 14.
June 7.	Dyed, Mary, wife of Thomas Price, *Goldsmith*, bur. June 11.
July 16.	A male stillborne child of Mr. Evans.
July 18.	Dyed, Henry, son of Edward Fenwick, *Upholster*, bur. July 19.
July 23,	Dyed, Thomas Weld, Esq., at Richmond, in Surrey, bur. Aug. 1.
Aug. 1.	Dyed, Thomas, son of Thomas Woodlaw, *Barbour*, bur. Aug. 2.
Aug. 6.	Dyed, Jane Pembrook, *servant* to Walter Hoare, *Tallow-chandler*, bur. Aug. 7.
Aug. 8.	Dyed, Robert, son of Joseph Cozens, *Barbour*, bur. Aug. 9.
Aug. 23.	Dyed, Michaell Steere, *aprentice* to Mr. John Thursbey, *Goldsmith*, bur. Aug. 23.
Aug. 21.	Dyed, Giles Bloomer, at Low Layton, Essex, bur. Aug. 27.
Aug. 25.	Dyed, Sarah, wife of Robert Kinge, *Silversmith*, bur. Aug. 27.
Sep. 3.	Dyed, John Heard, bur. Sep. 4.
Sep. 22.	Dyed, Phillip, son of Phillip Frowd, *Esqr*.
Sep. 23.	Dyed, Ann, daughter of Mr. Peter White, *Goldsmith*, bur. Sep. 25.
Oct. 20.	Dyed, William, son of Richard Harvey, *Silversmith*, bur. Oct. 21.
Dec. 16.	Dyed, Samuell Simonds, *Druggest*, bur. Dec. 19.
Dec. 19.	Dyed, John, son of Allexander Pollington, *Haberdasher of Hatts*, bur. Dec. 20.
Jan. 4.	Dyed, Maudlin Crainsly, *Widdow*, bur. Jan. 7.
Jan. 5.	Dyed, Ann, daughter of Joshua Bolt, *Druggist*, bur. Jan. 7.
Jan. 20.	Dyed, John, son of Richard Hawkins, bur. Jan. 21.
Jan. 30.	Dyed, Ahashuerus Bulker, bur. Feb. 2.
Feb. 13.	Dyed, Elizabeth, daughter of George Sheepshide, bur. Feb. 16.

Feb. 26.	Dyed, Mary, daughter of John Inns, *Goldsmith*, bur. Feb. 28.
Mar. 11.	Dyed, Hannah, daughter of Thomas and Frances Folic, bur. Mar. 14.
Mar. 27.	Dyed, William Foster, att Mile End, in the Parish of Stepney, bur. April 1.

1679

April 5.	Dyed, Martha, daughter of John Temple, *Goldsmith*, bur. April 18.
April 9.	Dyed, Elizabeth, daughter of Anthoney Storey, bur. April 11.
April 12.	Dyed, Richard, son of John Coleman, *Merchant*, bur. April 14.
April 13.	Dyed, John Steele, *Vintner*, bur. April 16.
April 20.	Dyed, Joseph, son of Joseph Cozens, *Barbour*, bur. April 20.
April 26.	Dyed, Elizabeth, daughter of Singleton Veale, bur. April 27.
Jan. 5.	Dyed, Edward, son of Peter Wade, *Goldsmith*, bur. June 6.
July 17.	Dyed, Hannah, daughter of Benjamine Combs, bur. July 18.
July 18.	A female abortive child of Jonathan Whaley.
Aug. 9.	Dyed, Mrs. Alice Sandis, *Widdow*, bur. Aug. 14, in the Chancell.
Aug. 27.	Dyed, Rebecca, wife of John Hillman, and bur. Aug. 29.
Sep. 17.	Dyed, Mary, wife of Thomas Williams, *Goldsmith*, bur. Sep. 22.
Sep. 21.	Dyed, Rowland, son of Thomas Flowerdew, *Merchant*, bur. Sep. 22.
Oct. 10.	Dyed, Daniell Bennett, *Cutler*, bur. Oct. 12.
Oct. 15.	A male stillborne child of Michaell Collard.
Oct. 20.	Dyed, Mary, daughter of Edward Fenwick, bur. Oct. 23.
Oct. 23.	A female chrisom child of ——— [*sic*] Churchman.
Nov. 7.	Dyed, Elizabeth, daughter of Edward Fenwick, *Upholder*, bur. Nov. 8.
Nov. 10.	Dyed, Elizabeth Gardner, *Widdow*, bur. Nov. 13, at the Quaker ground near Bunhill.
Nov. 15.	Dyed, Mrs. Mary Cleark, relict of Mr. Abraham Cleark, bur. Nov. 21, in Sir Thomas Ramsey's vault.
Dec. 3.	Dyed, Joane, wife of Alexander Ward, *Taylor*, bur. Dec. 4, in New Churchyard by Bethlem.
Dec. 6.	Dyed, Sarah, daughter of John Temple, *Goldsmith*, bur. Dec. 9.
Dec. 10.	Dyed, Francis Partridge, *man servant* to Thomas Garway, bur. Dec. 10.
Dec. 15.	Dyed, Elizabeth, daughter of Thomas Burford, *Factor*, bur. Dec. 17.
Dec. 18.	Dyed, Suzanna, daughter of Daniell Lord, *Barbour*, bur. Dec. 19.
Dec. 29.	Dyed, John, son of John Salendine, bur. Dec. 30.
Dec. 31.	Dyed, Constance, daughter of Peter White, *Goldsmith*, bur. Jan. 2.
Jan. 1.	Dyed, John Pullen, *Victualler*, bur. Jan. 4.

Jan. 5.	Dyed, John Hind, *servant* to Mr. Thomas Le Mon, *Scrivener*, bur. Jan. 8.
Jan. 12.	Dyed, Thomas Bonner, *Druggest*, bur. Jan. 14, in the New Churchyard, by Bunhill.
Jan. 24.	Dyed, Ann, daughter of John Sutton, *Goldsmith*, bur. Jan. 25.
Feb. 11.	Dyed, Anne, daughter of Henry Lambe, *Goldsmith*, bur. Feb. 12.
Feb. 17.	Dyed, Rebecca, daughter of Thomas Bowyer, bur. Feb. 18.
Feb. 21.	Dyed, Elizabeth, daughter of Joseph Cozens, *Barbour*, bur. Feb 23.
Mar. 11.	Dyed, Nicholas, son of Austin Ballow, *Merchant*, bur. Mar. 13.
Mar. 27.	Dyed, John, son of Paule Ridley, bur. Mar. 28.
Mar. 28.	A male abortive child of Samuell Jermyn.

1680

April 16.	Dyed, Peter Elliston, *apprentice* to Mr. William Browne, *Merchant*, bur. April 19.
May 2.	Dyed, Jame, son of Thomas Rooks, bur. May 5, in the New Churchyard, by Bethlehem.
May 5.	Dyed, Benjamin, son of Benjamin Combs, bur. May 5.
May 4.	Dyed, Samuell, son of John Archer, *Poulterer*, bur. May 5.
May 11.	Dyed, Edmund, son of Edmund Halfheid, bur. May 11.
May 22.	Dyed, Robert Fox, *Boxmaker*, bur. May 23.
May 23.	Dyed, John Aindowne, *servant* to John Rennalls, bur. May 24.
May 28.	Dyed, John Man, *Coffeeman*, bur. May 30, in the New Churchyard, by Bethlehem.
June 27.	Dyed, Thomas Rushworth, bur. June 28, in New Churchyard, by Bethlehem.
July 20.	Dyed, Elizabeth Richer, *Widdow*, of the Parish of St. George in Buttolph Lane, bur. July 23.
July 25.	Dyed, Rebecca, daughter of James Sibley, bur. July 27.
Aug. 28.	Dyed, Moise Edwards, *Hosier*, bur. Aug. 31.
Sep. 9.	Dyed, Elizabeth, daughter of Edward Gladwin, *Goldsmith*, bur. Sep. 10.
Sep. 14.	Dyed, Margarett, daughter of John Coleman, *Merchant*, bur. Sep. 16.
Sep. 25.	Dyed, Alice, daughter of John Sallendine, bur. Sep. 26.
Sep. 27.	Dyed, Richard Butler, *Barbour*, bur. Sep. 29.
Oct. 3.	Dyed, Anne, wife of John Bolitho, *Goldsmith*, bur. Oct. 8.
Oct. 14.	Dyed, John, son of Thomas Price, bur. Oct. 16.
Oct. 14.	Dyed, Margarett Hooper, *Widow*, bur. Oct. 17.
Oct. 24.	Dyed, Edmund, son of Nicholas Smith, *Goldsmith*, bur. Oct. 25.
Nov. 12.	Dyed, Ann Browne, *servant maid* to John Broughton, *Victualler*, of a hurt receaved by a fall into a vault or seller in Woolchurch Markett place, bur. Nov. 13, in the New Churchyard, by Bethleham.
Nov. 20.	Dyed, Bollingham, son of Phillip Frowd, *Esq.*, *Master of Post Office*, bur. Nov. 21,
Dec. 11.	Dyed, Jane Alleine, *Widdow*, bur. Dec. 12.
Dec. 21.	Francis Hayes, *Apothecarie*.
Dec. 24.	A female chrisom child of Joane Phee.

Dec. 28.	Dyed, Mary Steele, *Widow*, bur. Dec. 30.
Dec. 29.	Dyed, Richard Butler, *Merchant*, late of St. Clement's Eastcheap, bur. Jan. 3.
Jan. 5.	Dyed, Edmund, son of Edmund Pike, bur. Jan. 6.
Jan. 15.	Dyed, John Marshall, *aprentice* to Mr. Augustine Ballow, *Merchant*, bur. Jan. 16.
Jan. 16.	Dyed, Mary, daughter of Mr. John Tenysle, *Goldsmith*, bur. Jan. 18.
Jan. 25.	Dyed, John, son of James Sibley, bur. Jan. 26.
Jan. 28.	Dyed, Mary, daughter of Ambros Lightefoote, bur. Jan. 30
Jan. 29.	Dyed, Nathaniel, son of Mrs. Jane Payne, *Widdow*, of the Parish of St. Bennett Gracechurch, bur. Feb. 1, in Sir John Percivall's vault in the Chancell.
Feb. 1.	Dyed, Hannah, daughter of ——— [*sic*] Deard, bur. Feb. 2.
Feb. 1.	Dyed, Thomas, son of James Sibley, bur. Feb. 3.
Feb. 6.	Dyed, Mary, daughter Harbey, bur. Feb. 7. [*sic*]
Feb. 5.	Dyed, Elizabeth, daughter of George Sheepheid, bur. Feb. 10.
Feb. 10.	Dyed, Bridgett, daughter of John Snell, bur. Feb. 11.
Feb. 17.	Dyed, Samuell, son of Anthony Storey, bur. Feb. 19.
Feb. 19.	Dyed, Dorothe, daughter of George Sheepsheid, bur. Feb. 20.
Feb. 20.	Dyed, Joane Acklaw, *maid servant* to William Kirton, bur. Feb. 29.
Mar. 12.	Dyed, William Rawlingson, *Milliner*, bur. Mar. 16.
Mar. 18.	Dyed, William, son of Allexander Ward, bur. Mar. 20.
Mar. 22.	Christopher, son of John Thursbey, bur. Mar. 23.
Mar. 24.	Dyed, Dorothe Hooper, bur. Mar. 26.
Mar. 26.	Dyed, Elizabeth, daughter of Thomas Burford, bur. Mar. 29.
Mar. 27.	Dyed, Mary, daughter of Humphrey Bouldron, bur. Mar. 29.

1681

April 19.	Dyed, Mary, daughter of Edward Gladwin, *Goldsmith*, bur. April 20.
April 27.	Dyed, Rogger Browne, *aprentice* to Mr. John Snell, bur. April 28.
May 27.	Dyed, Elizabeth, daughter of George Twine, *Vintner*, bur. May 29.
May 30.	Dyed, Hannah daughter of Richard Burford, bur. May 31.
June 7.	Dyed, Thomas son of Edward Fenwick, *Upholder*, bur. June 8.
June 9.	Dyed, Thomas, son of William, *Merchant* [*sic*] bur. June 10.
June 10.	Dyed, George, son of Nicholas Love, bur. June 11.
June 11.	Dyed, Elizabeth Pew, *maidservant* to Mr. Robert Seigior, bur. June 12.
June 12.	Dyed, Alice, daughter of Mr. Augustin Ballow, *Merchant*, bur. June 15.
June 19.	Dyed, James, son of John Church, bur. June 20.
June 25.	Dyed, Thomas Ap Thomas, at Mr. Sandis, bur. June 26.
June 26.	Dyed, Samuell, son of John Tassell, *Goldsmith*, bur. June 28.
July 6.	Dyed, Mr. Nicholas Phillpots, *Gentleman*, of the County of Hereford, bur. July 14.

July 12.   Dyed, George Hunt, *servant* to Mr. Michaell Hodgkins, *Warehouseman*, bur. July 13.

July 22.   Dyed, Hannah, daughter of John Harleing, *Goldsmith*, bur. July 24.

July 26.   Dyed, Henry, son of John Coleman, *Merchant*, bur. July 28.

July 27.   William Jeanes, *aprentice* to Richard Franckling, *Packer*, bur. July 28.

Aug. 2.   Dyed, Henry Huntly, *coachman* to Mr. Charles Duncomb, *Goldsmith*, bur. same night.

Aug. 6.   Dyed, Anne, daughter of William Browne, *Merchant*, bur. Aug. 7.

Aug. 16.   Two abortive children, one male, one female, of Mr. Edmund Pikes.

Aug. 20.   Dyed, John Poult, *servant* to Mr. Anthony Storey, bur. Aug. 20.

Aug. 23.   Dyed, Suzanna, wife of Mr. John Tassell, *Goldsmith*, bur. Aug. 25.

Aug. 27.   Dyed, Frances, daughter of Henry Aynscomb, bur. Aug. 28.

Sep. 8.   Dyed, Christopher, son of Christopher Toms, *Barbour*, bur. Sep. 11.

Sep. 23.   Dyed, Elizabeth, daughter of John Rigden, bur. Sep. 25.

Sep. 24.   Dyed, William Child, *servant* to John Beamont, *Tallow-chandler*, bur. Sep. 26.

Sep. 24.   Dyed, Elizabeth, daughter of Mr. Barnard Eels, *Goldsmith*, bur. Sep. 30.

Sep. 29.   Dyed, Olliver, son of Jonathan Whalcy, *Victualler*, bur. Sep. 30.

Oct. 13.   Dyed, Hannah, wife of Paule Ridley, bur. Oct. 14.

Oct. 22.   Dyed, Elizabeth, daughter of Mr. Thomas Sandis, *Merchant*, bur. Oct. 23.

Oct. 27.   Dyed, Hannah, daughter of Paule Ridley, bur. Oct. 28.

Nov. 16.   Dyed, Thomas, son of Nicholas Smith, *Goldsmith*, bur. Nov. 18.

Dec. 8.   Rose Rushworth, at Newchurch Yard by Bethlehem.

Dec. 14.   A female stillborne childe of Thomas Brown.

Dec. 22.   Dyed, William, son of Samuell Jermyn, bur. Dec. 23.

Jan. 1.   Dyed, Elizabeth, daughter of Henry Lamb, *Goldsmith*, bur. Jan. 2.

Jan. 4.   Dyed, James Allalay, *Bricklayer*, bur. Jan. 5.

Jan. 29.   Dyed, Claude, son of Mrs. Anthoniett Griell, *Widdow*, of the Parish of St. John, Hackney, bur. Feb. 1.

Jan. —[*sic*] John Percivall, late of St. Georges in Southwark, and bur. the 3 of Feb. in the North Ile.

Feb. 7.   Dyed, Richard, son of Christopher Woodhouse, *Docter of Phisick*, bur. Feb. 9, of Berkhampstead in the County of Hartford.

Feb. 8.   Dyed, Mary, daughter of John Tassell, *Goldsmith*, bur. Feb. 9.

Feb. 10.   Dyed, Thomas Constable, bur. Feb. 12.

Feb. 14.   Dyed, Elizabeth, daughter of Alexander Ward, bur. in the New Churchyard by Bethlehem.

Feb. 24.   Dyed, Judith, wife of Caleb Westbrook, bur. in the middle Ile, from St. Stevens Coleman Streete.

Mar. 9.   Dyed, Mary, daughter of Thomas Webster, bur. Mar. 11.

1682

April 6.	Dyed, Alice, daughter of Nicholas Love, bur. April 7.
April 21.	Dyed, Thomas, son of Thomas Browne, *Victualler*, bur. April 23.
April 26.	Dyed, Adam, son of Adam Tingley, *Taylor*, bur. Ap. 27.
May 14.	Dyed, Hester, wife of Adam Tingley, bur. May 17.
June 12.	John Seed, son of Widdow Allalay.
June 20.	Dyed, Mr. James Hobland, bur. June 28, in the Chancell north side of the Communion Table.
Sep. 8.	Dyed, Margarett, wife of John Batch, *Silversmith*, bur. Sep. 11.
Sep. 9.	Dyed, William Lodsam, belonging to the Post Office, bur. Sep. 12.
Sep. 10.	Dyed, Elizabeth, daughter of Mr. Howell, *Perwigemaker*, bur. Sep. 11.
Sep. 10.	Dyed, Edward Pect, *aprentice* to Daniell Lord, *Barbour*, bur. Sep. 11.
Sep. 24.	Dyed, Mr. John Sealy, *Goldsmith*, bur. Sep. 24.
Sep. 29.	Dyed, Harwood, son of William Cooper, *Silkstockin Trimmer*, bur. Sep. 30.
Oct. 9.	Dyed, Gabriell, son of Mr. Gabriell Smith, *Druggist*, bur. Oct. 11.
Nov. 7.	Dyed, Elizabeth, daughter of Margrett Fox, *Widdow*, bur. Nov. 11.
Nov. 8.	Dyed, Sarah, wife of George Capall, *Packer*, bur. Nov. 10.
Nov. 10.	Dyed, Samuell, son of Mr. Allexander Pollington, *Haberdasher of Hatts*, bur. Nov. 12.
Dec. 3.	Mary and Grace, daughters of Mr. Richard Guy, *Vintner*.
Dec. 24.	Dyed, Elizabeth, daughter of John Golding, *Victualler*, bur. Dec. 25.
Dec. 26.	Dyed, Thomas, son of Leonard Sutton, bur. Dec. 27.
Jan. 25.	Dyed, Edward, son of E——— [*sic*] Veale, bur. Jan. 27.
Jan. 31.	Dyed, Elizabeth, wife of Gray Lord, *Vintner*, bur. Feb. 14.
Feb. 8.	Dyed, Cicalie Howard, *Widdow*, bur. Feb. 10.
Mar. 7.	Dyed, William, son of Thomas Pashlar, bur. Mar. 8.
Mar. 14.	Major Samuell Putt.
Mar. 17.	Dyed, Mary, wife of Mr. Thomas Seymour, *Goldsmith*, bur. Mar. 21.
Mar. 20.	Dyed, William Dey, bur, Mar. 22.

1683

April 20.	A female abortive child of Mr. John Smith, *Scrivener*.
April 28.	Ann Wild, *Widdow*.
May 14.	Dyed, Elizabeth, daughter of John Chambers, *Scrivener*, bur. May 16.
May 21.	Dyed, Elizabeth, daughter of William Cooper, bur. May 22.
May 25.	Dyed, Jonathan, son of Jonathan Whaley.
May 27.	Dyed, Suzanna, daughter of Mr. Thomas Sandis, *Merchant*, bur. May 28.
June 5.	Suzanna, wife of Mr. ——— [*sic*] Singleton, of the Parish of St. Mildred in the Poultry, bur. June 5.
June 4.	Dyed, Thomas, son of Thomas Manwood, *Bookebinder*, bur. June 5.
June 5.	Dyed, Charles, son of Mr. Barnard Eales, *Goldsmith*, bur. June 6.

June 5.	Dyed, Dorothe, daughter of Georg Sheepsheid, bur. 16 [*sic*]
June 13.	Edward Backwell, *Esq.* [see entry Oct. 20, 1685].
June 27.	Dyed, Mary Fletcher, *Widdow*, bur. June 30.
July 25.	Dyed, John, son of Thomas Pashlar, bur. July 27.
Aug. 1.	Dyed, Henry, son of Mr. Augustine Ballow, bur. Aug. 2.
Aug. 24.	Dyed, Richard, son of Richard Franckling, *Packer*, bur.
Aug. 26.	Dyed, Sara, daughter of Daniell Lord, *Barbour*, bur. Aug. 28.
Sep. 6.	Dyed, Edward Olton, *Vintner*.
Sep. 7.	Dyed, John, son of John Rennalls, *Apothycary*.
Sep. 13.	Dyed, Francis Eads, *Doctor in Phisic*.
Sept. 22.	Dyed, John, son of Mr. John Temple, bur. Sep. 23.
Oct. 2.	Dyed, Anthony Storer, *Upholder*, bur. Oct. 5.
Oct. 3.	Dyed, Elizabeth, daughter of Maurice Tipper, *Confectioner*.
Oct. 20.	Dyed, Mr. John Sweethin, bur. Oct. 25.
Oct. 26.	An abortive child of Thomas Block.
Oct. 28.	Dyed, Robert, son of John Maurice, *Merchant*, bur. Oct. 29.
Nov. 2.	Dyed, Jane, wife of Jarvis Baker, bur. Nov.
Nov. 13.	Dyed, Honour, daughter of Georg Beare, *Vintner*, bur. Nov. 15.
Dec. 2.	Mr. John Portman, *Goldsmith*, from the Parish of St. Brides London, in Sir John Parcivall's Vault.
Dec. 13.	Dyed, Elizabeth, wife of Thomas Manwood, bur. Dec. 15.
Dec. 17.	Dyed, Mr. John Child, *Grocer*, bur. Dec. 23.
Dec. 21.	Dyed, Sara Wallis, of the Parish of Greate Allhallowes, bur. Dec. 24.
Dec. 24.	Dyed, Henry, son of Mr. Thomas Williams, *Goldsmith*, bur. Dec
Dec. 26.	Dyed, Elizabeth, daughter of Abraham Catlett, bur. Dec. 30.
Dec. 31.	Dyed, Richard Smart, bur. Jan. 1.
Jan. 1.	Dyed, Mr. Charles Gossling, bur. Jan. 3.
Jan. 13.	Dyed, Robert, son of Robert and Annie Taylor, bur. Jan. 15.
Jan. 19.	Caleb Gravenor, in the New Churchyard by Bethlehem.
Jan. 20.	Dyed, Benjamine, son of ——— Brodwick, *Shoemaker*, bur. Jan. 22.
Feb. 6.	A female abortive child of Henry Lamb, *Goldsmith*.
Feb. 13.	Dyed, William, son of William Denne, *Goldsmith*, bur. Feb. 15.
Feb. 13.	Dyed, Jacob, son of John Farmere, bur. Feb. 17.
Feb. 15.	Dyed, Mr. Giles Conger, bur. Feb. 19.
Feb. 27.	Dyed, Anna, wife of John Wilson, *Vintner*, bur. Mar. 2.
Mar. 7.	Dyed, Melior, daughter of Richard Benskin, *Gold Ring Maker*, bur. Mar. 9.
Mar. 13.	Dyed, Isaac, son of Mr. John Coleman, *Merchant*, bur. Mar. 15.
Mar. 19.	Dyed, Elizabeth, wife of Capt. John Hillman, bur. Mar. 28.
Mar. 25.	Dyed, Mary Jones, *Widdow*, of the Parish of St. Gregories, London, bur. Mar. 23.

1684

April 2.	Caleb Nicholas, *Chiergeon*.
April 6.	Dyed, Edward, son of Edward Gladwin, *Goldsmith*, bur. April 9.

April 19.	Dyed, Mary, wife of Mr. Daniel Morris, *Plaisterer*, bur. April 23.
April 25.	Dyed, Richard Franckling, *Packer*, bur. April 27.
April 28.	Dyed, Thomas, son of Mr. Allexander Pollington, *Haberdasher of Hatts*, bur. April 30.
May 29.	Jane, wife of Mr. Nicholas Collett, from the Parish of St. Bottolph, Aldersgate.
June 18.	Dyed, Mary Day, bur. June 20.
June 21.	A male stillborne child of ――― [*sic*] Underwood.
June 7.	Dyed, Margerett, daughter of Mr. Peter Wade, bur. June 9.
June 22.	Dyed, Sara, daughter of Maurice Tipper, bur. June 24.
June 27.	Dyed, Faith, wife of Thomas Gibson, *Taylor*, bur. June 28.
July 25.	Dyed, Thomas Goade, *Gentleman*, bur. July 27.
July 31.	Dyed, William, son of Mr. Barnard Eales, *Goldsmith*, bur. Aug. 2.
July 31.	Dyed, Henry, son of Richard Guy, bur. Aug. 3.
Aug. 11.	Dyed, Martha, daughter of John Cooke, bur. Aug. 13.
Sep. 5.	Dyed, William Gladwin, *Wine Cooper*, bur. Sep. 7.
Sep. 11.	Dyed, Hester, wife of Thomas Pashlar, *Claspmaker*, bur. Sep. 14.
Sep. 14.	Dyed, William Searle, *apprentice* to Mr. John Chambers, bur. Sep. 16.
Sep. 18.	Benjamine, son of Mr. Augustine Ballow, *Merchant*.
Sep. 17.	Dyed, Martin, son of Edmund Halfheid, bur. Sep. 21.
Sep. 28.	Dyed, John, son of Edmund Pike, bur. Sep. 30.
Oct. 4.	Dyed, Sarah, daughter of Thomas Pashlar, bur. Oct. 5.
Oct. 18.	Charles and James, sons of Joseph Hindmarsh, *Bookseller*.
Nov. 4.	Dyed, James, son of Mr. Edward Fenwick, *Upholder*, bur. Nov. 5.
Nov. 5.	Margerett Kemp, *maidservant*, to Mr. William Bigg, *Vintener*, buried in New Churchyard by Bethlehem.
Nov. 23.	Grace Coale, *Widdow*.
Nov. 26.	Dyed, Edmund Halfheid, bur. Nov. 28.
Nov. 28.	Dyed, Mary, daughter of Thomas Woodlaw, *Barbour*, buried Dec. 2.
Dec. 3.	Dyed, Richard Benskin, *Gold ring maker*.
Dec. 12.	Dyed, Hannah Bushell, *maidservant* to Mr. John Wilson, *Vintner*, bur. at the New Churchyard by Bethlehem.
Dec. 15.	Margarett Moore, *maidservant* to Johathan Miles, *Coffeeman* at the New Churchyard by Bethlehem.
Dec. 27.	Dyed, Mr. Edward Barwell, bur. Dec. 31.
Jan. 11.	Dyed, Richard Harloe, bur. Jan. 12.
Jan. 17.	Dyed, Sara Bayley, *Widdow*.
Jan. 18.	Dyed, Mrs. Jane Welden, late of the Parish of St. Mary-at-Hill, London, bur. Jan. 21.
Jan. 28.	John, son of Georg Morey, bur. in the New Churchyard by Bethlehem.
Feb. —	Ellizebeth, wife of Mr. Alexander Pollington.
Feb. 8.	Dyed, Mrs. Ann Love, in the Parish of Allhollowes Staineing, London, bur. Feb. 11.
Feb. 22.	Dyed, Mr. John Haynes, *Wax Chandller*, bur. Feb. 26.
Mar. 16.	Dyed, Francis Nicholson, bur. Mar. 18.

1685

April 1.	Dorrothœ, daughter of John Golding, *Victualler*.

April 10. A male stillborne child of Mr. Peter White, *Goldsmith.*

May 6. Ann Pembrok, *maidservant* to Walter Hoare, *Tallow Chandler*, bur. in the New Churchyard by Bethlehem.

June 2. Dyed, Singleton Veale, bur. June 5.

July 9. Dyed, Elizabeth Hinson, *servant* to Mr. Henry Aikeroids, *Vintner*, bur. July 10.

July 12. Mr. William Duncker, in the Parish of St. Mary Stayneing, London.

July 13. Dyed, Ellizabeth, wife of Thomas Burford, *Warehouseman*, born July 16.

July 20. Dyed, Benjamin, son of John Archer, *Powlterer*, bur. July 22.

Aug. 3. Dyed, Peter, son of Peter Farmer, bur. Aug. 4.

Aug. 1. John, son of Christopher Smeeton, *Writeing Master*.

Aug. 15. Mrs. Ellizabeth Norton, wife of Carah Norton, of the Parish of St. Michael in Crooked Lane, London, bur. in Sir Thomas Ramscy's vault.

Aug. 9. Dyed, John, son of Mr. John Smith, *Scrivener*, bur. Aug. 16.

Aug. 20. Dyed, Suzanna, daughter of Thomas Manwood, *Bookbinder*, bur. Aug. 21.

Sep. 1. Jonathan, son of Jonathan Miles, *Coffeeman*.

Sep. 3. Elizabeth Goodwin.

Sep. 2. Dyed, Ann, daughter of John Golding, *Victualler*, bur. Sep. 4.

Sep. 3. Dyed, Henry, son of Mr. John Smith, *Scrivener*, bur. Sep. 6.

Sep. 5. Dyed, Sarah, daughter of Melior Benskin, *Widdow*, bur. Sep. 7.

Sep. 9. Dyed, Mr. William Pighte, *Gent.*, *Strainger*, bur. Sep. 10.

Sep. 25. Dyed, Sarah, wife of William Bigg, *Vintner*, bur. Sep. 27. A stillborne male child taken up out of the churchyard and put into her coffin, buried with her.

Oct. 20. The corps of Edward Backwell, Esq., was taken out of the vault under the Vestrey and carried to Terringham in the county of Buckingham to be buryed there ; who was brought from Holland where he dyed, and buryed the 13 of June, 1683, as above said.

Oct. 24. Dyed, Ann Veale, *Widdow*, bur. Oct. 27.

Nov. 1. Peter Fanquett, *Frenchman*, at New Churchyard by Bethlehem.

Nov. 23. Dyed, Hellena, daughter of Joseph Hindmarsh, *Bookseller*, bur. Nov. 24.

Nov. 28. Dyed, Isaack, son of Mr. Thomas Williams, *Goldsmith*, bur. Nov. 30.

Dec. 1. Dyed, Richard, son of Nicholas Marriott, bur. Dec. 2.

Dec. 1. Dyed, Mary, daughter of John Campin, *Ship Carpenter*, bur. Dec. 3.

Dec. 10. Dyed, Audre, wife of Joseph Cozens, *Barbour*, bur. Dec. 13.

Dec. 19. Dyed, Edward, son of Edward Chadcey, *Baker*, bur. Dec. 20.

Dec. 24. Dyed, Richard Poyner, *Apothycary*.

Jan. 1. Dyed, Ann, daughter of Mr. John Wilson, *Vintner*, of the Parish of St. Ethelboroughs, London, bur. Jan. 4.

Jan. 11. Dyed, Christopher Hooper, bur. Jan. 12.

Feb. 16. Mrs. Issabell Moore, *Widdow*, in the Parish Christchurch, London.

Feb. 17.	Dyed, Edward Fisher, *servant* to Mr. John Snell, *Goldsmith*, bur. Feb. 18.
Feb. 18.	Dyed, George Walker, *aprentiz* to Mr. Robert Moore, *Goldsmith*, bur. Feb. 21.
Mar. 10.	Dyed, Edward Accrees, bur. Mar. 12, at New Churchyard by Bethlehem.
Mar. 15.	Dyed, Lettis, daughter of Jonathan Whaley, bur. Feb. 16.
Mar. 19.	Dyed, Mary Cook, *servant* to Mr. Dorrington, bur. Mar. 20.
Mar. 24.	Dyed, John, son of Richard Guy, *Vintner*, bur. Mar. 25.
Mar. 26.	Dyed, Edward Evans, *Hotpresser*.

1686

April 8.	Mary Ward, at New Churchyard by Bethlehem.
April 20.	Dyed, Michaell, son of James Sibley, *Glassman*, bur. April 23.

[*End of the Burials in the 2nd Volume of the Registers.*]

[Vol. iij.]

THE Names of such as have bine buried in the Parish of St. Mary Wolnothe in London, sithence the twentieth day of April, Anno Domini 1686.

1686

June 20.	Dyed, Judith, daughter of Richard Peck, bur. June 21.
June 25.	Dyed, John, son of Mr. John Grosvenor, *Upholder*, bur. July 4.
July 9.	Dyed, Arabella, daughter of Mr. Phillip Scarth, *Druggest*, bur. July 10.
July 29.	Dyed, Blaney, son of Mr. Blaney Sandford, bur. July 30.
July 31.	Dyed, Mr. Salmon Willett, of Fulham, *Gentleman*, bur. Aug. 4.
Aug. 8.	Dyed, Richard, son of Mr. Thomas Williams, *Goldsmith*, bur. Aug. 10.
Aug. 16.	Dyed, Rebecca Tingnall, bur. Aug. 18.
Aug. 25.	Dyed, William, son of William Browne, bur. Aug. 26.
Aug. 28.	Dyed, William, son of Mr. Barnard Eales, *Goldsmith*, bur. Aug. 30.
Aug. 30.	Dyed, Mary, daughter of Mr. Peter Wade, *Goldsmith*, bur. Sep. 1.
Sep. 20.	Dyed, Henry Aickeroid, *Vintner*, bur. Sep. 23.
Oct. 1.	Dyed, Paule Giles, *Brewer*, bur. Oct. 4.
Oct. 8.	A stillborne of Robert Abbis, *Goldsmith*.
Oct. 6.	Dyed, Richard Burford, *Warehouse Keeper*, bur. Oct. 10.
Oct. 8.	Dyed, Ann, daughter of Daniell Lord, *Barbour*, bur. Oct. 10.
Oct. 30.	Dyed, John Goare, *Victualler*, bur. Oct. 31.

Nov. 4.	Dyed, John Buggin, *Minister and Stranger*, bur. Nov. 7.
Nov. 9.	Mr. John Lloyd, *Merchant* at Mr. Morgans, late of Bristow.
Nov. 16.	Dyed, Mr. Daniell Morris, *Plaisterer*, bur. Nov. 20.
Nov. 17.	John Lee, *aprentice* to Mr. Robert Willson, *Vintner*.
Nov. 27.	Thomas, son of Mr. Henry Lamb, *Goldsmith*.
Dec. 1.	Mrs. Margarett Wintley, wife of Mr. William Wintley, of the Parish of Allhallowes the less, *Silkdyer*.
Nov. 30.	Dyed, John, son of Mr. Edward Fenwick, *Upholder*, bur. Dec. 2.
Dec. 3.	Dyed, Sarah, daughter of Mr. Edward Fenwick, *Upholder*, bur. Dec. 4.
Dec. 7.	Dyed, Ann Harward, *Widdow*, bur. Dec. 9.
Dec. 21.	Dyed, Willmore, son of Mr. Peter Wade, *Goldsmith*, bur. Dec. 23.
Dec. 26.	Dyed, Margarett Browne, *Widdow*, at Mr. Richard Burfords, bur. Dec. 29.
Dec. 26.	Dyed, Mr. Peter Herringhook, *Merchant*, late of St. Antholins, London, bur. Dec. 31.
Jan. 8.	Dyed, Rebecca Baker, daughter of Jane Baker, *Widdow*, bur. Jan. 9.
Feb. 2.	Dyed, Jane, daughter of Edward Chadcey, *Baker*, bur. Feb. 4.
Feb. 8.	Dyed, Mr. John Willson, *Vintner*, of the Parish of St. Ethelburgh, London, bur. Feb. 11.
Feb. 15.	Dyed, Johanna Brackens, *maid servant* to Mr. Robert Peck, *Hosier*, bur. Feb. 16, in the New Churchyard by Bethlehem.
Feb. 18.	Dyed, John Peter, son of Mr. Peter Lauz, *French Merchant*, bur. Feb. 19.
Mar. 9.	Dyed, Hannah, daughter of Hannah Burford, *Widdow*, bur. Mar. 11.
Mar. 11.	Dyed, Edith Terwhitt, *Widdow*, bur. Mar. 13.
Mar. 13.	Dyed, William Courtney, bur. Mar. 15.

1687

April 3.	Dyed, Margaret wife of John Smith, *Scivener*, bur. April 8.
May 7.	A ——— [*sic*] abortive child of Mr. Peter White, *Goldsmith*.
May 9.	A ——— [*sic*] abortive child of Mr. Blaney Sandford.
May 21.	Dyed, James, son of Mr. James Thompson, bur. May 22.
May 26.	Margarett, daughter of Mr. John Smith, *Scrivener*.
May 26.	Dyed, Anna, daughter of John Smith, *Packer*, bur. May 27.
May 26.	Dyed, Mrs. Joyce Weld, *Widdow*, of Richmond, Surrey. bur. May 31.
July 6.	Dyed, Henry, son of Henry Robinson, *Goldsmith*.
July 30.	Dyed, Mr. John Sayer, *Vintner*, bur. Aug. 5.
Aug. 3.	Dyed, Elizabeth, daughter of Mr. John Knap, *Merchant*, bur. Aug, 4,
Sep. 20.	Dyed, Mr. Rowland Dee, *Merchant*, bur. Sep. 28.
Sep. 30.	Dyed, Mrs. Margarett Dyc, *Widdow*, bur. Oct. 3.
Oct. 12.	Dyed, George Tingnall, *Victualler*, bur. Oct. 14.
Nov. 6.	Dyed, Ann Seed, bur. Nov. 7.
Nov. 18.	Dyed, Sarah, daughter of Abraham Catlett, bur. Nov. 20.
Nov. 20.	Georg Chapman, *aprentice* to John Batch, *Silversmith*, bur. Nov. 22.

Nov. 26.	Dyed, William, son of Nicholas Love, bur Nov. 28.
Dec. 20.	A male infant being murtherd by the mother, Sina Jones, *servant* to Joseph Cozens, *Barbour*, brought to bed there.
Dec. 25.	Dyed, Mary, daughter of Mr. Edward Fenwick, *Upholder*, bur. Dec. 27.
Jan. 23.	Dyed, Suzanna, daughter of John Golding, *Victualler*, bur. Jan. 24.
Jan. 23.	Dyed, Mrs. Mary Ward, *Widdow*, bur. Jan. 27.
Feb. 7.	Dyed, Dorothoe, daughter of Robert Cox, *Bookbinder*, bur. Feb. 8.
Mar. 6.	Dyed, Charles, son of Mr. John Coleman, *Merchant*, bur. Mar. 8.
Mar. 8.	Dyed, William Juxson, bur. Mar. 11, in Finsbury Ground.
April 22.	Dyed, Samuell Symonds, *Clerk* to Mr. Woodward, *Attorney at Law*, bur. Mar. 23.
Mar. 31.	Dyed, Margarett Chettleburgh, bur. April, 11.

1688

May 18.	A female abortive child of John Moor, *Cook*.
May 20.	Dyed Browne, son of Mr. Thomas Sandis, bur. May 23.
June 6.	Dyed, Charles Banar, bur. June 7 in the New Churchyard by Bethlehem.
June 6.	Dyed, Justinian, son of George Sheepside, bur. June 10.
June 9.	Dyed, Suzanna, daughter of Mr. Barnard Eales, *Goldsmith*, bur. June 12.
June 18.	Dyed, Katherine, daughter of Henry Robinson, bur. June 19.
June 28.	Charles Viner, Esq., in Sir Robert Viner's vault.
July 1.	Dyed, Jane, daughter of Mr. John Chambers, *Scrivener*, bur. July 3.
July 12.	John England, *Gent.*, in the Parish of St. Andrew, Holborne.
July 17.	Dyed, William Gray, at the Widdow Evans' house, bur. July 19.
July 25.	Dyed, Joseph, son of Mr. Joseph Moore, *Goldsmith*, bur. July 27, in the New Churchyard by Finsbury.
Aug. 24.	Dyed, Sarah Cole, *servant* to Mr. Wood, *Fishmonger*, bur. Aug. 26.
Aug. 28.	Dyed, Mr. Thomas Symonds, *Merchant*, bur. Aug. 30.
Sep. 2.	Dyed, Sir Robert Viner, *Knt. Barrt.*, at Windsor Castle, and bur. the 16th day in his vault in the South Chapple.
Sep. 21.	Dyed, Mr. Thomas Watkins, *Leatherseller*, bur. Sep. 23.
Sep. 22.	Dyed, John Daniell, *Gold Ring Maker*, bur. Sep. 23.
Sep. 29.	Dyed, Henry, son of Mathew Shepherd, *Skinner*, bur. Oct. 2.
Nov. 2.	Dyed, William Harrison, *Vintner*, bur. Nov. 4.
Nov. 12.	Dyed, Andrew Denison, *Taylor*, bur. Nov. 14, at New Churchyard by Bethlehem.
Nov. 11.	Dyed, Ann, daughter of Mr. John Temple, bur. Nov. 13, from White Fryers, London.
Nov. 15.	Dyed, Rebecca Mordan, bur. Nov. 18.
Dec. 4.	Dyed, Mrs. Mary Dunckar, *Widow*, bur. Dec. 7.
Dec. 8.	Dyed, Ann, wife of ———— [*sic*] Tobin, of the Savoy Parish, bur. Dec. 11.

Dec. 23.	David and Rebecca Children.
Dec. 28.	Jonathan, son of George Childrens.
Dec. 30.	Mrs. Elizabeth Deale, from the Parish of St. Bridgett, London.
Jan. 7.	Dyed, Richard, son of William James, *Washballmaker,* bur. Jan. 9.
Jan. 9.	Dyed, Ann Jarvis, *servant* of Thomas Jarvis, *Coffeeman,* bur. Jan. 10.
Jan. 20.	Dyed, Thomas Parks, *Coachman* to Charles Duncomb, Esq., bur. Jan. 21.
Feb. 2.	Dyed, William Lambert, bur. Feb. 5.
Feb. 11.	Dyed, Mrs. Mary Haywood, bur. Feb. 13.
Feb. 17.	Dyed, Thomas, son of John Bach, *Working Goldsmith,* bur. Feb. 18.
Feb. 20.	Dyed, Claudius, son of Mr. Peter Lauz, *French Merchant,* bur. Feb. 21.
Feb. 20.	Dyed, Mr. Andrew Crisp, *Rector of the Parish,* bur. Feb. 25, in the Chancell.

1689

April 3.	Dyed, Isaack, son of Isaack Moorloe, in the Finsbury Ground, April 5.
April 3.	Dyed, John, son of Edward Paine, bur. April 4.
May 7.	Dyed, John, son of George Cooke, *Instrument Maker,* and was bur. the 10th in Bethlehem Churchyard.
June 18.	An abortive child of Mr. Peter White, in the same Churchyard.
June 22.	Dyed, Samuell Jermyn, *Cleerke of this Parish,* bur. June 25.
June 28.	Dyed, Thomas Green, bur. June 30.
July 14.	Miles Fletcher, in Bedlam Churchyard.
July 16.	Mr. Homes man.
July 16.	A Frenchman who lodged at the Rose and Crowne in Sherburne lane.
July 22.	Lidia, daughter of Mr. John Coleman.
Aug. 14.	Mary, wife of Thomas Winkfield, and was carried out of the Parish.
Aug. 15.	Dyed, Ellen, wife of Edward Pilkington, and was carried out of the Parish.
Sep. 4.	Dyed, Elizabeth, wife of John Travell, and was carried out of the Parish.
Sep. 19.	Richard Poole.
Sep. 20.	Benjeman Fenwick.
Oct. 12.	[*sic*] Godfrey Beck, dyed and was bur. the 13.
Oct. 20.	Dyed, Richard Poulter, and was carried out of the Parish to St. James's, Duke Place.
Oct. 25.	Adam Children.
Nov. 2.	Dyed, John Painter, and was buried at St. Michaell's Cornhill.
Nov. 3.	Dyed, Ann Brown.
Nov. 10.	Ann, wife of [ink faded] Kelley.
Nov. 11.	Dyed, Ellinor, wife of Thomas Winfield, and was carried to Croydon.
Nov. 20.	Ann Becoe.
Nov. 23.	Dyed, Peter Colly, bur. Nov. 26.
Nov. 25.	Dyed, Ann, daughter of Joseph Cossens.

Nov. 30. Robert Knap.

Dec. 1. Dyed, Even Gardner, bur. in Bethlehem Churchyard, Dec. 3.

Dec. 3. Dyed, Jane, [this has been written over, apparently Anah] Vanbesber, [*sic*] daughter of Thomas Weld, Esq.

Dec. 3. Dyed, Henry Williams, bur. Dec. 4.

Dec. 21. Stephn Venables, in Bedlam Churchyard.

Dec. 30. Dyed, Lawrence Weld, bur. Jan. 2.

Jan. 9. Jeshua Marloe, buried at Finsbury.

Jan. 10. Dyed, Benjiman, son of Mr. John Coleman, bur. Jan. 12.

Jan. 20. Dyed, Mary, daughter of John Moore, bur. Jan. 28.

Feb. 7. Dyed, Thomas Travvis, *Bookeseller.* bur. Feb. 9.

Feb. 12. Dyed, Joseph Moore, *Chasser*, bur. Feb. 14.

Feb. 24. Dyed, Sarah, wife of Mr. Alexander Pollington, *Haberdasher*, bur. Feb. 27.

Feb. 24. Dyed, Mr. Robert Viner, *Goldsmith*, and was carried into Warwickshire to be buried.

1690

April 1. John Ilattsom [or Hattsom.]

April 27. Dyed, Elizabeth, wife of Peter White, *Goldsmith*, bur. April 30.

April 27. Was borne Robert, the son of Peter White, *Goldsmith*, and Elizabeth, his wife, and buried 2nd of May following.

May 7. John Solloman.

May 13. Sarah, wife of Godfrey Beck.

May 16. Elizabeth, daughter of Edward Gladding.

June 9. Thomas Sands.

June 11. Richard Woolnoth.

June 23. Died, Elinor Seiks, at Mr. West, *Scrivener*, interred at St. Christophers, June 24.

July 13. Robert Ewling, of the post house.

July 17. Mr. Nathaniell Pool, *Goldsmith*.

July 17. Cornelius, son of Mr. John Coleman.

July 28. Departed this life Thomas Gregory, interred same day.

Aug. 6. Departed this life John Love, interred Aug. 7.

Aug. 17. Departed this life William Trinder, and was carried into Oxfordsheir to be buried, Aug. 21.

Sep. 1. Departed this life Mrs. Jeane Spinks, interred Sep. 4.

Sep. 17. Mr. William White, of St. Georges, Southwark, was brought and interred.

Oct. 3. Interred, Mr. Isaac Clark, of St. John at Hackney, in Sir Thomas Ramsey's vault.

Oct. 5. Interred, Mary, daughter of John Hawley, *Haberdasher of Hatts*.

Oct. 9. Departed this life Mary Cattlett, interred Oct. 10.

Oct. 14. Joane Woolnoth, a parish child, was interred.

Oct. 17. Dyed, John Chadsey, bur. in the Churchyard neare the Post house, Oct. 19.

Nov. 5. Departed this life Dorothy Wicks, interred at Finsbury, Nov. 7.

Nov. 17. Departed this life, Jediaell Turner, interred Nov. 18.

Nov. 28. Interred, Joan Hall.

Nov. 29. Interred, Isaac Le Blone.

Dec. 11.	Dyed, William Hawkins, interred at St. Sweetings, Dec. 15.
Dec. 22.	Dyed, a poor woman, and was buried in Bethlehem.
Dec. 24.	Interred, an abortive child of Edward Edwards.
Jan. 1.	Interred, Thomas Townsend.
Jan. 2.	Interred, William Burfoot.
Jan. 2.	Interred, Samuell Shipley.
Jan. 4.	Luke Jones was buried at Stepney.
Jan. 6.	Dyed, Abraham Catlett, interred Jan. 8.
Jan. 15.	Dyed, Timothy Bebb, interred Jan. 18.
Feb. 4.	Departed this life Susanna Downing, interred in Bethlehem Churchyard, Feb. 5.
Feb. 9.	Dyed, Thomas Churchy, and was carried to Somersett there to be burried, Feb. 16.
Feb. 12.	Departed this life Mary Browne, interred Feb. 15.
Feb. 15.	Departed this life Hannah Dewit *Widdow*, interred at Christchurch Feb. 19.
Mar. 5.	Dyed, Sarah Beach, interred Mar. 6.
Mar. 17.	Departed this life, Elizabeth Giles, interred Mar. 20.

1691

April 3.	Died, Edward Bringley, interred April 5.
April 4.	Dyed, William Guy, interred April 5.
April 12	Dyed, Charles Browne, interred April 15.
April 17.	Dyed, Elizabeth Cockerill, interred at Finsbury, April 20.
April 22.	Dyed, Mary, wife of Henry Bradley, interred April 26.
May 20.	Dyed, John Inns, interred April 26.
June 8.	Dyed, Ellinor Booker, interred June 9.
July 10.	Dyed, John Robinson, interred July 12.
July 14.	Jane Holbrook, interred July 16.
July 28.	Nicholas Williams, interred
Aug. 27.	Dyed, Gibson Lucas, and was carried into the Cemetery Aug. 28.
Sep. 2.	Mr. David Clark, of St. John, Hackney, interred in Sir Thomas Ramsey's vault.
Nov. 1.	Departed this life Ann, wife of John Hillman, interred Nov. 5.
Nov. 7.	Departed this life John Sommerton, *a Scotch Minister*, interred Nov. 9.
Nov. 18.	Richard Woolnoth, interred
Nov. 15.	Dyed, Alice Tuenell, interred Nov. 18.
Nov. 20.	Dyed, David Howling, interred Nov. 22.
Nov. 29.	Dyed, Ann Moss, and was carried to the Anna Baptist Ground in the Park in Southwark, Nov. 30.
Dec. 2.	Dyed, Henry Hoskins, of Woolwich, interred Dec. 4.
Dec. 6.	Dyed, John Chambers, interred Dec. 10.
Dec. 24.	Dyed, Jemimah Temple, interred Dec. 25.
Dec. 29.	Dyed, John Eldridge, interred Jan. 1.
Jan. 3.	Dyed, William Knap, interred Jan. 4.
Jan. 3	Dyed, Robert Barlow, interred in Bethlehem, Jan. 4.
Jan. 10.	Dyed, John Harling, interred Jan. 13.
Jan. 26.	Dyed, John Harling, senior, interred Feb. 3.
Jan. 28.	Dyed, Sarah North, interred Jan. 31.
Feb. 5.	Dyed, Elizabeth Staples, interred Feb. 8.
Feb. 5.	Dyed, Bridgett Eales, interred Feb. 10.
Feb. 8.	Dyed, Richard Holdbrook, interred Feb. 10.

Feb. 11.   Dyed, Elizabeth Perkins, *Widdow*, interred Feb. 13.
Feb. 13.   Dyed, Elizabeth Cooper, interred Feb. 16.
Feb. 23.   Dyed, Maurice Tipper, interred Feb. 24.
Feb. 28.   Dyed, Francis Hawand, interred Feb. 29.
Mar. 7.   Dyed, Thomas Smith, interred Mar. 10.
Mar. 15.   Dyed, Charles Goure, interred Mar. 16.
Mar. 25.   Dyed, Martha Cosens, interred Mar. 27.

1692

April 2.   Dyed, Phillip Dacres, interred April 5.
April 28.   Dyed, John and Abigaill Woolnoth, both parish children, interred April 29.
June 2.   Dyed, Mary Huggins, interred June 5.
July 7.   Dyed, Helener Hindmarsh, interred July 8.
July 28.   Dyed, Francis Hindmarsh, interred July 29.
Aug. 2.   Dyed, Hannah Pashler, interred Aug. 4.
Aug. 6.   Dyed, Susanna Wynn, interred in Bethelem Churchyard, Aug. 7.
Aug. 15.   Dyed, John Johnson, interred Aug. 16.
Sep. 3.   Dyed, Elizabeth Peck, interred Sep. 5.
Sep. 8.   Dyed, Sarah Holmes, interred Sep. 9.
Sep. 10.   Dyed, Ann, a *blackamoor servant* to Mr. Pollington, interred in Bethlem Churchyard, Sep. 11.
Sep. 16.   Dyed, Alexander Tayes, interred Sep. 21.
Nov. 13.   Interred, Jeane Collett, of St. Clement Dane.
Nov. 16.   Dyed, Joshua Catlet, interred Nov. 17,
Nov. 18.   Dyed, Elizabeth Marlow, interred Nov. 19.
Dec. 8.   Dyed, Elizabeth Smith, interred Dec. 10.
Jan. 6.   Dyed, John Hilman, interred Jan. 11.
Jan. 28.   Dyed, Phebee Lumin, interred Jan 29.
Jan. 27.   Dyed, John Gardner, interred Jan. 30.
Feb. 10.   Dyed, Jean Barber, interred Feb. 12.
Feb. 12.   Dyed, Johns Sands, interred Feb. 14.
Feb. 11.   Dyed, Samuell Sweeting, interred Feb. 23.
Feb. 22.   Dyed, Ann Sutton, interred Feb. 24.
Feb. 21.   Dyed, Mary Yates, interred Feb. 26.
Feb. 26.   Dyed, William Rose, interred Feb. 27, a poor woman's child, delivered in the street.
Feb. 27.   Interred, an abortive child of Mr. Richard Lawrence.
Mar. 3.   Dyed, Hannah Marlow, interred in Mr. Tindall's ground at Bunhill, Mar. 6.
Mar. 5.   Dyed, John Woolnoth, interred Mar. 7.
Mar. 6.   Dyed, Mary Knapp, interred Mar. 7.
Mar. 7.   Dyed, Katherine Scott, interred Mar. 9.

1693

April 11.   Dyed, Joseph Archer, interred April 13.
April 19.   Dyed, Elizabeth Woolnoth, interred April 20.
May 14.   Dyed, Mary Edwards, interred May 15.
May 17.   Dyed, Robert Bache, interred May 18.
June 5.   Dyed, John Yates, interred June 10.
June 12.   Dyed, Thomas Batch, interred June 14.
June 20.   Dyed, Mary Harling, interred June 23.
June 22.   Dyed, John Robinson, interred June 24.

July 17.	Dyed, Thomas Blyde, interred July 19.
July 21.	Dyed, Richard Venables, interred in Bethlehem Church-yard, July 23.
July 27.	Died, Mary Buckworth, a parish foundling child, interred July 29.
July 29.	Dyed, Charles Hord, interred in Oxfordsheir, Aug. 2.
Aug. 2.	Dyed, Joan Haynes, interred Aug. 3.
Aug. 9.	Dyed, George Hands, interred Aug. 10.
Aug. 16.	Dyed, George Signol, interred Aug. 17.
Aug. 16.	Dyed, Joseph Church, interred Aug. 17.
Aug. 20.	Dyed, Sarah Chase, interred Aug. 21.
Sep. 26.	Dyed, Sarah Peck, interred Oct. 1.
Oct. 6.	Dyed, Christopher Toms, interred Oct. 8.
Oct. 15.	Dyed, Thomas Hinmarsh, interred Oct. 16.
Oct. 25.	Dyed, Mary Bradbury, interred Oct. 29.
Oct. 24.	Dyed, Abraham Mackland, interred Nov. 2.
Nov. 13.	Died, John Ruston, interred Nov. 14.
Nov. 27.	Died, Mary, wife of John Browne and daughter of Jacob Gildersleeve, late of Amsterdam, *Milliner*, interred Nov. 28.
Nov. 27.	Dyed, James Dacres, interred Nov. 29.
Nov. 29.	Dyed, Alice Harding, *Widow*, interred Nov. 30.
Nov. 30.	Interred, John Storer.
Nov. 29.	Dyed, Elizabeth, the reputed daughter of Samuell Fisher, *Hosier*, on the body of Elizabeth Lane, interred Nov. 30.
Nov. 30.	Died, Edward Paine, interred Dec. 3.
Dec. 7.	Died, Mary Taylor, interred with her child, Dec. 10.
Dec. 18.	Peter Grill, of St. Leonard, Shoreditch, interred
Jan. 27.	Dyed, Mary Handcock, interred Jan. 29th.
Jan. 31.	Dyed, John Ladyman, interred Feb. 1.
Feb. 5.	Dyed, Mrs. Elizabeth Sands, wife of Mr. Thomas Sands, interred Feb. 10.
Mar. 9.	Dyed, Michaell Drake, interred in Bethlehem Churchyard, Mar. 10.
Mar. 9.	Dyed, John Puffey, from Mrs. Rawlinsons, interred Mar. 12.
Mar. 13.	Dyed, Katherine Eller.

1694

April 23.	Dyed, Sarah Moor, interred April 25.
May 23.	Dyed, Sarah Burford, interred May 26.
July 5.	Dyed, Mr. Barnard Eales, interred July 10.
July 10.	Dyed, Edmund Ryley, Mr. Perkin's man, *Druggist*, interred July 11.
July 23.	Dyed, Eleanor Turner, *Widdow*, at Mr. Peter Whites, interred July 25.
July 28.	Dyed, William Browne, interred July 29.
Aug. 11.	Dyed, Judith Scrivens, at Mr. Gibbs's, and was carried into Kent to be interred, Aug. 13.
Aug. 11.	Ann Jakeman, was kild by a cart, and was interred Aug. 11.
Aug. 14.	Dyed, Susanna Sutton, interred Aug. 16.
Aug. 28.	Dyed, Isaac Parsons, interred Aug. 29.
Aug. 30.	Dyed, Elizabeth Roe, interred Aug. 31.
Sep. 16.	Dyed, Anne, daughter of George Cooke, bur. Sep. 18.
Sep. 16.	Dyed, Mr. John Beamont, bur. Sep. 19.

Sep. 18.	Dyed, Thomas Sargeant, bur. Sep. 20.
Oct. 26.	Dyed, John, son of Augustin Ballow, bur. Oct. 27.
Nov. 9.	Dyed, Mr. John Grosvener, interred Nov. 13.
Nov. 18.	Dyed, John Gilbert, interred Nov. 19.
Nov. 22.	Dyed, John Venables, interred in Bethlem Churchyard, Nov. 23.
Dec. 3.	Katherine Farmers, was brought from St. Bennett Finch, and interred.
Dec. 7.	Dyed, Thomas Clay, and was carried into the Poultry to be interred, Dec. 7.
Dec. 9.	Dyed, George White, interred Dec. 10.
Dec. 11.	Dyed, Ann Toms, bur. Dec. 12.
Dec. 20.	Dyed, William Ferrall, interred Dec. 21.
Jan. 16.	Dyed, Frances, wife of John Travell, and was carried to Redding to be interred, Jan. 21.
Jan. 22.	Dyed, Margrett Beals, interred Jan. 23.
Jan. 23.	Dyed, Thomas Cook, son of Widdow Cook, interred Jan. 25.
Jan. 25.	Dyed, Sarah Barker, *servant* to Mr. Bates, interred in the Churchyard under Maddam Lucye's window, Jan. 27.
Feb. 18.	Dyed, Sir William Phipps, and was interred in the vault under the organ gallery, Feb. 21.
Feb. 20.	Dyed, Katherine Wooley, interred Feb. 23.
Feb. 26.	Dyed, Edward Waring, interred Feb. 27.
Mar. 6.	Dyed, Mary Stoatsbury, interred Mar. 8.
Mar. 12.	Dyed, Earle Auger, interred in the chancell Mar. 13.
Mar. 12.	Dyed, Abraham Wilcox, bur. Mar. 14.

1695

April 5.	Dyed, Thomas Taylor, interred April 7.
April 9.	Dyed, Samuel White, interred April 11.
April 23.	Dyed, Mr. Anthony Storer, of the Inner Temple, *Gent.*, interred April 27.
May 1.	Dyed, Elizabeth Paine, interred May 2. S. M. W. N.
May 2.	Dyed, Richard Bolt, interred May 5. S. M. W. C.
May 13.	Interred, John Richardson, a Parish child. S. M. W. N.
May 14.	Dyed, Hannah Fenwick, daughter of Mr. John Fenwick, interred May 17. S. M. W. C.
May 19.	Dyed, John Peck, interred May 20. S. M. W. N.
June 23.	Dyed, John Roker, interred June 25. S. M. W. N.
June 27.	Dyed, Thomas Block, interred June 30. S. M. W. C.
July 19.	Dyed, Mary, wife of John Simpson, and was carried to Enfield to be interred, July 23. S. M. W. C.
Aug. 7.	Buried, a stillborne child of Mr. Abraham Willcox. S. M. W. N.
Sep. 5.	Dyed, Robert Bridges, *servant* to Mr. Toms, *Barber*, bur. Sep. 6. S. M. W. C.
Sep. 21.	Dyed, Mr. Phillip Scarth, and was carried to be interred to Hatfield, in Essex, Sep. 25. S. M. W. N.
Sep. 26.	Dyed, Samuell Chadwell, and was carried to St. Tooleys, in Southwark, to be buried. S. M. W. C.
Oct. 16.	Dyed, Henry Osborne, Nephew to Thomas Guy, Esq., bur. Oct. 17. S. M. W. C.
Oct. 17.	Dyed, John Davis, *Clarke of this Parish,* bur. Oct. 19. S. M. W. C.

Oct. 21.	Dyed, Mary Hindmarsh, interred Nov. 1.
Nov. 2.	Dyed, John Roe, interred Nov. 5. s. m. w. c.
Nov. 3.	Dyed, Richard Henly, interred Nov. 6. s. m. w. n.
Dec. 1.	Dyed, Row Thorpe, interred Dec. 4. s. m. w. n.
Dec. 4.	Dyed, Jeams Sexton, interred Dec. 6. s. m. w. c.
Dec. 16.	Interred, a female child of Mr. Edward Jones. s. m. w. c.
Dec. 23.	Dyed, Elizabeth Browne, *Widdow*, relect of William Brown, of this Parish, *Shoomaker*. s. m. w. n.
Dec. 30.	Ann Browne, *Widdow*, *Darywoman*, bur. Jan. 2. s. m. w. n.
Feb. 1.	Dyed, Mary, daughter of Mr. John Holmes, of St. Mary Woolchurch.
Feb. 1.	Dyed, Beata, daughter of Joseph Tovey, of St. Mary Woolchurch Haw, and was carried to be interred in the Quaker ground in Cripplegate Parish.
Feb. 3.	Dyed, Richard Turner, *servant* to Mr. Samuell White, *Factor*, interred Feb. 5, St. Mary Woolchurch Haw.
Feb. 15.	John Woolnoth, a foundling.
Feb. 16.	Mr. Joseph Hindmarsh, *Bookseller*, of St. Mary Woolchurch Haw.
Feb. 21.	Dyed, Daniel, son of Daniel Puckle, *Gent.*, lodging at Madam Platts, in the Parish of St. Mary Woolchurch Haw, and carried to be interred at the Parish Church of St. Albans, Wood Street.
Mar. 18.	Dyed and was buried, Thomas, son of Thomas Cleave and Mary his wife, *Millinor*, lodgers at Mr. Maddisons in Sherborne lane.
Mar. 21.	Dyed, Robert Batho, the elder, father to Robert Batho, of this Parish, *Confectioner*, bur. Mar. 25.

1696

Mar. 30.	Dyed, Joseph, son of John and Mary Bolton, of St. Mary Woolchurch Haw, *Mealeman*, bur. Mar. 31.
April 8.	Dyed, William, son of Richard and Sarah Guy, of this Parish, *Vintner*, bur. April 10.
April 22.	Dyed, John Lambert, *apprentice* to Mr. Edward Lamber, of this Parish, *Goldsmith*, lodger at Mr. Stanton, bur. April 24.
May 13.	Dyed, Laud Doyley, *Goldsmith*, was carried to the Parish Church of Turvill, Oxfordshire, to be buried, May 16.
May 18.	Buried, William, son of John Giles, *Packer*.
June 5.	Dyed, Robert, son of Robert Abbis, of St. Mary Woolchurch Haw, bur. June 7.
June 16.	Was brought from Peckham, in Surrey, Mr. John Howard, *Apothecary*, and was buried.
June 22.	Mary, wife of Mr. Edward Fenwick, of St. Mary Woolchurch Haw, *Upholster*.
June 25.	Buried, Jonas Horton, a foundling, of St. Mary Woolchurch Haw.
June 28.	Buried, Nathaniell Watts, *servant* to Mr. Speeding, of St. Mary Woolchurch Haw.
July 22.	Buried, Mrs. Sarah, wife of Mr. Godfrey Woodward, *Attorney*, of St. Mary Woolchurch Haw.
July 26.	Buried, a female stillborne child of Mr. Gilling, lodging at Mr. Shadseys, *Baker*.
Aug. 19.	Buried, John Haw, foundling of St. Mary Woolchurch Haw.

Aug. 24. Buried, William Leton, late of the Parish of Grayes, Essex, *Baker*, died in St. Mary Woolchurch Haw.

Sep. 19. Buried, Victor Draper, a foundling of St. Mary Woolchurch Haw.

Oct. 7. Dyed, Mr. Thomas Cockerill, of St. Mary Woolchurch Haw, *Bookseller*, and carried to be interred at Tindall's ground, Finsbury, Oct. 9.

Oct. 8. Dyed, John, son of Richard Gilbert, of St. Mary Woolchurch Haw, *Norwich Factor*, bur. Oct. 9.

Oct. 21. Dyed, Edward Howell, *servant* to Mr. Silvester, of St. Mary Woolchurch Haw, *Linendraper*, interred Oct. 23.

Nov. 5. Dyed, Hester Oldsworth, *servant* to Mr. Edward Ambrose, of St. Mary Woolchurch Haw, *Gent.*, bur. Nov. 7.

Nov. 20. Buried, William Wood, of St. Mary Woolchurch Haw, *Fishmonger*, in the chancell.

Nov. 20. Interred, Charlotta, wife of John Whitehorne, daughter to Mr. Brindley, at the Post Boy.

Dec. 13. Dyed, Francis son of Mr. Edward Jones, of St. Mary Woolchurch Haw, bur. Dec. 15.

Dec. 15. Dyed, Dorcas Urds, *Widdow*, lodging at Deputy Moors, and was carried to be interred in the vault at St. Swithin's Church.

Dec. 24. Buried, Anne, daughter of Robert Wayfield, *Scrivener*,

Dec. 26. Dyed, Mr. William Gladwin, *Goldsmith, Batchelor*, bur. Dec. 30.

Jan. 24. Dyed, Ellinor, daughter of Mr. Phillip Roaker, *Goldsmith.*

Feb. 20. Dyed, Mr. Henry Aynscombe, of St. Mary Woolchurch Haw, *Distiller*, interred Feb. 24.

Mar. 2. Dyed, Sarah, daughter of Martin Beamond, of St. Mary Woolchurch Haw, *Tallow Chandler*, bur. Mar. 3.

Mar. 11. Dyed, John, son of Captain John Passell, *Goldsmith*, lodger at Mr. Meads, of St. Mary Woolchurch Haw, was carried to the Parish Church of St. Vedast, alias Foster Lane, to be interred the same night.

1697

April 5. Dyed, Samuel, son of Martin Beamond, of St. Mary Woolchurch Haw, *Tallowchandler*, bur. April 6.

April 9. Dyed, Robert Cotton, Esq., son of Sir Robert Cotton, *Knight, one of his Majesties Post Masters General*, carried, April 14, to Cunnington, Cambridgeshire to be interred.

April 27. Buried, Susanna Woolnoth, a Parish Child, brought from Nurse Hunt at Ponder's End, in Edmunton Parish.

May 14. Was carried to Hull, in Yorkshire, Anthony Iveson, *Woollen Draper*, who dyed at Mr. Toms, *Barber*, in St. Mary Woolchurch Haw.

June 9. Buried, Katherine Price, *servant* to Mr. Joseph Archer, *Victualler.*

June 14. Dyed, Elizabeth, daughter of Mr. Samuel Shipley, of St. Mary Woolchurch Haw, *Fishmonger*, bur. June 15.

June 16. Dyed, Mary, daughter of Mr. Bolton, *Mealeman*, of St. Mary Woolchurch Haw, bur. June 17.

June. 20. Buried, Elizabeth, wife of Capt. George Twyne, of St. Mary Woolchurch Haw, *Vintner.*

June 25.   Dyed, Seymore, son of Alexander Pile, of St. Mary Woolchurch Haw, *Gent.*, bur. June 27.

July 1.   Dyed, Mary, daughter of John Taylor, of St. Mary Woolchurch Haw, *Cheesemonger*, bur. July 2.

July 5.   Dyed, Mary, daughter of Thomas Chippins, of this Parish, *Cooke*, bur. July 6.

July 25.   Buried, an abortive child of Mr. Henry Wilson, *Goldsmith*, of St. Mary Woolchurch Haw.

July 8.   Dyed, Mr. Thomas Williams, *Goldsmith*, at Westham in Essex, and was interred July 13.

July 6.   Dyed, Margaret, Evans, *Widdow*, interred July 10.

July 14.   Dyed, James Price, son of Mr. John Sebelle, *Gent.*, and Mary his wife, interred July 17.

July 22.   Dyed, Daniel Wingfield, *servant* to Mr. Robert Westcott, of St. Mary Woolchurch Haw, *Vintner*, bur. July 23.

July 27.   Dyed, Mary, daughter of John Evans, *Porter at the Post Office*, interred July 29.

Sep. 5.   Dyed, John, son of George Cooke, *Razormaker*, bur. Sep. 8.

Sep. 23.   Dyed, Sarah Farrington, *Widow*, and lodger, was carried to St. Swithins to be interred, Sep. 26.

Oct. 21.   Was brought from Hackney and buried, Mrs. Ann Elliot, *Widow*, only mother to the now wife of Mr. Robert Baskett, of St. Mary Woolchurch Haw, *Apothecary*.

Nov. 10.   Dyed, John, infant and son of Mr. John Ladyman, *Silversmith*, bur. Nov. 11.

Nov. 12.   Dyed, Mr. Thomas Burford, of St. Mary Woolchurch Haw, *Factor*, bur. Nov. 17.

Nov. 23.   Buried, Anne Lambert, *servant maid* to Mr. Chippins, *Cooke*.

Nov. 30.   Dyed, James Dalton, *servant* at the Post Office, bur. Dec. 1.

Dec. 5.   Dyed, Hannah Parker, *servant to* Daniel Quare, *Watch Maker*, carried, Dec. 6, to the Quakers ground in Cripplegate to be buried.

Dec. 6.   Buried, Henry Johnson, *apprentice* to Mr. Gabriel Smith, *Druggest*.

Dec. 12.   Dyed, Mr. James Blaygrave, *Goldsmith*, bur. Dec. 17.

Dec. 16.   Dyed, Rebecca, daughter of Thomas Farrer, *Fruiterer*, of St. Mary Woolchurch Haw, bur. Dec. 19.

Dec. 25.   Dyed, Richard Coate, nephew to Mr. Richard Smith, *Goldsmith*, bur. Dec. 27.

Jan. 2.   Buried, Richard, son of John Giles, *Packer*, in Sherborne Lane.

Jan. 2.   Dyed, Mr. Nicholas Mawbert, *Jeweller*, lodger at Mr. Griells, of St. Mary Woolchurch Haw, bur. Jan. 4.

Jan. 12.   Buried, Mary, daughter of Benjamin Tudman, *Goldsmith*.

Jan. 12.   Buried at Bedlam Churchyard, Elizabeth, wife to William Sabell, lodger in St. Mary Woolchurch Haw, *Chandler*.

Jan. 13.   Dyed, Elizabeth, daughter of John Best, of St. Mary Woolchurch Haw, *Razormaker*, bur. Jan. 16.

Jan. 25.   Dyed, John Browne, *servant* to John Browne, *Parish Clarke*.

Jan. 16.   Dyed, Thomas Fox, of St. Mary Woolchurch Haw, *Boxmaker*, bur. Jan. 19.

Jan. 17.   Dyed, Manny, daughter of Mr. Thomas Manwood, *Bookebinder*, bur. Jan. 18.

Feb. 28.	Dyed, Elias, son of John Malpass, lodger in St. Mary Woolchurch Haw, bur. same night.
Feb. 28.	Buried, Mary Bates, *Pensioner*, of St. Mary Woolchurch Haw.
Mar. 5.	Dyed at the house of Mr. Stephen Ram, Anthony Ram, *Esquire*, bur. Mar. 8.
Mar. 8.	Dyed, Robert Robinson, *Tayler*, lodger at Mr. Gibbs, of St. Mary Woolchurch Haw, bur. Mar. 9.

1698

Mar. 26.	Buried, a stillborne child of Mr. Charles Kinges, of St. Mary Woolchurch Haw.
April 3.	Dyed, Jane, daughter of Thomas Parr, of St. Mary Woolchurch Haw, *Surgeons' Instrument Maker*, bur. April 6.
April 14.	Dyed, Isabella Cooke, of St. Mary Woolchurch Haw, bur. April 16.
April 17.	Dyed, Jane, wife of Thomas Haywood, of this Parish, *Tillett Painter*, bur. April 19.
April 17.	Dyed, Katherine, daughter of Mr. Joseph Grosvenor, of St. Mary Woolchurch Haw, *Scrivener*, bur. April 19.
April 21.	Dyed, Ann, daughter of Charles Jennings, *Victualler*, of St. Mary Woolchurch Haw, bur. April 24.
April 23.	Buried, a stillborne male child of Mr. John Silvester, of St. Mary Woolchurch Haw.
May 7.	Dyed, Margery Corbett, *servant* to Mr. Joseph Tovey, of St. Mary Woolchurch Haw, *Tallowchandler*, bur. May 8.
May 11.	Dyed, Sarah, daughter of Mr. John Knapp, of St. Mary Woolchurch Haw, *Merchant*, bur. May 12.
May 20.	Dyed, Mr. John Smith, of this Parish, *Victualler*.
May 29.	Was brought from Eltham, in Kent, Mr. Rowland Dee, *Gent.*
May 29.	Dyed, Mr. Thomas Seymour, of this Parish, *Goldsmith*, bur. June 4.
June 21.	Dyed, Mary, daughter of Joseph Archer, of this Parish, *Victualler*, bur. June 22.
June 23.	Dyed, John, son of John Evans, deceased, lodger at Mr. Giles Parker, bur. June 24.
June 25.	Dyed, Mr. Thomas Bird, *Gent*, lodger at Mr. Platts, of St. Mary Woolchurch Haw, carried, June 30, to be interred at the Parish Church of Ware, Hertfordshire.
June 27.	Dyed, Richard, son of Thomas Farrer, of St. Mary Woolchurch Haw, *Fruiterer*, bur. June 29.
June 26.	Buried, Samuel Haw, a foundling of St. Mary Woolchurch Haw.
July 23.	Dyed, Melior, wife of Mr. Mathew Shute, of this Parish, *Jeweller*, bur. July 25.
July 25.	Dyed, Mr. James Anderson, of this Parish, *Apothecary*, carried to Tindall's ground in Finsbury, July 28.
Aug. 7.	Buried, Mrs. Abigail, wife of Mr. Edward Lloyd, of this Parish, *Coffeeman*.
Aug. 8.	Buried, Charity Woolnoth, a foundling.
Aug. 21.	Dyed, Richard, son of William Barrwell, of this Parish, *Milliner*, carried to Tindall's ground in Finsbury.

Sep. 25.   Buried, William Shrewsbridge and John Satchell, *Carpenters*, killed by the fall of a scaffold, pursuant to the Coroner's warrant.

Oct. 16.   Dyed, Hester, daughter of Michaell Wilson, of St. Mary Woolchurch Haw, *Goldsmith*, bur. Oct. 18.

Nov. 23.   Dyed, Martha Day, *servant* to Mr. Ambrose, *Attorney*, in St. Mary Woolchurch Haw, bur. Nov. 24.

Nov. 16.   Buried, John Elliott, of this Parish, *Sword Cutler.*

Dec. 7.   Dyed, Margarett, wife of Francis Jones, of this Parish, *Victualler*, carried to St. Clement, Eastcheap, Dec. 9.

Dec. 11.   Dyed, Thomas, son of Mr. George Ceorge Cook, of this Parish, *Razormaker*, bur. Dec. 14.

Dec. 24.   Was brought from Eltham, in Kent, Mrs. Jane Dee, bur. in the chancell.

Jan. 2.   Dyed, Mr. Samuell Moss, *Batchellor and Norwich Factor*, lodging at Mr. John Hawleys, *Haberdasher*, bur. Jan, 5.

Jan. 3.   Dyed, Elizabeth, daughter of Mr. Marke Gilbert, of St. Mary Woolchurch Haw, *Norwich Factor*, bur. Jan. 4.

Jan. 24.   Dyed, Ann, daughter of Mr. Richard Gilbert, of St. Mary Woolchurch Haw, *Norwich Factor*, bur. Jan. 25.

Jan. 27.   Dyed, Major John Manlove, lodger at Mr. Griels, in St. Mary Woolchurch Haw, bur. at St. Stephens, Walbrook, Jan. 31.

Feb. 15.   Dyed, Mr. John Whitehorne, of this Parish, *Victualler*, bur. Feb. 17.

Feb. 17.   Dyed, Elizabeth, daughter of Mr. George Smith, *Poulterer*, of St. Mary Woolchurch Haw, bur. Feb. 19.

Feb. 24.   Buried, William Tachell, *servant* to Sir Robert Cotton.

Mar. 5.   Brought from Bishosgate and buried, Katherine Jermyn, *Widdow*, mother of Mr. Samuel Jermyn, *our late Parish Clarke.*

1699

April 11.   Dyed, Charles, son of John Shales, *Mariner*, lodger at Wilcox, the *Barbers*, bur. April 13.

May 1.   William, infant son of William Woolston, lodger at Mr. Jediall Turndie, in Sherborne Lane, bur. May 2.

May 7.   Brought from Mr. Goodman, *Wine Cooper*, in Mark Lane, St. Olave Hart Street, Mrs. Mary White, *Widdow.*

May 22.   Dyed, Mr. Edward Lambert, *Goldsmith*, bur. at Clapham, Surrey, May 26.

June 20.   Buried, Ann, daughter of Mr. Joseph Archer, *Victualler.*

June 29.   Dyed, Thomas, son of John Stanton, *Jeweller*, bur. June, 30

July 22.   Dyed, Mr. Richard Smith, *Goldsmith*, bur. in Northwood Church, Isle of Wight, July 28.

July 28.   Was taken up, the body of Jane, wife of Mr. Elmes Spincke, *Goldsmith*, and sister of the aforesaid Mr. Richard Smith, by faculty from the Bishopp of London's office to be interred with Mr. Smith at the Isle of Wight, in Northwood Church, she having been bur. Sep. 4, 1690.

July 27.   Dyed, Elizabeth, daughter of Phillip Roaker, *Goldsmith*, bur. July 28.

Aug. 2.   Dyed, Elizabeth, daughter of Mr. Robert Westcott, of St. Mary Woolchurch Haw, *Vintner*, bur. Aug. 4.

Aug. 28.   Dyed, Jane, daughter of Thomes Kimberley, *Boxmaker*, lodger at Mr. Giles, *Packer*, bur. Aug. 20.

Sep. 1.   Buried, George, son of Mr. John Knapp, of St. Mary Woolchurch Haw.

Sep. 5.   Brought by Nurse Bramwood, at Newhall, in Edmonton, Joseph Woolnoth, a foundling, and was buried.

Oct. 5.   Dyed, Sarah, wife of Mr. Thomas Handcock, *Goldsmith*.

Oct. 5   Dyed, Thomas, son of Thomas Kimberley, *Boxmaker*, bur. Oct. 8.

Oct. 9.   Dyed, Elizabeth Higgins. *servant* to Mr. Robert Westcott, *Vintner*, of St. Mary Woolchurch Haw, bur. Oct. 10.

Oct. 10.   Dyed, Joan, wife of Mr. Jonathan Whalley, of St. Mary Woolchurch Haw, *Cooke*, bur. Oct. 11.

Oct. 17.   Brought from Mr. Vyners, in Tufton Street, St. Margarets, Westminster, Honour, wife of ———— [sic] Leigh, *Gent.*

Oct. 20.   Dyed, Mr. John Archer, *Poulterer*, of St. Mary Woolchurch Haw, bur. Oct. 22.

Nov. 5.   Dyed, Henry Mansell, *Merchant*, lodger at Mr. Lucys, bur. Nov. 9.

Nov. 11.   Dyed, Mr. Jonathan Millner, *Cutler*, in Popehead Alley, bur. Nov. 17.

Nov. 18.   Dyed, Anne, daughter of Mr. Robert Abbis, *Engraver*, bur. Nov. 19.

Nov. 24.   Buried, Mary, daughter of William Wollastone, *Yeoman*.

Dec. 1.   Dyed, Mr. Peter Cary, *Guernsey Factor*, lodging at Mr. Browne, *Parish Clerk*, bur. Dec. 3.

Dec. 7.   Mr. William Edmunds, *Victualler*, of St. Mary Woolchurch Haw, bur. Dec. 14.

Dec. 16.   Dyed, Sarah, daughter of Mr. John Simpson, of St. Mary Woolchurch Haw, *Victualler*, bur. Dec. 17.

Dec. 30.   Buried, Stephen Haw, a foundling.

Dec. 31.   Buried, Samuel Brightland, nephew to Godman the *Baker*.

Jan. 24.   Brought from Mr. Robinson, *Ringmaker*, St. Michael, Bishsishaw, Mary Hide, *Widdow*.

Feb. 4.   Buried, Elizabeth Haw, a foundling.

Feb. 6.   Buried, Sarah Woolnoth, a foundling.

Feb. 12.   Buried, James, son of Mr. Joseph Archer, of this Parish, *Victualler.*

Feb. 15.   Brought from Whitefryers, St. Dunstans in the West, Mary Whitter, *Widdow and Pensioner*, of St. Mary Woolchurch Haw.

Mar. 1.   Buried, Mary, daughter of Mr. George Reed, *Goldsmith*, of this Parish.

Mar. 7.   Buried, Elizabeth, daughter of Mr. Augustin Ballows, brought from St. Leonards, Shoreditch.

Mar. 9.   Brought from Spittlefields, Stepney Parish, Mrs. Sarah Seymour, *Spinster.*

1700

May 22.   Mr. John Weld, *Druggest*, brought from Mr. Ashbys, of Woodford, Essex.

May 28.   Buried, Mr. Humphrey Seymour, *Gent.*, brought from Mr. Lovedays, in Stoake Newington.

June 5.   Buried, Arthur, son of Thomas Woolley, of St. Mary Woolchurch Haw, *Linendraper.*

June 7.	Buried, Mr. Thomas Horne, *Gent.*, lodger at Mr. Courtneys, in Exchange Alley.
June 12.	Buried, Mary, wife of Mr. Samuell Lynn, *Millinor*, lodger at Mr. Waterer, *Carpenter*.
June 16.	Buried, Mr. Walter Wareing, *Reader to this Parish*, lodger at Mr. Taylors, *Cheesemonger*, in St. Mary Woolchurch Haw.
June 23.	Buried, Ellinor Launder, *Burnisher of Plate, and an ancient maide.*
June 28.	Buried, Mr. Thomas Brown, *Victualler*, of St. Mary Woolchurch Haw.
June 30.	Buried, Martha, daughter of Mr. John Giles, of this Parish, *Packer*.
Aug. 4.	Buried, Elizabeth Lomex, *servant* to Mr. Skelton, *Vintner*.
Sep. 13.	Buried, Jane, wife of Mr. Robert Abbis, *Engraver*, of this Parish.
Sep. 22.	Buried, William Radford, a poor Parish boy.
Sep. 30.	Buried, Elizabeth, daughter of Mr. Samuel Augier, *Rector of the United Parishes.*
Oct. 4.	Dyed, Mr. John Hawley, of this Parish, *Habberdasher of Hatts*, bur Oct. 8.
Oct. 14.	Brought from St. Andrews, Holborn, Mrs. Mary Crisp, *Widdow* of Mr. Andrew Crisp, *late Rector of this Parish.*
Oct. 17.	Carried out of this Parish and buried in Tendall's ground in Cripplegate, Frances, daughter of Mr. William Barwell, of this Parish, *Vintner*.
Oct. 22.	Buried, Katherine, daughter of Mr. James Sibley, of St. Mary Woolchurch Haw, *Glassseller*.
Oct. 31.	Buried, Mary, daughter of Mr. Robert Lowth, of this Parish, *Coffeeman*.
Nov. 1.	Brought from St. Palchres, Mrs. Grace Webb, *Widdow*.
Nov. 10.	Buried, William, son of Mr. Robert Lowth, of this Parish, *Coffeeman*.
Nov. 21.	Buried, Mr. Edward Burlton, *Student in Physick*, hee lodged at Mr. Dawkins, *Apothecary*, at the White Swan in Walbrook, of St. Mary Woolchurch Haw.
Nov. 21.	Buried, Rebeccah, daughter of Mr. Robert Lowth, *Coffeeman*, of this Parish.
Nov. 28.	Buried, Margaret, wife of Mr. Edward Morris, *Taylor*, lodging at Mr. Giles, *Packer*.
Dec. 3.	Buried, Margarett Jones, *servant* to Mr. Wood, *Fishmonger*, of St. Mary Woolchurch Haw.
Dec. 14.	Mr. James Field, *Distiller*, of St. Mary Woolchurch Haw, carried and buried in St. Giles, Cripplegate.
Dec. 25.	Buried, Mr. Robert Abbis, *Engraver*, lodger at Mr. Stantons, *Jeweller*, of this Parish.
Dec. 28.	Buried, Mr. John Thursbey, of this Parish, *Goldsmith*.
Jan. 19.	Buried, Mr. John Avent, *Clerk to the Commissioners of the Post Office.*
Jan. 27.	Buried, Edward, son of Mr. John Moore, of this Parish, *Apothecary*.
Feb. 3.	Brought from St. Lawrence Jury, Mr. Samuell Sandys, *Bookkeeper*.
Feb. 17.	Brought from Eltham, Kent, Mr. Thomas Flowerdew, *Merchant*, and buried upon Mr. Rowland Dee, his father-in-law.

Feb. 18. Buried, Mary, daughter of Mr. John Giles, *Hottpresser*, of this Parish.

Feb. 28. Carried to Abchurch, Mrs. Mary Everard, *Widdow* of Samuel Everard, Esq.

Mar. 2. Buried, William, son of William Beach, *Porter*, and lodger at the Royal Oake Lottery house, Bearbinder Lane, and a stillborne childe.

Mar. 4. Buried, Mary Thorpe, *Spinster*, lodger at Godmans, the *Bakers*.

Mar. 13. Buried, Samuel, son of Mr. James Taylor, *Cheesemonger*, of St. Mary Woolchurch Haw.

1701

April 13. John, son of John Wynn, *Cheesemonger*, of St. Mary Woolchurch Haw, buried at Bethlem Churchyard,

April 21. Carried to Bethlem Churchyard, Sarah Butterworth, *servant* to Mr. John Stanton, of this Parish, *Jeweller*.

April 27. Buried, Dorothy, daughter of Mr. John Stanton, of this Parish, *Jeweller*.

April 28. Was taken up, Arthur, son of Mr. Thomas Woolley, by the request of Mrs. Arabella Woolley after all duties paid, delivered to Mr. Reed, her servant, in order to be interred with Mr. Woolley, in Darbyshire.

May 6. Buried, Robert, son of Mr. Thomas Farrell, of St. Mary Woolchurch Haw, *Fruiterer*.

May 8. Buried, Richard, brother and *servant* to Mr. John Sevelle, *Merchant*, of this Parish.

May 10. Buried, Robert Newham, *servant* to Mr. Johnson, *Linnendraper*, of St. Mary Woolchurch Haw.

June 10. Carried to East Greenwich, Francis, son of Mr. William Jones, *Apothecary*, of St. Mary Woolchurch Haw.

July 4. Buried, Patience Woolnoth, a foundling.

July 26. Brought from the Fleete Prison, Henry Lewis, *Goldsmith*, and buried.

July 31. Buried, George, son of George Tyler, *Watchmaker*, lodger at Waghorne's Coffee-house, Pope's Head Alley.

Aug. 1. Buried, Hannah, daughter of Mr. Thomas Faulkeringham, at the Golden Ball, corner of Bearbinder Lane, *Goldsmith*.

Aug. 6. Buried, John, son of John Wyberne, *Scrivener*, lodger at Mr. Bradburys, of St. Mary Woolchurch Haw.

Aug. 11. Samuel, son of Samuel Shipley, of St. Mary Woolchurch Haw, *Fishmonger*, by order of the Coroners warrant, he being accidentally drowned at Three Cranes Wharfe.

Aug. 22. Brought from Nurse Bramwood, in Edmunton, Rhoda Woolnoth, a foundling, and buried.

Aug. 25. Carried from this Parish and burried at Cunnington, Cambridgeshire, Dame Gertrude Cotton, the wife of the Right Hon. Sir Robert Cotton, *Knight, one of His Majesties Post Masters General*.

Aug. 26. Buried, Ann Haw, a foundling.

Aug. 28. Buried, Thomas Holmenden, *servant* to Mr. Thomas Chipping, of this Parish, *Cooke*.

Sep. 22. Buried, Katherine, daughter of Mr. George Reed, of this Parish, *Banker*.

Oct. 29.	Buried, a male child, a foundling.
Oct. 2.	Buried, Mr. Thomas Munday, of St. Mary Woolchurch Haw, *Victualler*.
Oct. 6.	Buried, James, son of Mr. John Bach, of this Parish, *Silversmith*.
Nov. 11.	Buried in Tindall's ground in Bunhill Fields, Sarah, wife of Mr. Joseph Moore, of this Parish, *Goldsmith*.
Dec. 7.	Buried, Sarah, wife of Mr. Benjamin Gough, *Butcher*, of St. Mary Woolchurch Haw.
Dec. 7.	Buried, William Blakestone, *Batchellor, one of the Clerkes at the Post Office*.
Dec. 17.	Buried, Mary, the second wife of John Browne, *Clerke of this Parish*.
Jan. 2.	Buried, Thomas Hall, *Barber*, (who dyed by excessive drinkeing) by a report of the Coroner's warrant.
Jan. 9.	Buried, Mr. Mathew Stanton, of this Parish, *Factor and Batchelor*.
Jan. 25.	Buried, Stephen, son of Mr. George Cook, of this Parish, *Chirurgions Instrument Maker*.
Jan. 25.	Buried, a male child of Mr. George Knapp, *Merchant* of St. Mary Woolchurch Haw.
Feb. 3.	Buried, Mary, daughter of John Boulton, of St. Mary Woolchurch Haw, *Mealeman*.
Feb. 6.	Buried, a foundling.
Feb. 18.	Carried to be buried in the Quaker's ground in Cripplegate, Mary, daughter of Daniel Quare, *Watchmaker*, of this Parish.
Feb. 22.	Carried to be burried in Stepney Churchyard, Mrs. Elizabeth, wife of Mr. John Chambers, of this Parish, *Scrivener*.
Feb. 22.	Buried, Featherstone Nelson, a poor child, on the charge of the Parish of St. Mary Woolchurch Haw.
Feb. 27.	Buried, Mary Coherne, lodger at Roberts, the *Fishmonger*, in St. Mary Woolchurch Haw.
Mar. 7.	Buried, Rebecca Woolnoth, a foundling.

1702

April 5.	Buried, Martha, daughter of John Moicier, *a French Master of the Matthew Matticks*, [*sic*] lodger at Mr. Garrards, *Barber*.
April 10.	A female child of Mr. Michaell Wilson, *Engraver*, of St. Mary Woolchurch Haw.
April 29.	Carried from Mr. Joshua Both, *Drugster*, of St. Mary Woolchurch Haw, and buried in St. Stephens, Walbrook, Susanna Piggott, *Widdow* and lodger.
May 2.	Brought from Barkeing, in Essex, and buried, Mr. Augustin Ballow, *Merchant*.
June 22.	Buried, Shafto, son of Mr. Richard Gilbert, of St. Mary Woolchurch Haw, *Factor*.
June 28.	Buried, Bridgett Robinson, *servant* to Mr. Bogenmaker, of this Parish.
July 5.	Buried, Rebecca, wife of Mr. John Malshstede, *Bookkeeper*, from her father's house, Mr. Cole, in Sherborne Lane.

July 7.   Buried, Thomas, son of Daniell Ashworth, *Butcher*, and lodger at the Globe, alehouse in St. Mary Woolchurch Haw.

Aug. 17.   Buried, Katherine Lyddell, *servant maid* to Mr. Eaton, *Linnendraper*, of St. Mary Woolchurch Haw.

Sep. 20.   Buried, Mr. Harmonius Bogenmaker, keeper of the Dutch ordinary, in this Parish.

Sep. 30.   Buried at Eltham, Kent, Mary, daughter of Mr. William [News?] of this Parish, *Factor*, [N.B.—The surname is written above the line and is very indistinct.]

Oct. 3.   Buried, a stillborne male child of Mr. Lawrence Martin, *Vintner*, of St. Mary Woolchurch Haw.

Oct. 10.   Buried, Susanna, a foundling.

Oct. 29.   Buried, Mr. Thomas Handcock, of this Parish, *Engraver*.

Nov. 14.   Buried at Wimbledon, Surrey, Margarett, wife of ———— [*sic*] Robotham, lodgers in Dove Court, at Deputy Moores.

Nov. 20.   Buried, a stillborne child of Mr. John Rogers, lodger at Mr. Cozens, *Barber*.

Nov. 22.   Buried, Martha, wife of Mr. Thomas Chippins, *Cooke*.

Dec. 27.   Buried at Clapham, Surrey, Nathaniel Mathew, son of Mr. Nathaniel Woolfrey, of this Parish, *Goldsmith*.

Jan. 19.   Brought from St. Stephens, Coleman Street, and buried, Mr. John Smith, *Scrivener*.

Jan. 25.   Buried at Mitcham, Surrey, William, son of Mr. Edward Drayner, of this Parish, *Vintner*.

Feb. 7.   Buried, Elizabeth, daughter of Mr. Robert Conant, of St. Mary Woolchurch Haw, *Linnendraper*.

Feb. 15.   Buried, Edward, son of Mr. John Moore, of this Parish, *Apothecary*.

Feb. 23.   Buried, Sarah Nethercoate, *servant* to Mr. Silvester, of St. Mary Woolchurch Haw, *Linnendraper*.

Feb. 25.   Buried, Michael, son of Michael Kent, *Basketmaker*, and lodger at the King's Arms, St. Mary Woolchurch Haw.

Mar. 1.   Buried, Peter Williams, *servant* to Mr. Thomas Chippins, of this Parish, *Cooke*.

Mar. 2.   Buried, Mary, daughter of Mr. John Baldock, *one of the Clerks at the Post House*.

Mar. 4.   Buried, Edward Robinson, nephew to Mr. Peter Robinson, of this Parish, *Bricklayer*.

Mar. 23.   Buried, Martha, daughter of Mr. Abraham Wilcox, of this Parish, *Barber*.

1703

April 2.   Buried, Goddard, son of Mr. Richard Nelthorp, of this Parish, *Goldsmith*.

April 3.   Buried, Elizabeth, daughter of Mr. John Baldock.

April 12.   Buried, Suzan, daughter of Martin Beamond, late of St. Mary Woolchurch Haw, *Tallowchandler*.

April 21.   Buried at Tamworth, Staffordshire, Mary, wife of Thomas Hurt, *Bookseller*, dyed at Thomas Guy, Esq.'s house.

April 22.   Buried, Mr. John Constance, *Taylor*.

April 29.   Buried, Elizabeth, wife of Edmund Goldgrey, *Confectioner*, of St. Mary Woolchurch Haw.

May 1.   Buried at Barcham, Kent, Mrs. Elizabeth Elcock, *Spinster*.

May 3.	Buried, Mr. John Cole, of this Parish, *Porter.*
June 1.	Buried, Hardie Moor, a bastard male child.
June 2.	Buried, Ann, daughter of Mr. John Rogers, *Attorney.*
June 13.	Buried at Hatfield, Hertfordshire, Thomas Shatterden, Esq., lodger at Waghorne's Coffeehouse, dyed June 11.
July 2.	Buried, Edith Beamond, of St. Mary Woolchurch Haw.
July 15.	Buried, John, son of Robert Nicholls.
Aug. 6.	Buried, Ann, daughter of Mr. George Read, *Bancker.*
Sep. 1.	Buried, James, son of Mr. John Moore, *Apothecary.*
Sep. 8.	Buried, Mary, daughter of Daniel Stephens, *Coffeeman.*
Sep. 18.	Buried in the Quakers' ground Cripplegate, George Stevens, *servant* to Daniel Quare, *Watchmaker.*
Sep. 19.	Buried, John, son of Mr. Joseph Archer, *Victualler.*
Sep. 25.	Buried at Hambleton, Bucks., Charles Gregory, *apprentice* to Mr. Stephen Ram, *Bancker.*
Oct. 6.	Buried, Michael, son of Michael Wilson, *Goldsmith,* of St. Mary Woolchurch Haw.
Oct. 20.	Buried, Ellinor Wright, niece to Mr. Jonathan Kirke, of this Parish, *Goldsmith.*
Oct. 26.	Buried at Chiddington, Kent, Mr. Robert Stretfeild, *Seedsman.*
Oct. 26.	Buried, William, son of William Brightwell, *Barber.*
Nov. 3.	Buried at Hatfeild Broadoak, Essex, Dame Dorothy Barrington, Widdow of Sir Charles Barrington, *Knight and Barronett,* dyed Oct. 27.
Nov. 4.	Buried, Mr. Thomas Westall, *Gent.*
Nov. 9.	Buried, Mary, daughter of Mr. Robert Lowth, *Coffeeman.*
Nov. 20.	Buried at Bareham, Kent, George Elcock, Esq.
Nov. 30.	Buried, George, son of Mr. Francis Jones, of Falmouth, Co. Cornwall, *Gent.*
Dec. 15.	Buried, Margaret Fleming, *servant* to Mr. Xpher Tome, of Mary Woolchurch Haw, *Barber.*
Dec. 30.	Buried, Mary, daughter of Mr. George Tyler, *Watchmaker.*
Jan. 20.	Buried at Much-Haddam, Herts., Abigal, relict of *Dr.* John Goodman, *of Divinity.*
Feb. 8.	Buried, Mary Smart, *Spinster.*
Feb. 26.	Buried, John, son of Mr. John Stanton, of this Parish, *Jeweller.*
Feb. 27.	Buried, Mr. Benjamine Gough, *Victualler* at the Globe Alehouse, St. Mary Woolchurch Haw.
Mar. 8.	Buried at Tindall's ground, in Bunhill Fields, Susanna Blandford, *Widdow.*
Mar. 15.	Buried at Stoake Newington, Anne, wife of Mr. Edward Ambrose, *Attorney-at-Law.*
Mar. 20.	Buried, John, son of Mr. John Baldock.
Mar. 27.	Buried, Philadelphia, daughter of Mr. Richard Nelthorp, of this Parish, *Goldsmith.*

1704

April 12.	Buried at St. Mary Magdalene, Old Fish Street, Elizabeth, wife of Mr. William Bennet, of this Parish, *Blacksmith.*
April 29.	Buried, Mr. Phillip Avent, *an Attorney's Clerk,* from St. Mary, Islington.
May 27.	Buried in Bethlem grounds, Susanna, daughter of Mr. John Wynne, *Cheesemonger,* of St. Mary Woolchurch Haw.

June 7.　Buried, Thomas, son of Mr. John Rogers, *Attorney-at-Law*.

June 8.　Buried, Mrs. Margaret Symonds, *Widdow*, brought from Mr. John Symonds, *Attorney*, Tower Street, Allhallows, Barking.

June 20.　Buried, Mary, daughter of Mr. Robert Conant, *Linnen-draper*.

July 16.　Buried, Thomas, son of Mr. George Cook, *Chirurgeons Instrument Maker*.

July 21.　Buried, Richard, son of Robert Gill.

Aug. 3.　Buried, Caleb, son of Mr. Caleb Morgate, *Scrivener*.

Aug. 18.　Buried, Mr. John Rogers, *Attorney*, brought from Chelsea. Anne, his daughter, and Thomas, his son, being by permission taken out of the vault and interred in the same grave with him.

Aug. 18.　Buried, Mrs. Jane Cook, Widow of Mr. —— Cooke, *Instrument Maker*, brought from Hackney.

Aug. 23.　Buried, Mr. William Bradbury, of St. Mary Woolchurch Haw, *Millener and Upper Churchwarden*.

Aug. 30.　Buried, Judith, wife of Mr. Phillip Waite, *Victualler*, of St. Mary Woolchurch Haw.

Aug. 31.　Buried, Anthony Farlow, lodger at the Eagle and Child, of St. Mary Woolchurch Haw.

Sep. 6.　Buried in Tindall's ground, Cripplegate, Elizabeth Gipps.

Sep. 7.　Buried, John, son of Mr. John Moore, of this Parish, *Apothecary*.

Sep. 21.　Buried, a female stillborne child of Mr. John Godman, of this Parish, *Baker*.

Sep. 30.　Buried, Hannah Dove Woolnoth, a foundling.

Oct. 19.　Buried, Mary Haw, a foundling.

Nov. 7.　Buried, Hannah Archer, *Widdow*, of St. Mary Woolchurch Haw.

Nov. 9.　Buried at Battersey, Surrey, Mrs. Margareta Maria, wife of Mr. Thomas Adams, *Merchant*, lodger at Mrs. Foleys, in this Parish.

Nov. 24.　Buried, Ellinor, wife of Robert Fletcher, *Doctor of Physic*, brought from Dover Street, Spittlefields.

Dec. 5.　Buried, John Derrick, *apprentice* to Deputy John Moore, of this Parish, *Goldsmith*.

Dec. 19.　Buried, in the Cathedral Church, Salisbury, Richard Drake, *Merchant*, and lodger at Mr. Pattisons, in the Parsonage house of this Parish

Jan. 16.　Buried, Mrs. Dorothy Willians, *Widdow*.

Jan. 17.　Buried, Thomas, son of Mr. Edmund Bick, *Waxchandler*.

Jan. 28.　Buried, Benjamin, infant son of Benjamin Gough, *Butcher*, lately dead.

Feb. 21.　Buried, Urith [*sic*] wife of Mr. Thomas Powell, *Pewterer*, of St. Dionys Backchurch, and eldest daughter of Mr. Robert Baskett, *Apothecary*, of St. Mary Woolchurch Haw.

Feb. 4.　Buried, Mr. George Children, *one of the Bearers of this Parish*.

Feb. 13.　Buried, Samuel, infant son of Samuel Feild, *Cheesemonger*.

Feb. 25.　Buried, Susannah, infant daughter of Mr. John Stanton, of this Parish, *Jeweller*.

Mar. 15.　Buried, Frances Haw, a foundling.

Mar. 16.　Buried, upon her grandfather, Mr. Aynscombe, Elizabeth, infant daughter of Mr. Marke Gilbert, *Norwich Factor*.

1705

April 24.	Buried, Sarah, daughter of Mr. John Best, of St. Mary Woolchurch Haw, *Chirurgions' Instrument Maker.*
May 4.	Buried, a stillborne male infant of Mr. Stephen Child, *Goldsmith.*
May 5.	Buried, Susanna, daughter of Mr. George Halse, *Merchant,* of St. Mary Woolchurch Haw.
June 7.	Buried, Elizabeth, daughter of Mr. Robert Conant, *Linen-draper.*
June 12.	Buried, Margaret Mathew, *servant* to Mrs. Rogers.
June 26.	Buried, Beenoni Woolnoth, a foundling.
June 19.	Buried, Elizabeth, wife of Mr. Robert Batho, of this Parish, *Confectioner.*
Aug. 10.	Buried, Mr. Adriaen Courtney, *Batchelor,* of this Parish, *Goldsmith.*
Aug. 12.	Buried, John Baldock, *Lodger.*
Aug. 14.	Buried, Gregonia, daughter of Mr. George Reed, of this Parish, *Bancker.*
Aug. 28.	Buried, Charles, son of Mr. Thomas Webb, *Mariner.*
Aug. 31.	Buried, Mr. John Hudson, *Batchellor,* of this Parish, *Goldsmith.*
Sep. 2.	Buried, John, son of Mr. Robert Pattison, of this Parish, *Factor.*
Sep. 11.	Buried, Elizabeth, daughter of Phillip Frowde, *Porter,* of this Parish.
Sep. 18.	Buried, Martha Gender, *Spinster.*
Sep. 29.	Buried, Grace, wife of Mr. John Silvester, of St. Mary Woolchurch Haw, *Linendraper.*
Oct. 9.	Buried at Daggenham, Essex, Edward, son of Mr. William Exton, of St. Mary Woolchurch Haw, *Linendraper.*
Oct. 12.	Buried, Martha Montaine, *Spinster, servant* to Mr. John Knapp, *Merchant.*
Nov. 8.	Buried at St. Leonard Shoreditch, Susanna, daughter of Richard Cock, of St. Mary Woolchurch Haw, *Linen-draper.*
Nov. 10.	Buried at Spencehurst, Kent, Mr. William Waghorne, of this Parish, *Confectioner.*
Nov. 15.	Buried, Jane, daughter of Mr. Thomas Parr, of St. Mary Woolchurch Haw, *Chirurgion Instrument Maker.*
Nov. 24.	Buried, Susanna, daughter of Mr. Richard Godman, of this Parish, *Baker.*
Nov. 26.	Buried in Bethlem Churchyard, Mr. David Venables, *Goldsmith.*
Dec. 7.	Buried, Elizabeth, wife of Mr. William Denny, of this Parish, *Goldsmith.*
Dec. 18.	Buried, Hester Walker, daughter to Mr. Charles Latham, of this Parish, *Drugster,* long since deceased, brought from Wentworth Street, Whitechapple.
Dec. 31.	Buried, Anne, wife of Mr. Christopher Toms, *Barber.*
Jan. 15.	Buried, at Popler, Rachell Skinner, *Widdow.*
Jan. 23.	Buried, John, son of Mr. Thomas Chadwell, of this Parish, *Jeweller.*
Feb. 17.	Buried, Mathew, son of Mr. Edmund Meekins, *Vintner.*
Feb. 28.	Buried at St. Buttolph Without Aldgate, Frances, wife of Robert Sheene, *servant to the Post Office.*

Mar. 11.	Buried, Benjamin, son of Mr. John Knapp, *Merchant,* of St. Mary Woolchurch Haw.
Mar. 26.	Buried, Anna, daughter of Mr. Thomas Chadwell, *Jeweller.*
Mar. 19.	Buried, a female stillborne infant of Mr. Richard Gilbert, *Factor.*
Mar. 28.	Buried, Elizabeth, daughter of Mr. Thomas Faulkeringham, of this Parish, *Goldsmith*

1706

April 8.	Buried, Mr. Jonathan, son of Mr. Robert Baskett, of St. Mary Woolchurch Haw, *Apothecary.*
April 25.	Buried, Charles Flowerdew, brought from Stratford, Essex, drowned.
April 27.	Buried, Margaret Haw, a foundling.
June 1.	Buried, Mary Smart, *servant* to Mr. Greenhill, *Factor.*
May 17.	Buried, Charles, son of William Mooreing, *Cooke,* found dead in the River Thames.
July 19.	Buried, Benjamin, son of John Bolt, *Mealeman.*
July 22.	Buried, Jane, wife of Mr. Thomas Parr, *Instrument Maker.*
July 11.	Buried, Elizabeth, daughter of William Lawe, *Confectioner.*
Aug. 14.	Buried at Alton, Middlesex, Mary Knight, *servant.*
Aug. 22.	Buried, at Bunhill Fields, Frances Gibbes, *Widdow.*
Sep. 11.	Buried at Bunhill Fields, Mrs. Ann Lippingwell.
Oct. 7.	Buried Mr. Bobert Batho, *Confectioner.*
Oct. 20.	Buried, Olive, daughter of Mr. John Best.
Oct. 11.	Buried, Margaret Barnes, a foundling.
Nov. 14.	Buried, Ellinor Johnson.
Nov. 13.	Buried at Daggenham, Essex, Robert, son of Mr. William Exton, *Linnendraper.*
Nov. 21.	Buried, John Chambers, Esq., *Scrivener,* brought from Lime Street Square, St. Andrews Undershaft, the coffin covered with velvet.
Nov. 22.	Buried, Susanna, daughter of James Thomason, *Goldsmith.*
Dec. 16.	Buried, Grace, daughter of Mr. Jonh Knapp, *Merchant.*
Dec. 29.	Buried, Rachell, daughter of Thomas Gibbs.
Jan. 4.	Buried, Anne, daughter of Mr. Joseph Cozens, *Barber.*
Jan. 7.	Buried at the Quakers Ground, near Bunhill Fields, Susanna Beare, *Widdow.*
Jan. 7.	Buried, Mary Sharpe, *Infant.*
Jan. 12.	Buried at the Quakers Ground, Bunhill Fields, Deborah Gerrard, *Widdow.*
Jan. 12.	Buried, Mr. William Sampson, *Perriwigg Maker.*
Jan. 30.	Buried, Mr. William Denny, *Goldsmith.*
Feb. 2.	Buried, Mr. Thomas Chippin, *Cooke.*
Mar. 1.	Buried, William, son of Mr. William and Anne Fisher, *Shipwright.*
Mar. 3.	Buried, William, son of Mr. John and Katherine Foster, *Stationer.*
Mar. 9.	Buried, Mr. John Lathby, *Exchange Broaker.*
Mar. 15.	Buried in Creed Churchyard, Mrs. Alice Herringman, *Widdow.*

1707

April 5.	Buried, Mr. William Hayes, *Apothecary*, from the Savoy Parish.
May 6.	Buried, Martha, daughter of Mr. Joseph Cozens, *Barber*.
May 25.	Buried, Mr. Thomas Haywood, *Widdower, Tillett Painter*.
May 25.	Buried, Lydia, daughter of Mr. Soloman Swayle, *Strong-waterman*.
May 28.	Buried, Mrs. Mary, wife of Mr. Benjamin Tudman, *Goldsmith and Bancker in Linnen*.
May 3.	Buried, Mr. Richard Scarth, *Batchellor*, son of Mr. Phillip Scarth, *Druggest*, deceased.
June 5.	Buried at Hambleton, Hampshire, Ursula Symonds, *Spinster*, daughter of Capt. Symonds, *Vintner*, at the Popes Head Taverne, deceased.
June 12.	Buried, Christian, wife of John Palmer, *Victualler*.
June 18.	Buried, Elizabeth Alcock, *servant* to Mr. John Knapp.
June 30.	Buried at St. James, Duke Place, Mary, wife to Mr. Jonathan Kirke, *Goldsmith*.
July 2.	Buried, Thomas, son of Mr. Bryan Robinson, *Turner*.
July 15.	Buried, James, son of Mr. James Stannyland, *Blacksmith*.
Aug. 1.	Buried, a stillborne child of Mr. Petty, *Tallowchandler*.
Aug. 8.	Buried, Mr. William Browne, *Merchant*.
Aug. 8.	Buried, Jane Faith, *Widdow*, a poor woman.
Aug. 14.	Buried, Mr. Soloman Swayle, *Strong waterman*.
Oct. 2.	Buried, Sarah Brimmer, *servant maid* to Mr. Phillip Dacres, of St. Mary Woolchurch Haw, *Drugster*.
Nov. 4.	Buried, Mrs. Mary Catchpole, *Widdow*, mother of Mrs. Rebecca, wife of Mr. Robert Lowth, of St. Mary Woolchurch Haw, *Coffeeman*.
Nov. 16.	Buried at St. Martin, Ludgate, Frances, daughter of Capt. Symonds, at the Popeshead Tavern, *Vintner*.
Nov. 20.	Buried at Walthamstow, Essex, Mrs. Elizabeth, wife of Mr. Jeremy Stokes, *Coffeeman*.
Nov. 20.	Buried, Mr. William Moore, *Perriwigmaker*, of St. Mary Woolchurch Haw.
Dec. 2.	Buried, John, son of John Baldock, of this Parish.
Dec. 13.	Buried, William, son of Hilliard, lodger at Mr. Charles Kerby, *Clasper of Books*, of this Parish.
Dec. 23.	Buried, Mary Parkis, *servant maid* to Mr. Charles Shales, of this Parish, *Goldsmith*.
Dec. 26.	Buried, Thomas, son of Mr. Samuel Gibson, of this Parish, *Drugster*.
Jan. 15.	Buried at Hatfield Broadoak, Essex, Charles, son of Mr. Charles Shales, of this Parish, *Goldsmith*.
Jan. 17.	Buried at St. Leonard, Shoreditch, Martha, daughter of Mr. Richard Cock, *Linnendraper*.
Jan. 25.	Buried at Bethlem Churchyard, Mr. John Reynolds, *Gent*, of St. Mary Woolchurch Haw.
Feb. 4.	Buried at St. Pancras, Soper Lane, Mrs. Sarah Kenrick, *Widdow*, aunt of Mr. Kenrick, *Grocer*, of St. Mary Woolchurch Haw.
Feb. 4.	Buried, Mr. Thomas Grosvenor, *Batchelor, and Upholder*, of St. Mary Woolchurch Haw.
Feb. 4.	Buried, Mary Poole, *Spinster*, daughter of Mrs. Mary Poole, *Widdow*, at the Postboy Alehouse, in this Parish.

Feb. 5.   Buried, Jane, wife of Mr. Thomas Allcroft, *Cutler*, paid double duty [in margin].

Feb. 16.   Brought from Low Layton, in Essex, and buried, Mrs. Jane Vincent, *Widdow*, and only mother to John Chambers, *Esquire*, sometime *Scrivener* of this Parish.

Feb. 18.   Buried, Mrs. Elizabeth, wife of Mr. Richard Beezer, of St. Mary Woolchurch Haw, *Distiller*.

Feb. 27.   Buried, Jane, daughter of Capt. John Dorrell, and grand daughter to John Chambers, *Esquire*, brought from the Parish of St. Katherine, Coleman, and buried in Linnen ; paid double duties as a stranger.

Mar. 10.   Buried, Thomas, son of Thomas Alcroft, *Cutler*, paid double duty.

Mar. 19.   Buried, Mr. James Sibley, of St. Mary Woolchurch Haw, *Potter*.

1708

Mar. 28.   Buried, Martha, daughter of Mr. Richard Godman, of this Parish, *Baker*.

Mar. 30.   Buried, Ellinor, daughter of Mr. Samuel Chase, of St. Mary Woolchurch Haw, *Sword Cutler*.

April—[*sic*] Buried, Daniell, son of Gerrad Roberts, of St. Mary Woolchurch Haw, *Fishmonger*.

April 12.   Buried, Mr. John Palmer, *Victualler*.

April 19.   Buried, Mary, foundling.

May 19.   Buried, Susanna, daughter of William Brightsdell, *Barber*, of St. Mary Woolchurch Haw.

May 23.   Buried, Elizabeth Littlewort, alias Howard, *servant* to Mr. Mason, *Sexton*.

May 29.   Buried, an Abortive Child of Mr. Robotham, of this Parish.

June 16.   Mary Jones, *Widdow*, in the family vault, Great St. Helens.

June 11.   Buried, Alice, daughter of Mr. William Spencer, *Victualler*, of St. Mary Woolchurch Haw.

June 13.   Buried, Elizabeth, daughter of Mr. Timothy Rutter, of St. Mary Woolchurch Haw, *Upholder*.

June 21.   Buried, Mrs. Mary, *widdow* of Mr. Richard Holdbrook.

June 25.   Buried, Mr. Feelis Overton, *Gent*, *Widdower*, lodger at Mr. Gabriel Smith's, *Drugster*.

July 5.   Buried, Mrs. Elizabeth Devenish, *Spinster*.

July 10.   Buried, Timothy, son of Timothy Rutter, *Upholsterer*.

July 18.   Buried, John Browne, *Parish Clerk*.

Sep. 28.   Buried, Mary, daughter of Mr. John Bolton, of St. Mary Woolchurch Haw, *Mealman*.

Nov. 6.   Buried at Greenwich, Mrs. Mary Mayor, aunt to Madam Jones, of St. Mary Woolchurch Haw.

Nov. 7.   Buried, Edward Fenwick, *Upholster*, of St. Mary Woolchurch Haw, died Nov. 1.

Nov. 14.   Dyed, Susanna, daughter of Martin Beamont, *Marriner*, of St. Mary Woolchurch Haw, bur. Nov. 16.

Dec. 13.   Brought from St. Andrew's Parish and buried, Madam Sarah Cooke, daughter to the late Mr. Godfrey, *Woodward*.

Dec. 22.	Buried at Cripplegate, Mrs. Ann Edward, mother to Mrs. Chadwell.
Jan. 26.	Died, Samuel, son of Joseph Fielder, *Poulterer*, of St. Mary Woolchurch Haw, bur. Jan. 28.
Feb. 2.	Francis Fifield, Mrs. Staniland's apprentice. [Written in the Margin.]
Feb. 18.	Died, William Cater, father-in-law to Mr. Godman, of this Parish, bur. Feb. 24.
Feb. 22.	Died, William Langbridge, a lodger's child.

1709

Mar. 28.	Died, Sarah Cater, mother-in-law to Mr. Godman, bur. April 2.
April 2.	Dyed, Mrs. Katherine, daughter to Mr. Ralph Garrard.
April 4.	Buried, Edward, infant son of Mr. Nelthrop, of this Parish.
April 16.	Died, Joseph ——— *servant* to Mr. Harrison, buried at Tindall ground.
Mar. 22.	Died, Elizabeth, daughter of Mr. Tiler, bur. Mar. 24. S.M.W.N.
Mar. 21.	Died, Mary, daughter of Mr. Godman, buried Mar. 24.
April 2.	Died, Mary Wightman, carried to Bedlam to be buried.
Mar. 26.	Died, Mathew Palmer, a Parish child.
Mar. 31.	Buried, Tabitha Smith, mother to Mrs. Stannyland.
Mar. 20.	Died, Mary, daughter of Mary Spencer.
May —. [*sic.*]	Died at Hackney Mr. Robert Baskett, *Apothecarry.*
May 6.	Died, Francis Powell, *servant* to Mr. Jonathan Miles, bur. May 9.
May 7.	Died, Mr. Jonathan Whaley, *Cooke*, bur. May 10.
May 8.	Died, Sarah Eaton, buried at Dagnam, May 11.
June 1.	Died, John, brother to Thomas Guy, *Esquire*, of St. Mary Woolnoth, bur. June 4.
Aug. 23.	Died, Herman Dwaris, kinsman of Mr. Barnard, of St. Mary Woolchurch Haw, bur. Aug. 28.
Sep. 1.	Buried, Dorothy Coleman, brought from St. Catherines.
Sep. 9.	Died, Joseph Wilson, of St. Mary Woolchurch Haw, and buried with his brother, Michael Wilson, brought from St. Edmund the King, Sep. 13.
Sep. 27.	Buried, Mrs. Elizabeth Sherrington, brought from Ho, in Hampshire.
Oct. 18.	Died, Elizabeth, wife of Mr. William Lawe, *Confectioner*, bur. Oct. 21.
Oct. 28.	Died, Margret, wife of Mr. Wynne, *Cheesemonger*, bur. Oct. 30.
Oct. 27.	Died, Thomas Freeman, bur. Oct. 31.
Nov. 3.	Buried, Lidia, daughter of Mr. Ballow.
Nov. 13.	Died, Mr. Edward Drayner, buried at Micham, Surrey.
Dec. 11.	Buried, Richard, son of Mr. Scot, at Tindall's ground.
Dec. 29.	Buried, Elizabeth Bradley, daughter of Sir William Humble, from York.
Dec. 29.	Died, Ann, daughter of Mr. William Laws, bur. Jan. 1.
Jan. 1.	Died, Thomas Sweeting, *Gent.* bur. Jan. 9.
Jan. 9.	Died, Elizabeth Humpston (a relation of Mr. Lowths), in Cripplegate Parish, bur. Jan. 12.
Jan. 9.	Died, Margret Eales, bur. Jan. 19.

Jan. 15.   Died, Joseph, infant son of Mr. Fielder, bur. Jan. 16.
Jan. 19.   Died, Edward Drayner, junr., buried at Mitcham.
Jan. 26.   Buried, a stillborn child of Mr. Foster, *Stationer.*
Feb. 2.   Died, James Archer, an infant, a lodger's child, bur. Feb. 3.
Feb. 15.   Died, Jane, daughter of Mrs. Poole, bur. Feb. 19.
Mar. 9.   Died, David Baschard, a lodger's child at Mr. Stegers, in the Poultry, bur. Mar. 12.

1710

Mar. 26.   Died, Mary Cannum, Mrs. Poole's sister, bur. Mar. 29.
April 12.   Buried, Mary Phillips, a relation of Mr. Ballow.
April 27.   Died, Jeremiah Hilton, son of Mr. Keynton, bur. April 28.
April 23.   Died, Mr. Daniel Perkins, bur. April 28.
May 8.   Died, Phillip, son of Mr. Frowde, *Chandler*, bur. May 9.
May 9.   Died, Francis, son of Mr. Barrwell, bur. May 10.
May 18.   Died, Sarah, wife of Mr. Deputy Moor, bur. May 24.
May 24.   Buried, Alice Rose, Mr. Paines *Housekeeper*, brought from Hoxton.
May 22.   Died, Michael, son of Mr. Kent, bur. May 24.
June 5.   Died, Richard, son of Mr. Godman, bur. June 7.
June 7.   Buried, Phœbe, a parish child.
June 9.   Died, William Buck, an infant, bur. June 10.
June 13.   Died, William Alnut, a lodger, bur. June 15.
June 20.   Died, George, son of Mr. Thomas Deard, bur. June 23.
June 28.   Died, George Fulbrook, Mr. Robinson's *servant*, bur. June 30.
July 3.   Buried, Thomas Flowerdew, *Gent*, brought from Eltham, Kent.
July 10.   Died, Thomas Patterson, bur. July 12.
July 19.   Died, Mary, daughter of Mr. Bolton, *Mealman*, bur. July 21.
July 26.   Died, Hannah Woolnoth, a parish child, bur. July 27.
Aug. 4.   Died, Elizabeth, daughter of Mr. Lowth, bur. Aug. 6.
Aug. 5.   Died, Theodosia Skelton, Mr. Parker, *Bookseller, servant*, bur. Aug. 8.
Aug. 12.   Died, Jonathan, son of Mr. Roberts, *Fishmonger*, bur. Aug. 14.
Aug. 14.   Buried ——— Woolnoth, a parish child.
Aug. 14.   Died, Elizabeth, daughter of Mr. William Hudson, *Instrument Maker*, bur. Aug. 15.
Sep. 10.   Died, Stephen Billson, *apprentice* to Mr. Hayes, bur. Sep. 12.
Sep. 18.   John Studell, *footboy* to *Esquire* Evelyn, bur. Sep. 19.
Sep. 21.   Died, Edward Mansell, *apprentice*, bur. Sep. 25.
Oct. 3.   Died, John, son of Bryan Robinson, bur. Oct. 4.
Oct. 13.   Died, John Hart, a lodger, buried at Cripplegate, Oct. 15.
Nov. 5.   Died, Dorathy Puckford, a lodger's wife, bur. Nov. 8.
Nov. 4.   Died, Robert, son of Capt. Dorrell, in Fenchurch Street, bur. Nov. 8.
Nov. 8.   Died, Joseph Cooke, Mr. Childs *servant*, buried in Christ Church, in Newgate Street.
Nov. 30.   Died, John, son of Mr. Alcroft, *Cutler*, bur. Dec. 1.
Dec. 4.   Died, Pegge, daughter of Mr. Child, bur. Dec. 6.
Dec. 4.   Died, Maria, daughter of Mr. Tyler, *Watchmaker*, bur. Dec. 6.

Jan. 14.	Died, Charles, son of Mr. Robert Abbot, bur. Jan. 15.
Jan. 21.	Died, Robert Abbot, *Barber*, bur. Jan. 25.
Jan. 25.	Died, Dorothy Eaton, Mr. Eaton's mother, buried at Daggenham, Essex, Feb. 1.
Feb. 27.	Died, John, son of Mr. Lyde, *Linnendraper*, bur. Mar. 1.
Mar. 1.	Died, William Hudson, *Instrument Maker*, bur. Mar. 6.
Mar. 1.	Died, Henry, brother to Mr. Thomas Streetfield, *Drugist*, buried in Kent, Mar. 8.
Mar. 6.	Died, Mary, daughter of Mr. Nelthorp, *Goldsmith*, bur. Mar. 8.
Mar. 22.	Died, William, son of Mr. Buck, lodger, bur. Mar. 23.

1711

April 6.	Died, Mary, daughter of Mr. Kent, bur. April 8.
April 8.	Died, Sir Richard Guy, bur. April 15.
May 7.	Died, Katherine, daughter of Mr. Rutter, bur. May 8.
June 8.	Died, William Laws, an infant, bur. June 9.
June 9.	Died, Clare Elizabeth Sarjant, Mr. Read the *Tinman's* granddaughter, bur. June 11.
June 9.	Died, Joseph, son of Mr. Fielders, *Poulterer*, bur. June 12.
June 15.	Died, Theodosia, daughter of Mr. Jones, bur. June 17.
July 11.	Died, Mary, wife of Mr. Barrwell, burried St. Stephen, Coleman Street.
July 27.	Died, James, son of James Sewdall, at the Eagle and Child, bur. July 31.
Aug. 8.	Died, Jane, daughter of Mr. Blinkhorne bur. Aug. 9.
Aug. 15.	Buried, a stillborne child of Mr. Tonkes, the *Apothecary*.
Sep. 4.	Died at Stratford by Bow, Mr. Richard Gilbert, *Norwich Merchant*, in Bearbinder lane, bur. Sep. 7.
Sep. 8.	Died, Judith Norgate, a lodger's daughter, bur. Sep. 11.
Sep. 16.	Buried, Earle, son of Mr. Samuel Angier, *Rector*, in the chancel, brought from Kirby Street, Hatton Garden.
Sep. 17.	Died, John, son of Widdow Freeman, bur. Sep. 21.
Sep. 21.	Died, Sarah Knot, a lodger, bur. Sep. 23.
Sep. 28.	Died, Giles Cox, Mr. Payner's man, bur. Sep. 30.
Oct. 5.	Died, Susanna Sedgewick, Mr. Gilbert's aunt, bur. Oct. 7.
Dec. 8.	Died, Elizabeth Chapple, Mr. Barker's sister, bur. Dec. 11.
Dec. 14.	Died, John, son of Mr. Edmund Meekins, bur. Dec. 16.
Jan. 1.	Buried, Mary Farrow.
Jan. 2.	Died, Elizabeth Worrell, a lodger, bur. Jan. 4.
Jan. 3.	Buried, Alexander Pollington, brought from Newington.
Jan. 8.	Buried, Jonathan Tookie, a lodger.
Feb. 10.	Died, Edward, son of Mr. Nelthorp, bur. Feb. 11.
Feb. 14.	Died, John Booth, bur. Feb. 17.
Feb. 16.	Died, Jane Deard, bur. Feb. 19.
Feb. 24.	Died, John, son of Mr. Boddicot, bur. Feb. 26.
Mar. 2.	Died, Rachell Porch, buried at St. Pancras.
Mar. 6.	Buried, Rachell Knapp.
Mar. 11.	Died, John Moulding, a lodger's son, bur. Mar. 13.
Mar. 16.	Died, Thomas Payne, *Goldsmith*, bur. Mar. 19.

1712

April 9.	Buried, Mercy Wright.
April 14.	Buried, Rachell Thurburne.

April 21.   Buried, Mr. Kirby's mother.
April 24.   Buried, John, son of Mr. Mackay.
May 20.   Buried, Mr. Golding's wife.
May 23.   Buried, Christian Harris.
May 29.   Buried, Hester Fidge (brought out of the country).
June 6.   Buried, Thomas, son of Mr. Gibson.
June 14.   Died, Margaret, daughter of Mr. Hawkins, bur. June 17.
June 19.   Buried, Henry Philpot, (brought from St. Giles).
June 28.   Buried, ———· Watkins, (brought from Debtford).
July 16.   Buried, Mary, daughter of Mr. Child.
July 16.   Dyed, Israell, son of Mr. Samuell Keynton, bur. July 18.
Aug. 11.   Buried, Katherine Woolnoth, a foundling.
Aug. 21.   Died, Elizabeth, wife of Mr. Tyler, bur. Aug. 24.
Aug. 24.   Buried, Deputy John Moore.
Aug. 24.   Died, John Prosser, *servant* to *Esquire* Evelyn, bur.
                    Aug. 26.
Aug. 26.   Buried, Francis, son of Mr. Robotham.
Sep. 5.   Buried, Berny, an infant.
Sep. 9.   Died, James, son of Mr. Best, bur. Sep. 11.
Sep. 18.   Buried, Dorothy, daughter of Mr. John Knapp, brought
                    from Richmond.
Sep. 19.   Buried, Margret Grimston, a *Pensioner.*
Sep. 29.   Buried, Anne and Rebecka Fenwick, (both brought from
                    Edmonton.)
Oct. 1.   Buried, Mary Fenwick (brought from·Edmonton).
Oct. 7.   Died, Elizabeth, wife of Mr. Edward Loyd, bur. Oct. 10.
Nov. 4.   Buried, Benjamin Tudman, (brought from St. Edmunds
                    the King).
Dec. 20.   Died, James Skinner, carried to Walton, Hampshire.
Dec. 26.   Died, Richard Lock, carried to Shoreditch.
Jan. 10.   Buried, a female child of Mr. Richard Scots, at Tindall's
                    ground.
Jan. 15.   Died, Henry, son of Mr. Loyd, bur. Jan. 17.
Jan. 22.   Dyed, Mary North, a lodger, bur. Jan. 24.
Feb. 10.   Died, Sarah Turner, bur. Feb. 11.
Feb. 15.   Buried, William Browne.
Feb. 15.   Died, Edward Loyd, bur. Feb. 17.
Mar. 1.   Died, Judith Drayner, Junr., carried to Micham, Surry.
Mar. 5.   Buried, Mary Brown, (brought from Clapham).
Mar. 10.   Buried, Mary, daughter of Mr. Bryan Robinson.
Mar. 15.   Died, Elizabeth Cooksin, Mr. Booth's kinsman, bur.
                    Mar. 17.
Mar. 15.   Died, John, son of Mr. Child, bur. Mar. 17.

1713

Mar. 29.   Buried, Elizabeth Toms, Mr. Toms's granddaughter,
                    (brought from Westminster).
Mar. 29.   Died, Richard Iles, infant, Mr. Bracey's grandson, carried
                    to Barkin Church.
April 1.   Died, Philadelphia, daughter of Mr. Nelthorp, bur.
                    April 3.
May 13.   Buried, Martha Willett (brought from Kensington).
June 4.   Died, James Tonkes, *Apothecary*, bur. June 10.
June 8.   Died, Joseph Cousins, *Barber*, bur. June 11.
June 15.   Died, Samuel Chase, *Sword Cutler*, bur. June 18.

June 17.	Died, Elizabeth Caswell, infant, carried to Allhallows, Lombard Street.
June 23.	Buried, William Deard, brought from the Old Jury.
June 24.	Buried, a stillborne child of Mr. John Manly's.
July 22.	Buried, Rebecca Beard.
Aug. 13.	Buried, John, son of Mr. John Knap.
Aug. 20.	Buried, James Tonkes, an infant.
Aug. 25.	Buried, Mary Blake.
Sep. 1.	Buried, Katherine Rutter, an infant.
Sep. 11.	Buried, James Best.
Sep. 20.	Buried, Thomas Law, an infant.
Oct. 22.	Captain Fry, a lodger at Mr. Pattisons, was carried to Bristol to be buried.
Oct. 28.	Buried, Ann, daughter of Mr. Poole, at the Postboy.
Nov. 18.	Buried, Elizabeth Brinley.
Nov. 18.	Buried, Mary Streatfield, an infant.
Nov. 25.	Josiah Eaton was carried to St. John's at Hackney.
Nov. 27.	James, son of Mr. George Caswell, *Goldsmith*, was carried to Allhallows, Lombard Street.
Dec. 28.	Buried, Ann Hillyard, infant.
Jan. 6.	Buried, Samuel Child, an infant.
Jan. 14.	Buried, Stephen Maylard, an infant.
Jan. 21.	Buried, Thomas Harrison, a *Bookseller*.
Jan. 28.	Buried, Henry Sandtman, a *Forreigner*.
Jan. 28.	Buried, John Nelthorp, an infant.
Feb. 11.	Buried, Elizabeth Herring, a lodger's child.
Feb. 26.	Buried, John Blake, *Victualler*.
Feb. 28.	Stephen Venables was carried to old Bedlam Ground.
Feb. 28.	Buried, Elizabeth Thomson.
Mar. 11.	George Evelyn, son of Sir John Evelyn, *Bart.*, was carried to Debtford to be buried.
Mar. 12.	Buried, Rebecca Tipping, mother-in-law to Mr. Silvester.

1714

Mar. 25.	Frederick Herne, *Esq.*, a lodger at Mr. Barnards, Bearbinder Lane, was carried to St. Stephens, Coleman Street, to be interred.
Mar. 27.	Buried, Thomas North.
April 13.	Buried, Richard Brookes.
April 15.	Buried, Martha Latham, brought from St. Catherine Coleman.
April 23.	Buried, William Laws, an infant.
April 30.	Buried, Sarah Wellins.
May 13.	Buried, Martha Wightwick, brought from Kensington.
May 16.	Buried, a stillborn child of Mr. Scotson's daughter.
June 8.	Buried, John Yersin.
July 4.	Buried, Martha Heard.
July 6.	John Potter.
July 6.	Ann Branfill was carried into Essex to be buried.
July 18.	Buried, John Bromfield.
July 11.	Benjamin was carried to Whitechaple to be buried. [*sic.*]
Aug. 17.	Buried, William Newboll.
Aug. 21.	Buried, Martha Knap.
Sep. 5.	Buried, Alexander Pollington.
Sep. 9.	Buried, Joseph Thurborne.

Sep. 11.	Benjamin Waterhouse.
Sep. 13.	Buried, Joseph Thurborne, Sen.
Sep. 23.	Anne Caswell was carried to All Hallows, Lombard Street, to be buried.
Nov. 5.	Buried, Jonathan Herring.
Nov. 7.	Buried, Mary Baker.
Nov. 8.	Buried, John Morris.
Nov. 20.	Buried, John Robotham.
Nov. 23.	Buried, Dorothy Venham.
Dec. 25.	Buried, Elizabeth Venham.
Jan. 3.	Buried, John Oldesworth, in the country.
Jan. 3.	Buried, Thomas Roberts.
Jan. 13.	Carried to Chiswick, Christopher Franckland, to be interred.
Feb. 4.	Buried, Lionell Willis.
Feb. 27.	Buried, Mary Rutter.
Mar. 24.	Buried, Mary Bryan.
Mar. 27.	Buried, Elizabeth Boddicote.

1715

April 9.	Buried, Samuel Webster.
April 13.	Buried, Richard Snagg.
April 20.	Buried, Daniell Biddulph.
April 20.	Buried, Anastatius Hatton.
April 29.	Sarah Tax, taken to Kensington.
May 13.	Buried, Anne Knapp.
May 17.	Buried, George Yersin.
June 6.	Buried, Richard Cullam.
June 27.	Buried, Martha Berney.
June 28.	Buried, James Grogan.
June 28.	Buried, Praise Thomason.
July 19.	Buried, John Russell.
July 19.	Buried, Mary Sibley.
Aug. 14.	Buried, Anne Guy.
Aug. 14.	Buried, Henry Blaney.
Aug. 21.	Buried, James Mackay.
Aug. 30.	Buried, John Powell.
Oct. 9.	Buried, Christopher Toms.
Oct. 19.	Buried, was carried to Clerkenwell to be interred, Dorothy Nelthorp.
Nov. 2.	Buried, Elizabeth Lawrence.
Dec. 2.	Buried, The Lady Sarah Guy.
Dec. 15.	Buried, Mary Keynton.
Dec. 28.	Buried, Rebecca Farrell.
Jan. 23.	Buried, William Egerton.
Jan. 25.	Buried, Martha Veazy.
Jan. 26.	Buried, Peter Courtney.
Jan. 29.	Buried, Susan Kirby.
Feb. 2.	Buried, Mary Sweeting.
Feb. 9.	Buried, Richard Godman.
Mar. 3.	Buried, Anne Waterhouse.
Mar. 9.	Buried, Elizabeth Cheltenham.

1716

May 14.	Buried, Olave Best.

May 20.	Buried, Samuel Fenner.
May 29.	Buried, John Keynton.
June 23.	Buried, Sarah Turner.
June 30.	Buried, John Loyd.
July 5.	John Freshmaker carried away.
July 5.	Buried, Leonard Best.
July 21.	Buried, Adam France.
Sep. 16.	Buried, Anne Mayland.
Sep. 23.	Buried, Elizabeth Harris.
Sep. 28.	Buried, Cornelius Cheltenham.
Oct. 12.	Buried, Philadelphia Nelthorp.
Oct. 17.	Buried, Thomas Mence.
Oct. 30.	Buried, William Goodwin.
Nov. 20.	Buried, Elizabeth Ballow.
Nov. 22.	Buried, Robert Teblet.
Nov. 25.	Buried, Elizabeth Mence.
Jan. 17.	Buried, Thomas Veazy.
Jan. 21.	Buried, Jane Dingley.
Feb. 22.	Buried, Esther Davis.
Feb. 27.	Buried, Elizabeth Fuller.
Feb. 28.	Buried, John Hitchcock.
Mar. 2.	Buried, Eleanor Lucket.
Mar. 10.	Buried, John Jesse.

1717

Mar. 31.	Buried, John Collins.
April 14.	Buried, Samuel Gibson.
May 12.	Buried, Robert Collins.
May 12.	Buried, Elizabeth Kenwick.
May 13.	Buried, Mary Yersin.
May 16.	Robert Mitchell was carried to Stepney.
May 23.	Buried, Mary Alport..
May 26.	Mary Beeby was carried to Crutched Fryers.
June 8.	Buried, Godfrey Webster.
June 26.	Buried, John Veazy.
July 4.	Buried, Sarah Guy.
July 19.	Buried, Thomas Davis.
Aug. 22.	Was carried away, Katherine Teate.
Sep. 1.	Buried, Francis Watson.
Oct. 4.	Buried, James Jackson.
Oct. 11.	Was carried away, John Cooper.
Oct. 17.	Buried, Michael Kent.
Oct. 27.	Was carried away, Thomas Kellway.
Nov. 23.	Buried, an abortive child of Mr. Russell.
Nov. 25.	Buried, Margret Lang.
Dec. 1.	Buried, Rebecca Julian.
Dec. 22.	Buried, William Wood.
Jan. 19.	Buried, John Law.
Jan. 21.	Buried, John Dent.
Jan. 28.	Buried, Elizabeth Robotham.
Feb. 1.	Was carried away, Jonathan Kilby, and was buried, Edward Spurling [*sic*].
Feb. 8.	Was carried away, John Horseman.
Feb. 27.	Was carried away, Lawrence Preston.
Feb. 8.	Buried, Edward Spurling [*sic*].

1718

Mar. 25.	Buried, Mary Hayward.
April 9.	Was carried away, Mary Wynne.
April 17.	Buried, Elizabeth Keynton.
April 24.	Buried, Thomas Varnam.
May. 3.	Buried, Joseph Watson.
May 23.	Buried, Elizabeth Young.
May 29.	Buried, Elizabeth Yard.
June 7.	Buried, James Thomason.
July 12.	Buried, George Dawson.
July 16.	Buried, Dr. Robert Fletcher.
July 28.	Buried, George Cabriere.
Aug. 5.	Buried, Anne Dorrell.
Aug. 7.	Buried, William Jones.
Aug. 10.	Buried, John Rowley.
Aug. 13.	John Branfill, carried to Upminster.
Aug. 16.	Buried, Henry Guy.
Sep. 13.	Buried, Elizabeth Cheltenham.
Oct. 15.	Was carried to Wimbleton ——— Scarth.
Oct. 17.	Buried, Praise Thomason.
Nov. 7.	Buried, Lucy Collins.
Nov. 16.	Buried, Walter Thomas.
Nov. 20.	Was carried away, Elizabeth Gifford.
Nov. 23.	Was carried away, Margaret Palmer.
Nov. 23.	Buried, William Reesse.
Jan. 6.	Buried, John Vassall.
Jan. 10.	Buried, Joseph Woodley.

1719

Mar. 26.	Carried away, Diana Nicholls.
April 8.	Buried, Barbara Jakeman.
April 12.	Buried, William Morris.
April 21.	Buried, William Woolaston.
April 25.	Carried to Greenwich, Mary Jones.
May 6.	Buried, Anthony Evans.
May 12.	Buried, Susanna Bache.
May 25.	Buried, Elisabeth Homer.
May 25.	Judith Sanderson, carried to Michem.
June 1.	Buried, Alice Watson.
June 3.	Buried, Mary Watson.
June 11.	Buried, Thomas Wescomb.
June 24.	Buried, John Jeale.
June 26.	Buried, Joseph Stanton.
June 28.	Buried, Mary Fearne.
July 1.	Buried, Nathaniell Denny.
July 9.	Buried, Elizabeth Grosvenor.
July 15.	Buried, Charles Guy.
July 27.	Buried, Margret Cooke.
July 29.	Buried, Joseph Fielder.
Aug. 2.	Buried, William Cheltenham.
Aug. 8.	Buried, James Thomason.
Aug. 16.	Buried, Martha Rowley.
Dec. 3.	Buried, Thomas Toms.
Dec. 3.	Buried, Mary Dingley.

Dec. 17.	Buried, William Weston.
Dec. 20.	Buried, John Gibbon.
Dec. 27.	Buried, John Russell.
Dec. 30.	Buried, Martha Constable.
Dec. 31.	Buried, Mary Cabriere
Jan. 11.	Buried, James Wallis.
Jan. 15.	Rowland Williams, carried to Stepney.
Jan. 24.	Buried, John Robothan.
Feb. 9.	Buried, Anne Cricle.
Feb. 14.	Buried, Arthur D'arcy.
Feb. 28.	Buried, Elizabeth Venables, carried to Old Bethlehem.
Mar. 20.	Benjamin Branfill, carried to Upminster.

1720

Mar. 27.	Buried, George Cooke, junr.
Mar. 31.	Buried, John Taylor.
April 1.	Carried into the country, Elizabeth Wood.
May 26.	Buried, Elizabeth Goodshaw.
May 27.	Buried, Samuel Keynton.
May 27.	Buried, Edward Cooke.
May 27.	Buried, George Blany.
June 9.	Buried, Handy Shephard.
June 12.	Buried, Edmund Eades.
Aug. 3.	Carried to St. Benedicts, Sophia Pinney.
Aug. 17.	Buried, Andrew North.
Aug. 17.	Buried, Margret Ford.
Aug. 23.	Buried, Roger and Sarah Middleton, in one coffin.
Aug. 28.	Carried to Edmonton, Anne Morrell.
Sep. 11.	Buried, John Keynton.
Sep. 21.	Buried, John Eldridge.
Sep. 26.	Buried, Anne Cheltenham.
Oct. 3.	Buried, Peter Robinson.
Oct. 5.	Buried, John Jackson.
Oct. 8.	Buried, John Knapp.
Nov. 22.	Buried, Thomas Davis.
Dec. 16.	Carried to Jugby in Leicestershire, Joseph Wilson.
Jan. 16.	Carried to St. Mary le Bow, Anne Barnard.
Jan. 19.	Buried, Anne Falkingham.
Feb. 15.	Buried, Captain John Dorrill.
Feb. 20.	Buried, William Menzies.

1721

Mar. 28.	Was carried to Charlton in Kent, James Craggs, *Esquire.*
April 15.	Buried, Paul Hillton.
April 28.	Buried, Martha Webster.
June 25.	Was carried to Mile End . . . [*sic*] De Pive, *Jewwoman.*
June 28.	Was carried to College Hill, Mary Wareing.
Aug. 4.	Buried, Dorothy Knapp.
Aug. 23.	Buried, Dorothy Robotham.
Sep. 6.	Was carried to Stratford, William Stevenson.
Sep. 17.	Buried, Hamlet Toone.
Sep. 15.	Buried, Robert Pattenson.
Sep. 22.	Buried, Sarah Cheltenham.
Dec. 3.	Buried, Elizabeth Cooper.

Dec. 13.   Buried, Elizabeth Pollard.
Jan. 25.   Buried, Mary Hilton.   Placed wrong, as under [*sic*]
Jan. 28.   Buried, John Morris.
Feb. 25.   Buried, Mary Hilton.
Mar. 2.   Buried, William Davis.
Mar. 10.   Buried, Thomas Sperinck.
Mar. 12.   Buried, Henry Blaney.
Mar. 13.   Buried, Thomas Samadine.

1722

May 19.   Was carried to Upminster, Charles Branfill.

[End of Burials in 3rd Volume.]

No Register is to be found of the Burials between May 19, 1722, and December 15, 1744.

[𝔙𝔬𝔩. 𝔦𝔦𝔦𝔧.]

THE REGISTER of Burials in the Parish of St. Mary Woolnoth, London, since the First of December, 1744.

The Rev. SAMUEL ANGIER, A.M., *Rector.*
The Rev. CHARLES PLUMPTRE, D.D., *Rector.*
The Rev. JOHN NEWTON, *Rector.*

1744

Dec. 15.   Buried, Samuell, son of Mr. William Baker, *Stationer*, of St. Mary Woolnoth.
Dec. 19.   Buried, John Barber, of the General Post Office.
Dec. 29.   Buried, Elizabeth, daughter of Brough Maltby, *Linnen-draper.*
Jan. 20.   Buried, Richard, son of William Webster, *Watchmaker*, in Exchange Alley.
Jan. 31.   Buried, John Slaney, of St. Mary Woolnoth Parish.
Feb. 6.   Buried, John Cooper, *a Mason employed at the Mansion House.*
Feb. 7.   Buried, Mary Sturgiss, was brought from St. Giles in the Fields.
Feb. 14.   Buried, Peter, son of John Langley, *Haberdasher of Hatts*, in Exchange Alley.
Feb. 22.   Buried, Miss Eunice Gilbert of Bear-binder Lane.
Mar. 10.   Buried, Joseph, son of Marmaduke Westwood *Apothecary*, in Fenchurch Street or Buildings.
Mar. 14.   Buried, John Maxwell.

1745

April 1. Buried, Elizabeth, wife of Joseph Brown, a *Barber*, in Sherborne Lane.
May 26. Buried, Sarah Shuttleworth.
May 31. Buried, Mary Robinson, was brought from the Old Jewry.
Sep. 1. Buried, David Dennison.
Sep. 27. Buried, Miriam, daughter of Joseph Marsh.
Nov. 17. Buried, Elizabeth Bick, of St. Mary Woolchurch Haw.
Nov, 20. Buried, Samuel Russell, of St. Mary Woolchurch Haw.
Dec. 13. Buried, Elizabeth Dennison, of St. Mary Woolchurch Haw.
Feb. 2. Buried, Isabella Collins.
Feb. 27. Buried, Catharine Price (*housekeeper* at Mr. Stone's).
Mar. 12. Buried, Sarah Bleving.

1746

April 6. Buried, Ann Maltby, a child
June 8. Buried, Mary Strong, of St. Mary Woolchurch Haw.
Oct. 15. Buried, Ann Hieron.
Dec. 21. Buried, George Hindmass (late of the Post Office).
Dec. 31. Buried, Hannah Thompson.
Feb. 14. Buried, Miriam Marsh (a child).
Feb. 17. Buried, James Hodges (a child).
Mar. 5. Buried, Thomas Cooke (a child).
Mar. 5. Buried, Ann Hasell.

1747

April 19. Buried, Miss Ann Highmore and Mrs. Sarah Palmer.
May 1. Buried, James Eldridge (a child).
June 3. Buried, Dinah Willson (a child).
June 25. Buried. Hannah Manning (a child).
Aug. 12. Buried, Sarah Willson (a child).
Sep. 12. Buried, Margaret Rushton.
Oct. 4. Buried, Daniell Miles Webster (a child).
Jan. 15. Buried, Elizabeth Brown (a child).
Jan. 21. Buried, Mary Collins.
Feb. 19. Buried, Mr. John Ward.
Feb. 28. Buried, Catherine Church.
Mar. 17. Buried, Mary Hudson, (from Mr. Stantons, Lombard Street).

1748

April 24. Buried, Nathaniel Edwards.
May 4. Buried, Sarah Robins.
May 17. Buried, Affiah Maltby, (sister to Mr. Maltby, *Linnendraper*).
May 20. Buried, Elizabeth Bache, (a lodger at Mr. Moys).
May 27. Buried, Richard Baker, (*Churchwarden of St. Mary Woolnoth*).
July 27. Buried, Joseph Archer, (*Clerk of this Parish*),
July 29. Buried, Susannah Cooke.
Nov. 11. Buried, Elizabeth Blandford, (a child).
Dec. 9. Buried, Hannah Bentley, (a child).

Dec. 11.	Buried, Lucretia Walne.
Feb. 6.	Buried, Margaret Bradbury.
Feb. 19.	Buried, Charles Littleton.
Feb. 19.	Buried, Ursula Eldridge.
Feb. 20.	Buried, Mary Webb, (child).
Mar. 25.	Buried, Mary Collins.

1749

April 4.	Buried, William Daviss, (of Bearbinder Lane).
May 4.	Buried, Margaret Moseley.
May 12.	Buried, Mary Moss.
Aug. 22.	Buried, Rebeccah Jayes, *(Searcher)*. S. M. W. N.
Sep. 3.	Buried, a man unknown. S. M. W. C.
Oct. 8.	Buried, Maria, infant daughter of William and Elizabeth Baker. S. M. W. N.
Sep. 11.	Buried, Godfrey, infant son of William and Sarah Webster. S. M. W. N.
Sep. 14.	Buried, Robert Meades Prince, of Sherborne Lane. S. M. W. N.
Sep. 24.	Buried, Rebeccah Pile, *(Spinster)*. the corner of Little Lombard Street. S. M. W. C.
Oct. 9.	Buried, Edward Fenwick, from Tottenham, Middlesex.
Dec. 23.	Buried, John, infant son of John and Mary Griffiths. S. M. W. N.

1750

May 2.	Buried, Richard Barnard, from Cornhill.
May 13.	Buried, John Morris, Popes Head Alley. S. M. W. N.
May 18.	Buried, Hester Wilson, from Hoxton.
May 29.	Buried, Mercy Gerrard, from St. James.
July 7.	Buried, John Bosanquet, *Esquire*, from Warnford Court, Throgmorton Street.
July 13.	Buried, John Wakefield, opposite the Mansion House. S. M. W. C.
Aug. 7.	Buried, John Prince, an infant, from Sherborne Lane. S. M. W. N.
Aug. 15.	Buried, Hannah, wife of William Manning, in Lombard Street. S. M. W. N.
Sep. 25.	Buried, William Tolme, infant son of John Bentley, near the Mansion House. S. M. W. N.
Oct. 19.	Buried, John Reithugsen, from Whitechapel.
Nov 2.	Buried, Anne Davis, of Bearbinder Lane. S. M. W. C.
Nov. 4.	Buried, John Marley, of Little Lombard Street. S. M. W. C.
Nov. 13.	Buried, Letitia, wife of John Smith, *Sadler*, in Lombard Street. S. M. W. N.
Nov. 30.	Buried, Charles Wood, *Poulterer*, from Walbrook.
Dec. 3.	Buried, George Blanchard, from the Post Office. S. M. W. N.
Dec. 23.	Buried, George, infant son of Henry Haskey, in Little Lombard Street. S. M. W. N.
Dec. 27.	Buried, Robert, son of Robert Webb, *the Clerk*. S. M. W. N.
Jan. 1.	Buried, Hugh Powell, *a Waiter* from Jonathan's Coffee House. S. M. W. N.
Jan. 21.	Buried, Rebecca Bickerdike (an infant), from St. Sepulchres.

Jan. 30. Buried, Ann Barnard (an infant), from St. Michael's, Cornhill.

Feb. 10. Buried, George Barrett, from the Corner of Cornhill. S. M. W. C

Feb. 10. Buried, Faith, wife of John Brown, in Sherborne Lane. S. M. W. N.

Mar. 7. Buried, Penelope (infant) daughter of George and Mary Hodges. S. M. W. C.

1751

Mar. 31. Buried, Elizabeth Wood, *Widow*, from Walbrook.

April 10. Buried, William Collins, the elder, from Sherborne Lane. S. M. W. N.

May 14. Buried, Thomas Blaney, the elder, *Sexton of this Parish.* S. M. W. N.

June 1. Buried, Jane, wife of Samuel Hall, of Bearbinder Lane. S. M. W. C.

June 5. Buried, George, son of William Baker, the corner of the Post Office, Lombard Street. S. M. W. N.

July 24. Buried, Elizabeth, infant daughter of Henry Haskey, Little Lombard Street. S. M. W. N.

Sep. 29. Buried, Dorothy Palmer, *a servant* from Sam's Coffee-house. S. M. W. N.

Oct. 12. Buried, Catherine, infant daughter of Joseph and Eleanor Martin, in Lombard Street. S. M. W. N.

Oct. 16. Buried, James, infant son of Andrew and Catherine Moffatt, in Lombard Street. S. M. W. N.

Oct. 16. Buried, Richard Palmer, an *Apprentice* to Mr. Cook, in Sherborne Lane. S. M. W. N.

Dec. 10. Buried, Thomas, infant son of Henry and Anne Jones, opposite the Mansion House. S. M. W. N.

Dec. 18. Buried, William Ford, (a lodger), from the Postboy Alehouse, in Sherborne Lane. S. M. W. N.

Jan. 11. Buried, Mary, wife of George Lee, in Lombard Street. S. M. W. N.

Jan. 14. Buried, Susannah Gilbert, *Widow*, from Warneford Court.

Feb. 11. Buried, Sarah, wife of William Sanderson, opposite the Mansion House. S. M. W. C.

Feb. 23. Buried, Thomas, infant son of William and Mary Austin, from Allhallows the Great.

1752

Mar. 16. Buried, The Rev. Samuel Angier, A.M., *Rector of these United Parishes.* S. M. W. N. and S. M. W. C.

April 5. Buried, Gaius Alley. S. M. W. C.

April —. Buried, Beata, infant daughter of Joseph and Herman Blandford. S. M. W. C.

May 13. Buried, Thomas Taft, of Dove Court. S. M. W. N.

May 19. Buried, Samuel Newey, from opposite the Mansion House. S. M. W. C.

May 30. Buried, Robert James, of Little Lombard Street. S. M. W. C.

Aug. 4. Buried, Thomas Davis, of Bearbinder Lane. S. M. W. C.

Oct. 6. Buried, Sarah, infant daughter of Joseph and Ann Brown. S. M. W. N.

Oct. 27.   Buried, John Shuttleworth, opposite the Mansion House. s. m. w. c.

Nov. 11.   Buried, William Law, of Little Lombard Street.   s. m. w. n.

Nov. 12.   Buried, Joseph, son of Joseph and Eleanor Martin. s. m. w. n.

Dec. 19.   Buried, John Brown, *servant* to Mr. Brumfield.   s. m. w. n.

Dec. 28.   Buried, Sussanah, wife of Timothy Cook, near the Mansion House.   s. m. w. c.

1753

Jan. 18.   Buried, Mary, daughter of Rebecca Price, of Thomas Nathan's Coffee-house in Exchange Alley.   s. m. w. n.

Jan. 24.   Buried, James Pitman, late *servant* to Messrs. Ransom & Hodges.   s. m. w. c.

Jan. 27.   Buried, Ann, daughter of John Martin, *Woollendraper*, in Lombard Street.   s. m. w. c.

Mar. 15.   Buried, Sarah, infant daughter of Henry and Ann Jones, opposite the Mansion House.   s. m. w. c.

April 18.   Buried, Thomas, infant son of Thomas and Mary Brown, of Sherborne Lane.   s. m. w. n.

April 20.   Buried, Esther, infant daughter of William and Elizabeth Baker, *Stationer*, in Lombard Street.   s. m. w. n.

May 24.   Buried, Dionisia, daughter of Samuel Pafflin, of St. Giles Cripplegate.

June 9.   Buried, Mary, infant daughter of William and Mary White, in Little Lombard Street.   s. m. w. n.

June 23.   Buried, Catherine Beckett, from Mrs. Wakefield.   s. m. w. c.

Oct. 14.   Buried, John Edwards, the corner of Bearbinder Lane. s. m. w. n.

Oct. 29.   Buried, Lucy, infant daughter ——— [*sic*] Brown, at the Postboy.   s. m. w. n.

Dec. 9.   Buried, Samuel Stringer.   s. m. w. c.

1754

Jan. 5.   Buried, Elizabeth Fielder.   s. m. w. c.

Feb. 6.   Buried, Elizabeth Martin, from St. Peter's, Cornhill.

Feb. 13.   Buried, John Southen James, from Mr. Wade's, Change Alley.   s. m. w. n.

Mar 19.   Buried, Hannah, infant daughter of Thomas and Mary Parsons.   s. m. w. n.

April 10.   Buried, Sewster Savage.   s. m. w. n.

May 22.   Buried, Charlotte, infant daughter of Alexander and Ann Smith.   s. m. w. n.

May 22.   Buried, Samuel Pufflin, an infant.

June 14.   Buried, Thomas Waltering.   s. m. w. n.

June 17.   Buried, Elizabeth Seymour.   s. m. w. n.

June 21.   Buried, John Ismay.   s. m. w. n.

Aug. 7.   Buried, Elizabeth, infant daughter of Henry and Elizabeth Baldero.   s. m. w. n.

Aug. 8.   Buried, Catherine Shuttleworth.

Sep. 15.   Buried, Sarah Webb.

Sep. 26.   Buried, John Price.

Oct. 5.   Buried, Peter Rivalier.

Nov. 9.   Buried, Mary Ballow, from Richmond.

Nov. 13.   Buried, Joseph Bentley, an infant.

1755

Jan. 1.	Buried, Moris Davis, an infant. s. m. w. n.
Jan. 5.	Buried, a poor woman, name unknown.
Jan. 22.	Buried, John Leadbeater.
Jan. 23.	Buried, Joseph, son of Joseph and Eleanor Martin. s. m. w. n.
Jan. 26.	Buried, Joseph Cass. s. m. w. n.
Feb. 14.	Buried, Thomas Merrifield. s. m. w. n.
Mar. 20.	Buried, Robert, infant son of R. P. and Lucy Finch.
May 28.	Buried, Elizabeth Rivalier. s. m. w. n.
Aug. 12.	Buried, John, infant son of Andrew and Katherine Moffat. s. m. w. n.
Aug. 12.	Buried, John, infant son of Joseph and Ann Brown. s. m. w. n.
Aug. 28.	Buried, Joyce Guy, from Abchurch Parish.
Sep. 4.	Buried, Godfrey, infant son of William and Sarah Webster. s. m. w. n.
Nov. 27.	Buried, John Tysoe. s. m. w. n.

1756

Jan. 4.	Buried, Hanna Keeling. s. m. w. c.
Jan. 7.	Buried, Katherine Gardiner, from Richmond.
Mar. 7.	Buried, Thomas Roscow. s. m. w. c.
April 2.	Buried, William Collins. s. m. w. n.
May 26.	Buried, Francis Roscow. s. m. w. c.
May 28.	Buried, William Manning, an infant. s. m. w. n.
June 25.	Buried, Rachel Cook, an infant. s. m. w. c.
July 2.	Buried, Mary Denovan Brown, an infant. s. m. w. n.
July 5.	Buried, Esther Cheeseling. s. m. w. n.
Nov. 11.	Buried, John Shuttleworth.
Nov. 25.	Buried, Mary Beach. s. m. w. n.
Dec. 19.	Buried, William Pamfling.
Dec. 19.	Buried, Frances Baker, an infant. s. m. w. n.
Dec. 23.	Buried, Elizabeth Dalling. s. m. w. c.

1757

Jan. 28.	Buried, Samuel Keynton.
Mar. 21.	Buried, Ann Godly. s. m. w. c.
June 19.	Buried, James Richmond. s. m. w. n.
July 1.	Buried, John Baker. s. m. w. n.
Aug. 31.	Buried, Jane Cook and Ann Webb, two infants.
Sep. 21.	Buried, Edmond Gilbert.
Nov. 14.	Buried, Henry Jones. s. m. w. n.
Dec. 11.	Buried, William Best. s. m. w. c.
Dec. 12.	Buried, Richard Wilding. s m. w. n.
Dec. 23.	Buried, Sarah Hall. s. m. w. n.

1758

Jan. 18.	Buried, Ann Cooke. s. m. w. c.
Feb. 2.	Buried, William, son of ——— [*sic*] and ——— [*sic*] Saunders. s. m. w. n.
Mar. 2.	Buried, Elizabeth Boldero. s. m. w. n.
April 2.	Buried, Sarah Taft. s. m. w. n.

April 8.	Buried, Robert Jones, an infant. s. m. w. n.
April 12.	Buried, Thomas Gilbert, from St. Margaret, Westminster.
April 26.	Buried, Thomas Brown, an infant. s. m. w n.
May 10.	Buried, Henry Quantito. s. m. w. n.
June 27.	Buried, Sarah Hodgkins. s. m. w. c.
July 5.	Buried, Hannah Manning, an infant. s. m. w. n.
Aug. 22.	Buried, Mary Gannell, an infant.
Sep. 1.	Buried, Frances Cook, an infant. s. m. w. c.
Oct. 6.	Buried, John Arnold, an infant. s. m. w. c.
Oct. 15.	Buried, Richard Bentley, an infant. s. m. w. c.
Oct. 17.	Buried, James Peachy, an infant. s. m. w. n.
Dec. 6.	Buried, Mary Andrews, from Bow, Middlesex.
Dec. 31.	Buried, Sarah Neale. s. m. w. n.

1759

Jan. 19.	Buried, Randall Boldero. s. m. w. n.
Jan. 25.	Buried, Elizabeth Cook. s. m. w. n.
Jan. 25.	Buried, Thomas Sewell. s. m. w. n.
Feb. 18.	Buried, Judith Manning. s. m. w. n.
April 1.	Buried, Thomas Geary. s. m. w. n.
April 2.	Buried, Robert Dodson.
April 5.	Buried, Leonard Wooddeson. s. m. w. n.
May 11.	Buried, William Winchester. s. m. w. n.
June 24.	Buried, Richard Yarrow. s. m. w. n.
July 5.	Buried, Mary Savage. s. m. w. n.
Aug. 19.	Buried, Elizabeth Parsons. s. m. w. n.
Aug. 25.	Buried, Deneven Brown. s. m. w. n.
Aug. 28.	Buried, Robert Evans. s. m. w. n.
Aug. 30.	Buried, Patience Story. s. m. w. n.
Aug. 30.	Buried, Thomas Greenhill, infant. s. m. w. c.
Sep. 20.	Buried, Robert Theophus Jones. s. m. w. n.
Sep. 25.	Buried, Alexander Foreman. s. m. w. n.
Sep. 30.	Buried, Griffeth Roberts.
Sep. 30.	Buried, Thomas Woodeson, an infant. s. m. w. n.
Oct. 9.	Buried, James Brown. s. m. w. n.
Nov. 14.	Buried, William Hurford. s. m. w. n.
Nov. 23.	Buried, Letitia, from Westminster. [*sic*]
Nov. 23.	Buried, Mathew Testas. s. m. w. n.
Nov. 30.	Buried, Ann Wilding. s. m. w. n.

1760

Feb. 15.	Buried, Jonathan Chambers, from St. George's Parish, Queen's Square.
Feb. 17.	Buried, Samuel Bowditch. s. m. w. c.
Feb. 28.	Buried, William How. s. m. w. c.
Feb. 29.	Buried, Robert Simpson, from St. James, Garlick Hithe.
May — [*sic*]	Buried, Sarah Jones, an infant.
June or July — [*sic*]	Buried, Daniel Bowdich, an infant.
Dec. 21.	Buried, John Webb, *Parish Clerk.*

THE following list of persons connected with and in most cases buried at St. Mary Woolnoth, has been compiled from Wills and other documents, and has been printed as likely to prove interesting.

1338.	From Robert at le Hyde to the Churchwardens, quit rent of houses in the Parishes of St. Mary Abchurch and St. Laurence Candlewick Street, for the soul of Sywatha, the *Cornmonger*.
1396.	Thomas Noket, "*Pannarius*" to be buried "in cancello int. sum. altar. et sepulturam Petri Whappelod in fine boreali dicti Altaris."
1399.	Johannes Lenne, "*Clericus, Civis Lon.*" to be buried " in Capella Sancti Johannis Bapt. in ecclesia Beatoe Marioe de Wolnoth " "Emmam uxorem meam."
1411.	John Barnevyle, *Citizen and Pewterer*, to be buried in the Lady Chapel. A bequest made to Wickhambreaux Kent.
1418.	John Potter, *Citizen and Shoemaker*, to be buried in St. Mary Woolnoth Church.
1423.	Peter Ay'rall *Citizen and Vintner*, to be buried in the Lady Chapel by Julian his wife.
1425.	Alice Okely, *Widow*, to be buried in the Church.
1426.	Alice Ayrell, [*sic*] Widow of Peter Ay'rall, to be buried next her husband.
1429.	Thomas Roche, *Citizen and Vintner*, to be buried in St. Mary Woolnoth.
1434.	William Fitzhugh, *Goldsmith*.
1442.	Joan Eyr, to be buried "in Cancello" by her husband, Thomas Eyr.
1444.	Andrew Michell, *Citizen and Vintner*, to be buried in St. Mary Woolnoth.
1453.	Joan Michell, to be buried with Thomas Roche and Andrew Michell her two husbands.
1453.	Johannes Petworth, *Rector of Denge*, co. Essex, to be buried in St. Mary Woolnoth.
1465.	John Wellesbourne, *Esquire*, of Wycombe, Co. Bucks, to be buried in St. Mary Woolnoth.
1496.	Thomas Wymond, *Citizen and Fuller*, to be buried with his wife Joan. A perpetual obit. *
1500.	Robert Weston, *Citizen and Mercer*, to be buried in the Chancel, near Elizabeth his wife.
1503.	George Lovekyn "*Tayllour to our Soveraigne Lorde the Kinge*," " to be buried afore the fonte thereundre the Chapell of St. George by me there late made, that is to sey in or by the burying place of Jane my first wife."
1504.	William White, *Draper and Alderman*, a native of Tickhill, Yorkshire.
1511.	Robert Norreys, *Mercer*, to be buried " beside the holy water stok in the Cloyster where my brother and my master Weston children were buried."
1516.	George Harware, *Taylor*, of London, to be buried in St. Mary Woolnoth.

* His Second (?) wife, who survived him, was Elizabeth, daughter of ——— Tenacre, and cousin of William Tenacre, *Citizen and Mercer*, from Kent (Will 1494), she married secondly Sir John Thurston, Knight, *Citizen and Goldsmith*.

1519.   William Hilton, *Citizen and Merchant Tailor, and Tailor to the King.* †

1520.   Nicholas Warley, *Citizen and Goldsmith*, to be buried near daughter Elizabeth. ‡

1521.   John Garrard, *Citizen and Goldsmith*, to be buried in St. Mary Woolnoth.

1523.   Richard Peppes, of London, *Scryvener*, to be buried in St. Mary Woolnoth. §

1524.   John Molder, M.A., *Vicar of Wolford, Co. Warwick*, to be buried in St. Mary Woolnoth "if he die in London." There is a bequest to Evesham, where his parents lived.

1525.   Sir John Skevington, *Knight*, of this Parish, *Alderman, Sheriff* 1520, his wife was Elizabeth, daughter of William Brett, he was born at Skeffington, Co. Leicester.

1531.   Elizabeth Warley, Widow of Nicholas Warley, to be buried in St. Mary Woolnoth.

1533.   Robert Amadas, *Citizen and Goldsmith*, to be buried in St. Mary Woolnoth. ‖

1538.   Roger Towneshende, *Priest, Chancellor of Sarum, Rector of North Creke, Sault and Heyden, Co. Norfolk, Vicar of Lydd, Co. Kent*, "to be buried in my Parish Church of St. Mary Wolnoth. *

THE following, though later than the commencement of the Church Registers, may be of interest,

1541.   John Barnes, *Citizen and Goldsmith*, son-in-law of Sir Martin Bowes, apparently buried elsewhere.

1549.   Thomas Stephyns, *Citizen and Goldsmith*, to be buried in St. Mary Woolnoth, and to have a monument. (See p. 182.)

1552.   Edward Barbor, *Citizen and Scrivener*, to be buried in St. Mary Woolnoth, near his father. (See p. 183.)

† His Will mentions Lufkyns Chapel dedicated to St. George, also "The fraternitie of our blessed Lady and Corpus Christi over the Church doore . . . . wherof the bachelors of the said parish be rulers and wardens."

‡ He was a brother of Alderman Henry Warley, and had property in Shropshire.

§ Son of John Peppes, thelder, of Braintree. There is a Will of a John Peppis, of Braintree, 1519.

‖ See " Extracts from Church Accounts."

* He was the son of Sir Roger Towneshend.

Sainte Marie Woolchurche Hawghe

THIS booke was bought in the one and fortieth yeare of the reigne of our Sovereine Ladie Elizabeth by the grace of god Queene of England France and Ireland defender of the faith etc.

1599

Steven Some *Grocer Knight Lord Maior of this citie of London the same yeare*

Edward Holmden *Grocer* ⎫ *sheriffes of London*
Robert Hamson *Merchanttayler* ⎭ *the same yeare*

Richard Bancroft *doctor of divinitie Lord Bishop of London the same time*

Theophilus Elmer *doctor of divinitie Archdeacon of London the same time*

Edward Stanhope *doctor of the civil lawe chanceler of London the same time*

John Hayward *bachelour of divinitie parson of this church the same time*

John Dauies and ⎫ *Haberdashers churchwardens*
Robart Rainton ⎭ *the same yeare*

Quo baptizatus, nuptus sit, siue sepultus
tempore quis quæris? hæc liber iste docet.
Quo moriere die, caro mortua quoue resurget,
dicere quærenti pagina nulla potest.
Fixa tamen et certa manet mortalibus hora,
qua moriturus erit, quaque resurget homo.

ergo ⁓ ⁓ plus vigila semper.   Laus deo Amen.

J. H.

Baptisms

ELIZABETH, our Gracious Queene, happilie began hir reigne on the sevententh daie of November in the yeare of our Lord one thowsand fyve hundred fiftie and eight, since which time there have bene in the parishe of St. Marie Woolchurch Hawghe in London these christenings followinge.

1558

Dec. 14.	Jone Basford.
Dec. 21.	Agnes Kindrike.
Jan. 9.	Blanche Travall.
Feb. 7.	George Skegs.

1559

July 30.	Sara Ebbe.
Oct. 26.	Jone Smith.
Oct. 31.	Blanche Babissedike.
Nov. 17.	Thomas Staynye.
Feb. 11.	Alexander Best.
Mar. 10.	Richard Skeks.

1560

Mar. 27.	Peter Travell.
Mar. 31.	Gawin Shakilton.
April 28.	Thomas Bening.
April 30.	Jone Crewe.
May 18.	Sara Bonde.
May 23.	John Mason.
June 23.	Anne Gunstone.
July 25.	Arthur Basford.
Oct. 26.	{ William Bludwicke { Sibill Bludwicke } "Twines" of John Bludwicke.
Nov. 10.	Ursula Cudner.
Nov. 24.	Edward Salter.
Dec. 3.	{ Marie Holmes { Ales Holmes } "twines daughters" of Edward Holmes.
Mar. 15.	William Cater.

1561

Mar. 30.	Robarte Swaine.
April 13.	Marie Allen.
April 20.	Susan Sparrowe.
April 20.	William Daie.
April 27.	Jane Best.

May 15.	Richard Crewe.
May 23.	John Hobson.
June 8.	John Walker.
June 29.	Martha Shakilton.
July 5.	Richard Harrison.
Aug. 17.	Samuell, son of George Anthonie.
Sep. 7.	Grace, daughter of Richard Bradlie.
Oct. 12.	Jone, daughter of Thomas Mason.
Oct. 19.	Jeremie, son of William Lewes.
Oct. 25.	Thomas, son of Robart Cudnar.
Nov. 2.	Elizabeth, daughter of Richard Travell.
Nov. 14.	Robarte, son of Robart Partridge.
Dec. 14.	Brian, son of Edward Holmes.
Dec. 28.	Ales, daughter of John Webbe.
Jan. 1.	George, son of William Page.
Jan. 4.	Thomas, son of William Handford.
Jan. 6.	Sara, daughter of John Sharp.
Jan. 25.	James, son of James Wrenche.
Feb. 12.	Roger, son of John Shard.
Mar. 15.	William, son of Edward Skegs.

1562

June 21.	Susan, daughter of Thomas Walker.
July 1.	Jone, daughter of William Powle.
July 8.	Joseph, son of John Crewe.
Aug. 22.	Ales, daughter of Thomas Gun.
Sep. 6.	Anne, daughter of Thomas Allen.
Oct. 1.	Margaret, daughter of John Fabian.
Oct. 10.	Anne, daughter of Lawrence Harrison.
Oct. 11.	Edward, son of James Willan.
Oct. 21.	John, son of William Cater.
Jan. 10.	Francis, son of Edward Holmes.
Jan. 17.	Francis, son of George Anthonie.
Feb. 21.	Marie, daughter of John Sharp.

1563

June 20.	Edmund, son of Robart Cudner.
July 12.	Blanch, daughter of John Crewe.
July 25.	Sibille, daughter of Steven Wilson.
Aug. 8.	William, son of Richard Harrison.
Aug. 29.	Thomas, son of Richard Andlebic.
Sep. 12.	Margerie, daughter of William Powle.
Oct. 6.	John, son of Thomas Allen.

1564

Mar. 25.	Thomas, son of Thomas Gunne.
April 3.	Ester, daughter of Edward Holmes.
Sep. 17.	Ales, daughter of Adam Powell.
Oct. 1.	Thomas, son of William Cater.
Oct. 15.	Emme, daughter of John Crewe.
Oct. 28.	Thomas, son of John Sharpe.
Nov. 1.	Humfrie, son of Thomas Walker.
Nov. 4.	Susan, daughter of Thomas Allen.

Nov. 19.	Barbara, daughter of James Willan.
Feb. 11.	Thomas, son of Richard Briggs.
Feb. 18.	Thomas, son of Laurence Harrison.
Mar. 11.	Humfrie, son of William Handford.

1565

Mar. 25.	Elinor, daughter of Richard Sharp.
May 27.	Jonathan, son of Edmond Creswell.
June 3.	Jone, daughter of Francis Dedicote,
July 7.	Marie, daughter of Robart Cudner.
Aug. 12.	John, son of William Swaine.
Sep. 9.	Thomas, son of John Tayler.
Sep. 30.	Thomas, son of Richard Wade.
Oct. 10.	Bridget, daughter of Thomas Walker.
Oct. 14.	Rose, daughter of Thomas Copcote.
Dec. 29.	Marie, daughter of William Cater.
Jan. 12.	Edward, son of James Willan.
Feb. 10.	Katherin, daughter of Robart Yarington.
Mar. 3.	Margaret, daughter of Thomas Allen.

1566

April 25.	Thomas, son of William Shorley.
May 19.	William, son of William Handford.
May 23.	Margaret, daughter of Richard Sharp.
June 2.	Marie, daughter of John Crewe.
July 21.	Bartholomew, son of Richard Brigges.
July 21.	Thomas, son of Edmond Creswell.
Aug. 17.	Thomas, son of George Mason.
Sep. 29.	Ales, daughter of Richard Hale.
Oct. 4.	Abell, son of John Maysham.
Oct. 18.	Thomas, son of William Swaine.
Dec. 4.	John, son of Richard Wade.
Dec. 22.	John, son of Thomas Copcote.
Jan. 10.	Anne, daughter of John Sharpe.
Jan. 29.	George, son of Lawrence Harrison.
Feb. 5.	Edward, son of Edward Stephanson.
Feb. 9.	Elinor, daughter of William Keale.
Feb. 12.	Anne, daughter of William Spencer.
Feb. 14.	Thomas, son of Thomas Walker.
Feb. 23.	Anne, daughter of Adam appoell.
Mar. 9.	Bridget, daughter of Thomas Allen.

1567

May 11.	Lewis, son of William Cater.
May 18.	Humfrie, son of Robart Yarrington.
Aug. 23.	Elizabeth, daughter of Richard Harrison.
Aug. 28.	James, son of Anthony Vanhoven.
Sep. 17.	Jane, daughter of Robert Perpoint.
Oct. 5.	Thomas, son of Thomas Wilkinson.
Oct. 19.	Edmund, son of Edmund Creswell.
Jan. 1.	Humfrie, son of Francis Dedicote.
Jan. 11.	John, son of John Sharpe.
Jan. 18.	James, son of William Sharlie.

Feb. 16.	John, son of Edward Holmes.
Mar. 21.	Marie, daughter of John Maie.

1568

June 29.	Judith, daughter of Lawrence Harrison.
Aug. 24.	Brigit, daughter of Thomas Smith.
Sep. 18.	Elizabeth, daughter of Thomas Filian.
Sept. 29.	Dorithie, daughter of John Maskall.
Oct. 3.	Richard, son of Robart Perpointe.
Oct. 3.	Rafe, son of Griffith Kenricke.
Oct. 10.	William, son of Humfrie Dedicote.
Oct. 10.	Marie, daughter of Robart Yarington.
Oct. 18.	Thomas, son of Thomas Wilkinson.
Nov. 14.	William, son of Richard Hale.
Nov. 17.	Francis, daughter of Peter Lide.
Nov. 28.	Anne, daughter of William Cater.
Dec. 12.	Rose, daughter of Thomas Allen.
Dec. 19.	John, son of William Jones.
Dec. 28.	Katherine, daughter of Adam Appoell.
Jan. 31.	Jone, daughter of William Spencer.
Feb. 1.	John, son of William Spencer.
Mar. 13.	Daniel, son of Thomas Hasell.

1569

Mar. 27.	Robart, son of Thomas Gun.
May 22.	Arthur, son of William Handford.
June 5.	Marie, daughter of Edmund Creswell.
July 3.	Brigit, daughter of William Sharlie.
July 31.	Sara, daughter of Richard Wade.
Sep. 4.	John, son of Thomas Walker.
Sep. 4.	Katherin, daughter of Henrie Shepard.
Sep. 21.	Susan, daughter of Robart Perpoint.
Sep. 29.	Emerie, daughter of Humfrie Dedicote.
Dec. 4.	Ellin, daughter of John Sharp.
Dec. 11.	Thomas, son of Thomas Allen.
Jan. 15.	Phillip, son of Robart Wighthand.

1570

Mar. 27.	Robart, son of Robart Yarington.
April 9.	Georg, son of John Maskall.
July 14.	Jeronimie, daughter of William Spencer.
July 23.	Marie, daughter of Adam appoell.
Aug. 19.	William, son of Griffith Kenrick.
Sep. 10.	Jane, daughter William Keale.
Sep. 13.	Elizabeth, daughter of Nicholas Stanes.
Oct. 29.	Sara, daughter of Richard Sharpe.
Nov. 5.	Anne, daughter of Robart Perpoint.
Nov. 5.	Ellin, daughter of Peter Lide.
Jan. 21.	Dwell, daughter of John Ringes.
Feb. 9.	Marie, daughter of Thomas Filian.
Feb. 11.	Humfrie, son of Thomas Allen.
Feb. 25.	John, son William Handford.
Mar. 7.	Henry, son of Michael Abdie.
Mar. 11.	Katherin, daughter of Robert Smith.
Mar. 17.	John, son of Edmund Normanvill.

1571

Mar. 25.	Rychard, son of Robart Wighthand.
May 6.	Sarah, daughter of Richard Wade.
May 13.	Michael, son of John Maskall.
May 20.	Jone, daughter of Robart Yarrington.
June 10.	Robart, son of George Baker.
Aug. 10.	William, son of William Spencer.
Sep. 1.	Joyce, daughter of William Keele.
Sep. 9.	Sara, daughter of Thomas Hasell.
Nov. 20.	Elizabeth, daughter of William Sharlie.
Nov. 25.	Susan, daughter of William Keningham.
Dec. 5.	William, son of Robart Perpoint.
Dec. 9.	Nicholas, son of Nicholas Stanes.
Jan. 6.	Thomas, son of Henrie Shepard.
Feb. 8.	Henrie, son of Robart Smith.
Mar. 19.	John, son of John Keighlie.
Mar. 22.	John, son of Edmund Normanvile.

1572

April 7.	Humfrie, son of Thomas Walker.
April 16.	Henrie, son of George Fenne.
Aug. 27.	Edward, son of Michael Abdie.
Sep. 3.	Theophilus, son of Richard Sharpe.
Sep. 7.	Pernel, daughter of William Handford.
Oct. 4.	Richard, son of Richard Harris.
Oct. 12.	Elizabeth, daughter of Thomas Healde.
Oct. 26.	Ales, daughter of Robert Wighthand.
Nov. 29.	Jone, daughter of William Kele.
Dec. 12.	Dorcas, daughter of William Keningham.
Jan. 4.	Robart, son of Robart Yarrington.
Jan. 4.	Judith, daughter of Robert Smith.
Jan. 18.	Judith, daughter of John Ringes.
Feb. 7.	Henry, son of Will Spencer.
Mar. 8.	Robart, son of Robart Brooke.

1573

June 7.	Martha, daughter of Robart Perpoint.
Aug. 30.	John, son of Griffith Kenrick.
Oct. 2.	John, son of William Keighlie.
Oct. 18.	John, son of William Kenningham.
Dec. 27.	John, son of John Maskall.
Jan. 3.	Jone, daughter of Nicholas Stanes.
Jan. 6.	Jane, daughter of Robart Smith.
Feb. 21.	Thomasin, daughter of William Handford.
Feb. 28.	Jereme, son of James Allen.

1574

April 11.	Marie, daughter of Robart Brooke.
April 13.	Ester, daughter of Thomas Healde.
April 18.	William, son of Robart Linge.
April 23.	George, son of George Fenne.
May 16.	John, son of Robart Yarrington.
May 17.	Walter, son of Edward Leastede.

May 23.	Richard, son of Richard Harris.
Aug. 8.	John, son of John Sharpe.
Sep. 20.	Giles, son of Michael Abdie.
Oct. 3.	Elizabeth, daughter of Thomas Allen.
Nov. 6.	Robart, son of Richard Westerne.
Dec. 7.	Jane, daughter of Giles Crowche.
Dec. 27.	Rebecca, daughter of Thomas Hasel.

1575

Mar. 27.	Simon, son of Robart Perpointe.
April 10.	Mary, daughter of John Bradlie.
April 11	Thomas, son of Robart Linge.
April 24.	Sara, daughter of William Keningham.
May 27.	Elizabeth, daughter of George Fenne.
June 12.	Ester, daughter of Robert Smith.
June 24.	John, son of John Brakenberie.
July 24.	Martha, daughter of Robert Brook.
July 24.	Blanche, daughter of John Maskall.
July 25.	Basill, son of William Spencer.
Sep. 7.	William, son of Daniell Andros.
Oct. 9.	George, son of George Harman.
Dec. 25.	Philip, son of Thomas Walker.
Jan. 8.	Thomas, son of James Allen.
Jan. 8.	Judith, daughter of Nicholas Stanes.
Jan. 15.	Elizabeth, daughter of Thomas Jakman.
Jan. 29.	Benjamin, son of Thomas Healde.
Feb. 4.	Elizabeth, daughter of William Fosse.
Feb. 5.	John, son of Henrie Shepard.
Mar. 18.	William, son of Richard Westerne.

1576

July 15.	Anne, daughter of Giles Crowche.
July 22.	Richard, son of Robart Smith.
May 6.	Elizabeth, daughter of William Shakleton.
Sep. 2.	William, son of Richard Witterins.
Sep. 24.	William, son of William Keale.
Sep. 30.	Anne, daughter of Daniel Andros.
Oct. 20.	Anne, daughter of John Maskall.
Oct. 28.	Cecelie, daughter of Robart Perpoint.
Nov. 20.	Samuel, son of Robart Yarrington.
Dec. 23.	John, son of John Tredwine.
Feb. 3.	Marie, daughter of John Chambers.
Feb. 17.	Hanna, daughter of William Handford.
Mar. 17.	Thomazine, daughter of George Fenne.

1577

May 24.	Ellin, daughter of Richard Westerne.
May 26.	John, son of William appoell.
June 13.	Richard, son of Nicholas Stanes.
July 7.	Joseph, son of Robart Smith.
Aug. 11.	Elizabeth, daughter of William Keningham.
Aug. 18.	William, son of Robart Witcherlie.
Sep. 8.	Susan, daughter of William Shakilton.

Oct. 28.	Thomas, son of Christopher Rielie.
Nov. 3.	Henry, son of Raphael Smith.
Nov. 30.	Peter, son of Robart Perpointe.
Dec. 1.	Theophilus, son of Rafe Ewer.
Dec. 25.	Elizabeth, daughter of Henrie Shepard.
Dec. 29.	Benjamin, son of Robart Barnard.
Feb. 16.	Daniel, son of Daniel Andros.
Mar. 9.	Margaret, daughter of John Chambers.

1578

April 11.	Humfrie, son of Davie Evans.
May 4.	Richard, son of John Butford.
June 28.	Judith, daughter of William Spencer.
July 6.	William, son of Robart Smith.
July 25.	James, son of John Sharpe.
Aug. 8.	Isaac, son of Thomas Hasell.
Sep. 14.	Thomas, son of John Bradlie.
Sep. 28.	Francis, son of Francis Longworth.
Oct. 12.	John, son of Richard Witterens.
Oct. 22.	Christopher, son of Robart Ling.
Oct. 31.	Nicholas, son of Raphael Smith.
Dec. 3.	Peter, son of Nicholas Stanes.
Dec. 28.	Thomas, son of John Maskall.
Feb. 4.	Jane, daughter of Steven Brogden.
Feb. 22.	Robart, son of William Shakleton.
Feb. 27.	Rafe, son of Robert Marsham.
Mar. 8.	Jonathan, son of Leonard Page.
Mar. 22.	Hewe, son of William Handford.
Mar. 23.	Susan, daughter of Leonard Wraxham and Isabel Wilcocks, borne out of matrimonie.

1579

May 24.	Samuel, son of Samuel Chamberlaine.
June 28.	Peter, son of Peter Dens.
Aug. 2.	Thomas, son of John Brownlie.
Aug. 30.	Henrie, son of John Richardes.
Sep. 20.	William, son of William Strange.
Oct. 25.	Elizabeth, daughter of Robart Norton.
Nov. 1.	Hewe, son of Francis Longworth.
Nov. 1.	John, son of Rafe Ewer.
Nov. 4.	Robart, son of William Spencer.
Nov. 8.	Thomas, son of Robart Smith.
Nov. 16.	Margerie, daughter of Robart Chauntrell.
Feb. 14.	Jeremie and George, "twinnis" sons of Henrie Butler.
Feb. 14.	Ellin, daughter of Henrie Shepard.
Feb. 21.	Humfrie, son of Daniel Andros.
Dec. 26.	Marie, daughter of Edward Noble.
Mar. 16.	Robart, son of Robart Barnard.

1580

Mar. 30.	Joyce, daughter of John Sharp.
April 25.	Anne, daughter of John Whetstone.
July 11.	Nathaniel, son of Leonard Page.

July 16.	Sibill, daughter of Robart Linge.
July 31.	John, son of Robart Brooke.
Aug. 28.	Richard, son of Davie Evans.
Sep. 4.	Thomas, son of Edward Holmeden.
Sep. 6.	Daniel, son of John Maskall.
Sep. 11.	Jane, daughter of Robart Perpoint
Oct. 16.	Marie, daughter of Isaac Norton.
Oct. 23.	John, son of John Brownelie.
Nov. 2.	Wenefred, daughter of James Ladbrooke.
Nov. 21.	Edward, son of Edward Jux.
Jan. 1.	Susan, daughter of William Shakleton.
Jan. 15.	Jeronimie, daughter of William Handford.
Mar. 1.	Henrie, son of Daniel Andros.
Mar. 14.	Alice, daughter of Francis Longworth.

1581

April 22.	John, son of Robart Barnard.
May 12.	Edward, son of Robart Marsham.
July 9.	Jonathan, son of Robart Smith.
July 30.	John, son of Edward Noble.
July 31.	Elizabeth, daughter of John Phillipps.
Aug. 11.	Elizabeth, daughter of William Keale.
Oct. 15.	Henrie, son of Nicholas Stanes.
Nov. 1.	Clare, daughter of Robart Perpointe.
Nov. 19.	Lidia, daughter of Rafe Ewer.
Dec. 17.	Sara, daughter of Robart Race.
Dec. 26.	Steven, son of William Straunge.
Dec. 31.	Rafe, son of Richard Horton.
Jan. 7.	Daniel, son of Mr. William Charke.
Jan. 16.	Hector, son of John Whetstone.
Mar. 18.	Marc, son of Marc Norton.

1582

April 1.	Andrewe, son of Leonard Page.
April 16.	Gregorie, son of Lionel Wombell.
June 17.	Daniel, son of Robart Smith.
June 29.	Elizabeth, daughter of John Brownelie.
July 15.	Edward, son of Robart Barnard.
July 29.	Sara, daughter of William Turner.
Sep. 2.	Elizabeth, daughter of Thomas Lillie.
Oct. 21.	Elizabeth, daughter of Thomas Hill.
Oct. 21.	Elizabeth, daughter of Isaac Norton.
Nov. 11.	Israel, son of Daniel Andros.
Dec. 16.	John, son of John Bradlie.
Dec. 16.	Joshua, son of Rafe Ewer.
Feb. 10.	Margaret, daughter of William Keale.
Feb. 17.	Margaret, daughter of Cutbert Boothe.
Feb. 25.	Ellin, daughter of Thomas Fox.
Mar. 3.	Susan, daughter of Robart Race.
Mar. 13.	Anne, daughter of Richard Horton.
Mar. 20.	Helena, daughter of Robart Perpoint.

1583

Mar. 31.	Lidia, daughter of Antonie Martin.
April 6.	Gregorie, son of John Sharpe.

V

April 7.	Agnes, daughter of Henrie Shepard.
May 19.	Martha, daughter of John Kettlewood.
May 31.	Dorithie, daughter of John Dove.
June 9.	Anne, daughter of Richard Westwood.
June 16.	Martha, daughter of Marc Norton.
Aug. 11.	Elizabeth, daughter of John Whetstone.
Aug. 18.	Robart, son of Robart Keningham.
Sep. 15.	Brigit, daughter of John brownelie.
Oct. 20.	Judith, daughter of Francis Puckering.
Nov. 3.	Edward, son of Edward Noble.
Dec. 15.	John, son of Francis Longworth.
Jan. 12.	Isaac, son of Isaab Norton.
Jan. 22.	Anne, daughter of Jeffrie Hall.
Feb. 2.	John, son of Barnabie Allen.
Feb. 23.	Abigail, daughter of Nicholas Stains.
Mar. 15.	Joyce, daughter of William Shakleton.
Mar. 22.	John, son of John Martin.

1584

April 11.	John, son of Edward Hill.
April 12.	Ezechiel, son of Mr. William Charke.
April 21.	Susan, daughter of Mr. Edward Holmden.
May 23.	Ellin, daughter of Cutbert Booth.
July 5.	John, son of Edward Whorewood.
July 26.	John, son of Robart Barnard.
Aug. 2.	Penelope, daughter of Richard Westwood.
Aug. 9.	Elizabeth, daughter of Leonard Page.
Sep. 4.	Marie, daughter of Walter Meeres.
Oct. 11.	Roger, son of Thomas Hill.
Oct. 18.	Robart, son of Mr. Fenne.
Nov. 7.	Elizabeth, daughter of John Dove .
Nov. 29.	Caleb, son of Rafe Ewer.
Dec. 27.	Constance, daughter of John Leg.
Jan. 1.	Nicholas, son of John Bradlie.
Jan. 3.	Rebecca, daughter of Marc Norton.
Jan. 26.	Arnold, son of Henrie Shepard.
Jan. 27.	William, son of Daniel Andros.
Feb. 14.	Richard, son of Richard Hunt.

1585

April 12.	Marie, daughter of William Turner.
April 25.	Elizabeth, daughter of John Martin.
May 2.	Marie, daughter of Isaac Norton.
May 23.	Edward, son of Robart Smith.
June 29.	Elizabeth, daughter of Edward Hill.
July 19.	Jone, daughter of Cutbert Boothe.
July 25.	Richard, son of Edward Whorewood.
Aug. 6.	Elizabeth, daughter of Mr. Edward Holmeden.
Aug. 22.	Richard, son of Richard Westwood.
Sep. 5.	Henry, son of Garret Warde.
Sep. 26.	Thomas, son of Samuel Munger.
Sep. 28.	Alice, daughter of Thomas Fox.
Oct. 17.	John, son of Robart Race.
Oct. 24.	John, son of Francis Longworth.

Nov. 14.	William, son of Walter Meeres.
Dec. 5.	John, son of John Whetstone.
Dec. 6.	Marie, daughter of Edward Noble.
Dec. 12.	Margaret, daughter of Thomas Hill.
Dec. 26.	Rafe, son of Thomas Rookesbie.
Dec. 27.	Thomas, son of John Dove.
Jan. 1	Henry, son of Robart Barnard.
Jan. 30.	John, son of Francis Puckering.
Mar. 13.	Thomas, son of Barnabie Allen.

1586

April 4.	Christian, daughter of Henrie Shepard.
May 1.	Anne, daughter of Edward Juxe.
May 1.	John, son of William Judde.
July 3.	Steven, son of Daniel Andros.
July 3.	John, son of Richard Hunt.
Aug. 14.	Dorithie, daughter of Robart Rainton.
Aug. 28.	Ellin, daughter of Marc Norton.
Sep. 4.	Martha, daughter of Isaac Norton.
Sep. 13.	Edward, son of Edward Hill.
Sep 18.	Josias, son of Leonarde Page.
Oct. 30.	Adrian, daughter of Garret Ward.
Nov. 13.	Thomas, son of Mr. Edward Holmden.
Dec. 3.	Francis and Edward, "twinnes sonnes" of Francis Puckering.
Dec. 11.	Gerarde, son of Samuel Munger.
Dec. 21.	Marie, daughter of Cutbert Boothe.
Jan. 29.	James, son of William Shakleton.
Feb. 26.	Andrewe, son of Richard Westwood.
Mar. 12.	Marie, daughter of Rafe Ewer.

1587

May 7.	Anne, daughter of Walter Meeres.
May 14.	William, son of John Maskall.
May 24.	Marie, daughter of Thomas Fox.
May 24.	Ruth, daughter of an Irishwoman, *beggar*, borne in the streete.
June 25.	Elizabeth, daughter of Edward Jux.
June 25.	Anne, daughter of William Judde.
July 2.	John, son of Richard Cavell.
Aug. 30.	Edward, son of Barnabie Allen.
Sep. 6.	John, son of John Martin.
Nov. 5.	Benjamine, son of Mr. William Pearson.
Nov. 5.	Rebecca, daughter of Isaac Norton.
Nov. 12.	Nicholas, son of Robart Rainton.
Jan. 6.	George, son of Garret Ward.
Jan. 21.	Robart, son of Edward Noble.
Jan. 24.	Nicholas, son of Edward Hill.
Mar. 3.	Elizabeth, daughter of Richard Westwood.

1588

Mar. 31.	Luke, son of Marc Norton.
April 18.	Steven, son of Robart Barnard.
April 10.	Thomas, son of Thomas Chambers.

April 28.   Richard, son of John Whetstone.
April 28.   Anne, daughter of Thomas Rookesbie.
June 16.   Edward, son of Mr. Edward Holmeden.
July 20.   Paule, son of Francis Puckering.
July 28.   Elizabeth, daughter of Edward Whorewood.
July 28.   Marie, daughter of Richard Cavell.
Aug. 18.   Marie, daughter of Edward Jux.
Oct. 18.   John, son of John Balie.
Nov. 17.   Marie, daughter of Robert Rainton.
Dec. 15.   Sara, daughter of Mr. William Charke.
Dec. 15.   John, son of George Redburne.
Jan. 18.   Elizabeth, daughter of Mr. Esaie Bewers.
Jan. 19.   Silvanus, son of Isaac Norton.
Mar. 16.   Thomas, son of Walter Meeres.
Mar. 23.   Marie, daughter of Thomas Stevenson.

1589

April 4.   Edward, son of William Jud.
April 20.   Thomas, son of Thomas Rookesbie.
May 4.   Edward, son of Edward Noble.
May 11.   Rebecca, daughter of John Norman.
June 8.   Anne, daughter of Thomas Chambers.
July 6.   Elizabeth, daughter of Marce Norton.
Aug. 3.   Thomas, son of Richard Westwood.
Oct. 12.   Thomas, son of Edward Hill.
Oct. 12.   Henrie, son of Mr. Henrie Wall.
Oct. 26.   Margaret, daughter of Robart Rainton.
Nov. 16.   George, son of Mr. Edward Holmden.
Nov. 20.   John, son of Hughe Brinkhurst.
Dec. 15.   Chiddocke, son of William Shakleton.
Jan. 11.   Ezekiel, son of John Balie.
Jan. 11.   Dorcas, daughter of Mr. John Scot, *Counselor.*
Jan. 18.   Elizabeth, daughter of Richard Hunt.
Jan. 18.   William, son of George Redburne.
Feb. 13.   Marie, daughter of Martine Smith.
Feb. 15.   Timothie, son of William Wortlie.
Mar. 5.   Richard, son of William Jud.
Mar. 10.   Thomas, son of Thomas Ward.

1590

Mar. 29.   Elizabeth, daughter of Luke Smith.
April 12.   Chrystyon, daughter of Isaac Norton.
May 3.   Thomas, son of Thomas Chapman.
May 7.   Thomas, son of Thomas Stevenson.
May 24.   Martin, son of Edward Whorewood.
June 29.   Elizabeth, daughter of Thomas Sharlie.
Aug. 9.   Anne, daughter of Edward Puckering.
Nov. 1.   Thomas, son of Thomas Chambers.
Nov. 8.   George, son of George Balie.
Nov. 15.   William, son of Edward Hill.
Feb. 5.   Robarte, son of Robart Barnard.
Feb. 21.   Nathanael, son of Robart Andros.
Mar. 3.   Anthonie, son of Richard Hunt.
Mar. 8.   Anne, daughter of Thomas Rookesbie.
Mar. 21.   Alice, daughter of Luc Smith.

1591

May 5.	Prudence, daughter of Thomas Chapman.
June 6.	John, son of Mr. William Charke.
June 20.	Arthur, son of Arthur Kinge.
July 4.	Hester, daughter of Edward Whorewood.
July 14.	Andrew, son of Edward Noble.
Aug. 15.	William, son of John Balie.
Aug. 22.	Katherine, daughter of John Watkinson.
Sep. 5.	Mary, daughter of Giles Blake.
Sep. 17.	Robart, son of George Redburne.
Sep. 19.	Walter, son of Walter Meeres.
Seb. 19.	Sara, daughter of Richard Hall.
Sep. 19.	Elizabeth, daughter of Mr. Edward Holmden.
Oct. 24.	William, son of Richard Westwood.
Oct. 30.	John, son of Isaac Kilburne.
Nov. 1.	Elizabeth, daughter of Hugh Venables.
Jan. 9.	Elizabeth, daughter of Garret Ward.
Jan. 30.	Marie, daughter of Thomas Rookesbie.
Mar. 5.	Anne, daughter of Luke Smith.

1592

April 23.	Mary, daughter of Thomas Chambers.
May 7.	Paule, son of Edward Hill.
May 7.	Elizabeth, daughter of Thomas Steventon.
June 4.	Samuel and Susan, twines, son and daughter of Robart Barnard.
Aug. 20.	Rebecca, daughter of Richard Hall.
Sep. 8.	William, son of Richard Mooreland.
Oct. 4.	Richard, son of George Belie.
Oct. 8.	Richard, son of George Gesling.
Oct. 15.	Isaac, son of John Belie.
Oct. 31.	Francis, daughter of William Baites.
Feb. 14.	Martha, daughter of John Smith.
Feb. 18.	Dorithie, daughter of Luke Smith.
Feb. 18.	Alice, daughter of Robart Dodson.
Feb. 25.	Edward, son of Edward Whorewood.
Feb. 25.	Giles, son of Giles Blaage.
Feb. 25.	John, son of George Redburne.
Mar. 18.	Elizabeth, daughter of William Peate.

1593

April 8.	Henry, son of John Watkinson.
April 8.	John, son of Robart Andros.
April 8.	Richard, son of Richard Smith.
May 27.	Henrie, son of Henrie Braiton.
July 28.	John, son of John Lewis.
Aug. 12.	Steven, son of Arthur King.
Aug. 15.	William, son of Thomas Chambers.
Aug. 31.	Henrie, son of Walter Meeres.
Sep. 26.	Jonathan, son of Isaac Norton.
Oct. 17.	Elizabeth, daughter of Isaac Kilburne.
Oct. 6.	[*sic*] Michael, son of John Whelcr.
Nov. 4.	Isaac, son of John Balie.
Nov. 18.	Marie, daughter of Georg Gesling.

Dec. 12.	Anne, daughter of Thomas Stevenson.
Dec. 30.	Sara, daughter of Georg Belie.
Jan. 13.	John, son of John Dewaters.
Jan. 27.	George, son of Edward Hill.
Mar. 3.	Wenefride, daughter of John Chatwin.
Mar. 16.	Anne, a maide child, three months old, left in the streetes of this Parish, not borne here.
Mar. 17.	William, son of Giles Blaage.

1594

June 9.	Mary and Sara, twins, daughters of Robart Dodson.
June. 30.	Nathanael, son of Richard Hall.
July 7.	John, son of Garret Warde.
Oct. 6.	Gregorie, son of Luke Smith.
Dec. 5	William, son of Isaac Kilburne.
Dec. 15.	Anne, daughter of George Gesling.
Dec. 17.	Edward, a man childe, left in our streetes, not borne here.
Jan. 20.	Charles, son of Mr. Richard Blunte, my Lord Buckhurst, and my Lord Montjoye being godfathers, my Lady Montague, godmother.
Jan. 22.	William, son of Thomas Chambers.
Feb. 6.	Emanuel, son of William Horton.
Mar. 5.	Henrie, son of John Hill.
—— 16.	Mary, daughter of William Wilson.

1595

Mar. 27.	Clement, son of John Balie.
April 17.	Sibilla, daughter of Dudlie Hawkes.
May 4.	Martha, daughter of Robert Andrews.
June 22.	Nicholas, son of Edmond Palmer.
July 26.	Elizabeth, daughter of Jane Sharlie, *Widoe.*
Aug. 15.	William, son of John Smith.
Aug. 17.	Henrie, son of William Cotton.
Sep. 7.	Barbara, daughter of Richard Trowt.
Sept. 18.	Thomas, son of Robart Hill.
Sep. 21.	Giles, son of Robart Dodson.
Sep. 28.	Susan, daughter of Richard Harrison.
Nov. 23.	George, son of Giles Blaage.
Nov. 24.	John, son of Mr. Edward Holmden.
Dec. 8.	Margaret, daughter of Nicholas Draper.
Feb. 8.	Giles, son of John Dewaters.
Mar. 13.	Elizabeth, daughter of George Belie.

1596

April 7.	Thomas, son of John Balie.
April 18.	John, son of John Pedlie.
May 2.	Thomas, son of Thomas Hill.
June 14.	Anne, daughter of Richard Scot.
June 21.	Jone, daughter of Isaac Kilburne.
July 5.	William, son of William Horton.
Aug. 13.	Thomas, son of William Eltington.
Sep. 7.	James, son of James Sharlie.
Sep. 12.	Reinald, son of Dudlie Hawkes.

Sep. 12.	Thomas, son of William Cotton.
Oct. 10.	Mary, daughter of John Hill.
Oct. 24.	Nicholas, son of Robert Barnet.
Oct. 24.	Martha, daughter of William Wilson.
Nov. 10.	Thomas, son of Anthonie Crew.
Jan. 17.	Mildred, daughter of Robart Dodson.
Feb. 20.	Nathanael, son of Edward Whorewood.

1597

April 17.	Edward, son of Thomas White.
May 1.	William, son of William Harrison.
May 5.	Thomas, son of John Colte.
May 15.	Mary, daughter of Thomas Faldoe.
May 29.	Anna, daughter of John Pereson.
July 31.	Thomas, son of William Bisband.
Aug. 28.	Martha, daughter of William Croslie.
Sep. 6.	Sara, daughter of Isaac Kilburne.
Oct. 9.	Sara, daughter of John Werton, borne in blakfriers.
Oct. 9.	Bettrice, daughter of Robert Andrews.
Feb. 5.	Marie, daughter of Edward Whorewood.
Feb. 19.	Thomas, son of Michael Tempest.
Feb. 26.	Dorithe, daughter of Thomas Harwar.
Mar. 12.	Richard, son of Richard Trowte.

1598

April 30.	Elizabeth, daughter of Robart Dodson.
May 1.	Ellin, daughter of James Sharlie.
May 28.	John, son of James Jhonson.
May 30.	Marie, daughter of Abraham Grening.
June 4.	Richard, son of Thomas Hill.
June 4.	John, son of George Belie.
June 4.	Thomas, son of Thomas Faldoe.
June 11.	Anne, daughter of Thomas Chambers.
July 28.	Richard, son of John Peerson.
Sep. 17.	Humfrie, son of Richard Bill.
Oct. 8.	John, son of John Colte.
Oct. 15.	Thomas, son of Edward Hill.
Oct. 28.	John, son of William Harrison.
Nov. 26.	Edith, daughter of Giles Blaake.
Dec. 10.	Isaac, son of Isaac Kilburne.
Jan. 4.	John, son of Dudlie Hawkes.

1599

May 1.	Sara, daughter of John Nevell.
June 3.	James, son of John Pedlie.
June 24.	Simon, son of John Balie.
July 15.	Elizabeth, daughter of James Sharloe.
July 25.	Theophilus, son of Robart Dodson.
July 30.	Jasper, son of John Waters.
Aug. 26.	Richard, son of Richard Webbe.
Sep. 9.	Marie, daughter of John Hayward.
Oct. 7.	William, son of William Wylson.
Nov. 18.	Susan, daughter of Thomas Harwar.
Dec. 2.	Anne, daughter of Abraham Grening.

Oct. 14.	[*sic*] Marie, daughter of William Crosselie.
Dec. 9.	Elizabeth, daughter of William Harrison.
Dec. 24.	Richard, son of William Nicholas.
Jan. 20.	William, son of John Colte.
Feb. 13.	Francis, son of Michael Tempest.
Mar. 9.	John, son of John Peerson.

1600

April 13.	Martha, daughter of William Legate, Anabaptiste, baptized by my Lord Bishop his comandment in the fyfte yeare of her age.
April 16.	Robart, son of William Keale.
June 22.	An, daughter of William Mathewes.
July 20.	Rebecca, daughter of George Belie.
Sep. 20.	Anthonie, son of Edward Greente.
Sep. 21.	Humfrie, son of Humfrie Walwin.
Oct. 5.	Roger, son of Rowland Sadler.
Oct. 12.	Marie, daughter of John Balie.
Oct. 19.	Robart, son of Garret Ward.
Nov. 9.	Martha, daughter of Thomas Faldoe.
Nov. 16.	John, son of John Nevel.
Nov. 30.	Robart, son of Robart Dodson.
Dec. 7.	Millicent, daughter of William Nichols.
Dec. 13.	Judith, daughter of Dudlie Hawkes.
Dec. 28.	Elizabeth, daughter of William Harper.
Jan. 4.	Thomas, son of Mr. John Culpepper, of Fointon, in Sussex.
Mar. 15.	James, son of Criamour Shawe.

1601

April 19.	Sara, daughter of Humfrie Handford.
April 26.	Marie, daughter of John Pedlie.
May 3.	Peter, son of William Harrison.
May 14.	Samuel, son of Clement Webster.
June 28.	Katherin, daughter of John Peerson.
Aug. 2.	Marie, daughter of James Forde.
Aug. 16.	Thomas, son of Robart Androwes.
Aug. 23.	Thomas, son of Isaak Kilburne.
Sep. 20.	Elizabeth, daughter of William Crosley,
Oct. 14.	Philip, daughter of Edward Greente.
Oct. 18.	Susan, daughter of William Wilson.
Oct. 23.	Elizabeth, daughter of Rowland Sadler.
Nov. 11.	Thomas, son of John Dewaters.
Nov. 29.	Marie, daughter of John Squire.
Dec. 20.	Henrie, son of Christofer Mitchel.
Dec. 27.	William, son of James Sharlie.
Feb. 1.	Robart, son of William Goffe.
Feb. 7.	John, son of Thomas Faldo.
Feb. 21.	Katherin, daughter of William Harper.

1602

June 6.	John, son of Humfrie Handford.
June 13.	Elizabeth, daughter of William Harrison.
June 20.	Katherin, daughter of Thomas Harwar.

July 18.   Martha, daughter of John Pedlie.
Aug. 15.   An, daughter of Robart Dobson.
Aug. 15.   Elizabeth, daughter of William Mathewes.
Sep. 12.   Martha, daughter of John Nevel.
Sep. 19.   Arthur, son of Anthonie Crewe.
Oct. 28.   Anthonie, son of Rowland Sadler.
Dec. 5.   James, son of James Ballard.
Dec. 21.   Marie, daughter of Edward Houghton.
Jan. 16.   Richard, son of Richard Battie.
Feb. 20.   An, daughter of Edward Greente.
Mar. 13.   Samuel and An, twines of John Peerson.

moritur serenissima Regina Elizabetha die mensis martii 24 eodem die
foelicissimis auspiciis imperium potentissimi Regis Jacobi inchoatur.

1603

April 8.   Oliver, son of William Harper.
April 17.   Marie, daughter of Thomas Godfrie.
April 17.   Elizabeth, daughter of William Nichols.
April 17.   An, daughter of Thomas Leeche.
May 1.   Thomas, son of George Belie.
June 26.   Morton, son of Thomas Plat.
July 21.   Marie, daughter of Mr. Jeremie Rawston.
July 31.   Marie, daughter of William Harrison.
Aug. 4.   Thomas, son of Thomas Hawsar.
Aug. 4.   Sara, daughter of William Croslie.
Jan. 19.   Jane, daughter of Clement Webster.
Feb. 26.   Elizabeth, daughter of John Warren.
Mar. 1.   Robart, son of William Fermor.
Mar. 4.   Marie, daughter of James Sharlie.
Mar. 11.   Marie, daughter of Edward Clark.

1604

April 1.   Margaret, daughter of William Nichols.
April 27.   Elizabeth, daughter of Edward Grente.
May 6.   Elizabeth, daughter of Thomas Kobstuke.
May 15.   Mawd, daughter of Rowland Sadler.
June 17.   Richard, son of Thomas Balle.
July 15.   Marie, daughter of Mr. Robart Cox.
Aug. 17.   Sara, daughter of John Nevel.
Aug. 19.   Thomas, son of Richard Robinson.
Aug. 19.   Jane, daughter of ——— [*sic*] Hunt.
Sep. 2.   Elizabeth, daughter of John Peerson.
Sep. 21.   Elizabeth, daughter of John Wolliston.
Oct. 7.   William, son of Thomas Leeche.
Oct. 21.   William, son of William Mathews.
Dec. 2.   Daniel, son of Daniel Darnelie.
Dec. 9.   Elizabeth, daughter of Humfrie Handford.
Dec. 9.   Elenor, daughter of Edward Houghton.
Dec. 25.   Elizabeth, daughter of ——— [*sic*].
Dec. 26.   Edward, son of Josias Soame.
Feb. 17.   Henrie, son of Thomas Hill.
Mar. 3.   Martha, daughter of Thomas Godfrie.
Mar. 3.   Elizabeth, daughter of William Nichols.
Mar. 10.   Marie, daughter of Robart Knight.

1605

April 21.   John, son of Anthonie Crewe.
May 5.   Henrie, son of Richard Lanman.
June 9.   Sara, daughter of Robart Dodson.
June 12.   William, son of Thomas Harwar.
June 16.   Thomas, son of John Warren.
July 28.   Barbara, daughter of ———[*sic*] Vaghan.
July 31.   Dorithie, daughter of Jeremie Rawstone.
Aug. 4.   Abagail, daughter of Thomas Kobstake.
Aug. 11.   Marie, daughter of Thomas Plat.
Sep. 29.   Martha, daughter of Richard Robinson.
Oct. 6.   Richard, son of Isaak Kilburne.
Oct. 6.   Rebecca, daughter of Henrie Squire.
Oct. 13.   Sara, daughter of Edward Clarke.
Nov. 3.   Thomas, son of Thomas Ball.
Nov. 1.   Elizabeth, daughter of James Lasher.
Nov. 10.   Edward, son of William Harrison.
Dec. 4.   Humfrie, son of Humfrie Handford.
Dec. 10.   Elizabeth, daughter of Anthonie Calcot.
Dec. 26.   Thomas, son of Thomas Martin.
Feb. 12.   William, son of William Nichols.
Feb. 26.   Thomazin, daughter of Thomas Leeche.
Mar. 2.   Marie, daughter of Richard Smith.

1606

April 6.   Martin, son of John Wolliston.
Maie 4.   Elizabeth, daughter of John Newehouse.
June 8.   Josias, son of Josias Soane.
June 22.   Henrie, son of Garret Ward.
June 29.   John, son of Daniel Denbrooke.
July 13.   Edward, son of Daniel Darnelie.
July 30   Elizabeth, daughter of Robart Cox.
Aug. 1.   Robart, son of Robart Walthewe.
Sep. 21.   Arthur, son of Thomas Plat.
Sep. 28.   Thomas the elder, and John the younger, sonnes of Robart Dodson.
Oct. 28.   Ales, daughter of Edward Clarke.
Nov. 28.   Margaret, daughter of Thomas Ball.
Nov. 30.   Mathew, son of James Laiton.
Dec. 7.   Samuel, son of Leonard Brushford.
Dec. 18.   Marie, daughter of Humfrie Handford.
Dec. 21.   John, son of Thomas Godfrie.
Jan. 20.   John, son of Henrie Squire.
Feb. 1.   Josceline, son of Edward Gates.
Feb. 22.   Susan, daughter of Thomas Leeche.
Mar. 15.   Christofer, son of Robart Andrewe.

1607

April 10.   Marie, daughter of Thomas Martin.
May 18.   Anthonie, son of Anthonie Calcot.
July 5.   Daniel, son of Daniel Denbrooke.
July 5.   Jane, daughter of John Peerson.
July 19.   Hannah, daughter of Mr. William Fermor.
July 26.   Marie, daughter of William Goodyeare.

July 20.   An, daughter of Josias Some.
Aug. 18.   William, son of Robart Knight.
Oct. 4.   Anthonie, son of Anthonie Crewe.
Oct. 15.   Dorithie, daughter of Jeremie Rawston
Oct. 18.   John, son of Richard Robinson.
Oct. 18.   Thomas, son of Thomas Kobstake.
Oct. 25.   Dorcas, daughter of Anthonie Sturtivant.
Nov. 8.   Henrie, son of John Wolliston.
Dec. 20.   Marie, daughter of Thomas Ball.
Dec. 20.   An, daughter of Thomas Godfric.
Jan. 10.   Nathianael, son of Christofer Lanman.
Jan. 19.   Martha daughter of Edward Clarke.
Mar. 6.   Elizabeth, daughter of Edward Houghton.
Mar. 13.   Henrie, son of Henrie Squire.
Mar. 13.   Susan, daughter of Mark Humble.

1608

April 3.   Joseph, son of Richard Lanman.
April 28.   Marie, daughter of William Chapman.
May 1.   Humfrie, son of Edward Ditchfield.
May 1.   George, son of William Harrison.
May. 1.   Marie, daughter of John Warren.
May 22.   Elizabeth daughter of Humfrie Handford.
May 22.   Marie, daughter of William Moselie.
June 5.   Isaac, son of John Nevel.
June 12.   Marie, daughter of Daniel Denbrooke.
June 19.   Susan, daughter of Thomas Harwar.
June 26.   An, daughter of Robart Cox.
July 3.   John, son of William Rogers.
July 19.   Thomas, son of Thomas Martin.
Aug. 7.   John, son of John Moise.
Aug. 7.   Elizabeth, daughter of John Collins.
Aug. 14.   Marget, daughter of Griffith Morgan.
Aug. 28.   Joseph, son of Joseph Rite, of St. Swithines, their Church
              was then in mending.
Sep. 1.   Walter, son of Walter Cade.
Oct. 25.   Elizabeth, daughter of Robart Walthewe.
Nov, 23.   John, son of William Croslie.
Dec. 18.   James, son of Josias Some.
Nov. 26.   Marie, daughter of James Laiton.
Jan. 1.   Marget, daughter of John Wolliston.
Jan. 22.   Robart, son of Robart Knight.
Feb. 5.   Elizabeth, daughter of Mathew Hillar.
Feb. 6.   James, son of Anthonie Calcok.
Mar. 12.   Elizabeth, daughter of Thomas Kopestake.

1609

April 15.   Marie, daughter of William Nicholls.
April 30.   Sindome, daughter of Edward Clarke.
May 17.   Leah, daughter of Jeremie Rawston.
May 14.   William, son of Henrie Squire.
May 25.   Elizabeth, daughter of Edward Hammond.
July 2.   Robart and Jone, twines of Mark Humble.
Aug. 13.   John, the son of Edmund Dawnie, born 1 Aug.
Aug. 17.   John, son of Anthonie Sturtivant.

Sep. 10.	Sara, daughter of Thomas Harwar.
Oct. 22.	Richard, son of William Harrison.
Nov. 25.	Marie, daughter of Edward Ditchfield.
Dec. 20.	Marie, daughter of John Wolliston.
Jan. 1.	An, daughter of Thomas Martin.
Feb. 2.	James, son of James Laiton.

1610

April 25.	Susan, daughter of Edward Clark.
Aug. 2.	Elizabeth, daughter of Richard Bennett.
Sep. 10.	Lettice, daughter of Griffith Morgan.
Sep. 23.	Robart, son of Robart Knight.
Oct. 21.	Marie, daughter of Mark Humble.
Nov. 18.	John, son of Thomas Harwar.
Nov. 18.	Edward, son of Edward Sugden.
Dec. 16.	Sara, daughter of Mathew Hillar.
Dec. 23.	Samuel, son of William Rogers.
Dec. 23.	Samuel, son of Thomas Kopestake.
Dec. 30.	Marie, daughter of John Woollistone.
Jan. 2.	Elizabeth, daughter of James Haies.
Jan. 13.	Joseph, son of Robart Hammond.
Jan. 13.	Isaak, son of Daniel Denbrooke.
Jan. 20.	An, daughter of William Harrison.
Feb. 17.	John, son of Humfrie Hanforde.
Feb. 17.	Thomas, son of James Laiton.
Feb. 24.	Briget, daughter of Thomas Martin.
Mar. 24.	Elizabeth, daughter of Edmund More.

1611

April 28.	Marie, daughter of Thomas Hocket.
May 17.	George, a child left in our parish, not borne here.
June 6.	Edward, son of Edward Hammond.
June 23.	An, daughter of Edward Clarke.
Aug. 25.	Samuel, son of Edmund Dawnie.
Aug. 25.	Edward, son of Thomas Ball.
Oct. 30.	Marie, daughter of William Fermor.
Nov. 17.	Abirgail, daughter of ———[*sic*] Waller.
Nov. 21.	An, daughter of William Nichols.
Dec. 8.	Ellen, daughter of Anthonie Earth.
Dec. 22.	William, son of James Haies.
Dec. 22.	Francis, son of John Nevill.
Jan. 12.	Francis, daughter of Edward Snoden.
Jan. 24.	Annie, daughter of Anthonie Calcok.
Jan. 26.	Sara, daughter of Daniel Denbrooke.
Jan. 26.	Margit, daughter of John Wollistone.
	Mergœret [Written in the margin].
Feb. 16.	William, son of Edward Houghton.
Mar. 16.	Sara, daughter of John Clenche.
Mar. 22.	Thomas, son of Thomas Harwar.
Mar. 24.	Thomas, son of Edmund More.

1612

April 5.	An, daughter of Daniel Darnelie.
April 5.	Jone, daughter of Thomas Martin.

April 26.	Sara, daughter of Edward Ditchfield.
May 3.	Thomas, son of William Harrison.
May 10.	Abigail, daughter of Mark Humble.
May 30.	Sara, daughter of William Moseley.
June 20.	Augustine Dawnie,
July 19.	John, son of John Prince.
Aug. 2.	John, son of Robart Hammond.
Aug. 9.	Margaret, daughter of Robart Cox.
Aug. 16.	An, daughter of Mr. John Downes.
Aug. 18.	William, son of Robart Knight.
Aug. 30.	Mathew, son of Mathew Hillar.
Aug. 30.	Katherine, daughter of Thomas Hocket.
Sep. 13.	Joane, daughter of Richard Hill.
Oct. 18.	Laurence, son of Edward Clarke.
Nov. 15.	Abigail, daughter of Richard Bennett.
Dec. 3.	Francis, daughter of William Nichols.
Dec. 20.	Francis, son of Robart Neave.
Mar. 7.	Erasmus, son of John Moyse.
Mar. 7.	Leonard, son of James Layton.

1613

May 1.	Katherine, daughter of John Woollistone.
July 11.	Robart, son of James Haies.
July 18.	Richard, son of Daniel Darnelie.
Aug. 29.	Elizabeth, daughter of Francis Browne.
Sep. 5.	James, son of Edward Hammond.
Sep. 26.	Rebecca, daughter of Thomas Harwar.
Oct. 15.	Helen, daughter of Mr. William Browne.
Oct. 20.	Marie, a child left in the parish.
Oct. 31.	Abigail, daughter of Edmund Dawnie.
Nov. 7.	John, son of Edward Snoden.
Nov. 7.	Ales, daughter of Robart Neave.
Dec. 21.	Thomas, son of Edward Ditchfield.
Dec. 26.	Edward, son of Edward Clarke.
Jan. 23.	John, son of Thomas Kopestaken.
Feb. 13.	Isaak, son of Robart Knight.
Feb. 27.	George, son of Francis Britridge.
Feb. 27.	Marie, daughter of Daniel Denbroke.
Feb. 27.	Rebecca, daughter of William Harrison.

1614

Mar. 27.	Marie, daughter of John Downes.
April 6.	Elizabeth Reade, a child left in our parish, not borne here.
April 17.	Antonie, son of George Ward.
April 17.	Ales, daughter of Robart Aske.
May 1.	Ester, daughter of Thomas Hocket.
May 8.	Nathanael, son of Thomas Milles.
May 15.	Dorcas, daughter of John Wollistone.
July 10.	Dorithie, daughter of Francis Southworth.
July 28.	Thomas, son of Matthew Hillar.
Aug. 28.	Edward son of William Nicholls.
Aug. 30.	Edward, son of Thomas Martin.
Sep. 7.	Peersee, daughter of Francis Browne.
Oct. 2.	An, daughter of Edward Haughton.

Oct. 19.	Elizabeth, daughter of Roger Nightingale.
Dec. 11.	Elizabeth, daughter of Erasmus Grenewaie.
Dec. 18.	Deborathe, daughter of Edward Clark.
Jan. 15.	William, son of John Nevel.
Jan. 15.	Marie, daughter of Edward Hammond.
Jan. 20.	An, daughter of William Fermor.
Feb. 5.	An, daughter of William West.
Mar. 12.	John, son of John Herring.
Mar. 19.	John, son of John Sawnders.

1615

April 9.	Elizabeth, daughter of Daniel Denbroke.
May 21.	Henrie, son of Robart Neave.
June 20.	Simon, son of James Laiton.
July 16.	Richard, son of Thomas Milles.
July 16.	Anna, daughter of Francis Southworth.
Aug. 31.	John, son of James Haies.
Sep. 24.	Richard, son of Roger Nightingale.
Oct. 8.	Simion, son of Simion Sutton.
Oct. 20.	Robart, son of Francis Browne.
Jan. 7.	Daniel, son of Thomas Jackson.
Jan. 10.	Thomas, son of Edward Clarke.
Jan. 21.	John, son of Thomas Martin.
Jan. 21.	Martha, daughter of Edward Ditchfield.
Feb. 6.	Francis, son of Thomas Evans.
Feb. 15.	Jonathan, son of William West.
Feb. 25.	James, son of Mathew Hillar.
Feb. 25.	Mathew, son of William Harrison.
Mar. 17.	George, son of Thomas Bracie.
Mar. 17.	Jane, daughter of Thomas Harwar.

1616

Mar. 21.	Ester, daughter of Erasmus Grenewaie.
May. 21.	Ester, daughter of Thomas Marshall.
June 16.	Richard, son of Richard Bennet.
June 16.	Ester, daughter of Robert Neave.
June 23.	Thomas, son of Francis Southworth.
June 23.	William, son of Thomas Yeorth.
July 7.	Margarie, daughter of Robert Aske.
Aug. 4.	Francis, son of Thomas Milles.
Sep. 4.	Sara Woolchurch, a childe left in our parish, not borne here.
Oct. 27.	Robart, son of Robart Knight.
Nov. 10.	George, son of William Walton.
Nov. 10.	Thomas, son of Francis Browne.
Nov. 10.	Sara, daughter of Hugh Handford.
Dec. 22.	George, son of George Warde.
Jan. 12.	Briget, daughter of John Sawnders.
Jan. 19.	Anthonie, son of John Moise.
Mar. 27.	John, son of Simon Sutton.
Mar. 9.	Jonathan, son of Mathew Hillar.

1617

April 22.	Rebecca, daughter of John Marsh.
April 27.	Thomas, son of Thomas Martin.

July 6.	Elizabeth, daughter of William Nicolls.
July 6.	John, son of Edward Hammond.
July 13.	George, son Robart Neave.
July 20.	Elizabeth, daughter of Thomas Bracie.
July 27.	George, son of George Ballarbie.
July 18.	Ann, daughter of William and Marie Foster, of Newcastle.
Aug. 4.	Francis, son of Francis Sowthworth.
Sept. 7.	Robart, son of Thomas Evans.
Sep. 14.	Samuel, son of Thomas Harwarr.
Sep. 14.	Elizabeth, daughter of William West.
Sep. 21.	John, son of Edmund Dawney.
Sep. 21.	Mary, daughter of Thomas Yeorth.
Sep. 27.	John, son of Thomas Milles.
Nov. 23.	John, son of Danyell Danbrooke.
Nov. 23.	Melior, daughter of William Walton.
Jan. 10.	John, son of Edward Ditchfield, the elder of two twins, Humfrie, the younger of those twyns was the same day baptized.
Feb. 1.	Humphrey, son of Humphrey Hanford.
Feb. 11.	Judith, daughter of Mr. Thomas Leeche and Judith his wife.
Mar. 8.	Robert, son of Robert Aske.
Mar. 15.	Thomas, son of George Balie.

1618

April 2.	Marie, daughter of Thomas Marshall.
April 20.	Elizabeth, daughter of Thomas and Anne Wright.
April 26.	Elizabeth, daughter of John and Meriall Best.
May 31.	Danyell, son of Mathew Hillar.
June 7.	Danyell, son of Robart and Mildred Barloe.
June 18.	John, son of John Fish, *our Clarke.*
June 24.	Edward, son of Richard Bennett, was baptized on midd-sommers daie, beinge wedensdaie.
July 1.	Francis, son of Francis Browne.
July 19.	Martha, daughter of George Warde.
Aug. 10.	William, son of Edward Snoden.
Sep. 13.	Ester, daughter of Robart Neave.
Sep. 27.	Francis, son of Francis Towers.
Oct. 7.	Richard, son of Thomas Martin was baptized at home.
Nov. 8.	Marie, daughter of Robart Knight.
Nov. 8.	Marie, daughter of John Hayes.
Nov. 15.	Anne, daughter of Henrie Marsh.
Jan. 8.	John, son of Joseph Hopkinson.
Jan. 17.	Edmund, son of Lewis Swayne.
Feb. 2.	Marie, daughter of Richard Chamberlin.
Dec. 13.	Susanna, daughter of Thomas Harwarr.

1619

April 7.	Nicholas, son of John and Margrett Marsh.
April 11.	Mary, daughter of Abraham and Mary Greeninge.
April 25.	Susana, daughter of Thomas and Margrett Jackson.
May 9.	Mary, daughter of John and Emma Sanders.
June 6.	Judith, daughter of Raphe and Judith Merrifield.
Aug. 15.	Mathias, son of Francis and Susan Browne.
Aug. 18.	Dorethy, daughter of Mathew and Saray Hillard.

Aug. 19.   William, son of John and Barbara Tayler.
Dec. 29.[sic] Mary, daughter of William and An Walton.
Sep. 29.   Thomas, son of Nicholas Whitfeild, was born in the
                streete.
Nov. 7.   Saray, daughter of Thomas and Mary Marten.
Nov. 13.   Garrett, son of George and Elizabeth Ward.
Nov. 21.   Saray, daughter of John and Melior Best.
Dec. 12.   William, son of Edward and Elizabath Hammond.
Jan. 9.   Jane, daughter of Richard and An Chamberlayne.
Feb. 13.   John, son of John and Elizabeth Baker.
Feb. 25.   Bennonie, son of Daniel and Saray Danbrooke.

1620

Mar. 29.   Anne ——— [sic] a child borne in the streete.
April 11.   Mary, daughter of Erasmus and Barbara Grenewaye.
May 14.   William, son of Francis and Elizabeth Tower.
July 5.   Elizabeth, daughter of Robert and Elizabeth Neave.
Aug. 2.   Debora, daughter of Edward and Katherine Ditchfeild.
Sep. 3.   Mary, daughter of John and Martha Foster, Dwelling in St.
                Lawrence in ——* Lane, was baptized in Woolchurch,
                (Bercause Bowechurch was repairinge).
Sep. 27.   Elizabeth, daughter of John and Mary Petus.
Oct. 1.   Abraham, son of Raphe and Judith Merrifield.
Oct. 1.   Richard, son of Henrie and Ann Marsh.
Oct. 8.   Benjamin and Joseph, twinn sons of Mathew and Saray
                Hillard, born Oct. 2.
Oct. 15.   Mary, daughter of John and Katherine Perry.
Jan. 14.   Anne, daughter of Thomas and Anne Brace.
Feb. 11.   Elizabeth, daughter of William and Jane Smith.
Feb. 19.   Edward, son of Henry and Katherine White beinge
                strangers was Baptized in the house of William
                Stavenson.
Feb. 15.   Thomas, son of William and Ann Nichols.

1621

April 18.   Robert, son of John and Elizabeth Carwithin.
April 21.   Elizabeth, daughter of Thomas and Mary Martin.
April 22.   John, son of Robert and Mildred Borlowe.
July 15.   Thomas, son of Thomas and Elizabeth Cadell.
July 27.   John, son of John and Barbara Tailer.
Sep. 2.   Ann, daughter of John and Emm Sanders.
Sep. 23.   Thomas, son of George and Anne Ward.
Oct. 28.   Richard, son of James and Margrett Woolhouse.
Nov. 4.   John, son of John and Katherine Exlebie.
Oct. 17. [sic] John, son of John and Marie Pettus.
Nov. 23.   John, son of William and Jeane Yower.
Nov. 25.   Henery, son of Thomas and Elner Pearson.
Nov. 28.   Jeames, son of Richard and Anne Write.
Dec. 27.   Susanna, daughter of Francis and Anne Browne.
Jan. 6.   Edmond, son of Mathew and Sara Hillare.
Jan. 13.   Anne, daughter of Richard and Anne Chamberline.
Mar. 7.   Anna, daughter of William and Anne Nicholls.
Mar. 10.   Marie, daughter of Thomas and Marie Steevens.
Mar. 17.   Henery, son of Ralph and Judeth Merifold.
Mar. 17.   Joane, daughter of Edward and Elizabeth Hammond.

* The word " foster " has had the pen drawn through it.

1622

May 13.	Umphry, the son of William and Anne George.
May 14.	Martha, the daughter of Robert and Persis Knight.
June 13.	Judith, the daughter of Thomas and Mary Martin.
Aug. 18.	Erasmus, the son of Erasmus and Barbara Greenway.
Sep. 19.	A child left in our parish was Baptized and Named Stephen Woolchurch.
Sep. 20.	Anne, the daughter of John and Francis Brooks.
Oct. 6.	Anne, the daughter of John and Mary Pettis.
Oct. 13.	Richard, the son of Abraham and Mary Greeninge.
Oct. 13.	Margrett, the daughter of John and Katherine Perry.
Oct. 14.	John, the son of Thomas and Easter Marshall.
Jan. 12.	Edward, the son of Thomas and Anne Brace.
Jan. 19.	Mary, the daughter of George and Elizabeth Warde.
Jan. 26.	Margrett, the daughter of Robert and Elizabeth Neave.
Jan. 31.	A child left in our Parish and named Henry Woolchurch.
Feb. 2.	Elizabeth, the daughter of Mathewe and Elizabeth Hillard.
Feb. 9.	Richard, the son of John and Sara Wilkinson.
Feb. 16.	Francis, the daughter of Francis and Anne Browne.
Mar. 24.	A child left in the Parish, Named William Woolchurch.

1623

April 6.	Rebecca, the daughter of Raph and Judith Merifeild.
April 6.	Elizabeth, the daughter of John and Alice Fishe.
April 16.	John, the son of John and Margarett Marshe.
May 14.	William, the son of William and Sara Harrison.
July 13.	Thomas, the son of Edward and Peninah Snowdon.
Aug. 24.	Josuah, the son of Thomas and Mary Stevens.
Oct. 23.	Humfry, the son of Edward and Katherine Ditchfield.
Nov. 30.	Robert, the son of Erasmus and Barbara Greenway.
Nov. 30.	Sara, the daughter of William and Ellin Webb.
Dec. 26.	Ruth, the daughter of Gilbert and Ann Rigsby.
Dec. 28.	Elizabeth, the daughter of Sir Robert and Dame Elizabeth Brooke.
Jan. 25.	Elizabeth, the daughter of John and Em Saunders.
Feb. 22.	Theophilus, the son of Mathew and Elizabeth Hiller.
Mar. 14.	Elizabeth, the daughter of Francis and Ann Browne.
Mar. 17.	Luce, the daughter of John and Grace Lee.

1624

April 11.	Thomas, the son of William and Barbara Copeland.
May 6.	Minnion, the son of William and Ann Nichols.
June 17.	Hanna, the daughter of John and Margrett Marsh.
July 18.	Elizabeth, the daughter of George and Elizabeth Ward, at St. Christopher.
Aug. 25.	A child born in the parish, was named Mary.
Oct. 1.	Mary, the daughter of William and Jane Traeston, at St. Christoshers Church.
Oct. 17.	Robard, the son of Mathew and Elizabeth White.
Nov. 11.	Raphe, the son of Raphe and Judith Merifeild.
Nov. 28.	Phillip, the son of Thomas and Anne Brace.
Jan. 1.	Steeven, the son of Richard and Elizabeth Matchett.
Jan. 4.	Richard, the son of John and Mary Pettus.

Jan. 12.   John, the son of Richard and Elizabeth Hamden.
Mar. 15.   Ann, the daughter of James and Mary Hubland, was
               baptized at the French Church, and was borne in this
               parish.

1625

June 8.   Ann, the daughter of John and Ales Fish.
July 29.   Mary, the daughter of Henry and Ann Marsh.
Sep. 16.   John, the son of Thomas and Easter Marshall.
Dec. 4.   Nicholas, the son of Nicholas ———— [*sic*] Mager.
Dec. 4.   Warner, the son of Raphe and Judith Merifeild.
Jan. 12.   William, the son of John and Mary Pettus.
Jan. 15.   Margrett, the daughter of Gilbert and Ann Rigsbee.
Jan. 29.   Edward, the son of Mr. William and Ann Nicholls.
Jan. 29.   Ales, the daughter of William and Ellin Webb.
Mar. 12.   Edward, the son of William and Barbara Copeland.
Mar. 12.   Allexander, the son of Thomas and Isabell Dalley.

1626

April 9.   Abigale, the daughter of Anthony and Abigale Light.
April 16.   Thomas, the son of Thomas and Ann Hockett.
June 4.   John, the son of Mathew and Elizabeth White.
Sep. 24.   Ann, the daughter of Thomas and Ann Brace.
Sep. 24.   Mary, the daughter of William and Ann Hooke.
Oct. 20.   Samuell, the son of George and Ann Steevenson, dwelling
               in St. Steevens parish.
Nov. 15.   William, the son of William and Ann Stookes.
Feb. 18.   Sara, the daughter of Mr. William and Ann Nicholls.

1627

April 13.   John, the son of John and Emma Sanders.
April 25.   Nicholis, the son of Robert and Joane Jackson.
May 10.   Suzan, the daughter of Edward and Rose Chamberlin.
May 20.   Elizabeth, the daughter of William and Ann Webster.
June 20.   Mary, the daughter of John and Margaret Noodes.
July 15.   Mary, the daughter of Elias and Ann Watson.
Aug. 23.   John, the son of Mathew and Elizabeth White.
Sep. 16.   Francis, the son of John and Alis Fish, *our Clarke.*
Sep. 30.   Prudence, the daughter of Miles Codd.
Nov. 4.   John, the son of Hugin Hovell.
Nov. 18.   Grace, the daughter of Mathew and Elizabeth Hiller.
Dec. 2.   Ann, the daughter of Hughe and Mary Owen.
Dec. 5.   Mary, the daughter of John and Mary Pettis.
Dec. 9.   Daniell, the son of Robert and Ellin Thomson.
Jan. 1.   Thomas, the son of John and Judith Seed.
Feb. 3.   Elizabeth, the daughter of William and Ann Hooke.
Mar. 2.   Lovday, the daughter of Henry and Sara Ware.

1628

April 2.   Robard, the son of Robard and Martha Lander.
April 3.   Thomas, the son of Anthony and Abigale Light.
April 6.   Margrett, the daughter of William and Ann Stoakes.
June 19.   Jane, the daughter of William and Ellin Webb.

June 26. Martha, the daughter of Sir Robard Brookes and Elizabeth his wife.
June 29. Basill, the son of Richard and Elizabeth Kennitt.
July 15. John, the son of John and Margrett Noodes.
July 27. Margrett, the daughter of of Thomas and Ann Hackett.
Aug. 13. George, the son of William and Barbara Copeland.
Sep. 18. Mathew, the son of Mathew and Elizabeth White.
Sep. 28. Henry, the son of Anthony and Francis Needam.
Oct. 5. Elizabeth, the daughter, of Thomas and Isabell Dalley.
Oct. 7. William, the son of William and Ann Webster.
Oct. 28. Elizabeth, the daughter of Hugh and Mary Owen.
Nov. 30. Sarah, the daughter of Francis and Ann Brown.
Dec. 24. John, the son of Robard Jackson.
Jan. 14. Ann, the daughter of Edward and Rose Chamberlen.
Mar. 8. Steeven, the son of John and Mary Pettis.
Mar. 15. Mary, the daughter of John and Elizabeth Grantt.

1629

Mar. 1. Margrett, the daughter of John and Dorithie Scott.
April 7. William, the son of Samuell and Tomizin Small.
May 14. John, the son of Robard and Margrett Pascall.
May 17. Elizabeth, the daughter of Anthony and Abagaile Light.
June 24. Elizabeth, the daughter of Elias and Ann Watson.
July 1. Mary, the daughter of Hugin and Mary Hovell.
July 14. John, the son of John and Margrett Nodes.
July 26. Elizabeth, the daughter of William and Elizabeth Smith.
Sep. 22. Ann, the daughter of Robard and Martha Lander.
Sep. 29. Samuell, the son of John and Em Sanders.
Nov. 1. Sara the daughter of Hugh and Mary Owen.
Nov. 19. Andrew, the son of Thomas and Elizabeth Yeardley.
Feb. 17. Hanna, the daughter of William and Ann Hooke.
Mar. 18. Mary, the daughter of John and Judith Seed.
Mar. 25. Sara, the daughter of Henry and Sara Ware.

1630

April 8 Edward, the son of John and Alis Fish *our Clarke.*
May 30. Samuell the son of Samuel and Tomizine Small.
June 27. Ann, the daughter of John and Dorithie Scott.
Aug. 11. Margrett, the daughter of Gilbert and Margrett Rigbee.
Sep. 26. Richard, the son of Robard and Ellin Tompson.
Sep. 26. Merian, the daughter of William and Ann Gullson.
Oct. 1. Robard, the son of Robard and Margrett Pascall.
Oct. 3. Francis, the son of John and Mary Pettis.
Oct. 10. Ann, the daughter of Anthony and Francis Needam.
Oct. 10. Barbara, the daughter of Edward and Rose Chamberlen.
Nov. 7. Ann, the daughter of John and Ann Freeston.
Nov. 10. Martha, the daughter of Hugh and Mary Owen.
Nov. 14. John, the son of William and Ann Webster.
Dec. 15. Peeter, the son of Peeter and Martha Calvey.
Dec. 28. Mary, the daughter of John and Margrett Nodes.
Jan. 12. Thomas, the son of Mr. Water Longe, *Gentleman,* and Mary his wife, daughter to Mr. Cox of this Parish.
Jan. 14. Allin, the son of Raphe and Ann Boyse.

Jan. 23.　　Ann, the daughter of William and Ann Stoakes.
Mar. 13.　　Henry, the son of Anthony and Abigale Light.
Mar. 20.　　Suzanna, the daughter of Robard and Martha Lander.

1631

May 29.　　Judith, the daughter of John and Judith Seed.
June 23.　　Elizabeth, the daughter of Mathew and Elizabeth White.
June 9. [*sic*] Rebecca, the daughter of Thomas and Mary Steephens.
June 23.　　Rebecca, the daughter of Richard and Elizabeth Kennitt.
July 10.　　Elizabeth, the daughter of George and Phillip Winzer.
Sep. 13.　　Andrew, the son of Robard and Margrett Pascall.
Oct. 12.　　Samuell, the son of Samuell Bayley.
Oct. 15.　　Ruth, the daughter of Robard and Joane Jackson.
Nov. 16.　　Katherine, the daughter of George and Suzan Horton.
Nov. 18.　　Mary, the daughter of Hugh and Mary Owen.
Nov. 21.　　Suzan, the daughter of William and Ann Butterworth.
Nov. 27.　　John, the son of Hugin and Mary Hovell.
Dec. 1.　　Marie, the daughter of Jeremie and Abigale Briges.
Jan. 11.　　Katherine, the daughter of John and Katherine Fowler.
Jan. 22.　　John, the son of Zachary and Jane Worth.
Feb. 2.　　Elias, the daughter of Elias and Ann Watson.
Mar. 5.　　Thomas, the son of William and Mary Doolfin.
Mar. 15.　　Elizabeth, the daughter of Steeven and Elizabeth Charlton.

1632

April 11.　　Henry, the son of Gilbert and Margrett Rigbee, the first
　　　　　　　of three twines, the other two buried the same day.
April 22.　　Anna, the daughter of Tobias and Joane Shorley.
May 6.　　Elizabeth, the daughter of Samuel and Thomizin Small.
May 10.　　Mary, the daughter of Anthony and Francis Needam.
May 27.　　Sara, the daughter of Anthonie and Abigaile Light.
June 3.　　John. son of John and Ann Freeston.
Aug. 15.　　Francis, daughter of William and Barbara Copeland.
Aug. 19.　　John, son of Edward and Rose Chamberlin.
Sep. 19.　　Nathaniell, son of Robert and Margerett Pascall.
Oct. 17.　　John, son of John and Judith Seed.
Nov. 4.　　Love, daughter of Henrie and Sara Ware.
Nov. 9.　　Marie, daughter of Morgaine and Elizabeth Owen.
Nov. 11.　　Ann, daughter of Leonard and Marie Buckner.
Nov. 11.　　Katheren, daughter of Hugh and Mary Owen.
Nov. 11.　　Susan, daughter of John and Sara Questenbury.
Nov. 18.　　Mary, daughter of Thomas and Ann Brace.
Nov. 25.　　John, son of John and Dorathy Scott.
Nov. 25.　　An, daughter of George and Susan Hawton.
Nov. 30.　　John, son of William and Ann Webster.
Jan. 13.　　Milse, son of Jeremy and Abigall Briggs.
Jan. 13.　　Barbara, daughter of Samuel and Margaret Bayly.
Jan. 13.　　A childe borne in our parish whose mother was delivered
　　　　　　　in the streete, and was named Hanna Woolchurch.
Feb. 10.　　Steephen, son of Robert and Ellen Tomson.
Feb. 17.　　Alice, daughter of John and Joyce Search.
Mar. 3.　　Martha, daughter of Robert and Martha Lander.
Mar. 20.　　Zachary, son of Zachary and Joan Worth.

1633

Mar. 31.	Thomas, son of Mathewe and Elizabeth White.
May 15.	Sarah, daughter of Richard and Jane Hunte.
June 9.	Elizabeth, daughter of John and Elizabeth Grant.
Aug. 11.	Suzana, daughter of Thomas and Mary Land.
Sep. 6.*	John, son of William Prichard.
Sep. 5.	William, son of William and Mary More.
Sep. 26.	Elisha, son of Elisha and Ellen Robins.
Oct. 11.	George, son of George and Phillipp Winser.
Oct. 18.	Francis, son of Gilbert and Margrett Rigbee.
Oct. 27.	Martha, daughter of John and Martha Seed.
Nov. 13.	A child left in our parish named Symon Found.
Nov. 15.	William, son of William and Mary Doolfin.
Nov. 17.	Christopher, daughter of Miles and Elizabeth Codd.
Nov. 24.	Elizabeth, daughter of John and Ann Freeston.
Nov. 30.	John, daughter of Hugh and Mary Owen.
Jan. 5.	Jeremy, son of Jeremy and Abagaile Briges.
Jan. 6.	Raphe, son of Urias and Barbara Cissell.
Feb. 2.	Mary, daughter of Anthony and Abagaile Light.
Mar. 30.	Tymothie, son of Robard and Ellin Tomson.

1634

May 11.	Anthony, son of Thomas and Susan Ardin.
May 22.	Sara, daughter of William and Sara Curtis.
May 29.	Hanna, daughter of Moyses and Sara Fox.
July 6.	Suzana, daughter of John and Sara Fisher.
July 13.	William, son of William and Marie Fox.
Aug. 10.	Henry, son of William and Ann Stookes.
Aug. 15.	Rebecca, daughter of Richard and Jane Hunt.
Aug. 24.	George, son of Samuell and Tomizin Small.
Aug. 29.	Edward, son of Robard and Margrett Pascall.
Aug. 29.	Elizabeth, daughter of Robard and Martha Lander.
Aug. 31.	Raphe, son of Raphe and Isabel Durantt.
Sep. 17.	John, son of Tobias and Joane Sherly.
Sep. 28.	Elizabeth, daughter of Henrie and Sara Head.
Oct. 12.	Elizabeth, daughter of Morgin and Elizabeth Owen.
Dec. 26.	Ann, daughter of John and Elizabeth Fawrest.
Jan. 11.	Hugh, son of Hugh and Marie Owen.
Jan. 11.	Francis, son of John and Ann Freestone.
Jan. 29.	William, son of Mr. John Finch and Elizabeth his wyfe, *stranger*, was borne in Mr. Charleton's house, bearebinder-lane.
Feb. 8.	Stephen, son of Francis and Elizabeth Marbere.
Mar. 6.	Josias, son of George and Phillip Winzer.
Mar. 18.	Marie, daughter of George and Christian Wright.
Mar. 27.	Thomas, son of hugh Owen, baptised Mar. 27, 1635, this childe was left out of the register by the former clarke. [Written at the top of the page in a different hand.]

1635

April 9.	Thomas, son of Samuell and Barbare Baley.
May 1.	Dorithie, daughter of John and Dorithie Scott.
May 1.	Judith, daughter of Gilbert and Margrett Rigbee.
July 12.	Thomas, son of Zacharie and Joane Worth.

*The word "fifte" scored out and the figure "6" written above.

July 19.	William, son of Thomas and Marie Land.
July 27.	Frances, son of Francis and Elizabeth Clay.
Aug. 16.	Martha, daughter of Robert and Elin Swan.
Sep. 3.	Theophilus, son of William and Sarah Curtis.
Sep. 17.	William, son of Elisha and Ellin Robins.
Oct. 4.	Sarah, daughter of Henery and Sarah Head.
Oct. 9.	Grisegon, daughter of Robert and Margrett Pascall.
Nov. 13.	Margrett, daughter of Stephen and Elizabeth Charlton.
Nov. 25.	Thomas, son of Robert and Martha Lander.
Dec. 26.	Stephen, son of Mr. Mathew and Elizabeth White.
Dec. 21.	A child that was borne in our Parish and lay above in the Stocks was named Francis ——— [*sic*].
Mar. 2.	Nathaniell, son of William and Elizabeth Richeson.

1636

Mar. 25.	George, son of Mr. John Boyse and Marie his wife.
June 1.	Josiah, son of Mr. Richard Hunt and Jane his wife.
Aug. 11.	John, son of Mr. Samuel Small and Tomizin his wife.
Aug. 24.	Thomas, son of Thomas and Marie Fawson.
Sep. 25.	Marie, daughter of Henery and Easter Hemlock.
Dec. 26.	Grace, daughter of Gilbirt and Margrit Rigbi.
Jan. 4.	Ann, daughter of Jeffry and Ann Bathe.
Jan. 9.	Samuell, son of Robert and Margrit Pascall.
Jan. 11.	John, son of John and Elizabeth Eatton.
Jan. 12.	Sarah, daughter of Robert and Frances Gravner.
Feb. 15.	Marie, daughter of Mr. Elisha Robins and Ellin his wife.
Feb. 23.	Richard, son of Mr. Mathew White and Elizabeth his wife
Mar. 12.	Honnor, daughter of Thomas and Marie Land.

1637

April 4.	Samuel, son of Mr. John Trevitt and Sarah his wife.
April 9.	Marie, daughter of Pharow and Marie Humphary.
April 18.	John, son of Mr. Francis Clay and Elizabeth his wife.
April 27.	Ales, daughter of Mr. Forth Goodday and Sarah his wife.
April 27.	Peeter, son of Edward and Clement Phillips.
July 7.	Thomas, son of John and Elizabeth Barnwell.
July 7.	Katherine, daughter of John and Elizabeth Fawcet.
Aug. 1.	Marie, daughter of Mr. Richard Hunt and Jane his wife.
Aug. 4.	John, son of John and Judeth Seed.
Aug. 23.	Edward, son of John and Ann Freeston.
Sep. 6.	Amey, daughter of George and Phillip Winsore.
Sep. 13	Marie, daughter of Mr. James Beaumont and Ellen his wife.
Oct. 22.	Marie, daughter of Mr. John Boyse and Marie his wife.
Nov. 5.	Jeremie, son of Mr. William Price and Marie his wife.
Feb. 28.	Jefrey, Underbench, a child that was lefte at Mr. Hovel's dore in our parish.
Mar. 4.	Marie, daughter of Mr. Leonard Buckner and Marie his wife.
Mar. 4.	Thomas, son of Thomas and Sara Croudson.

1638

May 2.	Margaret, daughter of Robert and Margrett Pascall.
June 7.	Sara, daughter of Edward and Clement Phillips.

July 8.   Isaiah, son of John and Mary Faucett.
July 13.   Marie, daughter of Thomas and Marie Fawson.
July 19.   Thomas, son of Mr. Henery Head, and Sara his wife.
Oct. 9.   Mihell, son of John and Elizabeth Eatton.
Oct. 12.   Elizabeth, daughter of Mr. John Boyse and Marie his wife
Oct. 13.   Barbara, daughter of John and Elizabeth Ward.
Nov. 13.   Isaac, son of Mr. Richard Hunt and Jane his wife.
Nov. 29.   Susan, daughter of Mr. John Freeston and Ann his wife.
Nov. 30.   Andrew Stone, a child found on a stone at Mr. Crook's
              dore.
Dec. 2.   John, son of James and Ellin Beaumont.
Dec. 19.   Francis, daughter of Pharo and Marie Humphary.
Dec. 30.   Samuel, son of Mr. William Richardson and Elizabeth
              his wife.
Jan. 24.   Lawrance Mr. Forth Goodday and Sarah his wife.
Jan. 31.   Mathew, son of Mr. William Curtis and Sarah his wife.
Jan. 31.   Thomas, son of Thomas and Marie Land.
Feb. 21.   Samuell, son of Mr. Robert Gravner and Frances his wife.
Feb. 24.   Humphary, son of Edward and Anne Chamberlin.

1639

May 21.   Marie, daughter of Mr. Thomas and Jane Coats.
July 21.   Francis, son of Mr. Francis and Elizabeth Clay.
Aug. 14.   William, son of Gilbirt and Margrit Rigbey.
Aug. 30.   Marie, daughter of Mr. Zachrey and Joane Worth.
Sep. 22.   Dorcas, daughter of George and Margrit Cony, borne in
              the Parish of Marie Colechurch and was baptized in
              our Church by reson there owne Church was
              Reparing.
Oct. 11.   Thomas, son of Mr. Richard and Jane Hunt.
Oct. 20.   Marie, daughter of Mr. William and Elizabeth Pinckney.
Nov. 9.   Edward, son of George and Phillip Winser.
Dec. 15.   William, son of Thomas and Sarah Crowdson.
Jan. 15.   William, son of Mr. John and Ann Freeston.
Jan. 24.   Elizabeth, daughter of Mr. Elisha and Ellin Robins.
Jan. 29.   Martha, daughter of Mr. Samuel and Tomazin Small.
Feb. 14.   Michel, son of Robert and Margrit Paschall.
Feb. 18.   John, son of Mr. Leonard and Marie Buckner.

1640

May 1.   Ann, daughter of Mr. Stephen and Elizabeth Charlton.
June 12.   Frances, daughter of Mr. John and Marie Boyse.
June 12.   Benjamin, son of Hugh and Marie Owen.
June 23.   Elizabeth, daughter of Mr. Edward and Elizabeth
              Hurdman.
June 24.   Phillip, son of Mr. Mathew and Elizabeth White.
July 2.   James, son of John and Elizabeth Ward.
July 5.   Margret, daughter of Mr. William and Phillipa Medley.
July 12.   Marke, son of John and Ann Hall, of the Parish of
              Mildred, in the Poultrey, there owne Church repairing.
Aug. 12.   Martha, daughter of Mr. Firth and Sarah Goodday.
Aug. 25.   Joseph, son of Mr. Rober and Frances Gravner.
Aug. 30.   Elizabeth, daughter of Thomas and Ailse Rie.
Sep. 6.   Thomas, son of Robert and Jane Harbert.

Sep. 18.	Marie, daughter of Mr. William and Sarah Curtis.
Sep. 29.	William, son of Mr. William and Elizabeth Pinckney.
Oct. 3.	Marie, daughter of Mr. Edmund and Marie Paig.
Dec. 24.	Kathorin, daughter of Mr. Richard and Jane Hunt.
Dec. 26.	Samuell, son of John and Elizabeth Eatton.
Dec. 27.	Elizabeth, daughter of Mr. Humphary and Jane Richardson.
Dec. 30.	William, son of Mr. William and Elizabeth Richardson.
Jan. 10.	Ann, daughter of Thomas and Mary Fawsen.
Feb. 10.	Robert, son of Edward and Ann Chamberlin.
Feb. 28.	Thomas, son of Mr. Francis and Elizabeth Clay.
Feb. 28.	Martha, daughter of James and Ellin Beaumont.

1641

May 25.	Marie, daughter of George and Melier Carlton.
April 14.	Pharow, son of Pharow and Marie Humphary.
April 30.	Marie, daughter of Mr. William and Susan Brisco.
June 16.	Margret, daughter of John and Margret Duncom.
July 15.	Jane, daughter of Thomas and Jane Coates.
July 22.	Marie, daughter of Thomas and Marie Land.
Aug. 20.	Ann, daughter of Mr. John and Marie Boyse.
Sep. 10.	John, son of George and Phillip Winsor.
Sep. 19.	Richard, son of Edward and Margrit Moore.
Sep. 30.	Humphary, son of Mr. Samuell and Tomizen Small.
Nov. 23.	Roberte, son of Robert and Frances Gravener.
Jan. 7.	Nathaniel, son of Mr. Richard and Jane Hunt.
Jan. 13.	Sarah, daughter of Mr. Mathew and Elizabeth White.
Feb. 7.	John, son of George and Christian Wright.
Feb. 11.	Sibbell, daughter of Richard and Ann Nightingal.
Feb. 18.	Edward, son of Edward and Ann Chamberlin.
Mar. 23.	Thomas, son of George and Melior Carlton.

1642

April 3.	John, son of James and Ellin Beaumont.
April 13.	Thomas, son of Mr. John and Judeth Seed.
April 15.	Easter, daughter of James and Frances Whitehead.
May 11.	Sarah, daughter of Thomas and Sarah Croudson.
June 14.	Phillipa, daughter of Mr. William and Phillipa Medley.
July 22.	George, son of Mr. Forth and Sarah Goodday.
Aug. 5.	Daved, son of Mr. Thomas and Jane Coates.
Aug. 19.	Susan, daughter of Hugh and Marie Owen.
Sep. 2.	Sibbell, daughter of Mr. Humphary and Elizabeth Richardson.
Sep. 7.	John, son of Mr. John and Phillip Garrat.
Sep. 8.	James Monday, a child found one Monday night 5th of Sep. one Mr. Thompsons stall.
Oct. 20.	Nicholas, son of Mr. John and Ann Freeston.
Nov. 11.	Sarah, daughter of Alexander and Sarah Cartmell.
Nov. 22.	John, son of Mr. William and Sarah Curtis.
Dec. 12.	Robert, son of Robert and Susan Gaite.
Feb. 8.	Richard, son of Mr. Richard and Jane Hunt.
Mar. 16.	Richard, son of Isaac and Margret Sall.
Mar. 22.	Rebekah, daughter of Mr. Edmund and Marie Paige.
Mar. 21.	Marie, daughter of Mr. William and Elizabeth Pinckney.

1643

April 21.	Marie, daughter of Mr. John and Marie Boyse.
May 18.	Samuell, son of John and Susan Stringer.
May 19.	John, son of Mr. George and Melior Carlton.
June 22.	Joseph, son of Mr. Robert and Frances Gravener.
June 24.	Zachary, son of Thomas and Sarah Croudson.
Aug. 8.	Ann, daughter of Mr. Leonard and Marie Buckner.
Aug. 9.	Ann, daughter of Mr. Joseph and Ann Litlewood.
Aug. 21.	Marie, daughter of Thomas and Marie Allen.
Aug. 27.	Ann, daughter of Richard and Susan Tiller.
Sep. 14.	John, son of Mr. William and Phillipa Medley.
Nov. 3.	Jane, daughter of George and Marie Hill.
Dec. 8.	George, son of Mr. George and Marie Bayly.
Jan. 4.	Thomas, son of Thomas and Marie Land.
Jan. 22.	Ruth, daughter of George and Phillip Winser.
Feb. 16.	Nathaniell, son of Mr. George and Christian Wright.
Mar. 7.	Thomas, son of Mr. Thomas and Jane Coats.
Mar. 14.	Lattes, daughter of Mr. Thomas and Marie Fawson.

1644

Mar. 28.	Thomas, son of Mr. Francis and Elizabeth Clay.
May 27.	Jane, daughter of Edward and Ann Chamberlin.
June 29.	John, son of Mr. John and Marie Boyse.
July 4.	John, son of Robert and Susan Gaites.
Aug. 14.	Thomas, son of Thomas and Sara Croudson.
Oct. 25.	Marie, daughter of Alexander and Sarah Cartmell.
Oct. 31.	John, son of blanche Land, was borne in the street by the stocks.
Nov. 30.	John, son of Mr. Joshua and Joan Fowler.
Dec. 11.	Isabella, daughter of Mr. William and Phillipa Medley.
Dec. 19.	Hanna, daughter of Mr. William and Sarah Curtis.
Dec. 22.	William, son of Mr. William and Jane Bennet.
Jan. 9.	John, son of Mr. Humphary and Elizabeth Richardson.
Jan. 27.	Richard, son of Richard and Mary Cawthorne.
Mar. 1.	Winefred, daughter of Mr. Joseph and Ann Littlewood.
Mar. 2.	Elizabeth, daughter Edward and Elizabeth Adams.

1645

Mar. 31.	John, son of John and Phillipa Garrat.*
April 13.	James, son of George and Melyer Carlton.
June 4.	Marie Hay, a child found in the street one Mr. Harwars stall.
June 26.	Job Poore, a child found one Mr. Medley his stall.
Aug. 8.	Edward, son of Mr. Edward and Ellin Pilkington.
Oct. 4.	John, son of William and Susan Stringer.
Nov 3.	James, son of James and Ellin Beaumont.
Nov. 6.	Ann, daughter of Mr. Edmund and Marie Payge.
Nov. 6.	Sarah, daughter of Mr. George and Marie Bayly.
Nov. 17.	Ann, daughter of Hugh and Marie Owen.
Dec. 5.	Robin, son of Pharoh and Marie Humfrey.
Dec. 14.	Richard, son of Richard Tiller, desesed, and of Susan his wife.
Jan. 4.	John, son of Mr. William and Sarah Curtis.

* In this and the following year the day and hour of birth are frequently given at some length, these I have not thought it necessary to insert.—*Editor.*

Jan. 22.	John, son of Thomas and Mary Land.
Feb. 19.	William, son of Mr. William and Phillipa Medley.
Mar. 24.	Elizabeth, daughter of Mr. Francis and Elizabeth Clay.

1646

April 3.	Ellin, daughter of Mr. Humphary and Elizabeth Richardson.
April 23.	A child found at Mr. Sawyers in the street one a place to whet knives and was named Edward Sharp.
May 1.	Richard, son of Richard and Jane Lawson.
May 10.	Sarah, daughter of Mr. George and Christian Wright.
June 19.	Christian, daughter of Mr. John and Ann Freeston.
July 11.	Ann, daughter of Edward and Ann Chamberlin.
July 11.	Jane, daughter of Thomas and Sarah Crowdson.
Aug. 23.	Jane, daughter of Mr. William and Jane Bennet.
Aug. 23.	John, son of Alexander and Sarah Cartmell.
Sep. 1.	A female child found one Mr. Hovell his bench and named Mary Buck.
Sep. 6.	Elizabeth, daughter of Mr. George and Melior Carlton.
Feb. 22.	Bridget, daughter of Mr. John and Mary Boyse.
Nov. 20.	Edward, son of Mr. Edward and Ellin Pilkington.
Nov. 22.	Elizabeth, daughter of Mr. Robert and Frances Gravener.
Dec. 23.	John, son of Mr. Elisha and Ellin Robins.
Feb. 5.	Mary, daughter of Mr. Mathew and Elizabeth White.
Mar. 4.	Rebeckah, daughter of Mr. Joshua and Joan Fowler.
Mar. 14.	Elizabeth, daughter of Mr. William and Elizabeth Richardson.
Mar. 23.	Mary, daughter of Mr. William and Philippa Medley.

1647

May 18.	Jane, daughter of Richard and Jane Lawson.
June 17.	Nathaniell, son of William and Suzan Stringer.
July 6.	John, son of Mr. Robert and Anne Holmes.
July 30.	Frances Fryday, a child found on a stall at the East end of Woolchnrch.
Aug. 25.	Elizabeth, daughter of John and Phillipa Garrett.
Aug. 31.	William, son of Mr. Thomas Weatley, *Minister of Mary Woolchurch*, and of Sarah his wife, was borne in the Parish of Michaell Royal, Aug. 23, 1647, about 6 of the Clock at night.
Sep. 2.	Thomas, son of Pharoah and Mary Humphreys.
Oct. 19.	Reginald, son of Reginald and Jane Horne.
Dec. 9.	Judith, daughter of James and Ellin Beaumont.
Dec. 7.	Att home, James, son of Mr. James and Mary Cutler.
Jan. 13.	Ellin, daughter of Edward and Hellen Pilkington.
Jan. 16.	Judith, daughter of Mr. William and Jane Bennett.
Jan. 19.	John, son of Mr. John and Jane Sexton.

1648

April 3.	Henry, son of Mr. Henry and Phebe Flower.
April 25.	Anne, daughter of Edward and Anne Chamberlin.
May 14.	Robert, son of George and Melior Carlton.
June 6.	Mary, daughter of Mr. William and Phillipa Medley.

June 13.	Samuel, son of Alexander and Sarah Cartmell.
July 3.	Christian, daughter of Mr. George and Christian Wright.
July 19.	Edmond, son of Mr. Humphrey and Susan Hall.
July 20.	John, son of Mr. Joseph and Anne Littlewood.
Sep. 14.	Anne, daughter of Richard and Joan Nicholson.
Oct. 7.	Richard, son of Mr. John and Anne Freestone.
Oct. 20.	Ruth, daughter of Mr. Joshua and Joan Fowler.
Nov. 22.	Sarah, daughter of Mr. Thomas and Sarah Wheatley, *Minister of Mary Woolchurch*, borne in the Parish of Michael Royal.
Dec. 8.	Samuell, son of Mr. Richard and Jane Lawson.
Dec. 28.	At home, Richard son of Hugh and Ursula Handford.
Mar. 15.	Sarah, daughter of Reginald and Jane Horne.

1649

Mar. 27.	Elizabeth, daughter of Mr. Richard and Anne Gower.
April 2.	Phebe, daughter of Mr. Henry and Phebe Flower.
April 8.	Elias, son of Mr. George and Mary Bailey.
April 14.	John Wallstone, a male child found in the ally by the Church door laid on a stone in the wall.
April 12.	Charles, son of Thomas and Anne Fitton.
May 20.	Nathaniell, son of Mr. William and Elizabeth Richardson.
May 31.	Sarah, daughter of John and Philippa Garrett.
July 6.	Edmond, son of Edmond Hiller.
July 30.	Jane, daughter of Mr. John and Jane Sexton.
Aug. 9.	Mathew, son of Mr. George and Melior Carlton.
Aug. 21.	Dulsabella, daughter of Mr. Edward and Rebeckah Love.
Aug. 28.	Elizabeth, daughter of Mr. William and Elizabeth Pinckney.
Aug. 28.	Henry Penny, a male child about the age of 3 years was found in our Parish with a penny in his hand.
Aug. 30.	Anne, daughter of John and Margarett Clarke.
Sep. 18.	Ellin, daughter of Mr. Edward and Ellin Pilkington.
Oct. 23.	Isabella, daughter of Mr. William and Phillippa Medley.
Dec. 27.	There was a male child found att Mr. Paschalls stall before day and was named John Beforeday being St. John's day.
Mar. 16.	Anne Munday, a female child found in the ally between the Church and the Stocks.

1650

April 7.	John Bynight, a male child left in our Parish att Mr. Garretts doore.
April 25.	Thomas, son of Mr. Richard and Anne Gower.
May 16.	Alexander, son of Alexander and Sarah Cartmell.
May 19.	Judith, daughter of John and Ellin Beaumont.
May 21.	Elizabeth, daughter of Richard and Jane Lawson.
May 28.	Hannah, daughter of Mr. Edmond and Mary Page.
May 29.	Rachell, daughter of Mr. Mathew and Elizabeth Wright.
Aug. 21.	Christian, daughter of Mr. George and Christian Wright.
Oct. 18.	Margaret, daughter of Mr. William and Philippa Medley.
Nov. 9.	Mary Evening, a female child found att Mr. Morris doore in Cornhill.
Dec. 20.	Anne, daughter of Mr. John and Elizabeth Warren.

Jan. 28.	Jonathan, son of John and Phillippa Garrett.
Feb. 12.	Elizabeth, daughter of Mr. Joshua and Jane Fowler.

1651

June 6.	Elizabeth, daughter of Mr. John and Jane Sexton.
July 1.	Thomas, son of Mr. Richard and Jane Lawson.
July 3.	William, son of William and Anne Paybody.
Sep. 1.	Elizabeth, daughter of Mr. Mathew and Elizabeth Wright.
Sep. 15.	Thomas Munday, a child found in our Parish on Munday night att Mr. Conys doore.
Sep. 19.	Reginald, son of Reginald and Jane Horne.
Sep. 22.	Elizabeth Munday, a child found in our Parish att Mr. Morris doore, on munday night.
Oct. 22.	Barbara, daughter of Mr. Edward and Ellen Pilkington.
Nov. 18.	Margarett, daughter of Mr. John and Margarett Clarke.
Nov. 20.	Anne, daughter of Alexander and Sarah Cartmell.
Nov. 24.	Elizabeth, Munday, found att Mr. Allens doore on Munday night.
Nov. 29.	Richard, son of Mr. Richard and Anne Gower.
Feb. 16.	Edward Munday, found on a Munday night att Mr. Wrights stall.

1652

June 17.	Anne, daughter of Mr. William and Sarah Sawyer.
June 22.	Vincent, son of James and Ellin Beaumont.
June 24.	Mary, daughter of Thomas and Mary Cony.
July 25.	Nicholas, son of Nicholas and Suzan Clarke.
July 30.	James, son of George and Melior Carlton.
Aug. 17.	John, son of Richard and Jane Lawson.
Oct. 1.	Richard, son of Mr. John and Katheren Best.
Nov. 3.	Elizabeth, daughter of John and Mary Garrard.
Nov. 5.	John, son of John and Elizabeth Savage.
Dec. 3.	Sarah, daughter of Mr. John and Jane Sexton.
Jan. 12.	Bernard, son of Mr. Mathew and Elizabeth Wright.

1653

Mar. 26.	Joshua, son of Mr. Joshua and Joan Fowler.
April 20.	Bethia, daughter of John and Philippa Garrett.
May 22.	Stephen, son of Thomas and Margarett Billington.
May 30.	Andrew, son of Augustine and Mary Brower.
June 14.	Richard, son of Thomas and Mary Cony.
July 15.	John, son of Thomas and Frances Langley.
Sep. 1	Richard, son of Mr. Edward and Ellen Pilkington.
Sep. 8.	Martha, daughter of Edmond and Katherin Wanlees.
Oct. 1.	James, son of John and Margarett Clarke.
Oct. 15.	John, son of Robert and Elizabeth Martin.
Oct. 23.	John, son of Mr. John and Katherin Best.
Dec. 25.	Elizabeth, daughter of John Wright.
Jan. 7.	Mary Gold, a female child found on a Goldsmith's stall, in Lombard Street.
Feb. 9.	Thomas, son of Thomas and Sarah Birch.

1654

April 24.	Edward, son of Reginald Horne.

May 2.	John, son of Rowland and Elizabeth Stead.
Feb. 22.	165¾, John Broadboard was found.
Mar. 1.	165¾, Mary March was found.
May 15.	Isaac Whitmunday, found on Whit-Monday.
June 15.	Thomas Storme, was found in our Parish.
June 15.	1653, Elizabeth, daughter of Edward and Elizabeth Thursfeild.

This child is not entered in the right place, by reason the Register was not present at the baptizing, but is since well satisfied by severall witnesses. Witness my hand. Edward Philips, *Register*.

April 8.	Elizabeth, daughter of John and Edith Beaman.
May 8.	Sarah, daughter of Mr. Mathew and Elizabeth Wright.
May 16.	Mary, daughter of William and Mary Perkins.
May 25.	Nathaniell, son of Thomas and Anne Godfrey.
June 1.	Rebeckah, daughter of Alexander and Sarah Cartmell.
July 26.	Daniell, son of Richard and Jane Lawson.
Sep. 10.	Margery, daughter of Robert and Margery Swan.
Nov. 19.	Mary, daughter of William and Mabell Wels.
Nov. 28.	Anne, daughter of Mr. Richard and Ann Thompson.
Dec. 24.	Benjamin, son of Nicholas and Suzan Clarke.
Jan. 1.	Richard, son of Arthur and Mary Capell.
Jan. 18.	Martha, daughter of Mr. Richard and Martha Smith.
Jan. 21.	Mary, daughter of Francis and Elizabeth Dimmock.
Jan. 25.	Anne, daughter of Mr. Richurd Ball, *our Minister*, and Suzan his wife.
Feb. 7.	John, son of James and Mary Cutler.

1655

May 14.	Elizabeth, daughter of Mr. William and Sarah Sawyer.
June 17.	Elizabeth, daughter of Mr. Edward and Ellen Pilkington.
June 26.	Anne, daughter of Mr. Richard and Anne Gower.
July 30.	Jonathan, son of James and Ellen Beaumont.
Aug. 12.	Mary, daughter of Rowland and Elizabeth Stead.
Sep. 1.	Richard, the bastard son of Margarett Rigby.
Sep. 4.	Francis, son of Edward and Elizabeth Thursfeild.
Sep. 18.	Ellinor, daughter of Mr. John and Isabell Lilburne.
Sep. 24.	Mary, daughter of Thomas and Frances Langley.
Jan. 28.	James, son of Mr. John and Jane Sexton.
Sep. 30.	Mary, daughter of Thomas and Magdalen Bruce.
Oct. 2.	Mathew Slip, a child found in our Parish.
Nov. 1.	Joshua, son of Joshua Hall.
Nov. 30.	Bethia, daughter of John and Phillippa Garrett.
Dec. 26.	William, son of William and Mary Perkins.
Jan. 9.	Robert, son of Mr. Richard and Anne Thompson.
Feb. 10.	John, son of Thomas and Sarah Birch.
Feb. 17.	Thomas, son of Mr. Arthur and Mary Capell.
Feb. 24.	John, son of Edward and Elizabeth Bowe.
Mar. 16.	Alexander, son of Nicholas and Susan Clarke.

1656

April 10.	Rebeckah, daughter of Mr. Robert and Rebeckah Webbe.
April 15.	Samuell, son of Reginald and Jane Horne.
April 27.	Margarett, daughter of Thomas and Margarett Billington.
—— [*sic*].	A child borne in the street, named Peter Harris.
May 25.	Anne, daughter of Thomas and Mary Cony.

July 7.	William, son of William and Sarah Sawyer.
Aug. 7.	Peter, son of John Grey.
Aug. 24.	Margarett, daughter of John and Elizabeth Wright.
Sep. 9.	Edward, son of Edward and Elizabeth Thursfeild.
Nov. 5.	Elizabeth, daughter of Mr. John and Margarett Worth.
Nov. 18.	Jeremiah, son of Thomas and Magdalen Bruce.
Dec. 5.	Judith, daughter of Mr. John and Jane Sexton.
Jan. 2.	Richard, son of John and Edith Beaman.
Jan. 22.	Robert, son of Robert and Margery Swan.
Feb. 3.	Richard, son of Mr. Richard and Anne Thompson.
Feb. 20.	Thomas Lane, a child found on Mr. Sexton's stall.
Mar. 13.	Francis, son of John and Elizabeth Story.

1657

May 8.	Thomas Slack, a child found in this Parish.
May 18.	Thomazin Broad, a child found in this Parish.
May 26.	Henry, son of Reginald and Jane Horne.
July 22.	Margarett, daughter of Mr. Richard and Elizabeth Price, borne in St. Stephen's Parish.
Aug. 3.	Elizabeth, daughter of John Briscoe.
Aug. 17.	John, son of Edmond and Judith Hills.
Sep. 15.	Robert, son of Mr. Robert Webbe.
Sep. 17.	George, son of Mr. John and Isabell Lilburn.
Oct. 22.	John, son of Mr. John and Sarah Grey.
Nov. 21.	Mary, daughter of Mr. Edward and Elizabeth Thursfeild.
Dec. 25.	John, son of Mr. John and Margarett Worth.
Mar. 9.	John, son of Mr. John and Jane Sexton.
Mar. 20.	John Stoneway, was found in the freestone alley by the Church.

1658

April 1.	George, son of Mr. George and Rebeckah Compeere.
April 7	Elizabeth, daughter of Mr. Richard and Martha Smith.
April 8.	John, son of Mr. Richard and Anne Thompson.
April 22.	John, son of John and Mary Beresford.
May 12.	Rachell, daughter of Mr. Mathew and Elizabeth Wright.
May 16.	John, son of John and Sarah Moore.
June 27.	Francis, son of John and Elizabeth Wright.
July 2.	Rachell, daughter of John and Philippa Garrett.
July 12.	Margarett, daughter of William and Mary Perkins.
June 20.	John, son of James and Mary Cutler, borne June 19, baptized as they say I saw it not baptized.
Aug. 13.	William, son of William and Mabell Wells.
Jan. 2.	Rebeckah, daughter of William and Rebeckah King.
Feb. 22.	Rachell, daughter of John and Margrett Worth.

1659

April 12.	Jane, daughter of Mr. John and Jane Godsall.
May 8.	John, son of Mr. John and Elizabeth Story.
May 12.	Mary, daughter of Mr. George and Rebeckah Compeere.
May 17.	Susanna, daughter of William and Anna Blackborne.
May 22.	Mary, daughter of Mr. Arthur and Mary Capell.
May 30.	Roger Munday, was found at Mr. Sexton's doore.

June 8.   John, son of Giles and Mary Blomer.
July 3.   Richard, son of Mr. Richard and Anne Thompson.
July 17.   Joseph and Benjamin, twins sons of Robert and Margery Swan.
Aug. 10.   Sarah, daughter of Thomas and Sarah Birch.
Aug. 28.   Elizabeth, daughter of John Reyley, as the mother, Andrey, saith, who is of Boston, in Lincolnshire, was borne in the street.
Sep. 22.   Barbara, daughter of Mr. John and Jane Sexton.
Sep. 13.   Judith, daughter of Edmond and Judith Hills.
Nov. 12.   Anne, daughter of Thomas and Anne Child.
Dec. 4.   Thomas, son of Mr. Robert and Rebeckah Webbe.
Dec. 22.   Katherin, daughter of John and Edith Beaman.
Dec. 30.   Elizabeth, daughter of Edward and Elizabeth Thursfeild.
Jan. 18.   Elizabeth, daughter of William and Mary Wells.
Jan. 3.   John, son of Reginald and Jane Horne.
Jan. 29.   Elizabeth, daughter of Mr. John and Mary Aylworth.
Feb. 5.   Burnell, son of Mr. Richard and Susan Ball.
Feb. 22.   Mary Poore, a child found in the street.
Feb. 23.   Thomas, son of Mr. John and Margarett Worth.
Feb. 26.   Susannah, daughter of Nicholas and Susannah Clark.
Mar. 4.   Peter, son of Mr. John and Sarah Grey.
Mar. 7.   Sarah and Rebeckah, twins, daughters of Mr. Richard and Martha Smith.
Mar. 15.   Rebeccah, daughter of Mr. John and Margarett Clark.

1660

Mar. 11, 165$\frac{4}{9}$, Anne, daughter of John and Mary Child, born Mar. 3, 165$\frac{4}{9}$.
Oct. 30, 1656, Mary, daughter of John and Mary Child, born Oct. 30, 1656.
June 28, 1658, Martha, daughter of John and Mary Child, born June 28, 1568.
Jan. 11, 16$\frac{58}{60}$, John, son of John and Mary Child, born Jan. 3, 16$\frac{58}{60}$.

These four children before-mentioned were not entered in their due places in the yeares and daies of their births and baptisms, by reason the Register was not informed by the father in due time of their respective births and baptisms, but now, at the father's request (certified by his subscribing hereof with two more witnesses), they were all four registered together this 31 March, 1660, per me, Edward Philips, *Register*.

Witness hereof,
Jno. Child.
John Burton.
Wm. Thomlinson.
[All the signatures are in good bold hand.]

April 22.   Leonard, son of John and Hester Baines.
May 1.   Charles, son of Thomas and Mary Cony.
July 1.   Charles, son of William and Rebeckah King.
July 10.   Roger Quick, a male child found on Mr. Seeds stall.
July 7.   Anne, daughter of Thomas and Mary Sedgwick.
May 2.   John, son of Henry and Mary King.
Aug. 5.   Thomas, son of Thomas and Margarett Billington, his father being first deceased.
Oct. 26.   Rebeckah, daughter of Mr. George and Rebeckah Compeere.
Dec. 20.   Samuell, son of Samuell and Elizabeth Stone.
Dec. 25.   Cæsar, son of Cæsar and Elizabeth Willis, borne in St. Saviour's, in Southwark.

Dec. 27.   Anna, daughter of William and Anna Blackborne.
Jan. 25, 1659, Robert, son of Mr. Robert and Ruth Smith, born Jan.
        25, 1659.
           [Misplaced, due notice not having been given].
Feb. 1.   Elizabeth, daughter of Nicholas and Susan Clarke.
Feb. 13.   Charles, son of Robert and Rebeckah Davis.
Feb. 19.   Mary, daughter of Robert and Mary Dawson.

1661

April 29.   Thomas Munday, a child found at Mr. John Wrights
        doore.
May 8.   John, son of John and Hester Baines.
May 12.   Edmond, son of Edmond and Judith Hills.
May 14.   Lettice, daughter of Thomas and Anne Child.
May 14.   Thomas Merryman, a child found by Mr. Thomas Childs
        doore.
May 16.   Edward, son of John and Margarett Borth.
May 21.   John, son of Edward and Elizabeth Thursfeild.
June 16.   John, son of Mr. John and Mary Aylworth.
Aug. 2.   Gailbetty, daughter of Mr. Richard and Elizabeth Smith.
Sep. 8.   William, son of William and Mary Wells.
Sep. 22.   Charles, son of Thomas and Margaret Desborough.
Sep. 22.   Judith, daughter of Robert and Sibilla Carpenter.
Sep. 30.   Dudle Munday, a male child found att Mr. Blomers door
        in Cornhill.
Oct. 6.   Charles, son of John and Elizabeth Wright.
Oct. 6.   Michaell, son of John and Edith Beaman.
July 30.   Thomas, son of John and Sarah Moore.
Oct. 19.   Ellen Broadboard, found on Mr. Bothams stall.
Oct. 27.   Jane, daughter of Reginald and Jane Horne.
Nov. 19.   Peter, son of Robert and Ruth Smith.
Nov. 23.   Mary, daughter of Edward and Arabella Skinner.
Nov. 27.   Robert, son of John and Kathcrin Grosvenor.
Nov. 28.   James, son of Henry and Mary King.
Dec. 1.   Elizabeth, daughter of John and Sarah Grey.
Dec. 22.   Fox, the bastard son of Thomasin Woodbine.
Jan. 15.   Mary Harrow, a child found at Mr. John Clarkes stall.
Feb. 9.   Mary, daughter of John and Mary Harling.
Feb. 11.   John, son of Jonathan and Mary Botham.
Feb. 26.   Mary, daughter of George and Joan Million, *free Scrivner.*
Mar. 2.   Margarett, daughter of Mr. Arthur and Mary Capell.
Mar. 6.   John, son of John Freestone, junr., and Mary his wife.
Mar. 12.   Samuell, son of John and Mary Childe.

1662

April 2.   Mary, daughter of John and Mary Dawson.
April 7.   Samuell, son of John and Mary Berrisford.
April 8.   Elizabeth, daughter of Mr. John and Margarett Clarke.
May 5.   Andrew Munday, a child found on Mr. Blackebornes stall.
June 3.   Zakeriah, son of John and Margrett Worth
Aug. 5.   Mary, daughter of Henry and Ann Orpin.
Aug. 15.   Katherine, daughter of Mr. Richard and Elizabeth Smyth.
Sep. 21.   Charles, son of Captaine Robert and Margret Morris.
Sep. 23.   Thomas, son of William and Anna Blackeborne.

Oct. 27.	Mary Munday, a child found on Mr. Blackbornes stall.
Jan. 6.	Mary, daughter of John and Katherine Grasvenor.
Jan. 15.	Joanah, daughter of Edward and Elizabeth Thursfeild.
Mar. 8.	Elizabeth, daughter of John and Mary Harlinge.
Mar. 10.	Thomas, son of Thomas and Elizabeth Gardiner.
Mar. 11.	Sarah, daughter of John and Sarah Moore.
Mar. 12.	Mary, daughter of Mr. Edward and Mary Rich.

1663

April 12.	Ann, daughter of Mr. Richard and Ann Thompson.
April 12.	Susan, daughter of John and Mary Dawson.
April 14.	Arabella, daughter of Edward and Mary Skinner.
July 8.	Samuell, son of Samuell and Elizabeth Stone.
July 15.	Mary, daughter of Mr. Richard and Elizabeth Smith.
Aug. 9.	Pricillæ, daughter of William and Rebecka King.
July 25.	James, son of William and Prœcilla Smith.
Aug. 10.	Henry, son of George and Joane Million.
Oct. 4.	Edward, son of John and Ales Tempest.
Oct. 6.	John, son of William and Katherine Gillmore.
Oct. 11.	Sarah, daughter of Nicholas and Susannah Clarke.
Oct. 27.	Ann, daughter of John and Sarah Gray.
Nov. 1.	Heaster, daughter of John and Heaster Baines.
Nov. 24.	Simond, son of John and Margrett Worth.
Feb. 7.	Robert, son of Thomas and Margrett Dessborough.
Feb. 7.	Susanna, daughter of William and Judeth Farnham.

1664

April 10.	Ann, daughter of Anthony and Mary Male.
April 10.	Ester, daughter of William and Mary Wells.
April 12.	Gervaies, son of Edward and Elizabeth Thursfeeld.
April 21.	John, son of John and Mary Elton
April 24.	James, son of James and Dorothy Walldegrave.
May 1.	Rebecka, daughter of George and Rebecka Compeere.
May 3.	Edward, son of Edward and Mary Rich.
May 20.	John, son of William and Ann Forest.
May 21.	James, son of Godfrey and Elizabeth Beck.
July 6.	Sarah, daughter of Edward and Sarah Flaxmore.
July 10.	Hellen, daughter of William and Dorothy Palmer.
July 26.	Rowland, son of John and Katherine Grosvener.
July 30.	Margaret, daughter of Jerome and Phillippia Collins, borne at Mr. Medley's house.
Aug. 14.	Thomas, son of John and Margarett Clarke.
Aug. 25.	Elizabeth, daughter of Samuel and Elizabeth Stone.
Sep. 1.	Ann, daughter of Samuel and Rhoda Toft.
Sep. 18.	Elizabeth, daughter of John and Mary Dawson.
Sep. 25.	Ralph, son of William and Rebecka King.
Oct. 4.	Susanna, daughter of John and Sarah Moore.
Oct. 13.	Rebecka, daughter of John and Elizabeth Bentley.
Oct. 23.	Hanna, daughter of John and Mary Harling.
Nov. 3.	Martin, son of Thomas and Elizabeth Gardiner.
Nov. 9.	Ann, daughter of John and Ann Farrington.
Nov. 10.	James, son of Jonathan and Mary Botham.
Dec. 11.	Elizabeth, daughter of Richard and Katherine Philips.
Dec. 11.	Simon, son of Simon and Ann Hunt.

Jan. 8.	William, son of William and Ann Blackbourne.
Feb. 7.	Katherine, daughter of William and Katherine Gillmore.
Feb. 26.	Ann, daughter of John and Edeth Bamam.

1665

April 9.	Hester daughter of Reginald and Jane Horne.
April 16.	George, son of John and Ann Dorney.
April 18.	Jane, daughter of Catherine and Richard Hare.
July 2.	Isaiah, son of Isaiah and Mary Fossett.
July 13.	Eliz, daughter of Abraham and Lettis Sheares.
Aug. 1.	Nicolas, son of Nicolas and Susan Clarke.
Aug. 1.	Catherine, daughter of Edward and Sarah Flaxmore.
Aug. 28.	Thomas, son of Thomas and Mary Desborough.
Oct. 10.	George, son of Thomas and Mary Cony.
Jan. 31.	Catherine, daughter of John and Catherine Pearson.
Feb. 1.	Susan, daughter of John and Elizabeth Bentley.
Feb. 19.	Ann, daughter of Samuell and Elizabeth Stone.
Mar. 18.	Mary, daughter of William and Mary Wells.

1666

April 6.	John, son of John and Catherine Gravener.
April 15.	Francis, daughter of William and Rebecca King.
July 31.	Isaac, son of John and Margarett Worth.

1670

July 15.	Samuel, son of Moses and Mary Lowman.
Dec. 3.	Anthony, son of Anthony and Elizabeth Storer.
Jan. 6.	Joseph and Benjamin, sons of Robert and Elizabeth Watkins, by Dr. Charles Mason.
April 8.	Francis, son of Francis and Ann Heys, by Dr. John Merriton.
Dec. 3, 1669.	Ann, daughter of Samuel and Ann Terricke, by Mr. Crispe.
Jan. 20, 1669	Samuel, son of Richard and Jane Northan, by Mr. Wattson.
Feb. 2, 1671.	Elizabeth, daughter of Richard and Dorothy Thompson.
May 2, 1672.	Elizabeth, daughter of Gyles and Mary Blomer, by Dr. Charles Mason.
Aug. 21, 1671.	William, son of John and Alice Tempest, by Dr. Charles Mason.
June 26, 1672.	Francis, son of John and Margarett Farrington.
April 30, 1673.	William, son of Francis and Ann Heyes.
Nov. 1, 1671.	Elizabeth, daughter of Henry and Elizabeth Aynscombe.
Feb. 30, 1674.	Daniell, son of John and Mary Harling.
June 11, 1674.	Thomas, son of Sir Robert Markham, *Baronet,* and the Lady Mary, his wife, borne June 1, baptized by Mr. Williams, of St. Mildred, Poultrie.
Dec. 21, 1674.	Thomas, son of John and Jane Cooke.
Oct. 19, 1671.	Mary, daughter of Thomas and Mary Nutt.
Nov. 2, 1674.	Anne, daughter of Francis and Anne Hayes.
Nov. 11, 1672.	Anne, daughter of Henry and Elizabeth Aynscombe

Nov. 29, 1674.	Thomas, son of Henry and Elizabeth Aynscombe.
Mar. 29, 1676.	Margret, daughter of John Heard.
Nov. 9, 1676.	Sarah Perkstall, was found in the market place.
May 31, 1672.	Borne, Elizabeth, daughter of Anthony and Elizabeth Storer.
Aug. 10, 1673.	Borne, Samuel, son of Anthony and Elizabeth Storer
Dec. 3, 1674.	Borne, John, son of Anthony and Elizabeth Storer.
July 19, 1676.	Roger, son of ——— [*sic*] being borne upon the market place.
Aug. 25, 1676.	Sarah, daughter of John and Mary Harling.
Aug. 20, 1676.	John, son of John and Jane Cook.
Feb. 12, 1665.	Elizabeth, daughter of John and Elizabeth Scotson.
Dec. 10, 1676.	Susanna, daughter of John and Elizabeth Scotson.
Jan. 17, 1676.	Elizabeth, daughter of Joshua and Elizabeth Bolt.
May 7, 1673.	Mary, daughter of Edward and Mary Fenwick.
Jan. 11, 1674.	Edward, son of Edward and Mary Fenwick.
Nov. 10, 1676.	Anne, daughter of Edward and Mary Fenwick.
Mar. 4, 1676.	Sarah, daughter of John and Katherine Gravenor.
Mar. 12, 1675.	Thomas, son of Henry and Sarah Wybert.
Mar. 13, 1676.	Henry, son of Henry and Sarah Wybert.
May 31, 1677.	Mary, daughter of John and Hanna Archer.
Aug. 10. 1677.	Thomas, son of John and Ann Heard.
Sep. 8, 1677.	Pheby, daughter of William and Martha Taylor.
Feb. 11, 1677.	Sarah, daughter of Henry and Sarah Wybert.
Feb. 12, 1677.	Isabella, daughter of John and Jane Cooke.
Jan. 17, 1677.	Joshua, son of Joshua and Elizabeth Boult.
May 6, 1670.	Thomas, son of John and Katherine Gravenor.
Nov. 12, 1671.	Kathrine, daughter of John and Katherine Gravenor
Sep. 8, 1674.	Mary, daughter of John and Katherine Gravenor.
Jan. 10, 1678.	Richard, son of John and Sarah Hawkins.
Jan. 12, 1678.	Hannah, daughter of John and Hannah Archer.
Feb. 8, 1678.	Robert Entry, found in Dr. Tabor's entry, Mr. Philips baptized it.*
April 19, 1678.	Hannah, daughter of John and Mary Harling.
April 8, 1679.	Oliver Wolstock, a foundling.
June 25, 1679.	Daniell, son of John and Izabell Broughton.
Sep. 21, 1679.	Elizabeth, daughter of John and Jane Cooke.
Jan. 18, 1679.	Robert, son of Robert and Mary Irosbey.
Aug. 19, 1680.	Thomas, son of Michaell and Rebecca Hodgkins.
July 21, 1680.	William son of Joshua and Elizabeth Boult.
Aug. 18, 1680.	Elizabeth, daughter of Thomas and Mary Nutt.
Nov. 29, 1680.	Christopher, son of Christopher and Ann Tomes.
Nov. 30, 1680.	Elizabeth, daughter of John and Isabella Broughton.
Dec. 17, 1680.	John, son of James and Rebecca Sibley.
Dec. 19, 1680.	Sarah, daughter of Morrice and Sarah Tipper.
July 3, 1681.	Mary, daughter of John and Hannah Archer.
July 17, 1681.	Honour, daughter of William and Elizabeth Rawlinson.
July 20, 1681.	Frances, daughter of Henry and Elizabeth Aynscombe.
Sep. 26, 1681.	Mary, daughter of John and Jane Cooke.
April 11, 1682.	Jane, daughter of Morrice and Sarah Tipper.
April 23, 1682.	Rebecca, daughter of Michaell and Rebecca Hodgkins.
Nov. 14, 1682.	Sarah, daughter of John and Jane Cooke.
Dec. 3, 1682.	Jacob, son of John and Katherine Farmery.

* Mr. Philips was the Registrar. See page 335.

X I

Dec. 5, 1682.   Mary, daughter of Alexander and Margery Ward.
Mar. 7, 1682.   Marck Anthony, an Indian, by Mr. Franck Sclater,
                    officiating for Mr. Crisp. The witnesses were
                    Mr. Thomas Raund, Mr. James Watkins, Mrs.
                    Elizabeth Howard.
May 10, 1683.   Ann, daughter of Michaell and Rebecca Hodgkins.
Sep. 10, 1682.   Joseph, son of Thomas and Mary Nutt.
Aug. 6, 1685.   Thomas, son of John and Dorothy Knap.
London, the 14 April, 1686, collected in the parish of St. Mary
                    Woolchurch Haw one a Breefe for the French
                    prodestants that have Lately Taken Reffuge in
                    his majestyes Kingdomes, Theirty Three Poundes
                    Fourteene shillings six pence, wee say
                    £33 14s. 06d.
  Collected by whos names are under written
                                ANDREW CRISPE.
                                HENERY AYNSCOMBE, ⎫ *Church*
                                THOMAS SANDES,   ⎬ *Wardens.*
Sep. 5, 1686.   Christopher, son of Christopher and Ann Tooms.
Feb. 14, 168⁶⁄₇. Samuell, son of Samuell and Mary Shipley.
May 10, 1687.   Elizabeth, daughter of John and Dorothy Knapp.
May 26, 1687.   Katherine, daughter of James and Rebeccah Sibley.
June 26, 1687.   Sarah, daughter of Thomas and Elizabeth Sandes.
Sep. 18, 1687.   George, son of George and Anne Beate.
April 19, 1688.   Mary, daughter of Morrice and Sarah Tipper.
April 19, 1688.   Ann, daughter of John and Dorothy Kapp [*sic*].
April 19, 1688.   Mary Starr, left within Mrs. Andrews' doore.
Sep. 13, 1688.   Jane, daughter of Samuel and Mary Shipley.
June 1, 1689.   Anne, daughter of Thomas and Rebecca Farrell.
June 23, 1689.   William, son of William and Jane Hackett.
June 28, 1689.   Miles, son of Miles and Katherine Fletcher.
Aug. 13, 1689.   Sarah, daughter of Mathew and Ann Sheppard.
Nov. 15, 1689.   William Haw, a foundling. [In margin.]
Oct. 19, 1689.   William Haw, a foundling. [In margin.]
Oct. 20, 1690.   Rebecca, daughter of Mathew and Ann Sheppard.
Dec. 31, 1690.   Mary, daughter of Samuell and Mary Shipley.
Feb. 9, 169½.   Thomas Haw, a foundling.
July 16, 1692.   William Haw, a foundling.
July 29, 1692.   Samuel, son of Samuel and Mary Shipley, *Fishmonger.*
April 26, 1693.   Thomas Haw, a foundling.
Feb. 7, 168⅞.   George, son of John and Hanah Holmes.
Mar. 9, 1688.   John, son of John and Hanah Holmes.
April 6, 1690.   Benjamin, son of John and Hanah Holmes.
May 24, 1691.   Elizabeth, daughter of John and Hanah Holmes.
Mar. 4, 169¾.   Thomas, son of John and Hanah Holmes.
May 28, 1699.   John, son of John and Frances Travell.

[*End of the Baptisms.*]

Mariages

ELIZABETH our gracious Quene happelie began hir reigne the seventeth daie of november in the yeare of our Lord one thowsand fyve hundred fyftie and eighte since which tyme there have bene in the parish church of Saint Marie Woolchurch hawe in London these mariages following.

1558

*　　　*　　　*　　　*

1559

June 22.	Richard Grene and Margaret Malison.
July 9.	Charles Durand and Marie David.
July 16.	John Ragen and Anis Battell.
July 17.	William Tomkins and Elizabeth Dawkes.
Aug. 3.	William Serchfield and Edith Neve.
Nov. 13.	John Awsten and Margerie Dormer.
Nov. 19.	John Bludwicke and Alice Parker.
Nov. 29.	Anthony Allen and Elizabeth Mansie.
Jan. 13.	Edward Barber and Margerie Lame.
Jan. 13.	Rychard Auroll and Margaret Hampson.
Jan. 23.	Dunstone Walton and Blanche Vateson.
Jan. 28.	James Willian, and Annis Heward.

1560

May 6.	Richard Williams and Elizabeth Gyttins.
July 1.	Robart Travell, and Elizabeth Reve.
Aug. 26.	Thomas Mitchell and Jane Graie.
July 7.	Richard Sparrowe and Margaret Wemes.
Oct. 21.	Richard Farmer and Martha Ducket.
Oct. 21.	John Freyke and Margaret Trolop.
Oct. 22.	Robart Farrar and Marie Wanton.
Feb. 1.	William Kelcie and Elizabeth Banister.

1561

May 1.	Thomas Atterbie and Isabell Brigges.
June 1.	John Newes and Ellin Swanson.
Sep. 1.	Edward Southwarke and Jane Llwed.
Oct. 12.	Roger Peerboe and Elizabeth Krumblocke.
Oct. 26.	Edmund Crosfeld and Agnes Whelpsdale.
Nov. 16.	Humfrie Theare and Emme Tyrrel.
Nov. 29.	Peter Forman and Jone Moore.
Nov. 30.	Humfrie Smith and Sence Smith.
Jan. 18.	Henrie Jones and Elizabeth Becket.

1562

Sep. 13.   Richard Hewes and Dorithie Handford.
Feb. 13.   Adam Willison and Agnes Burrowes.

1563

May 3.   John Senclore and Elizabeth Copcote.

1564

May 3.   Robart Yarington and Alice Anthonie.
July 4.   Edward Wemmes and Timothie [sic] Cotton.
July 22.   Hughe Yarington and Elizabeth Lygham.
Aug. 13.   Richard Wade and Agnes Shard.
Oct. 15.   Raphael Smith and Agnes Coleman.
Nov. 5.   Richard Adames and Elizabeth Rice.
Feb. 18.   Robert Kennigham and Elizabeth Andlebie.
Jan. 23.   John Homes and Ann Outreed.

1565

May 6.   John Woolward and Ellin Ebbes.
May 7.   Richard Mathew and Philip Mericke.
July 8.   John Browne and Margerie Agard.
Nov. 4.   Willam Spencer and Pernel Collet.
Nov. 5.   Edward Winstanlie and Margerie Haworth.
Nov. 5.   Robart Peerpoint and Millicent Grene.
Nov. 6.   Richard Hale and Marie Wilson.

1566

April 27.   William Keale and Margaret Bradlie.
May 12.   Thomas Smith and Agnes Smith.
July 7.   Adam Dublington and Jone Holowaie.
Jan. 27.   William Haines and Jone Pellerfer.
Jan. 27.   William Langlie and Margaret Best.

1567

April 20.   David Noke and Julian Crokford.
July 15.   Edward Pridie and Ellin Fairman.
Sep. 8.   Thomas Peerpoint and Agnes Bradlie.

1568

July 25.   Nicholas Wallhill and Sence Steven.
Feb. 8.   William Rolph and Ellin Dawson.

1569

June 26.   John Moore and Lucrece Kettleware.
June 26.   Oliver Thurston and Margaret Cocker.
Oct. 30.   John Mulling and Jane Brightman.

1570

April 9.   Michael Abdie and Joyce Cater.
June 11.   George Smith and Elizabeth Vaughan.

June 11.   Samson Farnam and Jone Vaughan.
Oct. 15.   Edward Eaton and Clemence Jordan.
Oct. 16.   John Keighlie and Elizabeth Huckell.

1571

May 14.   Henrie Kecher and Judith Riche.
Feb. 18.   Peter Hunningburne and Margaret Hickes.

1572

this yeare were none maried in this churche

1573

—— [*sic*]   Rafe Rowlins and Sence Walhill.
Aug. 5.   Robart Linge and Anne Rut.
Dec. 13.   Henrie Roe and Susan Keighlie.

1574

April 25.   Thomas Ikin and Elizabeth Smith.
May 16.   John Bradlie and Magdalene Honie.
May 26.   Thomas Colis and Jone Chaptman.
July 12.   William Manlie and Jone Simson.
July 18.   Basill Turbervill and Mrs. Spurrier.
Aug. 30.   Henrie Kendall and Marie Anton.
Oct. 28.   Lancelot Lakin and Ellinor Morecok.
Nov. 14.   George Holman and Alice Staper.
Nov. 23.   Emanuel Cole and Margaret Ingram.
Nov. 28.   Thomas Wainewrighte and Dorthie Farmar.
Feb. 6.   James Perin and Joane Moorar.
Feb. 13.   John Roffe and Ellin Madder.

1575

April 18.   Richard Smith and Alice Sowth, both of Cambridge.
April 30.   Richard Witterens and Agnes Lide, Widoe.
May 15.   Rafe Yarlie and Agnes Abbot.
Sep. 11.   Robart Danbie and Jone Webbe.
Sep. 12.   John Hawkins and Elizabeth Sharp.
Oct. 9.   Edward Milward and Marie Parker.
Nov. 26.   Randal Bevington and Emme Ewer.
Nov. 27.   George Hewes and Rose Jenninges.
Nov. 28.   George Nailer and Jone Mune.
Dec. 5.   Gabriel Grimstone and Emme Best.
Feb. 12.   Lawrence Smith and Elizabeth Rey.

1576

May 20.   Steven Porter and Margaret Smith.
July 8.   Arthur Watson and Anne Wright.
July 22.   Robart Richardson and Margaret Brigges.
July 23.   Lancelot Young and Sence Rowlins.
Aug. 12.   Thomas Palmer and Margaret Harris.
Nov. 10.   Thomas Finnard and Margaret Haines.

1577

June 23.	Roger Yomanson and Anne Burrall.
Nov. 24.	Francis Longworth and Sicelie Holdernes.
Jan. 26.	David Evans and Ellin Pelter.

1578

April 21.	Thomas Savage and Julian Hatton.
June 21.	William Tomson and Agnes Eliot.
June 22.	Clement Bancks and Ellin Lockwood.
June 30.	Rodulph Warcop and Katherin Masham.
Sep. 13.	Richard Hancokes and Margaret Ditchfield.
Sep. 21.	Cutbert Boothe and Margaret Crowchman.
Nov. 3.	William Ellerker and Margerie Wighthand.

1579

June 21.	James Pemberton and Joyce Abdie.
July 19.	Robart Browne and Ales Rowe.
Sep. 6.	John Crane and Katherin Hasel.
Oct. 12.	Josias Carelesse and Sibil Hunt.
Oct. 19.	Richard Snelling, of Postlade in Sussex, and Margaret Maie, of Burtwash, in the same countie.
Jan. 25.	Baltazar Zanches and Elizabeth Orrell.
Jan. 31.	Roger Preest, of Stratford Bowe, and Jane Knevet.

1580

May 12.	Nicholas Honor and Anne Curtis.
Aug. 8.	John Legget, of Thedon Garland in Essex, and Margaret Archer, of Epping in Essex.
Aug. 29.	William Malden and Jone Ashlie.

1581

April 11.	John Foote and Margaret Brooke.
Sep. 18.	Henry Browne and Agnes Walker.
Nov. 6.	Walter Ward and Anne Smith.
Nov. 12.	Humfrie Tandie and Agnes Coleman.
Feb. 5.	Caleb Crewe and Grace Hurst.

1582

May 1.	Nicholas Drinkell and Elizabeth Warre.
May 1.	Albane Swaine and Margerie Smith.
Jan. 4.	Paule Steade, of Harrison in Kent, and Mary Gardiner of Lencham in Kent.
Feb. 17.	Peter Hart and Amerie Grace.

1583

June 10.	William Holman and Margaret Welber.
Sep. 5.	Richard Ible and Beatrice Barnes.
Oct. 19.	Edmond West and Marie Fayrecloe.
Oct. 20.	John Pridgen and Anne Lancaster.
Dec. 21.	Barnard Hide and Agnes Bate.

Jan. 23.	William Slacke and Elizabeth Henlie.
Jan. 30.	Alexander Williams and Anne Swinsto.
Feb. 3.	Thomas Farrington and Alice Taylor.
Mar. 2.	John Davies and Marie Best.

1584

Oct. 18.	Thomas Webbe and Barbara Hudsford.
Jan. 23.	William Yarrington and Jone Rufford.
Feb. 14.	Erasmus Pratchet and Mary Kendell.

1585

Oct. 3.	John Waters and Elizabeth Temes.
Dec. 20.	John Sappes, of Lawton in Sussex, and Elizabeth Brat, of Watline in Sussex.

1586

June 20.	Humfrie Dutton and Mary Spencer.
June 25.	Robart Smith and Susan Munsey.
Oct. 24.	Daniel Betnam, of Pluklie in Kent, and Marie Cambrocke were married by the Deane of Paules in this church.
Oct. 2.	John Barker and Anne Randall.
Jan. 16.	Alexander Cox, and Magdalen Smith.
Jan. 25.	Thomas Bosvill and Awdrie Overton.
Feb. 12.	Edward Manfelde and Mary Russel.
Feb. 22.	John Jacob and Elizabeth Chapman.

1587

June 11.	John Evans and Mary Burton.
July 11.	Esaie Bewers, *Minister*, and Kathern Thornton.
Nov. 30.	Thomas Brewer, and Ellin Smith.
Feb. 4.	Edward Nicholls and Agnes Russel.
Feb. 19.	Daniel Tilman and Judith Brooke.

1588

May 1.	Richard Jenner and Jane Bateman.
Aug. 4.	Meredith ap Jones and Alice Flewellins.
Oct. 27.	Simon Garret and Lettice Jones.
Feb. 24.	Anthonie Rookesbye and Elizabeth Dethick.

1589

May 12.	Thomas Ward and Susan Allen.
July 8.	George Brooke and Alice Reinaldes.
Jan. 1.	Anthonie Cowper and Sarah Leyfeild.
Feb. 1.	Peter Venables and Jane Rogers.
Feb. 24.	Christopher Scurroe and Amerie Orrell.

1590

June 8.	Thomas Kempe and Dorithee Maskall.
Aug. 30.	Steven Davies and Grace Hill.

1591

April 6.	Georg Rone and Margaret Hill.

April 26.	James Melson and Anne Spencer.
June 1.	William Peake and Margaret Steventon.
June 14.	Humfrie Simson and Thomazine Lambe.
Oct. 24.	Richard Moreton and Jone Keele.
Nov. 7.	John Cox and Margerie Brian.
Nov. 21.	William Lane and Elizabeth Grave.
Jan. 30.	John Hole and Alice Bennet.

1592

April 2.	Robart Dodson and Anne Parkins.
April 19.	Gabriel Warcop and Mary Worthington.
May 29.	Thomas Axam and Jane Terrie.
June 12.	George Solime, Joan Plat.
Aug. 13.	John Morgan and Ellen Keale.
—[*sic*]	Richard Glover and Mary Holmden.

1593

May 6.	Giles Eden and Anne Lanfere.
June 24.	Anthonie Durbidge and Anne Foster.
July 1.	Richard Sabine and Dorathe Bateman.
Dec. 10.	Cutbert Haselwood and Anne Cooke.
Feb. 10.	Henrie Adams and Magdalen Willis.

1594

April 1.	William White and Anne Melsam.
May 5.	Robart Wilmot and Margaret Halles.
Aug. 15.	Thomas Write and Anne Culliver.
Oct. 27.	Maurice Guillam and Alice Welles.
Nov. 24.	William Harrison and Sara Keningham.
Jan. 20.	George Wood and Margaret Write.

1595

Nov. 11.	George Dibine and Francis Peercson.
Dec. 8.	Humfrie Gunstone and Jane Gibbons.
Dec. 7.	William Cox and Elizabeth Gardiner.
Jan. 2.	Robart Jennie and Marie Smith.
Jan. 27.	Miles Hubbart and Elizabeth Thorpe.
Feb. 16.	Richard Webbe and Elizabeth Belie.
Feb. 16.	Henric Shepard and Jane Davies.
May. 28.	Henrie Baldwin and Catherine Duffeild, of east wingstead, in sussex.

1596

June 24.	Thomas Jaie and Susan Garret.
May. 8. [*sic*]	Thomas White and Dorcas Keningham.
Oct. 10.	Edward Eateridge and Ellin Deane.
Dec. 12.	William Sweting and Susan Perce.

1597

June 9.	Richard Chappel and Mary Wentworth.
Sep. 12.	Francis Willson and Ellen Morgan.

Sep. 16.	Thomas Yonge and Jone Clarke.
Oct. 2.	Allan Baker and Jone Carter, *by banes.*
Oct. 9.	Thomas Burton and Mary Wilkinson, *by banes.*
Nov. 20.	Robart Brooke, *Minister*, and Susan Perpoint.
Dec. 12.	Vincent Gunson and Margere Taylor.
Feb. 13.	William Wiseman, of Steventon in barkshire, and Sara Crowche.
Feb. 13.	John Bargar, of Kent, *Gentleman*, and Jane Crowche.

1598

May 21.	Rice Maddocks and Alice Salter, *by banes.*
Aug. 8.	Thomas Maxfeild and Joyce Morris, by Mr. Biddle.
Oct. 8.	John Smashie and Margerie Bland.
Dec. 1.	Richard Tumber and Mary Kennard, both of Kent.
Jan. 9.	Humfrie Walwyn and Pernel Handford.
Jan. 15.	Henrie Archer and Anne Crowche.
Jan. 21.	Thomas Sherle and Elizabeth Lacke.
Feb. 19.	John Jakson and Francis Lanman both of Greenwich.
Mar. 20.	Philip Browne and Sara Evered, both of Walsingham.

1599

April 15.	William Hawlie and Elizabeth Bye.
May 16.	William Water and Elizabeth Hoopes.
June 21.	William Brewster and Mary Welles.
July 29.	Samuel Browning and Elizabeth Salsberie.
Aug. 16.	Edmond Chamberlaine and Anne Moulton.
Sep. 24.	Rafe Davenant and Jane Herring.
Jan. 20.	John Richardson and Anne Foster.
Jan. 26.	Richard Best and Elizabeth Encrones.

1600

May 1.	William Carter and Mary Kenrick.
Aug. 10.	Robart Smith and An Chrichloe.
Sep. 14.	John Elmer and Susan Jones.
Sep. 22.	James Ford and Elizabeth Johnson.
Sep. 29.	John Squire and Mary Averill.
Dec. 2.	Thomas Godfrie and An Ewer.
Jan. 1.	William Leeche and Margerie Shawe.
Feb. 12.	William Hall and Elizabeth Edmondes.

1601

July 15.	Thomas Heaton and Marie Jarvis.
Nov. 24.	Christofer Price and Elizabeth Sleventon.
Dec. 2.	Robart Hutchinson and Elizabeth Shepard.
Dec. 15.	Robert Walthew and Elizabeth Lanman at Grenewich, in the Quenes Chappell.
Feb. 7.	Thomas Stockelie and Martha Jakson.

1602

May 16.	John Woollison and Agnes Ward.
June 29.	William Fermor and An Brooke.
June 29.	Edmund Awsten and An Bennet.

Aug. 16.	Edward Granger and An Martin.
Sep. 28.	Thomas Horneblowe and Barbara Waters.
Nov. 31.	Edward Tubman and Alice Martin.
Nov. 23.	Peter Pickering and Jone Blowe.
Dec. 14.	Chrystofer Tomson, Clemence Sharles.
Jan. 16.	Martin Weaver and Jone Cox.
Feb. 8.	John Collins and Catherine Jarvis.
Feb. 16.	William Awstin and Katherin Keale.
Mar. 7.	John Robinson and Susan Holmden.
Mar. 7.	Thomas Ball and Margaret Bowch.

moritur serenissima Regina Elizabetha die extremis mensis martii 24 eodem die foelicissimis auspiciis imperium potentissimi regis Jacobi inchoatur.

1603

April 27.	John Hodson and Alice Michel.
May 22.	John Wilkins, Margerie Scutte.
June 1.	John Blewet and Martha Pine.
Dec. 14.	Francis Furre and Bridget Stoke.

1604

April 9.	Daniel Enzor and Elizabeth Wimple.
April 10.	William Bullok and Millisent Saint.
May 31.	Jacob Welden, of the Savoie, and Margaret Cherrie.
June 7.	Mr. John Grene, of Cliffords In, and An Baker.
June 21.	Samuel Weekes, of Fotescraie in Kent, and Susan Munke.
Sep. 27.	Mr. Oliver Harvie, of thurlie in bedfordshire, and Mrs. An Clarke.
Sep. 27.	Richard Brooke and Rachel Germaine.
Nov. 19.	James Lasher and An Chambers.
Feb. 8.	William Litchfield and Elizabeth Sanders.

1605

April 1.	John Willis and Hellin Sawberie.
May 19.	Thomas Hudson and Jane Croftes.
Sep. 8.	George Cotton and Jane Woodward.
Jan. 6.	James Laiton and Elizabeth Barnes.
Feb. 2.	John Slie and Elizabeth Barrett.
Feb. 9.	Emanuel Castleman and Elizabeth Hopes.
Feb. 11.	Thomas Highehowe and Rebecca Averill.
Feb. 17.	Orlando Gibbons and Elizabeth Patten.
Mar. 2.	John Cole and Margarie Wilkinson.

1606

May 15.	Brian Lake and Elizabeth Robartes.
June 22.	Daniel Russell and Susan Shelden.
Sep. 29.	Edward Smith and Dionise Johnson.
Oct. 9.	Alexander Annand and Marget Sampson.
Nov. 23.	John Grenesmith and Elizabeth Smith.
Dec. 20.	Mr. William Button and Mrs. Anne Fermido.
Dec. 2.	John Chaltie and Marie Chapman.
Jan. 1.	Christofer Lanman and Elizabeth Whorewood.
Jan. 18.	William Eastlake and Elizabeth Davies.
Jan. 21.	Christofer Stubbs and Sara Smith.

1607

April 7.	Edmund Dawenie and Marie Daniel.
April 19.	William Moselie and Katherin Clifford.
May 25.	John Collins and Elizabeth Andrewe.
May 26.	William Brigges and Anne Newton.
June 15.	Henrie Broadstok and Dorcas Snowde.
Nov. 4.	Henrie Caustin and Jane Sanders.
Nov. 29.	John Prince and An Greene.
Dec. 4.	Jeremie Werge and Agnes Underwood.
Jan. 6.	Richard Whorewood and Em More.
Feb. 7.	Thomas Lambart and Marget Valour.
Feb. 9.	Edmund Palmer and Marget Thrale.

1608

April 7.	Richard Ballard and An Helie.
April 19.	Thomas Booker and Judith Hillar.
May 17.	Walter Maie and Marie Williamson.
June 12.	John Wendeslie and An Davies.
Nov. 2.	John Mosse and Marie Welding.
Dec. 13.	Nicholas Hasborough and An Hawke.
Dec. 18.	Richard Osburne and Elizabeth Gibbins.
Feb. 9.	Robart Hughes and Jone Lucket.

1609

May 29.	Samuel Johnson and Grizzell Stutville.
Aug. 17.	John Salter and Sara Robinson.
Nov. 20.	Christofer Watson and Marie Snelling.

1610

April 24.	Mr. Robart Holt and Mrs. Avis Robartes.
May 28.	Edmund More and Elizabeth Kilburne.
Aug. 5.	Nicholas Hughes and Joise Knowles.
Sep. 10.	Adam Wright and Elizabeth Elliot.
Oct. 4.	Henrie Horningold and Rebecca Holt, by Mr. Cheston.
Nov, 30.	Richard Tailor, of Edgworth, and An Prat, of Finchlie.
Dec. 11.	Edmund Dawnie and Margaret Linnis.
Jan. 31.	Laurence Adams and Elizabeth Mitchell.

1611

April 23.	Richard Waterfal and Elizabeth Bashford.
May 5.	Reinold Horslie and Martha Garret.
Sep. 5.	Radulph Page and Alice Colt.
Oct. 22.	Thomas Glascok and Frances Williamson.

1612

April 7.	John Clenche and Sara Bowier.
May 3.	Richard Smith and Elizabeth Fancot.
June 20.	Thomas Godfrie and Agnes Rickarde.
June 25.	William Foster, *Doctor of Phisick*, and Alice Baker.
July 19.	Robart Owen and Elizabeth Convaise.
Sep. 29.	John Slater and Marie Bradbelt.

Nov. 8.	John Bradshewe and Margaret Everiste.
Nov. 15.	Richard Courtnie and Elizabeth Smith.
Dec. 29.	Thomas Munnes and Ursula Malcote.
Jan. 24.	John Fish and Margaret Stevens.
Feb. 15.	John List and Marie Manninges.

1613

April 6.	Mr. Peter Hall and Mrs. Marie Sherrate.
April 6.	John Herring and Marie Neale.
April 6.	Gilbert Pickering and Isabel Winterfall.
April 8.	Mr. Robart Clarke, of Goodcastor in Essex, and Mrs. Judith Daniel, of St. Stevens in Colman Streete.
July 29.	Roger Nightingel and Sibilla Hawkes.
Sep. 2.	Edward Curtis and Elizabeth Enzor.
Nov. 4.	John Grace and An Downinge.
Dec. 15.	Edward Willes and Judith Masters.
Jan. 23.	George Write and An Huswife.
Mar. 6.	Peter Whaire and Jone Bewchere.
Mar. 7.	Joseph Bingham, of Bexlie in Kent, and Elizabeth Kettle, of Crayford in Kent.

1614

May 8.	John Richards and Judith Shonke.
May. 15.	Oliver Cake and Elizabeth Zeowch.
July 21.	Robart Brooke and An Cox.
July 25.	Raphael Goodwine and Rebecca Gaites.
Oct. 2.	George Fallowfield and An Brigge.
Nov. 15.	Steven Acton and Judith Sansum.
Dec. 27.	Simon Sutton and Lidia Draper.
Feb. 21.	John Gipkin and Agnes Burbie.

1615

Mar. 20.	Thomas Marshal and Ester Wachter.
May 7.	Robart Swan and Ellin Southworth.
May 16.	Thomas Brace and An Scot.
May 22.	John Robartes and Joise Flete.
July 20.	Thomas Love and Margret Palmer.
July 23.	Francis Acton and Christian Reinalds.
Oct. 12.	John Sidnaie and Francis Benham.
Jan. 20.	Nicholas Shakelford and Margaret Barwik.
Jan. 24.	Richard Billedge and Sarah Sharpe.

1616

April 22.	Zacharie Coleman and An Edwards.
Dec. 7.	Robart Allis and Lidia Curtis.
Feb. 2.	John Carter and Margaret Woolrite.
Feb. 27.	Thomas Fles and Sarah Atkins, *by license facul.*

1617

May 6.	Richard Brewer and Elizabeth Philpott, *by banes.*
Sep. 6.	Edward Coker and Martha Browne.
Sep. 20.	Edward Goodriche and Joane Waddall.
Jan. 15.	Sir George Gunter, *Knight*, of Rackton, in the parish of Lislewood in Sussex, and Purnell Walwyn.

1618

On Easter Tuesday, April 7. Joseph Hopkinson and Marie Hayward.
April 19. William Wasdall and Joane Bradburie.
April 27. Anthonie Peede and Eulalia Upcott.
April 30. John Tailor and Barbara Jegon.
June 18. William Stanton and Esther Birde.
July 19. Hugh Robarts and Margrett Boier.
Aug. 1. John Upcher, of Dedham, and Marie Hedgman.
Aug. 17. Richard Bernard, of Erith, and Jane Stepper.
Dec. 3. Nathaniel Catline, of Lincoln's Inn, and Mary Turner, of Trinity Lane.

1619

Feb. 7. Edward Simpson and Mary Snyder, *by banes.*
June 19. Robert Page and Margaret Broome.
Jan. 9. Nicholas Packer and Alice Brittan.
Feb. 27. Thomas Honburough and Jane Doe.

1620

June 1. Thomas Dauson and Elizabeth Beather, *with a licence.*
Aug. 10. Robert Smith and Francis Flood, *with a licence.*
Nov. 22. John Lane and Elizabeth Locke, *with licence.*

1621

April 20. Henry Merry, of this Parish, and Connice Hadsell, of St. Michael's, Cornhill.
April 8. Richard Edwards, of St. Michael's, Crooked Lane, and Mary Lightfoote, of this Parish.
May 1. John Watkins, of St. Olives, Southwarke and Hester Gui, of this Parish.
May 22. John Grant and Margerie Williams.
Aug. 6. Mr. William Proctor and Rachell Spight, both of St. Buttals, Aldersgate.
Aug. 26. William Webster and Anne Shears.
Dec. 6. Mr. John Beale, of St. Buttals, Aldersgate, and Jeane Elmor, of St. Marie, Bowe.
Feb. 20. Robert Froman, of St. Gilses, Cripplegate, and Marie Patrige, of this Parish.
Feb. 28. Anthonie Baines, of this Parish, and Marie Keyne, of Westminster.
Feb. 28. Henery Bonis, of Gillingham in Kent, and Elizabeth Harrison, of this Parish.

1622

Aug. 13. Mr. John Williams, *Parson,* of Duddinghurst in Essex, and Pricilla Howland, of London.
Dec. 3. Thomas Benn, of the Parish of St. Brides, and Ann Goodwin, of Henley in oxfordshire.
Dec. 3. Theophilus Eaton and Grace Hiller, both of this Parish.
Dec. 5. Joseph Denman and Hanna Eaton, both of this Parish.
Jan. 14. William Seath, of Gravesend, and Sara Ambris, of Milton in Kent.
Feb. 8. John Bludder, of the Parish of Buttolps Aldgate, and Alice Forman, of the Parish of St. Peters Cornehill.

1623

May 11.   Michael Collins, of Eastamsted in Berkshire, and Susan Stoake, of Windsore.

June 10.   Percivall Wylie, of St. Andrews Holborne, and Ellen Congden, of St. Clemente Eastecheape.

June 17.   William Copeland and Barbarie Booth, both of this Parish.

July 22.   Thomas Strowde, of Burling in Essex, and Jane Seaborough, of Wakering in Essex.

Aug. 9.   Rowland Smith and Elizabeth Busby, both of Stepney.

Oct. 16.   Mr. John Bond, of Westminster, and Jone Aske, of this Parish.

Nov. 11.   William Hayne, of the Parish of Sepulchers, and Ann Pedwell, of St. Aldhage.

Nov. 27.   Raphe Pettitt, of the Parish of Sepulchers, and Exhan Okeley, of Cornehil

Dec. 4.   James Porter, of Wakering in Essex, and Grace Robgon, of Barking in Essex.

Dec. 11.   William Holliock, of St. Andrews Holborne, and Mildredd Dodson, of this Parish.

Jan. 6.   Mathewe White and Elizabeth Aske, both of this Parish.

Jan. 8.   Mr. John Spencer, of West Tilbery in Essex, and Jone Cawston, of St. Buttolph Bishopsgate.

Jan. 15.   Henry Haley, of Hendon of Middlesex, and Elizabeth Marshe, of the same towne.

Jan. 27.   Andrew Burton, of Greis Inn, and Ann Fairmedow, of this Parish.

Jan. 29.   Thomas Dorrell and Margery Vawdrie, both of this Parish.

Feb. 4.   Thomas Burhey, of Oxford, and Mary Mosley, of this Parish.

Feb. 23.   Robert Langley, of St. Buttolph Bishopsgate, and Francis Clarke, of Stepney Parish.

1624

April 5.   William Steedman, of St. Mary's Maudlins in barnsbee Street, and Alis Puckmer, of this Parish.

April 8.   William Donn and Elizabeth Hebb, both of this Parish.

May 25.   William Martin, of the Parish of St. Martins orgains, and Margarett Mather, of this Parish.

Sep. 22.   Joseph Freind and Jane Archer, both of the Parish of South Shoobery in Essex.

Nov. 30.   Nicholis Morgan, of St. Olives, Southwork, and Jane Fretwell, of this Parish.

Dec. 5.   Randle Monshaw, of the Parish of St. James Garlickhill, and Ursley Flint, of this Parish.

Dec. 14.   Charles Mallery and Jane Mallery, both of the Parish of Papworth in Cambridge.

Dec. 16.   John Harrison, of the Parish of Great St. Hellins, and Ann Tuchin, of the same Parish.

Mar. 1.   Robert Farrand and Ann Newton, both of the Parish of St. Larrence, of Old Jury.

1625

Mar. 22.   Robard Bishop, of St. Leonard, Shorditch, and Elianor Weston, of St. Buttolph without Bishopsgate.

June 30.   Edward Hyett, of Westham in Essex, and Ellin Rogers, of this Parish.

Aug. 16.   Richard Moyle and Katherin King, both of the Parish of St. John Zacharie.

1626

June 14.   Nicholas Hinge and Margarett Wood, both of the Parish of Becknam in Kentt.

July 9.   Elias Watson and Ann Lander, both of this Parish.

Oct. 15.   John Hince, of St. Savours, Southwork, and Margrett Bastwell, of this Parish.

Jan. 23.   Mr. John Pasmore, of St. Michaels, Cornhill, *Widoer*, and Margery Aske, *Widdow*, of this Parish.

Jan. 28.   Robert Thomson and Ellen Dornelly, *by licence*.

1627

April 16.   Edward Pilkington, of St. Bothalls, Aldgate, and Mary Picott, of the same Parish, *by licence*.

April 16.   Richard Nicholls, of St. Michaels, Cornhill, and Margrett Hopkinson, of the same Parish, *by licence*.

June 26.   Richard Rea, of the Parish of St. Brides, and Jane Greenway, of this Parish, *by licence*.

Memorandum quod undecimo die mensis Decembris 1627 matrimonium fuit solemniter celebratum in Ecclesiâ parochiali Sanctœ Mary Woolchurch inter Thomam Sheppard de Lincolnes Inne in com Middlesex Armigerum et Margaretam filiam Johannis Hemings geuerosi juxta formam et effectum cujusdam facultatis siue Licentie inde parish.

Dec. 20.   Mr. George Fenn, of Clavering in Essex, *Gentleman*, and Catherin Harker, *Widdow*, *by licence*.

Feb. 4.   Mr. Godwyn Tattliff, *Gent.*, and Bennett Hailes, *Widdow*, both of the the parish of St. Peeters, Canterbury, *by licence*.

1628

April 1.   John Gibson and Jane Warner, both of the Parish of St. Michaels, Cornhill, *by licence*.

Oct. 30.   Richard Clarke, of the Parish of St. Mildreeds in bred Streete, and Elizabeth Gould of this Parish, *by licence*.

Jan. 8.   William Hollies, of the Parish of St. Martins Ironmonger, and Mary Hockett, of this Parish, *by licence*.

Feb. 16.   Arthur Manley and Katherin Bayley, *Widdow*, *by licence*.

1629

June 6.   William Baynard and Mary Nodes, *Widdow*, both of this Parish, *by licence*.

Nov. 6.   Thomas May, of the Parish of St. Bothalls, Aldgate, and Mary Jacklow, of the Parish of St. Alphage, by london wall, neere Criplegate, *by licence*.

Feb. 2.   George Haughton, of the Parish of St. Margeretts, new fish streete, *Fishmonger*, and Susan Marven, of this Parish, *by licence*.

1630

Mar. 30.   Edmund Penson, of the Parish of St. Mary Maudlins Barnsbee Street, and Dorothie Borowes, of the Parish of St. Mildreeds in the Poultry.

Dec. 23.   Nicholas Gibson, of the Parish of St. Giles in the feild, and Ann Haynes, *Widdowe*, of the Parish of St. Pulchers, *by licence.*

Dec. 12 [*sic*] Mathew Cox and Francis Richardson, both of this Parish, *by licence,*

Jan. 28.   Henry Henlock, of the Parish of Nicholas Cole Abby, and Easter Hockett, of this Parish, *by licence.*

Feb. 22.   John Tynte, of the Parish of St. Swithens, and Faith Dowger, of this Parish, *by licence.*

Feb. 24.   William Bainard, of the Parish of Christchurch, and Sara Mecoe, of this Parish, *by licence.*

1631

May 5.   Richard Coppin, of Sion Colledge London, and Dorothie Billard, of the Parish of St. Michael wood street, *by licence.*

May 5.   Thomas Hobbs, of the Parish of St. Margretts new fish street, and Mary Banes, *Widdow*, of this Parish, *by licence.*

June 23.   Edward Peach, of the Parish of Milbarstone in the County of Northampton, and Mary Dale, *Widdow*, of this Parish, *by licence.*

Oct. 2.   Edward Francke, *Widoer*, of St. Johns Zacharis, London, and Hester Marshall, *Widdow*, of this Parish, *by licence.*

Nov. 8.   Robert Symes, of barcomsted in the County of Harfordshire, and Dorothie Beninge of the same County, *by licence.*

1632

April 2.   Morgaine Owen, of the Parish of St. brides, and Elizabeth Marsh, of this Parish, being aske in the Church.

Nov. 7.   Isack Knight, and Dorothie Harwar, *by licence.*

Nov. 8.   Mr. Thomas Blemell, *Minister*, and Amee Robinson, *Widow*, *by licence.*

— *Dec.* [*sic*] Robert Gregory, of the Parish of St. Albanes, wood street, and Elizabeth——[*sic*] of this Parish, *by licence.*

1633

Oct. 20.   Richard Kicklinge, of the Parish of St. Stephens, Coleman Street, and Grace Carter, *Widdow*, of the Parish of Allhallows in the Wall, *by licence.*

Nov. 24.   William Snowe, of the Parish of St. Buttolph Algate, and Clemence Skyner, of this Parish, being askte in the Church.

Dec. 8.   William Boreham, of the Parish of St. Bothalls, Bishopsgate, and Pearseys Humble, of this Parish, *by licence.*

1634

May 1. Pearcivall Day, of the Parish of St. Michaels Crooked lane, and Anne Ellell, daughter of William Ellell, in the County of Southampton, *Yeoman, by licence.*

May 15. Jocob Pearce and Elizabeth Jackson, both of this Parish *by licence.*

May 15. Higate Parsons and Mary Sheppard, both of Hendon in the County of Middlesex, *by licence.*

June 3. Soloman Fountaine, of the Parish of St. Botholls Bishopsgate, and Jawline (? Jacqueline) Dillavalley, *by licence.*

June 19. Andrew Goscoigne, of the Parish of St. Bothalls Aldgate, and Elizabeth Cowdrell, of Whitechappell, *by licence.*

Nov. 13. John Ruben, of St. Bothalls Algate, London, and Mary Prust of this Parish, *by licence.*

Dec. 4. Joshua Mainett, of the Parish of St. Bartholomews Exchange, and Barbara Hornblow, of this Parish, *by licence.*

1635

Mar. 31. John Egge, of the Parish of St. Bothalls, Algate, and Ellizabeth Swallow, of this Parish, being asked in the Church.

April 15. Revell Roe, of the Parish of St. Bothalls, Bishopsgate, *Yeoman,* and Mary Banister, in the County of Shreosbery, *by licence.*

Aug. 20. John Frances, of the Parish of St. Anns, Blackfriars, and Easter Brinsley, of this Parish, *by licence.*

Sept. 18. Richard Tomkins, of the Parish of Abchurch, and Ann Swinbury, of New Castell, in the County of Durom, *by licence.*

Nov. 29. Robert Haesleton and Ann Rider, both of this Parish, *by licence.*

Dec. 17. Robert Dale, of the Parish of St. Butolph, Algate, and Christian Manly, of this Parish, *by licence.*

Feb. 29. William Beech and Dorcas Clarke, *by licence.*

1636

May 4. Frances Shuttlewood, of the Parish of St. Edmons the King, and Ann Lee, of this Parish, *by licence.*

May 17. John Winstanley, of Martin, in the County of Midclesex, and Dorithie Spicer, of the Parish of St. Butolph, Algate, *by licence.*

June 9. John Barnwells and Elizabeth Wright, of this Parish, *by licence.*

Oct. 18. Richard Cooke, of the Parish of St. Marie Magdelens, Bermonse, and Julan Joans, of this Parish, *by licence.*

Jan. 19. Hamnet Malbon, of this Parish, and Hanna Taner, of Wisden in the County of Midclesex, were married *by licence* the 19th of January, not by licence but by banes [*sic*].

Feb. 14. John Batho, of this Parish, and Ann Bodey, of East Tilbury, in the County of Essex, *by licence.*

Feb. 19. Henery Howell, of the Parish of St. Butolph, Algate, and Easter Francklin, of the Parish of St. John Zachries, *by licence.*

1637

July 6.   William Ardin, of the Parish of St. Andrew, Holborn, and Katherin Hockit, of this Parish, *by licence.*

Aug. 15.   Steven Moons, of the Parish of St. Andrews, Eastcheap, and Sarah Hains, *by licence.*

Sep. 21.   Lionell Pidgin and Joyse Palmer, being asked in the Church

Sep. 28.   Lancelot Tolson and Mary Hales, *by licence.*

Oct. 8.   Alexander Becham and Alice Beaman, being asked in the Church.

Nov. 29.   William Rowland, of the Parish of St. Martins in the feelds, and Jane Allin, *by licence.*

1638

Mar. 26.   Richard Vaughon, of the Parish of St. Swetins, and Susan Hamon, of this Parish, being asked in the Church.

July 4.   Frances Roberts, of the Parish of St. Andrews, Undershaft, and Jane Comin, of this Parish, *by licence.*

Aug. 16.   William James, of Reding, in the County of Bucks, and Katherin Godard, of dio County [*sic?* ditto]

Dec. 27.   John Higgs, of the Parish of St. Mary Aldermary, and Margrit Dunn, of the Parish of St. Stephens, Coolman Streete, *by licence.*

1639

May 1.   Mr. Edward Hardman and Mrs. Elizabeth Brace, both of this Parish, *by licence.*

July 9.   Mr. Robert Chamberlaine, of the Parish of Finsbury in Kent [*sic*], and Sibbell Dewrie, of the same place, *by licence.*

July 16.   George Sheffeild and Anna Phips, of the Parish of Sepuchers, London.

Oct. 20.   John Madley and Jone Morric *by banes.*

Dec. 17.   Mr. John Starland, of Chatham of the County of Kent, and Marie Chamberlaine, of Finsbury in ditto Countey, *by licence.*

Jan. 9.   George Browne and Elizabeth Franklin, *by licence.*

Feb. 13.   Michael Person and Ailse Shelley, *by licence.*

1640

April 5.   Richard Tapps and Hester Read, *by licence.*

April 7.   John Snooke, of the Parish of Bennets, Pales wharf, and Marie Revell, of this Parish, *by licence.*

July 20.   Mr. Francis Pellet, of Abinger in the County of Surrey, and Dorothy Hayne of Emerst, *by licence.*

Dec. 31.   William Lewer, of the Parish of Buttolph, Bushopsgaitt, and Sarah Rochester, *by licence.*

Mar. 5.   John Burrows and Marie Sherrard, of the Parish of All Hallowe, Honneylanc, *by licence.*

Mar. 7.   Francis Greene, of the Parish of Andrews Undershaft, and Susan Barnat, of this Parish.

Mar. 22.   Mr. Thomas Winspeare, and Mrs. Marie Sheffeild, of Waltham Abbey in the County of Essex, *by licence.*

1641

May 30.   Robert Lavender and Jane Eebey, *by licence*.

1642

May 10.   Richard Williams and Easter Morgin, single persons.
July 7.   Richard Smith and Margret Paynter.
Aug. 29.   George Kendall, of Hampstead, and Ann Walker of the Parish of Andrews, Holborn.
Sep. 11.   Richard Trap, of the Parish of John Evangelist, and Marie Deare, of the Parish of Andrews Wardrob.
Sep. 29.   John Fox, of the Parish of Giles Criplegat, and Ann Wedgborough, of Beadfant in the County of Midlesex.
Oct. 6.   Richard Wright, of the Parish Alhalos, Barkin, and Ann Robinson, of the Parish of Alhallows the Less.
Nov. 8.   Bezaliell Sarjant and Ann Tomson of the Parish of Crayford in the Countie of Sussex.
Dec. 15.   Christopher Pinchin, of the Parish of Martins in the Vintrey, and Marie Dauncey, of the Parish of Aldermans Burrey.
Feb. 16.   Richard Shelcok, in the Parish of Alhallows the Great, and Marie Merriden.
Mar. 7.   William Foster, of Enfeild in the County of Midlesex, and Elizabeth Pratt, of Margret in Lothbury ward.
Mar. 14.   Mr. Joseph Lovet, of the Parish of Larance Jury, and Mrs. Ann Mason of the Parish of Pancross, Soperlane.

1643

May 2.   Peeter Molley, of the Parish of Alhallows by the wall, and Marie Palmer, of the Parish of Buttalph Bushopsgatt.
June 29.   William Swan, of this Parish, and Kathorin Oram, of Peckham in the County of Surrey.
Aug. 19.   Mr. Humphary Bewatter, of the Parish of Bennet Sheerhog, and Mrs. Dorethe Norton, of the Parish of Michill, Cornhill.
Nov. 27.   Thomas Moodey, and Jane Martin, of the Parish of Buttolph, Bushopsgatt.
Jan. 1.   William Hoxbey, of the Parish of horn in the County of Surrey, and Ailce Roth, of dito Countey.
Jan. 4.   John Burcher and Sarah Einglish, of the Parish of Bartholomew by the Exchandg.
Jan. 23.   Mr. Benjamen Dukan, of the Parish of Stephens, Colman Streete, and Mrs. Olive Price, of this Parish.
Feb. 8.   Mr. Jonathan Elyot and Mrs. Ann Nelson, of the Parish of Katherin Cree Church.
Mar. 14.   Mr Jacob Jurin, of the Parish of pancros Sop Lane, and Mrs. Ann Hublon, of this Parish.

1644

April 11.   Richard Cranwell, of the Parish of St. Leonard, Shoreditch, and Anna Smith, of the Parish of St. Albans, Woodstreete.

April 22.   Thomas Hoult, of Enfeild in the County of Middlesex, and Elizabeth Greene, of the Parish of St. Bennetts, Gracechurch, London.

April 22.   Thomas Francis and Jane Chamberlin, both of this Parish.

June 4.   William Oberman, of Lynn in the County of Norfolk, *Esquire*, and Mrs. Elizabeth Trafford, of Trafford in the County of Lincolne.

Aug. 15.   John Aderton, of the Parish of St. Mildreds, Poultry, and Anne Tomson, of this Parish.

Nov. 25.   Edward Porter, of the Parish of St. Andrews Undershaft, and Harold Boswell, of this Parish.

Jan. 6.   William Nevett, of Christ Church Parish, and Jane Geismond, of St. Faiths Parish.

Jan. 20.   Adam Southam, of the Parish of St. Mary, Somersett, and Elizabeth Watly, of Staines in the County of Middlesex.

Mar. 4, 164⅘. Mr. James Lordell and Mrs. Sarah Houbelon.

1645

April 22.   Edmond Chapmen, in the Parish of Sevenock, in the County of Kent, and Susan Hare, of this Parish.

Aug. 5.   Mr. Samuell Travers and Mrs. Christian Sickes of the Parishes of Alhallowes Staining, and of St. Peter in Cornhill.

Aug. 20.   Mr. Stephen Simson, of the Parish of St. Giles, Criplegate and Dousabell House, of Stepney.

Oct. 16.   Thomas Hughes, of the Parish of Alhallows the great, and Marie Mathews, of this Parish.

Nov. 15.   Richard Sayres, of Worth in the co. Sussex, and Mary Teake, of Cousley, in the same County.

Jan. 1.   William Turner, of the Parish of St. Mary Whitechappell, and Mary Masters, of this Parish.

Jan. 19.   John Doore, of the Parish of St. Andrew Undershaft, and Ann Goult, of the Parish of St. Mary Woolnoth.

Feb. 11, 164⅘ George Shepheard, of Redrith, and Francis Crookhorne of this Parish.

1646

April 5.   William Nicholl, of the Parish of St. Bennett Finck, and Hannah Webbe, of the Parish of St. Giles, Cripelgate

May 19.   Richard Johnson and Rebeckah Phillips, of the Parish of St. Dunstans in the East.

Sep. 17.   Anthony Woodlow, of Islington, and Isabell Tomlinson, *servant* to Colonel Thomas Gower.

Feb. 14, 164⁶⁄₇ Joseph Golby and Mary Carrell, of St. Mary Woolnoth

1647

There was none married this yeare.

1648

May 3.   Richard Templer, of Glympton in the co. Oxon, and Alice Harris, of Glympton.

May 11.   Matthias Buckbird, of the Parish of Harrow, and Ruth Owen, of the Parish of Egdwar, both in the County of Middlesex.

June 4.　Thomas House and Elizabeth Bridges, both of the Parish of St. Gregories by Pauls.

July 13.　John Smith, of the Parish of St. Margarett, Lothbury, and Anne Chandler, of Havering, in the County of Essex.

Nov. 7.　Andrew English, of Berstead, in the County Sussex and Mary King, of this Parish.

Mar. 15,164⅞ Mr. John Glascock, *Minister*, of St. Andrew Undershaft, and of the Parish of St. Faithes, and Mrs. Margarett King, of the Parish of St. Saviours, Southwark.

1649

April 26.　Mr. Robert Winch, of the Parish of St. Martins Iron-monger, and Mrs. Sarah Head, of this Parish.

Nov. 29.　Thomas Dyton and Dorothy Hamerton, both of Sepulchres Parish.

Jan. 3.　Luke Holcraft, of Redrith, and Elizabeth Viney, of Stepney, married by Mr. Thurman.

Mar. 7.　Anthony Middleton, of the Parish of St. Dunstan in the West, and Elizabeth Phillips, of this Parish.

Mar. 8.　Daniell Watts, in the Parish of Martin, in the County of Surrey, and Joan Wright, of Harrow Parish in the County of Middlesex.

1650

April 30.　Charles Loveden and Ellen Ashwell, both of the Parish of St. Martins, Ludgate.

May 1.　Richard Sadler and Elizabeth Bernard, both of Savoy Parish.

May 23.　Mr. Jacob Stock, of the Parish of All Hallows, Lombard Street, and Mrs. Elizabeth Gower.

May 23.　Samuell Sharpe and Anne Phillips, of St. John Zachary.

June 6.　Richard Bernard and Elizabeth Robinson, of Staines in the County of Middlesex.

July 4.　Nicholas Burt and Jane Toms, both of Buttolph Aldgate Parish.

Oct. 8.　Symon Tyers and Susan Tayler, both of Christ Church Parish.

Oct. 11.　Henry Luther, of Debtford in the County of Kent, and Joyce Dally, of ditto place.

Nov. 5.　Andrew Sexton, of All Hallows, Stayning, and Ann Pallin, of Chiswick in the County of Middlesex.

Nov. 23.　Mr. John Colleson and Elizabeth Pritchard, of Allhallows the great.

Jan. 30.　Mr. Edward Sadler and Mrs. Susan Underwood, both of the Parish of Mary-le-bow.

1651

June 30.　Richard Mildmay, of Ozzed, in the County of Essex, and Mary Alsmore, of Little Thurrook, in the said County.

July 31.　Mr. Luke Barber, of St. Bennett Finks Parish, and Mrs. Elizabeth Hedge, of Mitcham in the County of Surrey.

July 31.   Mr. John Tyler, of Sepulchres Parish, and Mrs. Mary Smith, of Botolph, Bishopsgate Parish.

Aug. 7.   John Wilson, of Giles, Criplegate Parish, and Jane Moodey, of Botolph, Bishopsgate Parish.

Sep. 9.   Edward Pearin and Anne Johnson, both of Giles, Criplegate Parish.

Jan. 8.   Captaine John Ward and Mrs. Jane Andrewes, of Margaretts, Lothbury Parish.

Mar. 9.   Gerard Roberts, on Downgate Hill, and Sarah Jones, in Sething Lane.

Mar. 9.   George Erwin, of Wapping, and Mary Goodwin, on Downgate Hill.

Mar. 18.   John Jones, of Giles, Criplegate Parish, and Elizabeth Bulmer, of Savoy Parish.

1652

July 11.   William Capnes, of St. Anne, Blackfryars, and Anne Bell, of St. Faiths Parish.

July 26.   William Dove, of Gravesend in the County of Kent, and Jane Lelsden, of Wapping, *Widow.*

Aug. 5.   Mr. Adlard Cage, of Linsey in the County of Suffolk, and Mrs. Bridgett Hedge, of Micham in the County of Surrey.

Sep. 27.   Thomas Mills, of Wardsmill in the County of Hartford, and Elizabeth Tuckwell, of Wapping.

Sep. 20. [*sic*] Henry Kedgell and Abigaill Wright, both of Old Street, in St. Giles, Criplegate Parish.

Feb. 18.   John Sharpe, of White Chappell, and Anne Tillyer, of this Parish.

Jan. 13.   Timothy Clamp, of the Parish of St. Mary Magdalen in Bermondsey in the Burrough of Southwark, and Rebeckah Early, of the same Parish.

Mar. 6.   William Good, of the Parish of Sepulchers, and Sarah Fosbrooke, of Saviours Parish in Southwarke.

1653

Aug. 21.   John Dun, of the Parish of St. George in Southwarke and Jane Scott, of the same Parish.

Sep. 15.   Thomas Banbury, in the Parish of St. Saviors in Southwarke, and Mary Farmer, of this Parish.

Sep. 20.   Mr. Richard Smith and Mrs. Marth Seed, both of this Parish.

Sep. 25.   John Comberland, of this Parish, and Alice Kifferd, of Westminster.

Sep. 6. [*sic*] Henry Harman, of this Parish, and Elizabeth Andrewes, of Hatfield, in the County of Hartford.

Dec. 1.   Edward Phillips, of this Parish, and Margaret Cordwell of the Parish of Katherine Cree Church, were publisht three times and married the 1st December.

Dec. 1.   Cuthbert Ridley, of the Parish of Allhallows, Barking, and Mary Phillips, of this Parish, were publisht three times and married 1st December.

Feb. 2.   George Smith, of the Parish of St. Botolph. Aldersgate, and Mary Hetchman, of the Parish of Allhallowes, Lombard Street.

Mar. 7.   George Paybody and Anne Hunlock, both of this Parish.

1654

May 22.   Mr. John Fox, of Stradbrooke, in the County of Suffolk, and Mrs. Susan Girling, of the same place, and sojourned in the Parish of Sepulchers, London.

June 28.   Thomas Sparrow, of the Parish of St. Martins Ironmonger, and Katherin Hollis, of the same Parish.

Oct. 7.   Robert Watts, of Crole in the County of Lincolne, and Elizabeth Parker, of the Parish of St. Michaell Cornhill.

Oct. 17.   John Harrison, of this Parish, and Sarah Keftman, of the Parish of Aldermary.

Dec. 7.   Henry Goodhew, of the Parish of Bottolph, Billingsgate, Charity Challoner, of Linvell, in the County of Sussex.

Jan. 23.   The Worshipful Francis Rolle, *Esquire*, the son of the Right Honourable Henry Rolle, *Lord Chiefe Justice of the Court of Upper Bench*, and Mrs. Priscilla Foot, the daughter of the Worshipful Thomas Foot, *Esquire*, sometimes *Lord Maior of the Honourable City of London*, of the Parish of St. Olaves Jury, were married the 23rd January, he was of Sepulchers Parish, without Newgate.

Feb. 2.   William Burges and Anne Joiner, both of the Parish of St. Martins.

1655

Mar. 25.   John Wilson and Alice Bailey, both of the Parish of St. Mary Woolnoth.

May 28.   William Croudson, of this Parish, and Mary Browne, of St. Swithins Parish.

June 4.   Francis Heardson, of the Parish of St. Dunstans in the West, and Anne Notingham, of St. Hellens field.

June 5.   Thomas Hutchin and Elizabeth Oungly, both of the towne of Gingrave, in the County of Essex.

June 20.   John Clarke, *Yeoman*, and Elizabeth Carlton, both of the Parish of St. Andrew Wardrobe.

July 5.   John Dyson, of Redrith, in the County of Surrey, and Elizabeth Wagstaffe, of the Parish of St. Martin Ironmonger.

Sep. 26.   Peter, Fletcher, of the Parish of St. Margarett Pattons, and Mary Davis, of this Parish.

Sept. 28.   Walter Foot, of Allhallows, Barking, and Mary Crouch, of St. Mary Hill.

Sep. 30.   Richard Williams and Margarett Rigby.

Jan. 18.   Mr. John James and Mrs. Fraunces Townsend, both of the Parish of St. Andrews, Holborne.

Mar. 4.   Ambrose Davison, of Martin-le-grand, and Mary Lamott, of St. Leonard, Shoreditch.

1656

May 22.   Stephen Gasly, of the Parish of St. Lawrence Jury, and Anne Bickering, of the Parish of St. Greeories by Pauls.

July 3.	Mr. John Story, of the Parish of St. Dunstans in the East, and Mrs. Elizabeth Haswell, of this Parish.
July 24.	Mr. Daniell Lewin, of Broxburne, and Mrs. Mary Woodhall, of the Parish of Ware, both in the County of Hartford.
Aug. 15.	Mr. John Rock, of the Parish of St. Bennets, Pauls Wharf, and Mrs. Anne Rowe, of the Parish of St. Gregories by Pauls.
Aug. 17.	Francis ———. [*sic*] of the Parish of ——— [*sic*] and Bulcaliela Ealding, of the Parish of St. Christopher.
Sep. 25.	William Procter, of the Parish of Alphage, and Sarah Gooday, of the Parish of St. Leonard's, Fetter Lane.
Oct. 28.	Symon Reynolds, of the Parish of All Hallows, the Great, and Barbara Dyson, of this Parish.
Nov. 11.	Martin Smith, of the Parish of St. Mary Woolnoth, and Elizabeth Markham, of the Parish of St. Buttolph, Bishopsgate.
Nov. 13.	Mr. William Thorowgood, of the Parish of St. Michael, Cornhill, and Mrs. Theodosia Leventhorpe, of Lambeth.
Mar. 16.	Richard Garrett, of Northampton, and Hannah Wall, of Hackney.

1657

April 9.	Edward Harbert, of East Hornden, in the County of Essex, and Elizabeth Pocock, of the same place.
May 12.	Mr. Bedford Whiting, of the Parish of St. Gabriell, Fenchurch, and Mrs. Anne Porter, of the Parish of St. Martins Ironmonger.
May 26.	John Walcott, of Walcott, in the County of Salop, *Esquire*, and Mrs. Elizabeth Clerke, the daughter of Sir George Clerke, *Knight and Alderman of the City of London.*
Sep. 15.	Thomas Parson, of the Parish of All Hallows, Lombard Street, and Katherin Preston, of St. Olaves, Silver Street.
Oct. 8.	John Bide, *Esquire*, of the Parish of St. Leonards, Shoreditch, and Rose Atkinson, of the Parish of St. Giles, Criplegate.
Oct. 15.	George Farmer, *Esquire*, of the Parish of St. Andrew, Holborne, and Mrs. Anne Gates, of the Parish of St. Dunstans in the West.
Nov. 5.	John Hickes and Anne Costelo, both of the Parish of St. Peter the poore.
Nov. 5.	Mr. William King and Mrs. Rebeckah Carlton, both of this parish.
Dec. 17.	John Horne and Anne Brett, both of the Savoy Parish.
Dec. 27.	Mr. Rayner Harman and Mrs. Rebeckah Rogers, of the Parish of St. Bartholomews, Exchange.
Jan. 19.	Mr. Henry Orpin and Mrs. Anne Fawson.
Feb. 2.	John Moore, of the Parish of St. Anne, Aldersgate, and Alice Smith, of Dukes Place.

1658

June 7.	Richard Coster and Elizabeth Clarke, of the Parish of St. Sepulchers.

Oct. 10.	Mr. Richard Snowe and Mrs. Mary Sparks, of St. Michaell, Cornhill.
Oct. 21.	Daniel Grey, of the Parish of St. Brides, and Ellen Hinton, of Trinity Parish.
Dec. 9.	William Leigh, of the Parish of St. Michaell, Bassishaw, and Elizabeth Berman, of Margarets, Westminster.
Dec. 26.	Joseph Ward, of Christchurch Parish, and Mary Burton, of St. Martins Ironmonger.
Dec. 27.	Anthony Harward, of the Parish of St. Dunstans-in-the-West, and Barbara Notingham, of the Parish of St. Hellens.
Jan. 6.	John Ball, of the Parish of Abchurch, and Joan Haines, of the Parish of St. James, Garlickhithe.
Jan. 13.	William Wigge, of the Parish of St. Mary Woolnoth, and Mary Tonge of—[*sic*]
Feb. 10.	Henry Waller, of Westminster, *Esquire*, and Mrs. Dorothy Gale, the daughter of Mr. George Gale, of St. Stephens, Walbrooke.

1659

April 12.	Mr. Nevill Lorrimer, of the Parish of St. Clements, and Mrs. Anna Offly, of Battersy in the County of Surrey.
April 21.	Roger Arkinstall, of the Parish of John Baptist, and Katherin Knell, of the Parish of St. Giles in the Feilds.
June 30.	Mr. Edward Langford, of the Parish of Allhallows the lesse, and Mrs. Anne Dowse, of the Parish of Tilbury in the County of Essex.
July 5.	John Overing, of Edgerton in the County of Kent, and Elizabeth Warren, of the County of St. Brides.
July 6.	Robert Last and Anne King, both of the Parish of Sepulchers.
July 26.	Mr. Robert Beversham, of the Parish of St. Dionis Backchurch, and Mrs. Sarah Davie, of the Parish of St. Mary Aldermanbury.
July 28.	Hugh Middleton and Alice Haines, both of the Parish of Margaretts, Westminster.
July 31.	Edward Swinerton, of the Parish of Allhallowes the Great, and Hannah Lewin, of St. Lawrence Jury.
Aug. 23.	John Hoseman, of Chesthunt, and Mary Pennyfather, of Hartford, both in the County of Hartford.
Sep. 2.	Oliver Haselden and Jane Muckley, both of the Parish of St. Margaretts, Westminster.
Sep. 11.	Henry Eldridge, of the Parish of St. Mary Bothawe, and Mary Only, of the Parish of St. Buttolph, Aldgate.
Sep. 22.	Benoni Wallington, of Dionis Backchurch, and Anne Sadler, of St. Stephen, Walbrooke.
Oct. 4.	The Worshipful John Dawes, *Esquire*, of Putney in the County of Surrey, and Honoria Watkins, of Covent Garden, daughter to the Lady Watkins.
Oct. 17.	Edward Salkeld, of St. Michael Querne, and Elizabeth Hawley, of the Parish of Andrew Wardrobe.
Oct. 20.	George Reeve, of the Parish of Stepney, and Sarah Stiles, of the Parish of St. Giles, Criplegate.
Nov. 3.	Nathaniell Ball, of the Parish of St. Olaves, Hartstreet, and Martha Hadrian, of Rochester in the County of Kent.

Dec. 18.	Edward King, of Magdalene Laver, and Anne Bancks, of White Batling, both in the County of Essex.
Jan. 12.	Robert Serles, of St. James Garlichithe, and Elizabeth Nod, of Andrew, Holborn.
Jan. 19.	John Jesse and Elizabeth Woolf, of St. John Baptist Parish.
Jan. 19.	James Webbe, of St. Martins in the Feilds, and Joyce Smith, of St. John Baptist Parish.
Feb. 25.	Mr. John Frickley and Mrs. Magdalene Day, both of Stretham, County of Surrey.

1660

April 24.	William Waugh, of the Parish of Allhallows the Great, and Margarett Robinson, of this Parish.
May 10.	Marke Blissett and Mary Collyer, both of Greenwich in Kent.
May 29.	Thomas Storey, of the Parish of St. Andrew, Holborne, and Rebeckah Jones, of the Parish of St. Giles, Criplegate.
June 3.	John Palmer, of the Parish of St. Giles, Criplegate, and Fraunces Ap John, of the Parish of St. Michaell, Cornhill.
June 10.	William Bingham, of the Parish of St. Giles, Criplegate, and Anne Shipman, of the Parish of St. James, Dukesplace.
June 19.	John Hill, of St. Dunstans in the West, and Mary Trevett, of St. Mary Woolnoth.
June 21.	Samuell Pordege, of Lincolns Inne, *Esquire*, and Mrs. Dorcas Langham, of Peterborough in the County of Northampton.
Sep. 23.	Osmond Strickland and Susan Stephens, both of the Parish of St. John Zachary.
Sep. 28.	William Singer, of Shepheard in Middlesex, and Jane Lavender, of Spunger in Essex.
Nov 8.	William Rusten and Elizabeth Tittelo, both of the Parish of Stebunheath, alias Stepney.
Dec. 10.	Jarvis Price, of Whitehall, *Esquire*, and Martha Mayor, *Spinster*, of the Parish of St. Peters Paul's Wharf.
Dec. 13.	Mr. Thomas Vernon, of the Parish of St. Clements, Eastcheap, and Anne Weston, of Catham, in the County of Surrey.
Dec. 27.	Symon Smith and Elizabeth Stephens, as by a certificate approved at Westminster, were married.
Jan. 1.	Thomas Jenner, of the Inner Temple, *Gentleman*, and Anne Poe, of the Parish of St. Edmonds the King, in Lombard Streete.
Jan. 8.	George Knight, of St. Margarets Pattons, and Elizabeth Richardson, of this Parish.
Feb. 21.	John Hobson, of Syston, in the County of Lincoln, *Esquire*, and Mary Deligne, of Harlaxton, in ditto County
Feb. 23.	Mr. Henry Harbin, of the Parish of St. Bennett Pauls Wharf, and Elizabeth Warharn, of St. Giles in the feilds.
Mar. 16.	John Shipman, of the Parish of St James Dukes Place, and Isabell Bagley, of the Parish of St. Mary Abchurch

1661

May 7.	Richard Drew, of the Parish of St. Stephen Walbrook, and Rachell Pett, of the Parish of St. Buttolph Aldgate.
May 29.	Jeremiah Dodwell, of the Parish of St. Andrew, Holborne, and Elizabeth Mason, of the Parish of St. Clemente Danes.
June 24.	John Burton, of the Parish of St. Magnus the Martyr, and Dorothy Dyer, of the Parish of St. Thomas the Apostle.
Nov. 14.	Francis Frampton, of Warnham in Dorsett, and Anne Jackson, of St. Stephens, Walbrooke.
Nov. 19.	Mr. Owen Arthur, of the Parish of Mary le Savoy, and Julian Beane, of the Parish of St. Olaves, Hart Street.
Dec. 1.	William Hills, of the Parish of St. Katherin Coleman, and Elizabeth King, of the Parish of Allhallowes on the Wall, *Widdow.*
Dec. 3.	Daniel Harris, of the Parish of St. Margarett, Westminster, and Elizabeth Orett, of the Parish of St. Martins, Ongars.
Feb. 6.	William Mores, of Cunerton in the County of Somersett, and Martha Colston, of the City of Bristoll.

1662

April 1.	John Dayrley, of the Parish of St. Bartholomew the great, and Anne Beech, of the Parish of St. Martins in the feilds.
April 3.	John Dashwood and Anne Kirby, both of Walthamcrosse, in the County of Essex, *by baines*, three times asked in the said Parish Church as by certificate appeares.
May 20.	Henry Bingoe, of the Parish of St. Leonard, Foster Lane, and Dorathy Frances, of the same, *Widdow.*
May 22.	Phillip Davis and Joane Titcombe, of St. Margrets, Westminster.
July 15.	George Day and Mary Thruston, *Widdow*, both of the Parish of St. Mary Mattfellon, alias Whitechapell, *Widdow* [*sic*].
Aug. 6.	Mr. John Dauling, of Westram in the County of Kent, *Gent.*, and Mrs. Elizabeth Bret, of St. Bennett, Grace Church.
Dec. 9.	Edward Couling, *Gentleman*, and Mrs. Mary Benet, *Spinster*, both of the Parish of St. Dunstan in the West.
Dec. 14.	William Gilmore, of the Parish of St. Sepulchers, and Katherine Hunlock, of this Parish.
Dec. 23.	Mr. Martin Higgins, of the Parish of St. John Baptist, and Mrs. Sibbilla Richinson, of this Parish.
Jan. 1.	Thomas Warnes, of Deptford, in the County of Kent, *Mariner*, and Sarah Austine, of the Parish of St. John Baptist.
Feb. 10.	Thomas Kippington and Jane Hodgson, both of this Parish, *by publication of baines.*

1663

June 9.   James Redyinge, of the Parish of St. James, Clerkenwell, and Frances Willson, of the Parish of St. Andrews, Holborne, *was married by lycense.*   Gilbert, London.

Sep. 17.   Edward Flaxmore and Sarah Hunlock, *by publication of banes.*

Oct. 18.   Francis Sollis, of the Parish of St. Thomas the Apostle, and Benedicta Cowslip, of the Parish of St. Lawrence Pountney, *Spinster, by lycense.*

Feb. 9.   Mr. Joseph Hammon, of the Parish of St. Lawrance Pountney, *Merchant*, and Mrs. Elizabeth Standley, *Spinster*, the daughter of Mr. William Standley, *Gent.*

Mar. 1.   Mr. Peter Causton, of St. Thomas Apostle, London, *Marchant*, and Mrs. Martha Grafton, *Spinster*, of the Parish of St. Stephen, Collman Street.

Mar. 21.   Mr. Mathew Locke, of Westminster, *Gentleman*, and Mrs. Alice Smith, of Annables, in the County of Herford, *Spinster.*

1664

May 22.   Mr. John Vincent, *Marriner*, and Elizabeth Wyght, both of the Parish of Stepney, alias Stepinheth.

May 30.   Isaiah Fosset, of this Parish, and Mary Jackson, of the Parish of All Hallows, Hunney Lane.

Nov. 10.   Thomas Mudd, of the Parish of St. Mary le Bow, and Elizabeth Raines, of the Parish of St. Bartholomew Exchange.

Nov. 17.   John Butkin, of the Parish of St. Augustine, London, and Anna Watts, daughter of George Watts, of Hartly-now, in the County of South-ton.

Feb. 28.   Mr. James Miller, of Pearetree, in the County of South-amton, and Mrs. Martha Stanley, of the same County, *by lisence.*

1665

[*The date only is given, there are no Marriages.*]

1666

April 7.   Mr. John Smyth, of St. Botolph, Bushopsgate, and Ann Foxhall, of this Parish. Married by Dr. Charles Mason.

End of Marriages.

Burials

ELIZABETH our gracious Quene happielie began hir reigne the sevententh daie of November in the yeare of our Lord one thowsand fyve hundred fiftie and eight since which time there have been in the parishe of Saint Marie Woolchurch Hawe in London these burialls followinge.

1558

Nov. 20.	Beniamin Crocheman.
Nov. 25.	Allen More.
Dec. 5.	John Witte.
Jan. 4.	Elizabeth Dixon.
Jan. 9.	Agnes Pole.
Jan. 9.	Agnes Kenricke.
Jan. 20.	Leonard Mallison.
Jan. 22.	Margaret Lacie.
Jan. 26.	Thomas Courtis.

1559

May 21.	Hewe Becket.
June 19.	Jone Allen.
July 13.	John Filian.
July 14.	Margaret Crewe.
Sept. 9.	Thomas Mansel.
Dec. 3.	Henrie Baboro.
Dec. 4.	Margaret Allen.
Dec. 6.	Jone Bradlie.
Jan. 11.	Annis Hill.
Jan. 13.	John Crewe.

Griffith Jones, *Parson of this Church*, was buried the xxiiij. of January, and Thomas Jenkinson was inducted the xxij. of February nexte following.

1560

May 18.	John Best.
May 20.	Cicelie Todde.
May 26.	A boie named John.
July 3.	John, son of John Crowchman.
July 27.	Arthur, son of George Basford.
Aug. 13.	Jone Dale.
Sep. 12.	Mistress Alsop, *Widoe*.

A coliars boie falling dead sodenlie in the streete, was buried the eighte of October.

Oct. 30.	Sibill Bludwicke.

Nov. 1. William Bludwicke.
Dec. 5. William Hayles.
Dec. 13. Ales, daughter of Edward Holmes.
Jan. 13. William More.

1561

April 5. Ellin, wife of Thomas Gun.
April 24. Paule Chamber.
May 30. Barbara, daughter of Thomas Bering.
June 9. John, son of Thomas Walker.
June 21. Constance Bond, *Widoe.*
Aug. 5. Richard White.
Nov. 11. Samuel, son of George Anthonie.
Jan. 16. Thomas, son of Robert Cudnar.
Jan. 31. John Powel.
Feb. 1. William Lawne.
Feb. 2. Nicholas Dawson.
Mar. 6. Margaret Wilson.

1562

April 2. Thomas Runkhorne.
Aug. 25. Elizabeth, daughter of John Smith.
Oct. 31. Richard, son of Lawrence Harrison.
Nov. 20. Margaret Duffild.
Dec. 2. Jone Barnes.
Mar. 21. John Handford.

1563

April 30. Edward Babsdike.
May 2. Margaret, wife of Richard Carter.
June 28. Jone, daughter of William Powell.
July 31. Jone Linsey.
Aug. 7. Susan, daughter of Mr. Alexander Best.
Aug. 7. Ellin, sister of Adam Powell.
Aug. 9. James Pahen.
My Ladie Forman deceased in this Parishe the seventh of this monthe
    and was buried in St. Christofers the twelfth.
Jan. 24. Thomas Jones.
Aug. 24. Rohert Hinkes.
Aug. 27. Jone Poole.
Aug. 29. John Grise.
Aug. 31. Emme, daughter of Mr. John Smith.
Sep. 9. Elizabeth Lwide, kinswoman to my Lady Forman, and
    wife of Edward Lwide, *Gentleman.*
Sep. 13. Joane, daughter of Mr. John Best.
Sep. 13. Magdalene Suckley.
Sep. 16. Richard Locker.
Sep. 17. Elizabeth, daughter of Mr. John Best.
Sep. 17. Mary, daughter of Thomas Bowier.
Sep. 25. George Coverlie.
Sep. 26. Thomas, son of John Crowchman.
Sep. 26. Margaret Hartlie.
Sep. 27. Thomas, son of William Rydell.

Sep. 20.	Suzan, daughter of Thomas Walker.
Oct. 2.	Alice Richardson.
Oct. 2.	Thomas Bowyer.
Oct. 3.	John Shard.
Oct. 5.	William Canon.
Oct. 6.	Edward, son of James Willan.
Oct. 7.	Nicholas, a *servant* of John Rut.
Oct. 16.	George Allen.
Oct. 16.	Jone, daughter of Thomas Mason.
Oct. 16.	John, son of Margaret Hill.
Oct. 18.	Henrie, son of Martin Strong.
Oct. 18.	Elizabeth, daughter of Robart Fayrman.
Oct. 18.	Edward Glaig.
Oct. 20.	Sara Maior.
Oct. 23.	Margaret Fytch.
Oct. 23.	George Banister.
Oct. 23.	Arthur Parkhurst.
Oct. 25.	Edward Halworth.
Oct. 27.	John Dole.
Oct. 31.	John Banes, out of the stoks.
Nov. 2.	Magdalen, daughter of Thomas Walker.
Nov. 9.	Goodwife Mothe, wife of Arnold Mothe.
Nov. 14.	Richard Chambers.
Nov. 14.	Robert Hankin.
Nov. 18.	Jeffrie, son of John Rut.
Nov. 19.	Alis, daughter of John Web.
Nov. 21.	John Harding.
Nov. 26.	Thomas Hanlie.
Nov. 26.	Thomas Hitchcock.
Nov. 27.	Henrie Smith.
Dec. 2.	Augustine Linch.
Dec .7.	John Hodges.
Dec. 12.	George Anthonie.
Dec. 12.	Agnes Buckwell.
Dec. 16.	Alexander, son of Alexander Best.
Dec. 17.	Rafe Shawe.
Dec. 18.	Thomas Newman.
Dec. 20.	A new born child of William Shackletons.
Dec. 21.	Steven, the son of Robart ynnstone.
Dec. 22.	Isabel Frear.
Dec. 24.	Nicholas Renald.
Dec. 29.	Francis, son of George Anthonie.
Dec. 29.	Thomas Damport.
Dec. 31.	Thomas, the son of Richard Andlebie.
Jan. 7.	William Jefferson.
Jan. 12.	Roger Wood.
Feb. 19.	Anthony Fessie.
Feb. 26.	Richard Andlebie.
Mar. 2.	Richard, son of Richard Bradlie.
Mar. 5.	Thomas Bradlie.
Mar. 19.	Thomas Selbie, nephew and *servant* of Richard Selbie.

1564

Mar. 27.	Elizabeth and Agnes, daughters of Richard Bradlie.
Mar. 30.	Marie and Grace, daughters of Richard Bradlie.

June 27.	Jone, daughter of William Swaine.
Nov. 26.	Humfrie, son of Thomas Walker.
Nov. 30.	A childe of William Sharlie.
Dec. 25.	Barbara, daughter of James Willan.
Jan. 16.	Blanche, daughter of John Crewe.
Jan. 22.	Henry Tyas, *Haberdasher.*
Feb. 20.	Margaret Hill.

1565

May 11.	A child of Anthony van Hovens.
July 5.	A man child new borne sonne of William Chapman.
July 7.	Thomazin, daughter of John Tempest.
July 14.	Nicholas, son of Mr. John Best.
Aug. 23.	Margaret Skevington.
Nov. 18.	Edmond, son of Robert Cudner.
Nov. 21.	Mrs. Dissell, the wife of John Dissell.
Dec. 3.	Thomas, son of Richard Brigges.
Dec. 6.	Bridget, daughter of Thomas Walker.
Dec. 18.	Thomas, son of William Dawson.
Jan. 15.	Thomas, son of Richard Wade.
Feb. 20.	Robarte Fayreman, *Goldsmith.*
Mar. 3.	Thomas Wemes, son of Mrs. Andros.

1566

April 2.	Elizabeth Smith, *Widoe.*
May 22.	The child of Thomas Filians, borne before the time.
Aug. 1.	Bartilmew, son of Richard Briggs.
Aug. 14.	John Adams.
Oct. 17.	A child new borne of Anthonie van Hovens.
Nov. 6.	*Widoe* Runckhorne.
Dec. 20.	Mrs. Tego, wife of Steven Tego.
Dec. 22.	Margaret, daughter of Richard Sharp.
Jan. 10.	Anne, daughter of John Sharp.
Feb. 16.	John Dissell.

1567

Aug. 27.	A child of Anthonie van Hovens, new borne.
Sep. 16.	John, son of Richard Wade.
Sep. 24.	Margaret Whitfeild.
Oct. 28.	A childe of William Handford, new borne.
Jan. 15.	John, son of John Sharp.
Jan. 30.	Thomas Calton.
Feb. 9.	Arthur, son of Francis Dedicote.
Feb. 27.	Richard Carter.

1568

Mar. 25.	William Dawson, *Brewer.*
Mar. 25.	Humphry, son of Robart Yarrington.
April 12.	Mrs. Emme Bettinson.
July 4.	Elizabeth Rigsbie, *servant* to Mr. Edward Holmden.
July 16.	Elizabeth, wife of John Woodward.
Oct. 14.	Margaret Wood, *Widoe.*
Oct. 18.	Bartilmew Jhonson.

Nov. 7.	Mrs. Andros, wife of Mr. Steven Andros.
Nov. 25.	Thomas, son of William Swaine.
Dec. 22.	Mrs. Pelter, wife of Mr. Richard Pelter.
Jan. 25.	Mrs. Filian, wife of Thomas Filian.
Feb. 1.	Jone, daughter of William Spencer.
Mar. 3.	Mrs. Miller.

1569

July 19.	Briget, daughter of William Sharlie.
Oct. 19.	Nicholas Tuese.
Nov. 12.	William Cator.
Dec. 6.	Mrs. Smith, wife of John Smith.
Feb. 4.	Thomas Wanton, *Grocer.*

1570

May 5.	Hugh Mores, *servant* to John Alde, *Printer*, died in the stoks of the plage.
May 11.	Anthony Pavier.
July 23.	Susan Milles.
July 24.	Ellin Bourne, *servant* to Steven Andros, died of the plage.
Aug. 3.	Ales, daughter of John Parkins.
Aug. 4.	Henry Bullingham.
Aug. 11.	James Bore.
Sep. 26.	Thomas, son of Thomas Gun.
Dec. 23.	John Marshell, *Grocer.*
Jan. 5.	Sara, daughter of Richard Wade.
Feb. 6.	Mary, daughter of Thomas Filian.

1571

Mar. 31.	John, son of Edmund Normavell.
April 1.	Margaret, daughter of Henrie Jaye.
May 12.	Mr. Alexander Best.
Sep. 5.	Mr. John Jennings.
Sep. 6.	A new borne childe of John Sharpes.
Sep. 23.	William Lewis, *servant* to Griffith Kenrick, died of the plage.
Oct. 11.	Christopher Hastinge, *servant* to Griffith Kenrick, died of the plage.
Oct. 13.	William, son of Griffith Kenrick, died of the plage.
Oct. 22.	Elizabeth Jones.
Jan. 5.	John de Lee, *Pewterer.*
Mar. 16.	Richard Tayler, *Merchant.*
Mar. 18.	Richard, son of Robart Smith.

1572

May 10.	William Stile.
June 23.	Jone Everet.
Oct. 27.	A child, new borne, of John Sharpes.
Nov. 2.	Ales Browne, a maide.
Nov. 20.	John, son of Robert Wryghthouse.
Dec. 3.	Bennet Collet, *servant* to Peter Lide, died of the plage.
Dec. 4.	John Corney, *servant* to Peter Lide, died of the plage.
Dec. 20.	Mr. Lewis Spurrier, *Haberdasher.*

Dec. 27.	Peter Lide died of the plage.
Jan. 16.	Humfrie Lewson, *servant* to Rafe Gentle, died in the stockes of the plage.
Jan. 20.	Francis, the daughter of Peter Lide, died of the plage.
Feb. 8.	Mr. William Bening, *Grocer.*
Mar. 10.	Mr. Christofer Vaghan.
Mar. 13.	Mr. Edward Wanton.
Mar. 15.	Thomas Yates, *Skinner.*

1573

May 15.	Susan, daughter of William Keningham.
June 6.	John Emerie.
July 16.	William, son of William Spencer.
Oct. 31.	A childe, new borne, of Richard Sharpes.
Nov. 13.	Elizabeth, daughter of William Sharlie.
Nov. 20.	Henry Trowghton.
Jan. 29.	Jane, daughter of William Keningham.
Feb. 10.	John Cox, *Tayler.*
Feb. 11.	John, son of the forsayd John Cox.
Mar. 8.	Sara, daughter of William Keningham.

1574

Mar. 8.	Ellin Hall, a maide.
May 10.	George Wattes, *servant.*
July 27.	Thomas, son of William Handford.
Aug. 3.	John Smith, *Shearegrinder*, died at Wansworth, August 3rd, buried in this church August 6th.
Sep. 11.	Agnes Horne, a maide.
Oct. 31.	Alice, daughter of Thomas Gun.
Nov. 11.	Marie, daughter of William Keningham.
Nov. 28.	Richard Blackwall, *servant.*
Dec. 29.	Elizabeth, daughter of William Keningham.
Jan. 10.	Rose Williams, a *maidservant.*
Jan. 20.	Humfrie, son of Thomas Walker.
Jan. 22.	Rebecca, daughter of Thomas Hasell.
Feb. 11.	Anne Best, a *maid servant.*

1575

April 30.	Jone, wife of Thomas Gun.
May 12.	Henry Worthington, a *servant.*
May 23.	Mr. Steven Andros.
June 10.	Judith Masterson, a maide.
June 11.	Richard Sharp, *Goldsmith.*
July 28.	Blanche, daughter of John Mascall.
Sep. 14.	William, son of Daniel Andros.
Sep. 19.	John Crowchman, *Vintner.*
Oct. 10.	Edward Hill, a *servant.*
Jan. 19.	Henrie Slade, a *servant.*
Jan. 29.	Elizabeth Healde, the wife of Thomas Healde, was delivered of two boyes the 28 Januarie, the younger and she died within three howres after she was delivered, and were buried both in one grave, the day following.
Mar. 1.	William Draper.
Mar. 13.	Jane, daughter of Robart Smith.

1576

April 11.	Cicelie Cornelis, a *servant*.
April 15.	Mrs. Margaret Bening, *Widoe*.
April 28.	William Sandie, died of the plage.
June 6.	Anthonie Scurrie.
June 14.	Anne Kidland, *Widoe*.
June 16.	Reynald Jayke, *servant*.
Oct. 17.	Caywood, son of Marc Norton.
Oct. 30.	Nicholas Hale, *Clarke and Sexton to this Church*, dwelling in Scalding Allie, died sodenlie the 29 of October.
Dec. 5.	Jone Wilkinson, *servant*.
Dec. 18.	Agnes, wife of Rafe Yearlie, of St. Olaves, in Southwarke.
Jan. 19.	John, son of Henrie Shepard.
Jan. 31.	Thomas Hodgekins, *servant*.

1577

April 8	Richard Selbie, *Pewterer*.
April 9.	Mrs. Keningham, wife of Robart Keningham.
May 17.	Ellin, daughter of Richard Westerne.
May 19.	Mr. Wighthand, wife of Robart Wighthand.
June 20.	Robert Askewithe, of High Newestead, in the Countie of York and Parish of East Witton, died sodeinlie by the Churche.
July 2.	A new borne child of John Bradlie.
July 16.	William Dee, *Draper*.
July 25.	George, son of George Fenne,
Aug. 16.	Margaret Selbie, *Widoe*.
Aug. 30.	John Birkeheade, *servant*.
Sep. 13.	Samson Farnam.
Sep. 17.	William Smith, a boye, died of the plage.
Oct. 1.	Jane, daughter of William Keale, died of the plage.
Oct. 3.	William Swartbright, *Goldsmith*, died of the plage.
Oct. 28.	William, son of William Witterin.
Nov. 1.	Agnes Greenwood, *servant*, died of the plage.
Nov. 21.	Thomas Walker, *Clothworker*.
Jan. 31.	Frederick, brother to James Berisfourd, and William Crosbie, *servant* to the same James, died of the plage.
Feb. 25.	Henrie Willington, *an olde Bachelor*.
Mar. 16.	Mrs. John Crowchman, *Widoe*.

1578

July 12.	William, son of Mr. Robart Smith, *Draper*.
July 18.	John Wanton.
July 22.	Mr. Humfrie Fainfax.
Aug. 18.	Susan, daughter of William Shakleton, *Goldsmith*.
Sep. 8.	Richard Williamson, died of the plage.
Sep. 17.	Margaret Trice, *Widoe*.
Sep. 22.	A child of Daniel Andros, borne dead.
Sep. 25.	William Leach.
Sep. 25.	Mrs. Ingram, wife of Mr. William Ingram.
Oct. 2.	John Marshall, a *boie*, *servant* to Robart Yarrington, died of the plage.
Oct. 6.	Mathew Hill, *prentice* to Richard Wade, died of the plage.
Oct. 7.	Anne Kerian, *servant* to Thomas Hasel, died of the plage.

Oct. 16.	Robart Tailecote, *servant* to Thomas Allin, *Pewterer*, of St. Sepulchre Parishe, being sick of the plage was sent into the stockes, died there, and was buried 16th daye.
Oct. 16.	William, son of Robart Linge, died of the plage.
Oct. 16.	Steven Brogden, *Draper*, died of the plage.
Oct. 18.	Thomas Cator died of the plage.
Oct. 22.	Samuel, son of Robert Yarrington.
Oct. 23.	Thomas Hassell, *Clothworker*.
Oct. 24.	Nicholas De vere, *bachelor*.
Oct. 24.	Sara, daughter of Richard Wade.
Oct. 27.	Elizabeth Brimstone died of the plage.
Oct. 30.	Roger Sharde, sonne of Mrs. Wade by hir first husband.
Oct. 31.	John Moslie died of the plage.
Nov. 1.	William Saul, *prentice* to Mr. Richard Wade, died of the plage
Nov. 1.	Henrie, son of Michael Abdie, died of the plage
Nov. 3.	William Cator, sonne of Mrs. Abdie by hir first husband, died of the plage.
Nov. 5.	Anne Cator, daughter of the same Mrs. Abdie, died of the plage
Nov. 14.	Nicholas Robinson.
Nov. 16.	Michael Abdie, *Merchanttayler*, died of the plage.
Nov. 27.	Mr. Richard Pelter, buried in the south of the chancel.
Dec. 5.	Thomas, brother and *servant* to Cutbert Boothe.
Dec. 16.	Ellin Colvin, a *servant*.
Dec. 26.	A child, dead borne, of Harrie Shepardes.
Jan. 3.	William Shottesford, *servant*.
Feb. 4.	Ellinor Sharpe, daughter of Mrs. Hawkins by hir fyrste husband.
Feb. 6.	Sara Sharpe, another of hir daughters.
Feb. 7.	Jane, daughter of Steven Brogden.
Feb. 24.	A child, new borne, of Robart Perpoints.
Mar. 1.	Bettrice Morris, a child dieing in the mother's lappe in the streete.
Mar. 7.	Adam Sharpe, son to Mrs. Hawkins by hir first husband.
Mar. 7.	A child, newe borne, of the same Mrs. Hawkins.
Mar. 13.	John Clarke, dieing in St. Stevens Parish.
Mar. 19.	Henrie Sharp, sonne of Mrs. Hawkins.
Mar. 22.	Mrs. Horton, wife of Richard Horton.

1579

April 8.	John Hunte.
May 23.	Mrs. Keningham, wife of Robart Keningham.
Sep. 4.	Rafe Marsham, of Norwich.
Nov. 2.	Mrs. Riche, wife of Mr. John Ryche.
Nov. 21.	Margerie, daughter of Robart Chauntrell.
Mar. 19.	Jone, wife of George Benson.
May 23.	Robart, son of Robart Barnard.

1580

April 20.	Mrs. Jone Bradlie, wife of Richard Bradlie.
April 14.	Alles Eaton, *an old maide*.
July 7.	Judith, daughter of Elizabeth Temes.
Aug. 12.	Jane Jarvis, *a servant*.

Aug. 29.	William Caro, *Sheregrinder.*
Sep. 6.	Thomas, son of John Maskall.
Sep. 21.	Richard, son of Davie Evans.
Sep. 24.	Robert Wighthand, buried in the chancill.
Nov. 2.	A childe, new borne, daughter to Jonas Ladbrooke.
Nov. 8.	Giles Allington, *principall of Lions Inne,* died in this Parish and was buried in St. Clement Danes.
Dec. 18.	Henrie, son of Henrie Butler.
Jan. 29.	Thomas Goodale.
Feb. 16.	Walter Lancaster.

1581

April 25.	John, son of Robart Barnard.
June 14.	Thomas Gun.
July 23.	Raphael Smith.
July 25.	Henrie Barker.
Aug. 2.	Mrs. Turbervile, wife of Basill Turbervile.
Aug. 4.	John, son of Rafe Ewen.
Aug. 9.	Marie, daughter of Mr. Robart Brooke.
Aug. 11.	John Freman.
Aug. 22.	Edward, son of Edward Juxe.
Sep. 5.	Mrs Westwood, wife of Richard Westwood.
Oct. 28.	John Atkins.
Nov. 7.	A newe borne childe of John Sharpes.
Feb. 20.	Daniel, son of Robart Race.
Feb. 28.	Agnes Pavier.

1582

April 6.	Mrs. Wanton, *Widoe.*
April 20.	Robart Boswell, *Skinner.*
April 20.	Katherin Noble, *Widoe,* buried in St. Stevens, died in this parishe, in her sonnes house.
June 19.	Dorithie, daughter of Thomas Lillie.
July 14.	Rafe, son of Isaac Norton.
July 28.	Lidia, daughter of Rafe Ewer.
Aug. 11.	Francis Cole, *Armorer.*
Aug. 29.	Samuel Eliot, *servant* to Mr. Robart Brooke.
Aug. 29.	A newe borne child of Robart Jux.
Sep. 2.	Henrie Meller, *servant* to Mr. Robart Brooke.
Sep. 14.	Thomas, son of William Filian, was baptized [*sic*]
Sep. 30.	Ales, daughter of Kennes, *Widoe.*
Oct. 22.	Judith, daughter of Nicholas Stanns.
Dec. 6.	Michael, son of John Maskall.
Dec. 13.	William Smith.
Dec. 29.	George Dawkes.
Jan. 4.	Thomas Tomson.
Jan. 22.	Mr. William Handford.
Jan. 30.	Marie, daughter of Thomas Nicholls.
Mar. 29.	Elizabeth Dewberie.

1583

April 7.	Gregorie, son of John Sharpe.
April 25.	Mathew, son of Marke Norton.
May 13.	Elizabeth, daughter of William Keningham.

May 25.	Nicholas Huckle.
May 30.	Elizabeth Camock, *servant* to Mr. Ponsabie, of St. Mildreds, was brought sicke of the plage into the stockes, there died.
June 16.	Elizabeth Wicket.
June 30.	Ellin Batteridge.
Nov. 16.	A childe, newe borne, of Edward Juxes.
Nov. 18.	Mrs. Jux, wife of Edward Jux, *Goldsmith.*
Nov. 29.	John Morgane.
Feb. 15.	Edward, son of John Dove.
Feb. 24.	Mr. John Best, *Haberdasher.*

1584

July 7.	John, son of Edward Whorewood.
July 23.	James, son of Samuel Mounger.
Sep. 13.	Marie, daughter of Walter Meers.
Sep. 19.	A child borne to Robart Race.
Nov. 1.	Mrs. Sharp, wife of Mr. John Sharp, died in child bed, and together with hir newe borne childe was buried.
Nov. 7.	A child newe borne of Francis Puckering.
Feb. 12.	Katherin, daughter of John Legge.

1585

April 15.	John, son of Rafe Ewer.
May 1.	Sarah, daughter of Robart Race.
May 5.	Mr. Richard Bradlie, *Haberdasher.*
May 18.	A newe borne child of John Kettlewood.
May 18.	Robart Wig, *Grocer.*
Aug. 18.	Mr. Edmund Ansell, *Skinner.*
Sep. 20.	Mrs. Bowne, *Widow.*
Sep. 20.	Alles, daughter of Thomas Fox.
Oct. 20.	Agnes, wife of William Turner.
Nov. 9.	Mrs. Alice, wife of Robart Yarrington.
Dec. 6.	Thomas, son of Mr. Edward Holmeden, buried in the chancell.
Dec. 12.	Elizabeth, daughter of Mr. Edward Holmden, buried in the same grave.
Dec. 13.	Mrs. Thomazin, wife of Mr. Robart Smith, buried in the chancell.
Jan. 14.	Sarah, daughter of Robart Race.
Jan. 31.	Robart Delve.
Feb. 16.	Thomas, son of Edward Whorewood.
Mar. 4.	Katherin Stronge, *Widoe.*

1586

April 15.	A childe newe borne of Charles Locklie.
May 9.	Susan, daughter of William Smith.
May 20.	Elizabeth, wife of John Kettlewood.
June 8.	Marie, wife of John Davies.
June 28.	Rafe Ewer.
Aug. 16.	Dorithie, daughter of Robart Ranton.
Aug. 24.	Edward Maddersed.
Sep. 21.	Marian Parker, *servant* to Mr. Robart Brooke.

Nov. 8.   Francis West, *a maideservant.*
Nov. 29.   Margaret Smith, *Widoe*, of St. Mildreds Parish.
Dec. 12.   Francis and Edward, twinnes sons of Francis Puckeringe.
Dec. 26.   William Newell, son of Mrs. Monger, by hir first husband.
Jan. 27.   Annie, wife of John Crumpe.

1587

April 3.   Anne, wife of James Willan.
April 3.   Mrs. Rose Best, *Widoe.*
April 18.   Anthonie Buklie.
May 15.   William, son of John Maskall.
June 8.   John Tomson.
June 11.   A newe borne child of Edward Whorewood.
June 23.   John Wilson.
June 30.   Briget, daughter of John Brownelie.
July 13.   Mrs. Margaret Smith, wife of Luke Smith, *Goldsmith.*
July 26.   Mr. Hill, wife of Thomas Hill.
Sep. 4.   Mrs. Crowche, wife of Giles Crowche.
Dec. 9.   Katherin Wilnall, *servant* to Mr. Robart Brooke.
Dec. 18.   Grace Buclie.
Dec. 26.   John Follet.
Jan. 14.   Ellin Dixie.

1588

Mar. 31.   James Willan, *Sexton.*
June 18.   Katherin Linger.
June 24.   Arnold, son of Harrie Shepard.
Aug. 5.   Simon Ball.
Aug. 17.   Anne, daughter of William Jud.
Aug. 18.   Hughe Keershawe.
Sep. 10.   A childe newe borne to William Dutton.
Sep. 11.   Mrs. Dutton, wife of William Dutton.
Oct. 28.   Mrs. Pernel Spencer, wife of William Spencer.
Nov. 8.   Elizabeth, daughter of Edward Jux.
Feb. 10.   A childe newe borne to John Stones.

1589

April 5.   Edward, son of William Jud.
June 8.   Marie, daughter of George Redburne.
July 6.   Ellin Awdlie.
July 15.   A child newe borne of Robart Barnard.
Nov. 19.   Thomas, son of Thomas Chambers.
Nov. 28.   Thomas, son of Rychard Westwood.
Dec. 3.   Jaques Bigwood, *a frenchman.*
Dec. 17.   Jane Whorewood.
Dec. 18.   George Maddox.
Jan. 24.   Erasmus Walpoole, *Gentleman.*
Mar. 5.   Marie, daughter of Rafe Ewer.

1590

April 7.   Ellin, daughter of Cuthbert Bowthe.
April 18.   A child newe borne of John Chambers.

June 21.	Marie, daughter of Thomas Stevenson.
July 9.	Margaret Yates, *Widoe*.
July 9.	George Wilson.
Sep. 5.	Isabell Write, a girle.
Nov. 27.	Marie, daughter of Cuthbert Booth.
Dec. 2.	Daniel Andros, *Draper*.
Jan. 5.	Cicelie Best, *Widoe*, sometime wife of Alexander Best.
Jan. 25.	Mrs. Spencer, wife of William Spencer.
Mar. 7.	Thomas Scot, *Gentleman*.
Mar. 18.	George Hunt, brother and *apprentice* of Richard Hunt.

1591

May 10.	Mrs. Brumlie, wife of John Brumlie, *Baker*.
May 30.	A child newborne of John Chambers.
July 5.	Mr. Edward Puckering, *Gentleman*.
Oct. 19.	Francis Charleton, of east dearham, in norfolke.
Oct. 20.	Francis Saunders, *a servinge man*.
Jan. 27.	Christopher Verlie.
Feb. 10.	Anne, daughter of Thomas Brooke.
Mar. 10.	Mrs. Shackleton, *Widoe*.

1592

April 24.	Marie, daughter of Thomas Chambers.
April 27.	Edmund, son of William Swaine.
Mar. 20.	Giles Clutterbooke.
June 19.	Lidia, daughter of Anthonie Marlow.
June 25.	John, son of George Redburne.
Aug. 25.	Francis Bowton.
Oct. 5.	William Horseman.
Oct. 6.	Richard, daughter of George Belie.
Oct. 10.	Elizabeth Muddle.
Oct. 14.	John, son of John Perkin.
Oct. 30.	Mrs. Swaine, wife of William Swaine the elder.
Oct. 31.	A child newborne of William Baytes.
Nov. 19.	Mr. John Brooke, *Gentleman*, of chinkefard, in essex.
Jan. 27.	Isaac, son of John Balie.
Feb. 10.	Francis Harward.
Feb. 21.	Mr. William Sharlie.
May 6.	Mrs. Whetstone, mother Mr. John Whetstone.

1593

April 15.	Elizabeth, daughter of John Smith.
June 1.	Mr. John Maskall.
July 12.	Steven, son of Robart Barnard.
July 26.	Ellin Wrighte.
July 31.	Francis Coxe.
July 31.	James Buckstone.
Aug. 9.	Anne Sariaunt.
Aug. 10.	Christian, daughter of Harrie Shepard.
Aug. 11.	Ales Worthington.
Aug. 15.	Mary, daughter of Robart De Lew.
Aug. 16.	William Midgelie.
Aug. 20.	William, son of Thomas Chambers.

Aug. 22.	Agnes, daughter of Harrie Shepard.
Aug. 23.	Tannikin van Cowen Bargan, *a french maide.*
Aug. 23.	Thomas Midgelie.
Aug. 25.	John, son of Robert de Lewe.
Aug. 29.	Jeronimie, daughter of Mrs. Handford, *Widoe.*
Aug. 30.	Arthur Lowe.
Sep. 4.	Brian Gawnte.
Sep. 8.	Mr. John King died at Detford.
Sep. 11.	George Smar.
Sep. 15.	Margerie Yong.
Sep. 16.	Walter Carwarden.
Sep. 19.	Thomas Nichols.
Sep. 27.	Jone Barnard.
Nov. 1.	Mistress Nichols, wife of the above named Thomas Nichols, was buried in the chancell.
Nov. 3.	Mistris Hunt, the wife of Mr. Richard Hunt, was buried in the chancell.
Nov. 4.	William Wilkes.
Nov. 26.	Martha, daughter of John Smith.
Dec. 5.	Katherin Cotson.
Dec. 4 [*sic*]	Thomas Jenkinson, *Parson of this Church,* in whose place succeded John Hayward, *Parson.*
Jan. 25.	Ales, wife of John Watkinson.
Jan. 28.	Katherin, daughter of John Watkinson.
Jan. 28.	Marie Barne, servant with the sayd John Watkinson.
Jan. 23.	Anne Watkinson, daughter of the same John Watkinson.
Mar. 1.	Mistris Sharley, *Widoe.*

1594

April 6.	Rebecca, daughter of Richard Hall.
April 20.	John Turnar, *servant* to Mr. Alderman Brooke.
April 30.	Father Pinke, dieing in the stocks.
May 3.	Mrs. Anne Orrel, *Widoe.*
July 6.	Katherin Walters, *servant.*
July 6.	Mrs. Noble, wife of Edward Noble.
Aug. 10.	A childe of Robart Hilles borne dead.
Aug. 13.	A childe at Thomas Hilles borne dead.
Aug. 29.	A childe at Edward Hilles, the childe of a sister of his, borne dead.
Aug. 16.	Tobias, the son of John Waters.
Sep. 2.	Elizabeth, the daughter of Thomas Sharley.
Sep. 7.	A childe of one Smith, a *Taylor,* in bearbinder lane, borne dead.
Sep. 25.	John Glover, *servant* to Richard Hunt.
Oct. 2.	Martin, son of Edward Whorewood.
Oct. 17.	Edward, another son of the same Edward.
Oct. 25.	Mrs. Hall, wife of Richard Hall.
Nov. 5.	Mrs. Griffin, wife Mr. William Griffin.
Nov. 25.	Mrs. Whorewood, wife of Edward Whorewood, in the chancell.
Jan. 8.	Henrie, son of Walter Meares.
Feb. 5.	Ales, daughter of Luke Smith.
Feb. 22.	Mr. Nicholas Staines.

1595

Mar. 27.	Mr. Cherit, of St. Stevens
Feb. 22 [*sic*]	Avis Humbertstone, *an ancient maid*.
April 23.	William, son of Thomas Chambers.
April 30.	Mrs. Ansell, *Widoe*, in the chancell.
Aug. 17.	Bevis, son of Edmund Palmer.
Sep. 9.	Ursula, wife of Harrie Shepard.
Sep. 24.	Giles, son of Robart Dodson.
Nov. 12.	Walter, son of Walter Meares.
Nov. 24.	William Gibbins, of Sussex.
Nov. 26.	A stranger of Lincolneshire, slaine with a bearecarte.
Dec. 30.	John Lovet.
Mar. 6.	A yong childe of William Hayward, brother of John Hayward, *Parson*, borne before the time, buried in the chancell.
Feb. 20.	William Keningham.
Mar. 7.	Morgan Bishop.
Mar. 13.	A childe of Edward Spike, borne dead.

1596

April 5.	Nicholas, son of Robart Rainton.
April 25.	A child of George Gosling, borne dead.
May 20.	Mr. Henrie Quinbie, a *barbarie Merchant*.
June 30.	Jane Trayford.
Oct. 30.	Mrs. Tayler, *Widoe*, moother of Mr. Thomas Chambers wife.
Nov. 3.	Nicholas Draper, of Brumlie, in Kent.*
Nov. 19.	George, son of Mr. Edward Holmden.
Dec. 3.	Mrs. Tomson, *the Poulterer*.
Feb. 3.	A childe newe borne of Richard Web.
Feb. 24.	Mrs. Elizabeth Zanches, wife of Mr. Baltazar Zanches, in the chancell.
Feb. 25.	Nicholas, son of Robart Barnet.
Mar. 1.	Mr. Richard Hunt, in the chancell.
Mar. 12.	Marie, daughter of Robart Rainton.
Mar. 19.	Margaret, the William Keale [*sic.*]
Mar. 21.	William Freestone.

1597

Mar. 29.	Elizabeth, daughter of William Keale.
April 16.	Thomas Fox, *servant* to Mr. Awsten.
April 24.	Henrie, son of John Hill.
	A blakmore, belonging to Mr. John Davies, died in Whitechappel parishe, was laid in the ground in this Churchyard, sine frequentia populi et sine ceremoniis quia utrum christianus esset necne nesciebamus.
May 20.	Mr. John Handford.
May 22.	William Tate.
May 30.	A pore woman dieing here.
Sep. 14.	Mrs. Keningham, widow of William Keningham.
Oct. 13.	Edward Noble dieing here was buried in St. Stephens church.
Oct. 28.	Mr. John Hill.
Dec. 21.	Richard Wade.
Feb. 1.	Anne, daughter of Thomas Chambers.
Mar. 21.	Richard, a yong child of Richard Trowte.

* "Mr. Draper he being a straunger lyeing at Mr. Bettenshaws." Ch. Acc.

1598

April 26. Edward Hutches, of Kingstone.
May 24. Christopher Orwell.
May 31. Marie, daughter of Abraham Grening.
June 29. John Clough, *servant* to Mr. Stokelie.
July 21. Mr. Robart Cotton, *Upholder*.
July 28. Mrs. Cotton, his wife.
Aug. 10. Francis Carter, sister of George Belie.
Sep. 30. Hester, daughter of Edward Whorewood.
Oct. 5. Doctor Crooke, that sometime red the lecture in this church, buried in the chancell.
Oct. 20. John, the son of John Fullam and Elizabeth Sutton.
Oct. 28. Henrie Shepard.
Dec. 1. Edith, daughter of Giles Blake.
Jan. 9. Mr. Edward Whorewood, in the chancell.
Jan. 24. Mrs. Phillippes, sister to Edward Whorewood.

1599

May 31. Jone, daughter of Isaac Kilburne.
July 20. Ales, wife of Mr. Spencer.
July 28. A child of Mr. Whorewoods, newe borne.
Aug. 19. Mr. Giles Crowche, in the chancell.
Sep. 28. John, son of Robart Delewe.
Oct. 2. Mrs. Webster, wife of Mrs. Clement Webster.
Oct. 2. Francis Bretton, a wife out of the house of Mr. Wilkinson.
Oct. 13. Anne, daughter of Mr. Thomas Chambers.
Feb. 13. Isaak, son of Isaak Kilburne.
Dec. 1. [*sic*] Michael Tempest, *Upholder*.
Mar. 2. Elizabeth, daughter of William Harrison.

1600

April 12. Fortune, sister of James Ballard.
April 15. Susan, daughter of Robert Deleawe.
May 13. John Richardson, of Lin.
June 13. James Johnson.
Aug. 10. John, son of George Belie.
Sep. 13. Adam Baker.
Sep. 18. John, son of James Johnson.
Nov. 8. A newe borne childe of Mr. Mitchel.
Nov. 17. Ales Spraie.
Jan. 31. Peter, son of Walter Rode.
Feb. 2 Richard Hewet, *servant* of Luke Smith.
Feb. 3. An, daughter of Adam Baker.
Mar. 17. David Limkok.

1601

Mar. 25. John Car dieing in Mr. Belie's house.
Mar. 31. Marie, daughter of Adam Baker.
April 9. Mr. Robart Brooke, *Alderman*.
April 19. Elizabeth, daughter of Robart de leave.*
May 10. Peter, son of William Harrison.
Aug. 4. A son of Thomas Godfrie, dieing halfe howr after birth.
Aug. 17. Mr. Nicholas Scot, *Grocer*.

* "Mr. Deloie a stranger in Bucklesburie." Ch. Ac.

Sep. 19.	Ellin Parrie.
Nov. 23.	Elizabeth, daughter of Hugh Whitbroke.
Dec. 10.	Mr. William Wortley.
Dec. 17.	Ales Fin, widoe, mother to Mrs. Davies.
Feb. 1.	Giles, son of John de waters.
Feb. 5.	Thomas, son of William Bisband.
Feb. 8.	A childe of Tailors, *Bricklaier,* stilborne.
Feb. 10.	Nathaniel, son of Edward Whorewood.
Feb. 14.	A child of Mr. Nichols, stilborne.
Feb. 15.	John Wingate, *servant* to Mr. Robart Cox.

1602

May 29.	Mr. William Keale.
April 23.	Mr. Robart Bacon.
April 29.	Mr. Baltazer Zanches.
Maie 17.	John, son of John Pedlie.
June 13.	Robart Haughton, *servant* to Thomas Chambers.
June 16.	Marie, daughter of John Balie.
Sep. 1.	Mr. John Pedlie, in the newe churchyard.
Sep. 16.	Elizabeth, daughter of William Croslie.
Sep. 27.	Mrs. Bowth, the wife of Cutbart Bowth.
Nov. 6.	Richard, son of William Nichols.
Dec. 16.	Mr. Robart Rainton.
Dec. 19.	William Goffe.
Feb. 2.	John Squire.
Feb. 4.	Marie Alcock, *servant* to Mr. Nevell.
Feb. 14.	Anthonie, son of John Warren.

Moritur screnissima regina Elizabetha die proxm mensis martii 24 et eodem die foelicissimis auspitiis imperium potentissimi domini nostri Jacobi angliœ scotiœ franciœ et hiberniœ Regis inchoatur.

1603

Mar. 31.	Susan, daughter of Thomas Harwar.
April 11.	Oliver, son of William Harpar.
Maie 13.	Edward Beamont, *servant* to Mr. Houghton.
July 3.	Mr. William Wilson.
July 3.	Robart Shackleton.
July 15.	A newe borne childe of Mrs. Wilsons.
July 15.	Ales Wighton.
July 17.	Mrs. Wilson.
July 19.	William Wilsons sonne.
July 19.	Marie Wilson.
July 19.	Jane Sharpe.
July 21.	Mr. Blage.
July 24.	Mrs. Ware.
July 25.	An Wilkins.
July 26.	Brian White.
Aug. 2.	William Blage.
Aug. 5.	Giles Blage.
Aug. 6.	Jacob Ware.
Aug. 8.	Mr. Warrens mother.
Aug. 9.	George Blage.
Aug. 17.	Judith Salter.

Aug. 19.	Robart Cowell.
Aug. 27.	William Halsted.
Aug. 30.	Elizabeth Moulton.
Sept. 6.	Henrie Ward.
Sep. 11.	John Wilkins.
Sep. 12.	Henrie Clarke.
Sep. 12.	William Sharlie.
Sep. 13.	Edward Barnard.
Sep. 13.	Sara Smith.
Sep. 20.	Sara Daniel,
Sep. 20.	Marie Harpar.
Sep. 26.	Mr. Robart Barnard.
Sep. 28.	Ele Greene.
Sep. 24. [*sic*]	William Jones.
Sep. 30.	John Smalshewe.
Oct. 1.	Ales Jonson.
Oct. 1.	· Mr. George Belie.
Oct. 1.	Susan Barnard.
Oct. 1.	Robart Lodge.
Oct. 3.	Henrie Barnard.
Oct. 3.	Samuel Barnard.
Oct. 9.	John Briges.
Oct. 13.	William Balie.
Oct. 14.	Ezechiel Bailie.
Oct. 16.	Christopher Keies.
Oct. 20.	Dorothie Balie.
Oct. 30.	Mrs. Susan Foldo.
Oct. 31.	Elizabeth Harper.
Oct. 31.	Katherin Harper.
Nov. 3.	John Norton.
Nov. 3.	John Balie.
Nov. 18.	Crysogon Norton.
Nov. 29.	Mrs. Vaghan.
Dec. 4.	Mr. Isaak Norton.
Dec. 17.	Robart Palie.
Jan. 1.	William Tuckoe,
Jan. 17.	Mr. Luke Smith.
Mar. 2.	Robart Fermor.
Mar. 22.	Alexander Rosewel.

1604

April 8.	Thomas Daniel.
July 4.	Simon Balie.
July 6.	Mr. Odiern, *Curate in this church.*
Sep. 21.	Elizabeth, daughter of William Nichols.
Jan. 23.	Martha Andrewes.
Jan. 28.	old mystris Handford.
Feb. 27.	Elizabeth Johnson, out of Mr. Gales house.
Mar. 17.	Mrs. An Chamberlaine, the wife of Mr. Edmund Chamberlaine, of Compton Abdale, in Glostershire, was buried in our chancell.
Mar. 17.	A child of Mr. Sone, *Goldsmith*, not baptized.

1605

Maie 18.	Marie, daughter of Thomas Godfrie.

Maie 30.	Mrs. Fish, the wife of Mr. Cornelius Fish, chamberlaine of London, buried in the chancell.
June 20.	The Wido Davies, moother of Mr. John Davies.
Aug. 1.	Dorithie, daughter of Jerome Rawstone.
Oct. 28.	Alexander Parrie, *servant* to Mr. Crewe.
Nov. 6.	Daniel Gwin, *servant* to Mr. Fysh.
Nov, 6.	Marie, daughter of Daniel Fookes.
Jan. 4.	Mrs. Bird, of Walden, sometime wife of Mr. Nicholas Stanes, of the Parish, was buried in the chancel.
Feb. 15.	Mrs. Nichols, wife of Mr. William Nichols.
Feb. 17.	Mr. Henrie Lanman, in our chancel.
Mar. 24.	Mrs. Ditchfeild, wife of Mr. Edward Ditchfeild.

1606

April 4.	John, son of Mr. William Rogers.
April 28.	Richard Elmewood, *servant* to the same Rogers.
Maie 15.	Martha, daughter of Thomas Godfrie.
Maie 17.	A still borne childe of Mrs. Nevels.
June 4.	Francis Vaghan, *servant* to Mr. Hill in Lumbard Strete.
July 6.	Sara, daughter of John Nevel.
July. 21.	John, son of John Denbrooke.
July 22.	Maptha, daughter of Richard Smith.
Aug. 11.	Mrs. Marie Parkin (called Mrs. Barkabie) *Midwife*, dieing in St. Toolies.
Aug. 17.	Elizabeth Jones.
Sep. 18.	Marie, daughter of James Sharlie.
Oct. 26.	Mr. William Mathewes.
Sep. 15.	Samuel Brushford.
Jan. 23.	A still borne childe of Mr. Laskers.

1607

April 10.	Mrs. Bisband, wife of Mr. William Bisband, of the blackfriars.
June 24.	John Ward, *servant* to Mr. Soane, *Goldbeater.*
July 14.	Thomas, son of Thomas Martin.
July 20.	William, son of William Rogers.
Sep. 22.	Florence Caldwel, *servant* to Mr. Clarke.
Sep. 26.	Peter Poole, *servant* to Mr. Clarke.
Oct. 18.	Mr. William Austin.
Dec. 14.	Elizabeth, daughter of Mr. Humfrie Handford.
Dec. 16.	Peter, son of Richard Lambart.
Jan. 6.	Mathew, son of James Laiton.
Jan. 12.	Joane, the wife of Leonard Brushford.
Feb. 14.	Richard Bowne.
Mar. 1.	Robart, son of Robart Mathewe.
Mar. 11.	Robart Hutchinson.

1608

April 23.	Thomas Harris, *servant* to Mrs. Austin.
April 23.	Thomas, son of Thomas Kopestake.
Maie 20.	Marie, daughter of William Chapman.
June 20.	Susan, daughter of Thomas Harwar.
June 30.	Marget Ranton.

Sep. 25.	Elizabeth Waies.
Oct. 12.	Robart Holland*
Oct. 20.	Alice Wilkinson, *Widoe*.
Oct. 23.	Thomas King.
Nov. 3.	John Welner.
Nov. 6.	Josias, son of Josias Some.
Nov. 23.	John Reeve.
Nov. 24.	Elizabeth, daughter of John Collins.
Nov. 26.	Edmund Richardson.
Dec. 19.	Richard Ansterlie.
Dec. 29.	Edward Den.
Jan. 4.	Margret, daughter of John Wolliston.

1609

Mar. 29.	Jaspar, son of John de Waters.
April 22.	Susan, wife of Abednego Seagrave.
May 14.	Katherin, wife Henrie Squire.
May 20.	John Ellam.
May 27.	Marie Needes.
June 13.	Mrs. Baker, daughter of Mr. Garret Warde.
June 28.	Mr. John Peerson.
July 18.	Elizabeth, daughter of Thomas Kopstake.
July 20	Robart, son of Robart Knight.
Aug. 7.	William Brushford.
Aug. 17.	Marie, wife of Edmund Dawnie.
Aug. 23.	John, son of Anthonie Sturtivant.
Aug. 23.	George Smith.
Sep. 4.	Elizabeth Spragges.
Sep. 13.	Thomas, son of Thomas Martin.
Sep. 17.	Marie Cole.
Sep. 29.	Henage Ograve or Ogard [*sic*]
Oct. 14.	A newe borne child of Mr. Daniel Denbrooke.
Oct. 16.	Barbara Denbrooke, mother of the same child, was buried in the chancell.
Dec. 7.	Thomas, son of Thomas Harwar.
Jan. 3.	Marie, daughter of John Wolliston.
Feb. 15.	John Allen.
Mar. 3.	Thomas Hamson.

1610

April 11.	Jane Severie.
June 30.	Mr. William Crosslie.
Sep. 9.	An Tailer.
Sep. 17.	A stilborne maidchilde of Mr. Nevels.
Sep. 22.	Thomas Ranton.
Oct. 24.	Isaac, son of John Nevell.
Nov. 22.	Judith, wife of Robart Rawlins.
Dec. 30.	Thomas Savill, brother to Leonard Savill.
Dec. 30.	A stilborne child of Mr. Prince.
Jan. 5.	Elizabeth, daughter of James Haws.
Feb. 18.	Brian Watson, *servant* to Mr. Aske.
Mar. 5.	Agnes Tayler, Mrs. Handford's *nurse*.

* "Payde more the Goodman Redburne for a knell at the buryall of Robert Holland, a stranger." Ch. acc.

1611

Mar. 29.	Katherine Hitches, *servant* to Mr. Darnelie.
April 22.	Ursula Knight, mother of Mr. John Knight.
May 6.	James Pedlie, son of John Pedlie.
May 14.	Marie, the wife of Thomas Hocket.
May 16.	Joseph, the son of Robart Hammond.
June 2.	Sara, daughter of William Bispham
June 26.	Robart, son of Robart Knight.
July 14.	Richard, son of William Harrison.
Aug. 21.	Samuel, son of Edmund Dawnie.
Aug. 26.	Elizabeth, the wife Mr. John Hawkins.
Sep. 16.	Thomas Mighton.
Oct. 15.	Thomas Hawstede, *servant* to Mr. Kopestake.
Jan. 4.	Sindonie, daughter of Edward Clarke.
Feb. 4.	John, son of James Lasher.
Feb. 11.	An Harrington.
Mar. 3.	William, son of Robart Knight.

1612

Mar. 27.	John Slanison, out of Mr. Kopestake's house.
May 19.	Mr. Garret Warde.
May 25.	John Clench, brother-in-law to Mr. Moise.
June 19.	Augustine, son of Edmund Dawnie.
June 29.	Margaret, wife of Mr. John Davies.
Aug. 29.	Elizabeth, wife of John Fyshe, *our Parishe Clarke.*
Sep. 30.	A manchild stilborne, sonne of Mr. Richard Waterfall.
Oct. 16.	Mr. Henrie Nicholson.
Feb. 2.	Mark Humble.

1613

April 1.	Mrs. Sara Handford, wife of Mr. Humfrie Handford, her bodie lieth in the new vault in the north Ile by the chancell.
May 8.	Marie Greensmith.
July 6.	Robart, son of Mr. Artur Earth.
June 20 [*sic*]	Mr. William Moselie.
July 17.	A sonne of Mr. Martins, unbaptized, was buried.
July 20.	John Haselenie *servant* to Mr. Marsh.
Aug. 16.	Mr. Richard Scot.
Sep. 15.	Katherin, daughter of Thomas Hocket.
Oct. 4.	Mrs. Elizabeth Grenewaie, wife of Erasmus Grenewaie.
Oct. 14.	Joane, daughter of Richard Hill.
Nov. 29.	Jonas Odar, brother to Mrs. Trowte.
Feb. 18.	John Yonge, *servant* to Mr. Nightingale.
Mar. 7.	James, son of Edward Hammond.

1614

Mar. 25.	Ffrancis Marshe, father to John Marshe.
April 2.	John, son of Thomas Kopestake.
April 28.	John Wade, an aged man, out of Mr. Wollistone's house.
May 3.	Marget, daughter of John Wollistone.
June 4.	A stilborne child of Robart Hammond.
June 11.	Mrs. Hammond, mother of that child.
Aug. 11.	George, son of Thomas Milles.

Aug. 12.	Dorithie, daughter of Francis Stuchworth.
Aug. 20.	Richard Laicolt, out of the counter.
Sep. 1.	Edward, son of Thomas Martin.
Oct. 22.	Elizabeth, daughter of Roger Nightingale.
Oct. 23.	John, son of Edmund Dawnie.
Oct. 20.	An Vaghan, daughter of Robart Vaghan.
Dec. 12.	William, son of Robart Knight.
Dec. 18.	A stillborne childe of Richard Margerison.
Jan. 6.	Ales, daughter of Robart Aske.
Jan. 10.	Hanna, daughter of Mr. William Fermor.

1615

April 20.	An, daughter of Richard Bennet.
April 28.	William Norman, *servant* to Leonard Harbart.
July 5.	John Watkinson, *an aged man.*
June 5.	Marie, daughter of Mr. Humfrie Handford.
June 15.	A stilborne childe of Georg Ward.
Aug. 30.	Edward, son of William Nichols.
Sep. 20.	Marie, daughier of Thomas Godfrie.
Oct. 13.	Elizabeth, daughter of Richard Bennet.
Oct. 21.	An, wife of Edward Haughton.
Oct. 21.	Marie, daughter of Robart Vaghan.
Oct. 26.	William, son of Edward Haughton.
Nov. 9.	Elizabeth, daughter of James Laiton.
Nov. 12.	Peter Norwood, *servant* to James Chamberlaine.
Dec. 9.	James Laiton.
Dec. 13.	John, son of John Sanders.
Jan. 17.	Elizabeth, wife of Dudlie Hawkes.
Jan. 22.	Elizabeth, wife of Abraham Grening.
Jan. 26.	Margaret, wife of John Fish.
Feb. 7.	Jane, wife of Clement Webster.

1616

Mar. 25.	Henrie Grene, *servant* to Edward Clarke.
April 4.	Humfrie, son of Mr. Humfrie Handford.
April 25.	Isabel, wife of Mr. Anthonie Crewe.
May 8.	Thomas Chamberlaine.
June 20.	John Smith.
June 22.	Marie, daughter of Edward Hammond.
July 6.	William, son of John Nevel.
July 13.	Daniel Simcoks, *servant* to Thomas Harwar.
July 15.	John, son of Richard Eaton.
July 20.	Richard Eaton, the father.
Aug. 20.	Joane, wife of Georg Redburne.
Sep. 25.	Elizabeth, wife of Christopher Lanman.
Oct. 16.	Sindonie, wife of Edward Clarke.
Jan. 7.	Mr. Clement Webster.
Mar. 19.	Mr. John Nevel.

1617

Mar. 4.	Ales Norton, *Widoe.*
April 9.	Mr. James Haies.
April 21.	George, son of Thomas Bracie,

May 2.	Marie, daughter of John Wollistone.
June 2.	Mr. James Sharlie.
July 23.	Anne, daughter of William and Marie Foster, of Newcastle,
Aug. 22.	Ester, daughter of Robart Neaue.
Aug. 29.	Robart, son of Robart Knight.
Sep. 24.	Robart, son of Thomas Evans.
Sep. 28.	John, son of Thomas Milles.
Oct. 8.	Anne Balme, *servant* of John Sanders.
Nov. 15.	Samuell, the wife of Doctor Crooke, after of Mr. Leech, was buried in the chancell by her first husband.
Jan. 12.	Mr. Francis Suthworth.
Jan. 21.	Humphrey, son of Edward Ditchfield.

1618

June 20.	Magdalene, wife of Anthonie Bawes.
June 26.	George, son of George Ballarbie.
June 26.	Mr. John Moyse.
July 5.	Edward Finch, *servant* to Robart Andwres [*sic*].
July 23.	Mr. Roger Nightingale.
Sep. 4.	Marie, daughter of Thomas Marshall.
Sep. 24.	Richard, son of Mr. Richard Bennett.
Sep. 24.	Mr. John Hayward *Batchlor in Divinitie and Parson of Woolchurch* deceased the eleventh and was buried the 15th October after he had lived in this parrish fowre and twentie yeares and three quarters. Et in eius Locum institutus est Richardus Crooke, Rector huius ecclesiæ.
Oct. 16.	Richard, son of Thomas Martyn.
Dec. 2.	George Redburne. *sexton* of St. Marie Woolchurch.
Jan. 8.	Jane Harbert, wife of Leonard Harbert.
Jan. 18.	John Underwood, *servant* to Mr. Abraham Greeninge.
Mar. 11.	Jane, daughter of Mr. Thomas Harwas.
Mar. 18.	Ester, daughter, of Mr. Robat Dodson.

1619

April 15.	Philip Durant, *a stranger.*
May 12.	William Brockes, partner with Mr. Edward Ditchfeild.
June 10.	Elizabeth, daughter of John and Melior Beast.*
Aug. 1.	Melior, daughter of Mr. William Walton.
Aug. 19.	Susan, wife of Mr. Francis Brown, was buried at St. Michaels in Cornehill, out of our Parish.
Sep. 3.	Leonard Harbert.
Sep. 14.	Elizabeth Disbrough, *servant* Mr. Croker.
Sep. 18.	Emma Ashby, *Widdowe,* and *stranger* or *soinener* in this Parish.
Oct. 4.	A childe of Richard Crooke, *Parson* of St. Marice Woolchurch, being borne in St. Christopher's Parish, was buried in the quire of St. Mary Woolchurch.
Nov. 14.	Edward, son of Mr. Richard Bennett, and Judith his wife.
Nov. 15.	Justina, wife of Richard Troute.
Nov. 28.	John Jackson, *servant* to Mr. Thomas Jackson.
Dec. 12.	A child of Richard Wrighte, and Ann his wife, being still borne.
	[N.B. An entry erased, with marginal note, also erased.]

* *Meriall* has had the pen drawn through it.

Jan. 5.　　Jane, the widdowe of Leonard Harbert.
Feb. 19.　　John, son of John Duwaters,

1620

April 2.　　Alice Peasie, *servant* unto William Steevenson and Jane
　　　　　　his wife.
April 19.　　A child of George Baly and Katheryn his wife, being still
　　　　　　borne.
June 14.　　John, son of John Baker and Elizabeth his wife.
June 28.　　Martha, daughter of George Ward and Elizabeth his wife.
June 30.　　Christopher, son of Robert Androws and Ann his wife.
July 18.　　Easter, daughter of Robert Neave and Elizabeth his wife.
July 23.　　Mr. Dannil Danbrooke.
Aug. 24.　　Mary Warde, *servant* to Richard Jenkinson and Elinor his
　　　　　　wife.
Aug. 28.　　Edward, son of Lewis Swayne and Grace his wife.
Nov. 9.　　Ann Tenby, *servant* to Edmund Rufford, *stranger*.
Dec. 2.　　William Deacon, *Comfitt Maker*.
Jan. 26.　　Thomas, son of Thomas Martin and Mary his wife.
Feb. 21.　　Thomas Vaughan, *servant* to George Bayly and Kateryne
　　　　　　his wife.
Feb. 22.　　Richard Carrill, *servant* to Edward Hammond and Eliza-
　　　　　　beth his wife.
Mar. 2.　　William Molcott, *stranger* and *Goldsmith*.
Mar. 18.　　A child still borne of William Ratcliefe and Grissell his wife.

1621

April 30.　　Nicholas, son of John Marsh and Margrett his wife.
May 4.　　Mr. Richard Laurence.
May 10.　　Mary, daughter of John Perry and Kateryne his wife.
May 12.　　Adam Seatree, *servant* to Lewis Swayne.
June 1.　　Mary, daughter of Erasmus Greenway and Barbara his
　　　　　　wife.
July 14.　　A child still borne of Thomas Henborough and Joane his
　　　　　　wife.
July 18.　　Mr. Richard Trought.
July 19.　　Joane the wife of Thomas Henborough.
Aug. 23.　　Garratt, son of George Ward and Anne his wife.
Aug. 29.　　John Simons, *servant* to Mr. John Clarke.
Sep. 19.　　A child stilborne of Mr. John Fish and Alse his wife.
Oct. 29.　　Thomas Henborough.
Oct. 29.　　Richard, son of Henery Marsh and Anne. his wife.
Dec. 5.　　Mr. Robert Coxe, *gentleman*, deceased Nov. 21.
Dec. 11.　　A child stilborne of John Hoges and Bessie his wife.
Jan. 29.　　Margrett, wife of Mr. Thomas Ball.
Mar. 25.　　A child stilborne of William Weeb.

1622

April 13.　　Thomas, son of Mr. Thomas Harwar and Katerine his wife.
April 30.　　Mr. James Brooke, son of Sir Robert Brooke and Elizabeth
　　　　　　his Lady.
June 14.　　Thomas, son of Lewis Swaine and Grace his wife.
July 9.　　A child still borne of Edward Snowdon and Penina his wife.

Aug. 2.	John, son of Dudley Hawke and Elizabeth his wife.
Aug. 5.	Mrs. Jone Ward, *Wydowe.*
Sep. 11.	Margarett Silward, *servant* to Mr. Calcott.
Oct. 6.	Sara, daughter of John Best and Melier his wife.
Nov. 8.	Mary, daughter of John Saunders, and Em his wife.
Nov. 16.	Richard Owen, *servant* to John Perry and Katherine his wife.
Dec. 11.	Jane Sheppard, *Wydowe.*
Dec. 17.	A young child of Robert Lander and Martha his wife.
Jan. 9.	Mr. Cuthbert Booth.
Jan. 9.	Raph Kent, *servant* to Mr. Pollard.
Mar. 6.	Thomas Norman, *servant* to Mathew Hiller and Elizabeth his wife.
Mar. 15.	Henry, son of Richard Billedge, and Sara his wife.

1623

Mar. 29.	Edward Dally, *stranger* at our Parishe.
May 3.	John, son of John Fishe and Alice his wife.
May 24.	Mr. Daniel Darnelly, of Colchurch Parishe.
May 31.	John, son of John Marsh, and Margarett his wife.
Aug. 5.	Mrs. Neve, wife of Robert Neve.
Aug. 7.	Mr. Robert Knight of Abchurch Parishe.
Aug. 26.	Josuah, son of Thomas Stevens and Mary his wife.
Sep. 11.	A child still borne of John Pettus, and Mary his wife.
Sep. 19.	A child still borne of Richard Hamden and Elizabeth his wife.
Sep. 27.	Edward Smalshawe, *Apothecarie.*
Oct. 15.	A child still borne of Robert Lander and Martha his wife.
Sep. 27.	James Cleanes, *servant* to Mr. Little.
Nov. 5.	Ann, daughter of Abraham Greening,
Nov. 15.	John, son of John Fowler and Rebecca his wife.
Nov. 28.	John May, *servant* to Sir Robert Brooke.
Nov. 30.	Rebecca, daughter of Robert Knight and Percis his wife.
Dec. 12.	John, son of Thomas Marshall and Hester his wife.
Dec. 18.	Mrs. Fishe, wife to Mr. Cornelius Fishe.
Jan. 4.	Ann, daughter of Richard Chamberlin and Mary his wife.
Feb. 3.	A child still borne of Thomas Jackler and Mary his wife.

1624

June 25.	Elizabeth, daughter of John Fishe and Ales his wife.
Aug. 4.	John, son of Calibb Ewre and Sara his wife.
Aug. 24.	Richard Warren, *stranger.*
Aug. 26.	Elizabeth, wife of Thomas Copestake.
Sep. 7.	Judith Cooke, *servant to* Mr. Merifeild.
Sep. 8.	Mary, daughter of Abraham Greening, and Mary his wife.
Sep. 9.	Mrs. Austen, *Widdow.*
Sep. 29.	Edward Bell, *servant* to Mr. Nichols.
Oct. 1.	Mr. Abraham Greening.
Oct. 11.	William Harrison, *Sargion.*
Nov. 5.	Rutland, son of Edward Snoden and Pennia his wife.
Nov. 16.	Raphe, son of Raphe Merifeild and Judith his wife.
Dec. 23.	A childe, still borne of Richard Chamberlen and Mary his wife.
Dec. 28.	Mrs. Squyre, sister to Mr. Harwar, buried by night.

Feb. 4.	A child, new borne, William Douns, and Elizabeth his wife.
Feb. 4.	Mr. Thomas Copestake.
Feb. 11.	Katherin, wife of Thomas Whitborne, by night.
Feb. 24.	Mr. Robard Aske.

1625

April 15.	Isack Lander, brother to Robert Lander.
June 14.	Abednego Seagrave, dwelling with Mr. Seagrave.
June 16.	John Tidd, *servant* to Mr. Seagrave.
June 25.	Ann West, *servant* to Mr. Seagrave, of the plague.
July 19.	Mr. Anthony Calcock.
July 23.	Ann Chamberlen, *Widdow*.
July 27.	Mr. John Langley, of the plague.
July 31.	Mary, daughter of Henry Marshe and Ann his wife.
Aug. 5.	Mr. Abednego Seagrave.
Aug. 8.	Mr. William Traeston.
Aug. 9.	Mr. Richard Chamberlin.
Aug. 9.	Robard —— [*sic*] *servant* to Calibb Ure, of the plague.
Aug. 10.	Mrs. Hayward, *Widow*, of the plague.
Aug. 13.	Rowland Fisher, *servant* unto Calibb Ure, of the plague.
Aug. 13.	William Bond, *servant* unto Richard Chamberlin, of the plague.
Aug. 19.	Phillis, daughter of George Bayley, of the plague
Aug. 20.	Mrs. Harrison, *Widdow*, of the plague.
Aug. 22.	William Dickinson, dwelling with Thomas Dickinson his uncle, died of the plague.
Aug. 23.	Robard, son of Marke Humble, of the plague.
Aug. 27.	Sara, daughter of William Webb, of the plague.
Aug. 27.	Thomas Gayle, of the plague.
Aug. 27.	Ellen Watkins, *Widdow*, of the plague.
Aug. 27.	Margarett Usherwood, *servant* unto Richard Wright.
Aug. 29.	Elizabeth, wife of Richard Matchitt, of the plague.
Aug. 29.	Katherin Currim, *servant* to Mr. Seagrave, of the plague.
Aug. 30.	Abagaile, daughter of Marke Hamble, of the plague.
Sep. 2.	Richard Matchitt, of the plague.
Sep. 3.	Thomas Cockill, *servant* to George Bayley, of the plague.
Sep. 5.	Rebecca, daughter of William Harrison, of the plague.
Sep. 7.	Thomas, son of George Bayley, of the plague.
Sep. 7.	Henry Payres, *servant* to Mr. Nicholes.
Sep. 8.	Robard Edwards, *Gooldbeater*, of the plague.
Sep. 3 [*sic*]	Elizabeth, daughter of John Woollerstone, of the plague.
Sep. 8.	Grace Nash, mother to Mrs. Swayne.
Sep. 10.	Susan Waterhouse and Elizabeth Fawkner, both out of one house, of the plague.
Sep. 12.	Sara, daughter of Richard Matchett, of the plague.
Sep. 13.	Elizabeth, daughter of Richard Matchett, of the plague.
Sep. 15.	Michell Cuff, *servant* to Mr. Nicholes, of the plague.
Sep. 16.	Thomas Thomlin, *servant* to Mr. Buxton, of the plague.
Sep. 16.	Nicholas Mayer, *Gooldbeater*, of the plague.
Sep. 16.	Jacob Vanspeare, of the plague.
Sep. 17.	John Woollerston, *Sexton of our Parish*.
Sep. 22.	Easter, daughter of Thomas Marshall and Hester his wife, of the plague.
Sep. 23.	Daniell Sherley, *servant* to Mr. Slow, of the plague.

Sep. 24.	Mr. Thomas Marshall, of the plague.
Sep. 24.	Mr. Christopher Lanman.
Sep. 24.	Elizabeth, daughter of Robard Neve, of the plague.
Oct. 21.	Mr. Beniamyn Buxton.
Nov. 1.	Sir Humphrey Handford, dyed at Woodford and was buried in his vawte at Woolchurch.
Dec. 12.	Warner, son of Raphe Merifeild and Judith his wife.
Jan. 1.	Mr. Lanman.
Jan. 3.	John Smith, *servant* to Mr. Slow, of the plague.
Feb. 5.	Easter, daughter of Erasmus Greeenway and Barbara his wife.
Feb. 27.	Mrs. Eaton, wife of Mr. Theophilus Eaton, daughter to Mr. Hiller.
Feb. 30.	Margrett Smith, *Widdow.*
Mar. 2.	Mr. Richard Hamden.
Mar. 21.	Richard Hodgson, *servant* to Richard More.
Mar. 22.	Thomas, son of William Copeland and Barbara his wife.

1626

April 13.	Mrs. John Marsh, *Church Warden.*
April 27.	Mrs. Woolfall, wife of Mr. John Woolfall.
June 15.	Mrs. Whare, sister to Mr. Ball.
June 20.	A child still born of John Mayo and Ursley his wife.
June 24.	Ursley, wife of John Mayo, died in childbed.
Sep. 7.	Mr. Richard Boolton.
Sep. 16.	Mr. Cornelius Fish, *Chamberlin of London.*
Sep. 18.	Cicily Williams, *servant* to Mr. Nicholes.
Sep. 25.	Robard Andrewes, *Beadle of this Parish.*
Nov. 15.	A child still borne of William Stookes.
Dec. 11.	William, son of William Stookes,
Jan. 13.	Henry Hadsall, son of Mr. Hadsall.
Jan. 16.	Mr. John Daves, from broad street.
Feb. 5.	Fagain Gwin, *Widoer,* and dwelt above in the stockes.
Mar. 11.	Francis Smalley, *servant* to Mr. Greenway, in bearbinder lane.

1627

April 16.	Mrs. Eure, *Widdow.*
June 11.	Thomas, son of Thomas Hockett and Ann his wife.
July 8.	John, son of William Hooke and Ann his wife.
Aug. 24.	John Wild, *servant* to Mr. Brookes.
Sep. 24.	John, son of Mathew White and Elizabeth his wife.
Sep. 24.	Francis, son of John Fish and Ales his wife.
Sep. 26.	Mr. Edward Clarke, by night.
Oct. 27.	Mr. Georg Bayley.
Nov. 2.	Mary Pickering, *servant* Mr. Edward Salter.
Mar. 14.	John, son of John Saunders, and Emma his wife.

1628

May 22.	Mrs. Brookes, *widdow,* deceased 16th, buried by night.
June 21.	Ruth, daughter of John Fowler and Rebecca his wife.
July 3.	William Wortha, *servant* to Mr. Whare.
Aug. 13.	James Watson, *servant* to Mr. White.
Sep. 17.	William, son of Richard Kennett and Elizabeth his wife.

Oct. 11.	Henry Butler, *servant* to Mr. Woolfall.
Dec. 11.	Martha, daughter of Mr. Edward Ditchfield.
Feb. 17.	Suzan Willan, wife of Edward Willan.

1629

April 6.	Margrett, daughter of John Scott, and Dorithie his wife.
April 21.	Ann Rigbee, wife of Gilbert Rigbee.
April 26.	Mary, daughter of Miles Codd.
May 1.	Mary Warner, *servant* to Mr. Cox.
June 7.	Ann, daughter of John Fish and Ales his wife.
June 8.	Mrs. Ann, daughter of Sir Robard Brookes and the Lady his wife.
July 16.	Margeritt, daughter of Gilbert Rigbee and Ann his wife.
July 29.	Mrs. Boolton, *Widdow*, and pentioner of the Parish.
July 31.	Hanna, daughter of Robard Tompson and Ellin his wife, was baptized the 30th of July, and was buried the 31st July.
Aug. 1.	Mrs. Gayle, *Widdow*, and pentioner of the Parish.
Aug. 18.	Mr. Richard Wright.
Sep. 8.	Edmond, son of Martin Pollard, and Mary his wife.
Oct. 8.	Mr. John Webber, by night.
Nov. 5.	Mrs. Fowler, wife of John Fowler.
Feb. 4.	Mrs. Seale, wife of Robart Seale and daughter to Mr. Ball, died in childbed.
Feb. 19.	Sir Thomas Crooke, *Knight Baronett of Ireland*, and died in Coleman Street, was buried in St. Mary Woolchurch by night.
Feb. 25.	Mrs. Francis Brookes, the wife of Mr. John Brookes, died at Westminster.
Mar. 16.	A child still borne, Richard Kennett and Elizabeth his wife.
Mar. 19.	Thomas, son of John Seed and Judith his wife.
Mar. 20.	Martha Swan, died in Captain Ditchfield's house.

1630

April 6.	Mrs. Yeardley, wife of Thomas Yeardley.
May 4.	John Davis, an old man that lay above in the stockes.
June 19.	Water Browne, *stranger* and brother to Mrs. Grantt.
July 12.	Mrs. Banes.
July 28.	Thomas Nicholes, brother to Mr. William Nicholes.
Aug. 24.	Mary, daughter of Hugin Hovell, and Mary his wife.
Nov. 2.	Robard Hull, *servant to* Sir Robard Brookes.
Dec. 9.	Suzan, daughter of Edward Chamberlin and Rose his wife.
Jan. 3.	A child still borne of William Copeland and Barbara his wife.
Jan. 10.	John, son of John Nodes and Margrett his wife.
Feb. 11.	Suzanna, daughter of John Juman, *stranger*, baptized 10th February, buried 11th.
Feb. 24.	Edward Weekes, *Comfet maker.*
Mar. 10.	Mrs. Worthington, wife of William Worthington.
Mar. 15.	Henry, son of Anthony Light and Abigaile his wife.
Mar. 22.	Loveday, daughter of Henry Ware, and Sara his wife.

1631

April 19.	Mrs. Ditchfield, wife of Captaine Ditchfield.

April 23.	Mrs. Longe, wyfe of Mr. Valentyne Longe, *Gentleman.*
May 31.	Margrett Shrimshaw, kineswoman to Mr. Browne.
June 8.	Mrs. Avarell, mother to Mrs. Harwar.
June 22.	Mr. Roger Dagg.
Sep. 17.	Nicholas, son of Robard and Joane Jackson.
Sep. 17.	John Merbery, *servant* to Mr. Stookes.
Sep. 17.	Ann, daughter of John and Emma Sanders.
Oct. 22.	Joane, wife of Robard Jackson *our Sexton*, died in child-bed.
Oct. 31.	Mr. John Marshall.
Dec. 26.	A child still borne of John and Mary Pettis.
Jan. 1.	Bridgett, daughter of John and Emma Sanders.
Jan. 14.	Sibell Clarke, *servant* to Mr. Greenway.
Feb. 13.	Robard Jackson, *Sexton of this Parish.*
Feb. 17.	Samuell, son of John and Emma Sanders.
Mar. 6.	Elizabeth, daughter of Mr. John Brookes, dyed at Westminster, and was buried in St. Mary Woolchurch by night.

1632

April 6.	Richard, son of Mr. Richard and Mary Lee.
April 11.	Two twins, still borne, of Gilbert and Margrett Rigbee.
April 20.	Ruth, daughter of Nathanaell and Mary Seaman.
May 14.	Mrs. Ann Handford, died at Woodford, and was buried in St. Marie Woolchurch by night.
May 22.	Mrs. Morris, wyfe of John Morris, died at Westminster.
July 29.	Mrs. Kennett, wyfe of Richard Kennett, died in childbed, and was buried by night.
Aug. 1.	Mrs. Lewes Swayne.
Sep. 23.	Francis, daugher of William and Barbara Copeland.
Sep. 29.	Elizabeth, daughter of Mathew and Elizabeth White.
Oct. 11.	Barbara Pepp, *servant* to Mr. Robart Neave.
Oct. 30.	Martha, daughter of Mr. Robert and Pearsis Knight.
Nov. 24.	Elizabeth, daughter of Mr. William and Anne Nicholls.
Nov. 30.	Mr. Edward Agburrowe.
Dec. 14.	John, son of Huggin and Mary Hovell.
Jan. 1.	Daniell, son of Robert and Hellen Tomson.
Jan. 8.	Mr. John Duwaters.
Jan. 30.	A child of Tobias and Joane Sherly, still borne.
Feb. 20.	Isaack, son of John and Emma Sanders.
Feb. 22.	William, son of Richard and Mary Leigh.

1633

Mar. 27.	A child still borne of John and Mary Petis.
April 9.	Mary, wife of Mr. John Pettis.
May 4.	Mr. Lewis Marbury, of St. Martins, Ludgate, buried by night in our Church.
May 6.	Elizabeth, daughter of Hugh and Mary Owen.
May 7.	Edward Willand, *a Distracted Almsman.*
June 4.	Beniamine Marshe, *servant* to Mr. William Nicholes.
June 25.	Francis, daughter of Mr. John Brookes, died at Westminster.
July 10.	Elizabeth, daughter of Elias Watson.
Sep. 5.	William, son of William More, died in St. Olaves Jewry.
Feb. 2.	Anne, wife of Elias Watson.

1634

Mar 27.	Mary, daughter of Anthony and Abagale Light.
April 4.	Tobias Sherley.
May. 9.	A poor womans child that was borne in our parish and was baptized Edward, May 7.
May 31.	George, son of George and Phillis Winser.
June 11.	Katheren, daughter of George and Susan Haughton.
June 16.	Ann, daughter of John and Ann Freeston.
July 1.	John, son of Edward and Rose Chamberlen.
July 10.	Mr. Anthony Stertevant, was buried by night.
July 23.	Mr. Thomas Turpin.
Sep. 29.	Mrs. Rebecca Clark, sister to Mrs. Harwar, died in Mugwell Street.
Oct. 4.	Elizabeth, daughter of Henry and Sara Hedd.
Oct. 14.	Sara, daughter of Thomas Harwar.
Oct. 31.	Mr. Thomas Harwar.
Nov. 6.	Abagaile ——— [*sic*] *servant* to Edward Phillips.
Nov. 11.	Elizabeth, daughter of Morgin Lewes.
Nov. 3.	Mrs. Sheares, mother to Mrs. Webster.
Dec. 2.	Mrs. Tomson.
Dec. 3.	Timothie, son of Robard and Ellin Tomson.
Dec. 24.	Richard Steephens, *stranger*.
Jan. 3.	Barbara, Saughter of Samuell Baley.
Jan. 15.	Mary Dobery, *stranger*, died in Mr. Wards house.
Jan. 21.	John, son of John Fawcett.
Jan. 23.	Robard, son of Mathew and Elizabeth White.

1635

April 21.	Francis, son of Gilbert and Margrett Rigbee.
May 3.	Dorithie, daughter of John and Dorithie Scott.
Sep 11.	A child still borne of Mr. and Anne Wormell.
Sep. 28.	A child of John and Elizabeth Eaton.
Oct. 17.	William Lewis *servant* to Mr. Needham.
Dec. 19.	Martin Farr, *servant* to Mr. Buckner.
Jan. 7.	William Moore, dwelling in Olaves Jury Parish.
Jan. 30.	Judith, daughter of Gilbert and Margarett Rigby.
Feb. 15.	A child of William Moores, from the Parish of Olaves Jury.
Feb. 25.	Edward, son of Robert and Margarett Pascall.

1636

Mar. 26.	Anne, daughter of John and Elizabeth Fawcett.
April 12.	Francis, son of John and Anne Freestone
June 5.	A maid that was kild with falls.
Aug. 22.	A child of Mr. Thomas Fawsons, died presently after it was borne.
Sep. 14.	John Plummer, *servant* to Mr. Hovell, of the plague.
Sep. 10.	John Chestin, *servant* to Mr. Hovell, of the plague.
Sep. 25.	John Tomkins, *servant* to William Croudson.
Oct. 4.	Collett Woollard, Mr. Hovells sister, of the plague.
Oct. 12.	Thomas Lewis, *alias* Morgan, *servant* to Edward Chamberlin, of the plague.
Oct 24.	Anne, a child of Edward Chamberlin.
Oct. 27.	Rose, the wife of Edward Chamberlin, of the plague.

Dec. 15	John, son of Thomas Croudson.
Jan. 5.	A stillborne child of Mr. Jeffery Bathe.
Jan. 6.	Anne, wife of Mr. Jeffery Bathe, in child bed.
Jan. 13.	Anne, daughter of Jeffery Bathe.
Jan. 15.	Anne Andrew, *Widow*.
Feb. 2.	Mr. Robert Neeve.
Feb. 27.	A child still borne of Anthony Light.

1637

Mar. 27.	John, son of John Seed.
Mar. 28.	Mary, daughter of John Seed.
April 13.	Mary, daughter of James Houbelon.
April 18.	Mr. Thomas Fleetwood.
July 17.	Katherin, daughter of John and Elizabeth Fawcett.
July 30.	John Durbidge, from above in the stocks.
Aug. 31.	Mrs. Ashenden, wife of ——— [*sic*] Ashenden.
Sep. 1.	Mr. John Woolfall.
Oct. 3.	Davidson Kitchinson, *servant* to Mr. Allen.
Oct. 7.	A child still borne of Mr. Wormells, out of Mr. Browns house.
Jan. 13.	Edward, son of John Underwood.
Mar. 22.	A child still borne, of Edward Chamberlins.

1638

April 19.	Mary, daughter of Mr. Richard Hunt.
May 22.	Elizabeth, daughter of Mr. James Beaumont.
May 28.	John Fish, *the Clerke of this Parish*.
July 19.	Nathaniell, son of Mr. William Richardson.
Aug. 1.	Grace, daughter of Gilbert Rigby.
Aug. 13.	Mr. Henry Poole.
Aug. 14.	Mr. Nicholas Head.
Aug 10.	Sarah, daughter of Edward Phillips.
Aug. 30.	Sarah Mullinax, a *servant maide* to Mr. Erasmus Greenway
Sep. 3.	Anne Wollaston, *widow*.
Sep. 7.	Mary, daughter of Mr. Elias Watson.
Sep. 13.	William Stokes.
Oct. 3.	Susan Stoke, *servant* to Mr. James Houbelon.·
Nov. 10.	Mrs. Jane, wife of Mr. Thomas Arthington.
Jan. 22.	John Fawcett.
July 28.	Mr. Robert Walthew.
Feb. 15.	A female child still borne of Edward Chamberlins

1639

April 20.	A child of Mr. Wormell's still borne.
June 3.	Martha, daughter of Robert Swan.
June 6.	Roger Watts, *servant* of Mrs. Mary Cox.
June 30.	Mr. Richard Kent.
July 5.	William, son of Thomas Land.
July 25.	Thomas Anns, *servant* to Mr. Walthew.
Aug. 20.	Mr. Nicholas Parker.
Aug. 23.	Mrs. Mary Long.
Aug. 31.	Mary, daughter Zachery Worth.
Sep. 25.	John Halsted.

Oct. 19.   A male child, still borne of Thomas Fawson.
Nov. 6.   Mr. Henry Head.
Nov. 11.   Thomas, son Thomas Croudson.
Dec. 2.   Mary Nicholson, *servant* to Mr. William Medley.
Dec. 6.   Mrs. Mary Hungerford, daughter of Thomas Hungerford,
           Esquire, a stranger.
Feb. 5.   A male child still borne of Edward Chamberlins.
Mar. 13.   Laurence, son of Mrs. Forth Gooday.
Mar 23.   Mr. Humfrey Barnes.

1640

Mar. 31.   Thomas, son of Thomas Rye.
April 9.   William son of Thomas Croudson.
April 13.   John Dowson, *servant* to Mr. Erasmus Greenway.
July 10.   Richard, son of Mr. Forth Gooday.
July 14.   William Dawson *servant* to Mr. George Ward.
July 29.   Mr. Thomas Arthington.
Aug.—[*sic*]   Martha, daughter of Mr. Forth Gooday.
Sep. 5.   Mr. Thomas Ball.
Sep. 7.   Mr. William Traford, of Chester, dyed at Mr. Worths.
Oct. 17.   Mary, daughter of Mr. Edmond Page.
May 4.   James, son of Mr. John Ward.
Nov. 10.   A child of Mr. Winsors.
Dec. 31.   Mrs. Jane Richardson.
Jan. 9.   Mr. Thomas Manley.
Feb. 18.   Benjamin, son of Mr. James Houbelon.
Mar. 16.   Thomas Hunt, of the Parish of St. Olaves, Silver Street,
           dyed of a fall out of Mr. White's garrett.

1641

Mar. 29.   John, son of Mr. James Beaumont.
April 3.   Amy, daughter of George Windsor.
May 1.   Mr. Anthony Light.
May 18.   Thomas, son of Thomas Land.
May 24.   Mr. William Boyse.
May 29.   Grisogon, daughter of Robert Pascall, of the plague.
May 31.   Honnor, daughter of Thomas Land.
June 8.   John Yates, *servant* to Mr. Ratcliffe.
June 15.   Jone Whitson *servant* to Mr. Houbelon.
June 15.   Margarett, daughter of Robert Pascall, of the plague.
June 17.   John Eave, *servant* to Mr. John Duncum.
June 17.   John, son of Robert Pascall, of the plague.
June 25.   Mr. Richard Crooke, *Parson* of Woolchurch deceased
           the 20th.
June 25.   ———— [*sic*], son of Robert Pascall, of the plague.
June 28.   Robert Pascall, of the plague.
July 7.   Margarett, daughter of Mr. William Medley.
July 14.   Mr. Philip Watson, *a stranger.*
Aug. 3.   William Inns, *servant* to Mr. James Beaumont.
Aug. 14.   Mr. Henry Long.
Aug. 25.   Jane, daughter of Mr. Thomas Coates.
Sep. 29.   Katherin Artin.
Nov. 11.   Mary, daughter of Mr. William Pinckney.
Dec. 22.   William Kingum, *servant* to Mr. Stephens.
Jan. 21.   Sarah, daughter of Mr. Mathew White.
Jan. 31.   Mr. Wormells son.

1642

June 22.	Thomas Miller, *servant* to Mr. John Eaton.
July 23.	Mr. Samuell Major.
July 24.	Francis, son of Mr. George Haughton.
Aug. 15.	Mrs. Sarah Gooday.
Oct. 5.	Sarah Owen, of the plague.
Oct. 5.	Mr. Charltons child.
Oct. 16.	Mr. Robert Lander.
Oct. 16.	Mary Owen, of the plague.
Oct. 20.	Martha Owen, of the plague.
Nov 2.	Benjamin Owen, of the plague.
Nov. 12.	Phillip Bawtrey of the plague.
Nov. 16.	Anne, daughter of Hugh Owen.
Nov. 24.	Mary, wife of Stephen Vanspeare.
Nov. 27.	John, son of Mr. John Garrett.
Nov. 28.	Nathaniell Collyer.
Dec. 20.	Mr. John Fowler.
Dec. 26.	William Vanspeare.
Jan. 2.	Robert Ratcliffe, *servant* to Mr. Metcalf.
Jan. 14.	Francis, son of Mr. Francis Clay.
Jan. 17.	John, son of George Windsor.

1643

May 30.	Mr. William Butler, of Southwell, Nottinghamshire.
Aug. 14.	Joan Nicholls.
Aug. 15.	A child of James Beaumonts.
Aug. 25.	Mr. Richard Nightingall.
Sep. 20.	Mr. Eatons son.
Sep. 21.	Mr. Hill, his child.
Sep. 24.	Mr. Edward Dalley.
Sep. 28.	Thomas Arrthington.
Oct. 5.	John Nixon.
Oct. 12.	Francis Franklin.
Oct. 17.	A female child of Mr. Robert Turpins.
Oct. 26.	Mrs. Elizabeth, wife of Collonell Thomas Gower.
Jan. 24.	Mary, daughter of Thomas Allen.
Feb. 10.	Mr. Henry Marsh.
Mar. 2.	Mr. Robert Trelawny, *Merchant*, of Plymouth, was buried in the chancell.

1644

April 29.	George Bincks.
May 26.	A child of James Beaumonts.
June 24.	Arabella Highgate, died at Mr. John Vincents.
July 29.	John, son of Mr. William Curtis.
Aug. 14.	Mr. Stephen Darnella, of the Parish of Katherin Coleman.
Aug. 19.	Mrs. —— [*sic*] Darnella.
Aug. 23.	John Piddock.
Sep. 22.	Thomas Francis.
Oct. 25.	Mrs. —— [*sic*] wife of Mr. Hugh Handford.
Oct. 25.	Thomas Allen.
Dec. 2.	An abortive male child of Mr. Robert Turpins.
Jan. 2.	Thomas Clepten.
Jan. 15.	Mr. Humble.

1645

April 12.	—— [*sic*] son of Mr. John Freeston.
May 3.	Edward, son of Edward Chamberlin.
July 3.	The Lady Hanford, was buried in her husband, Sir Humfrey Handfords vault.
July 12.	Mr. —— [*sic*] Batt.
July 17.	A female child of Widow Francis.
July 18.	William, son of Mr. William Pinckney.
July 25.	Joseph, son of Mr. Robert Grosvenor.
Aug. 12.	Edward, son of Mr. Edward Pilkington.
Aug. 19.	Mr. Eatons child.
Aug. 25.	Richard Tiller.
Oct. 22.	Christopher Metcalf.
Nov. 12.	Mr. Joshua Fowlers son.
Nov. 14.	Mr. Goddards son.
Dec. 7.	A female child of Hugh Owens.
Dec. 8.	Charles Davis.
Jan. 5.	Reuben, son of Mr. Pharaoh Humphrey.
Jan. 6.	Mrs. Greenway.
Jan. 13.	A male child of Thomas Croudsons.
Feb. 9.	Mary Browne, *servant* to Mr. Manley.
Mar. 6.	Mr. Medleys son.
Mar. 21.	John, son of Thomas Land.

1646

May 5.	Richard, son of Richard Lawson.
May 11.	Elizabeth, daughter of Mr. Lander.
May 19.	Mr. William King.
June 20.	Mr. George Ward.
Aug. 27.	Mr. George Robins.
Aug. 30.	Samuell, son of Mr. James Houbelon.
Aug. 31.	Elizabeth, daughter of Mr. Head.
Sep. 15.	Mrs. Mary, the wife of Mr. James Houbelon.
Sep. 13.	A still borne male child of James Cutlers.
Sep. 18.	Mr. Hugh Handford.
Nov. 18.	Humfrey Chamberlin.
Nov. 13.	Mrs. Percis Marbury.
Nov. 22.	Mr. Pilkingtons son.
Mar. 12.	William, son of Mr. William Bennett.
Mar. 21.	A female child of Edward Chamberlins.

1647

Mar. 25.	An abortive child of Mr. George Bailys.
Mar. 25.	James, son of Mr. George Carlton.
April 5.	Shadrack, son of Captaine Richard Hunt.
June 21.	Nathaniell, son of William Stringer.
Sep. 13.	—— [*sic*] Tomlins, Mr. Grasvenors man.
Oct. 14.	Mary, daughter of Mr. Thomas Fawson.
Oct. 21.	Mr. Horne, his child.
Sep. 15.	Stephen Vanspeare, a man of above 100 years of age.
Nov. 23.	An abortive female child of George Baily.
Jan. 6.	Sarah, daughter of Mrs. Head.
Feb. 5.	Mr. Richard Moore.
Feb. 21.	Mr. William Bennetts daughter.

1648

Mar. 30.	A female child of Mr. Mathew White.
April 21.	Henry, son of Captaine Henry Flower.
April 22.	——— [*sic*] Feild, [written ffeild, and may be the end of a name]
May 3.	Elizabeth, daughter of Mr. Thomas Birch.
June 14.	William Copland.
June 25.	A male child of Mr. Hunlocks.
June 27.	A female child of Mr. Lawsons.
Aug. 29.	Mary, daughter of Mr. Coates.
Sept. 4.	Francis Lawson.
Sep. 14.	Ellin, daughter of Mr. Edward Pilkington.
Sep. 15.	Isabell, daughter of Mr. William Medley.
Oct. 18.	Edmond, son of Mr. Edmond Page.
Nov. 10.	Ruth, daughter of Mr. Joshua Fowler.
Nov. 13.	A female child of Joan Nicholls.
Jan. 26.	A male child of James Beaumonts.
	King Charles was beheaded the 30th of January 1648 after that he had reigned 23 years 10 months and 3 daies.
Feb. 7.	Widow Tillers daughter.
Feb. 26.	Mr. Robert Brookes, was brought from Westminster and buried.
Mar. 8.	Mrs. Elizabeth Carlton, mother to Mr. George Carlton.

1649

Mar. 28.	Elizabeth Garrett.
Mar. 29.	Mr. William Richardsons child.
April 18.	Sarah, daughter of Mr. Thomas Wheatly.
June 8.	George, son of Mr. George Baily.
June 16.	A female child of Edward Chamberlins.
July 28.	Christian, daughter of Mr. George Wright.
Aug. 27.	Widow Alice Fish.
Sep. 9.	Widow Bawtrey.
Oct. 14.	Daniell Williams, *servant* to Mr. Thomas Coates.
Jan. 5.	A female child of James Beaumont.
Jan. 11.	Robert, son of Mr. Humfrey and Anne Holcomb, buried in the Chancell.
Jan. 15.	George Land, *servant* to Mr. Worth.
Feb. 20.	Mrs. Sarah Hodsall.
Mar. 19.	John Hill, *servant* to Mr. Metcalf.

1650

Mar. 30.	Elizabeth, daughter of Mr. Robert Grasvenor.
April 11.	Mrs. Katherin Manley.
May 16.	Mrs. Mary, wife of Deputy Hobson, was brought from Hackney.
May 21.	Mr. William Webster.
May 27.	Ellen, daughter of Mr. Edward and Ellen Pilkington.
May 30.	An abortive female child of Mr. Robert Turpins.
June 18.	Hannah, daughter of Mr. Edmond Page.
June 19.	A male abortive child of Mr. John Freestones.

July 2.	Mr. John Brookes dyed att Westminster and was buried in the chancell.
July 2.	Edward Copland.
Aug. 3.	Sarah, daughter of Mr. Thomas Birch.
Aug. 28.	Samuell, son of Alexander Cartmell.
Sep. 23.	John Peet, *servant* to Mr. Morris.
Oct. 15.	Mr. George Baily.
Nov. 14.	Thomas, son of Henry Fairfax.
Nov. 18.	Mr. Zachary Worth.
Nov. 20.	Mary, wife of William Jellyman.
Dec. 5.	Mrs. Elizabeth, wife of Mr. Michaell Herring, buried in the chancell.
Dec. 21.	William Jellyman.
Dec. 28.	Mrs. Anne Marsh.
Jan. 1.	Mrs. Katherin Savage.
Jan. 16.	Mrs. Philippa Medley.
Mar. 7.	Edith Armsby, *servant* to Mr. Clay.

1651

April 14.	Elizabeth, daughter of Mr. Richard Lawson.
April 24.	A female child of William Paybody's.
May 9.	Alexander, son of Alexander Cartmell.
May 21.	Edward Agbrough.
June 6.	Richard Hebbe, *servant* to Mr. Durant.
June 19.	Mr. John Scott.
June 25.	Mr. Mathew White.
July 10.	Sarah Croudson.
July 15.	Mary, wife of Thomas Land.
Aug. 10.	Elizabeth Middleton.
Sep. 29.	Judith, daughter of James Beaumont.
Oct. 1.	Christopher Read.
Oct. 20.	A male child of Mr. Edmond Page.
Dec. 11.	Mr. Thomas Parker.
Dec. 21.	John Sexton.
Jan. 2.	Humfrey Griffith.
Jan. 22.	Mrs. Anne Vachell, in the chancell.

1652

Mar. 29.	A female child of John Collins.
April 9.	—— [*sic*]. Mr. Hovell's maid.
May 5.	Thomas, son of Mr. Richard Gower.
May 11.	Thomas, son of Thomas Birch.
July 6.	John Slowman, *servant* to Mr. Best.
Aug. 5.	George Kennett.
Aug. 18.	Henry Fairfax.
Aug. 31.	Christian Wright.
Sept. 20.	Anne, daughter of Mr. William Sawyer.
Sep. 21.	Mrs. Clement, wife of Edward Phillips.
Sep. 23.	Mrs. Elizabeth Ward.
Oct. 2.	Sarah Wright.
Oct. 8.	Mrs. Swan.
Oct. 13.	Hannah Turpin.
Nov. 19.	Phebe, daughter of Captaine Henry Flower.
Nov. 2.	Vincent Beaumont.

Dec. 10.	Susan Birch.
Dec. 30.	Widow Anne Stokes.
Feb. 12.	Mrs. Agnis Parker.

1653

May 13.	Mr. George Wright.
May 16.	Godfrey, son of Mr. Pinckney.
June 30.	An abortive male child of Mr. Richard Lawson.
July 1.	Collonell Edward Hutchinson, of Wicomb abby, in the County of York.
Aug 10.	——— [*sic*] Gilpin, dyed suddenly in the street, she was the wife of ——— [*sic*] Gilpin, in Cock and Key Ally, Fleet Street.
Oct. 14.	Richard, son of Mr. Edward Pilkington.
Oct. 24.	Mrs. Bow.
Nov. 20.	Bethia Garrett.
Feb. 2.	Richard, son of Mr. Richard Gower.

1654

April 23.	Richard Cony.
May 12.	Mr. Copland.
June 3.	Mr. James Knight, of Dover.
July 15.	Jacob Dyson.
July 18.	An abortive child of Mr. John Sextons.
Sep. 28.	A female stilborne child of Mr Towns.
Sep. 29.	Sarah Wright.
Nov. 1.	A stilborne male child of Mr. Robert Turpins.
Nov. 22.	Mary Owen.
Dec. 27.	A stillborne female child of Mr. Richard Smithes.
Jan. 8.	John, son of Mr. Richard Ball, in the chancell.
Jan. 25.	Anne, daughter of Mr. Richard Ball.
Jan. 26.	Elizabeth Thursfeild.
Feb. 15.	A child of ——— [*sic*] Bruces.
Feb. 21.	John Ramskar.
Feb. 25.	Hugh Owen.

1655

April 27.	A child borne in the street.
April 29.	A female child of Alexander Cartmells.
May 4.	A female child of Mr. Edmund Pages.
May 28.	Mr. Samuell Gooday.
May 29.	Ellinor Whittall.
June 8.	Edward Horne.
June 12.	Margaret Medley.
June 17.	Mr. John Worths child.
June 30.	Mrs. Hiller.
June 30.	Captaine Gooday.
Aug. 2.	Mrs. Margarett. Orell.
Aug. 12.	Mary Stead.
Oct. 7.	A male child of Thomas Billingtons.
Oct. 1J.	Jane Butt.
Jan. 8.	Mrs. Beaumont.
Jan. 31.	*Widow* Chamberlin.

Feb. 17.	A still borne male child of William Wells.
Feb. 28.	Mary Dimmoch.
Mar. 7.	Rachell, daughter of Mr. Matthew Wright.

1656

April 5.	William Fairfax.
April 20.	Samuel Horne.
April 25.	William Perkins.
May 19.	Elizabeth Pilkington.
May 25.	Bartholomew Singleton.
May 22.	Anne, daughter of Mr. Richard Ball, *Minister*.
May 31.	Mr. James Cutlers child.
Aug. 12.	Benjamin Clarke.
Aug. 13.	Mr. Greys child.
Sep. 3.	Henry, son of Mr. Henry Davy, of St. Dionis, Bachchurch.
Sep. 13.	Sarah, wife of Thomas Croudson
Oct. 10.	Mr. James Godscall, in the chancell.
Nov. 6.	Mr. James Lawson.
Dec. 27.	A male child of Rowland Steads.
Dec. 30.	A male child of Robert Swans.
Dec. 31.	Rebeccah, daughter of Mr. Robert Webbe.
Jan. 18.	Henry Stokes.
Jan. 29.	Thomas Ellis.
Feb. 17.	Barbara, wife of Symon Reynolds.
Mar. 19.	Francis, son of Mr. John Story.

1657

April 10.	Captaine Richard Lawson.
May 13.	Mr. William Pinckny.
May 25.	John Weekes.
May 28.	Deputy Hoogan Hovell.
May 31.	Thomas ——— [*sic*].
June 5.	Sibella, daughter of John Shelter.
June 9.	Thomas Birch.
June 17.	William Perkins female child.
June 21.	George Paybodys female child.
June 24.	James Beaumonts child.
July 5.	Thomazin Hodson.
July 12.	A stilborne childe of Francis Dimocks.
July 23.	Mrs. Mary Cox, in the chancell.
July 27.	John Lasco.
July 27.	Margarett Wright.
Aug. 5.	Mr. Davis female child.
Aug. 18.	Thomas Moores child.
Sep. 17.	Mr. Henry Tomkins.
Nov. 17.	Mr, Edward Baker.
Feb. 8.	Anne Blackborne.
Feb. 21.	Mr. Henry Hunlock.
Feb. 25.	Mr. Downs child.
Feb. 26.	Mr. Sawyers child.
Mar. 9.	Richard Beaumont.
Mar. 12.	Mr. Thomas Coats.
Mar. 13.	Mr. Thomas Conys child.

1658

April 30.	Mr. James Cutler.
May 10.	The Lady Elizabeth Eveling.
May 15.	Mr. George Haughton.
May 24.	Symon Alington.
Aug. 19.	Mabell, wife of William Wells.
Aug. 21.	William, son of William Wells.
Oct. 10.	Edward Cutler.
Oct. 27.	Elias Watson.
Nov. 12.	Willlam Meyline, *servant* to Mr. Batt.
Nov. 11.	Anthony Booth, *servant* to Mr. George Compeer.
Nov. 13.	Anne ——— [*sic*] *servant* to Mr. Samuell Stone.
Dec. 18.	Mrs. Anne Sparks.
Dec. 18.	Mr. John Wildman, of Langhborough, in the County of Leicester.
Dec. 30.	A stillborne male child of John Beamans.
Feb. 17.	Mr. John Seed.
Feb. 19.	Mrs. Mary Hovell.
Feb. 26.	Margarett Billington.
Mar. 9.	Mrs. Katherin Harwar.

1659

Mar. 31.	George, son of Mr. George Compeere.
April 18.	Mr. Daniell Darnella.
June 6.	Richard Fawson.
June 8.	John Cutler.
June 17.	Mary Hunlock.
June 30.	Mary Compeere.
July 7.	Richard, son of Mr. Richard Thompson.
July 8.	Mr. Moores child.
Aug. 11.	Joseph Swan.
Sep. 1.	John Kennett.
Sep. 8.	Mrs. Sarah Sawyer,
Sep. 12.	Dr. Christopher Bier.
Sep. 16.	Mrs. Martha Swall.
Oct. 23.	Thomas Moores child.
Nov. 28.	William Feilding.
Dec. 6.	Thomas, son of Mr. Robert Webbe.
Jan. 31.	Elizabeth Stint.
Feb. 4.	A male child of George Millions.
Feb. 8.	John, son of John Clarke.
Feb. 20.	Mrs. Mary Radclyffe.
Mar. 10.	Mr. Briscoes child.
Mar. 10.	Mr. Nicholas Clarkes child.
Mar. 23.	Mrs. Martha Smith, in the chauncell.

1660

April 23.	Leonard Baines.
April 30.	Thomas Billington.
June 13.	John Wright.
July 29.	William Nicholson, came sick into our parish the 28th of July and could not speake to reveale himself, he dyed the same night in Robert Swans house.

Aug. 28.	John, son of Henry King.
Aug. 31.	Elizabeth, daugher of Jonathan Botham.

The high borne prince Henry, Duke of Gloucester, departed this life, the 13 September.

Oct. 13.	Mrs. Jane Sexton.
Nov. 8.	Elizabeth Mabson, *servant* to Mr. Milliam Medley.
Nov. 9.	Elizabeth Robinson, mother to *widow* Fawcett.
Nov. 29.	Alexander Clarke.
Dec. 1.	Rebeckah Garrett.
Dec. 2.	Thomas Clarke.
Dec. 8.	Mr. Francis Aylworth.
Dec. 9.	A female child of Mr. Tempests.

The Royall Primrosse of Orrange, Mary, daughter to our late sovaigne Charles the 1st, deceased, departed this life 24 December.

Dec. 25.	A male child of Mr. Robert Smithes.
Dec. 28.	Mr. Thomas Kennett.
Jan. 5.	Elizabeth Beresford.
Jan. 20.	A female child of Mr. Ralph Stints.
Feb. 11.	John, son of Mr. John Child.
Feb. 14.	Mrs. Desboroughs child.
Mar. 23.	Mr. Thomas Birch.

1661

April 1.	Joseph Stead, buried in St. Bennett Sheerhogs parish.
April 7.	John, son of Mr. John Gray.
May 7.	Rebeckah, daughter of Mr. George Compere.
June 25.	Mrs. Mary Aylworth.
Sep. 11.	Thomas Harris, *servant* to Mr. John Child.
Oct. 5.	John, son of John Baines.
Oct. 10.	Mr. Arthur Manley, in the chancell.
Oct. 17.	Mary, daughter of Robert Dawson.
Oct. 29.	Charles Wright.
Nov. 2.	Mrs. Anne Hockett.
Nov. 4.	Mrs. Sarah Cooke.
Dec. 20.	Richard Aylworth.
Dec. 25.	Thomasin Woodferne.
Jan. 7.	Mr. Mathew Hillier.
Feb. 1.	James King.
Feb. 10.	Robert, son of Mr. Robert Webbe.
Feb. 11.	John, son of Giles Bromer.
Feb. 12.	Mary, daughter of Mr. Edward Skinner.

1662

April 5.	Anne, daughter of Edward Andrews, *Esquire*, and grandchild to to Sir Humphrey Handford, was buried in her grandfathers vault.
April 22.	A male child of Mr. Thomas Sidgweeke.
April 24.	Henry Crosfeeld.
June 23.	A female child of Mr. Millions.
June 28.	Mr. Ralph Stint.
July 12.	Margarett Perkins.
July 7.	Thomas Dallton.
July 13.	Mr. Perkins child.

Aug. 15.	Mr. Ruth Smith.
Aug. 27.	Mr. Thomas Day, of Croyden.
Sep. 4.	Mr. Thomas Moore, his son in the churchyard.
Oct. 7.	Thomas, son of William Blackboone.
Oct. 25.	Lieutenant Colonel Mr. Robert Thompson.
Oct. 31.	Elizabeth Wells.
Nov. 28.	Mr. Robert Smith.
Dec. 12.	Mr. Richard Smith.
Dec. 24.	Mr. Downes his child.
Jan. 26.	Mrs. Katherine Allington.
Mar. 14.	Robert Swan.

1663

April 17.	Arrabella Skinner.
April 23.	A male child, still borne, of Mr. Thomas Coney.
May 5.	Samuel Berisford.
May 19.	Mr. Robert Web.
May 22.	Richard Walker.
July 20.	Jane Horne.
July 23.	Mrs. Rebecka, wife of Mr. Charles Mitchell.
Aug. 11.	Mrs. Mary, wife of Mr. William Perkins.
Aug. 11.	Precilloe, daughter of William and Rebecka King.
Aug. 26.	A malle still borne child of John Downes.
Sep. 10.	Charles Desborow.
Sep. 26.	Thomas, son of of William Smith.
Oct. 14.	Charles Coney.
Nov. 12.	Mrs. Arabella Skinner.
Nov. 24.	Michaell Baman.
Dec. 18.	Beniamen Botham.
Jan. 23.	Mary Ward, daughter of Mr. Thomas Hockett.

1664

April 11.	Henry Clapton, *servant* to Captaine Robert Morris.
April 17.	William Smith.
April 20.	Sarah, daughter of Simond Hunt.
April 27.	Mrs. Susanna Haughton.
May 8.	Mr. John Mayson.
May 20.	Sarah, daughter of William Forest.
May 20.	Mr. William Michell.
June 8.	Mrs. Sarah Wattson.
June 17.	Sarah, daughter of Mr. Nicolas Clarke.
June 19.	Ferdinando Croke.
July 26.	Sarah, daughter of John Moore.
Aug. 5.	Robart, son of John Grosvener.
Aug. 6.	Mr. Francis Clay.
Sep. 22.	Richard Mottershed.
Oct. 14.	Elizabeth Heriford.
Oct. 7.	Philippa Collings.
Oct. 12.	Ralph, son of Mr. William King.
Oct. 17.	Mr. John Aylworth.
Nov. 9.	John, son of John Sexton.
Dec. 10.	Elizabeth, daughter of Richard Phillips.
Dec. 23.	Simon, son of Simon Hunt.
Jan. 18.	Elizabeth, daugher of John Tempest.

Jan. 22.	Edward Chamberlin.
Feb. 14.	Francis, son of Mr. Edward Thursfield.
Feb. 14.	John, son of Mr. William Forest.
Mar. 3.	William, son of Mr. William Blackbourne.
Mar. 19.	Katherine, daughter of Mr. William Gillmore.

1665

April 27.	Catherine Pearce.
May 1.	Richard Vaughan.
May 6.	John May.
May 27.	Edward, son of Edward Andrewes, *Esquire.*
July 31.	Jane, wife of Reginald Horne.
Aug. 2.	Mary, daughter of Mr. Thomas Langley.
Aug. 8.	James Beamond.
Aug. 9.	Sarah Downes.
Aug. 12.	Mr. Elias Watson.
Aug. 22.	Elizabeth Hog, that broke hir soul [?] in the streete.
Aug. 28.	Mr. Francis Tanner.
Aug. 31.	Mr. John Dod.
Sep. 2.	Anne, daughter of Mr. Alexander Cartmell, pl. *
Sep. 7.	Mr. William Peckett.
Sep. 11.	Henry, son of Reginald Horne, plague.
Sep. 12.	Martha Bidgood.
Sep. 12.	Sarah, daughter of Reginald Horne, pl.
Sep. 13.	John, son of Reginald Horne, plague.
Sep. 17.	Sarah, wife of Mr. Alexander Cartmell, plague.
Sep. 20.	Mr. Thomas Tempest, Senior, pl.
Sep. 20.	Thomas Tempest, Junior, pl.
Sep. 21.	Henry Raban.
Sep. 25.	Reginald, son of Reginald Horne, pl.
Sep. 26.	John Piearson.
Sep. 26.	Joseph Brookes, plague.
Sep. 26.	Venabeles Bowman, pl.
Sep. 27.	Margaret, wife of Mr. Thomas Croudson, pl.
Sep. 28.	Catherine Measure, pl.
Sep. 30.	Howell Price, pl.
Sep. 30.	Mary Perkins, pl.
Oct. 1.	Thomas Ranbon.
Oct. 2.	Ann, wife of Simond Hunt, pl.
Oct. 4.	Mr. Edward Phillips. *Parish Clarke,* and his wife, pl.
Oct. 4.	Dorothy, wife of James Waldegrave, pl.
Oct. 6.	Charles Crowder, died heare and was buried in Aldermanbury Church.
Oct. 7.	Mr. Thomas Perkins, pl.
Oct. 10.	Mr. Thomas Fosson, pl.
Oct. 10.	Doretheus Wharton, pl.
Oct. 11.	Mr. Thomas Desborough,
Oct. 14.	Hester, daughter of Mr. William Wells, pl.
Oct. 15.	Mary Baman, pl.
Oct. 15.	Zachery, son of Mr. Thomas Crondson, pl.
Oct. 15.	*Widow* Fossett, Senior, pl.
Oct. 18.	Nicholas Smyth, pl.
Oct. 20.	Mrs. Fossett, Junior, wife Mr. Isaiah Fossett, with hir young child, pl.

* In this and the following case a small " pl " or " plague " is written in much blacker ink.

Oct. 20.	Thomas, son of Thomas Desborough, pl.
Oct. 22.	Elizabeth, daughter of Mr. Abraham Sheares.
Oct. 25.	Mary, wife of Mr. Thomas Cony.
Oct. 25.	Sarah, wife of Mr. William Forrest.
Oct. 29.	John, son of Thomas Desborough, pl.
Nov. 4.	Mr. Richard Phillips, pl.
Nov. 8.	Mr. John Clarke, pl.
Nov. 10.	Richard Holloway, pl.
Nov. 11.	Mary, daughter of Mr. William Wells, pl.
Dec. 7.	Mr. Thomas Fitton.
Dec. 10.	A child of Mr. Edward Flaxmore.
Dec. 12.	*Widow* Phillips, wife of Richard Phillips, Junior, pl.
Dec. 20.	Edward, son of Mr. Hugh Thornely.
Dec. 27.	Thomas Ripenton.
Jan. 2.	Henry Milan.
Jan. 9.	Mary, daughter of Mr. Alexander Cartmell.
Jan. 19.	Mr. William Medley.
Feb. 12.	Mrs. Pricilla King.
Mar. 3.	Nicholas Rich.

1666

[*No more Burials.*]

THE following list of persons connected with and in most cases buried at St. Mary Woolchurch Hawe, has been compiled from Wills and other documents, and has been printed as likely to prove interesting.

1394.	Henry Weston, to be buried neare his master, Lawrence Barbour.
1400.	John Sevesterr *"Civis et braciator"* had property at Henxteworth, Gylden Morden and Ashwell.
1400.	Robert Horne, *Citizen and Vintner*, from South Fereby, Lincolnshire, to have a marble stone of the price of two marks.
1402.	Agnes, *widow* of Richard Fraunceys, to be buried in the Churchyard, before the Cross there.
1406.	Richard Michell, to be buried in the Chapel of St. Katherine.
1413.	William Knyght, *Citizen and Felmonger*, to be buried near John, his son.
1418.	Thomas Ive, *Citizen and Clothman*, to be buried with Emma, his wife.
1425.	John Massy, *Brewer*, to be buried "in Claustro . . ante crucem."
1428.	Guy Laurence, *Citizen and Grocer*, to be buried in the Ladye Chapel where William Laurence, his father, lies.
1431.	Christine Mallyng, *widow* of Thomas Cake, alias Mallying, to be buried near her said husband.
1432.	William Clyff, *Mynstrall*, to be buried in the Churchyard.

1434. William Hennore, *Citizen and Grocer*, to buried "in Herbario infra cimiterium," next to Isold his wife.

146⅞. Edward Doyle, *Squier*, to be buried "in the Church hawe before the Cross."

1468. Richard Hatfeld, *Squyer*, of Steeple Morden, Cambridge-shire, to be buried in the Church, and to have a tomb of stone. He bequeathed five marks "towardes the makyng of a glasse wyndowe."

1471. Margaret, *widow* of Edward Doyle, to be buried in the Church hawe.

1483. John Clerk, *Citizen and Grocer*, to be buried with Joan his late wife.

1487. Nicholas Archer, *Fishmonger*, brother of John Archer, *parson of this church*, to be buried in the Church.

1504. John Archer,* *Fishmonger*, to be buried if he dies in London in the chancell of St. Mary Woolchurch, by his brother Nicholas before the High Altar.

1506. John Golofer to be buried in the Churchyard "nygh by the Crosse there standing on the Southest side where my granfader and gramoder and brethern and sustern lyen buried."

1510. Richard Shore to be buried here—he founded a chantry.

1516. Water Maykin, *Citizen and Draper*, to be buried here.

1516. William de Beowpre, "*Priest Syngyng in St. Peters, Cornhill*," to be buried here.

1517. Nicholas Wyngar, *Citizen and Grocer*, to be buried " by the tomb where my father John Wyngar lieth buried."

1522. John Thrower, *Grocer*, to be buried here.†

152⅔. Agnes Wyngar, *widow* of John Wyngar, *Alderman*, to be buried here.

1523. Richard Folyat, *Grocer*, to be buried "nygh unto the fonte where both my fader and my moder ben buried." §

1525. John Hanford, *Citizen and Merchant tailor*, to be buried " with Alice my wife."

1525. Robert Hanford, the elder, to be buried "with Margaret my wife."

1538. John Mathew, alias Trystram, *Citizen and Grocer*, to be buried near his father and mother.

1544. George Okeley, *Citizen and Skinner*. to be buried here.

1545. Henry Clytherowe, *Citizen and Merchant tailor*, to be buried here. ||

1542. John Clarke, the elder, *Citizen and draper*, to be buried in the Chapel with Alice his wife,

1551. Richard Canysby, *Grocer*, to be buried here.

1559. William Dansy, *Citizen and Barbor Surgeon*, to be buried here Mentions his kindred buried here.

---

* Mentions in his Will Thomas and John, sons of his brother, William Archer, of Sudbury, directs that " xx^li that my lord Blythe, Bishop of Chester, oweth me" was to be forgiven "yf it will like my Lord of Chester to make Thomas Archer felowe of the Kinges Halle in Cambridge." N.B —Geoffrey Blythe was Bishop of Lichfield 1503-1534. Lichfield was often called Chester. Dr. Blythe was Master of the King's Hall, Cambridge. Le neves Fasti—dates not given.

† He had property at Little Dunmow, Essex.

§ "I will that my knyll be rong with Jhus bell." Mentions fraternities of St. Anne and St. Christopher.

|| A connection of Lord Mayor Draper.

General Index.

INDEX TO NAMES

ST. MARY WOOLNOTH REGISTERS.

* Should be "Roger," not "Robert," p. 36.

Hallsey, John, 52, 53, 56, 153, 228, 229
  ,,   Margaret, 53, 229
  ,,   Sarah, 52, 53, 56, 228, 229
Halton, Robert, 149
Halwood, Anne, 134
  ,,   Thomas, 134
Hamans, Margaret, 122
Hambleton, Mary, 227
  ,,   Thomas, 240
Hamden, ——— 22
Hammerton, Anne, 134
  ,,   Clare, 201
Hammon, Elizabeth, 158, 205
Hammond, Alice, 14, 117, 191
  ,,   Hellen, 132
  ,,   Richard, 14, 191
  ,,   Robert, 204
  ,,   Thomas, 14, 191, 192
  ,,   Walter, 169
Hamore, Alice, 212
  ,,   Anne, 29, 207
  ,,   Elizabeth, 27, 205
  ,,   Isaac, 27, 205
  ,,   Jane, 24
  ,.   John, 33, 211
  ,.   Katherine, 26, 207
  ,.   Lettis, 137
  ,,   Mary, 25, 202
  ,.   " Mr.," 203
  ,,   Robert, 23, 33, 145, 211
  ,.   Sarah, 22
  ,,   William, 22, 23, 24,* 25, 26, 27,
             28, 29, 202, 205, 207, 212
Hamson, Mary, 130
  ,,   Thomas, 165
Hampton, John, 214
  ,,   " Mr.," 202
  ,,   Thomas, 131
Hanbery, Agnes, 122
  ,,   Elinor, 131
  ,,   Richard, 125
Hancks, Elizabeth, 240
Handcock, Ann, 1
  ,,   Bridget, 4
  ,,   Dancer, 152
  ,,   Edmund, 1, 182
  ,,   Fabian, 3
  ,,   John, 6
  ,,   Margaret, 2, 179
  ,,   Mary, 2, 180, 260
  ,,   " Mr.," 179
  ,,   Robert, 162
  ,,   Sarah, 5, 267
  ,,   Susan, 149
  ,,   Thomas, 1, 2, 3, 4, 5, 6, 179, 180,
                  183, 267, 271
Handford, Robert, 184
  ,,   Thomas, 184
  ,,   William, 125
Handmore, Elizabeth, 203
Hands, George, 260
Hankins, Robert, 176
Hanley, Elizabeth, 163
Hanmer, Katherine, 150
Hannah, Elizabeth, 110
  ,,   James, 110
  ,,   Thomas, 110
Harbey, Anne, 61, 63, 66
  ,,   Elizabeth, 61
  ,,   Hannah, 63, 242
  ,,   John, 66
  ,,   Mary, 247
        * Not " Hams."

Harbey, Rachel, 61, 63, 66, 242
Harding, Alexander, 169
  ,,   Alice, 260
  ,,   Anne, 137
  ,,   Edward, 18, 19, 196
  ,,   Ellina, 232
  ,,   George, 135, 188
  ,,   Hezekiah, 144
  ,,   James, 19
  ,,   John, 232, 242
  ,,   Margaret, 18, 196
  ,,   Mary, 169
  ,,   William, 165
Hardy, Priscilla, 167
Hargrave, Alice, 197
  ,,   Bridget, 22
  ,,   Henry, 21, 22, 197, 199, 200
  ,,   Humphrey. 21
  ,,   Jane, 22
  ,,   Mary, 171
  ,,   Susan, 134
Harleing, Benjamin, 60, 243
  ,,   Hannah, 67, 248
  ,,   John, 59, 60, 67, 243, 348, 258
  ,,   Mary, 59, 60, 67, 259
Harley, John, 64
  ,,   Richard, 64
  ,,   William, 64
Harloe, Richard, 251
Harney, Charles, 135
Harper, Alice, 190
  ,,   Mary 165
  ,,   Sir William, 190
Harrington, Thomas, 165
Harris, Alice, 200
  ,,   Ann, 154, 158
  ,,   Christian, 281
  ,,   Christopher, 13, 191
  ,,   Cicily, 149
  ,,   Edward, 167
  ,,   Elizabeth, 156, 284
  ,,   Francis, 154
  ,,   John, 109
  ,,   Margaret, 109
  ,,   Mary, 145
  ,,   Mary Margaret,˙109
  ,,   " Mr.," 192
  ,,   Phillip, 242
  ,,   Richard, 140
  ,,   Robert, 166
  ,,   Thomas, 9
  ,,   William, 9, 13
Harrison, Ann, 33, 145, 211
  ,,   Arthur, 170
  ,,   Christian, 96, 98
  ,,   Edward, 22, 204
  ,,   Elizabeth, 27, 67
  ,,   Ellen, 31, 129
  ,,   Emma, 124
  ,,   Hugh, 200
  ,,   Jacob, 205
  ,,   Jeronomy, 20, 204
  ,,   John, 67, 96, 98
  ,,   Katherine, 129
  ,,   Margaret, 30, 202
  ,,   Mary, 23, 26, 27, 29, 205, 207
  ,,   " Mr.," 203, 204, 278
  ,,   Ralph, 26, 27, 28, 204, 205
  ,,   Richard, 19, 20, 21, 22, 23, 27,
           28, 30, 31, 32, 33, 135, 193,
          196, 198, 200, 202, 204, 205,
                 207, 211, 212

Juckes, Michael, 111
Judd, Anne, 29
,, John, 28, 30
,, Susan, 226
,, Valentine, 28, 29, 30, 208
Judy or Jewdy, Ann, 15
,, Elizabeth, 20
,, Joan, 16, 193, 195
,, Katherine, 21, 193
,, William, 15, 16, 18, 20, 21, 129, 193, 195, 196
,, ———, 199
Julian, Rebecca, 284
June, see Juns
Juns, David, 236
,, Jane, 236, 240
,, John, 236, 240
,, Morris, 240
Jurian, Frances, 150
,, Jacob, 223, 224
,, Mary, 224
,, "Mr.," 152
,, Peter, 153
Jurious and Jury, see Jurian
Jux, see Juce
Juxon, William, 255
Kaye, Robert, 124
Kayll, Hugh, 197, 198, 201, 204
,, Thomas, 201
Keale, Alice, 4
,, Anne, 2, 11, 17, 28, 157, 211, 213
,, Arthur, 204
,, Christopher, 3
,, Elizabeth, 13
,, Francis, 4
,, Hugh, 11, 13, 15, 17, 18, 19, 190, 192
,, John, 1, 2, 3, 4, 5, 6, 7, 13, 28, 178, 179, 190, 192, 209
,, Joshua, 6
,, Katherine, 29, 31, 207
,, Lancelot, 17
,, Margaret, 4
,, Marian, 1
,, Mary, 19
,, Richard, 2, 31, 180, 204, 207, 209
,, Robert, 13
,, Rowland, 18
,, Samuel, 6
,, Sarah, 5
,, Thomas, 4
,, William, 28, 29, 203, 208
Keepe, Bridget, 155
Keightley, Frances, 224
Kelinge, Alice, 184
,, Arthur, 5
,, Cecily, 12
,, Dorothy, 13
,, Edward, 6
,, Hannah, 175, 292
,, Jasper, 9
,, Joan, 10
,, John, 6, 11, 182, 188
,, Katherine, 10
,, Margaret, 5, 123
,, Mary, 7
,, Robert, 8
,, Thomas, 4, 5, 6, 7, 8, 9, 10, 11, 12, 13, 122, 182, 184, 188
Kelk, Robert, 124
Kelly, Ann, 256
Kellway, Thomas, 284

Kelsey, Elizabeth, 139
,, John, 124
Kempe, Andrew, 48
,, Dorothy, 49
,, Elizabeth, 50
,, Katherine, 50
,, Margaret, 251
,, Mary, 48, 49, 50
,, Samuel, 241
,, Thomas, 48, 49, 50
Kempton, see Kenton
Kenedy, James, 213
Kent, Anne, 78, 207
,, Dixey, 76, 77, 78
,, Hannah, 76
,, Jane, 76, 77, 78
,, Margaret, 138
,, Mary, 89, 95, 96, 97, 237, 280
,, Michael, 89, 95, 96, 97, 106, 271,
,, "Mr.," 279, 280 [279, 284
,, Rowland, 169
,, Sarah, 106
Kentish, Frances, 117, 118
,, George, 118
,, John, 117, 118
,, Thomas Wooley, 117
Kenton or Kempton, Adam, 161
,, Ann, 34
,, Dorothy, 33
,, Henry, 145
,, Jane, 135
,, John, 30, 31, 32, 33, 34, 212
,, Margaret, 36, 213
,, Martha, 31
,, Mary, 30
,, William, 32
Kenwick or Kenrick, Elizabeth, 284
,, Sarah, 276
Kerby, John, 200, 201
Kernal, Anne, 196
Kettlewood, Alice, 9, 11, 186
,, Anne, 13
,, Bridget, 184
,, Elizabeth, 19
,, Henry, 17, 19, 195
,, John, 5, 8, 9, 11, 12, 123, 184, 186, 196
,, Mary, 8, 17, 284, 196
,, Paul, 17, 195
,, Sarah, 5, 127
Kevall, see Revall
Keye, Elizabeth, 124
,, Henry, 181
Keyes, Dorothy, 141
,, Giles, 130
,, Nicholas, 141
Keyle, John, 131
Keymer, Audrey, 133
,, Roger, 133
Keynton, Elizabeth, 285
,, Jane, 98
,, Israel, 94. 281
,, Jeremiah Hilton, 95
,, John, 101, 284, 286
,, Katherine, 96
,, Mary, 94, 95, 96, 98, 99, 100, 101, 283
,, Samuel, 94, 95, 96, 98, 99, 100, 101, 281, 286, 292
Kidd, Anne, 11
,, Francis, 9, 11, 187
,, Thomas, 9

Viccars, Thomas, 19, 20, 25, 196, 197, 198, 199, 202
„ William, 11
„ ———- 201
Vincent, "Mrs.," 277
„ John, 141
Vinchowe, Chrystyan, 139
Ving or King, Frances, 31
„ Ralph, 31
Vinor, or Vynor, Abigail, Dame, 239
„ "Alderman, 224
„ Anne, 36, 218
„ Charles, 255
„ Elizabeth, 39, 149
„ George, 43
„ George, Sir, 239
„ Honor, 233
„ Honor, Lady, 228
„ Mary, 37, 146
„ Mary, Dame, 241
„ "Mr.," 267
„ Rebecca, 41
„ Robert, 257
„ Robert, Sir, 241, 242, 243, 255
„ Susan, 40, 217
„ Thomas, 35, 36, 37, 38, 39, 40, 41, 42, 43, 148, 211, 216, 217, 218, 227, 233, 239
„ Thomas, Slr, 155, 228, 234
„ William, 35, 211
Voue, Ann, 139
„ Richard, 139
Vutton, Jane, 138
Vynor, see Viner
Wade, Ann, 44, 220
„ Edward, 67, 245
„ Margaret, 71, 206, 251
„ Mary, 69, 253
„ Nicholas, 31, 208
„ Peter, 31, 33, 67, 69, 71, 72, 73, 208, 245, 251, 253, 254
„ Rose, 69, 72, 73
„ Sarah, 32
„ Thomas, 43, 44, 220
„ William, 32, 137
„ Willmore, 73, 254
Wadsworth, Richard, 180
„ Thomas, 157
Waferer, Clemence, 138
„ Thomas, 138
Wage, Ralph, 179
„ Reginald, 179
Waghorne, "Mr.," 269, 272
„ William, 274
„ ———, 87, 91, 94
Wagstaff, John, 160
Waite, Judith, 273
„ Philip, 273
Wakefield, Arthur, 145
„ Audrey, 204
„ Barnaby, 21
„ Elizabeth, 195
„ Jane, 109
„ John, 109, 289
„ Maynard, 204
„ Nicholas, 22, 31, 132, 204
„ Samuel, 131
„ William, 170, 204
Waker, Jane, 214
„ Mabel, 214
Waldron, Sarah, 168
Walford, Mary, 144

Walker, Alice, 154
„ Anne, 105
„ Bridget, 233
„ Chrrstopher, 133
„ Edward, 43
„ Elias, 146
„ Elizabeth, 168, 191
„ George, 253
„ Hester, 274
„ Isaac, 146
„ Jane, 43
„ John, 17, 195
„ Martha, 224
„ Mary, 164
„ Oliver, 125
„ Robert, 162
„ Samuel, 105
„ Sarah, 105
„ Susannah, 170
„ Thomas, 17, 195
„ Venice, 140
„ William, 125, 204
Wall, Eliachim, 127
„ Elizabeth, 210
Wallington, Ann, 102, 103
„ Edmund Bick, 108
„ Edward, 102, 103, 108
„ Elizabeth, 108
„ Mary, 103
Wallis, James, 286
„ Major, 240
„ Sara, 250
Walls or Watts, Anne, 194
„ Thomas, 194
Walne, Lucretia, 289
Walstead, Hester, 88
„ John, 88
„ Rebecca, 88
Walter, John, 233, 337
„ Joshua, 33
„ Mary, 233
„ Nicholas, 33
Waltering, Thomas, 291
Walton, Elizabeth, 154
„ Prudence, 217
„ Richard, 7
„ Samuel, 7
Wannerton. Sarah, 147
Waple, Ann, 87
„ Robert, 87
Waplod, Dunstan, 127
Warcop, Henry, 124
Ward, Agnes, 204
„ Alexander, 69, 245, 247, 248
„ Anne, 18
„ Charles, 204
„ Elizabeth, 20, 248
„ Esther, 25, 202
„ George, 22
„ Hugh, 178
„ Joan, 245
„ John, 16, 152, 219, 288
„ Judith, 161
„ Katherine, 24, 148, 204
„ Mary, 126, 219, 255
„ "Mr.," 16
„ Philip, 156
„ Rich, 167
„ Robert, 21, 171, 204
„ Sarah, 173
„ Thomas, 17, 143, 206

Williams, Phillip, 58
,, Raby, 101
,, Rebecca, 213
,, Richard, 71, 128, 253
,, Rowland, 286
,, Sarah, 72, 74
,, Stephen, 113, 114, 115, 118
,, Susannah, 115
,, Thomas, 60, 61, 62, 63, 65, 66, 71,
72, 74, 139, 171, 222, 237, 239,
243, 245, 250, 252, 253, 264
,, Timothy, 72
,, Vincent, 87
Williams, *alias* Comyns, Edith, 21
,, Richard, 21
Williams not Witham, 222
Williamson, Anne, 199
,, Elizabeth, 133, 148
,, John, 22, 199
,, Mary, 21, 199
,, Thomas, 21, 199
Willington, Anney, 47, 223
,, Christian, 47, 226
,, John, 47, 48, 52, 223, 225, 226, 227
,, "Mr.," 222
,, Temperance, 52, 227
,, Thomas, 48, 225
Willis, Ann, 169
,, John, 31
,, Lionel, 283
,, Margaret, 217
,, "Mr.," 219, 220, 223
,, Peter, 34, 211
,, Simon, 33, 211
,, Thomas, 31, 33, 34, 167, 211,
217, 220
Williscroft, Ellen, 199
Willoughby, John, 143
,, Katherine, 183
,, Thomas, 124
Wills, Amy, 235
,, Mary, 152
,, "Mr.," 240
Wilmer, Edward, 154
Wilmore, Ann, 225
,, Thomas, 235
,, William, 218
Wilshier, Reynes, 130
Wilson, Ann, 67, 109, 250, 252
,, Bryan, 180
,, Dinah, 111, 288
,, Edward, 192
,, Elizabeth, 73, 74, 76, 100, 101,
102, 103, 105, 108, 109, 111,
133, 174, 186
,, Ellen, 127
,, "Goodwief," 18
,, Hannah, 103
,, Henry, 135, 264
,, Hester, 82, 84, 90, 189, 266
,, Hugh, 133
,, James, 171
,, John, 3, 12, 73, 102, 250, 251,
252, 254
,, Joseph, 105, 108, 100, 111, 278,
286
,, Letys, 122
,, Margaret, 189
,, Mary, 74, 109
,, Michael, 84, 90, 174, 266, 270, 278
,, Morgan, 188
,, Owen, 124, 186, 188, 190

Wilson, Ralph, 100, 101, 102, 103, 105,
108, 109
,, Richard, 3
,, Robert, 73, 74, 76, 161, 254
,, Sarah, 111, 288
,, Stephen, 111
,, Susan, 140
,, Thomas, 11, 12, 139, 163, 187,
189, 191, 198
Win, Elizabeth, 229
,, Mary, 229
,, Owen, 229
,, Robert, 138
Winchester, Ann, 120
,, Sarah, 120
,, William, 120, 293
Winchfield, John, 155
Winchurst, Annie, 166
Winder, Thomas, 193
Winfield, Ellnor, 256
,, Thomas, 256
Wingfield, Daniel, 264
Winkfield, Edward, 207
,, Mary, 256
,, Thomas, 256
Winstanley, Anne, 121
,, Elizabeth, 64
,, James, 64
,, Thomas, 64
Winston, Delabar, 159
Winter, Sarah, 176
Wintley, Margaret, 254
,, William, 254
Wirgen, John, 63
,, Mary, 63
Wisbert, Henry, 65
,, Sarah, 65
Wiseham, Catherine, 113, 114
,, James, 114
,, Samuel, 113, 114
,, William, 113
Witham, Elizabeth, 239
Witham, 222, *see* Williams
Withip, Richard, 145
Witton, *see* Wytton
Wittridge, Henry, 101
,, Sarah, 101
Woare, Alice, 196
Wodsworth, Rebecca, 166
Wolfall, William, 214
Wollaston, Elizabeth, 228
,, Henry, 228
,, John, 26, 202
,, Mary, 86, 267
,, "Mr.," 209, 227
,, William, 86, 266, 267, 285
Wood, Ann, 114
,, Anne Isabella, 114
,, Charles, 289
,, Edward, 33
,, Elizabeth, 28, 31, 103, 132, 201,
206, 213, 286, 290
,, George, 33, 213
,, Gilbert, 140
,, "Goodwief," 192
,, Jenny, 105
,, John, 30, 100, 101, 103, 105
,, Joyce, 30, 206
,, Katherine, 31, 210
,, Loyce, 29
,, Margaret, 135
,, Mary, 30, 101, 208

Wulfride, Alice, 125
Wyar, Joseph, 240
Wyatt, Bryan, 194
Wybert, Henry, 64, 66, 241, 243, 244
,, Sarah, 64, 66, 244
,, Thomas, 64
Wyburne, Henry, 238
,, John, 269
,, Soloanus, 238
Wydders, Agnes, 122
Wye, John, 127
Wyes, John, 124
Wyer, Margaret, 182
Wylde, Clement, 3
,, Joyce, 47
,, Mary, 47
,, Richard, 3
,, Thomas, 47
Wylkes, Christopher, 132
Wyllett, Agnes, 191
Wyllowes, Benjamin, 122
Wylmer, Cicily, 132
Wymark, Joan, 125
Wymond, Thomas, 294
Wynard, Edward, 139
Wynn, John, 269, 272
,, Margaret, 278
,, Mary, 285
,, "Mr," 92, 96, 278
,, Susannah, 259
,, Tobyah, 83
Wynterfall, Mary, 127
Wythers or Wethers, Alice, 123
,, Cicily, 122
,, Fabyan, 1, 3, 4, 125, 178, 181, 181
,, John, 2
,, Richard, 1
,, Susan, 3
,, Thomasin, 4, 125
Wythro, Susan, 125
Wytton or Witton, Adrian, 10
,, Alexander, 12
,, Alice, 189
,, Ann, 4, 13, 126
,, Andrye, 188
,, Brysilla, 5, 183
,, Dorothy, 8
,, Edward, 3
,, Elizabeth, 12
,, Hellen, 195
,, Joan, 126, 183
,, John, 6, 121, 185
,, Katherine, 2, 4, 127, 179
,, Lancelot, 188, 189
,, Martha, 9
,, Oliver, 7

Wytton, Susan, 3, 179
,, Thomas, 2, 3, 4, 5, 6, 7, 8, 9, 10, 11, 12, 13, 121, 179, 183, 185, 188, 190, 195
,, William, 11
Yard, Elizabeth, 285
Yardly, Alice, 57
,, Dulcibella, 57
,, James, 57, 241
Yarrow, Richard, 293
Yates or Yeates, Elizabeth, 150
,, John, 259
,, Mary, 154, 259
,, Robert, 97
,, Thomas, 97
Yeane, Hannah, 167
Yedd, Richard, 155
Yeomans, Ann, 13
,, Hugh, 13, 190
,, John, 195
,, Roger, 126
Yerland, Robert, 184
Versin, George, 283]
,, John, 282
,, Mary, 284
Ynchorem, William, 124
Yngram, see Ingram
Ynse, Cecily, 126
Yonger, Margaret, 122
York, John, 121
Youdd, Elizabeth, 57
,, Margaret, 57
,, Richard, 57
Young, Ann, 203
,, Charity, 238
,, Edith, 121
,, Elizabeth, 285
,, Emma, 196
,, Hasden, 175
,, Henry, 238, 240
,, John, 203
,, Joyce, 235
,, Judith, 121
,, Letitia, 165
,, Thomas, 139
,, William, 123
Yrde, Elizabeth, 234
,, Margaret, 59, 234
,, Richard, 234, 235
,, William, 59, 234
Zacheverall, see Sacheverell
Zeskyns, Katherine, 180
Zimpany, or Lumpany, Ann, 49, 51
,, John, 49, 51
,, Robert, 49
,, William, 51

Index to Names

ST. MARY WOOLCHURCH HAW REGISTERS.

Crewe, Emme, 299
,, Isabel, 387
,, Joan, 298
,, John, 299, 300, 314, 367, 370
,, Joseph, 299
,, Margaret, 367
,, Mary, 300
,, "Mr,," 384
,, Richard, 299
,, Thomas, 311
Crisp, Andrew, 340
,, "Mr.," 340
Crofter, Jane, 348
Croke, Ferdinand, 406
Croker, "Mr.," 388
Crokford, Julian, 342
Crooke, "Dr.," 381, 388
,, "Mr.," 327
,, Richard, 388, 397
,, Samuel, 388
,, Thomas, Sir, 393
Crookhorne, Francis, 358
Crosbie, William, 373
Crossfield, Edmund, 341
,, Henry, 405
Crosslie, Elizabeth, 312, 382
,, John, 315
,, Martha, 311
,, Mary, 312
,, Sarah, 313
,, William, 311, 312, 313, 315, 382, 385
Croudson, Jane, 330
,, John, 396
,, Margaret, 407
,, Sarah, 326, 327, 328, 329, 330, 401, 403
,, Thomas, 326, 327, 328, 329, 330, 396, 397, 399, 403, 407
,, William, 327, 361, 395, 397
,, Zachary, 329, 407
Crowche, Ann, 303, 347
,, Giles, 303, 377, 381
,, Jane, 303, 347
,, Mary, 361
,, "Mrs.," 377
,, Sarah, 347
Crowchman, Benjamin, 367
,, John, 367, 368, 372, 373
,, Margaret, 344
,, "Mrs.," 373
,, Thomas, 368
Crowder, Charles, 407
Crumpe, Anne, 377
,, John, 377
Cudner, Edmund, 299, 370
,, Mary, 300
,, Robert, 299, 300, 368, 379
,, Thomas, 299, 368
,, Ursula, 298
Cuff, Michael, 391
Cullifer, Ann, 346
Culpepper, John, 312
,, Thomas, 312
Cnrrin, Catherine, 391
Cnrtis, Ann, 344
,, Edward, 350
,, Hannah, 329
,, John, 328, 329, 398
,, Lydia, 350
,, Mary, 328
,, Mathew, 327

Curtis, Sarah, 325, 326, 327, 328, 322
,, Theophilus, 326
,, Thomas, 367
,, William 325,326,327,328,329,398
Cutler, Edward, 404
,, James, 330, 333, 334,399,403,404
,, John, 333, 334, 404
,, Mary, 330, 333, 334
Dagg, Roger, 394
Daie, William, 298
Dale, Joan, 367
,, Mary, 354
,, Robert, 355
Dally, Alexander, 322
,, Edward, 390, 398
,, Elizabeth, 323
,, Isabel, 322, 323
,, Joyce, 359
,, Thomas, 322, 323
Dalton, Thomas, 405
Damport, Thomas, 369
Danbrook, Daniel, 319
,, John, 319
Danby, Robert, 343
Daniel, Judith, 350
,, Mary, 349
,, Sarah, 383
,, Thomas, 383
Darnella or Darnelie, Ann, 316
,, Daniel, 313, 314, 316, 317, 390, 404
,, Edward, 314
,, Ellen, 383
,, "Mr.," 386
,, "Mrs.," 398
,, Richard, 317
,, Stephen, 398
Dashwood, John, 365
Danling, John, 365
Dauncey, Mary, 357
,, William, 409
Davenant, Ralph, 347
David, Mary, 341
Davie, Henry, 403
,, Sarah, 365
Davis, Ann, 349
,, Charles, 336, 399
,, Elizabeth, 348
,, Jane, 346
,, John, 297, 345, 376, 380, 384, 315, 392, 393
,, Margaret, 386
,, Mary, 361, 376
,, "Mr.," 403
,, "Mrs.," 382
,, Phillip, 365
,, Rebecca, 336
,, Robert, 335
,, Stephen, 345
,, "Widow," 384
Davison, Ambrose, 361
Dawes, John, 363
Dawkes, Elizabeth, 341
,, George, 375
Dawnie, Abigail, 317
,, Augustine, 317, 386
,, Edmund, 315, 316, 317, 319, 349, 385, 386, 387
,, John, 315, 319, 387
,, Mary, 385
,, Samuel, 316, 386
Dawson, Elizabeth, 337

I H I

Horton, Richard, 305, 374
,, Susan, 324
,, William, 310
Houbelon, Ann, 322, 357
,, Benjamin, 397
,, James, 322, 396, 397, 399
,, Mary, 322, 396, 399
,, " Mr.," 397
,, Samuel, 399
,, Sarah, 358
Houghton, see Haughton
House, Dousabel, 358
,, John, 363
Housman, Thomas, 359
Hovell, Hugin, 322, 323,324,393,394,403
,, John, 322, 324, 334
,, Mary, 323, 324, 393, 394, 404
,, " Mr.," 326, 330, 395, 401
Howard, Elizabeth, 340
Howell, Henry, 355
Howland, Priscilla, 351
Hovens, Van. see Van Hovens
Hoxbey, William, 357
Hubbart, Miles, 346
Huckell, Elizabeth, 343
Huckle, Nicholas, 376
Hudsford, Barbara, 345
Hudson, Thomas, 348
Hughes, Nicholas, 349
,, Thomas, 358
Hull, Robert, 393
Humberstone, Avis, 380
Humble, Abigail, 317, 391
,, Joan, 315
,, Mark, 315, 316, 317, 386, 391
,, Mary, 316
,, " Mr.," 398
,, Persis, 354
,, Robert, 315, 391
,, Susan, 315
Humphrey, Francis, 327
,, Mary, 326, 327, 328, 329, 330
,, Pharoah, 326, 327, 328, 329, 333, 399
,, Reuben, 393
,, Robin, 329
,, Thomas, 330
Hungerford, Mary, 397
,, Thomas, 397
Hunlock, Henlock, or Hemlock,Ann, 360
,, Esther, 326
,, Henry, 326, 354, 403
,, Kathcrine, 365
,, Mary, 326, 404
,, " Mr.," 400
,, Sarah, 366
Hunningburne, Peter, 343
Hunt, Anne, 337, 407
,, Anthony, 308
,, Elizabeth, 308
,, George, 378
,, Isaac, 327
,, Jane, 313, 325, 326, 327, 328
,, John, 307
,, Josiah, 326, 374
,, Katherine, 328
,, Mary, 326, 395
,, " Mrs.," 379
,, Nathaniel, 328
,, Rebecca, 325
,, Richard, 336, 307, 308, 325, 326, 327, 328, 378, 379, 396, 399

Hunt, Sarah, 325, 406
,, Shadrack, 399
,, Simon, 337, 406, 407
,, Sybil, 344
,, Thomas, 327, 397
,, ——— 313
Hurdman, Edward, 327
,, Elizabeth, 327
,, Grace, 344
Huswife, Ann, 350
Hutches, Edward, 381
Hutchin, Thomas, 361
Hutchinson, Edward, 402
,, Robert, 347, 384
Hyett, Edward, 353
Ingram, Margaret, 343
,, " Mrs," 373
,, William, 373
Inns, William, 397
Ive, Emma, 408
,, Thomas, 408
Jackler, Mary, 390
,, Thomas, 390
Jacklow, Mary, 353
Jackson, Ann, 365
,, Daniel, 318
,, Elizabeth, 355
,, Joan, 322, 324, 394
,, John, 323, 347, 388
,, Margaret, 319
,, Martha, 347
,, Mary, 366
,, Nicholas, 322, 394
,, Robert, 322, 323, 324, 394
,, Ruth, 324
,, Susannah, 319
,, Thomas, 318, 319, 388
Jacob, John, 345
Jakmam, Elizabeth, 303
,, Thomas, 303
James, John, 361
Jarvis, Catherine, 348
,, Jane, 374
,, Mary, 347
Jay, Henry, 371
,, Margaret, 371
,, Thomas, 346
Jayke, Reynald, 373
Jefferson, William, 369
Jegon, Barbara, 351
Jellyman, Mary, 401
,, William, 401
Jenkinson, Elinor, 389
,, Richard, 389
,, Thomas, 367, 379
Jenner, Richard, 345
,, Thomas, 364
Jennie, Robert, 346
Jennings, John, 371
,, Rose, 343
Jesse, John, 364
Joans, Julan, 355
John, Ap Frances, 364
Johnson, Alice, 383
,, Ann, 360
,, Bartholomew, 370
,, Dionise, 348
,, Elizabeth, 347, 383
,, James, 381
,, John, 381
,, Richard, 358
,, Samuel, 349

Thomson, Anne, 333, 334, 335, 337, 357, 358
,,   Christopher, 348
,,   Daniel, 322
,,   Dorothy, 338
,,   Elizabeth, 331
,,   Ellin, 322, 323, 324, 325, 392, 395
,,   Hannah, 392
,,   John, 334, 377
,,   "Mr.," 328
,,   "Mrs.," 380, 395
,,   Richard, 323, 333, 334, 335, 337, 338
,,   Robert, 322, 323, 324, 325, 333, 353, 392, 395, 406
,,   Stephen, 324
,,   Thomas. 375
,,   Timothy, 325, 395
,,   William, 344
Thorneley, Edward, 408
,,   Hugh, 408
Thornton, Katherine, 345
Thorowgood, William, 362
Thorpe, Elizabeth, 346
Thrower, John, 409
Thursfield, Edward, 333, 334, 335, 336, 337, 407
,,   Elizabeth, 333, 334, 335, 336, 337, 403
,,   Francis, 333, 407
,,   Gervaise, 337
,,   Joanah, 337
,,   John, 336
,,   Mary, 334
Thurston, Mary, 365
,,   Oliver, 342
Tidd, John, 391
Tiller, Anne, 329, 360
,,   Richard, 329, 399
,,   Susan, 329
,,   "Widow," 400
Tilman, Daniel, 345
Tipper, Jane, 339
,,   Mary, 340
,,   Morrice, 339, 340
,,   Sarah, 339, 340
Titcombe, Joan, 365
Tittelo, Elizabeth, 364
Toddle, Cicily, 367
Toft, Anne, 337
,,   Rhoda, 337
,,   Samuel, 337
Tolson, Launcelot, 356
Tomes, Anne, Anne, 339, 343
,,   Christopher, 339, 340
Tomkins, Henry, 403
,,   John, 395
,,   Richard, 335
,,   William, 341
Tomlin, Thomas, 391
Tomlinson, Isabel, 358
,,   William, 335
Toms, Jane, 359
Tonge, Mary, 363
Towers, Elizabeth, 320
,,   Francis, 319, 320
,,   William, 320
Town, "Mr.," 402
Townsend, Frances, 361
Traeston, Jane, 321
,,   Mary, 321
,,   William, 321, 391
Trafford, Elizabeth, 358
,,   William, 397

Trap, Richard, 357
Travell, Blanche, 298
,,   Elizabeth, 299
,,   Frances, 340
,,   John, 340
,,   Peter, 298
,,   Richard, 299
,,   Robert, 341
Travers, Samuel, 358
Trayford, Jane, 380
Trelawny, Robert, 398
Trevett, John, 326
,,   Mary, 364
,,   Samuel, 326
,,   Sarah, 326
Trice, Margaret, 373
Trolop, Margaret, 341
Trowte, Barbara, 310
,,   Justina, 388
,,   "Mrs.," 386
,,   Richard, 310, 311, 380, 388, 389
Troughton, Henry, 372
Trystram, alias Mathew, John, 409
Tubman, Edward, 348
Tuchin, Anne, 352
Tuckoe, William, 383
Tuckwell, Elizabeth, 360
Tuese, Nicholas, 371
Tumber, Richard, 347
Turberville, Basil, 343, 375
,,   "Mrs.", 375
Turner, Agnes, 376
,,   Mary, 306, 351
,,   William, 306, 458, 376
Turpin, Hannah, 401
,,   Robert, 398, 400, 402
,,   Thomas, 395
Tyas, Henry, 370
Tyers, Simon, 359
Tyler, John, 360
Tynte, John, 354
Tyrrel, Emme, 341
Underbench, Jeffrey, 326
Underwood, Agnes, 349
,,   Edward, 396
,,   John, 388, 396
,,   Susan, 359
Upcher, John, 351
Upcote, Eulalia, 351
Ure, Caleb, 391
Ure or Eure, "Mrs.", 392
Usherwood, Margaret, 391
Vachell, Anne, 401
Valour, Margaret, 349
Van Cowen Bargan, Tannikin, 379
Van Hoven, Anthony, 300, 370
,,   James, 300
Vanspeare, Jacob, 391
,,   Mary, 398
,,   Stephen, 398, 399
,,   William, 398
Vateson, Blanche, 341
Vaughan, Anne, 387
,,   Barbara, 314
,,   Christopher, 372
,,   Elizabeth, 342
,,   Francis, 384
,,   Joan, 343
,,   Mary, 387
,,   "Mrs.", 383
,,   Richard, 356, 407
,,   Thomas, 389

* In some cases the name is written "Wright."

* Written occasionally for " White Mathew,"
see White

FINIS.

CPSIA information can be obtained
at www.ICGtesting.com
Printed in the USA
BVHW031755190819
556236BV00001B/137/P

9 789389 465297